German armies

Warfare and History

General Editor
Jeremy Black
Professor of History, University of Exeter

Published

European warfare, 1660–1815
Jeremy Black

The Great War, 1914–18
Spencer C. Tucker

German armies: war and German politics, 1648–1806
Peter H. Wilson

Forthcoming titles include

War and Israeli society since 1948
Ahron Bregman

Air power and total war
John Buckley

English warfare, 1511–1641
Mark Charles Fissel

Ottoman warfare, 1500–1700
Rhoads Murphey

European–Native American warfare, 1675–1815
Armstrong Starkey

Wars of imperial conquest in Africa, 1830–1914
Bruce Vandervort

German armies
War and German politics,
1648–1806

Peter H. Wilson
University of Newcastle upon Tyne

First published in 1998 by UCL Press

UCL Press Limited
1 Gunpowder Square
London
EC4A 3DE

and

1900 Frost Road, Suite 101
Bristol
Pennsylvania 19007-1598
USA

The name of University College London (UCL) is a registered trade mark
used by UCL Press with the consent of the owner.

British Library Cataloguing-in-Publication Data
A catalogue record for this book is available from the British Library.

ISBNs:
1-85728-105-5 HB
1-85728-106-3 PB

Typeset in Bembo.
Printed by
T.J. International Ltd, Padstow, UK.

For Eliane

Contents

Maps

1. *The* Reich *in 1745*

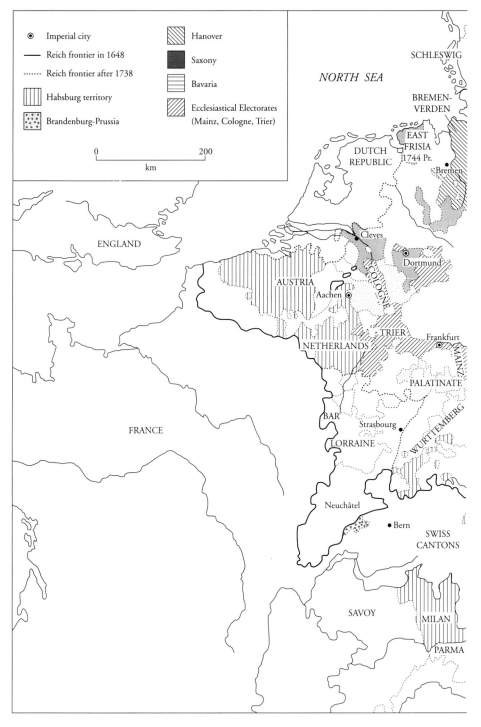

Imperial city

Reich frontier in 1648

Reich frontier after 1738

Habsburg territory

Brandenburg-Prussia

Hanover

Saxony

Bavaria

Ecclesiastical Electorates
(Mainz, Cologne, Trier)

0   200
        km

NORTH SEA

SCHLESWIG

BREMEN-
VERDEN

EAST
FRISIA
1744 Pr.

Bremen

DUTCH
REPUBLIC

ENGLAND

Cleves

COLOGNE

Dortmund

AUSTRIA

Aachen

TRIER

Frankfurt

MAINZ

NETHERLANDS

PALATINATE

BAR

Strasbourg

WÜRTTEMBERG

FRANCE

LORRAINE

Neuchâtel

Bern

SWISS
CANTONS

SAVOY

MILAN

PARMA

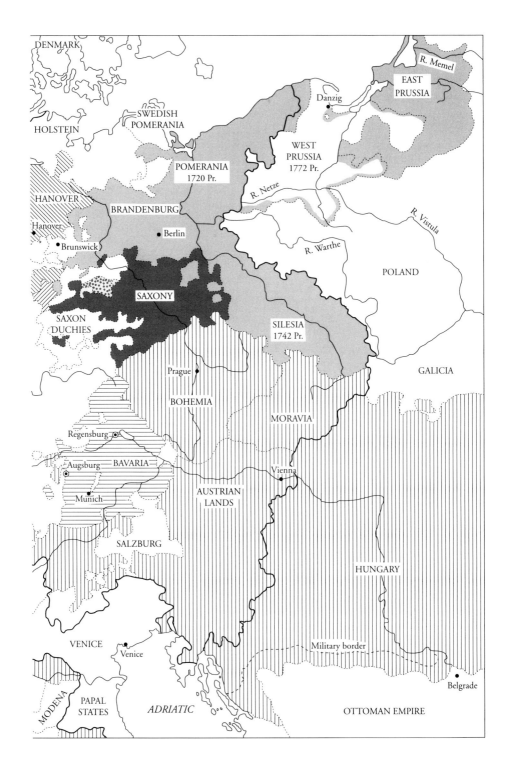

DENMARK

HOLSTEIN

SWEDISH
POMERANIA

HANOVER

Hanover

Brunswick

BRANDENBURG

POMERANIA
1720 Pr.

Berlin

SAXONY

SAXON
DUCHIES

Danzig

EAST
PRUSSIA

R. Memel

WEST
PRUSSIA
1772 Pr.

R. Netze

R. Vistula

R. Warthe

POLAND

SILESIA
1742 Pr.

GALICIA

Prague

BOHEMIA

MORAVIA

Regensburg

Augsburg   BAVARIA

Munich

SALZBURG

AUSTRIAN
LANDS

Vienna

HUNGARY

VENICE

Venice

Military border

MODENA

PAPAL
STATES

ADRIATIC

OTTOMAN EMPIRE

Belgrade

x

2. The Kreise

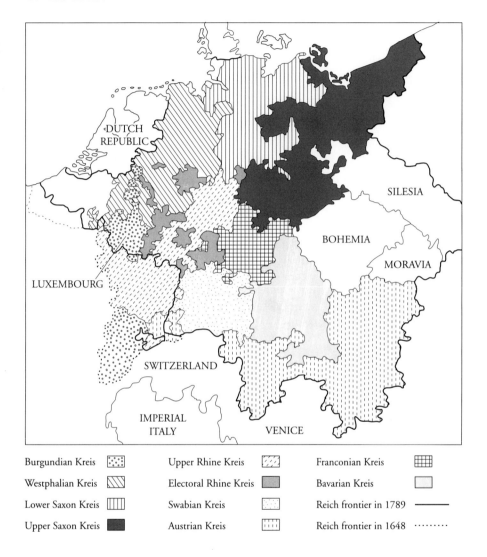

Burgundian Kreis	Upper Rhine Kreis	Franconian Kreis	
Westphalian Kreis	Electoral Rhine Kreis	Bavarian Kreis	
Lower Saxon Kreis	Swabian Kreis	Reich frontier in 1789	
Upper Saxon Kreis	Austrian Kreis	Reich frontier in 1648	

3. Western Germany in 1660

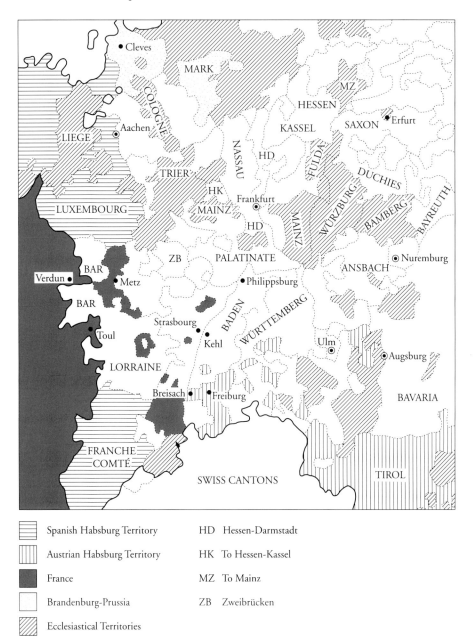

Spanish Habsburg Territory

Austrian Habsburg Territory

France

Brandenburg-Prussia

Ecclesiastical Territories

HD Hessen-Darmstadt

HK To Hessen-Kassel

MZ To Mainz

ZB Zweibrücken

4. *Northern Germany in 1648*

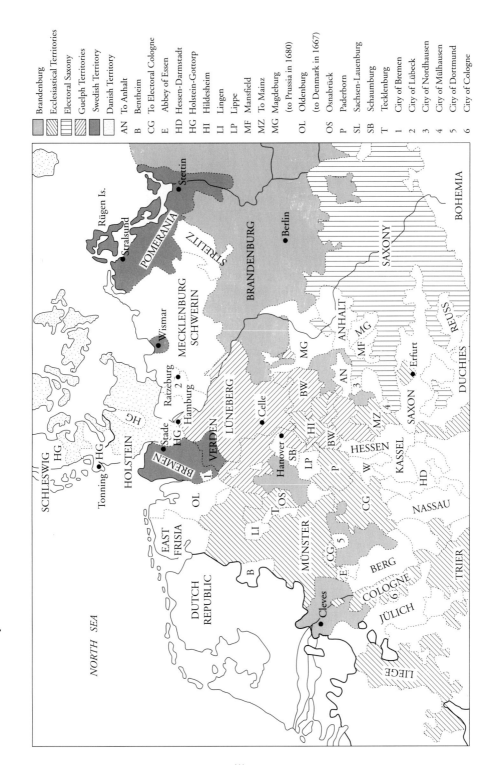

5. The battle of Rossbach, 1757

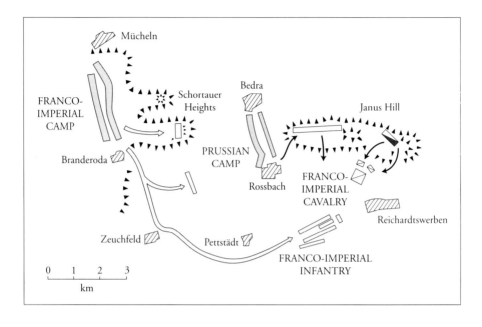

Preface

A few years ago in the helter-skelter of modern British higher education, I was pitched at short notice to teach a class of communication studies students following an option on modern European identity. Compelled to improvise, I began by asking them to list five things they associated with Germany. Depressingly, if perhaps not surprisingly, war featured prominently among the responses. However, the images and information upon which this was based derived overwhelmingly from twentieth-century events. The importance of war in the earlier German past, as well as German involvement in wider European conflict, was assumed rather than known. The students were far from alone in their beliefs, for much of the specialist literature conveys a similar impression, generalizing largely from the Prussian experience to chart the seemingly inexorable rise of German military power and bellicosity from the Great Elector, or at least Frederick the Great, through Bismarck and the generals of the Second Reich to Hitler and those of the Third.

This book challenges the assumptions behind these preconceptions. It had not been my original intention to do this, however, as I set out primarily to explore relations between German soldiers and society. Despite my continued fascination with this subject, which remains an ongoing concern, I kept returning to the basic question of why the numerous minor German rulers had armies at all. It is this issue that provides the starting point for a re-appraisal of German politics from the end of the Thirty Years War to the age of Napoleon.

During this transformation of my original research project, it has been my good fortune to benefit from the help and advice of many good people and institutions. In particular, I would like to thank Jeremy Black, Hamish Scott and my colleagues David Moon and Susan-Mary Grant for their encouragement and comments on draft chapters. John Childs cordially invited me to a seminar at Leeds University where some of the ideas were aired in public and received much constructive criticism. The directors and staff of the Public Record Office, Hauptstaatsarchiv Stuttgart, and Staatsarchiv Darmstadt provided invaluable assistance, while the inter-library loans section of the Robinson Library, Newcastle University, performed heroic feats in tracking down my more obscure requests. Julian Calvert furnished hospitality and unparalleled cuisine during a research trip to Germany. Eleanor Cunningham converted my barely legible scrawl into presentable typescript without protest at my ignorance of modern technology. To all these people and many others who assisted me I express my sincere appreciation.

Finally, I would like to thank Eliane, whose support and encouragement remained undiminished despite the birth of Alec, a far more worthy recipient of her time and attention than the problems of German history. Without her love this work would never have been finished.

Note on form

Names of places and people have been left in their German form unless there is a commonly used Anglicized version, when this is used instead. This mainly applies to the emperors and Brandenburg-Prussian rulers. Place names in Hungary and elsewhere in east–central Europe have varied considerably, so I have generally stuck to the German versions used at the time and in the subsequent historiography, with the modern usage in parentheses. Titles and technical terms are given in English except in cases where there is either no translation or the translation can be misleading. In such cases the German has been used throughout, but explained the first time the word appears.

Money is expressed as appropriate in the two main currency units used in the Reich, i.e., *Rhenish Gulden* (Rhenish florins, fl.) or *Talers* (tlr), with all fractions rounded up. As an indication of value, a foot soldier generally received under 4 fl. in pay and allowances a month throughout most of the period under review, equivalent to 20 days' wages of an unskilled labourer, or the price of 30–40 four-pound loaves of bread. It cost 34–40 fl. to recruit and equip an infantryman and 67–80 fl. to maintain him for a year in the eighteenth century. The figures for a cavalryman, including his horse, were 140–160 fl. and 135–155 fl. respectively.

Conversion rates for the currencies used in this book are set out below:

1 fl. Rhenish = 1.25 fl. Dutch
1.5 fl.   = 1 tlr
1 fl.   = 1.25 French livre (1660s)
1 fl.   = 1.5 French livre (1680s–90s)
1 fl.   = 2 French livre (*c.* 1700–50)
1 fl.   = 2.5 French livre (post 1750)

7.5 fl.   = £1 sterling (1680s)
8 fl.   = £1 sterling (1730s)
9.15 fl.   = £1 sterling (1780s)

List of abbreviations

AHR	*American Historical Review*
AHY	*Austrian History Yearbook*
AHVN	*Annalen des Historischen Vereins für den Niederrhein*
BBSW	*Besondere Beilage zum Staatsanziege für Württemberg*
BMWB	*Beiheft zum Militär-Wochenblatt*
bn	battalion
CEH	*Central European History*
coy	company
DBKH	*Darstellungen aus der bayerischen und Kriegs- und Heeresgeschichte*
EHR	*English Historical Review*
FBPG	*Forschungen zur brandenburgischen und preussischen Geschichte*
fl.	florin
GH	*German History*
HDM	*Handbuch zur deutschen Militärgeschichte, 1648–1939* [11 vols] (issued by the Militärgeschichtliches Forschungsamt, Frankfurt-am-Main, 1964–81, 1983 edn)
HJ	*Historical Journal*
HJb	*Historisches Jahrbuch*
HSAS	Haupstaatsarchiv Stuttgart
HZ	*Historische Zeitschrift*
IPO	Instrumentum pacis Osnabrugense (Treaty of Osnabrück, 24 October 1648, part of the Westphalian Settlement)
JMH	*Journal of Modern History*
JRA	Jüngster Reichsabschied (Latest Imperial Recess, 7 May 1654)
MGM	*Militärgeschichtliche Mitteilungen*
MIÖG	*Mitteilungen des Instituts für Österreichischen Geschichtsforschung*
MÖSA	*Mitteilungen des Österreichischen Staatsarchivs*

NASG	*Neues Archiv für sächsische Geschichte*
NF	Neue Folge (new series)
PJb	*Preussische Jahrbücher*
P & P	*Past and Present*
PRO	Public Record Office
REO	*Reichsexekutionsordrung* (imperial executive ordinance, 25 September 1555)
rgt	regiment
RHR	*Reichshofrat* (imperial Aulic Council)
RKG	*Reichskammergericht* (imperial Cameral Court)
RM	*Römer Monat* (Roman Month)
RVJB	*Rheinische Vierteljahrsblätter*
sqn	squadron
StAD	Staatsarchiv Darmstadt
tlr	taler
WF	*Württembergisch Franken*
WVJHLG	*Württembergische Vierteljahreshefte für Landesgeschichte*
WZ	*Westfälische Zeitschrift*
ZBLG	*Zeitschrift für bayerische Landesgeschichte*
ZGO	*Zeitschrift für die Geschichte des Oberheins*
ZHF	*Zeitschrift für historische Forschung*
ZHG	*Zeitschrift für hessische Geschichte und Landeskunde*
ZSRG	*Zeitschrift der Savignystiftung für Rechtsgeschichte, Germanistische Abteilung*
ZWLG	*Zeitschrift für Württembergische Landesgeschichte*

Introduction

This book attempts to solve one of the paradoxes of European history: why, when it was apparently weak and internally divided, did the Holy Roman Empire (*Reich*) survive in a hostile environment of centralizing belligerent states. The answers that emerge suggest a picture very different from the conventional image of war and German politics. The militaristic power state (*Machtstaat*) exemplified by Prussia is a crucial part of German history, but so too is a system of collective security and internal conflict and resolution that allowed a rich variety of political traditions to coexist relatively harmoniously. This system preserved the *Reich* against formidable attacks without making it a danger to the security of its neighbours. In contrast to the political culture of later German states, that of the *Reich* was inherently defensive, preferring peace to war in both domestic politics and external relations.

From the perspective of the 1990s it is tempting to compare this to recent efforts at collective defence and peacekeeping, such as the UN, NATO or the European Union. Certainly, the yawning gap between the utopian intentions and practical realities of these new world orders, along with the self-interested manoeuvrings of today's great powers in their painfully slow attempts to end the bloodshed in the former Yugoslavia encourage a more sympathetic treatment of princes and statesmen previously dismissed as petty despots and cynical opportunists. The apparently endless protocol disputes and inconclusive resolutions that have so exasperated earlier commentators on German politics seem both more tangible and understandable in a world where states with the capacity to destroy all known life cannot arrest men formally indicted as war criminals.

However, there is far more to a reappraisal of early modern Germany than viewing it with the concerns of the present rather than those of, say, 1933 or 1871. German involvement in European affairs needs to be seen within the context of imperial politics, or the relations between the component institutions and territories of the *Reich*. The *Reich* was never simply a subordinate adjunct of the Austrian Habsburg monarchy, nor was it a loose federation of independent states, even after the Peace of Westphalia (1648), which is often taken as signalling its terminal decline. Not only did it last for another 158 years, but it continued to evolve, providing a framework for its weaker elements to co-ordinate common action as well as a forum for European diplomacy.

Appreciation of these wider aspects has been inhibited by the lack of a suitable analytical structure to relate German politics to international relations. Chapter 1 attempts to remedy this by examining German political developments within the context of early modern state formation. In contrast to centralizing national monarchies like France, the *Reich* remained an area of fragmented sovereignty and overlapping jurisdictions, complicating its relationship to neighbouring states and its response to external aggression. Power remained unevenly distributed between the emperor and the princes and lesser authorities ruling the component territories without any single element ever gaining a decisive advantage. There was no single monopoly of warmaking, nor the right to conduct foreign relations, though each territory was bound by practical and constitutional restraints limiting its freedom of action. Survival of the traditional monarchical and hierarchical structure depended on the maintenance of this rough equilibrium, which could be disturbed either by the disproportionate growth of one or more of the German territories or by an external threat.

The following eight chapters examine the response to these threats as they developed after 1648. A roughly chronological approach has been adopted as this is a largely unfamiliar story. Germany's rich tradition of regional and constitutional history tends to produce detailed studies of individual territories and institutions, compounding the absence of the strong narrative line provided elsewhere in western Europe by the rough correlation between state formation and modern national boundaries. Most previous attempts to write a single account of this period distort events, either by concentrating on a single major territory like Austria, or by describing formal constitutional development devoid of the human element that gave it life, particularly at the level of local politics and personal ambition. States are not independent actors detached from society, nor did monarchs engage in international conflict without regard for their own populations, even in an age supposedly dominated by "limited" or "cabinet wars". The wider social dimension cannot be ignored, and though space precludes a full discussion here, it forms a constant thread running through this work. As it is helpful for the traveller to have some idea of the destination before beginning the journey, the remainder of this introduction sketches a rough map of the terrain to be encountered.

The Westphalian Settlement failed to resolve all the tensions that had caused the Thirty Years War (1618–48). The legacy of that conflict combined with a still troubled international environment to produce continued uncertainty within imperial politics until the 1680s. Though in fact no longer feasible, the possibility that the emperor might subordinate the *Reich* to some form of absolute authority remained a constant fear of many German princes and their European neighbours. The Austrian Habsburg dynasty did manage to retain their hold on the imperial title, as yet unbroken since 1440, and recover much of the influence they had lost during the recent war, but their authority within the *Reich* remained an extreme form of indirect rule, mediated by the princes and institutions. Even within their own hereditary lands, the Habsburgs' access to territorial resources was limited by the entrenched power of traditional elites and the practical difficulties associated with the limited effective reach of a still partially decentralized and underdeveloped state structure. Maintenance of their status as one of Europe's leading royal families depended on a constant process of bargaining with these elites and the German princes for access to men, money and influence.

Imposition of greater direct rule by force was virtually impossible, as the Thirty Years War had shown, though a number of leading princes were able to consolidate their hold over their own territories along increasingly absolutist lines. Assisted by subsidies from foreign powers eager to exploit their military potential and strategic importance, several of these princes began to engage actively in European conflicts, either as auxiliaries of other states or on their own account. Their activities stemmed from long-standing concerns for security and the need to establish their place in what was becoming a system of sovereign European states increasingly at odds with the medieval fabric of the *Reich*.

The need to combat external aggression, first in the form of the Ottoman Turks on the eastern frontier (1663–4) and later French expansionism to the west after 1667, forced the emperor into greater dependency on these militarizing "armed princes" (*Armierten*). The outbreak of the Dutch War in 1672 precipitated a political crisis, as the existing mechanism of mobilizing collective defence proved incapable of meeting the French challenge, pushing the emperor into a number of dangerous expedients at the expense of the weaker, unarmed territories (*Nicht Armierten*). Pressure mounted after the close of formal hostilities in 1679 as France and Denmark continued to encroach on German territory. The traditional structure was being eroded in favour of a looser federation of the larger territories, undermining both Habsburg authority and the autonomy of the lesser princes. This process was stemmed by a series of political compromises in 1679–84, defusing the external threat and revising collective security in a manner that consolidated the existing hierarchy and extended its life.

Crucially, this occurred prior to the Turkish onslaught on Vienna in 1683, enabling the *Reich* to survive the prolonged warfare that followed despite the coincidence of renewed dangers from the west with the start of the Nine Years War in 1688. However, the success of what became known as the Great Turkish War (1683–99) transformed Austria from a German to a European power, consolidated by further territorial gains during the War of the Spanish Succession (1701–14) and a further Turkish War (1716–18). The *Reich* preserved its territorial integrity throughout even in the face of additional tension in the Baltic during the parallel Great Northern War (1700–21), but the internal balance of power had been altered. For the first time since 1556 the centre of Habsburg political gravity lay outside Germany. As the emperor became less "German", he also became less able to deal with the latent tensions within the *Reich*. The geographical scope of his strategic interests after 1718 complicated his management of imperial politics, which displayed serious weaknesses during the War of the Polish Succession (1733–5). A serious defeat in the Turkish War of 1737–9 left the dynasty vulnerable at a critical time and contributed to the success of the Prussian seizure of Habsburg Silesia in 1740.

The victory signalled Prussia's emergence as a second German power of European stature, which was continued by its subsequent defence of Silesia throughout the War of the Austrian Succession (1740–8) and survival against a hostile coalition in the Seven Years War (1756–63). These two conflicts were as much German civil wars as international struggles, exacerbating the existing tensions and contributing to the incremental break-up of the constitutional mechanisms holding the *Reich* together. The continued political and military expansion of the two German great powers at the expense of Poland after 1763 overshadowed even the largest of the other territories, raising the possibility that Germany might also be partitioned. Preservation of the traditional structure depended increasingly on the fickle interest of foreign powers like France and Russia, who were concerned lest Austria or Prussia gain an international advantage through greater German domination. However, the *Reich* had far from collapsed and continued to exhibit a capacity for renewal into the 1790s. It took the appearance of a new external threat in the shape of revolutionary France to precipitate the final dissolution by 1806.

4

Chapter One

War and German politics

Aspects of state formation

In 1667 the German philosopher Samuel Pufendorf famously described the *Reich* as a "monstrosity", because it did not fit the normal categories of European political science.[1] Though possessed of sufficient human and material resources to hold the entire continent in awe, the *Reich* was scarcely able to defend itself, because it lacked the central co-ordination necessary to harmonize its disparate elements. Constant internal feuding, inflamed by sectarian hatred since the Reformation, further weakened it, contributing to the carnage of the Thirty Years War, which only served to widen the gap between it and its western European neighbours. Most subsequent commentators have agreed that the lack of a strong hereditary monarchy was a fundamental weakness, condemning Germany to a largely passive international role until Prussia and Austria acquired sufficient power to act independently and emerge as rivals for political leadership.

Though familiar, this picture no longer stands modern scrutiny, not least thanks to a fuller understanding of French, English and Dutch development as well as revisions to German history. New analytical devices, many of them borrowed from political science and social theory, have also led to a reappraisal of what constituted power and state formation in early modern Europe. This chapter begins by examining some of these ideas, which are then applied to German political developments and their place in international relations. German territorial fragmentation and its importance to regional politics is analyzed in the third section before concluding with an assessment of the mechanisms established before 1648 to co-ordinate collective security across the *Reich*.

States are characterized by their monopoly of powers denied to other institutions or organizations.[2] Chief among these is the monopoly of violence, meaning organized coercion or military power. Creation of such a monopoly involves a process of militarization whereby the central power not only establishes the exclusive right to wage war but creates the infrastructure necessary to do so. Vital to sustaining this is a monopoly of taxation to extract material resources from the economy and population through legally enforceable obligations. There are other monopolies, of which justice is probably the most important, enabling the state to regulate society and, depending on its application, reward clients and punish internal opponents.

Most of these monopolies are territorially bounded in that they apply only to the district geographical area controlled by the state. To be fully sovereign, the state must exclude all influence over its internal affairs from external agencies. Full sovereignty is attainable only in theory, and throughout Europe's history states have been subject to degrees of external influence, most notably papal authority over the Catholic Church. However, while the political power of one state is excluded from the territory of other sovereign states, its military power has the capacity to reach beyond its frontiers. Moreover, historically, organizations other than states have controlled coercive power, like the commercial trading companies of England and the Dutch Republic, which had their own armies and fleets in the seventeenth century. Establishing control over these forms of extra-territorial violence is an important element of the state monopoly of military power.[3]

The exercise of all monopoly powers is qualified by their level of legitimacy. Historically, legitimacy has been a highly flexible concept, dependent on what has been termed the "ideological power" of the political elite and the extent to which they can foster acceptance for their beliefs.[4] This has never been an entirely top-down, one-way process whereby those in authority imposed ideas on a subject population and enforced acceptance through direct coercion or manipulation of theology. Instead, legitimacy was established by a complex bargaining process as powerholders not only pushed as far as they could until they met popular resistance, but those below successfully compelled those above to take some account of their own desires. Throughout there were always people at all levels of society who disagreed with the broader consensus, expressed variously in terms of religious confession, social behaviour or political philosophy. The presence of such individuals ensured that the concept of legitimacy was never total but was constantly being subtly reworked, usually in opposition to, but sometimes in collaboration with, the dissenters.

If states are characterized by their possession of legitimate power monopolies, it follows that state development is a process of monopoly formation.

This process can be broken down into three stages, the first of which involves the establishment of an undisputed fiscal-military monopoly in the hands of a recognized central authority, generally a monarch who had defeated all other rivals for control over a specific area.[5] Most western European states reached this stage by the mid-fifteenth century, when the major monarchies like those of France and England had accumulated both significant executive or "despotic" power, recognized as the authority to rule, and built up an infrastructure of royal administration sufficient to put their commands into effect.[6] Their rule was still largely indirect in the sense that it was mediated by groups and institutions enjoying considerable autonomy. In addition to assemblies or estates that claimed the right to negotiate with the king on behalf of sections of the population, government also depended on an administration staffed not by salaried professionals but men who regarded their position as a right or privilege and who were integrated as much into civil society by informal patronage networks as they were tied by loyalty to the crown. Such ties were still personal, and the state powers, as far as they had been accumulated, were still essentially a private monopoly of the monarch.[7]

The existence and extent of these powers remained in dispute throughout much of the sixteenth and seventeenth centuries, a factor that accounts for much of the violent political turmoil troubling many parts of Europe, including the Thirty Years War. These internal struggles became part of the second stage of monopoly formation, and as it became obvious that the centralization of fiscal–military power could no longer be reversed, conflict centred on efforts to control it and distribute the associated benefits and burdens among different social groups. The varying outcomes of these struggles help explain the differing constitutions of European states, ranging from the Dutch republican government to the limited monarchy of England and royal absolutism in France by 1660.[8] Though formal power was already shifting to wider social groups in the former two cases, that of the latter and other absolute monarchies remained narrow private monopolies.

The final stage was a transition from personalized rule to wider public control, a change associated in France with violent revolution in 1789 and generally with profound consequences for the nature of the state. The state became an entity transcending the lives of individual monarchs and administrators, who became its servants rather than its "owners". Frequently, though not necessarily always, this transition was accompanied by the move to direct rule whereby the administrative apparatus required to sustain the power monopolies was fully integrated into the state and began for the first time to penetrate the previously largely private and autonomous spheres of everyday life through ever-increasing surveillance and regulation.[9]

The imperial constitution and international relations

Monopoly formation did not follow a simple path within the *Reich* due to a number of factors, not least the practical difficulties of establishing firm control over such a vast area. Despite considerable contraction since its fullest extent in the ninth century, the *Reich* still encompassed over 750,000 km^2 in 1648, inhabited by perhaps 18 million people, with an additional 2 million or so living in the further 65,000 km^2 of northern or Imperial Italy (*Reichsitalien*).[10] German politics fragmented into four distinct but related levels, and the easiest way to understand the otherwise baffling imperial constitution is to examine it on this basis.[11]

Unlike other European states, centralization at national level was paralleled by a similar development at that of the component territories, prolonging the medieval fragmentation of political and military power. As the emperor sought to concentrate power in his own hands as supreme overlord for the entire area, the individual territorial rulers were affecting the same within the areas under their authority, creating two distinct levels of monopoly formation. Control over the central mechanisms for raising money and men for common action was shared between the emperor and those princes and other lesser rulers who gained formal representation as *Reichsstände* (imperial estates) at national level through membership of the *Reichstag* (Imperial Diet).[12] Interposed between the national institutions and the princes was the secondary level of the *Kreise*, or imperial circles, acting as a forum for political co-operation on a regional basis amongst groups of territories meeting in their own *Kreis* Assemblies. Political activity within the territories constituted a fourth level when it took place within local institutions formally recognized in the complex web of imperial law. Chief among such institutions were the territorial estates or assemblies (*Landstände*), composed usually of representatives from the local clergy, nobility, towns and, in rare cases, villages, who claimed roughly similar powers in respect to negotiations with their own ruler as those exercised by the princes in the *Reichstag*.[13] Monopoly formation at territorial level thus involved a two-way process; on the one hand of bargaining between prince and estates for access to local resources, and on the other between prince and emperor to limit interference from either *Kreis* or national institutions.

Power and status were unequally distributed both between and within the different levels, reflecting the hierarchical character of the traditional constitution and German society as a whole.[14] An individual's place within the wider framework was decided primarily by birth and gender. With rare exceptions, only men had access to political power, and the level to which they could wield it varied largely according to which social group they belonged. Though practice deviated substantially from the ideals expanded by theologians and bureaucrats, society was still divided along functional lines, segregating people according to what role they performed to promote the wider common good.

In the most basic sense these divisions did not differ from those in other parts of Europe once touched by Roman Catholicism. Lowest in status was that broad section of society that corresponded to the Third Estate in France. Subdivided into numerous groups on the basis of occupation and further split by region and religion, this section was united by the common function of providing for society's material welfare and by the general absence of hereditary privileges associated with noble status. Also varying considerably in wealth, these commoners formed the bulk of the urban and rural population but had little access to formal political power beyond that at the most localized level. Most Germans lived in small communities governed by the heads of the richer well-established families, who normally controlled the election or appointment of the village council and law court, except in eastern Germany, where the nobility had greater influence over these affairs. Though territorial rulers were trying to bring these positions under their control by integrating them into their own administrative infrastructure, most communities retained considerable autonomy over their own affairs until well into the nineteenth century. Vital elements of the fiscal-military monopoly thus ultimately rested on these patriarchs upon whom most rulers depended to enforce orders to collect taxes, select militiamen, find recruits and billet soldiers. Though they had considerable scope in how they distributed these burdens within the community, most village headmen had little say in determining their level, as few territorial estates contained peasant representation. In comparison, the urban population, accounting for about a quarter of Germans by 1800, was often comparatively privileged, as most major towns were entitled to send one or two members of their council to sit in the local assemblies alongside the clergy and nobility. Those free imperial cities (*Reichsstädte*) that had escaped incorporation within the principalities continued to function as autonomous civic republics under their own magistrates also secured access to national politics by 1648.[15]

The clergy's function of praying for society's salvation gave them greater proximity to God and with it nominal social pre-eminence. They continued to recruit their members predominantly from the other social groups even after the Reformation, which introduced clerical marriage into the Protestant areas. Since that time German politics had been characterized by a process known as confessionalization whereby rulers sought to establish religious uniformity within their territories by excluding both dissenting minorities and external ecclesiastical jurisdiction as far as possible.[16] As a result, there was no national German church and the Protestants created their own distinct territorial institutions, while the Catholics remained subject to varying degrees of papal influence. Protestant clergy were subject to greater state supervision than their Catholic counterparts, but both enjoyed considerable autonomy, and many Protestant territories retained clerical representation in their estates as well as separate ecclesiastical foundations outside the reach of the princely treasury.

High clerics, especially in Catholic areas, were predominantly nobles who, as a group, enjoyed particular privileges associated with their nominal function as society's warriors in addition to the wealth they derived from land ownership. Socially, the German nobility belonged to the same broad group as their prince, but unlike him they lacked the special distinction of immediacy (*Reichsunmittelbarkeit*) indicating no other overlord than the emperor himself. Their political power derived less from their formal representation in territorial estates than their informal influence through patronage and control of economic resources. Even where peasants were not tied directly to the nobles as serfs, like those in parts in northern and eastern Germany, they were usually still bound by other feudal obligations in varying degrees of dependency and servitude.

Increasingly, the territorial ruler was intruding into these relationships in ways that were to influence war making. Often the prince himself was a major landowner and derived part of his income directly from exploitation of his own economic undertakings. In an age when state power was still largely a private monopoly, these domainal revenues formed a major source of military finance, supplemented by whatever the ruler could borrow or bargain in additional taxation from the estates. These bargains, often cemented in charters endorsed by the emperor, had consolidated the estates as a formal element of the imperial constitution since the late fifteenth century and contributed to the development of a parallel infrastructure to collect their tax grants and administer that portion of the prince's debts they had agreed to amortize. Such decentralization undermined princely power and ultimately threatened territorial monopoly formation, prompting moves to curb the estates' autonomy by assuming their functions where possible within the prince's own administration. The growth of this administration fostered the emergence of another distinct group, the state bureaucrats, who were often university-educated and enjoyed corporate privileges marking them out within the wider society, to which they remained related by marriage, kinship and patronage.

While the practical extent of each prince's power depended on the outcome of these developments within his territory, his position within the *Reich* was determined by a combination of his formal status and material resources. Land and formal political power were related with rule over specific areas conferring certain rights within the imperial constitution. The first broad distinction was between those whose territorial immediacy also brought voting rights within the *Reichstag* (*Reichstandschaft*) and those who lacked this quality. All princely land (*Fürstentümer*) enjoyed this privilege, but those of the counts (*Reichsgrafen*), prelates (*Reichsprälaten*) and imperial cities were slow to gain representation at national level. The counts and prelates failed to secure parity with their more illustrious neighbours and had to accept limited representation in six "banks", each sharing a single collective vote in the College of Princes (*Fürstenrat*) by 1654. The remaining 51 imperial cities eventually gained individual voting rights in 1648 but had to accept these within a third subordinate college of their own. The premier college was that of the electors (*Kurfürsten*), comprising a select group of princes with the privilege of choosing the emperor in what was an elective monarchy like that of Poland or the papacy.[17] The 350 or so families of imperial knights (*Reichsritter*) along with a few other small areas failed to gain any representation at all and remained under direct imperial overlordship.

The second distinction was between the territorial rulers, who were divided not only by rank and title but into spiritual and lay princes. The three most prestigious electorates (Mainz, Cologne, Trier) were ruled by prince-archbishops elected by their cathedral chapter, which was dominated by aristocratic canons who controlled considerable wealth within and outside the territory as well as many of the chief offices of state. About 21 of the princely territories were also ruled by bishops and archbishops similarly chosen by local chapters, while two of the collective votes were shared by 42 prelates who included a few abbesses, the only women to hold formal political power under the constitution. Together these territories comprised the imperial church (*Reichskirche*), solidly Catholic with the exception after 1648 of the bishopric of Osnabrück, and closely associated with the emperor's traditional pan-European pretensions as the secular defender of Christendom.[18]

Rule over the secular electorates, principalities and counties was decided by hereditary succession and the prevailing laws of inheritance, which permitted their accumulation and partition subject to formal imperial approval. Consequently, it was possible for a ruler to exercise different forms of power depending on the combination of land he had inherited. Princes, especially secular electors like those of Brandenburg, Bavaria and Saxony, often held several pieces of land qualifying for full votes along with shares in collective ones derived from possession of relevant counties, and they could also inherit or purchase property belonging to the imperial knights or within the jurisdiction of other rulers. Feudal ties were an imperfect match for this complex web of rights and privileges so that while most territories constituted separate imperial fiefs, held by their rulers as vassals of the emperor, others were dependencies of secular or ecclesiastical princes.

Imperial politics have often been misleadingly portrayed as a dualism of princes and emperor with the former seeking to escape the latter's control and establish their own independent states. Far from being in a state of dissolution, the *Reich* continued to evolve after 1648 when three possible paths of development remained open. The option preferred by the weaker territories and most of their European neighbours was to refine the internal equilibrium sustaining the existing hierarchy dependent on the emperor but not subject to his direct authority. Powers like France and Sweden, along with the majority of princes, were opposed to the alternative of greater central control represented by the spectre of "imperial absolutism" they had fought against during the Thirty Years War. Lying in the opposite direction was the federalist option of further devolution and autonomy to territorial level, possibly extending to the incorporation of the smaller, weaker elements within larger principalities like the secular electorates.

Throughout most of its existence the *Reich* had proved sufficiently flexible to absorb such contradictory tendencies, often accommodating varied development at different levels by constantly refining its internal equilibrium. However, when combined with other pressures, such as sectarian strife, the resultant tensions could prevent this process by partially paralyzing the constitution. This last occurred after 1608 as political and confessional polarization accelerated, linking national problems with internal territorial crises, most notably in the Bohemian revolt against Habsburg centralization after 1618, and fusing with wider European conflicts through the alliances between German rulers and foreign powers to cause the Thirty Years War.[19]

Although the Swedes, and to a lesser extent France, captured German territory in the course of the war, no one could establish hegemony over the *Reich*, nor did they wish to. The principal aim of the major powers was to oppose what was believed to be attempts by the Habsburg dynasty to establish an universal monarchy in the form of their pre-eminence within Europe.[20] This objective was secured in the Westphalian Settlement of 1648, intended not only to end bloodshed in Germany but to secure lasting peace throughout Europe.[21] The potential union of the two Habsburg branches ruling the Austrian and Spanish monarchies was inhibited by a formal division of the peace settlement into two parts. The *Instrumentum pacis Osnabrugense* (IPO), or Treaty of Osnabrück, secured peace for the *Reich* east of the river Rhine while that of Münster, the *Instrumentum pacis Monasteriense* (IPM) partially resolved the western European conflict by recognizing Dutch independence after their long struggle against Spain. The Austrian Habsburgs were forbidden to use their hold on the imperial title to facilitate German assistance to Spain, which remained at war with France, reinforcing the general intention that the *Reich* was to remain nonaligned with regard to its great power relations.

Though their formal powers were limited, the presence of France and Sweden as external guarantors of the IPO signalled the internationalization of imperial politics, which was to grow as the century progressed. Already Denmark had substantial territory in north Germany, entitling it to a formal presence in the constitution, while the Dutch retained garrisons in a number of Westphalian and Rhenish towns occupied during the war. Implementation of the peace treaty did secure the withdrawal of Swedish and French troops by 1653 but had serious repercussions for the Burgundian *Kreis* west of the Rhine, which was excluded by the IPM on the grounds that it consisted entirely of Spanish territory. In addition to foreign interference in imperial affairs, Habsburg and Hohenzollern possessions outside the formal *Reich* boundaries extended German interests into other parts of Europe; a factor that was to increase with the involvement of other dynasties in international affairs.

Despite the foreign guarantees to what was simultaneously an international treaty and an internal constitutional document, the IPO was not alien to imperial tradition. Since the so-called imperial reform movement of the late fifteenth century, all revisions to the internal political balance had been intended to reinforce the essentially pacific characteristics of imperial politics and German political culture. The *Reich* was to remain at peace with itself and its Christian neighbours to permit the emperor to fulfil his true function as supreme champion against the Ottoman Turks. Even though few believed this ideal could actually be achieved, maintenance of the internal "public peace" (*Landfriede*) declared by Emperor Maximillian I in 1495, along with avoidance of unnecessary foreign wars, remained the primary objective of imperial politics.

The internal structure of the *Reich* evolved to this end, with the emphasis being on peaceful conflict resolution and defensive collective security. A system of imperial justice developed after 1495, which, despite its subsequent reputation for pedantry and delay, was more concerned with arbitration than retribution. Two supreme courts were established at national level with the *Reichskammergericht* (RKG, Imperial Cameral Court) created in 1495 dominated by the princes, while the *Reichshofrat* (RHR, Imperial Aulic Council) based in Vienna from 1498, was more dependent on the emperor.[22] Though their influence was curtailed by the growth of autonomous territorial justice dependent on the princes, both courts could intervene in disputes between rulers and subjects as well as between the territories themselves. The *Reichstag* provided an additional forum encouraging compromise rather than conflict, as did the *Kreis* institutions, which were charged with enforcing court verdicts. Avoidance of bloodshed remained the priority, and in practice the courts struggled to find workable solutions rather than strict adherence to the law.

Collective security only emerged as a major issue from the early sixteenth century, for until the appearance of the Turkish threat on the eastern frontier, the greatest danger to peace appeared to come from the internal feuding of knights and princes. The same mechanisms developed to mobilize territorial resources for internal peacekeeping and peace-enforcement were adapted to provide defence against external threats whilst denying the emperor the opportunity to exploit them for his own offensive operations. Prohibitions to this effect were written into the electoral agreements (*Wahlkapitulationen*) containing concessions wrung from each new emperor by the electors, while the IPO imposed additional restrictions obliging him to seek *Reichstag* approval before sanctioning a full imperial war effort (*Reichskrieg*).

Federalism and imperial absolutism threatened this emphasis on peaceful adherence to accepted norms and collective neutrality because they both contained elements of particularism inclined to belligerence. In an example of how German political development could move in contrary directions simultaneously, the IPO, which strengthened the traditional structure by checking the growth of imperial power, also gave federalism a boost by confirming princely territorial sovereignty (*Landeshoheit*). Full sovereignty was still reserved for the emperor, who continued to act for the *Reich* in dealing with foreign powers and retained an exclusive veto on all *Reichstag* decisions. Nonetheless, the princes were identified as the sole representative of their territories, excluding local bodies like the estates, which had previously claimed the right to conduct external relations. Moreover, territorial rulers were permitted to make treaties with foreign powers provided these were not directed against the emperor in imperial constitution, an arrangement that in fact merely endorsed existing practice but, in doing so, lent it greater legitimacy.

Confirmation of territorial sovereignty consolidated the princes' monopoly of domestic power but left their international status still in doubt. After Westphalia it was clear that late medieval concepts of inter-state relations based on universal monarchy and united Christendom had been replaced by a new system of independent sovereign powers, but it was far from clear whether these would relate to each other as equals or in some form of hierarchical order. The ambiguous status of the lesser German dynasties as autonomous vassals of a man still claiming European overlordship made their position acutely vulnerable. Increasingly, it seemed that possession of a royal title, whether created within the *Reich* or acquired by inheritance or conquest outside it, offered the surest way to securing a place alongside the other sovereign powers, and this explains what has been labelled the "monarchization" of German dynastic ambition in the later seventeenth century.[23]

Achievement of such goals, along with long-standing dynastic objectives of additional security, land and titles, required resource mobilization, in turn fuelling the process of territorialization and the growth of princely absolutism. Far from being the cut-price Louis XIX's of popular mythology, German princes did not seek political change in emulation of foreign models but refashioned their territories by internal administrative consolidation and exclusion of external influence only when they encountered obstacles to the achievement of their ambitions. None of these went as far as desiring full independence since even the strongest prince still derived his security and prestige from continued membership of a polity ruled by Europe's premier monarch. What each sought was an adjustment of the territorial and political balance in his favour whilst denying similar advantages to his rivals. As such, German princely ambitions tended to cancel each other out, not only neutralizing tensions undermining the *Reich* but also providing opportunities for a skilful emperor to manipulate their rivalry to his advantage. In the longer term, however, it proved difficult to contain all ambitions, particularly when weak emperors required princely assistance against internal or external foes. Since the *Reich* did not acquire new land, the aggrandizement of one prince could only come at the expense of others within the existing frontiers. Apart from the imperial knights the most vulnerable potential victims were the counts, imperial cities and ecclesiastical princes, all of whom had diminished in numbers since the late middle ages through incorporation within expanding secular principalities. The IPO sanctioned further territorial redistribution, including the secularization of many ecclesiastical territories.

Such changes weakened the traditional hierarchy by reducing its principal supporters and undermining imperial authority. The emperor's prestige and power rested on his ability to manage imperial politics without alienating too many princes at any one time. This depended in turn to a large extent on his continued respect for the weaker territories, which, despite the annexations, still held the majority in the *Reichstag* and *Kreis* Assemblies. They continued to look to him as impartial judge and supreme guardian and their support for him was conditional on his adherence to this ideal. Redistribution of lands and tittles by the emperor even to reward his supporters tended to damage his long-term interests by arousing the jealousy and fear of others, while there was no guarantee that those who had benefited from imperial favour would remain grateful for long. A good example is the transferral of the electoral title along with the principality of the Upper Palatinate from Friedrich V in 1623 to the duke of Bavaria, the chief German ally of the Habsburg emperor in the Thirty Years War. Not only did Bavaria retain its gains in 1648 but a new eighth title had to be created to compensate the Palatinate, thus consolidating the power of the electoral college as well as embittering the rival branches of the Wittelsbach dynasty ruling these two territories.

Attempts to exploit imperial prerogatives for Habsburg objectives also provoked a backlash from the princes who opposed it as a misuse of power. Even Catholic rulers became concerned during the Thirty Years War at Ferdinand II's exploitation of the imperial ban (*Reichsacht*) to outlaw his Protestant opponents and confiscate their property to reward his supporters. From 1636 the emperor had been obliged to consult the electors before issuing a ban without a formal trial, and in 1711 a new electoral capitulation extended this to include formal agreement from the *Reichstag*.[24]

Nonetheless, some form of imperial absolutism remained an option after 1648 despite the defeat of all attempts to impose it by force during the war. Full transition to direct rule was neither feasible nor considered but the gradual erosion of princely autonomy was well within the bounds of possibility, provided the emperor avoided rash, provocative acts. Though their position as elective monarchs inhibited consolidation of power, the Habsburg dynasty had continued to secure re-election by cultivating their German clientele and through the widespread appreciation of their role in holding back the Turks. Including the third of Hungary they had obtained in 1526, their possessions were already three times the size of those of their nearest rivals, the Hohenzollerns of Brandenburg-Prussia, who in turn enjoyed a similar advantage over the Bavarian Wittelsbachs, the next most powerful dynasty after 1648.[25] These assets gave the Habsburgs an undoubted edge in imperial politics but were still insufficient to support a separate Austrian identity in international politics. The dynasty's position as an European great power continued to depend on prestige of the imperial title and the limited access it provided to wider German resources, forcing the emperor to concentrate on rebuilding his influence within the *Reich* after 1648. This process has become known as the "imperial reaction", though recovery would be a more apt term, and its success by the mid-1680s signalled that the emperor's position was far from being in decline after the Thirty Years War.[26] Nonetheless, the recovery depended ultimately on the emperor's ability to reconcile his dynastic ambitions, often involving external territorial aggrandizement, with the wider imperial interest represented by the common desire for domestic peace and collective security. The tensions inherent in this relationship will form a major theme throughout this book.

The Kreise *and regional politics*

Imperial influence varied considerably within the *Reich* due to the uneven pattern of political development. Nowhere is this better illustrated than in the evolution of the *Kreise*, which were to play a major role in organizing defence and conflict resolution after the Thirty Years War.[27] Discussion of their institutions and territorial composition also serves to introduce the dynastic and regional politics that will feature later in this work.

The *Kreise* had been established during the era of imperial reform by dividing the territories into initially six, from 1512 ten, regions to maintain the public peace and resolve common problems. Their structure reproduced and thereby reinforced the basic constitutional equilibrium, bringing both the strengths and weaknesses of national politics. The emperor's co-ordinating role was duplicated at regional level by the presence of one, two or occasionally three *Kreis* executive princes (*Kreisausschreibenden Fürsten*), who acted as the conduit for all official correspondence between the member territories and higher institutions. They had limited powers of initiative of their own, particularly in emergencies, but their authority was balanced by the mass of the other territories represented at the *Kreis* Assembly (*Kreistag*).[28] The appointment of the *Kreis* military commander (*Kreisoberst*), along with nomination of the region's judges in the RKG and the subdivisions of tax and other burdens assigned it by the *Reichstag*, were all subject to approval from the Assembly. How this worked in practice depended on the territorial composition and geographical location of each *Kreis*, particularly as the formal structure evolved in response to circumstances, allowing for considerable variations across the *Reich*.

The *Kreise* had the potential to further any of the three possible directions for future political development. Where they functioned best and achieved their fullest institutional growth, they strengthened the traditional hierarchy by compelling disparate territories to work together within the constitutional framework. However, they could also become vehicles of imperial absolutism through their role as tax and recruiting districts, which might, over time, erode the separate identity of their weaker members. Equally, they could serve as a convenient framework to project the influence of one or two more dominant territories, particularly if their rulers held the executive posts.

The Habsburgs enjoyed considerable advantages within this structure. Maximilian I had only agreed to its establishment on the condition that his hereditary lands around Austria were grouped into their own distinct *Kreis*, later extended to include the enclaves in south-western Germany and the Breisgau region on the Rhine. The few other princes included within the

Kreis had been reduced to the status of Habsburg territorial nobility by 1648, except for the bishops of Trent and Brixen, who were in no position to sustain an independent institutional identity alone. The Bohemian crown lands, including Moravia and Silesia, were not incorporated within the *Kreis* structure when they were acquired by Maximilian's successor in 1526, reinforcing the gradual separation of Habsburg territories from the *Reich*. The IPO confirmed this by exempting all but a small part of Silesia from the religious safeguards provided for the Protestants, permitting the emperor to continue the process of Catholic confessionalization he deemed essential to entrench his power. Habsburg territories were also outside the jurisdiction of the imperial courts, and since the emperor was his own overlord, interference from other institutions was virtually nonexistent. Nonetheless, the formal existence of the Austrian *Kreis* was preserved as a useful point to influence imperial politics without having to intervene directly in the capacity as emperor. As the later discussion of the Association Movement will show, this was to prove valuable in harnessing the resources of southern and western territories to Habsburg strategic objectives.

The Habsburgs also controlled the Burgundian *Kreis*, although this had passed to the Spanish branch when Charles V partitioned his possessions in 1556. Indirect rule from Madrid merely widened the separation of these areas from the rest of the *Reich*, already under way during Charles's reign and reflected in their exclusion from the jurisdiction of the imperial courts in favour of subordination to a separate institution based at Mechelen. The Westphalian Settlement reinforced this trend by omitting the *Kreis* from the German peace, leading many princes to dispute whether it fully belonged to the *Reich*. Though this condition ceased upon termination of the Franco-Spanish hostilities in 1659, doubts continued as to whether the more vulnerable provinces west of Luxembourg were entitled to assistance under imperial collective security. French diplomats skilfully exploited these ambiguities to isolate these and the equally exposed province of Franche Comté to the south before the War of Devolution, 1667–8. Though defeated, Spain recovered most of its Burgundian territory thanks to the diplomatic intervention of the Triple Alliance of England, Sweden and the Dutch Republic. The Germans also began to appreciate the area's value as a buffer zone, as the French threat continued to escalate after 1668. The *Reichstag* formally acknowledged that the *Kreis* was entitled to help in 1674 and empowered Emperor Leopold I to protect it two years later. By that time, as we shall see in a later chapter, much of the territory had already been lost to France. The possibility that the Spanish Habsburgs might die out entirely raised the question of the inheritance of Burgundy along with their other possessions and encouraged hopes, particularly among the Wittelsbachs, of the creation of a new German kingdom within at least part of these lands. The War of the Spanish Succession determined that the entire area should go to Austria, but confirmation of Habsburg control was to prove a mixed blessing for the emperor, bringing responsibility for defence of this vulnerable frontier zone along with exclusive control over a second *Kreis*.

Politics in the eight remaining *Kreise* were complicated by the imperfect match between *Kreis* and territorial boundaries. Several important rulers held land in more than one *Kreis*, including a number of the ecclesiastical princes, who were permitted to rule more than one bishopric simultaneously. It became possible for even comparatively minor dynasties to raise their political profile by manipulating their influence within the *Kreis* structure, especially where they held territory qualifying for one of the executive positions. The Wittelsbachs held considerable territory in five different *Kreise*, but their division into several rival branches prevented their maximizing this potential. The Bavarian *Kreis* was predominantly in their hands, as the electorate covered two-thirds of the total surface area, and most of the other secular territory was held by the junior branches of Sulzbach and Neuburg. The elector's relations often ruled the small bishoprics of Regensburg, Freising and Passau, but the presence of the large archbishopric of Salzburg, often controlled by an Austrian candidate, along with a few minor territories like the City of Regensburg, ensured sufficient political momentum to sustain a separate *Kreis* identity beyond total Wittelsbach control.

Wittelsbach influence was also present in the Electoral Rhenish *Kreis* on the middle Rhine in the shape of the Palatinate, but it was counterbalanced by the three ecclesiastical electorates and the fact that Mainz had an exclusive monopoly of executive authority. Possession of the small principality of Simmern secured the family control over one of the two Upper Rhine executive positions alongside the bishop of Worms. However, though the Wittelsbachs also held three other Upper Rhenish principalities, the largest territorial block within the *Kreis* was held by the two Hessian landgraves in Kassel and Darmstadt. The duchy of Lorraine was larger still, but had been excluded like Burgundy from the Westphalian peace because it was an ally of Spain. This ended its effective membership of the *Kreis* though the others continued to press for its reincorporation until 1738. The fragmented area of Alsace immediately to the west of the Rhine was also formally part of the *Kreis* but lost this connection after 1648. Though only the Austrian parts of Alsace had been ceded to France at Westphalia, Cardinal Mazarin skilfully exploited ambiguities in the peace treaty to loosen the ties of the entire region with the *Reich*. Louis XIV was to continue this policy with greater violence once he assumed personal rule in 1661, restricting the Upper Rhenish *Kreis* to the area east of the river by 1681. The presence of a large number of small counties and cities provided the basis for a viable collective culture particularly as the growth of the French threat forced the larger principalities to co-operate.

A similar potential existed in the Westphalian (also Lower Rhenish) *Kreis*, where the Wittelsbachs also claimed an executive position as part of the Jülich-Cleves inheritance. Jülich had been a major power within the Lower Rhine in the sixteenth century, when it controlled the duchies of Cleves and Berg and the counties of Mark and Ravensberg, but the extinction of its ruling family in 1609 led to a dispute between the Pfalz-Neuburg branch of the Wittelsbachs and the Brandenburg Hohenzollerns over possession of these strategic areas. The tension contributed to the outbreak of the Thirty Years War and the subsequent internationalization of imperial politics through the foreign alliances struck by the contending parties, as Spain backed Catholic Pfalz-Neuburg, the Dutch supported Protestant Brandenburg. The former connection did not survive beyond the war, but the latter was cemented by dynastic ties between the Hohenzollerns and the princes of Orange, who had considerable influence within the Republic as well as German possessions in Westphalia and the Upper Rhine. The prolonged inheritance dispute neutralized the most important secular power within the *Kreis*, permitting the bishop of Münster to establish an executive "directory" over Westphalian affairs. Whether this could survive beyond 1648 depended, like the other regional power struggles, on the growing interaction between German and European politics.

This was particularly pronounced in northern Germany, where both Sweden and Denmark had secured considerable influence. Sweden's formal position as guarantor of the IPO was underpinned by possessions in all three northern *Kreise*, totalling 16,351 km^2, or an area larger than most electorates. In addition to Western Pomerania in the Upper Saxon *Kreis* and the principality of Verden in Westphalia, Sweden held Wismar and the former bishopric of Bremen, entitling it to a share in the Lower Saxon *Kreis* executive. Denmark failed to match Sweden's formal constitutional position but nonetheless held significant parts of Lower Saxony and Westphalia, where it inherited Oldenburg and Delmenhorst (together 1,700 km^2) in 1667. The Lower Saxon territory was spread throughout the three strategic duchies of Schleswig, Holstein and Gottorp, totalling 18,050 km^2, astride the Danish border with the *Reich*. Sovereignty was fragmented, with the Danish king ruling 5,800 km^2 of Holstein (including 3,850 km^2 within the *Reich*), while the duke of Gottorp held the rest, which formed the narrow peninsula between Scandinavia and the European mainland. Schleswig, which lay outside the *Reich* immediately to the north, was also split, with the king owning one-third directly and exercising overlordship over the remainder. Though thwarted during the Thirty Years War, Denmark retained ambitions to impose rule over the entire region, including reactivating ancient rights over the great port city of Hamburg.[29]

Brandenburg and the Guelph dukes of Lower Saxony were the chief German opponents of the two Scandinavian kingdoms. Brandenburg had benefited from Swedish patronage during the Thirty Years War, which had secured over 24,000 km^2 of additional territory. This included the former bishopric of Minden, which reinforced its growing influence in Westphalia, along with that of Halberstadt and expectancy on Magdeburg, which gave it a presence in Lower Saxony as well. The bulk of the gains fell within the Upper Saxon *Kreis*, where Eastern Pomerania was added to the Brandenburg heartland. However, the Swedes thwarted attempts to obtain Western Pomerania and encroached on the elector's possessions outside the *Reich* in East Prussia, which was earmarked for possible inclusion in their expanding Baltic empire.[30]

Nonetheless, Brandenburg expansion had been considerable and alarmed the Guelph dukes, whose substantial holdings were fragmented by frequent dynastic partitions. By 1635 they had split into three pieces of unequal size each inhabited by between 150,000 and 200,000 people in the late seventeenth century: Dannenberg line in Brunswick-Wolfenbüttel (3,828 km^2), Calenberg in Hanover (3,850 km^2) and Lüneburg in Celle (13,470 km^2). Though they had collaborated during the war they had not matched Brandenburg's gains, obtaining only partial control of the Lower Saxon bishopric of Osnabrück (2,750 km^2), assigned by the IPO to a junior Guelph branch in alternation with Catholic bishops elected by the cathedral chapter.[31] They continued to exercise a protectorate over the town of Hildesheim, where they protected the Protestant citizens from their Catholic bishop, but they failed in their efforts to convert this into full secularization and annexation.[32] Nonetheless, they remained the dominant force within Lower Saxony, where the senior branch always held one of the executive posts. The other was exercised by the administrator of Magdeburg, who was in no position to oppose them, while the only other substantial territory, the combined duchies of Mecklenburg, had been devastated by the war. Increasingly, the Guelphs were to see the *Kreis* as a convenient mechanism to extend their regional influence and as a bulwark against Brandenburg, Sweden and Denmark.

This attitude was shared by the Wettin elector of Saxony, who monopolized the Upper Saxon executive and had acted as the political leader of the German Protestants since the Reformation. Brandenburg's expansion hamstrung the *Kreis*, effectively reducing it to the lesser territories immediately to the northwest and southeast of the Saxon electorate. Many of these were ruled by the Ernestine branch of the Wettins, who had been deprived of the electoral title in 1547 when Charles V transferred it to their Albertine cousins.

21

Rivalry amongst the Wettins remained an obstacle to co-operation, but the *Kreis* structure retained value to all as a check on Hohenzollern influence.

Both Swabia and Franconia benefited from the absence of a single domi-nant territory. Württemberg covered nearly one-third of Swabia, and its duke held one of the two executive posts, but his power was counterbalanced by the collective influence of 96 other member territories who held the majority in the region's assembly. Periodic rivalry with the much smaller margraviate of Baden-Durlach prevented Württemberg from exercising exclusive leadership of the Protestant members, assisting both the Catholic bishop of Constance to retain his executive position and reducing the likelihood of a permanent split along confessional lines. Similar factors were at work in Franconia, where the two Hohenzollern branches ruling Ansbach and Bay-reuth alternately exercised a secular Protestant executive while the bishop of Bamberg held the Catholic position. The power of both executive princes was offset by the presence of the large bishopric of Würzburg along with over 20 smaller territories sustaining regular Assembly meetings and a vibrant political culture.

Imperial collective security to 1648

Such a culture was vital to the effective operation of collective security, which had been severely strained by the recent conflict. The war had inflicted considerable material damage and although earlier estimates of the population losses are exaggerated, the psychological impact left on the survivors was still profound.[33] There was an acute sense of vulnerability along with an overriding desire to avoid such devastation in the future.

War had to be tamed if it could not be eliminated in order to limit the misery and suffering it entailed. Foreign armies were to be banished from the *Reich* and constitutional safeguards were written into the IPO to this effect, forbidding the emperor from inviting external military assistance without *Reichstag* approval. The transit of German troops across territorial frontiers and their billeting in areas other than their homeland also needed to be regulated. Probably even more pressing was the need to find some way of financing war to replace the violent extortion known as "contributions", whereby an army threatened to burn entire settlements unless these provided for its material needs.[34]

The political controversy centred on how these objectives might be best achieved, with three competing solutions corresponding to the possible direc-tions for constitutional change. The emperor favoured a single national army under his direct control maintained by cash contributions from the princes either directly or through the *Kreise*. The rulers of the larger principalities had already begun to maintain small permanent forces of their own before 1648 and favoured combining these as a collective army sustained by payments from their weaker unarmed neighbours. The emperor's monarchical solution equated with imperial absolutism while the arguments of the armed princes were in line with the federalist political option. Both solutions were variants of security through deterrence since they relied on the construction of an effective monopoly of violence, either at national or territorial level, complete with an infrastructure of permanent armed forces.

The alternative of the lesser unarmed territories sought peace through a form of unilateral disarmament. Like the estates in most territories, the lesser princes argued that permanent forces encouraged war by arousing the fear and jealousy of neighbouring states. In their opinion, it was far better to avoid involvement in other people's quarrels and attend to the immediate task of postwar recovery. Should a neighbouring state attack the *Reich*, defence could be organized by reviving the existing system intended to mobilize soldiers to enforce verdicts of the imperial courts and uphold the internal public peace.

These mechanisms rested in the matricular system (*Matrikelwesen*), used since the early fifteenth century to apportion the common military and fiscal burdens amongst the territories.[35] Each ruler was enscribed on a list specifying the number of men he was obliged to contribute and their cash equivalent expressed as the monthly wage bill of 12 fl. for a cavalryman, 4 fl. for a foot soldier. The *Reichstag* periodically revised the list, with that prepared by the meeting at Worms in 1521 becoming the benchmark for all subsequent modifications.[36] Subject to agreement with the emperor, the *Reichstag* could summon the territories to provide men, money or a combination of both. Cash payments were measured in units called a Roman Month (RM, *Römer Monat*) after the monthly wage bill of the armed escort accompanying the emperor to the traditional coronation by the Pope. The standard figure was calculated against the 4,202 cavalry and 20,063 infantry on the 1521 Worms list and amounted to about 128,000 fl. The *Reichstag* could sanction any number of RMs as well as multiples of the basic troop quota (*Duplum, Triplum*, etc.).

Inclusion on the list came to be regarded as a sign of *Reichstandschaft* and areas that were omitted found it difficult to acquire a separate identity and representation at the *Reichstag*. However, those on the list had little desire to shoulder a larger share of the burden and often sought to have their existing obligations reduced. Such revisions were formally subject to *Reichstag* approval but were frequently enacted without permission, especially as the *Kreise* began setting their own regional versions of the national list, which often placed their collective total considerably below the original figure. This practice of "self-moderation" (*Selbst-Moderation*) helps explain why the actual strength of the imperial army (*Reichsarmee*) generally fell below what the *Reichstag* had sanctioned.

Deployment of this force against external opponents depended on the same mechanisms that regulated its use against internal lawbreakers. Chief amongst these was the 1555 Imperial Executive Ordinance (*Reichsexekutionsordung*), which provided for an incremental mobilization through the *Kreis* structure to enforce the public peace and implement verdicts of the imperial courts.[37] If the forces of one *Kreis* proved insufficient, the executive princes could either summon others to assist or appeal directly to the emperor and *Reichstag* to declare a national emergency. Since the 1570 *Reichstag* meeting adopted this procedure to cope with external threats, military initiatives could come from either *Kreis* or national level, though both the emperor and the *Kreis* executive princes were prohibited from mobilizing for offensive action.

These mechanisms had been formally endorsed by the IPO but their detailed revision had been postponed to the next *Reichstag*, officially due to meet within six months but which finally opened in Regensburg in 1653. By seeking to strengthen the traditional mobilization structure, the lesser princes were promoting their continued membership of the political hierarchy, where they shared power with their larger and better armed neighbours. The latter's preference for a collective army composed only of their contingents was based on arguments inimical to the spirit of the old constitution. In place of the traditional association of political power with territorial status, the armed princes related it to military might. Their proposals made sense militarily in that they would provide larger, permanent forces but they would also end the separate identity of the lesser territories, which would be inexorably reduced to the level of those towns and nobles already subject to the princes' authority and paying for their soldiers. The emperor's ideas had similar implications for all territorial rulers, whose continued autonomy would rest solely on whatever influence they could retain through the *Reichstag*.

Of the three solutions, the emperor's stood the least chance of realization after 1648, as all previous attempts to centralize military power in his hands had failed and any fresh effort was likely to further undermine his fragile authority. Consequently, he was reluctant to promote the monarchical solution in formal discussions at the *Reichstag*, preferring instead discreet bilateral negotiations with leading princes to secure immediate assistance and rebuild his influence. By expanding his informal clientele the emperor could create a network of alliances that might later form the basis of a more formal monopoly of military power. In the meantime his reluctance to engage in open discussions discouraged the lesser princes who traditionally looked to him to take the initiative and were in any case opposed to any measures that might add to the claims on their meagre resources. While the armed princes were happy to back anything that lent further legitimacy to their own militarization, they had no desire to start a process that might equally end in greater constitutional restraints on their autonomy. It was these factors rather than a general lack of patriotism so bemoaned by nineteenth-century commentators that account for the long delay in completing defence reform. It remained to be seen which solution would prevail and whether the *Reich* would adopt a uniform structure across its territories or, as ultimately proved the case, combine elements of more than one in an irregular hybrid. One thing was clear: the choice would determine the future of the constitution, its ability to withstand external pressures and the nature of German involvement in international affairs.

Chapter Two

From Westphalia to the Réunions, *1648–84*

The growth of territorial armies

Several rulers had maintained small numbers of troops even before 1618, but it was not until after the Peace of Westphalia that the first true territorial armies emerged alongside the larger forces that had long existed in the Habsburg lands. The appearance of these armies had significant consequences for all levels of imperial politics as well as changing German relations with neighbouring states. Territorial absolutism was entrenched at the expense of estates' privileges and local particularism, while the gap between the armed and unarmed princes replaced sectarianism as the main division within imperial politics. With absolutism came a new belligerence inimical to the traditional pacific culture and reflecting the princes' determination to secure international recognition of their autonomy and ambitions.

Habsburg dynastic weakness contributed to these developments by undermining their already vulnerable position within Germany. Emperor Ferdinand III still appeared powerful, mounting a magnificent display at the 1653–4 *Reichstag* and securing the electors' recognition of his eldest son, Ferdinand Maria, as king of the Romans (*Römischer König*), or heir apparent, on 31 March 1653. However, the king died of smallpox in July 1654, and though the emperor persuaded the Bohemians and Hungarians to accept his second son, 14-year-old Leopold Ignatius, as their monarch, there was no possibility of him ruling the *Reich* before his 18th birthday. When Ferdinand III himself died unexpectedly at the age of 50 on 2 April 1657, formal Habsburg power ceased and the *Reich* entered an interregnum until his second son was elected as Emperor Leopold I on 18th July 1658.[1] The presence of Louis XIV as a prospective alternative candidate allowed the electors to impose a particularly harsh capitulation, binding the new emperor even more tightly to the IPO.

Leopold's unreserved acceptance of these conditions signalled a significant change in Habsburg management of imperial politics. Rather than seeking to overturn the constitution, the emperor now tried to work within it, manipulating its ambiguities and exploiting princely rivalry to enhance his practical power. These tactics required patience at a time when an uncertain international situation placed mounting demands on Habsburg resources and threatened to push Leopold into greater dependency on the militarizing princes. The result was a window of opportunity during which those princes who enjoyed certain strategic and material advantages were able to increase their power at the expense of local institutions and their weaker neighbours. Though this process threatened key elements of the *Reich*, contributing to a serious crisis after the start of the Dutch War in 1672, there were already signs that the chances for radical change were diminishing. The partial resolution of these tensions in a series of compromises in 1679–84 closed the window by reaffirming the traditional political hierarchy and its emphasis on adherence to established norms. Nonetheless, the intervening growth of the armed princes established a momentum that, though slowed, could not be reversed and ultimately contributed to the final disintegration of the *Reich* in 1806.

The armies that were created in this period contained structures that could trace their origins to the late fifteenth century and combined fortified installations, paid professional garrison troops and feudal levies. These elements were primarily defensive, reflecting not only the inability of any ruler to maintain large, combat-ready field forces, but the deeply rooted belief that starting offensive wars was un-Christian.[2] Campaigns to punish wrongdoers or fight the infidel Turk were mounted by mobilizing the levies, stiffened with additional mercenaries. The latter became more important with the spread of new weapons technology requiring large disciplined bodies of troops to be truly effective.[3] However, such professionals were expensive, and princes pressed their estates to increase their tax grant to cover the escalating costs of war. Old feudal obligations were gradually reworked, transforming limited personal service by noble vassals and peasants into either cash payments or enlistment in militias organized and trained to use the new tactics. Militiamen were embodied as emergency field units to supplement the mercenaries or, as they were increasingly from the 1660s, used as a recruitment pool for what were becoming permanent field formations. The mercenaries, meanwhile, were subjected to greater central control by subordinating the private military contractors, or "enterprizers", who recruited them, to princely authority.[4] Experienced contractors were retained on a semi-permanent basis in many larger territories from the early sixteenth century, either to ensure their services in the advent of a major war or to drill the remodelled militias. Frequently, small bodies of professional soldiers were also paid to garrison strategic castles and guard the magnificent new residences many princes were constructing to symbolize their growing power.

A basic pattern was in place by the 1590s and served as the core of the forces that fought the Thirty Years War. Large territories like the secular electorates already maintained small bodyguard and garrison companies that could be expanded, by inducting militiamen or recruiting additional mercenaries, to serve in offensive operations as field regiments. A minimum level of permanent defence was provided in both large and small territories by the trained militias, which could be mobilized to repel attacks or the transit of foreign troops by ringing the church bells. The estates generally contributed to the upkeep of the militia, though the local communities were often expected to bear part of the cost directly, while most princes maintained their professional forces from their domainal income. Old feudal obligations often still existed formally, including that of mass mobilization (*Landsturm*) as a last resort along with personal service by the nobility as cavalrymen (*Lehns-* or *Ritterpferde*). Although the latter was incapable of producing effective forces, the nobility jealously guarded this right as a defence of their traditional privileges and an excuse to avoid paying taxes.

Only the emperor had significant permanent forces before 1618, giving the Habsburgs the dubious distinction of founding the first German standing army, later claims by Prussian historians notwithstanding. In addition to a permanent militia organization along the eastern military frontier (*Militärgrenze*) with the Turks, the emperor maintained permanent garrison regiments in his Hungarian and Austrian fortresses from the 1580s. Other small field units existed, including the cavalry formations generally lacking in other territories, along with considerable stocks of weapons and artillery, a naval detachment on the Danube and a permanent administrative staff attached to the Court War Council (*Hofkriegsrat*).[5]

These forces were expanded after the outbreak of hostilities in 1618 by engaging military contractors like the famous Albrecht von Wallenstein to raise new regiments. Though Wallenstein was eventually murdered on the emperor's orders in 1634 when it was feared he might defect to the enemy, most contractors were already part of the Habsburg clientele bound to the emperor by ties other than cash payment. As they were slowly transformed into professional officers serving the state, they were joined by a growing number of the territorial nobility, who were gradually reconciled to the presence of a permanent Habsburg army by the career prospects and material rewards it offered. The same process took place in the other German territories that engaged actively in the war, regardless of which side they chose.

Attempts to integrate these other forces within a single imperial army failed despite a partial success in the Peace of Prague in 1635. The need to implement the Westphalian Settlement, together with the urgency of economic recovery, forced demobilization and partial disbandment of all territorial forces after 1648. The Bavarian army, which, at a peak of about 20,000 effectives, had been the largest and best of all non-Habsburg forces, was reduced to a few bodyguard and garrison companies, as were those of Saxony, Hessen-Kassel and the Guelph duchies, which had also mustered considerable numbers. Brandenburg, which had reorganized and increased its field forces from 1644, disbanded most of its regiments, especially the expensive cavalry, in 1649. Though Frederick William, later to be known as the Great Elector, still had more soldiers than any other prince, they did not yet constitute a permanent army. There was no unified organization as most of the remaining regiments had been reduced to a cadre of one or two companies and distributed amongst the provinces that maintained them. Combination of these garrisons into a single force, like the political integration of the Brandenburg-Prussian state, was a slow process that was only really begun in the mid-1650s.[6]

The Habsburg monarchy was characterized by a similar political fragmentation but in contrast retained a permanent army. The field forces under the emperor's direct command, which had numbered 37,000 effectives late in 1648, were reduced, but still totalled 25,000 in September 1650, rising again to over 30,000 by 1657. Moreover, these remained grouped into regiments already established before 1648, while the army remained supported by garrisons, naval forces and a permanent administrative infrastructure.[7]

Within six years of the Peace of Westphalia about ten territories were maintaining permanent forces of at least 1,000 men or more. By comparison, France still maintained 50,000 in 1665 even after considerable reductions from a wartime peak of 125,000 effectives. Nonetheless, the German totals were up to ten times what they had been before 1618 and represented a greater burden to what were much smaller territories. Moreover, most continued to expand into the 1660s. Though Lorraine ceased to be a significant military power by 1654, Münster emerged alongside Brandenburg and the Guelph duchies as a territory capable of fielding 18,000–20,000 men, though its average strength was closer to 5,000. Bavaria, Saxony and the Palatinate each had 3,000–5,000 more or less permanently under arms by the mid-1660s and retained the capacity to double this in an emergency with additional recruits and embodied militia. Pfalz-Neuburg and Holstein-Gottorp both had 1,000–2,000, while other middling secular principalities like Hessen-Kassel, Mecklenburg-Schwerin and the Ernestine duchies were beginning to add to their garrison companies.[8] Most imperial cities also maintained permanent infantry companies, though only Hamburg and to a lesser extent Nuremberg and Frankfurt ever had much more than 1,000 men at any one time.[9] In contrast to their later image as unmilitarized backwaters, several ecclesiastical states were at the forefront of these developments, with Mainz and Cologne emerging alongside Münster as those maintaining the most powerful forces. Both electorates were linked by personal rule to other bishoprics, expanding their resource base and permitting the maintenance of 1,000–2,000 men by the 1660s along with the construction of modern fortifications.[10]

The emergence of these armies depended on the princes' ability to secure regular funding from their estates, since traditional domainal income was insufficient, even in an area like Brandenburg where it represented a third of central government revenue. The estates generally opposed demands for increased military expenditure, not because they were insensitive to the presence of external dangers, but from a mixture of self-interest and political conviction. Their position within each territory and the wider imperial constitution rested on their ability to extract concessions from their prince in return for tax grants. If these grants were increased or, worse, became permanent, the estates would lose their main bargaining counter and with it their members' influence in local and territorial affairs. Like the lesser rulers in the wider national debate on defence reform, the estates based their position on tradition and the observance of ancient charters, looking to the emperor and imperial courts to protect these and punish princely transgressions. In contrast, the princes rested their case on expediency, emphasizing that the needs of the moment should take precedence over outdated customs and inappropriate practices. Both positions were elitist since both claimed they were the best judge of the common good, but whereas the estates argued that decisions should be taken in consultation with them, the princes claimed an absolute and exclusive right to determine what was necessary.[11]

Though they advocated change, the princes remained within the same broadly conservative philosophical framework as their estates so that a consensus remained possible. Moreover, the princes also looked to the emperor and imperial constitution to legitimize their accumulation of military power, arguing their forces were necessary to fulfil their obligations to uphold the public peace and contribute to collective security. Soldiers were often designated as *Kreistruppen* while performing police actions within the *Kreis* structure or forming part of a regional contingent to the *Reichsarmee*, even though they were in fact *Haustruppen*, or the household troops of the prince, who often referred to them as his private property (*Eigentum*).[12]

Local struggles between rulers and estates over access to territorial resources were thus linked to national politics by the princes' efforts to legitimize their own militarization within wider revisions to collective security. They scored a partial success at the 1653–4 *Reichstag* in Regensburg despite the general failure to agree a definitive reform. The concluding document was known as the latest imperial recess (*Jüngster Reichsabschied*, JRA) because the next meeting of the *Reichstag*, which opened in 1663, remained permanently in session.[13] Paragraph 180 of the JRA strengthened the princes' arguments by establishing a formal obligation of all territorial subjects to contribute taxes towards the upkeep of "necessary fortresses, fortified places and [their] garrisons".

The estates could no longer refuse all requests for military funding, but the deliberately vague wording permitted them to play a role in fixing the precise levels of funding and allowed the emperor to intervene when they could not agree. Moreover, by specifying only defensive installations and forces required to fulfil imperial obligations, the JRA denied the princes a firm basis for larger forces capable of independent action.

Renewed international tension increased the uncertainty of their position. The Swedes attacked the city of Bremen in 1654 in an unsuccessful attempt to deprive it of its autonomy and incorporate it into their own Lower Saxon territory. This was followed by the outbreak of a general Northern War in 1655 (see p. 35, this volume) at a time when the French and Spanish were still fighting in the Burgundian *Kreis*. The princes responded by forming alliances, either through the existing framework of the *Kreise* or by direct bilateral agreements. These were intended to enhance mutual security against external dangers and possible imperial absolutism, as well as providing a vehicle to carry demands for further constitutional revisions in their favour. The Habsburg dynastic crisis strengthened their position and the electors were able to insert further restrictions on the estates' rights of assembly into Leopold's capitulation in 1658. His election also saw the formation of the French-sponsored Rhenish Alliance (*Rheinbund*) led by the influential Johann Philipp von Schönborn, who, as elector of Mainz, was a natural focal point for princely interests (see Chapter 5). In addition to establishing its own assembly and defence structure independent of the formal institutions, the Alliance provided a framework for princely collaboration at the expense of their estates. Its collapse by 1668 encouraged the emergence of a new group known as the "Extensionists" (*Extendisten*) because they wished to widen the legislation of 1654 and 1658 to remove all restraints on the princely monopoly of taxation. Joined by Bavaria, Cologne, Brandenburg, Pfalz-Neuberg and Mecklenburg-Schwerin, the group carried the *Reichstag*, which endorsed their proposals. After this was vetoed by Leopold in 1671 the members agreed to establish a common force of 20,000 men to crush potential opposition within their territories and reinforce their lobbying of the emperor.[14]

These developments were accompanied by an escalating use of force within territorial politics, as the armed princes deployed troops to collect taxes and subdue recalcitrant towns and provinces. Christoph Bernhard von Galen, the belligerent bishop of Münster 1650–78, besieged his capital city twice in 1655, again in 1657 and finally successfully in 1661 with the help of the Rhenish Alliance.[15] Schönborn also called on Alliance support to deprive the enclave of Erfurt of its autonomy from Mainz control in 1664. The Guelph dukes assembled no less than 20,000 men and 100 cannon in June 1671 to bombard their town of Brunswick, which had refused to submit to their direct authority. These operations, along with the better-known use of force by the Great Elector against the East Prussian estates in 1661–3 and the city of Magdeburg in 1666, all ended in princely victories.[16]

Yet the appearance of violent arbitrary action is deceptive, and force proved a poor vehicle to impose absolutism. Schönborn's troops fled in their first attempt to seize Erfurt in 1663, while it had taken Galen over four years to break Münster's resistance. Military action was accompanied by concerted campaigns to sway public opinion and win diplomatic backing. Imperial support proved an essential prerequisite in each case, except East Prussia, which lay outside the *Reich*, and even here the Great Elector waited until after he had won full sovereignty from Poland to preclude the possibility of an appeal to Warsaw. Brandenburg repression in Cleves and Mark only proved successful after its alliance with the House of Orange in 1655 removed Dutch backing for the estates, and within eight months its troops had collected 300,000 tlr from the local population.[17] This represented a major gain, but in most cases direct military intervention brought only modest returns. The civic autonomy wrested from Münster, Erfurt, Magdeburg and Brunswick had never enjoyed firm foundation in imperial law and all were left with many of their local privileges intact. The Great Elector did not abolish the estates in his various provinces, but merely modified their constitutions, and even temporarily reduced taxes in East Prussia after 1663. Bargains, such as that struck with the Brandenburg estates in 1653, along with the co-option of their members and their integration into princely patronage networks, proved a more effective means of securing funding and advancing absolute rule.

The revival of the imperial courts after 1670 enhanced the ability of the emperor to intervene in local affairs and helped secure the survival of those estates that chose to oppose their prince. The long-term consequence, however, was to strengthen the German territorial state by forcing it to rely on nonviolent means to extend its authority. These tended to broaden its social base and make it more responsive to popular demands, even though it lacked a formal framework for democratic representation. Socially conservative and not without its critics, this German form of benevolent authoritarianism nonetheless remained sufficiently flexible to survive even beyond the Reich into the nineteenth century.

The use of force beyond territorial boundaries was also limited by practical and constitutional constraints. Despite the proliferation of forces, armed conflict between princes was rare and most preferred arbitration through the imperial courts to resolve their disputes. There were only two serious clashes before the early eighteenth century and both occurred prior to the revival of the imperial constitution from the 1670s.

The first centred on the disputed Jülich-Cleves inheritance in Westphalia and was begun by the Great Elector in 1651. Brandenburg had acquired Cleves, Mark and Ravensberg by 1614, but Pfalz-Neuburg still held Jülich and Berg along with the *Kreis* executive post. Though Frederick William eventually mobilized 16,000 men, he was only able to deploy 3,800 in the immediate vicinity, while Neuburg mustered 12,000. The conflict threatened to escalate as the duke of Lorraine backed Neuburg while the Orangist faction agitated for Dutch intervention in support of Brandenburg. However, actual operations were relatively bloodless, leading to the contemporary label "Düsseldorf Cow War", while the still-united Jülich-Cleves estates refused financial assistance to both sides. Brandenburg was forced to back down and the conflict was defused by imperial mediation. Further bilateral negotiations led to a split of the inheritance along the territorial *status quo* in 1666, lead-ing to the emergence of a *de facto* third Westphalian executive post for Brandenburg as well as joint co-operation to break estates' opposition to military taxation.[18]

Negotiation also resolved the second conflict, though less satisfactorily for the contending parties. Known as the Wildfang Dispute, the violence had its origins in a prolonged struggle for influence on the middle Rhine that initially involved Mainz and the Palatinate, began in 1651 and rendered the Electoral Rhenish *Kreis* inoperative until 1695. Backed by Lorraine and other lesser Rhenish territories, Schönborn launched an attack in 1665 that was intended to secure his hold on his secondary bishopric of Worms. A series of inter-mittent clashes followed until 1668 without either side achieving a decisive advantage. Franco-Swedish diplomatic intervention imposed a preliminary settlement, but the real reason for the end to violence was mounting fear of Louis XIV and greater trust in the imperial courts.[19]

If the *Reich* managed to limit the spread of violence within its frontiers, it found it impossible to prevent it emanating beyond them. The growth of extraterritorial violence stemmed from a coincidence of international and German factors. No territory, not even Austria, was capable of beginning a major war on its own but many were valued as potential allies by foreign powers engaged in their own conflicts and prepared to pay cash or offer a share in the spoils. These were the origins of what has come to be known as the German "soldier trade" (*Soldatenhandel*), a misnomer for what was a political relationship, where the financial element was primarily intended to subsidize the cost of military involvement rather than bring a profit.[20] Foreign powers had recruited soldiers in Germany since the early sixteenth century, though this was illegal without imperial permission, and was generally opposed by the princes, who needed all potential recruits for their own armies. France began payments to a number of Rhenish princes in the 1650s as part of its moves to win backing against a potential Habsburg revival, but the first treaty for offensive purposes was made by England with Münster on 13 June 1665.

At war with the Dutch since the previous year, Charles II wanted Galen's assistance to open a second front against the Republic by invading it from the east. Though the English promised £500,000, money was not Galen's primary motive since he was already opposed to the Dutch over frontier disputes and their support for the city of Münster.[21] Hoping to annex and re-Catholicize eastern Holland, the bishop invaded with 20,000 men in September. The Dutch responded by hiring 24,000 Brandenburg and Guelph troops, who massed on Münster's eastern frontier in March 1666 while France, then an ally of the Republic, moved reinforcements through Liege with the blessing of its ruler, Elector Max Heinrich of Cologne. In what was to become a feature of such arrangements, England failed to pay its subsidies in full and even made one instalment in the form of a shipload of lead. Galen extorted additional "contributions" from the Dutch provinces of Gröningen and Overijssel, but was clearly unable to continue the war against the opposition of his own cathedral chapter and the appearance of the Republic's auxiliaries. Though England fought on until July 1667, Münster made peace at Cleves on 18 April 1666, agreeing to reduce his army to 3,000 garrison troops.[22]

The bishop's reverse did not discourage him or his fellow rulers; on the contrary, German involvement in international conflict continued to increase, and Münster itself was one of the signatories to a string of treaties negotiated by French diplomats in 1667 to isolate the Spanish Netherlands as the intended target of Louis XIV's first major war. Like those with Pfalz-Neuburg, Mainz, Cologne and Brandenburg, Münster's new treaty was defensive, binding it only to hold troops in readiness to prevent possible Austrian assistance from entering the Burgundian *Kreis*. Nonetheless, these arrangements signalled a new departure for France, which had previously pursued a policy of containing the emperor by sponsoring large princely leagues anchored on the imperial constitution like the Rhenish Alliance. The switch to bilateral treaties gave French diplomats greater scope to tailor arrangements to suit their master's expanding ambitions. Spanish military preparations included the transfer into their own army of eight of the regiments Galen had been obliged to disband in 1666, along with the temporary hire of Celle auxiliaries in 1667–8, while Hanover and Osnabrück together provided 4,614 men to reinforce the Dutch as they joined Sweden and England in applying diplomatic pressure on France to abandon its operations in Flanders in 1668.[23]

The Northern War, 1655–60

Though they only remained the spear carriers of the great powers, the participation of the German princes in these conflicts indicated their growing political and military autonomy. The emergence of the territorial armies added to the pressures on the new emperor, whose election already coincided with a crisis on the *Reich*'s eastern frontier, as first Poland collapsed in the Northern War and then the Turks attacked Habsburg Hungary in 1663. These problems presented a severe test for the unreformed mechanism of conflict resolution and collective security, and though the *Reich* emerged relatively unscathed, the position of both Austria and Brandenburg underwent a significant transformation.

The Polish crisis was the direct result of the first German prince to succeed to a foreign throne.[24] Karl Gustav from the Kleeburg branch of the Palatine Wittelsbachs had been Swedish commander in the *Reich* before 1648 and became King Charles X following the abdication of Queen Christina in July 1654. Known as 'the northern Alexander', he was determined to consolidate Sweden's hold on the southern Baltic shore by closing the gap between the existing possessions in Pomerania and Livonia (modern Latvia) at the expense of the intervening Brandenburg and Polish territory. Coinciding with a Cossack revolt and a separate Russian attack in the east, the Swedish onslaught early in 1655 appeared to the Poles as "the Deluge", washing away their defences and precipitating a period of internal chaos.

Poland was nearly as large as the *Reich* and its imminent collapse threatened to create a power vacuum capable of destabilizing the whole of central Europe. The Great Elector was acutely vulnerable since his duchy of East Prussia outside the *Reich* was a dependency of the Polish crown, which he was obliged to assist. Military intervention was extremely risky because, despite the recent tax grant by his estates, the elector could only muster 8,000 men by September 1655, equivalent to less than a quarter of the Swedish force currently in Poland. Attempts to mediate a solution were brushed aside by the belligerents but at least met a sympathetic response in Vienna, where Habsburg ministers were growing alarmed, particularly as Transylvanian intervention in 1657 in support of the Swedes threatened to provoke a hostile Turkish response.

Faced with Polish reprisals for his continued inaction, Frederick William bowed to Swedish pressure and entered the war in support of Charles X. Subsequently praised as an astute move leading to East Prussia's independence, the Great Elector's action was more one of desperation and weakness than strength and cunning. Mobilization of peasant militiamen boosted the Brandenburg army to 27,000 by 1660, but this was still too small to play a fully independent role in the quarrels of major powers, especially as funding was far from secure. Nonetheless, Brandenburg intervention in June 1656 contributed to the Swedish victory at Warsaw the following month, raising the possibility that the Poles might be completely defeated. Alarmed, Russia temporarily changed sides in an arrangement brokered by the Austrians, who also promised limited military assistance for Poland. Meanwhile, Denmark and the Dutch Republic sent a fleet to the Baltic to protect the semi-autonomous port city of Danzig in a move that also threatened Charles X's communications with his homeland.[25]

The two major German princes were now allied to opposing parties in an international conflict that appeared to be sweeping westwards on to German soil. In autumn 1656 the Russians attacked East Prussia in an operation likened by contemporaries to a second invasion of the Huns. Meanwhile 3,000 Polish cavalry broke over the river Oder to raid Brandenburg itself. Faced with defeats in the east and Danish intervention in the west, Charles X pulled out of Poland to concentrate on a lightning strike against Denmark to gain mastery of the Sound. An alliance was struck with the duke of Holstein-Gottorp promising him full independence from Danish control in return for military assistance.[26] Charles struck in February 1658, crossing the frozen Baltic to attack Copenhagen, forcing the Danes to grant full sovereignty to the Gottorp parts of Schleswig as well as abandon the war.

However, the campaign left Charles weak elsewhere and he had been compelled to concede sovereignty to East Prussia by the Treaty of Labiau on 20 November 1656, reversing an earlier arrangement whereby the Great Elector transferred overlordship from Poland to Sweden. Frederick William now sought to escape Swedish domination altogether and reduced his involvement throughout 1657, particularly as 12,000 Austrians had arrived in Poland. Conscious of the need to retain the favour of key princes during the imperial interregnum, Austrian diplomats negotiated the Treaty of Wehlau on 19 September 1657 whereby Poland accepted an "eternal alliance" in place of its former overlordship over East Prussia. Following another treaty at

Bromberg in November, Brandenburg changed sides and joined the Poles in attacking Swedish positions in Pomerania. A further bargain was struck on 15 February 1658, when Frederick William traded his vote for Leopold in return for 10,000 Austrians to assist the 15,000 Brandenburgers and 3,000 Poles in Western Pomerania.

Though the recently formed Rhenish Alliance co-operated with the Guelphs in declaring most of Lower Saxony neutral, it proved impossible to prevent the conflict spreading to Mecklenburg and Holstein-Gottorp, particularly as the emperor himself was now a belligerent. People fled the area in terror as conditions returned to those experienced during the Thirty Years War. Denmark rejoined the war, overrunning Holstein-Gottorp in 1658 with Brandenburg and Austrian assistance, while Dutch and English warships re-entered the Baltic to block Swedish reinforcements. Leopold increased his forces to over 14,000 in 1659, hoping to drive the Swedes out of Germany before a Franco-Spanish peace enabled Louis XIV to intervene. Although a Swedish counterattack on East Prussia was repulsed, neither the Austro-Brandenburg forces nor their Danish and Polish allies could achieve decisive victory elsewhere. The conclusion of the Peace of the Pyrenees between France and Spain in November 1659 removed any chance of success, as Louis threatened to send 30,000 troops to support the Rhenish Alliance's efforts to restore peace to the north of the *Reich*.

As the Dutch withdrew their support for the Danes, the anti-Swedish alliance fell apart, and Frederick William had to relinquish hopes of acquiring Sweden's German possessions. French mediation secured the Peace of Oliva in May 1660, confirming sovereignty for both East Prussia and Gottorp-Schleswig but otherwise restoring the *status quo*. The retention of Swedish Pomerania by either Austria or Brandenburg would have placed the Westphalian Settlement in question, and the reluctance of the major powers to countenance this indicated that none was yet prepared to tolerate significant changes within the *Reich*. Austrian intervention had failed to improve Leopold's position in contrast to Frederick William, who had demonstrated Brandenburg military potential as well as secured East Prussia as an independent state. However, the war had drained the resources of both and indicated that neither could yet act independently in international affairs. French prestige had been enhanced within the *Reich* through Louis's role as a peacemaker, while the internationalization of imperial politics continued with the subsequent Anglo-Swedish guarantee for Holstein-Gottorp's territorial integrity in 1665 to counter potential Danish revanchism. Leopold's position declined still further as he became involved in the Transylvanian civil war after 1659 and so slid towards renewed confrontation with the Turks.

The Turkish War of 1663–4 and the Eternal Reichstag

The prolonged struggles known as the Turkish Wars (*Türkenkriege*) had been an important part of imperial politics since the collapse of Hungary as an independent buffer between the *Reich* and the expanding Ottoman empire. The Habsburgs were now responsible for Christian Europe's front line, defending not only their own hereditary lands in Austria but also Royal or western Hungary, which they secured when the rest of the kingdom fell to the Turks in 1526. Neither Christian or Islamic philosophy accepted the possibility of peace with the infidel, resulting in a semi-permanent state of war. Conflicts were only broken off, not terminated, so that when the last major war came to an end in 1606, the Treaty of Szitva Török regarded operations involving less than 5,000 men as not breaching the truce. Though the Turks refrained from renewing full hostilities during the Thirty Years War, constant skirmishing on the Hungarian frontier placed a strain on Habsburg resources.

Balkan politics added to the prevailing uncertainty.[27] Ottoman conquests had been rapid in the sixteenth century, partly because they did not destroy indigenous political and religious structures but incorporated them into their system of rule. Although the Hungarian and Serbian political elites were crushed or driven out, the Catholic and Orthodox Church leaders remained, retaining their authority and autonomy in return for acting as intermediaries for the new government. In Transylvania, Moldavia and Wallachia, the rulers and local elites were also retained in return for annual tribute to the sultan. The position of these Christian elites was ambiguous. Though many looked to the emperor (and later the Russian tsar) as a potential liberator, few were prepared to exchange the relatively loose Turkish control for Habsburg absolutism. Transylvania in particular enjoyed special privileges, including its own estates, thanks partly to its strategic situation between Poland and the Turkish and Habsburg parts of Hungary. Meanwhile, the nobles of Habsburg Royal Hungary tended to look to the Prince of Transylvania or even the Ottoman pasha of Turkish Hungary as guardians of their traditional constitution with its elective monarchy and right to resist tyranny. The intrusion of the Habsburgs thus represented what Orest Subtelny aptly describes as a clash of two opposing political philosophies.[28] On the one hand there was absolutism based on an organizing principle whose chief goal was power regulated by hierarchy and rational rules. On the other lay the indigenous estates system embodying an associative principle whose aim was the welfare of the privileged elites.

These tensions overlapped the eastern frontier of the *Reich* due to the cultural affinity amongst Austrian, Bohemian, Hungarian and even Polish nobles, was reinforced by the spread of Protestantism by the early seventeenth century, and helped start the Thirty Years War with the Bohemian revolt in 1618. Protestantism and noble particularism were brutally suppressed in Austria, Bohemia and Moravia, following the Habsburg victory on the White Mountain outside Prague in 1620, and the property of rebel noblemen was redistributed to Catholic loyalists to extend the basis of Habsburg support. However, there were limits to the consolidation of Habsburg executive power and the Bohemian and Moravian estates only received "renewed constitutions" rather than outright abolition. Consolidation of power through political centralization and Catholic confessionalization continued after 1648 as Leopold intensified Ferdinand III's efforts to subordinate the still largely Calvinist Magyar nobility.[29]

The emperor's position in the east thus represented an area where imperial and dynastic interests could coincide but one where defeat could also spell disaster. The presence of the "hereditary enemy of Christianity" so close to Vienna provided a major reason for the *Reich*'s existence and the emperor's authority within it. From Luther onwards, Protestant and Catholic clerics had propagandized against the Turks, encouraging the popular cliché of them as bloodthirsty infidels who murdered children and enslaved entire populations.[30] In an age where imperial generals could seriously consider liberating Jerusalem, the Turkish Wars took the character of Europe's last crusade. Though the absence of an active Turkish threat after 1606 had given the emperor a freer hand during the Thirty Years War, it also undermined German support for him. The renewed Ottoman advance in 1663 re-awakened German fears and permitted Leopold to assume the traditional imperial function as defender of Christendom, a task that he not only took seriously through personal conviction but one which re-emphasized the pan-European pretensions of his imperial title.

However, it seemed that even with divine blessing victory would prove hard to achieve. The Turks remained fearsome opponents despite the incipient decline of their political and military institutions. Even when this became obvious after the great Christian victory in 1683, German soldiers continued to fear the Ottomans as almost superhuman, although the growing overconfidence amongst Habsburg commanders led them to underestimate Turkish resilience. The geography and climate of the region added to the difficulties. The Hungarian Great Plain that stretched east and south from the Habsburg frontier was an arid and inhospitable environment at this time. A surgeon in the Brandenburg corps in 1686 described it as "a wilderness . . . for 30 miles and more there would be neither town nor village, and the grass was as tall as a man, so that we often had to clear a path for ourselves. As for the countryside it was full of wild dogs, which attacked men and cattle just as wolves do".[31]

Each spring and summer, as the mountain snows melted, the rivers draining into the Plain turned one-third of its area into malaria-infested swamp, generally killing a third or more of the undernourished soldiers who had the misfortune to serve there. Keeping the others alive proved even harder than in the west, as it was impossible to seize supplies in an area where banditry and cattle breeding were the mainstay of the local economy. Only 5 per cent of Hungary was arable land compared with 45 per cent of France, and there were only 9 to 10 inhabitants per km^2 in contrast to 37 in the *Reich*.[32]

Leopold encountered these problems as soon as he began his interference in Transylvania. Intending to curb Ottoman influence in this strategic principality on his northeastern frontier, he sent Marshal Montecuccoli and 15,000 men to support his own candidate as prince in September 1661. Decimated by dysentery, Montecuccoli's army proved no match for the Turkish counter-attack, which escalated to open war by April 1663. The situation became critical. The remaining Habsburg regular forces barely totalled 28,000, of whom only 12,000 could be deployed in Hungary, and even when backed by 15,000 "Insurrectionists" (Magyar feudal levies) were no match for the Turkish field army swollen to 100,000 by the arrival of Moldavian, Wallachian and Tatar auxiliaries. By August the Habsburgs had been driven from Royal Hungary and 70,000 people fled Vienna as panic spread throughout southern and eastern Germany.[33] As conditions worsened, Leopold became increasingly vulnerable to pressure from the princes, who, rallied by Schönborn, made their military assistance dependent on convening a new *Reichstag*. Scheduled for June 1662, this finally met on 20 January 1663 when it became clear that it could no longer be postponed. Exploiting his capacity as imperial chancellor to subvert procedural rules, Schönborn tabled reform of collective security for discussion alongside Leopold's simple call for cash contributions. Using the existing military framework of the Alliance as a model for a new army independent of direct imperial command, Schönborn proposed revising the matricular system to support a force of 4,000 cavalry and 10,000 infantry controlled by a war council of all imperial estates to be based in Frankfurt. Discussions were complicated by the parallel issue of a permanent electoral capitulation. Designed to fix the powers of all future emperors in a single document, it pushed by the Protestants, who threatened to withdraw unless it was considered.

Leopold was ill-prepared, having failed to sound out the key princes in private before the meeting convened. The panic following the rapid Turkish advance in July 1663 transformed the situation, and even the French envoys no longer believed the emperor was merely trying to turn the crisis to his advantage.[34] Leopold was compelled to compromise, agreeing to the Rhenish Alliance's terms on 11 July permitting the members to field their contingents as a separate army, which was immediately sent to the front. Louis XIV was included in these arrangements, contributing a contingent as an Alliance member rather than as a full belligerent, allowing him to honour his credentials as Most Christian King without formally breaking his *détente* with the sultan. In doing so he publicly humiliated the emperor, who was now seen as dependent on French help: to make sure everyone got the point, Louis unilaterally increased his contribution to 6,000 men including 300 aristocratic volunteers with the cavalry.

Meanwhile, the issue of reform remained stalled at the *Reichstag*, as many of the weaker territories opposed Schönborn's plan as too expensive, preferring instead the 1555 executive ordinance as a basis for mobilization against an external threat. Since Leopold was unwilling to divulge what plan he favoured, the *Reichstag* refused to make a decision. In a brilliant piece of stage management, Leopold broke the deadlock by arriving in person on 22 December 1663. Encouraged by his appearance and alarmed by the Turkish advance, other princes followed suit, gathering in Regensburg for personal talks with their supreme sovereign. By publicly thanking Schönborn for his efforts and promising further discussion on the outstanding issues, Leopold avoided the need for a final decision and secured substantial support from those territories that had not already sent troops with the Alliance army.

However, the mobilization of the *Reichsarmee* already displayed many of the features that were to characterize collective security after the great reform of 1681–2. First, the official strength of 30,000 decreed on 4 February 1664 was cut by the decision to deduct the contingents already serving in the Alliance corps. The remaining 20,993 men were apportioned to the individual *Kreis*, anticipating later mobilization arrangements, with the Austrian *Kreis* omitted because the emperor already had soldiers in the field. The distinction between armed and unarmed territories was already emerging, as many of the weaker princes paid stronger neighbours to take over their obligations. This occurred in Swabia, for example, where Württemberg, Baden, Fürstenberg, Ulm, Augsburg and Esslingen all fielded troops on behalf of other *Kreis* members, many of whom had been reluctant to contribute at all.

Nonetheless, *Reich* participation was fairly impressive (see Table 2.1). The Swabian imperial knights consented to the inclusion of their 220 infantry in the Swabian corps, although they were under no obligation to co-operate. Apart from the Burgundians, who failed to appear, the other *Kreise* turned out in force with the missing 5,000 men largely accounted for by the fact that Brandenburg, Saxony and Bavaria refused to intergrate their men with the *Kreistruppen*. Moreover, the appearance of the *Reichsarmee* in the field by June 1664 represented a considerable achievement for a force that had to be largely

Table 2.1 Imperial forces in 1664

Contingent	Official strength	Effectives
Reichsarmee		
Burgundian *Kreis*	2,022	None
Electoral Rhenish *Kreis*	505	476[1]
Westphalian *Kreis*	2,450	2,422
Lower Saxon *Kreis*	2,350	2,350
Upper Saxon *Kreis*	3,950	1,024[2]
Bavarian *Kreis*	2,461	1,060
Franconian *Kreis*	2,255	2,450
Swabian *Kreis*	3,500	3,512
Upper Rhenish *Kreis*	1,500	1,873
Subtotal	20,993	15,167
Rhenish alliance		
Mainz	900	1,200[3]
Trier	380	380[4]
Cologne	1,200	1,200[4]
Pfalz-Neuburg	1,100	1,110[5]
Sweden	650	?
Pfalz-Zweibrücken	150	?
Guelph duchies	1,320	1,320[6]
Württemberg	300	370[7]
Hessen-Kassel	300	460[8]
Hessen-Darmstadt	220	350[8]
Münster	1,200	1,200[9]
France	2,400	6,000
Subtotal	10,120	13,590
Independent contingents		
Brandenburg	2,000	2,088
Saxony	1,200	1,174
Bavaria	1,400	1,250
Subtotal	4,600	4,512
Total	35,713	33,269
Plus Habsburg army	62,000	51,000
Grand Total	97,713	84,269

Notes: Official strengths from Forst, "Reichstruppen", pp. 637, 639. Effectives from sources in note 35 and below.

[1] 400 Palatine troops and 76 Cologne cavalry. Bezzel, *Kurpfälzischen Heeres*, vol. I, pp. 91–6; Schempp, *Feldzug 1664*, pp. 202–6.

[2] Brandenburg and Saxony supplied their contingents independently. Anhalt, Reuss and the Ernestine duchies fulfilled their obligations. Patze (ed.), *Geschichte Thüringens*, vol. V, pp. 96, 202, 205, 237; Tessin, *Regimenter*, p. 65.

[3] Mainz replaced its 300 cavalry by twice the number of foot soldiers.

[4] Unclear whether all were sent.

[5] Bezzel, *Kurpfälzischen Heeres*, vol. I, pp. 151–5. Neuberg appears to have sent 55 additional cavalry later in 1664.

[6] Hanover, Brunswick and Celle. Sichart, *Hanoverischen Armee*, vol I, pp. 124–6, 345–9; Elster, *Braunschweig-Wolfenbüttel* vol. I, p. 76.

[7] Includes 70 *Kreistruppen*.

[8] Both landgraves replaced their cavalry with additional foot soldiers, sending a combined foot rgt. STAD E8 180/1; Keim, *Infanterie-Regiments Großherzogin*, p. 1.

[9] Not included in the original treaty with the emperor but marched with the Alliance corps. Münster also sent 50 cavalry and 651 infantry as *Kreistruppen*.

raised from scratch.[35] Energetic recruiting had increased Habsburg forces to 51,000 by February 1664, supported by 9,000 Hungarians, but disease and the need to garrison border fortresses reduced the combined force to 24,450 by the time Montecuccoli engaged the 50,000–60,000-strong Ottoman army at the monastery of St Gotthard on the river Raab on 1 August 1664.[36] As the Turkish elite forces crossed the river, the inexperienced *Kreistruppen* in the allied centre gave way and fled. The French and Alliance troops counter-attacked from the left while Montecuccoli's cavalry charged in from the right, just managing to stem the Turkish advance. Montecuccoli contemplated retreat but was persuaded by his subordinates to renew the attack. The *Kreistruppen* rallied and a general assault was launched, eventually driving the Ottomans back across the river. Though 30,000 of his troops remained unengaged, the grand vizier sensed the battle going against him and decided to retreat, leaving the Christians in possession of the field. Two thousand, mainly Germans, had been lost, along with a similar number of fugitives. Turkish losses are not known, but were probably less.

Somewhat surprisingly Leopold quickly agreed terms in the Peace of Vasvár (Eisenberg) on 10 August, surrendering several strategic border for-tresses, recognizing the Ottoman candidate in Transylvania and paying an indemnity of 200,000 fl. to the sultan in return for a 20-year truce. The Hungarian magnates were furious, accusing him of wasting his victory, but Leopold was conscious of how narrow the margin had been. Montecuccoli's army was already disintegrating, and though the *Reichstag* had granted military assistance for an unlimited period, the agreement with the Alliance had been for only one year. Leopold had also run out of money and wanted an excuse to remove the French from his territory where their presence was an affront to his dignity and an encouragement to the more independently-minded Hungarian nobles. Ottoman preoccupations elsewhere ensured that the truce nearly lasted its term, despite growing Hungarian discontent with Habsburg rule, culminating in open opposition to military repression in the period known as the Ten Dark Years, 1671–81.[37]

Further German conflict with the Turks was restricted to the provision of over 5,000 auxiliaries by Austria, Bavaria, the Guelphs and a number of ecclesiastical princes as part of the pan-European effort to assist the embattled Venetian Republic hold on to Candia (Iraklion) on Crete, which had been besieged intermittently since 1645. Though the Republic offered significant financial inducements, crusading zeal inspired the Germans to provide most of their men free of charge. Arriving in 1667 the soldiers had lost three-quarters of their complement to disease, unfamiliar climate and enemy action by the time the city fell after heroic resistance on 27 September 1668.[38]

The Dutch War, 1672–9

Leopold's involvement, restricted to under 600 men, had been intended to keep an eye on the other Germans and as a publicity stunt to counterbalance the presence of a large French contingent. The powerful French army, along with the construction of a magnificent new palace at Versailles after 1663, suggested that Louis XIV intended to displace the emperor as pre-eminent European monarch. However, the French threat derived not, as earlier nationalist historians maintained, from territorial ambitions at German expense, but from the king's determination to settle his differences with Spain and the Dutch Republic. His belligerence, obvious from 1667, impinged directly on the unfinished business of Westphalia by threatening the *Reich*'s nonaligned status in international affairs. Both Spain and the Dutch looked to Leopold and the German princes to assist their resistance to French expansion, while Louis's inability to prevent his military operations spreading to the *Reich* defeated his original intention of encouraging its continued neutrality. The fact that the French monarch was a Christian king and guarantor of the IPO added further complications not encountered during the earlier war with the Turks. In contrast to the eastern frontier, where peace with the infidel was considered impossible, Leopold was obliged by imperial and international law to avoid war with his western Christian neighbours. Any conflict with France would require the formal sanction of the *Reichstag*, something that seemed increasingly unlikely given the growing predilection of ambitious rulers like Ferdinand Maria of Bavaria to court Louis XIV's favour.

All this was doubly disturbing to Leopold because his own dynastic interests were at stake. The Spanish Habsburgs, now represented solely by the sickly Carlos II, were not expected to survive for long, raising the question of who should inherit their vast European and colonial empire. Louis had already advanced a claim on behalf of his Spanish-born wife and appeared the main challenger, raising the possibility that Leopold might be dragged into an international conflict for which he was ill-prepared.

These factors conditioned Leopold's response, the cornerstone of which was to reach an understanding with Louis that would avoid the need for war without compromising his claims to Spain. A secret bilateral deal struck on 19 January 1668 appeared the ideal solution. In the event of Carlos II's death, Leopold was to receive Spain, its American colonies and the northern Italian possessions, including Milan, while the Netherlands, Naples and Sicily fell to France. With the assurance of the essentials of the Spanish inheritance, Leopold refrained from intervening in the War of Devolution (1667–8) and subsequently negotiated a second treaty of neutrality in November 1671, undertaking not to interfere in Louis's planned attack on the Dutch

Republic.[39] Meanwhile, awkward questions about the extension of collective defence to the Burgundian *Kreis* were brushed aside and the princes denied a chance to repeat their efforts of 1663 to extract political concessions in return for military assistance.

However, it soon became impossible to pursue this line once Louis began his attack on the Dutch in April 1672. Not only did French troops infringe *Reich* neutrality by using the bishopric of Liège as an invasion route, but both Cologne and Münster actively assisted operations in return for subsidies and political support. While Bavaria, Hanover and Pfalz-Neuburg continued to remain unengaged, they also increased their forces with French help and began pressing for collective diplomatic intervention on behalf of Louis's claims. Brandenburg, followed by Trier, Celle, Wolfenbüttel and others, began providing auxiliaries for the Dutch and, later, Spain once it became involved in 1673. In a misguided attempt to deter such interference, Louis deliberately spread the war to western Germany, beginning systematic devastation in the Rhineland early in 1674.

This could not have come at a worse time for Leopold whose absolutist policies in Hungary had sparked a major revolt in 1672, tying down the bulk of his army. With leading princes actively supporting both sides and French armies occupying large parts of the Rhineland, it was impossible for Leopold to remain neutral. Between 1672 and 1674 he moved from passive bystander to active participant, involving the *Reich* in the first of a series of prolonged conflicts against French expansionism. After 1675 the war spread to northern Germany as Sweden intervened on Louis's behalf, though this failed to achieve the decisive breakthrough, compelling the king to rely on diplomacy to split the coalition that had formed against him. Continued French military efforts, especially in Flanders, assisted by holding operations in the Rhineland, held off his opponents until the diplomats secured peace at Spain's expense at Nijmegen in 1678–9.

Leopold's lacklustre handling of imperial defence during these years has drawn censure in the past from nationalist historians who have contrasted it with the more energetic involvement of the Great Elector. Even today the German dimension of this Dutch War is fundamentally misunderstood, extending beyond the almost universal mistaken belief that it involved a formal *Reichskrieg* to overlook the profound consequences of Leopold's war management. His decision to avoid a formal declaration of war compelled him to fight a defensive war with the assistance of the larger, militarizing territories at the expense of the weaker, unarmed ones. This expedient permitted the growth of the armed princes, who, with the onset of new French encroachments in the *Réunions* policy after 1679, looked set to implement their version of collective security after the war. Abandoned by an emperor, who was apparently unable to protect them against domestic and external opponents, the weaker territories revolted in the *Reichstag*, paving the way for the reforms that finally stabilized the imperial constitution after 1681 and provided the political and military framework that lasted until 1806. To put these later developments into their context we must return to the events of the war years and examine how Leopold sought to retain control over collective defence.

The direct involvement of Brandenburg on the side of the Dutch from May 1672, and the presence of the elector's soldiers in the politically sensitive city of Cologne, raised the possibility that Frederick William might steal Leopold's thunder and become leader of imperial opposition to French aggression. The decision to sign a military convention with the elector in June 1672, despite the treaties of neutrality with France, represented an attempt to influence the direction of Brandenburg involvement. The emperor's general, Montecuccoli, received secret orders to frustrate joint operations, while Leopold's chief adviser, Prince Lobkowitz, informed Louis that he should not take Austrian movements too seriously. The summer campaign of 1672 predictably failed to bring victory, leading to a Austro-Brandenburg withdrawal the following year and the penetration of French forces under Turenne as far as the river Main.

Leopold's inability to do more indicated his underlying weakness: Montecuccoli's meagre force of 15,000 men represented all that could be spared in 1672–3, given the emperor's other commitments, particularly in Hungary. In desperation, he resorted to illegal covert operations to neutralize troublemakers. In February 1673 imperial agents unsuccessfully tried to assassinate the bishop of Münster, who was still allied to France, while others did manage to abduct the chief minister of Cologne a year later.[40] However, none of this made up for the lack of manpower to confront Louis XIV, whose army grew to 253,000 effectives by 1678. The success of French diplomacy in manipulating the appeasement lobby amongst the princes ensured there was no prospect of persuading the *Reichstag* to declare war even if this had been Leopold's intention. Despite a public show of concern for the areas ravaged by France, the emperor had no desire to hand the princes another opportunity to extract formal concessions, while the lack of progress on matricular revision left it unlikely that such a move would produce the force required. Austrian military operations were portrayed simply as efforts to restore the public peace within the *Reich* rather than formal war against France. When renewed French depredations in the Palatinate early in 1674 made it impossible to ignore the obligation to assist, Leopold neatly sidestepped the issue by expelling the French ambassador from Regensburg and informing the *Reichstag* in March that, by their actions, the French had made themselves an enemy of the *Reich*. He then allowed the general mood of anti-French opinion to push the assembled delegates into sanctioning aid to the Palatinate and other threatened areas on 31 March. The subsequent decrees in April and May, widely taken by historians to be a formal *Reichskrieg*, were in fact merely elaborations of this instruction.[41]

In order to control Brandenburg, which was agitating to abandon its bilateral Peace of Vossem (1673) with France and re-enter the war, Leopold signed a new convention with the elector in July 1674. Linked to other arrangements with Spain and the Dutch to cover half of Brandenburg's expenses, the convention committed the Great Elector to providing 16,000 troops to act in concert with a reinforced Austrian army, now temporarily entrusted to Bournonville, to contain the French depredations. Appeasement had now been abandoned and Lobkowitz, its chief architect, was purged from the Austrian government in October.[42]

Imperial honour had been upheld without relinquishing the initiative to the princes, who were denied a say in the direction of the war. The significance of this became apparent in 1675–6, when the *Reichstag* considered sending an official delegation to the peace conference meeting at Nijmegen at Louis's insistence. Leopold responded vigorously to this challenge to his traditional prerogatives, exploiting the absence of a *Reichskrieg* to preserve his exclusive right to negotiate on the *Reich*'s behalf. An important precedent had been established, enabling the emperor to exclude the *Reichstag* from later negotiations in 1697 and 1713–14, despite formal declarations of war in 1689 and 1702.

However, the cost of preserving imperial influence was considerable. Continued postponement of defence reform left the mobilization sanctioned by the *Reichstag* dependent on the existing *Kreis* structure, where it could be derailed by the major princes. Though Franconia, Swabia, Upper Saxony and Upper Rhine sent forces to the Rhine after 1673, contributions from the Bavarian, Westphalian, Lower Saxon and Electoral Rhenish *Kreise* were virtually nonexistent due to the presence of French sympathizers. In fact the 15,000 or so *Kreistruppen* in the field by 1675 were far from insignificant, especially when seen in conjunction with at least as many militiamen and garrison troops retained for territorial defence, many of whom were performing vital frontline duty in outposts along the Rhine and fortresses like Mainz, Koblenz and Ehrenbreitstein (Table 2.2). However, they were still insufficient to hold the western frontier against Louis XIV, who could send as many as 50,000–70,000 men, while the opening of the second, northern front by Sweden only stacked the odds further against the *Reich*.

The unfavourable military balance left Leopold open to precisely the kind of pressure from the armed princes he was seeking to avoid. Adapting to Leopold's methods, such princes were already losing interest in the *Reichstag*

Table 2.2 *Kreis* contingents, 1673–8

	Contingent					
Kreis	1673	1674	1675	1676	1677	1678
Electoral Rhine						
Burgundy	No formal contribution					
Austria						
Westphalia	1,200	1,200	1,200	1,200	1,200	1,200
Upper Rhine	–	2,100	4,200	4,200	4,200	4,200
Franconia	2,151	3,000	6,000	6,000	6,000	–
Swabia	2,556	2,556	3,600	4,200	4,200	–
Upper Saxony	1,000	1,000	1,000	1,000	1,000	1,000
Lower Saxony	–	700	–	–	–	–
Bavaria	–	600	600	600	600	600
Total	6,907	11,156	16,600	17,200	17,200	7,000

Sources: Helmes, "Übersicht"; Tessin, *Regimenter*, pp. 65, 89–90, 153–5, 196–7; Tessin, *Mecklenburgischen Militär*, pp. 16–25; Schuster & Franke, *Sächsischen Armee*, vol. ι, pp. 87–93; Philippi, *Landgraf Karl*, pp. 17–19; Storm, *Feldherr*, pp. 261, 308–14.

Note: The Westphalian contingent garrisoned Cologne. The figure for Bavaria is an estimate based on the fact that Salzburg sent an infantry battalion.

as a vehicle for their aims,[43] seeking instead the opportunities offered by the war. By providing their armies under independent agreements with the major belligerents, they could aspire to far greater influence in European affairs than they could hope to achieve through their delegates in Regensburg. Already responsible for the involvement of German auxiliaries in the opening stages of the war, these considerations prompted other princes to hire their forces to the anti-French coalition of Spain, Denmark, Austria and the Dutch Republic that had formed by 1675. As both Cologne and Münster had been defeated in 1674, the latter transferring to the coalition, all German auxiliaries were now fighting the common enemy of the *Reich* (Table 2.3). The princes capitalized on this to dodge their contribution to the *Kreis* mobilization, claiming that the more numerous auxiliaries more than made up for the absence of their soldiers. From here it was only a short step to the argument that these should take the place of the *Kreis* contingents entirely and serve as the official forces of the *Reich* in return for cash payment from the unarmed territories.

This money was now urgently needed by the armed princes, who were

Table 2.3 German auxiliaries against France, 1674–8

Territory	Initial treaty	Partner	Contingent
Saxony	13 Aug 1673	Leopold I	2,848
Palatinate	10 Mar 1674	Austria, Spain Dutch Republic	2,500
Münster	12 May 1674	Leopold I	10,000
Celle	20 June 1674	Austria, Spain Dutch Republic	7,220
Wolfenbüttel	20 June 1674	Ditto	5,780
Brandenburg	1 July 1674	Ditto	16,000
Osnabrück	Dec 1674	Ditto	5,100
Pfalz–Neuburg	Jan 1676	Spain, Dutch Republic	8,500
Total 1673	2,848		
1674	53,448		
1675	47,100		
1676	55,600		
1677	59,660		
1678	61,692		

Note: The Saxon corps was reduced in 1674 and withdrawn entirely the following year. Münster's treaty was revised on 7 September 1674, cutting its obligations by 1,000 men. Spain and the Dutch shouldered part of the maintenance costs during 1675–7, while the Danes hired a further 4,060 from 1677, rising to 6,092 in April 1678. Brandenburg actually fielded 20,000 men, while the Pfalz–Neuburg contingent was reduced when three of its cavalry regiments were disbanded in 1678. It should also be remembered that all territories in the above table maintained further troops at their own expense.

finding their participation a serious strain despite the foreign subsidies. The post-1648 economic recovery was far from complete, while the failure of the Extensionists had left many still dependent on grants from their estates. Subsidies were scarcely lucrative, and though they paid for initial mobiliza-tion, they rarely covered the cost of long-term involvement. Barely able to pay its own army, Spain quickly defaulted on the money it promised, while the Dutch only agreed to cover half Brandenburg's expenses in their treaty of May 1672. Given the number of men they were obliged to contribute – Brandenburg was to field 20,000 – most rulers quickly experienced serious difficulties, especially as their foreign partners sought to reserve the best billets for their own men. Increasingly, the rulers of Brandenburg, Celle, Saxony and even Hanover, which was still neutral, began demanding billets and contributions from neighbouring German territories on the grounds that these were not pulling their weight for the common cause.

Faced with the need to assert his influence and obtain urgently needed additional forces, Leopold made a virtue of necessity by capitalizing on his prerogative to assign billets and arbitrate interterritorial disputes. To be successful, this tactic depended on balancing concessions to the armed princes with the need to maintain the loyalty of their unarmed victims, something that became very difficult after January 1675.

Following the *Kreis* mobilization and the emperor's second, agreement with Brandenburg, the common army had risen to over 50,000 men by the early autumn of 1674, making it the largest single force assembled by the *Reich* since 1648. Having crossed the Rhine at Strasbourg, the Germans hoped to winter in Alsace at their enemy's expense but were surprised by Turenne who burst through the Belfort gap, defeating them at Türkheim (5 January 1675) and sending them hurrying back into Swabia.[44] Leopold had to move quickly to prevent a return to the unauthorized billeting and requisitioning that had so undermined German life before 1648. Acting immediately and in contravention of his legal obligations to restrict billets and transit, Leopold distributed the retreating army throughout Swabia, Franconia and Thuringia, even assigning regiments to territories that were providing their *Kreis* contingents. The situation was exacerbated by the need to avoid the Bavarian *Kreis* so as not to push Elector Ferdinand Maria into declaring openly for France. Simultaneously, the Swedish assault on Brandenburg opened the northern front and led to the recall of the Brandenburg, Celle, Wolfenbüttel and Münster auxiliaries from the Rhine and Flanders and their concentration in the Westphalian and Lower Saxon *Kreise*, where similar arrangements had to be made not to antagonize Hanover.

The rapidity and scope of these movements fatally undermined Leopold's ability to retain direction of the war and the initiative passed to those armed princes who had secured influence within the *Kreise*, confirming the trend since the 1660s. Already in January 1664 Leopold, together with the *Reichstag*, had authorized *Kreis* executive princes to collect arrears of imperial war taxes by sending troops into offending territories. The door was opened to all sorts of malpractice, particularly where the executive princes were able to frustrate the efforts of *Kreis* Assemblies to establish accountability for their actions. Acting in the name of the Westphalians, the Great Elector was able to extract five times the amount of arrears actually owed from the county of Lippe by 1666.[45] The power of the executive princes was strengthened in this respect in 1673, and they began to influence the *Assignation* (distribution) of billets and cash contributions. Under this procedure, territories were assigned to an armed prince who was free to quarter his troops at his host's expense and to divert their war taxes directly into his own coffers in return for substituting his own soldiers for their missing contingent. While unscrupulous rulers like Bishop Galen of Münster were not above arbitrarily imposing themselves on their neighbours, most preferred to receive formal sanction for locally nego-tiated agreements as the best way of enforcing obligations and excluding interlopers. Intended principally to limit the excesses characteristic of the Thirty Years War, this practice was easily corrupted in the absence of firm imperial control into a semi-permanent form of taxation.[46]

Though both the *Reichstag* and the emperor attempted throughout 1675 to reassert central co-ordination, they were powerless to enforce it because implementation of their decrees rested with the executive princes. In serious financial difficulties and, in cases like Brandenburg, faced with foreign invasion, these were in no mood to respect the rights of lesser princes who appeared to be doing little for the war effort. Moreover, Leopold himself increasingly saw the practice as a convenient method of funding his own troops, attempting in the winter of 1675–6 to exclude all others from Swabian and Franconian billets.

The position of the weaker territories grew precarious. The billeting of winter 1674–5 already represented a considerable burden, with the cost of accommodating 12 Brandenburg regiments in Franconia for four months amounting to no less than 400,000 tlr, or nearly three times the annual tax receipts of Ansbach and Bayreuth combined.[47] The Swabians were even worse hit, with their unwelcome guests extracting well over 500,000 fl. more than they were entitled to from just 12 of the 97 member territories.[48] Moreover, the procedure set a precedent that was followed in the four subsequent winters of the war, as each time the imperial commanders failed to secure quarters outside *Reich* territory. While costs in Swabia remained roughly constant at 2–3 million fl. each time, they rose in Franconia to 2.1 million in 1675/6 and the subsequent winter. Altogether, billeting made up at least 8 million fl. of Swabia's total 21 million fl. war costs and dwarfed the annual cost of maintaining the 3,000 *Kreistruppen* which stood at 500,000 fl.[49] Adding insult to injury, the quartered troops became increasingly cavalier towards their hosts, the retreating Saxons simply commandeering the Swabians' field artillery in 1677.[50]

The situation in the north was worse, as Leopold was unable to stem the influence of Celle, Wolfenbüttel, Münster and Brandenburg, all of which enjoyed diplomatic backing from Spain and the Dutch in return for their renewed contribution to the allied effort in Flanders. On 21 September 1675, Münster, Brandenburg and Denmark agreed to Hanoverian billeting in large parts of Lower Saxony as the price of the duke's non-intervention in their operations against Sweden. This arrangement permitted Hanover to draw

33,500 tlr a month, while additional extortion in Hildesheim, for instance, had cost that bishopric no less than 973,000 tlr by 1677 alone.[51] Although Leopold sponsored a conference at Mühlhausen to regulate matters, he could not prevent the participants rearranging agreements to suit their political objectives. For example, the unarmed Westphalian territories of Essen, Werden and Dortmund were assigned to Münster in 1675 but the bishop traded them in March 1676 for Brandenburg's billets in the former bishopric of Bremen, which was earmarked for annexation from Sweden. Meanwhile, Brandenburg used its billeting rights in Westphalia to consolidate its hold on the area around Cleves and Mark.

Such measures played directly into the hands of Duke Georg Wilhelm of Celle, who hoped to displace both Brandenburg and Münster as the dominant power in northern Germany. With Hanover neutral and the other two Guelph rulers in Wolfenbüttel and Osnabrück following his lead, Georg Wilhelm exploited his influence in the Lower Saxon *Kreis* to buttress his ambitions. Already elected *Kreisoberst* in 1671, he exploited his mobilization powers to make policy without reference to the other members. The 3,000 *Kreistruppen* sanctioned by the Assembly in 1674 in response to the *Reichstag*'s call for assistance against France were in fact entirely provided by Celle and Wolfenbüttel at the others' expense. The doubling of official commitments by the *Reichstag*, following Swedish intervention in 1675, merely enabling the duke to off-load another 3,000 men on his neighbours. Backed by Magdeburg, the co-executive prince who also feared the Great Elector, Georg Wilhelm exploited growing anxiety at Brandenburg and Danish encroachments to stage manage the April 1677 Assembly meeting. Rejecting imperial claims to organize billeting, the delegates entrusted exclusive control to the duke as regional military commander. All "foreign powers" were ordered to remove their troops, a move designed to evict the Brandenburgers from Mecklenburg and other member territories, while a *Quindecuplum* of 20,000 *Kreistruppen* was authorized to cover Celle's continued extortion of cash from the unarmed areas.[52] Many of these were now opting for formal bilateral arrangements with Celle to assume their imperial obligations on a semi-permanent basis. Both dukes of Mecklenburg agreed to this in 1676 in an effort to avoid falling under Brandenburg influence, while Lippe in Westphalia entered into a similar contract in 1678 to escape the clutches of Münster.[53] Such agreements had the advantage of fixing limits on what an armed prince could extract from a territory but placed its status as a full imperial estate in question since it was no longer directly fulfilling its obligations.

These developments severely strained collective defence, and the lesson for the medium territories appeared to be clear: only through possession of their own independent forces would they preserve their political position and escape domination by their neighbours. From 1674, Würzburg, Bamberg, Eisenach, Gotha and Darmstadt made bilateral arrangements, supplying troops for Leopold's forces on the Rhine in return for limited cash assistance and exemption from billeting and provision of *Kreistruppen*. Despite the fact that Leopold defaulted on his subsidy and still assigned Austrian units to Würzburg and Bamberg in 1675–6, Bishop Peter Philipp von Dernbach believed he had struck a good deal, emphasizing to his cathedral chapters that the four auxiliary regiments cost only 265,000 fl. annually compared with 1,050,000 fl. spent previously in just six months for foreign billets. Imperial and papal support also compelled the querulous canons to suspend their opposition to Dernbach's absolutist domestic measures.[54] Unable to reach an agreement with Leopold directly, Regent Hedwig Sophie in Hessen-Kassel made a separate treaty with Denmark to achieve armed status by fielding 2,000 auxiliaries for its operations against Sweden in April 1677. As these were promptly destroyed by enemy action, a second force of 1,300 was despatched the following April, this time with formal imperial approval extending to exemption from billets (Table 2.4).[55]

The withdrawal of these territories from collective defence naturally angered their neighbours, who were still participating in the *Kreis* structure, while their exemption from billeting reduced the areas available for the emperor and armed princes. Matters reached crisis by October 1676, as shortage of assigned quarters and contributions began to undermine the Great Elector's war effort. Though Brandenburg received about 2 million tlr in

Table 2.4 Auxiliaries from the medium territories, 1674–8

Territory	Treaty	Contingent	Fate
Würzburg	Feb. 1674	2,140	Till 1675
Würzburg and Bamberg	Nov. 1675	6,000	Revised to 5,000 in April 1677. Till 1678
Eisenach	June 1674	1,000	Absorbed into 1676 treaty
Gotha and Eisenach	Nov. 1676	3,000	Till 1678
Hessen-Darmstadt	Aug. 1677	1,100	Till 1678
Hessen-Kassel	April 1677	2,000	Till 1678
Hessen-Kassel	April 1678	1,300	Till 1679

Sources: As notes 54 and 55.

Note: Hessen-Kassel's agreements were with Denmark; all the others were with the emperor.

Spanish, Dutch and Austrian subsidies in 1672–8, irregularities in payment caused acute cash flow problems, while Swedish intervention disrupted tax collection at a time when the army was expanding in line with political objectives.[56] Poised to drive the Swedes from Pomerania, the elector feared his operations would collapse unless he secured adequate resources, and, complaining bitterly that his demise was imminent, he took the law into his own hands. Four regiments were sent into Franconia to demand billets and contributions in October 1676, followed by another five to Hessen-Kassel, Fulda, Anhalt and the Thuringian states the next month, while two more occupied Cologne's Westphalian territories. Hessen-Kassel mobilized its militia to block the Brandenburgers' approach and opened talks with the Ernestine dukes for joint countermeasures while Hanoverians deployed nearby to protect their zone of contribution. Convinced that his patriotic efforts were going unrewarded, Frederick William was enraged that Celle then proceeded to close off Lower Saxony to his forces in April 1677. Determined not to lose revenue, the elector's agents engineered a mutiny in the newly-formed companies of the Administrator of Magdeburg to prevent him escaping exploitation under the guise of an armed prince.[57]

Believing that they were being sacrificed to preserve Leopold's relations with the elector, Franconia and Swabia decided to pull out of the war altogether, withdrawing their *Kreistruppen* by April 1677 and unilaterally declaring their neutrality.[58] Despite Frederick William's threat to pull out of the war in the west, Leopold could not ignore these continual affronts to his authority and the elector was forced to back down, withdraw his troops and levy an emergency poll tax on his own subjects instead. However, the damage had been done. Collective defence now existed only on paper, reducing the imperial army to Leopold's own contingent and the auxiliaries supplied under bilateral arrangement. Burgundy and large parts of the Electoral and Upper Rhine were occupied by the enemy, Swabia and Franconia refused to cooperate, while Bavarian participation remained restricted to Salzburg. Lower Saxony was almost exclusively controlled by the Guelphs, with Westphalia and Upper Saxony split between Münster and Brandenburg and Brandenburg and Electoral Saxony respectively.

The experience of the Dutch War had important implications for the security of the west and north of the *Reich*. Unlike the War of Devolution, France retained its wartime gains on a permanent basis in the Nijmegen Peace Settlement of 1678–9. While its northern frontier was consolidated at the expense of parts of the Spanish Netherlands, in the east France absorbed the entire Franche Comté, the ten Alsatian imperial cities known as the Decapolis, the strategic bridgeheads of Kehl and Freiburg as well as *de facto* control of Lorraine.[59] The latter was temporarily reversed in 1697–1738, while Kehl and Freiburg were permanently recovered for the *Reich* in 1698, but the fact remained that the Rhine was indefensible, confirming a trend since 1648. The loss of Metz, Toul and Verdun in 1552 only began to assume strategic importance with the cession of Upper Alsace to France in 1648. The Peace of the Pyrenees widened the gap in the *Reich*'s western defences by ordering the slighting of Nancy's fortifications and granting France a military corridor from Verdun to Metz, opening the route taken in the invasion of Lorraine in 1670. Acquisition of the Decapolis secured Alsace and the Vosges mountains for France, while their position was extended southwards by control of Franche Comté and the Belfort Gap.

The *Reich* had lost its protective glacis and the front line advanced to the upper reaches of the Rhine, where France now held the strategic advantage. In contrast to the Vosges, which were passable only east of Saverne and through the Belfort Gap, the Black Forest was traversed by several tortuous routes. While the French could manoeuvre on the broad Alsatian plain to defend their side of the river, the Germans were cramped on the narrow east bank, which was cut by numerous tributaries of the Rhine.

Contemporary opinion concurred that immediate defence behind the river was impracticable, and it was better to take up a central defensive position east of the Black Forest to see where the enemy would cross and then fall on him before he could deploy properly.[60] However, the French practice of raiding across the river to devastate the east bank made this politically impossible, since the emperor could not afford to abandon the Rhinelanders to enemy depredations.

Lacking the manpower for a successful push into Alsace, imperial generals were compelled to develop new methods to hold the river line by enhancing the natural protection afforded by the terrain. By 1675 Montecuccoli was conscripting thousands of peasants to construct field fortifications to bar possible crossing points and blocking the Black Forest passes. These defences, called "lines", were to become a major feature of imperial defence. In their most sophisticated form, as perfected during the War of the Spanish Succession, they consisted of interconnected earth walls and ditches, redoubts and gun batteries, palisades and blockhouses that stretched for 90 km or more. The impact on the local community and physical environment was considerable. No less than 1.6 million m^3 of earth had to be moved during the construction of the 86 km long Eppingen Lines in 1695–7. Traces of the ditches and banks survived into the twentieth century. Swaths of forest were cut down for use in construction or to create entanglements of sharpened branches up to 100 m across.[61]

Whole villages were deprived of the traditional sources of firewood, but the burden of labour service and guard duty proved even more onerous.

Utilizing existing feudal labour obligations and militia systems, commanders conscripted manpower from right across southwestern Germany. Villages were obliged to despatch work teams on a rota basis that had to be fed and paid at the community's expense. While the costs could sometimes be set against existing taxes, the *Kreis* Assemblies often sanctioned them as additional contributions to collective defence. Naturally the heaviest burden fell on the Breisgau and Baden as the areas in the immediate vicinity, but the Palatinate, Württemberg and even Franconian territories were also called upon to provide their share.[62] Militiamen were provided on the same basis to guard the extended defences. The Austrians had their own militia in the Breisgau, numbering 8,000–12,000 men divided into eight sections to patrol specific sectors. The Swabian *Kreis* was capable of mobilizing 4,000–8,000 more in addition to the local militias in Württemberg (4,800) and the two Badens (approximately 3,000). These forces represented significant proportions of the region's population, considering that the Breisgau and other Austrian dependencies had 290,000 inhabitants in 1700 and Württemberg only 10,000–50,000 more. The militia on guard duty in the Black Forest in 1696 amounted to one-quarter of the able-bodied male population.[63]

The defensive preparations were accompanied by an intensified use of outposts. Small detachments were scattered along the lines, natural obstacles and fortified towns to form a protective cordon to watch enemy movements and prevent contribution raids into the territory behind. Originally intended to screen winter quarters, this became a permanent part of imperial defence during the Dutch War and was continued in every conflict against France up to 1801. It involved co-ordination of the three elements of territorial defence (fortresses, garrisons, militias) at interregional level to ensure that every prince and city made sure its sector was not breached. The *Kreis* structure already provided the framework as it developed after 1673. While the Swabians and Franconians worked with the local Austrian authorities to watch the Rhine south of Philippsburg, the Upper and Electoral Rhenish *Kreise* guarded the stretch from there to Koblenz, where the Westphalians took over.

These factors help explain the varied pattern of *Kreis* development into the eighteenth century. Not only were Franconia and Swabia the most politically fragmented regions, they were also responsible for guarding the most exposed part of the Rhine. As the Nine Years War was to prove, once the French had broken through the Black Forest, they were free to ravage the relatively open country of the Swabian-Franconian basin. The Electoral and Upper Rhenish *Kreis* on the other hand were afforded some protection by the Palatinate and other German territories between the Rhine and the Saar. Even if the French crossed this ground, the going east of the Rhine was rendered more difficult by the wooded and broken country of the Taunus and Spessart. Further to the north, the Westphalians were protected by the wooded, hilly ground of the Ardennes, and beyond these to the west, the barrier fortresses of Brabant and Flanders.

These geo-strategic factors encouraged the coincidence of interest between the Swabians, Franconians, Rhinelanders and Austrians that established the basic pattern of imperial military effort till 1714. Re-emerging during the crises of 1733–5 and 1792–1801, this involved assembling a mixed force of Austrian, princely and *Kreis* contingents on the Upper Rhine, supported by militia and garrisons in key fortresses, to parry French thrusts across the river, while smaller detachments held positions further downstream in case of attack along the Saar, Moselle or Meuse.

In contrast, defence of the north had come to rest almost exclusively in the hands of the local armed princes who benefited from the underlying shift in the regional balance of power in 1675–9. The Swedish Baltic empire was overextended and under-resourced, contributing to regional instability both by encouraging Swedish attacks to find new resources as in 1655 and 1675 and by raising the possibility of a power vacuum should these attacks end in serious defeats.[64] Though far from decisive in military terms, the Great Elector's victory at Fehrbellin (28 June 1675) triggered a regional power struggle by exposing Sweden's weakness. Important as a demonstration of growing Brandenburg military power, the battle's true significance lay in encouraging Danish intervention against Sweden. Assisted by a Dutch squadron, the Danish fleet gained control of the Baltic, the essential prerequisite for the conquest of Sweden's German territories. Without hope of relief, the reduction of Stralsund, Stettin, Stade, Wismar and Sweden's other German fortresses became a matter of time provided Münster, Celle, Brandenburg and Denmark could sustain their co-operation.

Though French intervention in Westphalia early in 1679 compelled them to return their conquests, the underlying situation remained unchanged, for no amount of domestic reform after 1680 could alter Sweden's basic inability to defend its north German possessions, where the cost of maintaining a soldier stood at ten times the price of a native conscript.[65] It remained to see which territory would profit from this, but there were already signs that it would be the Protestant powers of Hanover, Celle and Brandenburg provided they could defeat Danish ambitions. Already the Dutch were showing less interest in the region, due to the more immediate threat to their southern frontier from France, while Münster's inability to make any permanent gains ensured its belligerence did not survive the death of its energetic Bishop Galen in 1678.

Réunions *and defence reform, 1679–84*

The conclusion of peace in 1679 brought little relief to the *Reich*, which remained confronted by two interrelated problems: preservation of territorial integrity and restoration of collective security. The first stemmed from the disappointment with the Nijmegen Settlement, which had robbed several major belligerents of important wartime gains. Chief among these was France, where Louis XIV remained dissatisfied despite making the largest territorial acquisitions in the last 250 years of the Bourbon monarchy. Louis felt that his security and *gloire* required more, especially as he wanted to be well placed to take advantage of the Habsburg's failing health: the death of Carlos II was widely predicted, while Leopold's sickly condition made an imperial election a distinct possibility.[66]

Between autumn 1679 and summer 1684, France used a mixture of real and invented claims, backed by the threat of renewed war, to extend its eastern and northern frontiers. Operating through the *Parlements* (regional supreme courts) of Metz and newly-acquired Besançon, as well as special *Chambres de Réunion*, French lawyers reinterpreted the peace treaties of 1648 and 1678–9 to "reunite" additional areas as alleged dependencies of the recent gains. Simultaneously a diplomatic offensive was launched to secure German and international recognition of the additional areas as permanent acquisitions and to sound out the possible candidacy of the Dauphin as king of the Romans.[67]

Not surprisingly, these actions proved highly controversial and have been hotly disputed ever since. There has been a tendency, still not entirely extinct, to interpret these events from nationalist perspectives as either justified expansion of France to its "natural frontiers", or as one in a long series of perfidious aggression against Germany. However, it makes as little sense to compare the *Réunions* of Louis XIV with the annexations of the revolutionary French Republic as it does to liken them to the French occupation of the Rhineland and Ruhr in 1919–23.[68] Instead, they need to be seen in a wider context, as Louis was neither unique in his motives nor methods. Heinz Schilling and John Stoye have drawn attention to similarities between the French *Réunions* and the aggressive policies of Denmark and the larger German territories, with Schilling noting the suppression of Münster, Erfurt, Magdeburg and Brunswick by their princes and Stoye referring to Danish designs on Hamburg as "Christian V's Strasbourg". It is irrelevant to argue like Aretin that Strasbourg's autonomy had better legal foundation (it was an imperial city) than the others, since all were victims of the same combination of intimidation, reinterpretation of old claims and the fabrication of new ones.[69] Moreover, such policies were only possible because of the same

58

fundamental weaknesses in the *Reich*. Significantly, these encroachments stopped as the *Reich* revived, first, in respect to internal juridification in the 1670s, and later, more fully with the reforms of the early 1680s. It's certainly no coincidence that it was precisely Denmark, Brandenburg, Hanover and Münster – all equally disappointed with Nijmegen – that conspired with France in 1679–84 to restart the war in northern Germany and counselled appeasement rather than resistance to French *Réunions* in the Rhineland.

Beginning in September 1679, French troops occupied territories on the left bank of the Rhine culminating in the seizure of Strasbourg on 30 September 1681. Thereafter, attention switched to the north, where incursions into Luxembourg escalated into full war with Spain in 1683–4, leading to the absorption of the duchy by France. The impression of French aggression was magnified by Louis's policies elsewhere. The first encroachments in the Rhineland were paralleled by the arrival of French troops in Monaco and Pinerolo; Casale in Mantua was seized at the same time as Strasbourg; the bombardment of Genoa, Chios and Algiers coincided with the capture of Luxembourg; papal supremacy was flouted by the Gallican Articles, as the king ignored the protests of Europe's secular overlord. Meanwhile, having failed to seize Hamburg in 1679, Denmark overran Holstein-Gottorp three years later. By 1684 large areas of the Lower Saxon, Upper and Electoral Rhenish *Kreise* along with the remainder of Burgundy were occupied by foreign powers who were unlikely to respect their continued integration within the *Reich*.[70]

These developments were compounded by the collapse of collective security and the rise of the armed princes. To them, though alarming, French and Danish belligerence provided a convenient excuse to continue the wartime exploitation of their unarmed neighbours, now all the more vital to their military finance given the end of Dutch, Spanish and Austrian subsidies in 1678. Some, however, clearly wanted more, intending like France to convert temporary occupation into permanent possession as compensation for the disappointing peace. Brandenburg pressed the *Reichstag* in 1679 to confirm its claims to East Frisia and permit the annexation of the imperial cities of Dortmund, Nordhausen and Mühlhausen as recompense for Frederick William's efforts on behalf of the common cause. Even more disturbing was Leopold's counterclaims for the city of Überlingen and the three Ortenau towns of Zell, Gengenbach and Offenburg in place of Freiburg lost to France. Though both sets of demands were rejected, the position of the weaker territories remained precarious. Having already suffered disproportionately during the war from enemy and allied depredations, they now found themselves the primary targets of their neighbours' reunion-style policies.

Leopold was caught at a disadvantage, as the peace settlement coincided with an escalation of the Hungarian revolt and the outbreaks of both a serious peasant rising in Bohemia and plague in Vienna. The war had demonstrated he could expect little from Spain, while attempts to continue co-operation with the Dutch broke down after fruitless negotiations during 1680–1. Diplomatic isolation was paralleled by dwindling support in the *Reich*, where it was obvious that Leopold could neither protect his traditional supporters nor satisfy the growing demands of the armed princes. Any solution to either the *Réunions* crisis or defence reform had to be linked to his attempts to rebuild Habsburg influence in the *Reich*.

For this reason it is necessary to reject the traditional interpretation of this period as a Habsburg sell-out of German interests, culminating in the Truce of Regensburg with France in August 1684, whereby Leopold recognized the validity of the *Réunions* for 20 years and pursued a war of conquest against the Turks instead. Far from abandoning the *Reich*, Leopold was preoccupied with restoring and upholding its integrity, recognizing the importance of this to his imperial recovery and turning eastwards only with reluctance when this became unavoidable with the Turkish attack on Vienna in 1683. The misunderstanding surrounding his actions stems from seeing war as the only reasonable response to French aggression. In fact, resistance would have been counterproductive, and Ernst Opgenoorth is correct in rejecting the notion that the *Réunions* could have been stopped if Brandenburg had joined Austria in a common effort.[71] The failure of the Great Elector to do this long exercised Borussian historians and has been attributed to the pernicious influence of French subsidies. Though Frederick William was prepared to fall in with French designs in order to advance his own interests, he also counselled appeasement as the only viable means of moderating Louis's demands. In view of the *Reich*'s military weakness prior to the reforms of 1681–2, this was a correct assessment. Moreover, the elector also appreciated the wider international situation. While it was significant that Louis turned his attention elsewhere after the Germans began to arm in 1681, the *Reich* was in no position to prevent the *Réunions* in Luxembourg or reverse those in Alsace without foreign assistance. Given Spain's chronic weakness, this could only come from the Dutch, but it was not until after 1684 that the Republic was prepared to take action, as William of Orange reasserted control over its foreign policy and anti-French feeling was stirred by Louis's revocation of the Edict of Nantes.[72] Meanwhile, continued Habsburg victories against the Turks after 1684 relieved the pressure in the east and placed Leopold in a better position to do something on the Rhine when war did finally break out in 1688. Rather than a sell-out, the Regensburg Truce is better interpreted as a damage limitation exercise that not only allowed the emperor to re-establish his position in the *Reich* but marked a major diplomatic reverse for French influence in Germany.

Despite suffering French belligerence, most imperial estates were prepared to co-operate with Louis after 1679 to preserve the peace, falling in with his requests to secure a *Reichstag* decision requiring Leopold to withdraw Austrian forces from the Rhineland. By complying, Leopold won support, in pointed contrast to Louis, who failed to withdraw his own troops and began the *Réunions*.[73] Co-operation between Leopold and the lesser territories grew as both sought diplomatic measures to ensure France honoured the Treaty of Nijmegen. Louis portrayed his annexations as simply the fulfilment of the peace terms, and it was far from clear how far his claims would extend or how ready he would be to resort to violence to enforce them. The prevailing attitude to war insisted on the peaceful settlement of disputes with the use of force only as the last resort.[74] Given the predisposition of the lesser princes to conflict resolution, it was natural that they should favour negotiation rather than armed resistance. The persistence of the French threat compelled a reluctant Leopold to continue the *Reichstag* and appoint the highly esteemed Theodor Heinrich Altet von Strattmann (1637–93) as his representative, enhancing the assembly's prestige and consolidating the trend towards permanence present since 1663.[75]

Continued co-operation between emperor and princes enabled the *Reichstag* to fulfil the role assigned it in the IPO to arbitrate international disputes involving the *Reich*. Responding to French offers, a *Reichsdeputation* was established in Frankfurt in March 1681, with representatives from all three colleges to assist the emperor's negotiators. Often dismissed as a pointless talking shop, the Deputation in fact served a useful purpose.[76] Using protocol disputes as an excuse, both sides spun out proceedings while they competed for the favours of key German princes. Leopold was considerably more successful in this than Louis by the time the Deputation broke up in December 1682. The compromise over defence reform in the meantime (see below) allayed the unarmed princes' fears without alienating too many of their armed neighbours. Leopold won respect through his obstinate refusal to recognize French annexations as permanent while the Laxenburg Alliance of June 1682 strengthened his position through a formal cross-confessional combination of armed and unarmed princes. Perhaps most significant was the role of the Deputation itself. By involving the *Reich*, Leopold demonstrated his credentials as an emperor who honoured tradition and the constitution at a time when French aggression was undermining Louis's credit in Germany. Leopold retained this support after 1682 by switching negotiations to the *Reichstag* and by capitalizing on the wave of imperial patriotism sweeping the German courts in the wake of the Turkish attack on Vienna. His position within the

Reich had been considerably strengthened by the summer of 1684 as France abandoned its original demands and settled for the 20 years' truce at Regensburg. Leopold and the war-weary lesser princes had drawn together in a new system of defence co-operation, the majority now recognizing his supremacy in foreign policy and ratifying the truce on 9 September. Meanwhile, the pro-French armed princes were isolated and forced to reconsider their opposition to Habsburg policy. Finally, all this had been achieved without undermining the *Reich*. Indeed, many of the federalist tendencies had been deflected, as the *Reichstag* realized its functions without impinging on the emperor's traditional authority and the French threat had been stemmed with the two in harmony rather than conflict.[77]

The extent of Leopold's recovery becomes clearer still when we examine his handling of defence reform over the same period. The shortcomings of his management of the war were obvious to ministers in Vienna by 1679, and, given continued French aggression and the fact that the Truce of Vasvar with the Turks was due to expire in 1684, the Austrian Court War Council (*Hofkriegsrat*) was entrusted with working out concrete reform proposals. The preferred option was the monarchical solution long desired by the emperor, with a permanent army (*Reichsarmada*) funded through a central war treasury (*Reichskriegskasse*), into which the princes were to pay war taxes. The second option was to endorse the armed princes' solution by sanctioning the continuation of assignations on a permanent basis. Alternatively, the *Reich* could strengthen the existing matricular system and oblige all to contribute actual contingents to a common army under overall imperial direction.

Whichever solution was adopted, Leopold was determined to retain full control over war management and peacemaking, and, as before, he concealed his true intentions, approaching the *Reichstag* in October 1679 only for general advice as to how the French threat might be confronted. In December, Mainz was prevented from tabling the question for open discussion on the grounds that the emperor wished to consult the electors first. Meanwhile, imperial diplomats negotiated separately with the leading armed princes, ostensibly for bilateral defensive pacts, but really to create an alliance network that could be converted into a new system of collective security. The others were simply expected to fall in with whatever was decided.

France sought to frustrate this plan by a mixture of bribes and intimidation, hoping also to win the key princes over to a permanent recognition of the *Réunions*. With French troops already across their frontiers, the four Rhenish electors of Mainz, Trier, Cologne and the Palatinate wished to do nothing that might antagonize Louis and so rejected Leopold's offers of an alliance. The role of Anselm Franz von Ingelheim, the new elector of Mainz from late 1679, was particularly important, since his inaction deprived the smaller territories of the traditional alternative to Habsburg leadership. Saxony, in receipt of French subsidies since November 1679, also refused to collaborate, while Brandenburg actively opposed Leopold's efforts. Encouraged by French money and diplomacy, Frederick William grew ever more disenchanted with Leopold, who rejected his claims to the Silesian Duchy of Jägerndorf and failed to help him recover his subsidy arrears from Spain. In response to imperial overtures, Frederick William argued that the emperor had brought the current crisis upon himself and the *Reich* by failing to secure a better peace in 1679, and he hinted darkly that the other electors could not be trusted. Only in Bavaria did imperial diplomats make headway, especially as Ferdinand Maria's death in May 1679 diminished French influence there. Believing Bavaria and Austria to be inveterate enemies, Louis underestimated their convergent interests and did little to prevent Max Philipp, regent for the new elector, Max Emanuel, moving over to Leopold. The *rapprochement* gathered pace in July 1680, leading to a firm Austro-Bavarian alliance by 1683.[78]

However, this was not enough to realize his plans and Leopold was compelled to change tack and consider the lesser princes' demands. One of the most vocal was Georg Friedrich of Waldeck, whose lands continued to suffer the depredations of the bishop of Münster. Predicting that France would exploit the disaffection of the lesser rulers to prevent unified opposition to the *Réunions*, Waldeck rallied ten of the worst affected in a mutual assistance pact known as the Wetterau Union or Frankfurt Alliance on 19 September 1679.

What made the Union significant was its unique military organization. Instead of relying on the traditional contingent system, each member paid into a central treasury in Frankfurt that maintained a single integrated army with common arms, uniforms and drill under the unified command of Waldeck himself. This scheme probably owed more to Waldeck's experience of re-forming the army of the similarly fragmented Dutch Republic after 1672 than his earlier career in Brandenburg. It offered a fresh alternative to the three ideas previously considered by Leopold and was quickly taken up by other princes. Not only did Catholic territories begin to join Waldeck's initially exclusively Protestant group, but the newly-emerging medium armed princes showed an interest. Among these was Peter Philipp von Dernbach, who till then had espoused reform solely along lines favoured by the larger, militarized princes. Though recent studies reveal that he was not the originator of the eventual reforms, they re-emphasize his role in bridging the gap between Leopold and the smaller princes. As both a loyal ally of the emperor since 1674 and Franconian co-executive prince, Dernbach had influence in both camps and was instrumental in extending Waldeck's Union into the later, broader Laxenburg Alliance by 1682. Encouraged by his success, Waldeck proposed in 1681 to expand his organization to cover the entire *Reich*, providing an integrated army of 90,000 based at *Kreis* level but responsible to a central imperial war council.[79]

By the end of 1680 it was obvious to Leopold that he was not going to achieve his monarchical solution and he decided to take matters to the *Reichstag*, where he hoped to neutralize electoral opposition by tabling a set of proposals carefully designed to rally majority support. The scheme announced on 17 January 1681 resembled Waldeck's project in many ways, for though Leopold continued to insist on a central war treasury and unified command, he was now prepared to devolve considerable powers to the *Kreise*. These were to establish their own war treasuries to maintain forces in the manner of the Union, with the central agency restricted to paying the general staff and siege artillery train. Aware that it would lead to endless delay, Leopold pre-empted attempts to discuss revision of the old matricular system by simply imposing quotas on the *Kreise*, leaving the detailed subdivision of cash and manpower contributions to future meetings of the *Kreis* assemblies.

This public initiative gave Leopold a decisive advantage over the armed princes, particularly since his proposals utilized the existing framework of the *Kreis*, whereas theirs merely emphasized their selfish ambitions. Ferdinand von Fürstenberg, the new bishop of Münster, pledged 25,000 men if Leopold assigned him the entire Westphalian *Kreis* as permanent billets. Frederick William boasted he would send twice as many troops as Bavaria and Saxony together, if he was made commander of the imperial army. Fearing it would mean the end of his exploitation of Lower Saxony, Ernst August of Hanover declined Waldeck's offers to head the Union, proposing the secret Herzberg Plan instead to Leopold in November 1681. This called for a set of alliances to provide 60,000 men from the existing armies of the larger territories for an immediate assault on the *Réunions*. The force was to be divided into three fully independent corps under Hanoverian, Brandenburg and Saxon command and be paid for by the unarmed territories.[80]

Such proposals indicate the growing self-confidence of the larger princes, now abandoning their earlier endorsement of reforms based on the *Kreis* structure to advocate solutions resting entirely on their own fully autonomous standing armies. However, they also indicate just how these princes were out of step with the prevailing mood in the *Reichstag*, which saw Leopold's proposals as the ideal answer to both French aggression and German encroachment. Brandenburg's association with France, which was opposed to any reform, also removed it as an active force at a crucial moment in the discussions. Indeed, the customary situation was reversed, with Leopold championing the role of the *Reichstag* while Frederick William urged the proceedings to be wound up.

With his chief opponents outmanoeuvred, Leopold's proposals were passed in stages between May 1681 and March 1682, establishing the structure that was to remain in place until the collapse of the *Reich*.[81] The first decision on 23 May fixed the army's basic strength (*Simplum*) at 40,000, considerably less than Dernbach and Waldeck had hoped for, but a figure that could be doubled (*Duplum*) or tripled (*Triplum*) as required. The *Dictatum Ratisbonne* of 30 August apportioned the total amongst the ten *Kreise* (Table 2.5) for subdivision amongst the territories pending a final revision of the 1521 matricular list by the *Reichstag*. A batch of decisions in September, December and January 1682 worked out much of the remaining detail, confirming unified command under imperial leadership and endorsing the two-tier financial structure with a central imperial War Treasury to maintain the general staff and artillery and separate *Kreis* war treasuries for the contingents. Payments, measured in Roman Months, could be levied with *Reichstag* agreement for the former, while the *Kreis* Assemblies controlled the operation of the latter.

In practice this meant that fiscal rather than military consideration guided the repartition within each *Kreis*. Although allocated a fixed share of cavalry and infantry, the *Kreise* apportioned these amongst their members in cash equivalents and left it largely up to the individual territories to provide their official contingents or convert their cavalry quota into infantry at the ratio of 1 to 3. In extreme cases involving tiny territories like those of the Swabian

Table 2.5 *Kreis* **quotas for the imperial army, 1681**

Kreis	Cavalry	Infantry	Total
Electoral Rhine	600	2,707	3,307
Upper Saxony	1,322	2,707	4,029
Austria	2,522	5,507	8,029
Burgundy	1,322	2,708	4,030
Franconia	980	1,902	2,882
Bavaria	800	1,494	2,294
Swabia	1,321	2,707	4,028
Upper Rhine	491	2,853	3,344
Westphalia	1,321	2,708	4,029
Lower Saxony	1,322	2,707	4,029
	12,001	28,000	40,001

Source: As note 81.

Note: 2,000 dragoons were included in the cavalry totals.

prelates, this led to some contingents being measured in fractions of men. Although the object of later ridicule, this was entirely in keeping with established practice to ensure that no one was unfairly burdened.

The *Kreise* were left with considerable freedom as to whether they collected money to maintain a regional army or expected their member territories to provide individual contingents that could be combined as integrated regiments. The ruling of 15 September 1681 permitted territories to opt out by paying cash contributions called *Relutionen* that could be used to hire substitutes either indirectly via the Imperial War Treasury or directly by separate agreements with a local armed prince. The final piece of legislation on 16 March 1682 concluded the financial arrangements by confirming JRA paragraph 180 that territorial subjects were to assist in paying for these forces.

The *Reich* had opted for a reform of its existing mobilization system and not, as is often stated, created a standing army. The size of the basic quota of 40,000 men was small, though, since this was purely an accounting device, comparisons with the larger, permanent forces of France are misleading. Mobilization would inevitably be slow, since many territories still lacked sufficient troops to fulfil even their minimum obligations, though the desire to escape continued exploitation by the armed princes was to encourage even small counties to establish permanent forces after 1681.

Implementation of the reforms remained patchy, however, given the loopholes intended to reconcile the armed princes to the legislation. The result was a hybrid structure, combining a contingent system organized by the active *Kreise* with the territorial armies of the electorates and larger principalities. The Franconians and Swabians, along with the lesser rulers on the Upper Rhine and in Bavaria, established integrated units roughly equating to their official quotas, whereas the electorate of Bavaria, along with the larger, militarized territories of northern and eastern Germany, kept their forces apart, sending either separate regiments designated as *Kreistruppen* or as auxiliaries under special arrangement with the emperor. Hessen-Kassel, Hanover, Saxony as well as Bavaria reorganized and re-equipped their forces during 1679–82, placing them on a permanent footing of 7,000–15,000 men each, underpinned by new funding agreements with their estates. It remained to be seen whether the weaker and largely still unarmed territories of Westphalia, Lower and Upper Saxony could free themselves from the grip of these larger territories by forming their own integrated *Kreis* forces. The Electoral Rhenish *Kreis* was still paralyzed by the regional power struggle between Mainz and the Palatinate and by common fear of French retaliation, while the remaining two *Kreise*, Austria and Burgundy, were entirely dominated by their respective Habsburg rulers, who were free to field their own forces.

The revised structure was undoubtedly flawed and became the subject of considerable criticism both at the time and subsequently. Nonetheless, it was the product of a political compromise that sacrificed military efficiency to prolong the life of the traditional imperial constitution. The emperor achieved his minimum objective of executive control over the force through what became a virtual monopoly of the imperial general staff (*Reichsgeneralität*), while his own forces remained beyond *Reichstag* control.[82] However, territorial political and military autonomy was also preserved, while the weaker princes and cities were given the opportunity to achieve collective armed status through the *Kreis* structure. Declaration of war along with the mobilization and deployment of the Reichsarmee was still subject to *Reichstag* approval, preventing a perversion of the reformed structure for Habsburg dynastic objectives. In short, the *Reich* had revised its military structure in line with its internal political equilibrium and defensive international orientation. Its primary task was to remain the repulse of external aggression, first through the mobilization of *Kreis* contingents to fight the Turks after 1683 and later by the deployment of a formal *Reichsarmee* to defend the Rhine against French attacks from 1688.

Chapter Three

War on two fronts, 1683–99

The Great Turkish War, 1683–99

The Turkish attack on Vienna in 1683 represented the most serious crisis of Leopold's long reign. For the second and only time since 1529 the Ottomans entered the *Reich* and besieged the imperial capital. The attack came before Leopold had recovered full control of imperial politics after the setbacks of the 1670s. The fate of his dynasty seemed to hang in the balance, yet by 1699 the situation had been transformed and Austria was well on the way to becoming a great power in its own right.

Leopold had expected a Turkish attack since 1680, but until spring 1683 it was not clear that Austria rather than Poland or Russia was the intended target. The growing threat, along with French aggression in the Rhineland, prompted him to take the then still rare step of augmenting his forces in peacetime, adding 30,000 men to the Austrian army between 1681 and February 1682 to give a total strength of 62,400. Though the defences of Vienna and the border fortresses were improved, security was undermined by the worsening situation in Hungary, where large sections of the Magyar nobility still resented Habsburg rule. Leopold had been forced to retreat from the repressive policies employed since 1671 and offer wide-ranging concessions at the Diet of Sopron in May 1681. Count Imre Thököly, who had led the earlier rebellion, refused to compromise and continued the armed struggle. His forces had grown to 20,000–30,000 men and had overrun most of Upper (northern) Hungary by September 1682, when they were joined by 12,000 Turkish auxiliaries. Buoyed up by successes elsewhere, Kara Mustafa, the new grand vizier, decided to escalate his support into open war, hoping the capture of the "golden apple" of Vienna would secure his position in the Ottoman court.[1]

Habsburg field forces numbered only 32,000 regulars and 6,000 insurrectionists deployed along the border between the Raab and Waag rivers, while Styrian militiamen and Croatian frontiersmen covered the area to the south. Command was entrusted to Duke Charles V of Lorraine, as an experienced general and member of Leopold's German clientele. Though they represented all that could be realistically achieved, these preparations were hopelessly inadequate to confront the Ottoman host, numbering anything up to 170,000.[2]

Hopes of delaying the enemy by a limited offensive were dashed by Kara Mustafa's decision not to waste time reducing the border fortresses as his predecessor had done in 1663, but to push on to Vienna directly. Leopold left the city on 7 July, three days after the first Tatar and Turkish light cavalry crossed the Austrian frontier. In strategic terms this was a wise move, and from his new post at Passau the emperor was free to rally the relief force, but the effect on morale was devastating. Peasants cursed him for abandoning them after starting (as they saw it) a war, while 60,000 people fled Vienna in a single day, cutting its population by two-thirds. A week later the main Turkish army arrived and began its siege while irregular forces devastated the surrounding countryside. Tall columns of smoke from burning villages marked the horizon, striking panic far beyond and magnifying the sense of danger felt throughout the *Reich*.

Although there has been some speculation whether the Ottomans could have held the city had they taken it, its loss, however, temporary, would have been a major psychological blow to Christian Europe and a serious dent in Habsburg prestige. The Ottoman frontier would have advanced 160 km into the *Reich*, making the Habsburg hereditary lands untenable and directly threatening Bavaria and much of southeast Germany. Though it is now clear that the Ottoman empire was showing signs of internal decay, these were far from obvious at the time. Vienna had to be saved.

The relief of Vienna was organized through the new Leopoldine system of collective security, combining the reformed mobilization structure with alliances with key princes. No *Reichskrieg* was declared, as this was unnecessary against the Turks, but the *Reichstag* sanctioned a triple quota of *Kreistruppen* under imperial command. Given the continued tension in the north and west due to Danish and French encroachments, it was obvious that the formal structure alone would not suffice. Though Swabia and Franconia mobilized in full, the Burgundian *Kreis* was paralyzed by the French invasion of Luxembourg that September. Fear of France kept the Electoral Rhenish and Westphalians at home, while the Lower Saxons remained preoccupied with the machinations of Denmark and Brandenburg. Waldeck's Union forces did arrive as substitutes for the Upper Rhenish *Kreis*, but the core of the German relief army was provided by Leopold's new understanding with Bavaria. Max Emanuel had already placed his army on standby following a defensive alliance on 26 January 1683, and a further agreement on 6 August signalled the immediate despatch of his entire army along with the Bavarian *Kreistruppen*.

Other assistance had to be bought with concessions that consolidated the privileged position of the armed princes within collective security. Though Anhalt and the Ernestine duchies provided their own contingents, Leopold permitted Elector Johann Georg III of Saxony to take over the financial contributions of the remaining lesser Upper Saxons on 7 June 1683, initiating a virtual monopoly of the *Kreis* that lasted till the end of the *Reich*. A similar arrangement was struck with Hanover on 14 January 1683. In return for holding 10,000 men in readiness, Duke Ernst August was authorized to collect 16,000 tlr a month from the Lower Saxon unarmed territories in addition to a down payment of 50,000 tlr from Austria to mobilize his troops. Saxony sent the largest single German contingent following a further agreement with Leopold on 30 July, but Hanover, along with Celle and Wolfenbüttel, was unable to assist for fear of Brandenburg, which was still allied to France and Denmark.[3]

The Great Elector was genuinely concerned at Vienna's plight and re-garded the Turkish threat as an issue for all Christians regardless of confession, but he was still deeply embroiled in French-sponsored plans to restart the war in northern Germany and was reluctant to assist Leopold without receiving something in return. Despite its considerable military potential, Brandenburg continued to remain a minor force in events, its subordinate status emphasized all the more by Frederick William's decision to honour his obligations under the Treaty of Bromberg (1657) and assist Poland instead. This had already occurred in 1672–4 during an earlier Polish conflict with the Turks and indicated that, despite the hard-won sovereignty for East Prussia, the elector was still tied to his former overlord.[4]

Polish involvement extended Leopold's system beyond the *Reich*. In a treaty signed on 1 April but backdated to 31 March to avoid the stigma of April Fools' Day, King Jan Sobieski pledged 40,000 men to help relieve Vienna in return for 200,000 tlr mobilization costs. Logistical problems asso-ciated with the 450 km march delayed their departure despite urgent appeals, and when they arrived the Poles probably numbered no more than 21,000. However, despite the absence of the Brandenburgers, 33,000 other Germans arrived in time to join the Poles and 21,000 Austrians near Vienna by 12 September (Table 3.1) It was not a moment too soon. That day a Turkish mine blew a hole in the city walls. The defenders were down to only 4,000 effectives and distress rockets were fired to hasten the relief. As the allies appeared on the Kahlenberg ridge above Vienna, the Turks launched a counterattack at 5 am.

Moving uphill across ground broken by vineyards and small woods they were at an immediate disadvantage. The Austrians and Saxons nonetheless had difficulty holding their ground, but an attack by the Poles on the right relieved the pressure. The entire Christian line gradually advanced down the slope, beating off repeated counterattacks. This time the *Kreis* contingents performed well along with the Bavarians. Once they reached the flatter, more open country of the plain, the Poles launched a massive cavalry attack. The Turkish line gradually disintegrated, and by 6 pm the entire force was in full flight, abandoning its artillery and huge tented encampment. In addition to the 40,000 already killed in the siege, the Turks had lost 10,000–20,000 men compared with only 2,000 of their opponents. Vienna was saved and the entire area between Austria and the Raab river was recovered by the Christians. It was a truly great victory.[5]

Given the divided command, the allies naturally fell out over claims to the glory, and the debate on the relative contributions of the heterogeneous forces has continued to the present. In retrospect it is clear that it was a genuinely combined effort. No single attack decided the battle alone, rather as each element of the army advanced it drew Turkish forces away from another part of the field permitting a fresh assault in that sector. Superior morale along with greater firepower and the tactical errors of their opponents decided the issue. Nonetheless, the arguments had a serious impact on the allies immediately after the battle. Indignation at Leopold's harsh treatment of the Hungarian Protestants, along with financial difficulties and the growing tension in northern Germany, prompted Johann Georg III to withdraw the Saxon corps within days of the victory. Leopold's tactless handling of the prickly Sobieski soured Austro-Polish relations. The situation was not helped by Sobieski's poor generalship during the pursuit of the Turks, nor the behaviour of his troops, who left a trail of destruction as they advanced into Hungary. Nonetheless the allies cleared all of Royal Hungary and even pushed over the frontier to seize Gran (Esztergom), a city of symbolic importance as the seat of the Catholic primate of Hungary, held by the Turks for nearly 150 years. For Kara Mustafa the consequences of these setbacks proved fatal. Despite blaming his subordinates and executing 50 regimental commanders, the sultan remained unimpressed and had the grand vizier garrotted and beheaded on Christmas Day 1683. Such exemplary punishment did little to improve the Ottoman military, which remained in poor shape into 1685.

The success in 1683 encouraged bold plans at the Viennese court but at first Leopold preferred to negotiate a quick peace as in 1664 to be free to deal with the growing French threat. Pope Innocent XI would have none of this,

Table 3.1 Imperial forces, 1683–99

Contingent	1683	1684	1685	1686	1687	1688	1689	1690	1691	1692	1693	1694	1695	1696	1697	1698	1699
Electoral Rhenish *Kreis*															1,200[20]	1,200	1,200
Westphalian *Kreis*						1,150[15]				3,500[17]							
Lower Saxon *Kreis*	600[1]		11,846[8]	1,000[12]						6,427[18]	6,427[18]	6,427[18]					
Upper Saxon *Kreis*		800	800	800	800	800	800										
Bavarian *Kreis*	2,300[3]	2,300	2,300	2,300	2,300	2,300	2,300										
Franconian *Kreis*	3,568	2,000	4,000[9]	2,300[13]	3,800[14]	4,700[14]										6,400[22]	6,400
Swabian *Kreis*	5,021	5,016	4,500[10]	4,000	4,000	3,300											
Upper Rhenish *Kreis*	2,400[4]	2,000	1,960[11]	1,960	1,960	1,960									2,400[21]	1,000[21]	
Bavaria	9,000	8,000	8,000	8,000	8,000	7,000	1,000	1,000	2,000	3,000							
Saxony	10,454			4,700		1,500	1,500	1,500	1,500	1,500	1,500	1,500	8,000	12,000	12,000	12,000[23]	
Brandenburg	1,200[5]	2,000	2,000[5]	8269					6,324[16]		6,000[19]	6,000	6,000	3,070	3,070	3,070[24]	
Würzburg-Bamberg	3,780[6]	2,000															
Total	39,123	24,116	41,906	33,329	17,260	22,710	5,600	2,500	9,824	14,427	13,927	13,927	14,000	15,070	18,670	23,670	7,600

Sources: Notes 3–5, 9–11.

Notes: [1] Hanoverian infantry.

[2] An estimate based on the organization of the corps into 6 companies (coys) from Gotha, Weimar, Meiningen and Coburg, 2 from Anhalt and some Anhalt cavalry.

[3] 1,000 men from Salzburg and 1,300 from Pfalz-Neuburg and the lesser territories. These served alongside the Electoral Bavarian corps.

[4] Forces of the Waldeck Union.

[5] Serving as auxiliaries with the Polish army. Withdrawn in February 1685.

[6] Provided separately but serving together with the *Kreis* corps in 1685.

[7] Max Heinrich of Cologne's corps of 1,500 cavalry and 5,000 infantry serving under special arrangement with the emperor. Cologne soldiers made up about a third of the force, with the rest coming from the elector's Westphalian and Lower Saxon bishoprics of Münster, Paderborn and Hildesheim. At least 4,600 were transferred directly into the Austrian army at the end of the year.

[8] 5,436 Hanoverian, 4,900 Celle and 1,510 Wolfenbüttel troops serving under special arrangements with the emperor. The corps included 108 infantry serving in lieu of Lippe-Detmold's *Kreis* contingent.

[9] Two bns and 1 sqn from the smaller territories, 8 infantry coys, 6 cuirassier coys and 4 dragoon coys from Würzburg and Bamberg. About 1,700 men were transferred directly into the Austrian army at the end of 1685.

[10] The *Kreis* unilaterally reduced its 2 infantry rgts to only 3,000 men. The 2 cavalry rgts retained their original strength.

[11] 1,600 infantry, 360 cavalry including a contingent from Hessen-Kassel that rejoined the *Kreis* organization.

[12] Provided by Sweden under special arrangement.

[13] 1,500 infantry and 800 cavalry. Effective strength was possibly only 2,000.

[14] 3,000 infantry and 800 cavalry. Pfister, *Infanterie-regiment Kaiser Wilhelm*, p. 51, gives field effectives in 1688 as only 1,700 men. An additional 900 infantry were transferred by Bayreuth directly into the Austrian army in 1688.

[15] 1,000 infantry and 150 cavalry provided by Mecklenburg-Güstrow under special arrangement with the emperor.

[16] Official strength was 6,100, but Brandenburg actually sent 1,036 cavalry, 409 dragoons, 4,809 infantry and 70 artillery men. Withdrawn May 1692.

[17] 3,000 infantry and 500 cavalry from Münster serving under special arrangement. They marched with the Guelph corps.

[18] 1,000 infantry from Celle and 5,427 horse and foot from Hanover serving under special arrangement. 2,000 men were transferred permanently to the Austrian army when the rest of the corps was withdrawn on 24 May 1694.

[19] Although the official strength was 6,000, Brandenburg actually sent 6,069 men in the first instance.

[20] Palatine infantry. They had served the emperor in Savoy in 1694–6.

[21] 1,000 Salzburg infantry plus 1,400 infantry recruits transferred directly to Austria in 1697.

[22] A composite force provided by Würzburg, Ansbach and Gotha (Upper Saxon *Kreis*) under special arrangement with the emperor.

[23] Withdrawn July 1698.

[24] Withdrawn June 1698.

73

believing the time was ripe for the total destruction of the Ottoman empire in Europe. Through his nuncio, Cardinal Francesco Buonvisi (1616–99), sent as the emperor's new confessor, Innocent induced Leopold to change his mind. Papal mediation secured the Regensburg Truce in August 1684 while other negotiations led to the formation of a Holy League on 5 March 1684 between Leopold, Poland and Venice. The latter took some persuading having lost every war against the sultan over the last 200 years, but, hoping to recover lost territory and increase its presence in the Aegean, the Republic declared war on 15 July 1684. Papal diplomacy secured promises of naval support from Tuscany and the Knights of Malta. Great faith was placed in uprisings from the Balkan Christians, but although the Venetians did secure limited co-operation from the Montenegrins, the initial response proved disappointing. The Catholic Republic of Ragusa (Dubrovnik) was persuaded to place itself under Leopold's protection and offer 5,000 ducats tribute. The money was never paid since it was dependent on Leopold capturing Herzegovina, while the Republic hedged its bets by never formally renouncing its ties to the Ottomans. More significant assistance was provided by Russia, which co-operated through a bilateral treaty with Poland after May 1686, formally becoming a member of the Holy League on 8 February 1697.[6]

None of this was much direct help for Leopold. The framework of the League consolidated the divided command structure of 1683. While agreeing not to negotiate separately with the Turks, each member was left to make what ever gains they could on their own front. The Russians confined their activities to the Ukrainian front, finally taking Azov at the mouth of the Don in 1696. Sobieski had high hopes of taking Transylvania, Podolia and part of Hungary, but these ambitions clashed directly with Leopold's intentions, and the king had to set his sights on Moldavia and Wallachia instead. Major attacks, launched in 1685 and 1686, failed, though Podolia was eventually recovered in 1699. Meanwhile, the Venetians became bogged down in Bosnia and the Morea (Peleponnesus), leaving Leopold alone on the central Hungarian front.[7]

Leopold's decision in 1684 committed him to long-term involvement in the Balkans at a time when the fate of the Spanish inheritance remained unclear. These preoccupations in both east and west shaped his attitudes to collective security and his policy in the *Reich*. Austria was too weak to fight on its own, and Leopold faced considerable difficulties funding his war effort. At least 500,000 fl. was needed to maintain the army for a year in Hungary, and additional money was required for arms, ammunition, operational costs and for troops deployed elsewhere. These costs soared after 1688, when Leopold was obliged to open a second front against France. A "Turkish tax" was introduced to boost revenue, but even with the rapid recovery of the devastated areas around Vienna and a revival of the Bohemian economy, the hereditary lands could only contribute 3.5 million fl. annually by 1686. This helps explain the repressive practices in Hungary, which was made to contribute an increasingly large amount to its "liberation". Initially, only 60,000 fl. could be collected each year. New indirect taxes were introduced, raising the total to 2 million fl. by 1686, which became the norm after 1693, when the nobility were compelled to contribute as well. Though the nobles persuaded Leopold to revise their assessment downwards, the entire country was obliged to find no less than 4 million fl. in 1698. The bulk of the burden fell on the peasants whose share rose to 3.5 million fl. Together with feudal dues, 20 million fl. was squeezed from them between 1685 and 1689 alone. After 1687 Transylvania was also compelled to provide 700,000 fl. as a lump sum in addition to maintaining 12 garrisons. Though these payments were lost temporarily in 1690, the principality was made to contribute 400,000 fl. annually after 1691. Even these sums proved insufficient, making external help all the more important. The *Reichstag* voted 2.75 million fl. in 1686, two-thirds of which was actually paid – a sure sign of imperial patriotism. The pope proved even more generous, taking the rare step of authorizing special taxes on the Austrian and Bavarian clergy in 1683. Not only did they now pay a third of their income to the war effort, but Leopold was empowered to appropriate a third of the land acquired by the Austrian church over the last 60 years. Innocent also authorized the sale of huge estates belonging to Archbishop Szelepcsényi and Bishop Sinelli after their deaths in 1685. Once disposed of, these assets raised 1.6 million fl. by 1687. In addition to 500,000 fl. sent to help Sobieski mobilize in 1683, the pope gave Leopold at least 1 million fl. A further 300,000 fl. was sent to Max Emanuel, while a detachment of Polish Cossacks was paid directly out of Innocent's own pocket. By 1686, however, Innocent was less forthcoming, partly because his own funds were nearing exhaustion, but also because he rightly suspected the corrupt Austrian financial administration of squandering the money. Aid was reduced and where possible now paid directly to the troops in the field.[8]

Even when the money was available, Leopold found it difficult to recruit sufficient troops. Only 34,000 regulars and 9,000 Hungarians could be found for the 1684 campaign. This rose to 60,000 in 1685 and 67,000 the following year, remaining roughly at this level till 1688. The start of the Nine Years War slashed this to only 30,000, including increasingly unwilling Transylvanian auxiliaries.

Lack of funds and manpower rendered assistance from the *Reich* essential. The defence of the Rhine was not neglected but it did assume second place to the war in Hungary. The *Reichstag* continued to sanction the deployment of the *Kreistruppen* at the expense of the contributory territories. Campaign losses and fear of the French delayed the return of most contingents, which had been withdrawn at the end of 1683 to recuperate, but after 1685 they wintered in Hungary and were replenished by fresh recruits sent from the home territories. However, the northern armed princes, along with the four Rhenish electors refused to contribute on the grounds of the persistant French and Danish threats, while the troops from the remaining four *Kreise* (Swabia, Franconia, Upper Rhine, Bavaria) proved insufficient, particularly as these were also anxious at sending soldiers so far east when the situation in the west seemed far from secure.

Leopold exploited these concerns in his efforts to tie all the princes to his strategy through a network of alliances. Intended to integrate both the armed princes and the collectively armed *Kreise*, this policy represented a modified version of his management of the Dutch War. Aware that the powerful northern princes were scarcely going to abandon their ambitions overnight, Leopold tried to win their support for his version of collective security, and, by offering minor concessions and limited subsidies in lieu of billets, he persuaded several key princes to contribute auxiliaries to Hungary far in excess of their nominal matricular obligations. Austria's special relationship with Bavaria was sustained by the exceptional expedients of direct subsidies and the marriage of Leopold's daughter Maria Antonia to Max Emanuel in 1685.[9] Meanwhile, the Laxenburg Alliance was extended as the League of Ausburg in 1686 to include large and small territories committed to defending the Rhine should Louis resume his aggression. The loyalty of the lesser rulers was retained by permitting collective membership of this new group through the *Kreis* structure. In return for fielding their contingents in the east and defending the Rhine if required, members were exempted from billeting, transit and other burdens equivalent to their level of military involvement (see Chapter 5). Only in the north, where the *Kreise* still lay largely in the hands of the major territories, did Leopold tolerate the continuation of wartime practices in return for assistance in Hungary.

The cost in men and money was considerable and no prince made a profit on the arrangements even if they considered the political benefits worthwhile. Hanoverian officials reckoned the cost of a soldier in the Hungarian theatre to be two to three times the expense of one serving on the Rhine, and the provision of the auxiliary contingent in 1685 cost Duke Ernst August 140,500 tlr over and above what he received from the imperial commissariat. Together with the Celle and Wolfenbüttel units, the corps lost 400 killed and 1,500 wounded, nearly a fifth of its strength, and 800 of the 6,000 sent in 1692 also failed to return. Over 3,000 men of the Brandenburg contingent of 1686 died within four months of their arrival, while that sent five years later lost over 4,000 or more than two-thirds of its original complement. These casualties represented a drain on the resources of even the largest territory and threatened to destroy the princes' chief policy instrument. Provision of the *Kreistruppen* also represented a considerable burden, particularly for the smaller territories, which shouldered the lion's share. Hessen-Darmstadt's contribution alone cost 103,710 fl. by 1685, equivalent to nearly half its annual revenue.[10]

Increasingly, many territories felt unable to continue and sought exemption from further obligations in return for transferring their soldiers directly to the Austrian army. Such transfers became Leopold's preferred way of obtaining military assistance and he often spun out negotiations for auxiliaries in the hope that financial exhaustion would force princes to sell him soldiers at less than it would cost his own officers to recruit them. He also offered to reduce *Kreis* obligations in return for drafting soldiers directly into his own army. This would have gone a long way towards achieving the monarchical solution, converting the *Kreise* into recruiting districts for the Austrian army. Not surprisingly, when this was put to the Upper Rhinelanders in 1687, Waldeck objected vehemently, claiming it would ruin their military structure and "be a gross ingratitude to the honest soldiers" to turn them over to the Austrians, whose pay and conditions were far worse.[11] However, the Franconians were less particular, already transferring part of their forces at the end of 1685 by which time Würzburg was in such dire straits it was no longer able to pay its own contingent. Together with units from Hanover, Cologne, Münster, Salzburg and elsewhere, about 11,000 men were drafted directly into the Austrian army by 1698. In addition, 11,000–14,000 *Kreistruppen* served each year until the outbreak of the Nine Years War forced their recall to the west in 1689. Despite this, Leopold's bilateral treaties still secured an average of 12,600 auxiliaries each year till 1699, considerably augmenting his own field forces, which generally numbered less than 30,000.

The scale of the German effort was magnified by the provision of further auxiliaries to the Venetian Republic, whose limited population did not permit the raising of substantial land forces of its own. As before, the Lion of St Mark turned to the German princes to provide its claws. The exact number of troops cannot be ascertained precisely but the available details are summarized in Table 3.2 Given that the figures are based on official strengths and do not include replacement recruits, the number sent probably approached the 18,500 cited by Andler, with total losses being near his figure of 14,000. As at Candia, the soldiers were ravaged by disease and the harsh climate rather than enemy action, and effective strength was often well below establishment. The five Hanoverian regiments totalled only 2,258 men in September 1686, of which over 1,700 were sick. The officers were not spared. The Hanoverian contingent alone lost 140, while all three Saxon colonels died.[12] Altogether

Table 3.2 German auxiliaries in Venetian service, 1685–89

Territory	1685	1686	1687	1688	1689	Losses
Bayreuth[1]		2,000	2,000	2,000		1,500
Waldeck[2]				1,000	1,000	?
Wolfenbüttel[3]				1,210	1,210	910
Württemberg[4]			3,144	4,532	4,532	2,769
Saxony[5]	3,000	3,000				2,239
Hessen-Kassel[6]			1,000	1,000		820
Hanover[7]	2,451	3,200	4,000	1,600	1,600	3,000
Sachsen-Meiningen[8]				100		?
Total	5,451	8,200	10,144	11,442	8,342	11,238

Sources: Notes 12–14.

Notes: [1] 2 infantry rgts hired for 3 years from 1686.
[2] 1 infantry rgt hired for 2 years late in 1687. Strength and losses unknown but possibly totalled 1,000 like the other units.
[3] 1 infantry rgt hired for 2 years late in 1687. Returned January 1690.
[4] $4\frac{1}{2}$ infantry rgts, including 1 provided by Hessen-Darmstadt under subcontract.
[5] 3 infantry rgts arrived summer 1685, departed March 1687.
[6] 1 infantry rgt hired in 1687 for 2 years. Returned early 1689.
[7] 3 infantry rgts in 1685, 4 in 1686, with a fifth arriving in September. Effective strengths were generally considerably below the totals shown.
[8] 1 infantry coy, probably 100 men like the other coys. It suffered unspecified heavy losses.

such losses far exceeded those suffered in the better-known campaigns in colonial America.

These atrocious casualties were not predicted when the first agreements were signed. The primary motive was financial, not in the sense of profit but simply to guarantee the soldiers' maintenance. It is not surprising that Ernst August concluded the first agreement in December 1684 following his mounting financial crisis in the wake of poor harvests and the end of French subsidies. Johann Georg III of Saxony also opened negotiations at the end of 1684 to secure employment for part of his expensive army. Both obtained relatively advantageous terms, encouraging others to follow their example, especially as it often proved difficult to cover costs in agreements signed with the emperor. Venetian service thus looked especially attractive to junior princes and rulers of small territories unable to supply large contingents for Hungary. Regent Friedrich Carl of Württemberg entered the scene initially as a subcontractor for Hanover, hoping to create appropriate employment for his growing family and to turn the regiments on the duchy's estates when they returned. Finding it difficult to meet his requirements, he also subcontracted the raising of a regiment to a man in a similar position, Prince Georg of Hessen-Darmstadt (1669–1705). As brother of the reigning landgrave, he had no immediate prospect of political power, and like many junior princes had served as a volunteer in Hungary in 1687. Obtaining command of a regiment was the logical next step to advance his military career. Similar motives seem to have prompted Bayreuth, Waldeck and Sachsen-Meiningen to provide troops. Landgrave Carl of Hessen-Kassel was initially less enthusiastic and rejected Venetian offers to hire four or five regiments after 1685 but eventually agreed to a single regiment in March 1687 once negotiations with the emperor had broken down.[13]

By the end of 1687 it was obvious that the expedition was proving a costly enterprise and a number of contracts were deliberately not renewed. The effective end of the Morea campaign coincided with the outbreak of the Nine Years War and resulted in the recall of the remaining units once their agreements also expired. The Venetians were left short of troops to maintain the position in the Morea and fend off attacks in Dalmatia and so recruited another seven German infantry regiments between 1690 and 1695. In contrast to the earlier ones, these came entirely from private military enterprizers, either experienced German officers or junior princes acting on their own account. Assuming that they had a similar establishment to the Württemberg regiment raised in 1695, the total would have been around 7,000 men, forming the backbone of the Republic's army, which otherwise rarely exceeded 20,000.[14]

Assistance from the *Reich* permitted Leopold to go over to the offensive in 1684 for the first time in any Turkish War, but the campaign revealed serious shortcomings in his forces. The target of the Hungarian capital Buda proved too ambitious, and the siege had to be abandoned after 108 days at the cost of 24,000 men. The debacle prompted reforms, particularly in the engineering and support services. The commissariat was improved and river transport increased to take advantage of the fact that most of the major rivers flowed in the direction of the Habsburg line of advance. By the 1690s even the German auxiliaries had their own floating bakeries and hospitals that accompanied them as they moved south down the Danube.[15]

Though the Turks had increased their field army to 80,000 by 1685, German contingents added 42,000 to the 60,000 Austrians, giving the imperialists a decided advantage. A more cautious strategy also brought results. The Turkish enclave around Neuhäusel was neutralized by the capture of that fortress, while a relief army was destroyed at Gran. These victories sealed Thököly's fate. A flying column was sent back into Upper Hungary, taking the last of his strongholds that autumn. Tied down elsewhere, the Turks were unable to assist, and once defeated, Thököly was seized by the pasha of Buda in a clumsy attempt to trade him for peace. Dispirited, his 17,000 warriors laid down their arms in October 1685 and were promptly re-enlisted into the Habsburg army by General Capara and Pál Esterhazy.

A renewed attempt was made against Buda in 1686, when the arrival of Bavarian, Brandenburg and Saxon auxiliaries again gave the imperialists a force of 100,000 men. What they lacked in expertise and equipment they made up in dogged determination, breaking into the city on the fourth attempt after a siege of 78 days. Although Buda burnt down in the process, its capture after 145 years of Ottoman rule was of huge symbolic and strategic importance, and the Turks fell back, abandoning most of southern and southwestern Hungary. The duke of Lorraine continued the offensive the following year by advancing westwards into Slovenia. The Turks, who still had 60,000 field troops, blocked his path at Mohacs (Berg Harsan), where they were decisively defeated on 21 August 1687. The victory secured the recent gains in Hungary and opened up most of Slovenia to Habsburg conquest later that autumn. More importantly, coming after several years of defeats Mohacs broke Turkish morale. Only 7,000 men remained under orders as the army dissolved in a mutiny that toppled Sultan Mehmed IV and led to the rule of his brother, Suleiman II. It took until 1690 before order could be restored, creating an unprecedented opportunity for Leopold in the meantime.[16]

Lorraine was already moving towards Timisoara, intending to isolate Transylvania, when he learnt of the Turkish collapse. Pushing on directly he quickly overran most of the principality by October. Max Emanuel, who replaced the ailing duke in 1688, built on these successes by seizing Belgrade on 6 September. It was indicative of the extent of Turkish weakness that this major fortress was taken after only three weeks. The line of the Danube was now secure, opening the way to Serbia. Three thrusts were sent, into Bosnia to the west, Serbia to the south and Bulgaria to the southeast. Ottoman authority disappeared almost completely as the long-awaited Christian uprisings now began. The Bosnian Serbs together with those in Banat declared openly for the emperor, the Bulgarian Catholics began the Ciprovci rising while the Armenian renegade Jegen (Devil) Osman Pasha controlled the area around Sophia with an army of Bulgarian and Greek Orthodox Christians. To add to the confusion, Djordje (George) Brankovic, a southern Hungarian landowner, declared himself hereditary despot of much of the Balkans. Meanwhile, Thököly was still at large with a force of 1,000 bandits.[17]

From primarily defensive operation, the character of the war had changed with profound consequences for Habsburg policy and relations with the princes. Even without the outbreak of the Nine Years War it is doubtful whether the *Reich* would have willingly supported what had become a war of Habsburg aggrandizement, and the concessions made by Leopold to secure continual support after 1688 were in part to reconcile the princes to assisting the enlargement of his Balkan domains. At no time did he consider incorporating the new territory into the *Reich*, seeking instead to strengthen his own direct rule over the new areas by curtailing the power of the local estates. This had begun in 1687, when the combined Hungarian–Croatian diet meeting at Pressburg was persuaded to make the Hungarian crown hereditary and annul their cherished right of armed resistance to arbitrary rule. With both the Turks and Transylvanians now powerless to intervene, the magnates' room for manoeuvre was extremely limited. Nonetheless, Leopold hung back from abolishing the rest of the traditional constitution for fear of repeating the mistakes of the 1670s. This proved a wise move, because it soon became obvious that military rule was counterproductive. The paranoid military governor, Count Antonio Caraffa, clung to the old belief that all Hungarians were potential traitors. Suspecting a new conspiracy, he began the infamous "slaughterhouse of Eperjes", a brutal six-month investigation that failed to discover any hard evidence. Only after Esterházy and other magnates secured his transfer in August 1687 did the murder and torture end. The so-called Dietrichstein Commission, established in July 1688, represented another throwback to the earlier repression. Staffed almost entirely by Austrians and Bohemians, this body was intended to oversee the recovery and administration of the new areas. There were no Magyars on its politically sensitive subcommittee, the *Commissio Neoacquistica*, set up to redistribute the captured property. Most of the original owners could no longer be traced, and even when they did appear, destruction of deeds and documents meant they could no longer prove their claims. Leopold was presented with a windfall opportunity to reward and repay key generals like Starhemberg, Heister and Prince Eugene, along with army contractors and senior court officials, by granting them huge estates in Hungary. Given the recent destruction and underdeveloped state of Hungarian agriculture, much of these lands were largely worthless, but their arbitrary distribution angered the local nobility. The Germanization of the area culminated with the disbandment of allegedly unreliable Hungarian garrison troops in the old border fortresses and their replacement by Austrian units. Mounting resentment had a debilitating effect on Habsburg administration until civilian officials began to replace military government and limit the abuses after 1695.

As a defeated country, Transylvania could do little to moderate military occupation. The local diet had tried to negotiate in 1685–6 but Prince Mihály I Apafi refused to endorse the preliminary agreement. His military collapse in 1687 left him no choice. In return for guarantees for his personal safety, he changed sides with the Treaty of Blasendorf (Blaj) on 27 October. Twelve fortresses were turned over to the invaders, rendering further resistance impossible. General Caraffa extorted another agreement at Hermannstadt (Sibu) on 9 May 1688, transforming Transylvania into a Habsburg protectorate. The emperor then issued the so-called Diploma Leopoldinum on 4 December 1691, establishing a Transylvanian constitution lasting until 1848. In return for renewed guarantees for their political and religious privileges, the Transylvanians transferred full control over their armed forces to the Habsburgs. The political implications of this arrangement far outweighed the military for the army numbered only 6,000 effectives, but its loss nonetheless deprived the country of its autonomy. Since his accession in 1690 the new prince Mihály II Apafi lived a virtual prisoner in Vienna. After his abdication in 1696 his homeland passed fully into Habsburg monarchy.[18] A major source of instability had been removed from Hungary's frontiers and Habsburg territory extended eastwards to the Carpathians.

This triumph was offset by the outbreak of the Nine Years War, caused partly by Louis XIV's mounting anxiety at Habsburg gains in the Balkans. The withdrawal of the *Kreistruppen* and most of the other Germans reduced the imperialist to barely 24,000 effectives and undoubtedly robbed Leopold of the best chance to extend his conquests. It was only thanks to the continuing chaos in the Ottoman empire that any further advance was possible. The margrave of Baden-Baden, the new field commander, pushed south seizing Niš (Nish) in Serbia in September 1689. Marshal Piccolomini was then detached southwards into Bosnia and Albania, while Baden captured Vidin in northwestern Bulgaria. Piccolomini was welcomed by the Serbian and Albanian Christians but had to abandon Skopje because of the plague. He succumbed on 9 November, robbing the imperialists of an able negotiator, skilled at striking deals with local leaders. By January 1690 the imperialist position was beginning to crumble when 2,200 men were lost at Kacanik, representing nearly a third of the force in Bosnia and a sizeable proportion of the now much-reduced army. To sustain the momentum, Leopold issued his famous declaration to the Balkan Christians guaranteeing them religious freedom and preservation of their privileges if they accepted him as hereditary ruler. The response was disappointing. The Bulgarian Catholics had been massacred after the failure of the Ciporvci rising and the Macedonians who rebelled in 1689 met a similar fate. The faltering Habsburg advance discouraged others from attempting the same. Meanwhile, the sultan had recovered control of his army and proclaiming Thököly prince of Transylvania, he sent 16,000 troops to overrun that country in August 1690. To counterattack Baden turned north with 18,000, defeating Thököly by September. It proved a pyrrhic victory. In his absence the Ottomans invaded Serbia with 80,000 men, recapturing all the towns along the lower Danube, including Belgrade guarding the entrance to the Hungarian Plain. The rapid loss of this great city was a major strategic and psychological blow, triggering a wave of refugees from the areas south of the Danube.[19]

By now, Leopold's western allies had become concerned that Austria had become too deeply embroiled in the Balkans to prosecute the war on the Rhine with the necessary vigour. However, the Anglo-Dutch-sponsored peace talks broke down in 1691 because both sides still believed they could win an outright victory. Determined to succeed, Leopold did just what William III feared and recalled all but five and a half regiments from his force on the Rhine. New treaties were concluded with Brandenburg and Bavaria to obtain additional assistance, and Baden advanced to defeat the 120,000-strong Ottoman army at Slankamen on 19 August 1691. Fought in almost unbearable heat, the action proved costly to both sides, Baden losing 7,000 to the 20,000 of his opponents. By the end of the year Baden's army had fallen to only 14,000 effectives, but the victory stabilized the Hungarian front and secured the imperial recovery in Transylvania.

Without adequate forces, Baden could do little more than hold the line and he was soon transferred to the Rhine for a similar holding operation against the French. The stalemate was sustained in the Balkans by the arrival of more German auxiliaries in 1692–6. Attempts to take Belgrade (1693), Peterwardein (1694) and Timisoara (1696) ended in failure, while the Turks continued to inflict minor defeats on isolated imperial detachments. Though the commanders were repeatedly blamed for the setbacks, the real problem was insufficient manpower.[20]

The prospect of peace with France transformed the situation, offering a real chance for a breakthrough. Not only could Leopold redeploy Austrian forces from the west, but other princes sprang to assist him with soldiers previously hired by William III. This gave the new commander, Prince Eugene, a paper strength of about 80,000 men. As in the campaigns of 1688–96 the army was split into three groups. Two corps covered the western and southern sections of Hungary while a third guarded Transylvania. Using the two Hungarian corps, Eugene moved against Peterwardein, a major Turkish fortress covering the lower reaches of the Drava just north of Belgrade. Under the personal command of the new sultan, Mustafa II (1695–1703), 100,000 Turks moved to outflank him to the north. Eugene turned to meet them at Zenta on 11 September 1697, defeating them just as they were crossing the Tisza (Theiss) river. Though the sultan escaped, 30,000 of his soldiers died, many of them drowning in the river, and the Janissaries suffered a blow from which they never fully recovered. The Austrians lost only 428 officers and men.[21]

This time Leopold wisely consented to peace. The end of the war in the west had spelt an end to Anglo-Dutch support, and, aware of the impending Spanish succession crisis, the emperor was also concerned at growing Russian influence in the Balkans. It was clear that his army was in no state to fight on, as two dragon regiments had mutinied and others were in a poor condition. After long negotiations, the sultan agreed terms at Karlowitz (Sremski Karlouici) on 26 January 1699, accepting the principle of permanent frontier with the infidel for the first time.

Though the Turks retained Timisoara and Belgrade, they confirmed Habsburg possession of Transylvania and the rest of Hungary. These conquests transformed the Habsburg monarchy, increasing its territory by 60 per cent and throwing its centre of gravity outside the *Reich* for the first time since Charles V. From a frontier city, Vienna now lay at the heart of a vast empire, the total extent of which was more than the other German territories combined.[22]

The war had been characterized by a level of brutality unknown in the west. Unlike those elsewhere, commanders of Balkan fortresses had rarely surrendered once the walls were breached, compelling their opponents to fight their way in. Generals quickly lost control of their men, who were enraged by the inevitable heavy losses and intoxicated by xenophobia and religious hatred. Johann Dietz's eyewitness description of the scenes following the capture of Buda in 1686 surpasses anything conjured up in Grimmelshausen's fictional account of atrocities during the Thirty Years War: "Not even the child in the mother's body was spared . . . Naked children of one or two years of age were spitted and flung over the city walls! I was amazed by what was done and to see that mankind shows itself far crueller to its own than the beasts."[23] The imperial victories at Slankamen and Zenta were concluded with massacres of their defeated opponents, and at the later engagement of Peterwardein (1716) only 20 Turks were taken alive. Often these actions were taken as reprisals for Ottoman atrocities, though it is pointless to speculate who began this vicious spiral of violence. German troops often went into battle fortified with drink, while their opponents used mild narcotics. Turkish soldiers were traditionally given a gold coin for each infidel head brought back from the field, encouraging them to mutilate corpses as well as decapitate prisoners. Hanoverian troops had watched powerless as the retreating Turks cut off the heads of 200 of their fallen and wounded comrades at St Gotthard in 1664. If anything, the level of inhumanity seems to have increased as the wars lengthened, suggesting that the participants experienced the same incremental brutalization witnessed among soldiers on the eastern front in the Second World War. A pair of Turkish kettledrums taken by Hanoverians at St Gotthard were found to be covered with human skin. Turkish soldiers trapped after a failed sortie from Buda "were massacred, and most were flayed, the fat was roasted out and the *membra virilia* cut off and great sacks full dried and stored; for of these that most costly preparation known as mumia was made".[24] Brutality was deliberately employed as a psychological weapon to terrify and intimidate an inveterate opponent. When Prince Eugene invaded Turkish Bosnia after Zenta, he left a trail of destruction far worse than anything the French had done in the Rhineland. Having burnt Sarajevo, he destroyed all Turkish settlements along his line of retreat, carrying off the women and children as slaves.[25]

Violent displacement of population had become a major feature of the conflict. Following the imperial collapse in Serbia in 1690, 200,000 Orthodox Christians fled into Habsburg territory to escape Ottoman reprisals. By 1699 130,000 Slavonian and Croatian Muslims had been driven to Ottoman Bosnia by the advancing imperialists. It would be easy to regard these events as an earlier version of the "ethnic cleansing" characterizing the recent war in the former Yugoslavia, but although they share similar brutality, they lacked the pseudo-historical nationalist justification and often derived from the varied fortunes on the battlefield. It is certainly not possible to trace the origins of nineteenth-century liberation movements to the earlier Turkish Wars, for although the various groups all claimed historic "homelands", no one could define precise boundaries given the high degree of ethnic intermingling and the absence of reliable maps. Regional autonomy and religious affinity rather than national identity proved the major influences behind the response of local inhabitants to invading armies. Population displacement was also driven by the need of all contending parties to secure captive labour for their underinhabited territories. The Turks raiding Lower Austria in 1683 carried off 81,200 people, mostly women and children, for ransom or sale as slaves, killing another 30,000 captives deemed of no value. During the reconquest of Hungary, advancing Habsburg troops skirted minor Turkish fortifications, evicting the local peasants as they went. Herded into Habsburg-controlled areas along with their livestock, these then fed Habsburg garrisons while their isolated opponents starved. Turkish prisoners of war were taken back to Germany as slave labour for fortification and construction projects in Vienna, Munich and other major cities.

Some of these captives eventually integrated into German society, in-dicating that the cultural importance of the Turkish War extended beyond brutality on the battlefield. General Schöning, the Brandenburg commander at Buda in 1686, made off with "two of the most beautiful women in the world", who subsequently converted to Christianity and "made distinguished marriages". Fatima, another such captive, became mistress to the Saxon Elector Friedrich August and was later ennobled. Her son, Friedrich August Count Rutowski, commanded the Saxon army in 1745–63. Twenty-eight Turks who converted to Christianity later settled in Württemberg, and such cases were probably not uncommon.[26] Though Turkish fashions were understandably not popular in Austria, other Germans were both fascinated and horrified by the Ottomans. The Saxons placed five tents and eleven cannon taken outside Vienna in 1683 on public display in Dresden. The elector also kept an elephant, which soon died, and experimented unsuccessfully with a stud farm using captured camels. A "Jamissary corps", resplendent in Turkish-style uniforms, was briefly attached to the army in 1699 and 1729–31. The eighteenth-century Prussian artillery also included musicians dressed in the Janissary style, while black African "Moors" were sought after as kettledrummers and trumpeters in German bodyguard units long before the soldiers returning from America in 1783 brought liberated slaves back to the *Reich*. The Turks' greater use of cymbals and brass instruments was copied in Germany, spreading elsewhere to become modern military music. Scientific and intellectual horizons were also broadened as, for instance, looted copies of the Koran were placed in the electoral library in Dresden, while Marsigli, an engineer officer in the Habsburg army, sought out Turkish and Hebrew manuscripts while his comrades plundered Buda.[27]

The gradual change in attitudes reflected the decline of the Ottomans as military opponents. Though beaten at St Gotthard in 1664, the Turks had retreated in good order, and Montecuccoli remained convinced of their formidable strength. However, at Kahlenberg they were routed for the first time in a major engagement, and similar disintegration at Mohacs, Slankamen, Zenta and the later battles of Peterwardein and Timisoara seemed to confirm their decline. The defeats weakened the army's material base – over 300 cannon were lost at Kahlenberg alone – and by 1715 the advance of a new Ottoman host inspired only derision among Christian observers. Popular enthusiasm for further "crusades" against the Turks remained high after 1699 but was clearly waning by the 1730s and dropped noticeably with the absence of an active threat from the 1740s. By the time of Austria's last Turkish War (1788–91), the author of the play "The War Tax" could portray Austrians and Turks as part of a common humanity, while the Janissary uniform was well on the way to being transformed into the modern clown's costume as Mozart's heroes in *Cosi Fan Tutti* donned the apparel of "Albanians" as comic disguises.[28]

The Nine Years War, 1688–97

Louis XIV's decision to settle a disputed election in the electovate of Cologne by invading the Rhineland in 1688 destabilized the entire imperial recovery and nearly cost Leopold his gains from the Turks. The new attack stemmed from the failure of France's imperial policy since the 1670s and indicated just how far Louis had moved from Mazarin's cautious and pragmatic approach to German affairs. In contrast to 1668, when ambassador Gravel had swayed opinion in the *Reichstag* with legalistic arguments to secure German neutrality, France had moved over to a combination of intimidation and bribes during the Dutch War. However, the less France adhered to the traditional categories of imperial politics, the more difficult it became to find German allies, particularly as Louis no longer wanted to become a member of a princely league tied to the imperial constitution like the old Rhenish Alliance. Increasingly, Louis was only interested in the larger armed princes, who could be manipulated through diplomacy, subsidies and coercion to act as French surrogates within the *Reich* and regarded their weaker neighbours merely as pawns that could be sacrificed in the interests of his wider objectives. This policy became counterproductive, particularly as it was obvious in the larger German courts by 1684 that France was never going to deliver the political rewards promised in return for tolerating the encroachments in the Rhineland. Though Louvois, the war minister since 1677, believed that "the Germans must from now on be considered real enemies" both he and his royal master failed to appreciate the impact of their policies on princely opinion.[29]

Louis grew concerned at the scale of Leopold's conquests in Hungary, especially after the capture of Buda in 1686, fearing it would remove the Ottomans as France's *Barriere de l'est*, or eastern counterweight to Habsburg power in central Europe. The formation of the League of Augsburg seemed to confirm Leopold's growing hold over the *Reich* and prompted intensified French efforts to win over the key princes during 1687–8. Despite renewing offers of diplomatic and financial ambitions for princely ambitions, negotiations in Bavaria, Brandenburg, Hanover, Württemberg and elsewhere failed to secure firm support. Louis continued to underestimate the resentment aroused by the *Réunions*, which had deprived several potential allies of parts of their territory. Ill-will was heightened by French interference in the Neuburg inheritance of the Palatinate in 1685, when Louis advanced claims to the electorate on behalf of his brother's German wife in an effort to force recognition of the *Réunions* as permanent. Revocation of the Edict of Nantes, terminating toleration for French Protestants, angered their co-religionists in Germany and contributed to Brandenburg's alienation from France and its subsequent alliance with the Dutch and *rapprochement* with Austria. Meanwhile, French support for Denmark, which had continued its *Réunion*-style policies after 1684, overrunning Holstein-Gottorp and briefly attacking Hamburg in 1686, prevented a firm understanding with the Guelph dukes despite Louis's backing for Hanoverian electoral ambitions.

However, French miscalculation had its most serious consequences in the case of the Wittelsbachs, whose support was essential for the formation of any credible anti-Habsburg bloc within the *Reich*. Rather than back Max Emanuel's brother, Joseph Clemens, as succesor to Max Heinrich of Cologne in June 1688, Louis opted for Wilhelm von Fürstenberg, whose previous support for French policy seemed to indicate greater loyalty. Not surprisingly, French offers to condone possible Bavarian annexations in southern Germany fell on deaf ears, particularly as Leopold lent his support to the Wittelsbach candidate. The final straw proved to be the result of another counterproductive French policy: angered by Louis's defiance of his ecclesiastical authority, Pope Innocent XI upheld the election of Joseph Clemens, despite his failure to secure the necessary majority, while Fürstenberg also failed to win Max Heinrich's other strategic bishopric of Liège.

Louis resorted to violence to redress these setbacks, calculating that a limited strike in the Rhineland would stiffen Turkish resolve in Hungary as well as intimidate the Germans into giving way to his demands over Cologne and the *Réunions*. Crossing the frontier on 24 September 1688, French troops rapidly overran Cologne and the Palatinate, taking Philippsburg, Mainz and other key fortified points. However, they failed to seize Cologne city, while the other successes merely masked their underlying weakness. French military preparations since 1685 had been primarily defensive, concentrating on fortifying points in areas annexed under the *Réunions*, and the army was ill-equipped for a protracted offensive war. For instance, the French were losing their technological and organizational edge, not adopting the socket bayonet and flintlock musket until 1697, long after the widespread use of these weapons in German armies. Vauban believed that the soldiers were now inferior in discipline and stamina to those of the early 1670s and doubted the army's ability to operate effectively in the winter. Already in December 1688 the high command felt it could not hold much of the area it had recently taken, while mobilization was placing a strain on a struggling economy. Combined with Louis's desire to force the Germans to concede his demands, these concerns led to a renewed policy of systematic destruction that had covered 15,000 km^2 of Palatine and Rhineland territory by early 1689. The level of violence exceeded that experienced in 1673–7, with Louvois insisting that his subordinates carry out their orders to burn German villages even if it meant killing the inhabitants. Though 2 million livres had been extorted by the end of 1688, the field commanders doubted the wisdom of these tactics, and Vauban urged "using more humane terms to explain the king's intentions". Growing French indiscipline removed the incentive to pay contributions that were supposed to guarantee good behaviour, and the local inhabitants either fled or joined the peasant guerrillas attacking isolated detachments. By February 1689 French raiding parties were no longer able to penetrate a cordon of German outposts, and their generals had to rely on covert agents to burn isolated buildings. Fürstenberg's government in Bonn remained a puppet of the French, who even sold off his wine cellar to pay their expenses, while other princes refused to be intimidated, despite such blatant coercion as directing artillery fire on their palaces. Intensification of the destruction as the French retreated before the German counterattack in May only reinforced the futility of the policy.[30]

When French troops entered the Rhineland in September 1688, the bulk of the German armies were still 800 km to the east. Though the north Germans had already disengaged from what was obviously a Habsburg war of conquest, most were no better placed to help collective security, having hired part of their troops to cover the Dutch Republic while William of Orange invaded England. Leopold had almost no soldiers within reach of the threatened areas, while the complete collapse of the mutinous Palatine army hardly inspired confidence in the Rhinelanders' ability to defend themselves. The situation had returned to that of the early 1670s, only that Leopold and the lesser territories were even more dependent on assistance from those who still had forces available. Saxony, Brandenburg and Hanover combined in a secret arrangement known as the Magdeburg Concert in October 1688 to defend the Lower and Middle Rhine at the expense of the local inhabitants. Though welcomed as liberators when they arrived to stem the French advance, the north Germans were soon resented, especially as they began to demand payment from the south Germans as well, despite the return of the Kreistruppen from Hungary in January 1689.

Leopold acted quickly to prevent his new security system fragmenting and with it, his leadership. Backed by Waldeck and the lesser princes in the Reichstag discussions from 11 December 1688, Leopold established the principle that all assigned billets and contributions were to be co-ordinated centrally. This was followed by a formal Reichskrieg against France on 3 April 1689, sanctioning the continued Kreis mobilization and its conversion into a full Reichsarmee. However, it was hardly inspiring that the man chosen to oversee assignations, General Caraffa, had just been recalled from his post in Hungary after the notorious Eperjes Bloodbath.[31] The arrangements were in any case soon thrown out of line by the escalation of the war after spring 1689.

William of Orange's unexpectedly rapid conquest of England late in 1688 forced Louis to widen his limited operations in the Rhineland to a full-scale attack on the Spanish Netherlands and the Dutch Republic. Both responded by augmenting their forces with German auxiliaries, while William brought over Danish troops to help defeat James II in Ireland at the Battle of the Boyne in 1690. Now crowned William III, the Dutch stadholder could draw on British financial and naval power to underpin the anti-French Grand Alliance established in 1689. Louis's attempt to strike at Spain by attacking the weakly defended Duchy of Milan was foiled by the defection of his Italian ally Duke Victor Amadeus II of Savoy to the Grand Alliance in June 1690.[32] Thus by the end of its third year the conflict resembled an enlarged version of the Dutch War, with heavy fighting in the Low Countries and secondary fronts along the Rhine, north Italy and the Pyrennes.

France made a major effort, boosting its army to an unprecedented 420,000 men of whom perhaps 340,000 were fully effective. The consequent diversion of resources depleted the navy and left command of the seas to the Anglo-Dutch fleet, but did give Louis numerical superiority on land.[33] The expansion of his forces compelled his opponents to do likewise, with William doubling the size of the British army to 63,000 by 1695. Of these only 20,000–40,000 could be sent to the continent in support of the Dutch, who also had 63,000 by 1695. The bulk of the Anglo-Dutch were deployed west of the river Meuse (Maas) to confront the main French effort in Flanders, leaving defence of the other areas to William's allies. Spain could barely muster 30,000 men, who were spread thinly between the Netherlands, Milan and the Pyrennes. The entry of Savoy into the Alliance added another 8,670 in north Italy, while further troops were obtained from Denmark and Sweden,[34] but the collective total was still less than half that of France, making German involvement vitally important.

William quickly secured the services of the north German armed princes by renewing the contracts made before his departure for England in 1688. Already nearly 15,000 Brandenburg, Celle, Wolfenbüttel, Hessen-Kassel and Gotha troops were serving west of the Meuse by 1690. Five years later these had risen to over 36,000 through the arrival of reinforcements and additional contingents from Hanover, Meiningen, Cologne and Münster, followed by another 2,130 Holsteiners in 1696. Brandenburg provided 21,000 men for the Luxembourg sector between the Meuse and the Rhine throughout the war in return for irregular Spanish subsidies and locally levied contributions. A further 2,800 Brandenburgers arrived to assist Savoy by 1694 along with a Bavarian contingent, while the remaining 8,000–10,000 Bavarians also returned from Hungary in 1689 and transferred to the Luxembourg sector in 1692 after brief service on the Upper Rhine. Max Emanuel lent other troops to rebuild the Cologne army once his brother Joseph Clemens triumphed over the French candidate in 1689. The Palatine army was also reformed in 1690, rising to 16,000 by 1696. Along with 3,000–4,000 men from Mainz, 6,000–7,000 from Hessen-Kassel, 1,600 from Hessen-Darmstadt and about 2,000 Trier garrison troops in Koblenz and Ehrenbreitstein, these forces held the Middle Rhine throughout the remainder of the war. Defence of the Upper Rhine fell to the *Kreistruppen* provided principally by Swabia, Franconia, Upper Rhine and Bavaria. Numbering under 20,000 in 1689, these had risen to 41,300 by 1695, including over 3,000 provided by Brandenburg, the Palatinate and Münster on behalf of Westphalia to hold the city of Cologne. Another 10,000–12,000 were periodically sent by Saxony until 1695, giving a total of approximately 140,000 German troops deployed in the west. Further troops were fighting in Hungary, where the number of auxiliaries rose from an all-time low of 2,500 in 1690 to over 14,000 after 1695. By that time Leopold's own army had risen to over 93,000, of which at least two-thirds were consistently deployed in the east (Tables 3.3–3.5). Additional German regiments served as integral elements of the Danish, Dutch and Spanish armies in the west and the Venetian in the east, while around 10,000–20,000 troops remained behind in the territories, particularly those in the north, to provide further security.

The spread in scale and scope of German involvement compelled Leopold to modify his war management, beginning in May 1689 with Austria's formal entry into William's Grand Alliance. Leopold had collaborated with Spain and the Dutch before in The Hague Alliance of 4 August 1672, which had underpinned the previous anti-French coalition, but his involvement in the current grouping was altogether more significant. Whereas the earlier combination could do little for Leopold, the new group, strengthened by British membership, was more able to help. Most important was the secret Anglo-Dutch undertaking, made without the knowledge of Spain, to back Leopold's claim to Carlos's inheritance, which eased his worries in the west despite the current conflict.[35] Membership also enabled him to outflank the ambitious northern princes, who were initially refused permission to join despite providing auxiliaries for Flanders, while the *Reich* as a whole was also excluded its formal declaration of war notwithstanding.

Nonetheless, in the long term the emperor's position became more complicated since he was now committed to a war fought by a coalition and had to take account of British and Dutch concerns when planning his operations.[36] His determination to continue his campaigns in Hungary caused particular problems, as William suspected him of neglecting his commitments in the west, while Leopold resented pressure to make a less than favourable peace with the Turks. Meanwhile, the importance of German auxiliaries to the war

Table 3.3 Grand Alliance forces in 1695

State	Army
Britain	63,000
Dutch Republic	63,000
Spain	30,000
Savoy	9,000
Swedish auxiliaries	9,700
Danish auxiliaries	7,540
German auxiliaries (Flanders)	36,100
German auxiliaries (Hungary)	14,000
Brandenburg	21,000
Brandenburg (with Savoy)	2,800
Bavaria	10,000
Saxony	12,000
Palatinate	10,000
Mainz	4,000
Armed Rhineland territories	10,100
Kreistruppen	41,300
Austria	93,000
Total	436,540
Against France	362,540
Against the Turks	74,000

Source: As note 34. More detailed breakdowns of the German contingents are given in Tables 3.4 and 3.5.

in Flanders and Luxembourg raised Anglo–Dutch interest in imperial politics and prompted growing interference in areas traditionally considered Habsburg preserves. This could be beneficial, as in William's help in the election of Archduke Joseph as king of the Romans in 1690, securing the Habsburg succession. However, William's obligations to the princes also inclined him to support their dynastic ambitions in the *Reich* and outside, as in their desire for a greater international profile through formal membership of the alliance.

Strategic planning now involved lengthy negotiations in The Hague, Vienna and the more important German courts each winter to co-ordinate action for the coming spring. Matters were complicated by the armed princes' dual role within imperial collective security and as auxiliaries of the Grand Alliance, which often placed them under obligations to provide more troops than they could afford. Though most were keen to play an active role in the defence of the Rhine and share the glory that would follow a successful

Table 3.4 German auxiliaries in Anglo-Dutch service, 1688–97

Territory	Initial treaty	Partner	1688	1689	1690	1691	1692	1693	1694	1695	1696	1697
Hessen-Kassel	10 July 1688	Dutch Rep.	2,442	2,442	2,442	2,442	2,442	3,804	4,670[1]	4,760	4,670	4,670
Württemberg	2 Aug 1688	Dutch Rep.	1,296[2]									
Brandenburg	18 Aug 1688	Dutch Rep.	6,000	6,000	6,000	6,000	6,000	6,000	6,000	6,000	6,000	6,000
Wolfenbüttel	18 Aug 1688	Dutch Rep.	1,388	1,388	1,404	1,404	3,023	3,093	5,091	5,091	5,091	5,091
Wolfenbüttel	19 Jan 1690	England			1,604	1,604[3]						
Celle	18 Aug 1688	Dutch Rep.	2,720	2,720	2,944	6,511[4]	6,511	6,793	6,793	6,793	6,793	6,793
Gotha	15 May 1689	Dutch Rep.	425	425	425	425	425	425	425	425	425	425
Gotha	21 Jan 1691	England				1,600[5]						
Hanover	20 June 1692	Dutch Rep. and England					7,949	7,949	7,949	7,949	7,949	7,949
Cologne	29 Sept 1693	Dutch Rep.						456	456	456	456	456
Saxony	23 Oct 1693	Dutch Rep.						396[6]	396	396	396	396
Meiningen	2 Dec 1693	Dutch Rep.							348	348	348	348
Münster	18 May 1695	Dutch Rep., England and Leopold I								4,000[7]	4,000	4,000
Holstein-Gottorp	14 May 1696	England									2,130	2,130
Total			14,271	12,975	14,819	19,986	26,350	27,484	32,128	36,128	38,258	38,258

Notes: [1] England became a partner in the arrangement from 16 January 1694.
[2] Passed directly into Dutch service.
[3] Joined the units hired by the Dutch in 1692 when England became a party to the 1688 treaty.
[4] Included 3,119 men that had been hired to Spain in 1690.
[5] Entered Franconian *Kreis* service in 1692.
[6] England also paid subsidies to the Saxon corps serving on the Rhine.
[7] An additional 3,300 men served under a parallel agreement exclusively with Leopold in 1695-7.

Table 3.5 Kreis contingents, 1689–97

Kreis	1689	1690	1691	1692	1693	1694	1695	1696	1697
Electoral Rhine[1]									
Upper Rhine[2]	4,720	4,720	4,720	4,720	4,720	8,000	8,000	8,000	
Westphalia[3]	2,400	2,400	3,075	3,075	3,075	3,075	3,075	3,075	3,075
Upper Saxony	2,648	2,648	2,648	2,648	2,648	2,648	2,648	2,648	2,648
Lower Saxony[4]	7,754	1,112		2,310	2,310	1,755	3,794	1,810	2,584
Swabia	4,000	4,000	5,500	12,000	12,000	12,000	12,000	12,000	12,000
Franconia	7,023	7,023	9,000	12,000	12,000	12,000	12,000	12,000	12,000
Bavaria	1,450	1,450	1,450	1,220	1,220	1,220	1,220	1,220	1,220
Total	29,995	23,353	26,393	37,973	37,973	40,698	42,737	40,753	33,527

Notes: [1] No official contingent was formed but the 4 Rhenish electorates maintained about 10,000 troops in garrisons and outposts by the early 1690s.
[2] Excluding additional Hessen-Kassel (c. 6,000) and Hessen-Darmstadt (560 rising to 1,600) contributions.
[3] In garrison in Cologne.
[4] Contingents from Hanover, Celle and Wolfenbüttel assigned to the *Reichsarmee* but outside a formal *Kreis* military structure.

recapture of Strasbourg and other areas lost to the *Réunions*, no one was prepared to entrust troops exclusively to imperial command. Men like Max Emanuel, Frederick III of Brandenburg, Ernst August of Hanover, Johann Georg III of Saxony and Landgrave Carl of Hessen-Kassel wanted an independent command of their own, preferably incorporating as many other princely contingents as possible and deployed on the Lower or Middle Rhine sectors from where they could intervene either in Flanders or south Germany. Neither Leopold nor William were prepared to sanction this since it would consolidate the influence of whoever took command and raise expectations of appropriate political concessions in any eventual peace.

The problem was temporarily resolved in 1689 by entrusting the *Reichsarmee* and associated forces to Duke Charles V of Lorraine, whose determination to recover his duchy ensured his political reliability, while his military talents commanded general respect. His death on 18 April 1690 reopened the issue and prompted Frederick III to direct his entire field army to the Meuse–Rhine sector to avoid it serving under either Bavarian or Saxon command. Matters were only settled when William persuaded Leopold to transfer Margrave Ludwig Wilhelm of Baden-Baden from Hungary to the Rhine early in 1693. Already famed as "Turkish Louis" (*Türkenlouis*) on account of his recent victories in the east, the margrave enjoyed considerable respect amongst the armed princes as well as the collectively armed *Kreise* whose forces he also commanded.

Divisions over command were exacerbated by the divergent interests of the allies. Though both king and stadholder, William had far from exclusive control over Anglo-Dutch policy, as his rule was limited by both parliament and the States General. Initially the dominant partner in the alliance, Dutch influence was already giving way to that of British by the mid-1690s, especially as the Republic coped less well with the mounting pressures of war. While both were primarily maritime powers and shared concerns over Louis's expansionist policies, the British were more preoccupied about the Channel coast and a potential Jacobite restoration, while Dutch anxiety extended deeper into the continent, as their security rested on the situation on the Lower Rhine and in Westphalia.[37] These differences were not yet as serious as they were to become later, but they did contribute to delays in Anglo-Dutch negotiations with Leopold and the princes as both London and The Hague struggled to harmonize policy.

Meanwhile, Leopold continued to prioritize the reconquest of Hungary despite his genuine commitment to reversing the *Réunions*. He lacked the troops to make a major contribution on the Rhine himself and was compelled to rely on the *Kreistruppen* and whatever men he could persuade the armed princes to spare. These reinforcements were invariably late, since the princes delayed until they knew both how many men the Anglo-Dutch wanted in Flanders and what billets Leopold was prepared to give them on the Rhine. If anything, things were worse in northern Italy, where Leopold was obliged by a treaty of 4 June 1690 to provide 6,000 to help Savoy. Together, with the Brandenburgers and Bavarians, there were about 30,000 German, Spanish and Savoyard troops in the region by 1691, rising to 40,000 three years later. Their operations depended on the ability of Victor Amadeus, Leopold, Frederick III and Max Emanuel to co-ordinate policy and funding with the local Spanish government in Milan, the north Italian territories and the Anglo-Dutch, who subsidized Savoyard and German expenses: it is scarcely surprising that the local commander, Prince Eugene, continually complained at the lack of recruits, money, supplies and equipment.[38]

Bavarian involvement in this sector was indicative of another of Leopold's problems. From being his main German ally, Max Emanuel was now causing increasing concern as, estranged from his Austrian wife, he intrigued on his own in Madrid for a share of the Spanish inheritance. It was particularly alarming that he gained admittance to the Grand Alliance on 12 April 1691, since this appeared to indicate possible Anglo-Dutch approval for his designs. Worse, the elector transferred the bulk of his army to Luxembourg, following his appointment as governor of the Spanish Netherlands on 12 December. Following a damaging French attack on Catalonia in 1693, the German rivals considered despatching troops there to boost their credit in Spain. Hearing in 1695 that Leopold was sending three regiments to advance the chances of Archduke Charles in Madrid, Max Emanuel also transferred a Bavarian regiment to Catalonia.[39]

Preoccupied by such problems, the allies often devised strategy with little regard to what their opponents might do. Elaborate plans for simultaneous offensives were frequently wrecked by the late arrival of important contingents or by unexpected French attacks, such as when the Dauphin crossed the Upper Rhine in 1690, outflanking the forces collecting for an attack on Alsace. Serious gaps opened along the allied front as detachments moved from one sector to another in accordance with princely intentions or bilateral deals made without the agreement of other partners. The Saxons repeatedly pulled out of the Rhine front in protest at the lack of assignations from Leopold, and their withdrawal late in 1692 was exploited by the French, who raided Württemberg and Swabia, causing considerable damage well into the following year.

Louis sought further advantage from this situation by negotiating directly with Hanover, Münster, Gotha, Saxony, Sweden and Denmark to establish a neutral "Third Party" to disrupt the Alliance and assist in securing a favourable peace.[40] Leopold and William were greatly alarmed when Münster followed

Hanover and cut its involvements in 1691, disrupting their plans and allowing the French to launch an offensive in Liége. Capitalizing on Münster's location near the allied winter quarters, the two planned to assemble their forces that September to intimidate the bishop into returning to the fold. Armed intervention eventually proved unnecessary thanks to the success of imperial diplomats in detaching Duke Ernst August from his secret French alliance. In fact the duke had never intended to ally openly with France, particularly as it became clear that Sweden would not intervene as it had done in 1675. Instead, he manipulated French efforts to force Leopold to pay a higher price for his loyalty. Encouraged by an offer of a substantial Hanoverian and Celle contingent for Hungary, Leopold conceded his main demand for a ninth electoral title early in 1692. The event was unprecedented, for earlier awards of electorates to the Albertine Wettins and Bavarian Wittelsbachs had involved the transfer of an existing title from one of the emperor's domestic opponents. The move did secure Hanover as a loyal ally till well into the eighteenth century, particularly as the new elector was also concerned at the rise of Brandenburg and remained dependent on the emperor to secure formal confirmation of his title from the *Reichstag*. Moreover, Ernst August's decision to hire other troops to the maritime powers to win their recognition bound him closer to the Alliance. Together with greater co-operation with the elector Palatine, this helped offset the loss of Bavaria as the lynchpin of Habsburg imperial policy. However, it also provoked a hostile reaction from a host of medium princes who all felt more deserving of imperial favour than the duke.

At the forefront was Anton Ulrich of Wolfenbüttel, who, as a representative of the senior branch of the Guelphs, felt the title should have gone to him and was concerned that Hanoverian arrangements to inherit Celle would marginalize his own duchy within the family's territories. Aided and abetted by Denmark, Anton Ulrich established the League of Corresponding Princes in May 1692, joined eventually by Münster, Gotha, Ansbach, Würzburg, Hessen-Kassel and other middling territories. France encouraged these developments, hoping to bring the Saxons on board, but it proved impossible to find a basis for a stable Third Party. The conflicting ambitions of France's potential allies were revealed in 1693, when they fell out over the duchy of Sachsen-Lauenburg on the Elbe in Lower Saxony. Claimed by Saxony on the death of its last duke in 1689, Lauenburg had been seized by the Guelphs, who had entrenched at Ratzeburg. Denmark also coveted the area, particularly after Hanover and Celle had first thwarted plans to seize Hamburg in 1686 and then joined Sweden and the maritime powers in forcing it to evacuate Holstein-Gottorp in the Treaty of Altona in 1689. Encouraged by France, the Danes struck in August 1693 by bombarding Ratzeburg, destroying most of the town and killing nine of its inhabitants. This failed to open a northern front, as Leopold and the maritime powers moved swiftly to negotiate a Danish withdrawal.[41] Anton Ulrich regarded Lauenburg as a common Guelph issue and temporarily swung behind Hanover. The controversy over the ninth electoral title continued unabated, but France was unable to persuade Münster or Wolfenbüttel to undertake anything. By 1695 negotiations for a Third Party had collapsed and Münster joined the Grand Alliance.

However, mounting princely ambition made it harder for Leopold to refuse demands for billets and contributions, and this in turn undermined his leadership of the weaker territories established since 1682. Though the Magdeburg Concert of 1688 fell apart through internal disputes over zones of contribution, the north Germans had sent sizeable forces to expel the French from Cologne and the Palatinate. It made sense for their troops to remain in outposts and quarters along the Rhine and its hinterland rather than go home each winter. The princes claimed such billets should be provided free, since their forces already exceeded their matricular obligations and those of the unarmed north Germans on whose behalf they were also serving. The arrival of 30,000 Austrians and Bavarians in the region in 1689 added to the demand, especially since these had previously lived at the Hungarian's expense and now had to be paid by the hard-pressed governments in Vienna and Munich. Under pressure, Leopold defaulted on his earlier promise to the southern *Kreise* not to assign them to the armed princes as long as they fielded their own troops. However, the lesser territories had learnt their lesson in the Dutch War and, instead of retreating into helpless passivity, met this affront head on. Beginning with Franconia and Swabia in 1691, the Kreise banded together in the Association Movement to sustain collective armed status and exclude all attempts at domination. Gathering pace from 1695 under the leadership of the new elector of Mainz, Lothar Franz von Schönborn, the Movement began to challenge both the northern princes and the emperor, coming to the assistance of the lesser Westphalians' demands to be rid of billeting and seeking a voice in the conduct of the war and making of the peace.[42]

Matters came to a head when peace became a real option after Louis agreed on talks at Rijswijk in 1695. In addition to Max Emanuel, Frederick III, Ernst August, the Schönborn-led Association joined the Grand Alliance and disputed the claim of Seilern, the Austrian representative, to act exclusively on behalf of the *Reich*. Leopold regarded this as a serious threat to his leadership and fought to exclude them from the talks. He was assisted by the reluctance of both the maritime powers and Louis to admit the princes as equal partners in the discussions. Consequently, the German presence resembled that of the associated powers at the Paris Peace Conference of 1919–20; largely honorific and excluded from the real negotiations. Schönborn played into Leopold's hands with his inept attempt to co-ordinate the princes' efforts, operating "for the most part, in a world of illusions and appearances, rarely crossing the line into the substantial world of political realities and only marginally or temporarily affecting the directions taken by the major powers".[43] The elector made a serious tactical error in opting for a formal imperial deputation to represent the *Reich*, hoping thereby to avoid involving the entire *Reichstag*, where discussions would inevitably become enmeshed in the furore over the Hanoverian electorate. However, since the *Reichstag* had to be consulted over the deputation's membership, the emperor was able to delay its formations and weaken its effectiveness. As at Nijmegen, Leopold managed to negotiate on the *Reich*'s behalf, simply presenting the *Reichstag* with a *fait accompli*.

He preserved his prerogative but he was unable to stem the growing internationalization of imperial politics already apparent during the war. Though frustrated in their attempts to have a full say in the proceedings, the princes realized that their membership of a European alliance offered better access to international decision-making than collective action through imperial institutions. The more ambitious among them redoubled their efforts to be noticed, concentrating on the acquisition of royal titles as passports to the conference table. Elector Friedrich August of Saxony secured his by election (as Augustus II) to the Polish crown in 1697, initiating a dynastic union that was to last until 1763. He was followed by Frederick III in 1700, who sold his military and political assistance over the Spanish succession to Leopold in return for the title of king, technically only valid in his sovereign duchy of East Prussia outside the *Reich*. They were joined by elector Georg Ludwig of Hanover, who inherited the British crown as George I in 1714, and Crown Prince Friedrich of Hessen-Kassel, who succeeded Charles XII of Sweden in 1718. However, of more immediate importance was Max Emanuel's desperation not to be left behind set him on collision course with the Habsburgs over the Spanish inheritance.

Meanwhile, Leopold's sole representation at Rijswijk merely emphasized his responsibility for a disappointing peace on 20 September 1697. Though Luxembourg was restored to Spain and Lorraine to its fugitive duke, most of the other *Réunions*, including Strasbourg, were retained by France, leaving the Rhineland under direct threat and the Burgundian *Kreis* still inoperable. Leopold had done his best to recover more but the lack of any clear military advantage over France rendered it impossible. Coming at a time when he was consolidating his personal hold over Hungary, it seemed to many that he was placing his dynastic interests above those of the *Reich*. Worse, his partisan involvement was magnified by the so-called Religious Clause of the peace treaty that stipulated that the German areas returned to their rulers were to retain Catholic worship forcibly reimposed during the French occupation.

This was actually the work of the Catholic Elector Palatine, Johann Wilhelm, who had negotiated secretly with Louis since November 1695 to recover those parts of his lands lost under the *Réunions* and recent French operations. The elector was keen to win imperial favour to advance his own ambitions, which centred on displacing Max Emanuel as potential ruler of a future kingdom in the Spanish Netherlands. Aware that the devoutly Catholic Leopold could not advance their shared faith openly within the *Reich*, Johann Wilhelm secured the Clause himself and then presented it to the Rijswijk Conference as a *fait accompli*. Whether this was made without Leopold's knowledge or consent is unclear but it was certainly followed by closer Austro-Palatine co-operation: on 17 December 1698 an alliance was concluded, continuing Austrian guarantees for Palatine security in return for Johann Wilhelm's backing over the Spanish Succession and the formal recognition of the Hanoverian electorate. Over the next two years the elector worked hard to extend the network of pro-Habsburg alliances to Trier, Würzburg and Saxony, in addition to strengthening ties with Hanover.[44] However, news of the Clause unleashed a storm of protest from the Protestants, doubly alarmed by the near-contemporaneous conversion of the Saxon elector to Catholicism in order to obtain the Polish crown. Coupled with the still unresolved issue of the Hanoverian electorate, the controversy paralyzed formal imperial politics between 1698 and 1702. *Reichstag* discussions came to a standstill, while the Upper Rhenish *Kreis* broke down over Hessian-led Protestant opposition to Johann Wilhelm's attempt to establish a Catholic directorship. None of this was convenient for Leopold, who now needed German harmony more than ever in light of the imminent demise of Carlos II.

Chapter Four

Habsburg strategy in continental conflict, 1700–21

Imperial Italy and the Spanish Succession

Concern over the Spanish inheritance lay behind Leopold's reluctance to push imperial interests at Rijswijk. While recovery of the entire empire once ruled by Charles V was an objective, Leopold was realistic enough to appreciate that a partition was a far more likely outcome. His willingness to negotiate over the issue had already been demonstrated in his secret understanding with France in 1668. This treaty was now clearly a dead letter, and Leopold was conscious of the need not to do anything that might prevent such an advantageous agreement being reached again with Louis. However, matters were now more complicated as the growing interest of the maritime powers in Spain's fate made an understanding with William imperative. Neither Britain nor the Dutch Republic was prepared to let Louis or Leopold obtain the entire inheritance alone, since this would create a territorial colossus capable of monopolizing trade and power in western Europe and the Mediterranean. Either the empire should be partitioned, with the proviso that on no account should France obtain the Spanish Netherlands, or it should go to some neutral third party. The later option was decided in the so-called First Partition Treaty on 11 October 1698, allocating Spain, the Netherlands, Sardinia and the colonial empire to the Bavarian Crown Prince Joseph Ferdinand, with France taking Naples, Sicily and part of the Basque country, and just Milan going to Leopold's younger son Archduke Charles. Though confirmed by the dying Carlos II, this arrangement between Louis and William greatly alarmed Leopold, particularly as he was only told about it in January 1699.

The commercial potential of the American colonies or Spain's control of Mediterranean access, which so exercised the minds of Anglo-Dutch statesmen, were of far less importance to the emperor, who, as a dynast, was more concerned with the fate of Italy, which now became his "most important objective".[1] Italy had been at the heart of the Franco-Habsburg struggles of the late fifteenth and early sixteenth centuries and had featured during the recent war. Its prestige as the cradle of Renaissance civilization, ancient Rome and the Christian Church magnified the tangible strategic value of its territory and resources and strengthened Leopold's resolve to revive his position in imperial Italy.

Although no Italian representative had attended the *Reichstag* since 1496, virtually all of northern Italy except Venice lay within the *Reich*. The study of the relationship of this area to imperial politics has been revived almost single-handedly by Karl Otmar von Aretin, who emphasizes its importance not just to Habsburg dynastic interests but to the standing of the emperor in the *Reich*.[2] Though they remained outside the *Kreis* structure and system of collective security, the north Italians still considered their ties to the *Reich* as important. Austrian attempts in the 1690s to renew oaths of allegiance from the emperor's Italian vassals were met by an unexpectedly enthusiastic response, with more coming forward than existed on the list in the imperial Chancellery. A growing number of Italians took their local disputes to arbitration in the RHR, the only supreme court with jurisdiction in imperial Italy. The emperor was seen as a traditional counterweight to papal influence and as defender of weaker territories from the encroachments of larger states like Savoy, Tuscany and Naples. He was represented by permanent legations in Rome, Milan, Pisa and Pavia and his officials had a role similar to that of the *Kreis* infrastructure in Germany in co-ordinating common efforts like famine relief. Italians continued to look to Vienna and Regensburg as well as Rome for leadership and assistance. A deputation from north Italy addressed Emperor Charles VII in 1742, while even in the late eighteenth century the *Reichstag* still discussed Italian affairs. Emperor Joseph II, otherwise not noted for an interest in imperial politics, occasionally took his Italian role seriously, and his decrees against banditry in 1767, 1777 and 1788 were appreciated by local rulers. Altogether, the Italian connection was important to the emperor's prestige, pan-European pretensions and role as supreme arbiter.

The imperial position in northern Italy had long been complicated by the presence of Spain in Milan, Finale and the Tuscan ports known as the Presidi, as well as further south in Naples, Sicily and Sardinia. Imperial Italy covered an area of 250–300 individual fiefs all ultimately dependent on the emperor, who thus shared overlordship of the peninsula with the pope, whose authority covered 296 fiefs in central Italy, as well as nominal supremacy over Naples–Sicily. Charles V's decision to assign his Italian possessions to Spain in 1556 interposed a third overlord in the form of the Spanish crown, which sought to detach its areas from imperial and papal control and establish its own network of dependencies based on existing feudal ties to Milan and Naples. This long proved a source of friction between the two Habsburg branches until 1648, when Ferdinand III extracted Spanish recognition for his position in Italy in return for covert support against France. Ferdinand and later Leopold capitalized on continued Spanish weakness after 1659 to intensify feudal ties to Italy as compensation for the recent setbacks in Germany. The advent of renewed French interference in the area with Louis's *Réunion* policy frustrated Spanish attempts to re-establish independent influence and left them reliant on Austrian protection after 1682. Spanish officials in Milan co-operated with Austrian efforts to revive imperial influence, while a growing number of Italian nobles entered Habsburg service in preference to that of Spain or the pope. Italy became an important recruiting ground for the Austrian army, and from 1690 Prince Eugene attempted for the first time to levy contributions from the Italian vassals towards the imperial war effort, with the collection rate of one-fifth of total sums demanded compared not unfavourably with that in Germany.[3]

The experience of the disappointing campaigns against France, which had ended with the defection of Savoy by separate peace in 1696, re-emphasized the strategic importance of Milan. As the Italian Wars of 1494–1559 had proved, whoever held Milan commanded the Italian side of the Alpine passes to France and Austria. Acquisition of the duchy along with Spain's other rights in northern Italy thus assumed first place in Leopold's calculations once the conquest of Hungary was confirmed by the Peace of Karlowitz with the sultan in 1699.

However, his chances of obtaining Milan looked slim once the unexpected death of Joseph Ferdinand through smallpox on 6 February 1699 invalidated the First Partition Treaty. Neither of the maritime powers were prepared to reassign his share to Max Emanuel, whose attempts to consolidate his hold on the Spanish Netherlands by promoting its trade through Ostende was detrimental to their commercial interests. A second Partition Treaty was drawn up on 11 June 1699, redistributing Spain, the Netherlands and colonies to Archduke Charles and all the Italian possessions to the Dauphin, with the option of Milan going to the duke of Lorraine if he could be persuaded to relinquish his own lands to France. It is quite possible that Louis agreed to these terms in the belief that Leopold was bound to reject them and abandon his earlier co-operation with William. Certainly, the emperor now regarded the latter's promises of 1689 to assist him as worthless and sought a direct understanding with France instead, prepared to let Louis obtain the rest of the empire as long as the Italian possessions fell to him.[4]

War in the west, 1701–14

Ultimately, Carlos II put an end to this disregard of Spanish interests by assigning his entire inheritance to Philippe d'Anjou, Louis's grandson. Louis accepted this, hoping to complete Leopold's isolation, and following Carlos's long-awaited death on 1 November 1700, d'Anjou was duly proclaimed King Philip V. When the Spanish governor of Milan recognized Philip as his sovereign, Leopold felt compelled to act. Despite the lateness of the year, Prince Eugene was placed in command of the only available Austrian field army, totalling 24,000 men, assembling in the Tirol. As French troops began to arrive in Milan while Victor Amadeus threw his lot in with Louis, Eugene moved across what were considered impassable mountains through neutral Venetian territory (without permission) in June 1701 to surprise them. In a series of brilliant manoeuvres, he drove superior numbers of Franco-Spanish deep into Milan, occupying the pro-French duchy of Mantua in the process.[5] Though Eugene's army swelled to 45,000 with the arrival of additional Austrian regiments, it still represented Leopold's only strike force. He had begun a war he had no hope of winning alone, making the reaction of the *Reich* and the maritime powers absolutely crucial.

Thanks to Louis's overconfidence, the gamble came off. William became alarmed as French troops were admitted to the Spanish Netherlands by Max Emanuel. Louis's confirmation of his grandson's rights to the French throne raised the spectre of a Bourbon superstate spanning the Pyrennees, and his decision to recognize the Old Pretender as James III in September 1701 directly challenged the Protestant succession in England. Meanwhile, Prince Eugene's success in northern Italy appeared to be evidence of Austria's military power and raised Leopold's credibility as a potential ally against France. The Grand Alliance reconvened on 7 September 1701 in an arrangement ideally suited to Leopold's intentions: all Spain's Italian possessions along with the Netherlands were to go to Archduke Charles, while Philip V was to be forced to accept trade concession to the maritime powers in return for keeping the rest of the empire. Crucially, the Alliance held despite William's death on 8 March 1702, since both Queen Anne and the Dutch States General confirmed it.[6]

Leopold was again a member of an international coalition pitched against France, a factor increasing his chances of military victory at the expense of complicating his position of emperor. The rapidly changing European situation found its echo within the *Reich*, as the leading princes sought to capitalize on the chance to realize their ambitions. By 1700, Saxony, Brandenburg, Hanover, Bavaria and the Palatinate each had well-drilled armies of over 10,000 that could be expanded with the injection of cash subsidies to 20,000–

30,000, or more in the case of Brandenburg. Augustus II decided to use his directly and joined Denmark and Russia in an ill-advised plan to dismember Sweden's Baltic empire in November 1700. Intended to secure his position in Poland, this rapidly proved a disaster, tying him down in a protracted conflict known as the Great Northern War till 1721 (see pp. 129–49). In contrast, Frederick I "in" Prussia and Georg Ludwig decided to profit from the turmoil in the west, the former hoping for international recognition for his new royal status while the latter wished to enhance his chances of succeeding Queen Anne should she die without heirs. Their entry into the Grand Alliance reinforced its military potential and confirmed their status as semi-independent German actors alongside Leopold. Worse, Max Emanuel was known to be negotiating with Louis, offering the strategic advantage of a pro-French Bavaria in return for a share of the Spanish inheritance. Only Johann Wilhelm appeared loyal, but he too demanded concessions at Spain's expense. Meanwhile, lesser rulers like Landgrave Carl of Hessen-Kassel and dukes Eberhard Ludwig of Württemberg, Anton Ulrich of Wolfenbüttel and Friedrich II of Gotha had established forces of 3,000–10,000 men each and also sought access to big power politics. Hessen-Kassel, Württemberg and a number of others signed treaties with the maritime powers to provide auxiliaries for the defence of the Dutch Republic and the conquest of the Spanish Netherlands.

As in the Nine Years War, German involvement became vital to the allied effort; the Dutch had only 45,000 men in November 1700, while the English mustered a mere 7,000 plus another 12,000 in Ireland. The Republic did increase its strength to 76,800 by 1707, including regiments recruited in Switzerland and Germany, but although the English establishment reached a peak of 69,095 in 1709, Queen Anne could never spare more than 50,000 for the continent, and frequently less, due to the threat of a pro-Jacobite landing.[7] In contrast, Louis still managed to raise no less than 380,000, of whom perhaps 255,000 were fully effective, despite the mounting strain on the French economy. The Spanish army, which theoretically numbered 44,000, had an actual strength of only 18,000 in 1703, and while subsequent totals rarely exceeded this, fighting efficiency improved with the injection of French cash, equipment and expertise. In addition, Louis could count on 9,000 Savoyards until the slippery Victor Amadeus changed sides again in 1704.[8] Anglo-Dutch subsidies enabled the duke to boost his forces to 22,412 by 1710, but while the entry of Portugal in 1703 added another 10,000–15,000 more men to the Grand Alliance this still left it with less than half the numbers fielded by its opponents.

Both Britain and the Dutch quickly came to rely on German auxiliaries to sustain their war effort, particularly in Flanders. The Dutch already had over 56,000 German hired troops by 1707, while the later stages of the war saw no less than 97,000 Germans and 12,000 Danes in joint Anglo-Dutch pay fighting in Flanders, with a further 10,600 Germans in Italy and 7,000 Palatine troops in Spain (Tables 4.1, 4.2).[9]

The diversion of German forces placed collective security under considerable strain just as Leopold's allies expected him to mobilize the *Reich* for a war against France. His own contribution was fixed by the Alliance at 82,000, equivalent to the entire paper strength of his army in 1700. Raised to 108,670 in 1701, the subsequent official figure fluctuated between 119,000 and 138,000 thereafter, but was probably never more than two-thirds effective, and not all these could be deployed directly against France.[10] In any case, Leopold was determined to concentrate the bulk of his available manpower in Italy, relying on the lesser territories to watch the Rhine.

Unfortunately, Louis had lost no time in exploiting the controversy surrounding the Hanoverian electorate and the Rijswijk Religion Clause to further the paralysis of the *Reichstag*. A serious effort had been made from 1698 to mobilize support for French-sponsored German neutrality in any conflict over the Spanish inheritance.[11] In addition to seeking bilateral alliances with leading German powers like Brandenburg, Bavaria and Saxony, Louis tried to use the *Kreis* structure to neutralize the weaker western and southern territories. Key figures like Lothar Franz von Schönborn and Turkish Louis were targeted by French diplomats seeking to use their influence in the *Kreis* assemblies to revive the Association Movement as a passive, unarmed bloc of neutral territories. Meanwhile, Louis exploited the revived opposition to the ninth electorate following Ernst August's death in 1698 to encourage the reestablishment of the League of Corresponding Princes as a framework to manipulate the medium territories. Angered by Leopold's opposition to his candidacy in the Polish election of 1697 and by Austria's failure to pay his general's salary, Turkish Louis went along with these plans, joining the revived League with the rulers of Durlach, Wolfenbüttel, Würzburg, Münster, Meiningen, Gotha, Anhalt and Denmark in August 1700.

However, Louis's diplomats ran into the same problems they had encountered earlier in the 1690s, as it proved impossible to harmonize German concerns and French ambitions. Again, Louis overplayed his hand by moving troops into Cologne to deter German intervention. The south Germans and Rhinelanders were not prepared to belong to an unarmed group after their earlier experiences and followed Lothar Franz in reviving the Association Movement. Attempts to cause a new distraction in the north by encouraging Danish and Saxon ambitions collapsed when these proved to be at crosspurposes with those of Sweden, France's main Baltic ally. Others continued discussions solely to force Leopold to make concessions, such as the enfiefment of Ludwig Wilhelm with the Ortenau district in 1701. French efforts to steer the League of Corresponding Princes into more obvious opposition to Leopold nearly caused its fragmentation by March 1701, leaving only Gotha and Wolfenbüttel allied to France. Hoping for electoral titles, both increased their armies but would take no action without the active support of other princes. Diplomatic activity increasingly focused on Bavaria, as Joseph Clemens was expected to follow Max Emanuel's lead. Before he could make up his mind, Leopold narrowed the odds by sanctioning joint Hanoverian and Celle invasion of Wolfenbüttel in March 1702. Surprised in its billets, the Wolfenbüttel army was partly disarmed and the duchy forced to adhere to imperial policy. Meanwhile, Prussian troops carried out a similar operation in Gotha, and both duchies were obliged to hire auxiliaries to the Grand Alliance to ensure their continued loyalty.[12]

Jospeh Clemens openly declared for France in May 1702 to avoid a similar fate at the hands of the Dutch and north Germans, leaving Max Emanuel little choice but to start operations of his own in the hope this would compel Leopold to grant him a share of the Spanish inheritance. Neither of the Witttelsbachs was prepared for a confrontation with the Habsburgs, despite receiving French subsidies to the total of 39.8 million fl. by 1714. Cologne could only muster 5,000 men, and these were riddled with plague, which struck their encampment in winter 1701. Bavaria nearly doubled its army to 23,000 by 1703 but costs ran to 3.4 million fl. a year and the soldiers were already owed 1.2 million fl. pay arrears. Even when backed by nearly 18,000 militia, Max Emanuel doubted he had sufficient forces for a full offensive and limited his first strike to seizing some Swabian imperial cities in September 1702.[13] In doing so he unwittingly came to the emperor's assistance, for his attack prompted the Protestants to drop their insistence on linking any discussion of national mobilization to a resolution of the religious controversy. Despite the possibility of a Bavarian attack on Regensburg, the *Reichstag* voted a triple quota as a *Reichsarmee* and declared war on France in September–November 1702.[14]

Leopold had overcome the first crisis of the war with his leadership of the lesser princes still intact, but he remained threatened by Bavarian troops, while his ability to sustain harmony between his dynastic and imperial interests was undermined by the continued escalation of the conflict. The British were largely responsible for this with their decision to extend operations to Spain itself in an alliance with Portugal on 16 May 1703. In return for naval bases, trade concessions and military assistance, King Pedro demanded territory from Spain, subsidies and an allied commitment to expel Philip V. Now the leading partner, Britain convinced the Dutch of the necessity of this expansion of their common war aims and together they compelled a reluctant Leopold to agree in July. Archduke Charles was now to go to Spain as king in return for making

Table 4.1 German auxiliaries in Anglo-Dutch Service, 1701–12

Territory	Initial treaty	Partner	1701	1702	1703	1704	1705	1706	1707	1708	1709	1710	1711	1712[1]
Mecklenburg	27 Mar 1701	Dutch Rep.	1,680	1,680	1,680	1,680	1,552	1,552	1,552	1,552	1,552	1,552	1,552	1,552
Ansbach	29 Mar 1701	Dutch Rep.	2,214	2,214	2,214	2,214	2,214	2,214	2,214	2,214	2,214	2,214	2,214	2,214
Hanover and Celle	23 Apr 1701	Dutch and Rep. England	6,000	16,000	16,000	16,000	16,000	16,000	16,800	16,800	16,800	16,800	16,800	16,800
Hessen-Kassel	24 Apr 1701	Dutch Rep. (and England from 1702)	2,000	8,460	9,360	9,360	9,360	10,080	10,080	10,080	10,080	10,080	10,080	10,080
Palatinate	27 May 1701	Dutch Rep. (and England from 1703)	4,400	4,400	7,000	7,000	7,000	10,000	10,000	10,000	10,000	14,400	14,400	14,400
Münster	17 Oct 1701	Dutch Rep. (and England from 1703)	2,020	2,020	4,420	4,420	4,420	4,420	4,420	4,420	5,500	5,500	5,500	5,500
Prussia	30 Dec 1701	Dutch Rep. and England		5,129	5,129	5,129	13,129	25,129	25,129	25,129	25,129	25,129	25,129	25,129

State	Treaty	Paid by												
Liège	Jan 1702[2]	Dutch Rep.	2,379	2,379	2,379	2,379	2,379	2,379	2,379	2,379	2,379	2,379	2,379	2,379
Trier	8 May 1702[3]	Dutch Rep. and England	2,000	2,000	2,000	2,000	2,000	2,000	2,000	2,000	2,000	2,000	2,000	2,000
Osnabrück	13 Mar 1703	Dutch Rep. and England			800	800	800	800	800	800	800	800	800	800
Holstein-Gottorp	15 Mar 1703	Dutch Rep. and England		2,872	2,872	2,872	2,872	2,872	2,872	2,872	2,872	2,872	2,872	2,872
Gotha	27 Mar 1703	Dutch Rep. and England		2,600	2,600	2,600	2,600	2,600	2,600	2,600	2,600	2,600	2,600	2,600
Württemberg	31 Mar 1704	Dutch Rep.				4,000	4,000	4,000	4,000	4,000	4,000	4,000	4,000	4,000
Saxony	24 Apr 1707	Dutch Rep. and England						5,000	5,000	5,000	5,000	5,000	5,000	5,000
Wolfenbüttel	25 Feb 1709	Dutch Rep.									1,500	1,500	1,500	1,500
Öttingen	30 May 1711	England (and Dutch Rep. from 1712)											800	800
Total			18,314	44,282	56,454	60,454	68,326	84,046	89,846	89,846	92,426	96,826	97,626	97,626

Sources: As n9 plus PRO, SP108/214, 217, 218, 220, 225, 227, 228, 234, 237, 240, 241, 244, 246, 247, 249, 251, 405, 406; HSAS, A6: Bü. 59; G. Brauer, *Die hannoversch-englischen Subsidienverträge, 1701–1748* (Aalen, 1962).

Notes: [1] Most troops were discharged by April 1713.
[2] 3 infantry rgts recruited in Liège with the co-operation of the local cathedral chapter and maintained at the bishopric's expense.
[3] 3 infantry bns garrisoning Trier, Ehrenbreitstein and Koblenz. 1 bn of 700 men served in the field under special arrangement with England from 1709.

Table 4.2 German auxiliaries in imperial, German and Danish service, 1701–12

Territory	Initial treaty	Partner	1701	1702	1703	1704	1705	1706	1707	1708	1709	1710	1711	1712
Prussia	16 Nov 1700[1]	Emperor	8,000	6,000	6,000	12,000	12,000							
Bayreuth	18 Jan 1701	Emperor	3,100	3,100	3,100	3,100	3,100	3,100	3,100	3,100	3,100	3,100	3,100	3,100[2]
Würzburg	27 July 1701	Emperor	4,000[3]	4,000	4,000	4,000	4,000	4,000	4,000	4,000	4,000	4,000	4,000	4,000
Saxony	16 Jan 1702	Emperor		5,000[4]	5,000									
Weimar, Eisenach and Weissenfels	c. Apr 1702	Emperor		2,300[5]										
Baden-Baden	1702	Emperor		2,300	2,300	2,300	2,300	2,300[6]						
Wolfenbüttel	c. Mar 1702	Emperor		3,200[7]			1,113	1,113	1,113	1,113				
Nassau-Dillenburg	3 Mar 1702	Prussia		600	600	600	600	600	600	600	600	600	600[8]	
Gotha	23 Mar 1702	Prussia		2,121[9]										
Osnabrück	12 June 1702	Emperor		2,300	2,300	2,300	2,300	2,300	2,300	2,300	2,300	2,300	2,300	2,300[10]
Hildesheim	18 Aug 1702	Emperor		800	800	800	800	800	800	800	800	800	800	800[11]
Schwarzburg and Reuss	8 Feb. 1703	Franconian Kreis		1,000	1,000	1,000	1,000	1,000	1,000	1,000	1,000	1,000	1,000	1,000[12]
Mecklenburg	13 Apr 1703	Prussia			253	253	253[13]				742[14]	742	742	742
Mecklenburg	23 Apr 1703	Denmark			505	505[15]								

Paderborn	1 May 1703	Palatinate			1,280[15]	1,280	1,280	1,280	1,280	1,280	1,280	1,280	1,280	1,280
Hessen-Darmstadt	28 Nov 1704	Hanover and Celle				1,582[16]	1,582	1,582	1,582	1,582	779	779	779	779
Hessen-Darmstadt	21 Mar 1710	Wolfenbüttel									641[17]	641	641	
Palatinate	24 May 1705[18]	Emperor					4,100	4,100	4,100	4,100	4,100	4,100	4,100	4,100
Mainz	5 Aug 1705	Emperor					800[19]	800	800	800	800	800		
Ansbach	14 Mar 1709	Saxony									1,344[20]	1,344	1,344	1,344
Total			15,100	31,721	27,138	29,720	35,228	22,975	20,675	20,675	20,845	21,986	20,686	20,086

Sources: As n9 plus StAD, E8 B258/1–14, 259/2–3; Wrede, *Wehrmacht*, vols. 1, II; Jany, *Preußische Armee*, vol. 1; Bezzel, *Kurpfälzischen Heeres*, vol. 1.

Notes: [1] The "Crown treaty" whereby Prussia received a royal title. Official strength was 8,000. The larger contingent in 1704–5 was in lieu of Prussia's contribution to the *Reichsarmee*.
[2] Fully taken over by Austria after 1712. Bayreuth also recruited 2 rgts for Saxony 1699–1703.
[3] The infantry served as substitutes for Austrian *Kreistruppen*, while the 800 dragoons served against the Hungarian rebels in 1706–10.
[4] Saxony was supposed to provide 8,000 but only 5,000 served November 1702 to April 1704. Austria continued paying subsidies till 1712.
[5] The rgt disintegrated and the remnants were absorbed into other units. Weimar also recruited at least 1 rgt for Saxony.
[6] Taken directly into Austrian service. The later contingent served in Italy.
[7] Seconded to Bayreuth in 1705–7 to further Prussian policy. Transferred to the Palatine army in 1711.
[8] Used to garrison Magdeburg. Transferred to Anglo-Dutch pay in 1703.
[9] Fully taken over by Austria in 1716.
[10] Provided by the cathedral chapter. Fully taken over by Austria in 1713.
[11] Hired to fulfil Franconia's Association quota. Discharged in 1714.
[12] Hired as substitutes for Prussia's contribution to the *Reichsarmee*.
[13] Hired to augment the Prussian corps in Anglo-Dutch pay.
[14] Hired to make up Denmark's 7,000-strong corps in Austrian pay in 1701–9. Destroyed in an engagement with the Hungarian rebels in May 1705.
[15] Hired as substitutes for the Palatine Westphalian *Kreis* contingent.
[16] Hired as substitutes for the Hanoverian *Kreis* contingent.
[17] Hired as substitutes for the Wolfenbüttel *Kreis* contingent.
[18] The Palatinate was bound to the emperor before this but provided no formal contingent under a treaty arrangement until 1705.
[19] A dragoon rgt serving against the Hungarian rebels. Fully taken over by Austria in 1710.
[20] Hired as substitutes for the Saxon *Kreistruppen*. Fully taken over by Saxony in April 1713. Saxony also hired 2,219 Ansbachers (previously in Dutch pay) from 10 July 1713 to February 1717.

appropriate concessions to Britain, Portugal and the Dutch, while Leopold was supposed to contribute one-third of Pedro's subsidy. The original utility of the Grand Alliance to Habsburg dynastic ambitions had been destroyed, and Leopold was now committed to sending his son on a dangerous mission that seemed only to serve English and Dutch commercial interests. Charles himself was unhappy at being made king of a Catholic country, the conquest of which was dependent on Protestant Anglo-Dutch troops, while relations with his elder brother Joseph were soured when the latter insisted that Milan and Finale be assigned to Austria.[15]

This widening of the Alliance's objectives had taken place against a mounting crisis in Austria that came to threaten the very foundations of Habsburg power. Leopold's initial success at securing allies had masked the fundamental weakness in his fiscal–military position. The initial mobilization in November 1700 had only been possible thanks to the help of the estates, who voted a 50 per cent increase in their military taxes and took over half of the total state debt of 40 million fl. These measures relieved the immediate pressures on the Austrian Treasury (*Hofkammer*), enabling it to float new loans. However, tax revenue covered only half the current outgoings, meaning that finances were already precarious when the country entered the war. Unlike Britain and the Dutch, Austria had no means of servicing long-term credit, forcing it to rely on high-interest loans from individual financiers. The death of Samuel Oppenheimer in May 1703 precipitated state bankruptcy when it was revealed that the Treasury could only repay half the 11 million fl. of cash and supplies he had advanced the commissariat since 1701. To make matters worse, this coincided with the outbreak of a new Hungarian revolt, depriving the Treasury of urgently needed tax revenue and threatening the eastern frontier of Austria itself. Forced loans from courtiers and the collection of all private and church silver could do little to remedy the underlying problem of inefficient resource mobilization and lack of secure credit.[16]

The effect on the army was already felt in 1702. In place of the 80,000 soldiers he hoped to have in north Italy, Leopold could only find 20,000 by December 1702, of whom only 7,400 remained effective by April. Though recruits soon raised the total to 20,000 again, there were only 32,000 field troops on the Rhine to deal with both the French to the west and the Bavarians to the east. Meanwhile, Leopold's refusal to honour his earlier promise to the Protestants to return to the religious question led to renewed paralysis in the *Reichstag*. Led by Prussia, the Protestants refused *en masse* on 20 January 1703 to take part in any further discussions until the matter was placed on the agenda. Though Swabia, Franconia and the Upper and Electoral Rhenish *Kreise* had now mobilized under the auspices of the Association, the formation of the Westphalian, Lower and Upper Saxon contingents was still incomplete. Lack of clarification of details remaining after the initial orders of September–November 1702 provided a convenient excuse for Hanover, Prussia and Saxony to continue blocking the provision of troops instead of cash by those lesser north Germans who remained unarmed (Table 4.3).

The Bavarian *Kreis* was unable to take any action owing to the activities of Max Emanuel, whose forces had now occupied parts of Swabia. An Austrian offensive against Bavaria in spring 1703 failed through lack of manpower, while the elector's position improved still further when Villars and 30,000 Frenchmen broke through the Rhineland to join him in April. The condition of the Austrian army was so parlous that resistance against the subsequent Franco-Bavarian invasion of the Tirol was largely left to the local peasants. The attack was repelled and an attempt by the French in Milan to cross the Alps was beaten off, but elsewhere Louis's armies scored notable victories. When the Austro-German forces in Swabia fell on Bavaria in Max Emanuel's absence in the Tirolean passes, they were decisively defeated at Höchstädt (20 September 1703). Their own departure from the Rhine allowed the French in Alsace to seize the key fortresses of Breisach (8 September) and Landau (21 November). An attempt by Hessian, Hanoverian, Palatine and other German contingents to relieve the latter was routed at Speyerbach (15 November). Meanwhile, Max Emanuel increased the pressure on Leopold and the *Reich* to offer better terms by occupying Regensburg (April 1703) and then Passau (January 1704), directly on the Austrian frontier. Leopold consistently refused Bavarian offers to treat Regensburg as neutral on the grounds there could be no compromise with lawbreakers, but his inability to protect the venue of the *Reichstag* merely symbolized his powerlessness.[17]

Austrian fiscal–military collapse left Leopold acutely dependent on the maritime powers, who were not slow in turning the crisis to their advantage. Though he had felt strong enough to resist their pressure to compromise with Max Emanuel in 1701–2, this became increasingly difficult thereafter. Discouraged by Austria's poor military performance, the Dutch wanted to cut their aid and pull out of the Alliance altogether. Britain prevailed, keeping the Dutch on line and using their combined influence to compel Leopold to reopen talks with Bavaria in 1703. Although having little desire to meddle in imperial politics, Britain inevitably became entangled in other issues, especially given the importance of Protestant princes like Frederick I and Georg Ludwig to the allied army in Flanders. In September 1702 London lodged a formal complaint at Leopold's treatment of Protestants, especially those in Silesia, followed by further protests in 1703. Anglo-Dutch sympathy for the plight of their Hungarian co-religionists, coupled with the imperative of avoiding a further distraction to the southeast, induced them to push Leopold to negotiate with the rebels under Rákóczi in January 1704. All of this was

Table 4.3 *Kreis* contingents, 1701–14

Kreis	1701	1702	1703	1704	1705	1706	1707	1708	1709	1710	1711	1712	1713[1]
Electoral Rhine		1,450	1,470	1,470	1,470	1,470	1,500	1,500	1,500	1,500	1,500	1,500	2,732
Upper Rhine		3,325[2]	3,325	3,325	3,325	3,325	3,325	3,325	3,325	3,325	3,325	3,325	3,325
Westphalia	4,026[3]	4,000	7,000	7,000	7,000	7,000	7,000	7,000	7,000	7,000	7,000	7,000	7,000
Upper Saxony			2,250	2,250	2,250	2,250	2,000	2,000	2,794	2,794	2,794	2,794	6,294
Lower Saxony			3,273	3,273	4,005	2,421	4,666	4,333	3,478	1,720	1,720	1,720	2,722
Swabia	10,718	10,718	12,000	11,351	11,351	11,351	11,351	11,351	11,351	9,812	9,812	9,812	9,812
Franconia[4]	7,940	7,940	9,580	9,580	9,580	9,580	9,580	9,580	9,580	9,580	9,580	9,580	9,580
Bavaria			1,500	1,500	2,250	2,250	2,250	2,250	2,250	2,250	2,250	2,250	2,250
Total	22,684	27,433	40,398	39,749	41,231	39,647	41,672	41,339	41,278	37,981	37,981	37,981	44,415

Sources: Table 4.2 plus Storm, *Feldherr*, Sicken, *Wehrwesen*; Helmes, "Übersicht"; *Feldzüge*, vols. IV–XIV.

Notes: [1] Excluding about 30,000 men previously in Anglo-Dutch pay who joined the *Reichsarmee* from June 1713 under special arrangements with the emperor. All contingents were stood down by December 1714.

[2] Excluding an additional 1,292 Hessen-Darmstadt troops attached to the *Reichsarmee* in 1702–4.

[3] Cologne garrison. From 1703 an additional 2,000–4,000 served in the field.

[4] Excluding 3,000 (1,600 from 1709) supernumaries largely retained for home defence.

most unwelcome to Leopold who resented their intrusion when their own military efforts in Flanders and Luxembourg were scarcely more successful. It was especially galling to see not only the maritime powers but his close German ally Johann Wilhelm of the Palatinate join the disaffected members of the so-called "Young Court" around Archduke Joseph in calling for a more energetic and efficient war management.[18]

Regarding his father's trusted servants as elderly incompetents, Joseph had grown impatient to replace them with his own protégés. The first round of this power struggle was decided on 30 June 1703, when Leopold gave way and appointed Prince Eugene as Court War Council President with Gundaker Starhemberg to head the Treasury. The change of personnel in fact did little to remove the underlying weakness in the fiscal–military infrastructure, but it went far in restoring confidence. The maritime powers responded by advancing 3.6 million fl., while further sums came from individual Habsburg aristocrats and officials.[19] Meanwhile, Austrian military priorities were reordered to direct the main effort at eliminating the immediate threat from Bavaria before resuming the offensive in Italy. Crucially, this decision was in line with the idea of the Duke of Marlborough, who was assuming greater influence in British war strategy. The result was the famous Blenheim campaign of 1704, which proved truly decisive not only for the war but also imperial politics.[20]

Determined to press home his military advantage and concerned lest Max Emanuel make peace, Louis had sent another 36,000 men to reinforce the Bavarians. Moving in two instalments in May and June 1704, the French under Tallard broke through the Rhenish defences to raise the total Franco-Bavarian force to about 60,000. Further French detachments to the south had meanwhile disarmed part of Victor Amadeus's army and bottled the rest in Turin. Though Guido Starhemberg struggled through with a few Austrian reinforcements, the duke's position looked precarious and it seemed likely that Savoy would fall along with Swabia and the Upper Rhine unless the Franco-Bavarian threat could be eliminated.

Without revealing his intentions, Marlborough pulled 19,000 Anglo-Dutch troops from the Flanders front and swung south along the Rhine, drawing in various Danish and German auxiliaries as he went to rendezvous with Eugene and Turkish Louis in Württemberg. Though too late to prevent the arrival of Tallard's second instalment of reinforcements, the appearance of Marlborough's army, now 40,000 strong, transformed the situation. Leaving detachments to cover the Rhine, the allies moved east into Bavaria, defeating a Bavarian corps on the Schellenberg hill by Donauwörth on 2 July. Nine days later the Bavarians evacuated Regensburg, releasing their grip on the *Reichstag*. The allied advance was assisted by Max Emanuel's consistent refusal to counterattack for fear of destroying chances of a compromise with Leopold.

Finally, abandoning last-minute negotiations, Max Emanuel placed his fate on the fortunes of the battlefield at Blenheim (13 August) and lost: three-quarters of the combined Franco-Bavarian army was killed, captured or scattered, with the remainder, the elector included, lucky to escape back over the Rhine.[21]

Although Anglo-Dutch soldiers comprised less than a fifth of the allied army at Blenheim, Marlborough's intervention in south Germany proved decisive. His personal authority allowed the temporary redeployment of over 25,000 Hessian, Hanoverian, Prussian, Mecklenburg, Württemberg, Gotha and Ansbach auxiliaries as well as 17 regiments of Danes to reinforce Eugene and Turkish Louis.[22] Probably more important still were the links he forged with the senior Habsburg personnel, not just Eugene, but other figures associated with the Young Court, like Count Johann Wenzel Wratislaw, soon to become Bohemian chancellor and a key figure in Emperor Joseph's government. He even became an imperial prince, being rewarded with the small Swabian lordship of Mindelheim, confiscated from Max Emanuel, and so responsible for providing his own contingent of 48 *Kreistruppen* to collective defence.[23] Along with Marlborough's growing contacts with individual princes, these personal ties were to prove vital in speeding the complex negotiations necessary to harmonize coalition warfare.

Blenheim's importance extended beyond the immediate military benefits to restore an element of political initiative to the Habsburgs. Though it had been made possible by Anglo-Dutch intervention, the victory actually lessened Leopold's dependency on the maritime powers by removing the immediate need for their aid. With Bavaria overrun, the Viennese court could breathe more easily and return to its earlier objectives. Beginning already in Leopold's final year, this more assertive Habsburg stance became more pronounced with Joseph's accession in May 1705. The peace talks that they had been obliged to start in Hungary were turned to their advantage as a device to split the rebel leadership. Combined with a more sophisticated use of limited forces available, these tactics proved successful by April 1711, when the rebels surrendered.

A Bavarian peasant rising was also suppressed. Beginning in October 1705, this constituted the most serious direct popular challenge to absolutist rule within the *Reich* since the Bohemian nevolt of 1618. Leopold had been careful after Blenheim to secure the support of the Bavarian estates in the administration of the occupied electorate and the extraction of its resources. The rising was thus not the patriotic movement of Bavarian mythology but an attack on the Austrian military government and its collaborators within the local elites. Joseph underestimated the initial reports of trouble and instructed his military governor to proceed with the conscription of 12,000 Bavarians as nominal *Kreistruppen* to reinforce his army in Italy. The peasants responded with armed resistance, utilizing the electorate's militia structure as a organizational frame-work. By mid-November Joseph decided that his garrison of 7,000 was insufficient and adopted a policy of moderation and negotiation to buy time for reinforcements. Four thousand Württembergers were pulled out of winter quarters in the Black Forest while other Austrian units were redirected to bring the occupying forces up to 12,000 by December. The peasants were branded rebels, thus legitimizing the military build-up, which won public backing within the *Reich* and from the Bavarian estates. The Austrian garrison in Munich sortied to drive off the 16,000 peasants converging on the city, surrounding 2,000–3,000 at the village of Sendlingen. Though the peasants surrendered, the Austrians fell on them, killing 1,034 in the infamous Sendlingen Christmas Massacre on 25 December. Resistance elsewhere within the electorate collapsed within two weeks, as most accepted an am-nesty. Though about 4,000 peasants had died, treatment of the remainder was comparatively mild. Most of the captured leaders were imprisoned rather than executed, conscription was stopped, the extra forces were withdrawn and the Austrian government even paid some compensation for its soldiers' worst excesses. The uprising had stood little chance against experienced professional soldiers, but the moderate punishment was an indication that repression had its limits. Joseph wanted to settle matters quickly in view of fresh unrest in Bohemia and the Hungarian revolt, which was then at its height. He was also fortunate that the Bavarian rising occurred in the winter and so did not disrupt operations on the Rhine.[24]

Although far from clear initially, the Habsburg's position in the *Reich* was also improving. By conceding the issue of religious parity in generals' appoint-ments, Leopold removed a key stumbling block to the finalization of the mobilization orders. The last instructions were confirmed by the *Reichstag* on 11 March 1704 despite the presence of Bavarian soldiers immediately outside. Two days after Blenheim Austrian troops occupied Regensburg. Although the Bavarians had left by then, General Herbeville felt obliged to use a ruse to enter what was a Protestant imperial city: his dragoons passed through the gates concealed in farm wagons. Joseph solved the religious and political objections to an imperial garrison by withdrawing them in 1705, handing over to the civic guard companies instead. His ally Johann Wilhelm mean-while worked hard to defuse the religious controversy he had helped unleash, reaching an agreement with the leader of the Protestant opposition, Frederick I, on 21 November 1705. Most of the remaining difficulties were removed by further concessions by Joseph after the Swedish invasion of Saxony in 1707, while the Association Movement continued to facilitate co-operation be-tween the lesser Catholics and Protestants throughout the war.[25]

Habsburg influence recovered in other areas too, with the RHR benefiting from the temporary closure of the RKG in 1704–11 to fill the vacuum in conflict resolution. Meanwhile, Austrian territorialization was given a further boost when Joseph reduced the role of the imperial Chancellery in the Habsburg government by excluding Lothar Franz, the imperial chancellor, from the key decisionmaking body and giving greater priority to purely Austrian institutions. The ministerial power struggle was not resolved, because members of the Young Court competed among themselves for influence once Joseph came to power, but at least he gave firmer backing to Eugene and helped sustain the vital links to Marlborough and other key figures in the Anglo-Dutch leadership. Marlborough's personal intervention in the customary round of winter war planning in 1704–5 secured the secondment of 8,000 Prussians to north Italy at the maritime powers' expense for the coming campaign.[26]

The defeat of Bavaria, along with that of Cologne late in 1703, opened up further possibilities in the *Reich* to recover the initiative and counter mounting foreign influence. By openly siding with France, Max Emanuel and Joseph Clemens had placed themselves clearly in the wrong under imperial law. Their defeats removed the practical obstacle to their formal deposition and the redistribution of their lands and titles as escheated fiefs. As in the case of the earlier Habsburg military ascendency in 1629, this was a situation pregnant with danger and opportunity as the emperor sought to derive maximum advantage without arousing princely jealousy.

Leopold quickly lost out in the case of Cologne and Joseph Clemens's other dependent bishoprics of Liege, Hildesheim and Regensburg, as, with the exception of the latter, these were all overrun by Dutch troops and their north German auxiliaries late in 1703. With few troops, Leopold was in no position to intervene directly and so endorsed the interim transfer of power to the cathedral chapters in each case. While their erstwhile ruler retired to exile in Nancy under French protection, the cathedral canons made sure of their new autonomy by complying with Dutch and imperial demands to provide troops and billets. Joseph's attempt to capitalize on the absence of Wittelsbach influence in the north German imperial church was blocked by Dutch, Prussian and Palatine interference in episcopal elections: in 1706 the Dutch candidate defeated the emperor's favourite in the strategic see of Münster.[27]

The case of Bavaria was rather different, since this was overrun with Austrian soldiers, who remained there after the Anglo-Dutch, auxiliary and *Kreistruppen* returned to Flanders and the Rhine. Immediate annexation, though theoretically possible once Max Emanuel was placed under a formal ban, was not feasible given the likely hostile reaction. Nonetheless, Austria could reasonably expect to acquire at least part of the electorate on a permanent basis, possibly in connection with a final peace settlement. In the meantime, both Leopold and later Joseph had good reasons to postpone a decision since this permitted them to delay final resolution on the fate of Joseph Clemens's bishoprics, leaving open the possibility that Austrian influence could be extended there under more favourable circumstances. It also allowed them to continue the ruthless exploitation of Bavarian resources, which compensated for the temporary loss of those in rebel-controlled Hungary and gave them a hold over Eberhard Ludwig of Württemberg, who had unwisely seized Max Emanuel's Swabian lordship of Wiesensteig without waiting for formal approval.[28]

Palatine pressure ensured that a decision could not be postponed indefinitely. Johann Wilhelm pushed for a formal ban as a legal basis for the restitution of the more prestigious fifth electoral title and the Upper Palatinate lost during the Thirty Years War, as well as additional lands and rights to create a new kingdom in the Lower Rhine. By 1705 Vienna was convinced that such concessions in the past had been a mistake and that above all elevations to royal dignity were to be avoided. Far from satisfying Frederick of Prussia, the new crown merely left him hungry for more and he now attempted to establish a foothold in south Germany by offering additional aid on the Rhine. Though suspicious of Palatine ambitions, Frederick encouraged Johann Wilhelm in the hope of raising the pressure in Vienna. Desperate for troops in both Italy and the Rhineland, it was obvious to Joseph that he could not refuse all these requests, yet to grant more concessions now would merely stir up another hornet's nest of aggrieved princes.

Joseph's response was to delay a decision as long as possible, making piecemeal concessions only when absolutely necessary and when he gained something in return. This inevitably led to disappointment on the part of those who expected more but secured the Habsburg recovery by 1708. Joseph began by issuing the ban on Max Emanuel and Joseph Clemens on 29 April 1706, thus demonstrating his authority, establishing a legal pretext for the continual exploitation of Bavarian resources and mollifying Johann Willhelm at a crucial moment when his troops were needed in Italy. However, this was not enough since the elector wanted to be enfiefed with the former Bavarian lands and titles and by 1708 was threatening to withhold his 10,000 men unless Joseph agreed. Joseph spun out the process, securing important advantages at each stage of a complex settlement of outstanding issues in 1708. The Upper Palatinate and the fifth title were conferred on Johann Wilhelm on 23 June 1708, but only after he despatched more troops to Italy and returned the city of Kaiserswerth his men had taken in 1702 to Cologne. In return, the Cologne canons paid another 30,000 tlr to the imperial war effort, while Johann Wilhelm assisted in a general settlement of arrangements in the electoral college, not only confirming the Hanoverian title but readmitting the Habsburg-controlled Bohemian vote that had previously been excluded.[29] The arrangements left Austrian control of the remainder of Bavaria unaffected, while Joseph defeated attempts by the Protestant electors to dictate the choice of future elevations to their college.

The unavoidable consequence of this more assertive policy was the alienation of Prussia; inevitable because neither Leopold nor Joseph could accommodate Frederick's mounting demands without undermining their own position. Already in 1704 Leopold had declined an offer of an extra 14,000 men to serve in the Rhine and blocked a proposal to send other forces to the Moselle the following year, since both plans would have involved acknowledging an independent Prussian command and confirming Frederick's considerable territorial claims, extending to Ansbach, Bayreuth, Nuremberg and the German parts of William III's former domains. Subsidy arrears and the emperor's refusal to concede billeting demands further antagonized the king, who repeatedly threatened to recall his contingents from the Austrian and imperial armies. When dark hints that he was also negotiating with France failed to move Joseph in 1706, Frederick redirected his 12,000 on the Lower Rhine to Flanders, effectively ending co-operation with the *Reichsarmee*. Having already placed 5,000 men in Anglo-Dutch service at the end of 1701, followed by the 8,000 he agreed with Marlborough for Italy in November 1704, Frederick proceeded to strengthen ties with the maritime powers in further agreements on 24 November 1706 and 12 April 1709, adding another 6,125 men to bring the total in Flanders to over 23,000. Meanwhile, the contract for the 8,000 in Italy was renewed throughout the war and the king joined the maritime powers in pressurizing Joseph to make concessions to his Protestant subjects. In return he received subsidies roughly covering his costs and political support for the acquisition of the German parts of the Orange inheritance and the principality of Neuchâtel on the Franco-Swiss border.

In view of this behaviour, Joseph regarded the Austro-Prussian understanding of 1700 as over and began blocking Frederick's other ambitions in south Germany. Relations polarized as Frederick refused to recall his former Rhenish corps of 12,000 when French troops broke through the *Reichsarmee* and raided Swabia in May 1707. The imperial ambassador left Berlin the next month, which was followed by the departure of Frederick's representative from Vienna in September.[30] Serious as they were, these developments did not mean that the breakdown in Austro-Prussian relations was irretrievable, as neither Frederick nor his son and successor after 1713, Frederick William I, were prepared to push things to an open breach. Moreover, Joseph's resolute opposition to Prussian plans won him sympathy from Georg Ludwig and from Lothar Franz, whose own influence was threatened by Frederick's designs in Franconia. Their continued support, along with that of an increasingly impatient Johann Wilhelm, helped sustain Habsburg influence in the *Reich*, enabling Joseph to seize the initiative in Italy.

Despite the victory at Blenheim the situation in north Italy still seemed hopeless at the beginning of 1705. When Eugene returned there to resume command he found only 8,000 of the 15,000 men fit for action. These were bottled up in the mountains near Lake Garda on neutral Venetian soil by Marshal Vendôme and 30,000 Frenchmen, while a second army under La Feuillade kept a beleaguered Victor Amadeus surrounded in Turin. Joseph immediately transferred troops from the Rhine, ignoring protests from Margrave Ludwig Wilhelm and the maritime powers, to give 30,000 effectives by the summer, including the 8,000 Prussians and 4,000 supplied by Johann Wilhelm. These still proved insufficient and Eugene's attempt to break out of Venetian territory was defeated at Cassano (16 August).

As in 1704, Austria's reverses worked to its advantage, because its allies regarded the emperor's near-collapse in north Italy as jeopardizing their own plans. It looked certain that, unless Turin was relieved in 1706, all of north Italy would fall to France, enabling Louis to redeploy troops to defend the Spanish Netherlands. Marlborough again played a crucial role in the winter shuttle diplomacy, convincing Frederick to leave his men in Italy and inducing Johann Wilhelm to send another 3,000 in return for his existing force passing into Anglo-Dutch pay. Further agreements were struck with Wolfenbüttel, Gotha and Hessen-Kassel for 1,000, 3,000 and 10,000 men respectively even though this meant withdrawing the latter from their existing role in Belgium. Excluding the Hessians, who were still *en route*, the combined army totalled 50,000 by summer 1706, a third of which were in Anglo-Dutch pay. In addition, Marlborough secured an emergency payment of 300,000 tlr in November 1705, followed by a loan of another £250,000 in February, which did much to restore Austria's battered finances. Though Joseph was obliged to confirm his commitment to the futile campaign in Spain, he now had the means to resume the offensive in Italy.[31]

Here the situation was much as it had been at the beginning of the previous year: La Feuillade and 48,000 blockaded Victor Amadeus's 16,000 in Turin while Vendôme and 44,000 barred Eugene's path from Lake Garda. However, Vendôme was suddenly recalled to Flanders to restore order after Marlborough's victory at Ramillies (23 May 1706) leaving command to the inexperienced duke d'Orleans. Eugene exploited the temporary distraction to dash to Turin, compelling Orleans to split his forces and follow him with part, leaving General Count Medavi and 23,000 near the Adige in case the Hessians and other reinforcements appeared through the gap in the Alps. Orleans and La Feuillade's armies were defeated by Eugene at Turin on 7 September, with the remnants retreating into France. It was a truly great victory but the results were less clear-cut than Blenheim since it coincided with Medavi's defeat of the Hessians at Castiglione (9 September).[32] Though both Savoy and Milan were cleared, Medavi remained in Cremona and Mantua astride Eugene's communications with the Alpine passes and further relief from the Tirol. Additional French troops still held other key towns, and there was the distant possibility that they might be reinforced by the 8,000 Spanish in Naples.

Joseph was determined to remove Medavi as soon as possible to clear the way for the completion of his Italian plans, which extended to a conquest of the Spanish possessions in the south. These plans ran counter to the intentions of the maritime powers, who wanted Eugene's victorious forces to push directly over the Alps in an invasion of Provence to secure allied control of the French naval base of Toulon and force Louis to make peace. The harmony between Habsburg and Anglo-Dutch war aims that had been re-established after the disagreements over operations in Spain in 1703, now broke down as Joseph proceeded to settle matters in Italy to suit himself. He knew that if he provided the 20,000 men demanded by his allies for the Toulon expedition, he would have insufficient forces to deal both with Medavi and invade Naples. Fortunately, Louis was equally short of troops and opened negotiations with Eugene in December 1706 to withdraw the garrisons to France. Despite Anglo-Dutch protests, Joseph agreed to the bilateral convention concluded in Milan on 13 March 1707 permitting the evacuation of Medavi's troops and paving the way for the invasion of the south.[33]

While Eugene and Victor Amadeus crossed the Alps with 35,000 for Toulon, Marshall Daun and 10,000 left Turin that April, advancing through the papal states to reach the Neapolitan frontier on 22 June. Spanish resistance collapsed by 7 July, yielding all Naples to Habsburg control. The presence of the Anglo-Dutch fleet in the western Mediterranean for the Toulon expedition assisted Daun by preventing any hope of relief from France or Spain. Despite their bitter disappointment over the failure of their operations in Provence, which collapsed that August, the maritime powers used their warships the following year to take Sardinia, completing allied control over Spanish Italy.

Joseph used his imperial powers to consolidate his hold over Italy, regarding dynastic and imperial interests as mutually reinforcing. Already in 1705 he tried to persuade the *Reichstag* to extend the scope of the *Reichskrieg* to include Italy and Hungary. Despite offering to lead the army in person, the delegates refused, since it was clear that it would merely provide cover for continued diversion of German resources from the Rhine front. Joseph was more successful in Italy, where the collapse of Spanish rule removed competition to his feudal overlordship. French troops had behaved badly in Milan, while the local elites grew restless as it became clear that Philip V was prepared to cede the duchy to his grandfather. This established a basis for an intensifi-cation of feudal ties in the wake of the Austrian victory in 1706. Italy was divided into the coastal status of Genoa, Tuscany, Lucca and Massa, which were compelled to pay a cash *contributio*, while the landlocked territories of Modena, Mantua, Mirandola, Parma and Guastella were assigned as billets to the Austrian troops. Since several of these preferred to buy off their obliga-tions, Joseph found another valuable source of revenue: around 20-30 per cent of the sums demanded were paid, amounting to 2 million fl. in 1707, rising to 5 million fl. annually thereafter.[34]

Habsburg authority was reinforced by the intervention of the RHR, which on Joseph's authority singled out pro-French Duke Charles Ferdinand Gonzaga of Mantua for exemplary punishment. The task was made easier by his flight to the pleasures of the Venetian carnival, allowing the Austrians to occupy his lands in 1707. As in the case of Bavaria, Joseph was in no hurry to execute the ban, which had already been prepared by May 1707, because he had no desire to cede the Gonzaga principality of Montferrat, which Leopold had promised to Victor Amadeus. The duke's death in 1708 removed his remaining excuse, and the ban was formally pronounced on 30 May, with Austria retaining possession of Mantua itself as an escheated fief and Montferrat going to Savoy. Duke Francis Maria of Mirandola was also placed under the ban in 1707 for having supported France and, along with the principality of Concordia, his lands were confiscated. Mirandola was later transferred to Joseph's main Italian supporter, Duke Rinaldo of Modena, whose wife, Charlotte Felicitas, was a Guelph princess and so a relation of the emperor's German ally, Georg Ludwig of Hanover. Meanwhile, Tuscany also recognized imperial overlordship, confirming the possibility that the emperor would be free to dispose of this territory as well once the ailing Medici line died out.

With his authority confirmed in the north and his troops in possession of the south, Joseph proceeded to consolidate control by taking on the pope, whose feudal jurisdiction overlapped Austrian-held areas. Evoking images of medieval papal–imperial conflicts as well as the struggles of the Reformation, Joseph won some support in the *Reich*, notably from Protestant powers like Prussia. The maritime powers were also sympathetic, as Clement XI was known as a Jacobite supporter, but they were anxious that Joseph did not push the pope into the arms of France. Catholic reaction was predictably hostile, especially after Clement threatened to excommunicate Joseph on 2 April 1707, and the ecclesiastical electors tried to mediate a compromise. In Italy only Modena and Savoy lent diplomatic support, but Joseph resolved to go ahead regardless, sending troops under Daun and Bonneval from Milan to attack the papal states in May 1708.

The Austro-Papal War has been portrayed as a rash miscalculation of an overconfident emperor,[35] but, though ill-advised, Joseph in fact took care to minimize damage to his international standing. Daun and Bonneval were instructed to avoid provocative attacks on Rome and other big cities to prevent a repeat of 1527, when Charles V's troops had ransacked the papal capital and taken the pope hostage. Meanwhile, Joseph improved his Catholic credentials by intervening diplomatically in the Toggenburg religious dispute in Switzerland on the side of the Catholic cantons, who obliged him by refusing papal request for 4,500 mercenaries.[36]

Clement's other military activities were hardly more successful. Though amounting to 25,000 men, the new Roman army under the disgraced former imperial general Marsigli failed to stem the advance of the numerically inferior Austrian forces and became known among the local inhabitants as the *Papagallini*, or "Pope's Chickens" on account of their constant retreats.[37] With no hope of victory, Clement avoided further humiliation by making peace in January 1709. Though he continued to prevaricate into 1710, he eventually conceded Joseph's main demands, recognizing Archduke Charles "III" as king of Spain and providing covert backing for the consolidation of Austria's hold over north Italy in return for an end to the suppression of papal feudal jurisdiction.

Concentration on Italy had strained relations with the maritime powers, who remained convinced, probably unfairly, that the Milan Convention of 1707 was responsible for the failure of the Toulon expedition. Certainly, Medavi's return allowed Louis to redeploy troops in Provence and Spain, where they contributed to the major allied reverse at Almanza. More seriously, Joseph's preoccupation with Italy undermined his position in the *Reich* by weakening defence of the Rhine. By 1705 there were only 5,900 Austrians serving with the *Reichsarmee*, falling to a mere 2,200 amongst 26,000 Germans there in May 1707. These were completely inadequate and failed to prevent the French breakthrough into Swabia later that month.[38]

Though the situation soon stabilized, it had become imperative for Joseph to silence mounting German and international criticism of his war management. Despite a still critical situation in Hungary, troops were withdrawn from there and Italy to give 20,000 Austrians on the Rhine in 1708. Johann Wilhelm was persuaded to redeploy 10,000 of his Palatine troops there, and together with other contingents, German forces rose to 80,000 or the largest so far in the war. However, Joseph also needed to win Anglo-Dutch confidence and so fell in with Marlborough's plan for a major offensive in the Spanish Netherlands. Eugene was entrusted with 33,000 men, including all the Austrians, and sent to the Moselle to co-ordinate an attack with Marlborough's push in Flanders, resulting in a string of victories (Oudenarde,

Lille, Ghent, Bruges). Though this left Georg Ludwig with insufficient manpower to achieve the desired breakthrough into Alsace, at least the Rhine was now secure and imperial prestige remained high.

By 1709 Joseph had achieved the major Habsburg objectives. All of Spain's Italian possessions were now in his hands, with the added bonus of the strategic duchy of Mantua. Marlborough's recent victories brought much of the Netherlands under his control, while the tide of the war in Hungary had turned and the defeat of the rebels was a matter of time. Habsburg imperial influence was riding high despite Prussian alienation, and the Baltic war had been kept at bay with Anglo-Dutch help in persuading Charles XII of Sweden to turn his attention eastwards instead. That winter had hit France badly and the mounting strain of war compelled Louis to open peace talks in spring 1709.

There was now a real chance of ending the war on advantageous terms, providing nothing disturbed Joseph's position in the meantime. Apart from a possible French military revival, threats came from two quarters: the demands of his brother Charles and pressure from the Association Movement for a permanent security barrier (*Reichsbarriere*) on the Rhine. Though Spain always remained a secondary objective, Joseph could not ignore it, since its capture had become a question of dynastic prestige and any failure would have serious repercussions for the family's future: Leopold's will specified that if Charles was unable to obtain Spain, he was to receive the Tirol and Outer Austria (*Vorderösterreich*) as an autonomous territory in the *Reich*.[39] Yet imperial prestige also rested on retaining the loyalty and confidence of Lothar Franz and the lesser princes, who remained convinced that their security depended on consolidating the western frontier at France's expense. Despite the recent victories, Austria lacked the resources to satisfy all these objectives alone, remaining dependent on the maritime powers to take both French and Spanish territory.

There is some controversy concerning Joseph's policies at this stage. His principal biographer, Charles Ingrao, takes a largely negative line, emphasizing the priority of purely dynastic considerations and arguing that the Habsburgs no longer regarded the *Reich* "as a functioning political body". Others, notably Aretin, have taken a more benevolent view, asserting that Joseph still took his duty as emperor seriously and stressing its importance to Habsburg dynastic power. Certainly, Ingrao's interpretation tends to anticipate the fragmentation of the *Reich* by at least 40 years: there was still far more holding it together in the early eighteenth century than "the chance coincidence of each princes' individual interests". Moreover, while the "politicization of imperial policy" was pronounced under Joseph, it was neither novel nor did it threaten to undermine "the image and sanctity of his legitimacy . . . [or]

125

suppress the last vestiges of loyalty among the larger German princes" in the way that Leopold's war management had nearly done in the 1670s.[40] In many ways, Joseph proved more successful at retaining German loyalty during a crisis than his father had done so that arguably the imperial recovery peaked during his reign. Yet Ingrao is surely right to draw a distinction between dynastic and imperial policies that Aretin tends to regard as synonymous: the key to Joseph's success was his ability to harmonize the two despite numerous points of tension and inherent contradictions.

Joseph did not ignore the lesser German's aims but sought to bring them in line with his own dynastic ambitions, adopting their programme for a *Reichsbarriere*, although it continued to rank a poor third behind Spain and Italy.[41] He was astute enough to see that the European powers would not countenance a permanent union of Austria and Spain but believed the Anglo-Dutch might at least support his brother's rule in return for guarantees of their trading interests. In this manner he believed he could still reconcile the contradictory interests of dynasty and *Reich*. He refused to increase the Austrian military presence in Spain or restore it on the Rhine, continuing to rely on Anglo-Dutch subsidies to sustain his efforts in Italy and Hungary while expecting their troops to win the war in Spain and Flanders. This proved a miscalculation.

He failed to realize that Anglo-Dutch, especially British, commercial interests could just as easily be satisfied by a Bourbon as a Habsburg king of Spain. Meanwhile, the Dutch increasingly regarded Joseph's expansive war aims as an obstacle to peace. The Republic would already have been satisfied by Louis's limited offer in 1706 and only their growing dependency on Britain had kept them in the war. By 1708 the feeling that this would only serve British interests led to secret Franco-Dutch peace talks. As long as Marlborough and the war party remained in power, Britain tolerated its allies' divergent aims to keep them in the war, but unfortunately this contributed to the failure of the 1709 negotiations, as its diplomats insisted on article 37 of the preliminary treaty requiring Louis to evict his own grandson from Spain. The entire negotiations collapsed, ending the best chance for advantageous peace. British public opinion grew hostile to the war, which it regarded as fought only for the benefit of continental powers. The Tory election victory of October 1710 led to growing demands for peace on exclusively British terms. Joseph's death on 17 April 1711 left Charles as the sole male Habsburg, raising the spectre of revived universalist pretensions and removing the last British doubts at bilateral negotiations with France. The Anglo-French peace preliminaries of 8 October 1711 signalled the break-up of the Grand Alliance as British cut its subsidy commitments from 1712 leaving the war-weary Dutch as the sole financial backers of the common effort. Only the injection of cash and the hope that their continued participation would secure their political objectives had kept minor powers like Savoy and Prussia in the Alliance. Also disillusioned with the war and fearing they would lose out, they too scrambled to join the negotiations before the major players concluded a deal at the Utrecht Peace Conference of 1712–13.[42]

The collapse of the Grand Alliance coincided with an intensification of the Great Northern War and the spread of hostilities to the Lower and Upper Saxon *Kreise*, distracting Hanover and Prussia as well as Saxony, which had been largely absent from the war in the west since 1709. Louis exploited the disarray amongst his enemies, reviving plans for a Third Party capable of preventing Charles from continuing the war. However, it is a sign of anti-French feeling that Louis could only make an indirect approach through German intermediaries, beginning in June 1711, when Count von der Mark secretly contacted Elector Johann Wilhelm. Other agents won the support of Christiane Wilhelmine von Grävenitz, the influential mistress of Duke Eberhard Ludwig of Württemberg and through her numerous Mecklenburg relations, negotiations were also begun with Duke Friedrich Wilhelm of Mecklenburg-Schwerin in spring 1712. The latter was well-connected, being brother-in-law to Frederick I of Prussia and son-in-law to Landgrave Carl of Hessen-Kassel, both of whom France also hoped to win over. In return for promises of French financial aid to free him from dependency upon his estates and diplomatic backing to preserve his territorial integrity, Friedrich Wilhelm was asked to further the formation of the Third Party. Though Johann Wilhelm steadfastly resisted French offers, some others, notably Eberhard Ludwig were tempted, but the inability of Louis XIV's armies to secure a decisive military advantage despite their victory at Denain (26 July 1712) discouraged the princes from following Max Emanuel's earlier example. As it became clear that Louis could never deliver his extravagant promises, the princes reaffirmed their loyalty to Charles with Eberhard Ludwig being content with promotion to imperial field marshal in place of the "kingdom" he had hoped France would create for him in Franconia.[43]

Nonetheless, Charles was increasingly hard-pressed, particularly as the Dutch accepted the Utrecht Settlement with France and agreed an armistice in Flanders. Charles refused to compromise, conscious of the need to retain German support by pressing demands for a *Reichsbarriere* and determined not to relinquish earlier Habsburg gains to France or Spain. Spain itself had to be abandoned, and on 11 March 1713 the emperor agreed an armistice, evacu-ating the 25,000 Austro-German troops with English naval assistance and securing neutrality for all of Italy. Operations were now restricted to the Rhineland where the interests of the *Reich* were directly at stake. The *Reichstag*, which had already voted 1 million fl. in 1712, granted another

4 million fl. on 18 January 1713 to take over the auxiliaries as they were discharged by the Dutch in April. Despite this patriotic gesture, the *Reichsarmee* was already disintegrating as the northern armed princes concentrated on seizing Sweden's German possessions. Hanover had already pulled out at the end of 1712, when it cancelled its arrangement with Hessen-Darmstadt, which had previously fielded the Guelph contingent. As the Ansbach and Bayreuth auxiliaries left Dutch service, they passed by prior arrangement into that of Saxony to reinforce its army in Poland. Charles moved quickly to prevent the loss of other units, negotiating a series of agreements between June and September 1713, permitting Württemberg, Hessen-Darmstadt, Münster, Paderborn, Wolfenbüttel, Würzburg and Gotha to set their share of the 4 million fl. tax against the provision of extra troops for the Rhine. Attempts to extract political concessions were beaten off despite the critical situation. Landgrave Carl tried to use Hessen-Kassel's strategic position near the Upper Rhine to establish an independent army by drawing on the Mecklenburg and Ansbach contingents to increase the bargaining power of the medium princes. His hopes for the acquisition of Rheinfels and part of either Italy or the Netherlands went unfulfilled and like the Palatinate and even Hanover, he eventually sent a large force for the 1713 campaign.

However, these negotiations consumed much of Prince Eugene's energy, and for most of the year he had only 60,000 men against 160,000 French. He was already displaying the caution that was to be criticized as excessive during his defence of the Rhine in 1734–5, and he refused to take steps to prevent the French capturing Landau (August) and then Freiburg (November).[44]

Though it was clear that the *Reichsbarriere* was now unobtainable, the German military effort at least prevented France making more serious gains. Louis was in no position to continue the war and was forced to abandon some of his more extravagant, though less vital, demands, such as the restitution of the exiled Prince Rákóczi to Hungary. A compromise was agreed at Rastatt on 7 March 1714, whereby Charles retained the Netherlands, Milan, Naples and Sardinia along with the Tuscan Presidi towns, Mantua and Mirandola, but otherwise accepted the 1697 frontiers with France. To the bitter disappointment of Johann Wilhelm and others, who had hoped to profit from Max Emanuel's and Joseph Clemens's misfortune, both electors were restored to their former domains. Apart from Landau, which was retained by France, the *Reich* lost no territory, while Austria gained another 142,873 km^2, equivalent to nearly half the pre-1683 extent of the Habsburg monarchy. Left with little choice, the *Reichstag* accepted this arrangement in the Treaty of Baden on 7 September 1714. Before we can assess the impact of these changes on German politics, we need to see how the emperor fared in his efforts to maintain peace in the north of the *Reich*.

The peace of the north, 1700–21

As the Spanish Succession was being settled in the west, an equally titanic struggle was deciding the balance of power in northern Europe. This Great Northern War signalled the decline of the Swedish empire and settled Poland's fate as a battleground of its neighbours. All these developments were of considerable long-term significance for the rise of Prussia and the future of German history. Of more immediate concern was the constant danger of this conflict merging with that in the west to spread the chaos ravaging Poland into the *Reich* just as Sweden's earlier Baltic wars had become enmeshed in the Franco-Habsburg struggles of the 1630s. That this danger did not materialize beyond a short but destructive series of campaigns in Mecklenburg, Pomerania and Holstein in 1711–15 owes much to the desire of all but France to keep the two wars apart. The Germans contributed to this as princely ambition helped ignite the northern war while fear restricted its scope. Imperial conflict resolution was tested severely, especially as the international power struggle inflamed local disputes within the German territories. Yet the survival of the *Reich* was also a triumph of its political culture, as peace in the north depended on more than a coincidence of international interest; it was also sincerely desired by most Germans, emperor and princes included.

The expansive ambitions of Friedrich August, elector of Saxony since 1694, contributed to the Great Northern War and revealed the discrepancy between goals and resources limiting the international role of even the strongest German prince. Better known as Augustus the Strong, the elector earned his sobriquet not through his territory's military potential but by fathering 355 children and his party tricks of straightening horseshoes and rolling silver platters.[45] Traditionally one of the leading German territories, Saxony was being overtaken by its regional rivals Brandenburg and Hanover, emphasizing its relative decline as German politics became internationalized and European monarchs cast their shadow over the *Reich*. Like their German competitors, the Saxon electors were not short on political ambitions within the *Reich*. In addition to dominating the Upper Saxon *Kreis*, they wished to annex the duchies of their Ernestine relations, who were to be compensated with either Jülich-Cleves (which the Wettins also claimed) or Naples and Sicily. Such intentions were hopelessly unrealistic, not only running contrary to Habsburg and Bourbon claims to Spanish territory but also necessitating a major redistribution of land within the Reich – something that was now clearly difficult to affect. In any case, Augustus was not the man to be limited by the narrow horizons of traditional Saxon policy, which offered little to improve his international standing.

Like many other German dynasts he turned his attention towards Poland's elective monarchy, which offered instant royal dignity to the successful candidate. The Neuburg Wittelsbachs had applied as early as 1667, while Augustus's elder brother, Johann Georg IV, had been preparing a possible Saxon candidacy since 1692. German interest increased when King Sobieski died on 17 June 1696 and Turkish Louis stepped forward as well as the French Prince de Conti. Later, as they found their ambitions frustrated in the *Reich*, the rulers of Württemberg and Hessen-Kassel also came to see Poland as the appropriate venue to realize their monarchical dreams. However, election was never easy and Augustus found himself defeated by a narrow majority of Polish nobles. Acting decisively, he invaded Poland with 8,000 Saxons on 26 July 1697. Distribution of 4 million zloties secured the loyalty of the badly paid Polish army while a further million induced the nobles to abandon Conti. The latter had never been keen on the idea and wisely turned back for France.[46]

Augustus's dubious victory was hugely important as the first major German involvement in the chaotic politics of the Polish–Lithuanian Commonwealth (*Rzeczpospolita*). In contrast to Brandenburg intervention in the Northern War of 1655–60, which had resulted in the separation of East Prussia from Poland, Saxon rule linked Polish internal affairs to those of the *Reich*, since it was clear that Augustus could only sustain his rule with German resources. Already, Saxon intervention had only been possible with Leopold's blessing, for the troops that had invaded Poland had been withdrawn from the emperor's army in Hungary and crossed Austrian Silesia. Polish politics were also increasingly permeable to external influence, and Augustus felt he could only consolidate his position by taking a more aggressive European role.

Initially, he had hoped to conclude Polish involvement in the Great Turkish War with acquisition of Moldavia, Wallachia and possibly even Transylvania and parts of Hungary, but this was clearly unrealistic given Leopold's recent victories and Sobieski's earlier defeats. Thinking Sweden was a weaker target, Augustus redirected his ambitions northwards, forming alliances with Denmark (1698) and Russia (1699) to dismember Charles XII's Baltic empire. The plan was essentially dynastic, intended to provide the material and political base to secure a permanent place for the Wettins amongst the European monarchs. Livonia was to be seized as a hereditary possession from which absolutism could spread like cancer to the rest of Poland, which would meanwhile acquire better access to the sea. Improved Polish and Saxon trade, protected by a navy, would free the electorate from imports subject to expensive German tolls and finance the consolidation of Wettin power. Though couched in terms of recovering a mythical lost Polish *dominium maris Baltici*, these objectives found little positive reception amongst most Poles, who preferred recapturing lands lost in 1667 to Russia. Moreover, Augustus was never serious about maintaining the territorial integrity of the sprawling Commonwealth, continually proposing partitions to win foreign backing for a truncated but absolutist Wettin Poland.[47]

Saxony's resources were far too limited to sustain such ambitions and would have been overstretched even if Augustus had simply tried to rule his new kingdom. With an area of 40,150 km^2 and a population of 2 million, Saxony was one of the largest German territories but still could not cope with the demands placed upon it. The estates granted over 1 million tlr annually, while the introduction of excise duties in 1702 and a poll and property tax in 1709 pushed total revenue to 6.7 million. The sale of rights and dynastic claims to other German rulers raised over 3.14 million, with a further 200,000 arriving annually in return for Wettin backing for Habsburg claims to Spain, but even these sums failed to cover the soaring expenditure, compelling recourse to expensive loans brokered by Jewish capitalists. Troops also had to be obtained elsewhere despite the introduction of conscription in Saxony in 1702. Already in 1697 Saxony tried to hire the German auxiliaries recently discharged by the maritime powers in addition to negotiating new contracts with Eisenach, Gotha, Weimar, Zeitz, Bayreuth, Mainz, Hanover, Mecklenburg, Wolfenbüttel and Denmark by 1702. Apart from temporary Danish assistance in 1698–9 and 1701, most of these deals fell through, because Augustus insisted on impossibly short deadlines and lacked the ready money to cover mobilization costs. Though his army's paper strength rose to 27,000 by 1702, the infantry alone were 31 per cent (5,000 men) below strength and in practice he never had more than 15,000 effectives in Poland, maintained by constant drafts from Saxony's dwindling manpower.[48]

These soldiers disappeared in the vast expanse of the Commonwealth, stretching for 733,500 km^2, nearly half as big again as France and eighteen times the size of the electorate. Though not as underpopulated as the campaign area of the Turkish wars, Poland–Lithuana was only inhabited by about 8 million people, generating an annual revenue of around 2.5 million tlr, of which a bare million seems to have reached Augustus. Royal rule was indirect, mediated by a powerful aristocracy that dominated the *Seym*, or Polish assembly, held power in the provinces and exercised most of the regional and local government functions. Though the *Seym* eventually authorized an increase in the royal army from 24,000 in 1699 to 64,000 by 1710, actual strength rarely topped 35,000 of whom no more than 20,000 were ever under Augustus's direct control. The Saxon military presence remained illegal under the Polish constitution and the *Seym* continually called for their withdrawal lest they become an instrument of absolutism. Though Augustus did win over Conti's supporters, he failed to resolve a civil war developing in Lithuania or quell peasant revolts in Byelorussia and noble discontent elsewhere.

Augustus was scarcely better placed diplomatically. The coalition he assembled resembled that pitted against the Turks a decade before in that each ally made war on a separate front. While Augustus invaded Livonia, Tsar Peter attacked Ingria and Frederick IV sent 18,000 Danes into Holstein-Gottorp. Augustus's operations hardly got off the ground and Peter's ended in defeat at Narva (20 November 1700), but the Danish action represented a direct threat to the imperial public peace as well as an attack on Sweden's main German ally.

Although the Holsteiners had built up a modest army since the last Danish occupation ended in 1689, their 5,300 men stood no chance against the invaders and bolted into the safety of their fortified base at Tönning. Sweden, which had already provided a third of the Holstein army, moved another 7,400 to assist. Celle and Hanover massed 9,650 further south in support of their traditional bulwark against Danish expansionism while the Dutch, who had brokered the last settlement, despatched 3,000 reinforcements. Frederick IV and Augustus took urgent countermeasures, trying to reactivate the League of Corresponding Princes to provide 20,000 Wolfenbüttel, Gotha, Ansbach and Würzburg soldiers to attack the Guelphs while Danish cash bought 8,000 Saxon reinforcements.

However, these attempts to spread the Baltic conflict to the *Reich* were at cross-purposes with German and European interests. Frederick of Brandenburg wanted to avoid anything that might disturb his negotiations with Leopold for the Prussian royal crown and so remained on the sidelines. Though German discomfort pleased Louis XIV, he had no desire to encourage Danish–Swedish hostility since he relied on both countries to sustain French interests in the north. Without French subsidies, the German princes could not mobilize and Münster's decision to seek security in a Dutch alliance while Würzburg sided with the emperor indicated that the old anti-Hanoverian league was no longer serviceable as an instrument of French or Danish imperial policy. Desperately short of troops himself, Augustus could only spare 3,185 men, many of whom were Sorb conscripts who could not speak German. These got as far as Celle but retreated as soon as Hanoverian reinforcements arrived. Isolated and confronted by a Swedish landing on Zealand, Frederick IV made peace at Traventhal on 18 August 1700.[49]

Brokered by the maritime powers, who also wished to be rid of the crisis, the treaty limited Gottorp and Danish military presence in their respective parts of Holstein and established a demilitarized zone along the strategic Flensburg–Rendsburg–Hamburg highway. International assistance helped preserve the Gottorp plug in the Danish bottle, preventing further spillage of Copenhagen's ambitions into northern Germany. To ensure adherence, Danish and Gottorp troops were hired by the maritime powers for the new war in the west, while further diplomatic intervention in 1705–7 helped the emperor defuse their dispute over the secularized bishopric of Lübeck. Other pressure was brought to bear on Sweden to prevent Charles XII from exploiting Denmark's departure from the northern war by launching the 19,000 men he had massed in his German territories directly at Saxony. The rise of Anglo-Dutch naval strength gave the maritime powers the potential to cut Swedish communications across the Baltic. The threat was enough and Charles took his men off to Poland instead.[50]

This decision spared Germany but spelt disaster for Augustus, who, deprived of Danish and Russian assistance, was incapable of withstanding the Swedish attack. By July 1704 Charles XII had taken Warsaw and installed his own candidate Stanislaw Leszczynski as king. Although Russia resumed war on its front and even sent 6,000–7,000 troops to reinforce the Saxons, Augustus was embroiled in a Polish civil war he stood little chance of winning.[51]

The immediate beneficiaries of the elector's predicament were his north German rivals Hanover and Prussia. By turning eastward to Poland, Augustus abandoned Saxony's traditional stabilizing role as a counterweight to these two territories, creating a power vacuum in northern Germany. Prussia acquired Saxon protectorate rights over Quedlinburg and the imperial city of Nordhausen in return for urgently needed cash, while Hanover assumed Saxony's claims to Lauenburg, Hanau and Schwarzburg-Sondershausen in addition to temporary possession of its share of Mansfeld in return for further sums. More important symbolically was the transfer of Saxon political leadership of the German Protestants, a constant factor since the Reformation, to the rival Ernestine branch in Gotha, pawned along with the district of Borna to raise more cash in 1697.[52]

Prussia quickly capitalized on its advantage, clearly intending to convert its new protectorates into permanent possessions and expand into other former Saxon preserves. The new assertiveness was clearly demonstrated at Nordhausen, which contracted Hanover to substitute its Lower Saxon *Kreis* contingent to balance expanding Prussia influence. Acting before this could be ratified, 1,100 Prussian troops rushed across a frozen lake to take the city by surprise at 3am on 7 February 1703. The gates were stove in, two cannon pointed at the mayor's house, the civic guard beaten up, all weapons confiscated and the public keys seized. After a further 500 Prussians arrived, the citizens were cowed by this intimidation and signed a treaty for ten years on 10 March, reinforcing Prussia's new protectorate with the right to garrison Nordhausen and provide the city's contingent at its expense.[53]

Dramatic and scarcely legal, the brutal subjugation of Nordhausen figured little in the grand canvas of European affairs and seemed a paltry gain for a state with twice as many troops as Saxony. This raises the question that has long vexed German historians as to whether Prussia could have extracted more from its strategic position between the two great wars. Since Droysen it has become customary to conclude that Prussia's first king pursued "war in the west without a policy and policy in the east without a war".[54] In place of the allegedly more independent and determined policies of the Great Elector, Frederick sold the services of his army for Anglo-Dutch subsidies to pay for his court, thus depriving Prussia of a chance to expel the Swedes from northern Germany and make gains at Poland's expense. Recently, Linda and Marsha Frey have done their best to rehabilitate the king, and though their efforts remain only partially convincing overall, their assessment of Prussia's precarious position is more sensitive to the prevailing circumstances than the earlier verdicts. Like his contemporaries, Frederick was certainly not short of territorial ambitions, principally desiring the Polish corridor of West Prussia, and throughout the war he was prepared to deal with whichever power offered the best chance of obtaining it. However, his natural hesitancy encouraged caution at a time when the high stakes required large risks.[55] Yet Frederick's vacillation, far from being fatal, preserved Prussia when Augustus's and Max Emanuel's rash policies were ruining their electorates.

Prussia was still a minor power in European terms, and though possessed of a larger army than Saxony, was no more capable of independent action. Frederick's new royal status, itself intended to raise Prussia's profile, had to be confirmed through international agreements recognizing its validity, necessitating in the meantime an appropriately magnificent court to sustain regal dignity and lend credibility to political aspirations. These objectives could only be achieved through good relations with the emperor and maritime powers, which Frederick cultivated, like Augustus and Georg Ludwig, by supplying auxiliaries for the war in the west.

This western orientation was also a German orientation, placing Frederick not as an exception among otherwise supposedly more dynamic Hozenzollerns, but very much in the traditional mould of expanding the family's influence within the *Reich*. The acquisition of West Prussia was a land bridge to connect East Prussia to the Brandenburg heartland and not as a launching point for further Polish annexations. The main northern target remained the realization of claims to all of Pomerania dating back to 1637, complemented by an intensification of the Great Elector's efforts to entrench a firm position in Westphalia. In addition to extending existing protectorates in that region, Frederick claimed William of Orange's German possessions, worth, according to his own estimate, 60 million tlr, generating 400,000 tlr annually, or over a third what Augustus received as king of Poland. Moers and Gelders were obtained with Anglo-Dutch backing, while Prussian influence was further consolidated in Westphalia with the acquisition of most of Tecklenburg after Frederick bought up the rights of the other claimants 1696–1700. Imperial confirmation of a locally negotiated agreement with the East Frisian estates was obtained in return for military support in 1694 and established the basis for eventual annexation of the principality in 1744. These objectives were pursued less successfully after 1713 by his son, Frederick William I, who also continued his father's extension of Prussian influence into southern Germany through closer ties to Hohenzollern-ruled territories in Swabia and Franconia. Frederick's treaty with the Swabian branch in 1695 eventually led to incorporation of Hohenzollern-Hechingen and Sigmaringen into the expanding Prussian state in 1848, while his negotiations in Ansbach and Bayreuth laid the groundwork for Frederick the Great and his successor, Frederick William II, to engineer Prussian inheritance in 1792. Though Max Emanuel beat him to the county of Wolfstein in the Upper Palatinate, Frederick secured Geyer and Limburg-Speckfeld in Franconia and pressed unrealized claims to Hanau, Mömpelgard and Jülich-Berg.[56] This was a challenge to traditional Habsburg predominance far greater than the acquisition of Polish wastelands, even if that had been possible.

Intervention in Poland before 1714 would have been disastrous. Lying between the Swedish and Russo-Saxon operational bases, Prussian territory was far more exposed than Hanover, or for that matter Saxony itself. Augustus and Peter were highly unreliable alliance parties only held together because their stubborn refusal to compromise prevented either of them reaching an advantageous peace with Sweden. A repeat of the earlier alliance with Sweden, which had led to joint intervention in Poland in 1655, was scarcely possible given that Frederick's ambitions directly contradicted those of Charles XII. In any case, it was obvious no outsider could gain a firm foothold in the commonwealth's anarchic politics. The difficulties that would have been encountered in holding on to any annexations that could have been made are amply illustrated by Frederick's experience over Elbing. This Baltic port had been pledged to Prussia by the Poles in the Treaty of Bromberg in 1657 as security for a 300,000 tlr loan that had never been repaid. With Augustus's permission, in October 1698 Prussian troops shelled and stormed the town, which quickly became a symbol for Polish discontent with their new king. Acting without Augustus's consent, Polish troops ransacked the

East Prussian town of Soldau in retaliation. Following Russian diplomatic pressure, Frederick evacuated Elbing in December 1699 in return for the Polish crown jewels as security for the loan. Using Augustus's inability to redeem them as an excuse, Frederick again occupied the town in 1703 but left quickly following Swedish pressure, since Charles XII was keen to assure the Poles that he would not permit a dismemberment of their country. Further intervention became almost suicidal soon thereafter, as plague spread to Poland in 1707 – as it was, 270,000 East Prussian civilians were killed by 1711, reducing the province's population by over a third.[57]

Frederick's abstinence, however unwilling, spared his subjects Saxony's fate. After Augustus's forces had been routed at Fraustadt on 3 February 1706, not even Anglo-Dutch pressure could prevent Charles XII launching a full-scale invasion of the electorate. The Saxon army disintegrated and fled into Thuringia along with streams of refugees, as 40,000 Swedes advanced westwards from Poland, establishing their headquarters at Altranstädt near Leipzig that spring.

The Swedish invasion posed the second major test for imperial conflict resolution to deflect the crisis from the *Reich* and prevent the juncture of the two European wars. Circumstances were more favourable to France than they had been in 1700, for Denmark and Sweden were now officially at peace. Augustus recalled his contingent from the Rhine, while other north German princes delayed the despatch of reinforcements to the *Reichsarmee*, weakening it and contributing to the French breakthrough in May 1707. Growing German sympathy for Sweden also raised the possibility that some princes might join the new "Northern Alexander", just as their predecessors had sided with Gustavus Adolphus in 1630. The Swedish royal house already had dynastic ties to Zweibrücken, Hessen-Kassel and Holstein-Gottorp, while Charles XII's personal charisma as a soldier-king and Protestant hero proved seductive to such would-be warriors as Georg Ludwig, Frederick I or Landgrave Carl. Hanover and Prussia also appreciated Charles's role as guarantor of the imperial constitution and, while harbouring designs on his German territory, had no desire to remove him entirely. Despite the decline of the Danish threat, the north Germans still valued Sweden's role as a counterweight to external dangers, a role that became ever more important with Russia's advance along the Baltic's southern shore. Hanover, especially, was keen to sustain its co-operation with Sweden within the system of imperial politics, renewing long-standing defensive arrangements in 1704 and extending them to include specific safeguards for the continued integrity of the north German imperial cities as well as Holstein-Gottorp. Moreover, these were put into effect when, for example, it appeared that Denmark would use the opportunity of renewed unrest in Hamburg to seize the city,

Wolfenbüttel co-operated with Prussia and Sweden to place 2,800 peace-keepers there in 1708–12.

There was a danger that this co-operation might extend to more ambitious projects, such as the scheme for a Triple Alliance of Sweden, Hanover and Prussia floated by Frederick to ensure better protection for German and Hungarian Protestants, possibly extending to a Protestant emperor to succeed Joseph I. A product of classic "Third Party" thinking, the Alliance was supposed to dictate a comprehensive peace in the west, ensuring that neither the Habsburgs nor the Bourbons gained a preponderance.[58]

In fact, such dangers were more apparent than real, for as in 1700 no one other than Louis XIV wanted the crisis, least of all Charles XII. There was never any chance that he would allow his intervention in the *Reich* to distract him from his principal objective of reducing Poland to a Swedish satellite capable of sustaining his Baltic empire. The invasion of Saxony was simply intended to finish Augustus and permit the concentration of all available resources on defeating Russia, which remained the main obstacle to this goal. These preliminaries were achieved in the First Treaty of Altranstädt on 24 September 1706, by which Augustus recognized Leszczynski as king of Poland but kept a courtesy royal title. Though he had no intention of pursuing Frederick's dangerous project, Charles manipulated the uncertainty surrounding his ultimate intentions to extract further concessions from Joseph in the Second Treaty of Altranstädt on 1 September 1707, confirming Leszczynski as king and Gottorp influence in the bishopric of Lübeck, along with permanent exemption for Sweden's German territories from all imperial defence obligations and an extension of religious toleration to Protestants in Upper Silesia under special Swedish guarantee.[59] With his prestige enhanced and Sweden's constitutional position in the Reich revised to its advantage, Charles left Saxony, having extracted 13–14 million tlr for his war effort and embarked on his fateful invasion of Russia.

North Germany was given three years breathing space before the war swept back into central Europe following the king's famous defeat at Poltava in 1709. As Charles fled to temporary exile in Turkey, the Russo–Danish–Saxon coalition reformed, supporting the tsar's invasion of Finland and Livonia with renewed Danish activity in the Baltic and a Saxon return to Poland. In addition to the 17,000 in Sweden and Finland, the regency council in Stockholm only had General Krassow's 10,000 men in western Poland and the 11,800 in the German garrisons. Krassow was already in full retreat, more from the plague than Augustus's reappearance, presaging a return to the situation after Fehrbelin in 1675, when Sweden's collapse opened a vacuum in the north of the *Reich*.[60]

International interest coincided with the German desire for peace, and the maritime powers assisted Joseph's efforts to establish formal neutrality for Sweden's territory within the *Reich*. This device had been used before in 1658, when the Rhenish Alliance guaranteed Bremen and Verden during the First Northen War. Now all of Sweden's German possessions were declared neutral by The Hague Convention signed by Joseph and the maritime powers on 31 March 1710, ratified by the *Reichstag* two days later and soon joined by the three members of the anti-Swedish coalition. Fear of Denmark prompted Prussia, Hanover and Münster to back the scheme, which was acknowledged by the Stockholm government, while the maritime powers opened negotiations to remove Krassow's army by hiring it as auxiliaries against France. Just as the earlier neutralization project rested on the armed might of the Rhenish Alliance, Joseph realized the need for peacekeepers to enforce the new arrangements. A second convention on 4 August projected an army of 15,000–16,000 Prussian, Hanoverian, Palatine, Münster and Wolfenbüttel troops funded by the maritime powers. About 3,000 Palatine troops, along with a small detachment from Mainz's enclave in Erfurt, did collect at Grünberg in Lower Silesia under imperial command, but the whole design was jeopardized by Charles XII's refusal to ratify it. Anglo-Dutch statesmen began to question the wisdom of depleting the forces facing the French, while some princes had doubts about sending their men close to plague-ridden Poland.[61]

Even with the peacekeeping force The Hague Convention's ability to preserve peace in the north was questionable, since this now rested on an artificial prolongation of a collapsed balance of power in the wake of Sweden's defeat. The situation became critical as the advance of the Russo-Saxon forces coincided with Joseph's death in April 1711, creating a second political vacuum until Charles VI's election in October. Under imperial law, the emperor's authority in an interregnum devolved on the two imperial vicars, Saxony for the north, the Palatinate for the south. Using these powers, Augustus gave permission for his allies to enter the *Reich*, collapsing the eastern half of the neutrality zone in Upper Saxony and Mecklenburg in August 1711. While 25,000 Danes swept through Holstein-Gottorp and Mecklenburg from the west, 6,000 Saxons, 12,000 Russians and 6,000 Poles pursued Krassow's retreating army through Brandenburg from the east. Trapped, the Swedes shut themselves up in their fortified positions in Stade, Wismar, Stralsund and Stettin. Neither the official peacekeepers in Grünberg nor the still substantial Prussian forces in Brandenburg were in any position to stop this, especially as Frederick felt unable to pull out reinforcements from Flanders without jeopardizing his case in the Utrecht peace talks that had just begun. While Sweden's Pomeranian forts were blockaded, their positions in Stade and elsewhere in Bremen and Verden were spared for the time being, because Denmark could not afford a campaign in Lower as well as Upper Saxony.

This opened the door to Hanoverian designs, which had incorporated the earlier intentions of Celle to annex these areas. Like Frederick I, Georg Ludwig's policy was Janus-faced, looking westwards to maintain Anglo-Dutch goodwill whilst also harbouring territorial ambitions in the east. If anything, the elector was even more cautious than the Prussian king and was especially unwilling to spill his subject's blood, preferring to exploit his rivals' weaknesses and share in their spoils without becoming actively involved himself. A reduction of Sweden's German presence in conjunction with Denmark became more realistic after 1706, when Frederick IV finally recognized the Hanoverian electorate. Talks intensified from autumn 1708 as it became clear that Charles XII was in serious difficulty in Russia, and Hanover did not renew its defensive alliance with Sweden when it expired in April 1709. No action was taken, but Georg Ludwig advanced Denmark part of his considerable financial reserves in 1711 in return for temporary possession of Delmenhorst and part of Oldenburg.

This destroyed the western half of the neutrality zone, as it permitted Denmark to invade Sweden's Lower Saxon possession, besieging and taking Stade (held by 2,600) on 16 September 1712, completing control over Bremen. Using the excuse that the Danes were carrying the plague, Hanover occupied Verden ostensibly to preserve it for Sweden.[62]

From here events rapidly spun out of German control as Sweden made a determined bid to recover its position by force. General Steenbock landed with 10,000 reinforcements on Rügen Island on 25 September, lifting the blockades of Wismar, Stralsund and Stettin. However, the Danish fleet promptly cut his supply lines, forcing him to leave 3,000 in Stralsund and break out with the remaining 16,000. Ignoring instructions to go to Poland, Steenbock turned west into Lower Saxony in search of supplies, returning north Germany to the state of the 1620s, when foreign armies chased each other looking for undamaged areas to exploit. Steenbock drove the remaining 15,000 Danes from Mecklenburg, defeating them at Gadebusch on 20 December as they crossed into Holstein. With 36,000 Russians, Poles and Saxons hot on his tail Steenbock had to follow the retreating Danes deeper into Lower Saxony, precipitating a local crisis.

Duke Friedrich IV had been killed serving the Swedes in Poland 1702, and since his death the affairs of his duchy had slowly slid out of control, as the Gottorp court and regency governments, split by faction, left the army and local authorities largely to their own devices. The ambitious minister, Baron von Görtz played a double game, outwardly professing neutrality to the Danes while secretly negotiating with the Swedes. Görtz permitted Steenbock's army to shelter in Tönning in February 1713, gambling that Prussia, Hanover and the maritime powers would come to Gottorp's aid as they had done in 1700. However, his hopes that the presence of the Holstein auxiliaries serving in Flanders would secure leverage in The Hague were dashed in April 1713 when the Dutch discharged them following the Peace of Utrecht. For lack of an alternative employer, the troops were transferred to Swedish pay in Pomerania once they returned via a circuitous route to northern Germany. Meanwhile, Tönning proved a death trap for Steenbock's army; bottled in a far more restricted area than at Stralsund, the Swedes quickly ran out of food. Three thousand had died and a further 2,800 were sick by the time the remaining 9,000 surrendered on 16 May. The Danes continued the siege of the 1,600 Holsteiners still in the fortress on the grounds that Görtz's action constituted an act of war. After heroic but futile resistance, they surrendered in February 1714 and, following the capture of the last Holstein units with the Swedes in 1715, Danish control over Gottorp possessions was complete.[63]

Once Steenbock had been trapped in Tönning, Menshikov led the Russian element of the allied army back into Pomerania, where it took Stettin with Saxon technical assistance on 29 September 1713. The remaining Swedes were then given an unexpected respite when Peter pulled his soldiers out of Germany and Poland in accordance with the Treaty of Adrianople, imposed on him by the sultan on 15 June, to reinforce his army attacking Finland. The conflict rolled back into the *Reich* for a fourth time, following Charles XII's personal appearance in Stralsund in November, 1714 after an adventurous journey from Turkey. Reinforcements were shipped over to bring the Stralsund garrison up to 17,000, while Charles negotiated for additional German troops to assume a new offensive.

As no help could be expected from his Gottorp relations, he intensified efforts in Kassel, where his diplomats had been active since 1709. Following a personal visit from the fugitive king in November, Landgrave Carl concluded a formal alliance on 30 January 1715 to hold his entire army ready to assist Sweden in Pomerania. On 15 April Crown Prince Friedrich married Charles XII's younger sister, Ulrike Eleonore, making him a potential candidate for the Swedish throne alongside the 15-year-old Duke Carl Friedrich of Holstein-Gottorp. The Swedish connection looked set to catapult the minor Hessian landgraves into the premier league of European dynasties. To be certain of succeeding the childless Charles XII, the Hessians intended to win French, Prussian and Saxon backing by offering their help in persuading Sweden to make peace in the north. Though the loss of Anglo-Dutch subsidies in 1713 had compelled the landgrave to reduce his own army to 6,000, he hoped to persuade Gotha, Darmstadt, Württemberg, Ansbach and Baden-Durlach to provide an additional 20,000 men. Darmstadt reluctantly agreed to contribute 300 cavalry, but none of the others were prepared to venture their now much-reduced forces in what seemed a hairbrained scheme to prop up Sweden's crumbling empire. Sweden's subsidies to Hessen-Kassel were already 855,000 tlr in arrears by 1717, and no money could be found to mobilize the others.[64]

Nonetheless, with Charles back in personal command, it was clear that a major military effort was needed to reduce the remaining Swedish garrisons. Denmark, now ravaged by plague and nearly bankrupt, could not do this alone, but Russian help was far away and little could be expected from Saxony. Augustus mustered only 9,000 soldiers when he re-entered the war in 1709, and though conscription and the hire of Ansbach, Bayreuth and Meiningen units raised this to a nominal 28,732 by November 1713, there were never more than 22,000 effectives, while the Poles barely numbered 12,000, whose pay arrears stood at a staggering 85 million zloties in 1717.[65] Augustus was far more concerned with consolidating his position in Poland and transferred the bulk of his forces there in summer 1714 in an attempt to impose absolutist rule. As usual this backfired; the Polish nobility formed a General Confederation at Tarnogród dedicated to expelling all Saxons and renewed the civil war in November 1715.

Weakness in the anti-Swedish coalition increased Hanoverian and Prussian bargaining power just as the return of their auxiliaries after Utrecht swelled the forces at their immediate disposal. In addition, the Act of Settlement placed Georg Ludwig on the British throne in August 1714, giving him access to vital naval strength, as long as he could persuade MPs that his Baltic interests coincided with theirs. Improved relations with Prussia, strengthened his position still further. It is easy to depict northern imperial politics as straight-forward rivalry between Hanover and Prussia, culminating in the eventual annexation of the former by the latter in 1866. While tension never disap-peared entirely, relations were not always antagonistic, as both appreciated that co-operation not only enhanced common security but political influence as well. Relations improved considerably since 1684, thanks to mutual recog-nition of new titles in 1692 and 1700 along with marriage alliances. Following Frederick I's death in February 1713, his son Frederick William I made an effort to resolve the remaining difficulties with Hanover, agreeing to preserve Holstein-Gottorp from outright Danish annexation, establishing a joint direc-torship of the Lower Saxon *Kreis* in May 1714 and deciding on military co-operation and a division of Swedish territory on 27 April 1715.[66]

The establishment of this working relationship emboldened both to enter the war as active belligerents, exploiting continued allied weakness to feed like parasites off the combined military effort. Following bilateral treaties with Russia in October 1713 and June 1714, Prussian troops occupied Stettin pending a final peace settlement in return for contributing 400,000 tlr to Peter and Augustus's war effort. Hanover struck a similar bargain with Denmark on 2 May 1715, paying 300,000 tlr and acknowledging permanent Danish possession of the Gottorp half of Schleswig in return for *de facto* control of Bremen as well as Verden. While Hanoverian troops replaced Danish garrisons in Bremen, 50,000 Prussian, Saxon and Danish troops besieged Stralsund assisted by the Danish fleet. Realizing the situation was hopeless, Charles XII slipped away by boat to Sweden on 21 December 1715, leaving his troops to surrender three days later.

Hanoverian and especially Prussian support enabled Denmark and Saxony to dispense with Russian help and so weaken the tsar's position within the coalition. However, Peter was determined to return to north Germany, hoping that Denmark would agree to his plan for joint invasion of Sweden to finish the war in a single strike. His troops were delayed in Poland by heavy rain, but the allies feared they would arrive before Wismar had fallen and so negotiated its surrender on 24 April 1716, returning it immediately to Sweden on condition its fortifications were slighted. Nonetheless, the worsening situation in Poland forced them to allow the Russians to winter in Mecklenburg before shipping over to Denmark in June 1716 preparatory to the final assault on Sweden itself.[67]

Wismar's fall ended the fighting on German soil but not the presence of foreign armies, which continued to menace the weaker northern territories. The Russians were especially feared, since their advance westwards after 1711 quickly outstripped Peter's rudimentary fiscal–military infrastructure, compelling them to live off the land and rely on extortion to raise the hard cash needed for equipment and war materials. The north German trading cities proved an attractive target, with Hamburg and Lübeck being compelled to contribute over 233,000 tlr in 1713 in addition to the 1 million tlr taken from Danzig in 1711–16. The similarly hard-pressed Danes also drew 250,000 tlr from Hamburg in 1712, while Steenbock burnt nearby Altona to the ground after it refused to pay the 100,000 tlr he demanded as he fled into Holstein in January 1713. As the main billeting and transit area between the Pomeranian and Polish fronts, Mecklenburg was particularly hard hit, with the damage amounting to 2.6 million tlr for 1711–13 alone.[68]

Charles VI had not neglected his imperial responsibilities during the mounting crisis. By the time of his election (October 1711) it was already clear that Joseph's policy of neutrality had collapsed, so that this priority became damage limitation with the ultimate goal of removing all foreign forces from the north. To these ends he sponsored the Brunswick Peace Congress of 1712–16, despatching Count Damian Hugo von Schönborn, brother of the imperial vice chancellor, as a high-profile troubleshooter.

Austria and the northern armed territories were to mobilize a substantial force of 30,000 men under Prince Eugene to enforce peace and sequestrate the Swedish territories to remove the cause of future conflict. If the Swedes did not leave voluntarily, they were to be placed under the imperial ban. This ambitious but otherwise not unsound project soon ran into difficulties. The Dutch refused to release their German auxiliaries until April 1713 by which time the immediate danger had passed. The final imperial campaign on the Rhine then kept the troops occupied until 1714, when Hanover and Prussia were edging towards active involvement in the war and opposed the deployment of peacekeepers. Hessen-Kassel, sympathizing with Sweden, objected to the sequestration of its territory and called for a general armistice instead. The worsening situation in the Balkans, culminating in the outbreak of a new Turkish War in 1716, finally deprived the project of any hope precisely when the Russians reappeared in Mecklenburg and Denmark.[69]

The Russians' return to the *Reich* in 1716 made a significant impact on imperial politics. In place of the 6,000 troops who participated in operations there in 1711–13, there were now 50,000, of whom 30,000 were temporarily ferried over to Denmark. The size of the Russian presence emphasized the tsar's growing importance in German politics and a further stage in the internationalization of imperial affairs. For most Germans their first contact with Russia had been Peter's brief visit on his Grand Tour of 1697, when his bizarre appearance and wild behaviour seemed to confirm the general prejudice against Moscovite barbarism. Though at least one Hanoverian managed to out-drink the Russian guests, most were pleased to see them depart for Holland. Amongst the princes, none saw the utility of political links: Georg Wilhelm of Celle commented that meeting the tsar had been worth 1,000 tlr but he would gladly pay twice that sum never to see him again.[70] Soon, however, they were to have little choice in the matter, for the establishment of Russian influence in the *Reich* was a lasting consequence of the Great Northern War.

To understand this fully, it is necessary to place Russia's relations with the German powers in the context of its general westward expansion. The tsar's empire could advance in three directions, all of which impinged on German interests. Movement southwest to the Black Sea and Balkans brought Russia into contact with the Habsburgs from 1686, by which time expansion directly westwards had led to interference in Poland's internal affairs. In the wake of Augustus's defeat in 1706, Peter even toyed with installing his own puppet ruler. The impossibility of directly controlling the anarchic Polish nobility led him back to the idea of indirect influence through Augustus, whose re-entry into the war in 1709 was dependent on Russian manpower. Many Poles now looked to the Tsar to protect their "liberties", giving Peter still greater leverage over Augustus, especially since it was his troops rather than the Saxons who eventually defeated the Confederation of Tarmogród in 1716. At the so-called Silent *Seym* of 30 January 1717, Peter imposed an internal balance between king and nobles that went well beyond anything France and Sweden had achieved at Westphalia. Army size and tax levels were severely restricted and Augustus was obliged to withdraw his Saxons from Polish soil. In contrast to the IPO, this settlement proved extremely damaging, because it left little flexibility for either king or nobility, who were barely able to work together on even the most pressing matters. Russian intervention remained a constant threat, especially as the tsar and his successors established a protectorate over Courland, a Polish dependency on the Baltic, now part of Latvia.[71]

Russian expansion to the northwest brought them directly into the *Reich*, which, along with the campaigns in Ingria, Livonia and Finland, formed the main area of interest during 1698–1727. The intrusion of the tsar introduced a novel factor into imperial politics because of Peter's unconventional approach to foreign policy. In contrast to Augustus's action in Poland, Peter's interests were primarily economic and strategic. The initial goal of access to the Baltic had been achieved by 1713, permitting the tsar to contemplate diverting European–Asian trade to Russia's benefit. Goods were to be shipped west via Russia's new Baltic ports and stockpiled in Mecklenburg for distribution through the north German trading cities. Peter happily fell in with the local duke's desire to recover the Mecklenburg port of Wismar, lost to Sweden in the Thirty Years War, as this would serve as a Russian mercantile and naval base to be linked by canal to the Elbe, enabling goods to avoid the Danish Sound dues. Along with Holstein, Mecklenburg meanwhile also assumed strategic importance as an operational base for the forces intending to invade Sweden.

However, Russia's entry into the *Reich* heightened the tsar's need for local allies and eventually compelled him to "westernize" his German policy. Unlike Sweden, France, Britain, or the Dutch, Peter was in no position to provide subsidies or political leverage in western and central European politics, forcing him to offer the only thing he had in relative abundance: manpower. For example, in 1708, when Georg Ludwig was imperial commander on the Rhine, he promised a large contingent to the *Reichsarmee* if Hanover would abandon its alliance with Sweden. Later, in 1712, he offered up to 60,000 men to replace the British, who had just withdrawn from the war, if Hanover and Austria would help him against Charles XII. Ultimately, this unconventional approach proved far less attractive to princely ambition than marriage alliances with the Romanovs. Dynastic ties to German families were sought since 1707, beginning with negotiations in Wolfenbüttel and extending later to Hessen-Kassel and Holstein-Gottorp. Regarded as short-term expedients to secure German allies, dynastic policy assumed greater importance as the tsar sought to be accepted on an equal footing with the major European monarchs, replacing commercial factors as the most important motive behind Russian intervention in northern Germany after 1716.[72] These dynastic, strategic and commercial interests intersected in Mecklenburg, where local politics provide a particularly dramatic illustration of key trends in the *Reich* since 1648.

Geography placed the duchy precisely where Danish, Swedish, Prussian and Hanoverian interests overlapped, laying it open to foreign interference. Having already become a battlefield in the Thirty Years War, the duchy was again overrun in 1675–9 and 1711–13, while throughout the 1680s and 1690s it suffered Prussian and Hanoverian exactions. Like their contemporaries in Holstein-Gottorp and other equally vulnerable territories, the Mecklenburg dukes had followed what appeared to be the only course of action, arming themselves and seeking powerful allies. Though they won sympathy from the peasants and smaller towns, they were opposed by most nobles and the Rostock magistrates, who dominated the estates and feared ducal policy would disrupt their grain trade and erode their political privileges.[73]

In addition to appealing to the RHR and the emperor, the nobles used their connections in the Hanoverian and Prussian governments to rally support when Duke Friedrich Wilhelm (1692–1713) levied taxes without consent to fund his involvement in the War of the Spanish Succession. The duke won imperial favour by supplying his *Kreis* contingent promptly, while other troops were placed under Dutch subsidy from 1701 to win wider international backing. The polarization of domestic politics thus meshed with imperial and international tensions, particularly as both Hanover and Prussia claimed the duchy. By 1708 Prussia had concluded a dynastic alliance with the duke whose sister married Frederick I while Hanover swung firmly behind the disaffected nobility known as the *Renitenten*.

Unlike many of his fellow rulers, Friedrich Wilhelm was not afraid to use force and borrowed a dragoon regiment from his brother-in-law in April 1708 to reinforce his peasant militia. The 830 dragoons were billeted on the nobles' estates while ducal peasants raided their villages to conscript the serf workers. The RHR reacted immediately, ordering the Prussians out and, short of troops elsewhere, Frederick I had little choice but to comply in April 1709. The failure convinced Friedrich Wilhelm and his successor after 1713, Carl Leopold, that they could only establish absolutism with foreign political and military backing. Such help was hard to find since they lacked the resources to compete with the well-established armed princes, and all attempts to win support by offering troops to the emperor, British and Dutch failed by 1713.[74]

The pace of events accelerated after Carl Leopold's accession, as this coincided with the return of the auxiliaries from the war in the west, enabling him to resume the offensive at home.

The new duke initiated a three-track programme designed to establish absolutism and enhance Mecklenburg's security and political autonomy. In addition to straightforward repression, including the occupation of Rostock and collection of taxes by force, Carl Leopold tried to win support through concessions to the smaller towns and attempts to reverse serfdom on the nobles' estates. Lack of time and mounting fiscal crisis frustrated this part of the programme, making the third element, powerful foreign support, all the more imperative.

Though he made periodic overtures to the emperor, even offering to convert to Catholicism, his unrealistic demands removed any chance of an Austrian alliance. As none of the other powers could be trusted, Russia seemed the only option, and within two months of his accession, Carl Leopold had opened negotiations with Peter. The result was a dynastic alliance on 7 April 1716, whereby Carl Leopold married the tsar's niece, Ekaterina Ivanovna, securing free military protection in return for commercial concessions and the use of Mecklenburg for Russian military operations.

The Russians' appearance in Mecklenburg and Denmark in 1716 was very alarming. With the Swedes now expelled from north Germany, Russian military assistance was less urgent, and the tsar's allies grew concerned that having invited him in they would not be able to get him out, while Britain feared he would replace Sweden as monopolist of naval stores. Personal motives matched these international interests, as the Hanoverian chief minister, Bernstorff, was closely allied to the *Renitenten* and resented the tsar's support for the duke. Increasingly, Sweden was seen in Hanover and London as a valuable counterweight to Russia, and after the formation of the Anglo-French alliance late in 1716, George I pushed for a compromise peace in the north, limiting Russian gains from Sweden in return for Swedish concessions to Hanover and its allies.

The growing tension within the anti-Swedish coalition was a factor behind Peter's abrupt decision to cancel the amphibious assault on Sweden in September 1716. Though the Russian army did winter in Mecklenburg, the basis of the tsar's new dynastic alliance with Carl Leopold had crumbled. As it became obvious that his soldiers would soon exhaust the local food supply, Peter bowed to Anglo-French pressure in August 1717 to evacuate Mecklenburg in return for an end to French financial assistance to Sweden. Most of the Russians had already gone by July, though a detachment of 3,300 was left at the duke's request to reinforce the Mecklenburg army.

The Russian withdrawal permitted Charles VI to resume efforts to end the

Mecklenburg dispute, beginning with a court order to prevent further violence. However, his policy indicates just how far official conflict resolution depended on the attitude of whoever was chosen as imperial commissioner to implement decisions in the affected locality. Both Hanover and Prussia vied to be appointed, hoping to use formal imperial authority to entrench their respective positions in the duchy. George I consistently based his policy on imperial traditions, the restoration of order and the preservation of the domestic *status quo* in contrast to Frederick William I, who backed the duke and his absolutist programme. In addition, Charles VI needed British help in the Mediterranean where Spain looked set to recover its former Italian possessions by force. The empowerment of Hanover and Wolfenbüttel to protect the Mecklenburg nobles coincided with the Anglo-Austrian treaty of 1716, whereby George promised 15 ships for the Mediterranean and a £200,000 loan.[75] Prussia was increasingly isolated, since its only ally, Russia, had not escaped its pariah status, forcing Frederick William to keep a foot in both camps, continuing to support Carl Leopold by diplomatic efforts intended to delay actual intervention whilst simultaneously petitioning Charles VI to be included in a formal imperial commission and even loaning the *Renitenten* money.

The Russian withdrawal left Carl Leopold in a precarious position and he gambled on increased repression to break his opponents before Hanover and Wolfenbüttel intervened. The army was increased to 9,000, and was backed by 1,200 militia and the 3,300 Russians in order to extort 35,000 tlr a month, which was equivalent to what the nobles had previously paid in a year. These measures were defended on the grounds of imperial legislation, including paragraph 180, whilst last-minute efforts were made to reach a compromise with at least some of the nobles. Ducal lawyers and Prussian diplomatic support did help delay Hanoverian and Wolfenbüttel action after Charles VI formally empowered them to execute the court verdict in October 1717, but the main factor holding them back was fear of Russia, which still had 30,000 men in Poland. Moreover, Charles VI wanted to be sure of full German support before giving the final go-ahead but his position was momentarily compromised by his partisan intervention in renewed religious controversy in the Palatinate.

In the end, the ground was cleared diplomatically rather than militarily, as Britain, France, Austria and Saxony converged to oppose Spain in the Mediterranean and demand a Russian withdrawal from Poland. Hanover and Wolfenbüttel, now full imperial commissioners, began assembling a provisional government and collecting an imperial execution force of 11,018 men from October 1718, beginning their advance in February 1719, a month after the Russians agreed to leave Poland. In a desperate attempt to starve off impending defeat, Carl Leopold tried to revive the Extensionist League. After this anachronistic plan met with universal rejection, the duke backed down, announcing on 27 February that he would submit to all imperial decrees, return property confiscated from the nobles and send the Russians home. Unfortunately, his field commander, General Schwerin, remained convinced a military solution was possible and ignored instructions not to resist. Finding his path blocked by Hanoverian troops at Walsmülsen on 6 March, Schwerin punched through, forcing the execution force to retire. However, the political will for further defiance was lacking, and Schwerin followed the duke into Prussia, leaving garrisons in the Dömitz and Schwerin castles. Much reduced by desertion, the Mecklenburg army then accompanied the Russians into self-imposed exile in the Ukraine, while the commissioners established their government in Rostock.

Armed intervention in Mecklenburg concluded the operations in northern Germany and secured the withdrawal of the last foreign soldiers, but the war still raged in Norway and Finland and the ultimate fate of Sweden's territories remained to be decided. George I, in his dual role as king and elector, took the lead, displacing the emperor as the chief peacemaker in the north. He was assisted by Charles XII's death in November 1718 and the continued rise of the Hessian Party in Stockholm, which favoured a negotiated settlement. Beginning with the Treaty of Stockholm in November 1719, British and Hanoverian diplomats secured a series of agreements with all of Sweden's opponents to end the war by September 1721. They first secured the permanent possession of Bremen and Verden in return for 1 million tlr and their good offices for the subsequent treaties. Saxony was bought off by Swedish recognition of Augustus as king of Poland. Prussia then paid 2 million tlr in February 1720 to keep Stettin and parts of Pomerania, returning Stralsund and the rest to Sweden. Five months later the Danes handed back Wismar and the areas under their occupation in return for financial compensation and Swedish recognition of full Danish possession of Schleswig. This last concession was a Hessian-inspired blow at their Gottorp rivals, which drove the now itinerant Duke Carl Friedrich firmly into the arms of the Russians. Hessian succession was assured and the Swedish diet recognized Friedrich as king in 1720. Using his German connections, Friedrich tried to assemble a coalition to protect the recovered territories from possible Russo-Prussian attack and force Peter to make peace. The religious controversy in the *Reich* fuelled Protestant sympathy for Sweden and raised hopes that the princes would volunteer their help. However, Sweden had no money for subsidies, and only 3,000 Kassel and 500 Darmstadt troops set out on 24 May 1721 to garrison Stralsund, returning soon afterwards once it became obvious that an agreement would be reached with Peter at Nystad.[76]

The brief Hessian mobilization in 1721 provide the last echo of a war that had troubled northern Germany since 1700. The relative success of the *Reich* in defusing tension and curbing German involvement showed the continued effectiveness of imperial institutions. Severe fighting had been restricted to 1712–13 and 1715, though 1700, 1706, 1711 and 1716–17 also witnessed considerable troop movements in parts of the region. The damage had been heavy, particularly in Mecklenburg, Pomerania and Holstein, but was no worse than 1675–9. Moreover, in contrast to the earlier conflict, the political autonomy of the lesser Westphalian and Lower Saxon territories was no longer under immediate threat from the German regional powers. Hanover and Prussia may have acquired Swedish territory but as pp. 281–25 will make clear, they were prevented by the emperor from infringing that of even the smallest of the northern principalities.

Nonetheless, the public peace was clearly breached, while Saxon adventurism in Poland indicated limits to the imperial control on extraterritorial violence. Moreover, it is significant that the official mechanisms to sustain public order functioned most efficiently when it suited international interests. The Peace of Travendahl, that of Altranstädt along with The Hague conventions, had all been achieved with foreign co-operation similar to that which defused earlier tension in the north on the eve of the Nine Years War. The collapse of northern neutrality after 1711 coincided with British indifference, Dutch distraction and Russian intervention, extending the internationalization of imperial politics and frustrating the genuine desire of the emperor and most Germans for peace. Internationalization continued with the Hanoverian succession to the British crowns to reach the stage by 1719 that even resolution of a local domestic dispute in Mecklenburg consumed the combined energies of some of Europe's best diplomats in addition to an English naval squadron cruising off the duchy's coast. Increasingly, these developments also rendered redundant the unofficial mechanisms of peace and security that form the subject of the next chapter.

Chapter Five

Princely leagues and associations

Methods and purpose of defence co-operation

The focus of the preceding four chapters has been on national politics and the relative success of the formal network of collective security and conflict resolution in preserving the *Reich* throughout the prolonged warfare of 1655–1721. It is now time to switch attention to an important aspect of war and German politics that has been largely ignored due to the parochial perspective of much of the writing on this period. Co-operation between individual territories had long existed alongside the formal mechanisms for peace and security, supplementing them or substituting for any breakdown in official structures. Such action was not in itself unconstitutional provided it remained within the spirit of imperial law and was intended to counter internal breaches of the peace and external threats to territorial integrity. It remained a key element of imperial politics after the revival of formal collective security after 1648, contributing to the preservation of the weaker territories and their participation in international relations.

Co-operation could take a number of forms that were not necessarily mutually exclusive. The oldest was the regional or cross-regional alliance of different types of territory, such as the Swabian League, which evolved from a group of imperial cities to include counties and principalities after 1488, and, by the time it collapsed in 1534, had expanded well beyond Swabia. The Reformation split such organizations along sectarian lines, with the Protestant Schmalkaldic League of 1531–48 facing a variety of Catholic groups.[1] The renewed political and religious polarization prior to the Thirty Years War witnessed the re-establishment of a Protestant Union (1608) and a Catholic

150

League (1609), neither of which survived the war. Thereafter, not only did religion decline as a criterion for co-operation but the composition of leagues became more exclusive. Schönborn's alliance projects of the early 1670s did include imperial cities as members, and Frankfurt joined the Laxenburg Alliance of 1682, but otherwise the cities that had once been at the forefront of such organizations were entirely absent, preferring to collaborate within the *Kreis* structure instead.

The trend towards leagues as vehicles for particular princely interests had begun early with Philipp of Hessen using the Schmalkaldic League to advance his own interests, including the forced restoration of his ally Ulrich to Württemberg in 1534.[2] The League of Princes established in 1552 was another early attempt, important also for its anti-Habsburg orientation. Both organizations also received backing from France, extending to more comprehensive foreign involvement during the Thirty Years War, including Sweden's ties to the Protestants. This remained a feature after 1648, but it would be wrong to interpret such leagues exclusively as platforms for selfish ambitions or their members as simply the dupes of cynical foreign powers. Though defence of religion ceased to be a major motivation, most groups remained dedicated to protecting their members' interests in an uncertain environment. Their stated intention was always to uphold the Westphalian Settlement and promote the common good; sentiments that cannot be entirely dismissed as rhetorical devices, since, as the previous chapters have indicated, these aims were open to different interpretations, some of which could also serve princely interests.

Alliances among members of the same dynasty, either by formal family compacts (*Hausunion*), or defence treaties helped offset the territorial fragmentation that had accompanied the frequent divisions in inheritance. Rulers from different families also banded together either on a regional or cross-regional basis to maximize collective potential for mutual defence or as a lobby group like the Extensionists or League of Corresponding Princes. A special variant was co-operation between ecclesiastical territories held in personal union by the same bishop.

The final form took place within the *Kreis* structure but independent of imperial or *Reichstag* initiatives. The *Kreise* provided a recognized basis for co-operation that could be extended across regions through associations. Although closely connected to the implementation of formal collective security, these also offered the potential to promote princely interests, particularly those ruling weak or vulnerable territories. The associations were by far the most significant form of co-operation and will form the main focus of this chapter. However, the next section will analyze the other types, beginning with that between ecclesiastical territories.

Princely leagues

The multiple holding of ecclesiastical territories provided the weakest basis for political and military co-operation. The lack of hereditary rule and the presence of a cathedral chapter in each territory, jealous of its own privileges, inhibited long-term collaboration. Nonetheless, their common religious and constitutional position encouraged such territories to draw together even after defence of Catholicism ceased to be of overriding importance.

The most important example is Johann Philipp von Schönborn, who ruled Mainz, Würzburg and Worms together between 1647 and 1673 and attempted to maximize their potential by co-ordinating their policies. An Union and Alliance between Mainz and Würzburg was established on 3 November 1656 to resolve mutual disagreements peacefully and facilitate political and military co-operation, supplemented on 26 January 1663 by a further agreement to collaborate on religious issues. Despite reluctance from the two cathedral chapters, Schönborn attempted to harmonize civil and military administration and introduced common regulations for both armies in 1655. A relatively high degree of military integration was achieved with the two forces co-operating against Erfurt in 1663–4 and sending a combined regiment to fight the Turks in 1663. Equipment and personnel were exchanged, including the Mainz General Kraft Kuno von der Leyen, who later transferred to command the Würzburg army.[3]

The connection with Würzburg, the largest (after Salzburg) and most heavily militarized south German bishopric, was a major factor in raising Schönborn's political profile but did not survive his death. His nephew, Lothar Franz, tried to revive it, standing as a candidate for coadjutor and later bishop in Würzburg in 1697–9 without success. Significantly, he referred to the advantages derived from the earlier connection in his efforts to win support from the emperor, pope and canons, but did not dwell on his uncle's centralizing measures for fear of alarming the Würzburgers. He genuinely believed that "combination", as he termed it, was the only way to save the ecclesiastical territories from secularization and international crises, but like other high clerics his main concern was to raise his own prestige and means to fund an appropriate lifestyle and did not extend to comprehensive or lasting integration of his sees.[4]

Subsequent ties with Worms (1673–5, 1729–32, 1756–1802), Speyer (1673–5) and Bamberg (1695–1729) did not compensate Mainz for the loss of Würzburg's resources. Other important links existed between Würzburg and Bamberg (1631–41, 1675–83, 1729–46, 1757–1802) and between Cologne and Münster (1583–1650, 1683–8, 1723–1802), enhancing the political and military influence in the joint ruler in each case. The Wittelsbach archbishops of Cologne were probably the most successful in collecting additional sees, particularly between 1688 and 1761.[5] In comparison, Trier was only connected to relatively unimportant bishoprics, a factor that reinforced its position as the weakest of the three ecclesiastical electorates.[6]

Co-operation could continue when there was not a formal link of a common ruler if other factors were conducive, as indicated by Münster and Cologne. Despite the determination of the Münster chapter not to elect another outsider after the death of Ferdinand of Bavaria in 1650, the new bishop, Christoph Bernhard von Galen, re-established links with Cologne through his friendship with its chief minister, Franz Egon von Fürstenberg (1626–82). Both regarded the position of the northwest German Catholic territories as vulnerable after the Westphalian Settlement, which had sanctioned Dutch independence and the secularization of Minden by Brandenburg and Bremen and Verden by Sweden. In addition to these fears, both shared common frontiers, as the duchy of Westphalia and enclave of Recklinghausen belonging to Cologne lay detached from the electorate by the secular Duchy of Berg. Cologne was initially the leading partner, with Fürstenberg providing artillery and other assistance for Galen's attempts to suppress the autonomy of his capital city in 1654–61. Thereafter, Galen's more forceful personality prevailed over both Fürstenberg and his master Elector Max Heinrich, particularly as Münster developed into one of the most heavily armed German territories by the 1670s. Galen took the lead in reorienting co-operation towards external aggression, beginning with his attack on the Dutch in 1665. Although Fürstenberg was encouraging at first, he refused to provide concrete assistance, but later concern at possible Dutch retaliation led to an agreement in 1670 to collaborate on strengthening Cologne's fortress of Dorsten near Recklinghausen. Galen's influence declined after the ill-fated joint attack on the Republic in 1672–4, but the incentives to co-operate remained undiminished by his death in 1678. Max Heinrich briefly gained control of the bishopric's still formidable army following his election there in 1683. Münster provided the military muscle needed to crush a revolt in Liège, another of the elector's secondary bishoprics, and together with Paderborn and Hildesheim sent a combined expeditionary corps against the Turks in 1685. Thereafter, Münster remained the natural choice for Cologne's electors when they needed help, regardless of whether they ruled it or not. Joseph Clemens hired Münster units to garrison Dorsten and Recklinghausen during the disputed Cologne election of 1688–9. Subsequently, Cologne never had more than half as many troops as Münster, and the political ambitions of later electors rested principally on their control of its forces during 1723–1802.[7]

However, such co-operation declined elsewhere amongst eccclesiastical territories after the 1680s due to the reluctance of cathedral chapters and estates to allow bishops to use their resources to further policies elsewhere. A further restriction came in 1731, when the pope limited multiple holding to no more than two sees simultaneously.[8] The parallel development of the *Kreis* structure and formal collective security offered an alternative, particularly as sectarian hostility declined. The Lutheran landgraves of Hessen-Darmstadt, for example, assisted the Catholic electors of Mainz to continue Schönborn's expensive fortification of the city, appreciating its value in defending the Middle Rhine.[9]

The oldest grouping of secular territories was the Union of Wetterau Counts, which had existed in various forms since the fourteenth century. Formed initially for common defence against Hessian encroachment and to lobby for full status of imperial estates, the Union became increasingly pre-occupied with repelling foreign threats from the late sixteenth century. Sandwiched between Mainz, Trier, Cologne and Hessen, the counties of Nassau, Hanau, Solms, Isenburg, Wied, Wittgenstein, Waldeck and Manderschied reduced their already small holdings still further by frequent dynastic partitions. Territorial fragmentation was exacerbated by the fact that many houses, especially those of Nassau, also held land in the Westerwald, which nominally belonged to the Westphalian *Kreis*, while their main lands lay in that of the Upper Rhine. Collaboration amongst themselves and with counts elsewhere ensured their survival and a collective voice alongside the princes in the *Reichstag*.

Mounting religious and political tension prompted closer co-operation after 1565, when Count Johann VI of Nassau-Dillenburg persuaded the others to agree a common police and defence policy. The outbreak of the Dutch Revolt heightened their insecurity, as their territories lay on the route of Spanish reinforcements, while the Nassau family was connected to the rebel leadership. After their peasant militia was defeated by the Spanish in 1574, the counts introduced regular training and drill, standardized uniforms and equipment and maintained a permanent cadre of experienced officers and NCOs to establish the basis for systematic territorial defence (*Landesdefension*). These reforms were continued by Count Johann VII of Nassau-Siegen, who related direct experience of modern warfare in the Netherlands to the reorganization of traditional German militia systems to produce a model of cheap, permanent defence that was to prove of lasting importance. The new ideas were publicized by the success of the reformed Dutch army led by Maurice of Nassau and the military academy established in Siegen in 1616 and inspired emulation in the Palatinate, Saxony, Brandenburg, East Prussia, Wolfenbüttel and Hessen-Kassel. Though ideally suited to the needs of impoverished areas like the Wetterau counties, territorial defence militias proved inadequate during the Thirty Years War, while political co-operation within the Union came under increasing strain with the policies of the Nassau leadership. Alliance with the Protestant-Swedish bloc ended in defeat in 1634, while sectarian strife split the membership as some Nassau branches converted to Catholicism.[10]

Nonetheless, the idea remained attractive to most counts, who still felt vulnerable after 1648. The Union was revived in 1652 under the leadership of the indefatigable Georg Friedrich von Waldeck, leading to a formal military alliance in 1670 as a substitute for the inoperative Upper Rhenish *Kreis*, riven by Worms–Palatine rivalry in 1664–95. The outbreak of the Dutch War encouraged the inclusion of larger territories for the first time. Following their failure to mediate a settlement of the disputed *Kreis* executive, the landgraves of Hessen-Darmstadt and Hessen-Kassel met the counts and the bishop of Fulda in a series of meetings in summer 1674. Together they mobilized 2,100 men that August as replacement *Kreistruppen*, doubling their force the following year in conjunction with official collective defence. Though this new group was significant in bringing together Catholics, Lutherans and Calvinists, it proved only partially successful, as both landgraves chose to establish their own armies to escape the oppressive assignations imposed on the region.[11]

Undeterred, Waldeck re-established his original Union at Frankfurt on 19 September 1679, including the Stollberg and Westerburg counts in addition to those of Nassau (most branches), Hanau, Solms, Isenburg, Wied, Wittgenstein, Waldeck and Manderschied. The revived Union was intended to protect its members against the *Réunions* and the armed princes by facilitating collective armed status. Waldeck built on the experience of the recent conflict and the Thirty Years War to establish a system combining 1,550 regular soldiers with a revived territorial defence militia of 2,000 men. When the *Reichstag* passed the defence reforms in 1681–2, the Union simply designated its existing forces as its members' *Kreistruppen*, providing the regulars in unbroken field service during 1683–97, first against the Turks and later against France.[12]

The Union expanded considerably beyond its original scope and purpose in the meantime as Waldeck sought to cross the sectarian divide and include Catholics as well as Protestants. First to join was Calvinist Landgrave Carl of Hessen-Kassel on 26 September 1679 on the condition that his 900 regulars remained outside the Union's existing integrated force. Max Heinrich of Cologne followed on 16 November, extending the organization outside the Upper Rhine for the first time. Fulda and Hessen-Darmstadt had joined by the end of September 1681, followed by the Thuringian territories of Schwarzburg, Gotha and Eisenach by March 1682, while the Westerwald counts agreed to collaborate until the Westphalian *Kreis* could organize its own force. However, the most significant new arrival was Bishop Dernbach of Würzburg, whose membership on 31 January 1682 was followed ten days later by the entire Franconian *Kreis*, enlarging the Union as the Kassel Defence Confederation, with a total strength of 17,000–18,000 men. By this stage, the organization represented a hybrid of newly-emerged armed princes like Dernbach and the Hessian landgraves, minor territories of the inoperative Upper Rhenish and Upper Saxon *Kreise* and the fully functioning Franconian *Kreis*. Dernbach now assumed joint leadership with Landgrave Carl and helped steer the new grouping into the imperial orbit, culminating in the Laxenburg Alliance with Leopold on 10 June 1682.[13]

These developments have often been portrayed as a valiant if utopian attempt by the lesser princes to put the defence reforms into practice, but closer examination indicates that Waldeck and his collaborators were more realistic but also more ambivalent in their approach to collective security. Rather than believing that either the Union or the recent imperial legislation could restrain the armed princes, Waldeck saw his alliance as a way that individually weak territories like his own could obtain parity with their larger neighbours by pooling their resources. From Leopold's lukewarm response to the reforms and the armed princes' refusal to countenance the wholesale loss of their contributions, Waldeck's policy was the only realistic option, especially for those areas where the *Kreise* had broken down.

In forming the Laxenburg Alliance, he secured a blanket exemption for all union members from billeting and contributions to the value of 130 Roman Months on the grounds that they now fielded troops whose maintenance was equivalent to this sum. Dernbach got the same for the Franconians, who likewise saw it as an opportunity to secure recognition for collective armed status. Its significant that the Alliance was the first agreement with the emperor to contain detailed rules governing transit and billeting in member territories and included rules on compensation for damage and unauthorized movements.[14] Not surprisingly this met with vehement protests from the armed princes. Frederick William called the actions of his erstwhile friend presumptuous on the grounds that Waldeck was a mere count and predicted they would lead to war with France. It is a measure of his success that Leopold already valued the Union's military contribution and not only ignored these protests but elevated Waldeck to the status of imperial prince in June 1682.[15]

However, in return Leopold extracted guarantees to ensure that the pool of potential billets available to appease the armed princes would not be further reduced by other minor territories sharing the Union's collective armed status. Henceforth, new members had to be approved by him, effectively restricting the Union to its original core of Upper Rhine territories, while those joining the Laxenburg Alliance did so under separate agreement. The Union's role diminished to that of a substitute for the still inoperative Upper Rhenish *Kreis*, leaving it vulnerable to the ambitions of Landgrave Carl of Hessen-Kassel.

The dispute between the executive princes neutralized the two most powerful rulers in the region, allowing Carl to step into the void, regarding the Union not only as a means to extend Hessian influence on the Upper Rhine but as a platform to give himself a more prominent political role. He intrigued in Vienna and even agreed in April 1684 to supply 4,000 auxiliaries to Spain, though the war with France ended before this could be carried out.[16]

Having persuaded Waldeck to make him Union director in 1681, Carl consolidated his position by at last securing his own bilateral agreement with Leopold on 26 January 1687. The deliberately vague wording permitted him to assume the vacant post of *Kreis* director, enabling him to coerce the remaining unarmed Upper Rhine territories into contributing about 200,000 tlr annually to his military expenses in 1689–97.[17]

The revival of the *Kreis* organization after 1698 put an end to both Hessian manipulation and the need for the Union, which had always been intended as a substitute and not a permanent replacement for the official structure. The Westerwald counts rejoined the Westphalian *Kreis* once this also established its own military organization in 1702, depleting the membership of the Wetterau group. Though the latter had continued to increase through the admission of further counts, its collective influence had declined not just with Hessian domination but because many of the original members, such as Waldeck and the Nassau houses, had now acquired princely status and felt that co-operation with lesser mortals was beneath them.

While the Wetterau Union was the prime example of regional co-operation, that between the Ernestine dukes is a good illustration of dynastic collaboration. The Ernestine Wettins remained in the shadow of their more prestigious Albertine cousins, who held the Saxon electoral title after 1547 and whose territory and resources far exceeded their own by 1648. Whereas the Albertines managed to keep their lands together and prevent cadet branches gaining full autonomy, the Ernestines fragmented through lack of primogeniture. Though reduced to two branches by 1672, they split again, with Weimar establishing two new lines in Eisenach and Jena, while Gotha broke into seven pieces in 1680–1 (Gotha-Altenburg, Coburg, Meiningen, Römhild, Eisenberg, Hildburghausen and Saalfeld). To make matters worse, the Wettin possession of Henneberg in Franconia was not only shared between the electoral and ducal lines, but the latter subdivided its portion amongst the various branches. Intended to provide adequate establishments for the numerous male offspring, this merely created family strife, with the main branches of Weimar and Gotha attempting to re-establish control of the cadet lines. Friedrich I in particular struggled to establish a *Nexus Gothanus*

Table 5.1 Ernestine territories in 1800

Branch	Main duchy		Share of Henneberg territory		Total	
	Area (km^2)	Population	Area (km^2)	Population	Area (km^2)	Population
Weimar	1,320	64,000	291.5	15,000	1,611.5	79,000
Eisenach	440	30,000			440	30,000
Gotha	1,540	82,000	33	1,800	1,577	83,800
Altenburg	1,430	104,000			1,430	104,000
Coburg-Saalfeld	841.5	49,300	148.5	7,600	990	56,900
Hildburghausen	563.75	30,000	41.25	1,800	605	31,800
Meiningen	330	25,000	709.5	34,000	1,039.5	59,000
Total	6,465.25	384,300	1,223.75	60,200	7,693	444,500

Sources: Patze (ed.), *Geschichte Thüringens*; V. Wallner, "Kreissässigen Reichsterritorien", pp. 709–11; W. H. Bruford, *Germany in the eighteenth century* (Cambridge, 1935), pp. 334–51, and his *Culture and society in classical Weimar, 1775–1806* (Cambridge, 1962), pp. 15, 56–9.

Principal changes prior to 1800:

(a) Eisenach fell to Weimar in 1741.

(b) Altenburg fell to Gotha in 1672.

(c) Absorption of junior branches (area and population included in the above totals):

  Jena (1672–90) to Weimar and Eisenach in 1690.

  Eisenach (1680–1710) to Gotha in 1707.

  Römhild (1680–1710) to Gotha, Meiningen, Hildburghausen and Saalfeld in 1710.

  Coburg (1681–99) Over 1,265km^2) to Saalfeld and Meiningen in 1699.

158

entitling him to exclusive exercise of territorial sovereignty on behalf of his younger brothers.[18]

Under such circumstances, co-operation though vital, was extremely problematic. Ernst the Pious of Gotha (1640–75) made the first attempt in response to the Turkish threat of 1663 by promoting the idea of common defence. Keen to establish leadership not only within the Upper Saxon *Kreis* but directly over the Ernestine duchies as well, Elector Johann Georg II took up the suggestion in 1669–70 by proposing a common Saxon army that could fulfil the region's imperial obligations. Ernst agreed but was overruled by Johann Ernst of Weimar (1662–83), who feared a loss of autonomy. However, Johann Ernst was unable to carry his younger brothers in Jena and Eisenach during the Dutch War, as his alternative based on a territorial defence militia proved incapable of preserving their lands from billeting and transit during 1673–7. Both Eisenach and Jena joined Gotha after 1672 in seeking a substitute for the Upper Saxon *Kreis* paralyzed by the conflicting ambitions of Electors Johann Georg and Frederick William. Like the Hessian landgraves, Johann Georg I of Eisenach (1671–86) chose the armed princes' route, signing a bilateral treaty with Leopold in 1674 to provide 1,000 men in return for exemption from billeting. Having been compelled to accommodate Austrian troops in 1672, 1675 and 1676, Weimar joined the others in an Ernestine alliance with the emperor in November 1676 to contribute to the upkeep of the Eisenach regiment and provide a further 3,000 men. As Leopold's war management collapsed in the quartering crisis of autumn 1676, the Ernestines extended their collaboration to include other rulers also suffering Brandenburg depredations. Though it did not survive the end of the war, this treaty of November 1677 with Saxony, Mainz and Würzburg-Bamberg provided a basis for future Gotha and Eisenach membership of the Laxenburg Alliance.

Meanwhile, negotiations continued to improve dynastic co-operation in the light of the breakdown of the Upper Saxon *Kreis*, following Brandenburg intransigence in 1682. All branches except Eisenach agreed to maintain a common army of 3,000 men in March 1681, but this collapsed the following year over the reluctance of Gotha and Jena to admit electoral Saxony. The death of the hesitant Johann Ernst II of Weimar removed a major obstacle in 1683, allowing the ambitious Friedrich I of Gotha to play a more prominent role. The armed status of the duchies was preserved by fielding a combined regiment against the Turks in 1683–5, while long negotiations led to all dukes joining Leopold's League of Augsburg in 1686. In return for pledging a joint regiment of 1,000 in any future war in the west, the dukes were promised exemption from all other military burdens. When war finally came in 1688, they responded to an imperial request by increasing their combined force to one cavalry and two foot regiments.

When Leopold reneged on his earlier promise and assigned the Upper Saxon *Kreis* to Elector Johann Georg III as a zone of contribution, the dukes escaped renewed billeting by signing the Treaty of Leipzig in 1689. In return for providing their 2,000 men to collaborate with the Saxon army, the elector released them from the obligation to provide cash and quarters and their men served on the Rhine until 1697. Though renewed in 1692, Gotha left the arrangement to pursue its own ambitions independently, initially in secret negotiations with France and later after 1693 in collaboration with Ansbach and Würzburg, which felt equally aggrieved at the new Hanoverian electoral title. Meanwhile, the other dukes were disappointed at the failure of Electoral Saxony to push the combined Wettin claim to Sachsen-Lauenburg and so let the Leipzig treaty expire in 1695.

Co-operation became increasingly difficult as Meiningen disputed the redistribution of land as the junior Gotha branches died out, while the main Gotha line continued to pursue its own policy elsewhere. Nonetheless, Weimar and Eisenach renewed their collaboration in 1696 and April 1700, agreeing to raise two regiments and seek better understanding with the Saxon elector. Weimar and Eisenach raised a new regiment as a joint *Kreis* contingent that served throughout the war, but their attempts to collaborate with the Saxon elector by providing further auxiliaries for Augustus's Polish adventure were frustrated by lack of money and recruiting difficulties during 1702–3.[19] Relations were further soured as it became clear that the elector was contemplating annexing all or part of their lands as compensation for defeat in Poland. Regular dynastic conferences were held after 1704, attended by Gotha, which had recovered from its ill-advised alliance with France two years previously, and led to a formal confederation in 1707 to provide a joint army of 3,074 men. As Augustus fled into their territories in the wake of the Swedish invasion of Saxony, the Ernestines co-operated, seeking Mainz, Hessian, Prussian and imperial help in getting him removed the next year. These diplomatic ties were extended after 1708 to include Hanover and the maritime powers, leading to a formal alliance with Hanover in 1711, whereby Georg Ludwig promised to protect the duchies in return for permission to recruit there. This expedient helped preserve the Ernestines as the Great Northern War rolled back into northern Germany in 1712–15.

By 1710 the incentives to co-operate had diminished as Gotha, Weimar and Eisenach reabsorbed the land of the cadet branches, dwarfing the remaining lines of Coburg-Saalfeld, Hildburghhausen and Meiningen. All three leading dukes believed they now had the basis to become fully independent armed princes in their own right, dreaming in the case of Friedrich II of Gotha

(1691–1732) and Ernst August II of Weimar (1728–41) of eventually subsuming the entire Ernestine lands and even recovering the electoral title. The latter duke, known as the *Soldatenherzog* on account of his passion for all things military, built up the Weimar army to over 3,000, while Gotha also mustered a similar total throughout much of this period. However, neither they nor the rulers of Eisenach could afford their inflated establishments, leaving them vulnerable to external manipulation. Though Gotha did place men in Anglo-Dutch subsidy even after 1713, Friedrich II was forced to establish better relations with Saxony. Negotiations, pursued jointly with other Ernestine dukes in 1720–7, acknowledged Augustus's formal leadership of the Protestant *Reichstag* bloc despite his personal conversion to Catholicism and saw Gotha and Weimar each providing about 800 men to the reconstruction of the electoral Saxon army after 1729. Gotha, Weimar and Eisenach all attempted to escape Saxon leadership by bilateral agreements with Charles VI after 1732, but this merely resulted in another overcommitment, ending the duchies as significant military powers after the mid-eighteenth century.[20]

In contrast, collaboration between the Guelph dukes was far more successful. Though possessed of a far greater territory than the Ernestines, dynastic fragmentation threatened to consign them to the same political obscurity, and all three were threatened when the Thirty Years War spread to the Lower Saxon *Kreis* in the mid-1620s. Despite the reluctance of Celle, the Guelphs began to co-ordinate defence policy, seeking to maximize their security and influence by pooling their resources. This led to the establishment of a common army in 1631–42, with a peak of 14,500 men by 1640, in addition to another 6,000 or so maintained separately by the three territories. The combined force was broken up after 1642, partly in response to imperial pressure, leaving the dukes without a significant military presence during the peace negotiations at Westphalia.[21] In the opinion of the Great Elector, this had weakened their bargaining power and contributed to why he and not they received the secularized bishoprics of Minden and Halberstadt.[22] The Guelphs appear to have concurred with the Great Elector, for they resumed their military co-operation, pooling their resources to become the leading north German Protestant power alongside Brandenburg and Saxony. Joint membership of military pacts with Sweden and Hessen-Kassel (1652) and Brandenburg (1654) was followed by collective affiliation to the Rhenish Alliance of 1658 and the provision of a combined contingent to the Turkish War in 1663–4. Meanwhile, when Duke Ernst August became bishop of Osnabrück in 1662, he received three companies from Duke August of Wolfenbüttel to found a new army.[23]

The fact that all this rested on shaky foundations was demonstrated by the inheritance dispute in 1665 that threatened to pull the Guelphs apart. Backed by Ernst August, Johann Friedrich seized the better parts of Hanover after the death of Christian Ludwig, while their brother, Georg Wilhelm, was away in Holland. Georg Wilhelm eventually settled for the larger but poorer areas of Celle in a settlement brokered by Georg Friedrich von Waldeck. Waldeck's entry into Guelph service in 1665 proved fundamental in revitalizing their territories and boosting their international prestige. In the seven years in their employ, he raised the combined strength of their forces from under 2,000 (1664) to over 19,000 (1671) (see Table 5.2) while his influence in the Dutch Republic led to the Guelphs becoming major suppliers of auxiliaries to that state. Following an agreement with the Dutch in 1665–6, the dukes went on to supply joint corps for Spain (1667) and Venice (1669), obtaining external funding for the build-up of their armies. These were used to further their political interests in warding off unwelcome Swedish encroachments on the city of Bremen in 1666 and suppressing the autonomy of their own town of Brunswick five years later.[24] The effectiveness of such collaboration freed the Guelphs from the need to co-operate with rulers elsewhere and preserved their freedom of action by remaining outside organization like the Extensionists.

Table 5.2 Growth of Guelph forces, 1665–1705

Date	Hanover	Celle	Wolfenbüttel	Osnabrück	Total
1665	5,322	4,980	4,400	2,500	17,202
1671	7,000	4,260	4,260	3,576	19,096
1674	13,000	7,220	7,749	3,864	31,833
1677	14,351	8,100	7,749	5,339	35,539
1679–80	3,675	5,000	1,972	2,894	13,541
1683	12,748	8,562	6,755		28,065
1684	14,448	8,964	4,540		27,952
1685	11,572	7,914	2,247		21,733
1688	8,440	5,060	1,800		15,300
1689	12,308	7,860	5,000		25,168
1692	14,300	9,577	6,720		30,597
1698–1700	7,000	3,820	3,960		14,780
1705	22,000		3,800		25,800

Sources: Sichart, *Hannoverschen Armee*, vol. I; Elster, *Braunschweig-Wolfenbüttel*, vol. I; Schnath, *Geschichte Hannovers* vol. I; HSAS A29: Bü. 168, lists of Guelph forces in 1700.

Note: Osnabrück's forces during the personal union under Ernst August (1679–98) are included in the Hanoverian totals.

Contemporaries were in no doubt that the military build-up facilitated the dukes' entry into European politics. By 1668 the French envoy in The Hague could write that they were

> now the most important princes in Germany. They possess all of Sweden's former credit. Even if they chose to mobilize 30,000 men they could do it within a few months. In the whole of the north there are no other princes who can pay their troops so punctually They now have 13,000 men, the best one can find, along with a large number of veteran officers.[25]

The collective total of the dukes' forces continued to rival that of Brandenburg and exceed those of all other armed princes throughout the remainder of the seventeenth century.

The new spirit of collaboration proved sufficiently resilient to survive Waldeck's departure for Dutch service in 1672 and the increasingly independent ambitions of Johann Friedrich, who had converted to Catholicism and forged a secret understanding with France. While his brothers tolerated Hanoverian extortion of billets and contributions, Johann Friedrich refrained from interfering in their military operations, which included provision of a combined auxiliary corps for the Dutch. Hanoverian–Celle tension mounted through mutual recriminations over the failure to emerge from the war with permanent gains, but common fear of Denmark forced them together again after 1684. In the meantime, Ernst August had succeeded Johann Friedrich, uniting the Osnabrück and Hanoverian forces between 1679 and 1698. Georg Wilhelm's prominence in the Lower Saxon *Kreis*, and the fact that the co-rulers of Wolfenbüttel, the two brothers Rudolf August and Anton Ulrich, followed his lead, also helped smooth co-operation. However, Ernst August had not abandoned his predecessor's ambitions and stole a march on his brothers by securing the electoral title exclusively for Hanover in 1692. Wolfenbüttel responded with immediate protests followed by an increasingly independent policy of its own, as Anton Ulrich began to ignore his more cautious elder brother. Nonetheless, co-operation continued as Georg Wilhelm, who had no children, accepted Ernst August's action and bequeathed his own lands to him. Hanover replaced Wolfenbüttel as Celle's partner in the provision of auxiliaries to the Dutch during the Nine Years War and Spanish Succession conflict, while even Anton Ulrich backed the others over the Lauenburg inheritance. By the time Celle passed to Hanover on Georg Wilhelm's death in 1705, the Guelphs had risen from marginalized, vulnerable north German princelings to a significant factor in European affairs, soon to be confirmed by the Hanoverian succession in England in 1714.

Although, at 61,215 km^2, the Wittelsbachs had three times as much land as the Guelphs, they were unable to maximize their potential through an inability to co-operate. In addition to the rival Palatine and Bavarian branches, there were ten other lines in 1648, of which Neuburg, Simmern, Sulzbach and Zweibrücken were the most important.[26] Religious differences between the different lines heightened the distance that geography already placed between them, denying the junior lines any significant role and preventing the senior ones from combining. Ironically, the very size of the Bavarian, Neuburg and Palatine holdings discouraged their rulers from collaborating, each thinking he already had sufficient resources for an independent policy. This reduced co-operation to within the Bavarian Wittelbachs, whose numerous offspring found suitable careers within the imperial church. In addition to providing several rulers for the local bishoprics of Freising and Regensburg, relations of ruling electors also governed Cologne consecutively from 1583 to 1761. Distance hindered this, but Ferdinand Maria did provide limited military assistance to Max Heinrich during the Dutch War, sending 1,360 infantry and dragoons to reinforce the Cologne army between 1672 and 1674, while another 1,700 infantry were sent to help his brother-in-law, Duke Charles Emanuel of Savoy, against Genoa in 1672–9. Further help for Savoy was provided in the Nine Years War by the next elector, Max Emanuel, who also loaned two infantry regiments to his brother, Joseph Clemens, to help rebuild the Cologne army in 1690. Little was achieved beyond this and Palatine–Bavarian rivalry continued to frustrate efforts to establish a family compact prior to the 1720s.[27]

The other examples were restricted to the rulers of the lesser territories, like Damian Hugo von Schönborn, bishop of Speyer, who transferred three infantry companies to his relation in Würzburg, Friedrich Carl, who was short of men to meet his treaty obligations to Austria in 1734. Similarly, the many branches of the much-fragmented house of Reuss in Thuringia had long collaborated to purchase expensive artillery and provide men to the *Reichsarmee*, and, together with their neighbours in Schwarzburg, often fielded joint regiments in the eighteenth century.[28] However, as the discussion of the Ernestines, Guelphs and Wittelsbachs has already indicated, these activities declined with the growth of princely absolutism. Political autonomy required military autonomy, and few rulers were willing to compromise their prestige and selfish aims by tying their army too closely to those of their neighbours. Co-operation was necessitated by individual weakness and was abandoned once sufficient resources became available. Those that were unable to follow this route fell back on the *Kreis* structure, which had greater potential to sustain co-operation beyond the medium term.

Kreis *Associations*

The possibility of using the *Kreise* as a basis for regional and non-regional alliances began to be appreciated after 1648. In many senses, the *Kreise* were ideal for this, since their main purpose was to facilitate such co-operation. In addition to the legislation entrusting them with upholding the peace, the imperial Currency Regulation (*Reichsmünzordnung*) of 1555 sanctioned regular interregional conferences to oversee a range of fiscal and economic activities. These functions were revived through their inclusion in the IPO and by the pressing need for post-war economic recovery and security.[29] Astute princes, such as Johann Philipp von Schönborn, recognized an opportunity to combine public spirit and personal ambition by using the *Kreise* as a ready-made structure to mobilize political alliances, capitalizing on the fact that reluctant or hesitant rulers were more likely to join an organization associated with the formal *Reich* constitution than an independent grouping. Moreover, the imperial executive ordinance permitted *Kreise* to compel member territories to take part in peacekeeping and defence, threatening sanctions on those who refused.

Though sharing the same defensive orientation of other princely leagues, these initiatives were always intended as the basis of more comprehensive co-operation, seeking not only to include all *Kreis* members, but to extend the alliance to other regions by associations of two or more *Kreise*. Likewise, the motives of the prime movers went beyond their immediate dynastic and security concerns to envisage a new form of imperial reform movement, sensitive to the needs of the medium and smaller territories, which had appeared to suffer most from the recent war. This characterized the Association Movement as a sort of "third way" between a potential resurgence of Habsburg dominance and the selfish particularism of the emergent armed princes, identifying it as the lobby group of those who were most concerned to retain the *Reich* in its traditional form.

The internationalization of imperial politics imparted a further dimension to this concept of a Third Party, projecting it on to the European stage in an attempt to mediate peaceful resolution to conflicts endangering the *Reich*. While this remained a feature throughout the Movement's existence, it was especially important in its initial Schönborn-led phase, drawing inspiration from imperial tradition and a variety of customary and novel attitudes to warfare. Like the late medieval public peace movement that had laid the foundations of the *Reich*'s system of conflict resolution, the Association built on the ideas of the laws of war (*bellum iustum*) deeply rooted in western Christian thought. These stressed the importance of a "just war", fought by a properly constituted and recognized political authority for the "right intention" of restoring peace and justice. War was thus the extension of a legal battle to be begun when all other attempts to redress an injustice had failed. This placed an obligation on both warring parties to accept the mediation of a third party, otherwise each could appear the aggressor by favouring continued conflict above peace.

The advent of more recent natural law philosophy reinforced these ideas through its emphasis on harmony and the obligation to attempt a peaceful solution prior to the resort to arms. The scientific discoveries and speculative metaphysics of the mid-seventeenth century encouraged the belief in a mechanistic view of international relations, operating through a set of under-lying laws designed to sustain states in perfect equilibrium like the planets in the universe. It seemed to follow that a neutral third party could intervene in conflict to secure peace by restoring the balance of power. All these ideas and traditions were intertwined in the IPO, which directly linked the *Reich*'s internal balance to that of European politics, and imposed a legal obligation not only on the emperor and two foreign guarantors, but on all princes and imperial estates to direct their alliance policies to upholding the constitution and political *status quo*.[30]

It is characteristic of the Third Party in imperial politics that it always occupied a weak position, regardless of whether it was attempting to mediate an inner German dispute or an international conflict, and it became the national refuge of those who stood to lose most if their more powerful neighbours came to blows. The recent struggles had indicated that passive neutrality was no safeguard against the adverse effects of someone else's quarrels so that self-interest reinforced the moral, theological and legal obliga-tions to intervene . Even comparatively powerful rulers took this seriously, with Frederick William telling the Brandenburg Privy Council in 1665 that "it is my duty as an elector to secure peace for the Reich" and seeking to arbitrate the Anglo–Dutch–Münster War that year, as well as remain on friendly terms with as many foreign powers as possible.[31] However, it was difficult to maintain impartiality without the political and military means to avoid being drawn into the conflict. The tendency to drift into either the Habsburg or Bourbon orbit dogged the Third Party throughout the later seventeenth century and helped explain why Schönborn sought a military basis for his policy. The independence and self-confidence that would accrue from a well-armed alliance made this a more attractive means for the weaker territories to preserve their security than the options provided by the formal constitution. Intervention through the imperial courts was not normally possible in international conflict, while "imperial mediation" (*Reichsmediation*) via collective action in the *Reichstag* was limited by the problems associated with that institution. In addition, an independent league offered a greater role to princes who might otherwise be lost in the mass of their fellows in the *Reichstag*, while also reaffirming their territorial sovereignty by providing a medium of negotiation with foreign powers.

There is some debate as to when the Association Movement emerged and how closely it was linked to reform and peacemaking. Most argue that the Association only began as an attempt to implement the 1681–2 defence reforms and see the alliance between Swabia and Franconia in 1691 as the true beginning of the Movements. Bernd Wunder sets the origins a little earlier in 1672, when the Dutch War exposed the failings of existing collective security and prompted some *Kreise* to co-operate.[32] The abortive attempts to establish Associations in the early 1650s are widely regarded as forerunners of the later efforts, but only Aretin argues that the intervening Rhenish Alliance (1658–68) was an integral element of the overall Movement, on the grounds that it was also a vehicle for collective security and imperial reform.[33] This is certainly correct, as it is possible to trace the long-term development of the Movement through a number of phases, distinguished primarily by changes in its membership and relationship to the emperor. However, we also need to remember that the Associations were never solely vehicles for collaboration for the common cause, but served to advance the interests of individual members, not only including attempts to raise their German and international profile, but also to enhance their personal power within their own territories.

It was not easy to mobilize sufficient support to establish a *Kreise* Association given the problems inherent in the *Kreis* structure. The emperor was naturally suspicious of any movement that might undermine his authority, and was generally opposed to initiatives emanating from amongst the princes without his prior consent. It was far from clear whether the IPO provisions governing alliances extended to the *Kreise* as unions of territories, although the Association supporters claimed that they did. However, the main obstacles to successful co-operation came from within, particularly as the larger, militarizing territories were already pursuing more independent policies by 1648 and had little desire to be subsumed within a wider movement they did not control.

Inclusion of *Kreise* dominated by one or two larger territories became almost impossible unless these were prepared to co-operate. Since Burgundy was already excluded on account of its ambiguous relationship with the *Reich*, while Austria was entirely dependent on the emperor, the number of potential members was reduced to the Electoral and Upper Rhine, Franconia and Swabia, with the possible addition of Westphalia, provided the majority of lesser potentates could assert their collective will. Thus, the prime movers behind the Association Movement were the medium-sized territories that controlled the executive positions in these *Kreise* and saw the Associations as a convenient means to consolidate their regional influence. Chief among these was Mainz, which, as the premier electorate strategically situated on the middle Rhine, already provided an alternative to the emperor's traditional leadership of the weaker territories.

Similarly, Württemberg, Würzburg, Bayreuth, Hessen-Kassel, the Palatinate and others also saw opportunities to find security and act as spokesmen for regional interests. However, without the agreement of the prelates, counts and cities, no *Kreis* Association could be formed, since success depended on incorporating all members into a common organization. The majority of these dwarf states wished to avoid anything that involved an additional drain on their meagre resources or might lead to conflict with more powerful neighbours. However, many also appreciated that they could only overcome their individual weakness through collective action and so remained receptive to schemes emphasizing security, peace and maintenance of the imperial constitution.

The Schönborn phase, 1648–72

Though far from being the only prince promoting such schemes immediately after the war, Johann Philipp von Schönborn came to personify the goals and methods of the initial stage of the Association Movement. Renowned as the "German Soloman", his general temperament inclined him towards peaceful resolution of conflict by acceptable compromise. Although Mainz had never been a major participant in the Thirty Years War, its elector played an important part in negotiating the final settlement.

Soon after his election as bishop of Würzburg in 1643, Schönborn began a three-track policy to establish the basis for a lasting peace. The first element, *Konjunktion*, involved the association of two or more *Kreise* for common defence and to assert collective influence on events. Though his first attempts in this direction failed, they were forerunners of the later Associations. The second policy of *Separation* was more successful, since it involved the detachment of the Franco-Spanish conflict from the German war, which was endorsed by the IPO. The last part, *Pazifikation*, was intended to remove all obstacles to peace by compromise solutions negotiated by all interested parties. Though his hope of detaching religion from politics was unrealistic, he made a major practical contribution to the agreement with the Protestants in March 1648. Despite his firm commitment to Catholicism, reinforced by his election to the see of Mainz and thus head of the imperial church, Schönborn remained convinced that permanent reconciliation of the different confession could be achieved and continued to work for this after 1648. He also remained a firm advocate of the concept of a general guarantee inherent in the Westphalian peace preservation programme, which he believed would prevent future conflict from destabilizing the *Reich*. Though not anti-imperial, Schönborn was opposed to the extension of Habsburg dynastic power, which he saw as partly responsible for the war. He was determined to realize a version of the traditional constitutional structure that combined elements of federalism with the desire to preserve the integrity of the existing institutions and the weaker territories. Princes like himself were to have a greater say in managing their own affairs without interference from above, but they were not to emancipate themselves from the overall framework or encroach on the interests of their neighbours. Both imperial absolutism and the aggression of the larger princes were to be contained by developing the constitutional checks and balances codified in the IPO.[34]

As institutions still largely untainted by Habsburg dynasticism, the *Kreise* were seen as ideal for his purpose, and Schönborn began negotiations in August 1650 for an Association of the Electoral and Upper Rhine to secure the region from the Franco-Spanish war still going on immediately to the west. The problem of convincing all members to participate emerged as a major obstacle at this early stage, since many of the smaller territories were reluctant to antagonize the emperor. Schönborn was left negotiating largely with princes in a similar position to himself: rulers of medium-sized territories that were beginning to militarize but were still too weak to act independently or as members of a more narrowly based princely league. Such princes provided the mainstay of the Associations in the early phase, in contrast to the heyday after 1691, when the initiative rested largely with the smaller territories. Nonetheless, the Palatinate also refused to co-operate on account of Elector Carl Ludwig's antipathy to Schönborn, while Hessen-Darmstadt was missing from amongst the Upper Rhenish participants. The others came together in a formal alliance known as the League of Frankfurt on 21 April 1651, agreeing to maintain one-and-a-half times their matricular obligations as a common defence force of 3,240 men. The lack of *en bloc Kreis* membership gave the new group the characteristics of a cross-regional princely alliance, but it has been correctly identified as an Association and indeed was referred to as a precedent by the later Schönborn elector of Mainz, Lothar Franz, in 1696.[35]

Franz Egon von Fürstenberg, the leading minister in Cologne, was enthusiastic about the new organization and hoped to extend it northwards to protect the electorate's exposed territories in Westphalia. He had already tried and failed to do this in 1650 by means of alliances with Brandenburg, Pfalz-Neuburg and the Dutch Republic and now saw the Association as a more promising alternative. Here he encountered another problem that was to dog the Movement, as the Westphalian rulers were reluctant to ally with the Rhinelanders in case it dragged them into a conflict outside their immediate region.[36]

These failures left northwest Germany exposed during a period of acute international instability. The Guelph dukes were in the midst of re-establishing dynastic co-operation after the Thirty Years War and regarded the Lower Saxon *Kreis* as too disunited to provide a framework for viable security. Their remedy was a traditional princely league formed at Hildesheim on 14 February 1652 with the rulers of Hessen-Kassel, Lippe, Bentheim-Tecklenburg, Oldenburg, East Frisia, Rietberg and Waldeck. Sweden joined on behalf of Bremen and Verden and all agreed to contribute to a joint force of 6,000 men. This grouping of Lower Saxons and Westphalians seemed to answer Cologne's security problems and Fürstenberg joined, linking the Hildeheim League to that of Frankfurt. However, though Paderborn followed suit, Münster and the other Westphalians remained outside, and neither group actually assembled their projected forces, though some members did augment their territorial garrison troops. The main significance of both leagues is that they served as precedents for cross-confessional alliances and demonstrated a willingness on the part of at least some rulers to use the *Kreis* structure as a framework for their security policies.

At first this was still far from clear, as both leagues broke up in 1654, with their members polarizing along sectarian lines. Swedish aggression towards the city of Bremen split the Hildesheim League, leaving the Guelphs without wider support. Help came from an unlikely source in the shape of Brandenburg, their chief Protestant north German rival. The Great Elector was also alarmed by the Swedish action, especially as he was isolated diplomatically after the failure of his attempt to settle the disputed Jülich inheritance by force in 1651. His protégé, Georg Friedrich von Waldeck, began promoting a plan for a new Protestant Union to provide general security and safeguard against potential Habsburg–Catholic resurgence. Although suspicious of the electors' ultimate intentions, the Guelphs agreed to an alliance in September 1654, pledging 1,500 men to Brandenburg's 2,000. The dukes also collaborated with a plan to create a formal Association of Lower Saxony and Westphalia, although the elector merely intended this as a means to secure a share of the Westphalian *Kreis* executive. Alarmed at this Protestant combination, the northern and Rhenish Catholics formed the Cologne Alliance on 15 December 1654, comprising Cologne, Trier, Münster and Pfalz-Neuburg.

However, whereas the latter two regarded it as an old-fashioned confessional bloc, Fürstenburg did not see it as incompatible with the new Protestant grouping and consistently sought to merge the two. Brandenburg gave some grounds for hope, as Frederick William was the only German ruler to come to Cologne's aid when its dependency of Liège was attacked by the duke of Lorraine in December 1653. Schönborn was pursuing a similar course, patching up local differences with Cologne to join Fürstenburg's new alliance in August 1655 as a preliminary step to linking it to the original, and now largely defunct Frankfurt League. The distraction of Brandenburg in the Northern War (1655–60) enabled Schönborn to emerge as the driving force behind all efforts to consolidate the alliances. He remained acutely aware of the dangers of a potential Habsburg revival and feared that the emperor might involve the *Reich* in a new war in support of Spain. It was clear that even if the existing groups could combine, they would lack the means to interpose themselves as a major factor in international relations. Sweden was now unacceptable to most Germans, including many Protestants, on account of its designs on Bremen, while an approach to the Dutch in 1657 failed to elicit a favourable response, leaving France as the only realistic partner. The guiding light of French policy was still Cardinal Mazarin, whose hand was strengthened when Habsburg's dynastic crisis precipitated new imperial elections in 1657. Membership of a German alliance suited his immediate objectives, which centred on neutralizing the Rhineland to be free to attack the Spanish Netherlands. Probably on the initiative of Pfalz-Neuburg, France was invited to join the new Rhenish Alliance (*Rheinbund*) established by Schönborn on 14 August 1658.[37]

French membership was welcomed by the Catholics as a counterweight to Sweden, which was also admitted for its north German possessions. The Guelphs were persuaded to join because France backed their policy of neutralizing the Lower Saxon *Kreis* during the Northern War to prevent either Brandenburg or Danes establishing a larger territorial presence there. Despite this and the fact that, like Trier and Münster, Frederick William refused to ratify the original treaty, Brandenburg, along with a number of other territories, joined by 1665, so that the Alliance successfully combined all the leading Protestant and Catholic princes, except the Bavarian, Saxon and Palatine electors. The two margraves of Baden also applied but were refused membership on account of their exorbitant demands (see Table 5.3)

At first sight there seems little to connect the Rhenish Alliance with either the earlier or later Associations, and it has often been dismissed simply as a device to advance French interests in the Rhineland. Certainly there was no formal *Kreis* membership, although it did preserve the neutrality of Lower Saxony as the Guelph's hoped. Nonetheless, there was more than just a coincidence of membership with the Frankfurt League of 1651 to link the new group to the broader Association Movement. As its founding treaty clearly stated, the alliance transcended traditional security concerns present in

Table 5.3 Rhenish Alliance membership, 1658–68

Territory	Date of membership	Military contingent Cavalry	Military contingent Infantry
Mainz	1658	300	600
Trier	1658[1]	180	400
Cologne	1658	420	800
Brandenburg	1658[2]	500	1,000
Münster	1658[3]	400	800
Neuburg	1658	400	800
Sweden	1658	420	1,000
Guelph dukes	1658	420	900
Hessen-Kassel	1658	180	400
France	1658	800	1,600
Hessen-Darmstadt	1659		
Württemberg	1660	100	200
Pfalz-Limburg	1660		
Zweibrücken	1663		
Strasbourg (bishopric)	1665		
Basel (bishopric)	1665		
Ansbach	1665		
Kulmbach	1665		

Notes:
[1] Only became a full member in 1661.
[2] Only became a full member in 1665.
[3] Only became a full member in 1660.

all princely leagues to see itself as a substitute for the inoperative national system of collective defence. It was expressly concerned to uphold the IPO and complete the unfinished business of Westphalia, including ending the excesses of war that still troubled parts of the *Reich*. To this end the Alliance immediately issued detailed instructions to its members to regulate transit, billeting and all matters of supply and payment of their contingents. Articles of war were issued to provide the basis of a disciplining code, while a general auditor was appointed to oversee a common system of martial law.[38] Provisions were also made for unified command and a central war council along with a congress based in Frankfurt. Significantly, the cross-confessional and cross-regional membership pointed to the future, since the ability to achieve both were essential prerequisites to the development of a fully fledged Association.

Despite its protestations to the contrary, the Alliance had a clear anti-Habsburg orientation and was regarded with suspicion by the newly-elected Emperor Leopold I. It was also a vehicle for particularist interests, including those of Schönborn himself, who saw it as a chance to develop the *Reich* along the lines of his modestly federalist programme. This provided one of the reasons for its collapse by 1668, since it was already clear to the elector five years earlier that the organization was incapable of serving as a viable alternative to established institutions like the *Reichstag*. As the Turkish Crisis mounted after 1662, Schönborn abandoned this element of his programme, joined the others calling for the *Reichstag* to reassemble and led the Alliance into its treaty, providing military support for the emperor. The disparate membership proved another problem, as serious tensions emerged between France, Münster and Bradenburg by 1665.

These difficulties coincided with the failure of Schönborn's efforts at international peacemaking, which were related to the Alliance's nominal stance as a neutral Third Party between the Habsburgs and Bourbons. The presence of France and Sweden as members compromised this from the start, but did not deter Schönborn from attempting to mediate an end to the Franco-Spanish conflcit in 1658–9, the Northern War in 1660, and Franco-Papal disputes after 1662. In all cases the warring parties made peace without reference to him and his fellow ecclesiastical electors, but it is still significant that the major powers avoided rejecting his efforts out of hand and felt obliged to make a show of seeking German arbitration. In the long run the connection with France proved a serious liability, especially after Louis XIV assumed personal rule in 1661 and began pursuing increasingly belligerent policies. French diplomats manipulated Schönborn's eagerness for peace as a cloak for their own objectives, using him as an unwitting front man in the 1666 Cleves conference to resolve the Anglo–Dutch–Münster War and after 1667 in Mainz and Cologne's efforts to end the War of Devolution.[39] The latter did not turn out as either Schönborn or Louis expected, as another, a more effective international Third Party in the form of the Triple Alliance of England, Sweden and the Dutch Republic, imposed peace on France and Spain in the Treaty of Aachen in 1668.

The War of Devolution revealed the fragility of Schönborn's system. Only by combining with others could medium territories like his own exercise influence outside their immediate vicinity and hold a balance between France, the emperor and the bigger, militarized powers like Brandenburg and Bavaria. This balance underpinned both the collective security of the Alliance members and Schönborn's efforts at conflict resolution, but it rested on a temporary convergence of interests. The French attack on the Spanish Netherlands removed the common ground by alarming the Rhinelanders, who feared they might be Louis's next victims, and signalling the start of the new French method of managing German politics through bilateral alliances with key princes. Louis not Leopold now seemed the main threat to the integrity of the *Reich*, and Schönborn rejected a French move to renew the Alliance in August 1668 with the reply that "there ceases to be a reason for such an alliance since there is nothing to fear from the emperor".[40]

Undaunted by these setbacks, Schönborn tried to link the Peace of Aachen with his old project of a general guarantee for the Westphalian Settlement to be signed by the Triple Alliance, emperor and the German princes. Princely interests were to be safeguarded by a new military alliance to uphold the guarantee which was to extend to both the Burgundian *Kreis* and the territory of his ally, the duke of Lorraine. It is only in retrospect that it is easy to dismiss these ideas as utopian: to Schönborn and many of his contemporaries, such schemes were the very essence of imperial politics. However, French opposition and the elector's own protracted dispute with the Palatinate condemned the plan to failure. Given its new priorities, France had no interest in the project and did its best to undermine it, exploiting Schönborn's partisan involvement to frustrate his efforts to mediate the Palatine–Lorraine dispute of 1668–9. The French invasion of Lorraine in August 1670 removed Schönborn's chief supporter and destroyed the only Rhineland army capable of serving as a core of his proposed military alliance.[41]

The elector was compelled to scale down his project and redirect it as much towards recovering Lorraine's territorial integrity as upholding peace in Europe. In its final version, as agreed at Bad Schwalbach in early August 1670, the proposed League, based partly on a plan devised by Leibniz, envisaged that each member should have one vote in return for providing 1,000 men to the common army. Though Leopold was offered two votes, the League was to keep its distance from imperial control by maintaining its own permanent directory in Frankfurt. Like the Rhenish Alliance, it was hoped that the new organization would allow Schönborn to preserve peace by holding the ring in imperial and international politics.[42]

Following the completion of the French occupation of Lorraine in October 1670, such hopes were clearly unrealistic. Even with the projected army of 12,000–20,000, the Schwalbach scheme had no chance of imposing its views on France. Whereas Schönborn had hoped to bind France to his system through its formal membership of the Rhenish Alliance, all association with that country had to be avoided if the league's peace initiatives were to be received as impartial. It became impossible to hold the centre ground, as prospective members diverged in their assessment of the best chances for peace and the advancement of their own interests. As Schönborn's project faltered and French diplomatic activity increased, many of those who wanted peace moved closer to France through the new bilateral subsidy treaties. The policy of the Third Party thus became one of appeasement, as individual princes bought their own security by promising neutrality or even active support for Louis's territorial ambitions on the Reich's western frontier. This new, loose group comprised Bavaria, Pfalz-Neuburg, Cologne, Münster, Brandenburg, Hanover and Osnabrück and was to form the basis for French attempts to influence imperial politics after the outbreak of war in April 1672.

The emergence of this new pro-French group is an indication that the Schönborn era was drawing to a close. His policy had depended on subsuming particularist ambitions in a single alliance, co-ordinating all efforts towards the twin goals of peace and security. For a time it looked as if he might achieve this, as he brought together the members of the earlier, disparate groupings in the Rhenish Alliance, but it proved impossible for him to reassemble the pieces after it collapsed in 1668.

Between 1670 and 1673 no less than seven different initiatives were launched by princes, all seeking a medium that would enhance their say in imperial politics whilst providing security against the risks that this inevitably involved. These included Schönborn's own Schwalbach project and his later Marienburg Alliance, along with the Extensionist League, the Brunswick Union of September 1672, a projected south German *Kreis* Association (1673), the northern Quedlinburg Association (1673) and a series of schemes sponsored by Pfalz-Neuburg.

Though they threatened Leopold's authority, these alliances also split opposition to the recovery of his influence. As the next section will show, Schönborn was marginalized as Leopold reasserted his leadership and defeated the federalist, centrifugal tendencies inherent in the early Association Movement. Undaunted, the archbishop–elector persevered despite the failure of one of the most far-fetched attempts hatched by his adviser Boineburg and the ever-inventive Leibniz. This "consilium Aegyptiacum", suggesting that Louis XIV direct his imperialism toward a colonial empire in Egypt rather than Holland, reached Paris after the king had began his attack. Schönborn died on 12 February 1673 amidst further efforts to push a scheme for a general peace guarantee.[43] His failure signalled more than the end of an era; it indicated that neither the emperor nor the king of France wanted minor potentates like him as arbiters of international conflict. Only briefly, during the later revival of the Association Movement, did the lesser German princes intervene as peacemakers when the ecclesiastical electors tried to end the Austro-Papal War of 1708–9 and the Nördlingen Association sought a collective voice at the Utrecht peace conference. The futility of these attempts discouraged further appearances on the European stage, restricting collective arbitration to that of imperial mediation through the *Reichstag* to resolve inner

German disputes. It seemed clear to the major princes at least that they would only be taken seriously by foreign powers if they intervened as belligerents, not mediators, a factor encouraging the long-term growth of subsidy politics and the provision of German auxiliaries for European conflicts.

The imperial ascendency, 1672–88

French belligerence and the growth of the armed princes, manifested in the Extensionist League of 1670, left the aging Schönborn no choice but to seek a better understanding with the emperor. The result of long negtiations was the Marienburg Alliance, assembled early in 1672 and comprising alongside Schönborn and Leopold, Saxony, Trier, Münster, and later Brandenburg-Kulmbach and Paderborn. This was but a hollow version of the original Schwalbach project. The membership was small and attempts to recruit others like Bavaria, Cologne and Hanover failed, as these were now secretly allied to France. More importantly, it lacked all the elements that had been intended to preserve princely autonomy and ensure Schönborn's leading role. There was no independent directory, and the projected joint army numbered only 8,000 and never actually assembled, particularly as Münster openly joined France in April 1672. Instead, Leopold's influence was paramount, and he manipulated Schönborn's diplomacy to marshall strategic princes into the imperial camp.[44]

Meanwhile, Leopold sought to rope in other territories by extending his own alliance network, particularly as it became clear that he could no longer hope to stay out of Louis XIV's Dutch War. Following his alliance with Brandenburg in June 1672, Leopold made his own treaty with the Dutch Republic on 25 July, placing him in a strong position to control the next princely initiative, which coalesced as the Union of Brunswick on 22 September 1672 (Table 5.4). Unlike the Marienburg Alliance, which was still attempting to incorporate imperial cities and minor principalities, this was an exclusive union of armed princes, pledging mutual assistance in the absence of a viable formal structure for common defence. Like Marienburg, the Union's importance was primarily political, serving as an umbrella organization to rally support behind the emperor. Denmark and Brandenburg quickly refused to co-operate unless their own territories were threatened, while Celle and Wolfenbüttel both made their own subsidy arrangements with the Dutch so that no Union army ever took the field. Nonetheless, Trier did join, creating the possibility that Leopold could merge the Union and the Marienburg Alliance under his leadership. This was vehemently opposed by Schönborn,

Table 5.4 German Alliances, 1671–2

Marienburg Alliance, 1671–2

Territory	Infantry	Cavalry	Dragoons	Total
The emperor	4,000	1,000	400	5,400
Mainz	1,000	150		1,150
Trier	500	75		575
Saxony	500	800	200	1,500
Münster	500	800	200	1,500
Brandenburg-Kalmbach	50	30		80
Paderborn				
Total	6,550	2,855	800	10,205

Brunswick Union, 1672

Territory	Infantry	Cavalry	Total
The emperor	6,000	3,000	9,000
Denmark	6,000	3,000	9,000
Brandenburg	6,000	3,000	9,000
Celle	1,200	600	1,800
Wolfenbüttel	1,000	500	1,500
Hessen-Kassel	800	400	1,200
Total	21,000	10,500	31,500

Source: As notes 44 and 45.

who found his own credibility as neutral mediator between Louis and the Dutch compromised by the emperor's entry into the war. His death and the temporary withdrawal of Brandenburg from the war by the Peace of Vossem (6 June 1673) removed both the Alliance and the Union as active elements of imperial politics.[45]

By this stage two new initiatives had emerged to challenge Leopold's control over events. Though both involved attempts to establish *Kreis* Associations, they were independent of Schönborn's earlier projects. Bavaria had been negotiating with Württemberg 1667 for a general pacification of southern Germany, but turned this scheme to suit French interests after its bilateral alliance with Louis in 1670. At a meeting at Dinkelsbühl in August 1673, Bavarian diplomats proposed an association of their own *Kreis* with Swabia and Franconia to provide a basis for armed neutrality during the Dutch War.

Meanwhile, the North Germans also moved closer within the *Kreis* structure, building on the ties that had existed before the formal separation of the Upper and Lower Saxon *Kreise* in the 1540s. Already in the Turkish War of 1664 the Upper Saxon Assembly had agreed to co-ordinate defence with the Lower Saxons, voting to continue this after the war in 1665. In 1672 both agreed to extend this to include Franconia, where the Saxon rulers shared territory in the Henneberg counties. The Upper and Lower Saxon Assemblies met in joint session in Quedlinburg in January 1673, formally establishing a common policy and sanctioning protection for the city of Hildesheim, which belonged to Cologne.[46] These developments highlighted the anti-Habsburg potential of the Associations because both threatened to remove large areas of the Reich from Leopold's war management. Leopold astutely struck a deal with the new Franconian executive prince, Dernbach, and so avoided the odium of direct intervention. Dernbach steered the Franconians into the Quedlinburg group at a meeting in Mühlhausen on 14 August 1673, thus frustrating Bavaria's efforts at Dinkelsbühl and providing a watchful eye on Hanover's activities in Lower Saxony. It was a partial victory for Leopold, who was now gradually committing himself fully to the war in the west and needed support to defend the Rhine.

The expanded Quedlinburg Association agreed a joint army of about 11,000 men in addition to their contribution to any *Reichsarmee*. Dernbach pushed for the immediate despatch of this force to the Rhine, but Swedish and Hanoverian machinations prevented agreement from the two Saxon *Kreise*. However, a bilateral agreement between Leopold and Elector Johann Georg II of Saxony was concluded on 3 August 1673, after the latter's failure to form a firm connection with France.[47] Franconia slipped increasingly into the imperial orbit, especially after Dernbach's election to Würzburg in 1675, giving him control of the largest territorial bloc in the region. The political dangers presented by the Associations had been neutralized, and although the two Saxon *Kreise* ratified their co-operation in 1674 and 1675, the Quedlinburg group ceased to function as an autonomous body, and the Saxons failed to respond to Franconia's call for assistance when Turenne's army appeared on the Main river in 1674.[48]

Unfortunately for Leopold, a new threat had emerged in the meantime in the form of the schemes promoted by Duke Philipp Wilhelm of Pfalz-Neuburg. Given the strategic importance of the duke's possessions on the Lower Rhine, his influence in Westphalia, dynastic connections and apparent readiness to treat with Louis, Leopold could not ignore this challenge. Philipp Wilhelm had been opposed by Austria during the recent Polish royal election and so was inclined to be more sympathetic to France, but still wanted to avoid direct involvement in a conflict that would inevitably have adverse repercussions for his own lands, given their proximity to Holland. Like Schönborn, he refused to accept French domination as the price for neutrality and pursued his own attempts at mediation when war broke out in April 1672. These were also based on the principle of a Third Party, which the duke hoped to form by calling on his Wittelsbach relations in Sweden, Bavaria and the Palatinate. As a first step he agreed a treaty of neutrality with Louis at Zeist on 24 July in the hope that through France he could reach an understanding with Sweden. He achieved a partial success when his help contributed to the Peace of Vossem, by which Brandenburg temporarily withdrew from the war in 1673.[49] Emboldened, he continued his negotiations for a Wittelsbach dynastic union to be enlarged by the inclusion of Cologne, Brandenburg, Hanover and Württemberg to create a group powerful enough to impose peace on the warring parties. These hopes proved illusory, and, like Schönborn, Philipp Wilhelm found himself manipulated by French diplomats to secure German nonintervention in their master's dismemberment of the Spanish Netherlands. He was compromised from the beginning by the Treaty of Zeist and his receipt of French subsidies between December 1672 and March 1675 in return for allowing transit to Turenne's army. Since virtually all the proposed members of the duke's Third Party were French clients, the whole thing was automatically suspect to both the Dutch and the emperor. Sweden's entry into the war in 1675 removed his last hope and left him completely isolated.

The duke was now vulnerable to a direct approach from Leopold, who had already negotiated a preliminary agreement on 16 July 1674. A favourable RHR verdict in the duke's dispute with his estates led to a better understanding in 1676 when Leopold married his daughter and initiated four decades of good relations with this strategic dynasty. Philipp Wilhelm now committed himself to the war, increasing his army and sending it to the front under Dutch subsidy.

However, the duke still hankered after the idea of a neutral Third Party as the best way to end the conflict that now spilled over his frontiers. The billeting crisis of winter 1676–7 encouraged him to seek the co-operation of territories in a similar position, and led to a project for a combination of Mainz, Trier, Würzburg–Bamberg, Hessen-Kassel, Hessen-Darmstadt, the Ernestine Saxons and himself with a common army of 30,000, partly funded by Spanish subsidies, to achieve collective armed status and end extortion by other powers. Although Hessen-Kassel and others opposed it, he got some support from Hessen-Darmstadt and elsewhere, encouraging him to continue with a variation of this idea after spring 1678 to include all the larger territories of Westphalia, Lower Saxony and the Electoral Rhine in an effort to impose peace west of the Rhine. This time he won the support of fellow Westphalian executive princes, Frederick William and Bishop Galen of Münster, who saw it as a means of protecting their gains in northern Germany from French intervention. It was agreed that the Westphalian *Kreis* should contribute 15,000 men to a common force under Duke Ernst August of Osnabrück. Some troops did assemble along the western frontier but were unable to prevent the French moving into Westphalia to compel Münster, Brandenburg and Celle to return their conquests to Sweden in 1679. Although causing momentary alarm, none of these schemes seriously disrupted Leopold's policies, especially as the duke remained within the emperor's preferred framework of loose alliances of medium territories and did not seek to create a vehicle for imperial reform.

With the conclusion of the defence reforms in 1682, Leopold shifted from a form of crisis management to more self-assured control of imperial politics. He did not lose interest in collective security,[50] but neither did he develop his alliance system to supplement it,[51] adapting instead his preferred policy of bilateral agreements with key princes to suit the new circumstances. The reforms now worked to Leopold's advantage by reducing the likelihood of autonomous princely alliances: who would want to enter into an arrangement obliging them to provide a contingent when they were already required to field one for the *Reichsarmee*? Only the larger princes, who were reluctant to contribute to the new defence structure, remained open to traditional alliances. Leopold now sought to bring them on board by inviting them to field their armies within the overall system of collective security but outside the restrictive structure of the *Kreise*. He was assisted by Dernbach and Waldeck, who realized that such alliances were the only way to make the new system work, seeing their Association of Franconia and the Upper Rhine Union in 1681 as a temporary expedient to assist the *Reich* rather than an alternative to the official structure

Leopold now brought this potentially dangerous autonomous group under his control by joining it on 10 June 1682 by the Treaty of Laxenburg, initially to last three years. Like most such combinations, the political implications were more important than the practical military results. Ironically somewhat similar to the Herzberg Plan of the previous year, the Alliance envisaged the formation of three corps to defend the western frontier. The Middle Rhine was to be held by the existing 18,000-strong Union and Franconian forces, assisted by 3,000 Austrian cavalry. A further 20,000 Austrians were to guard the Upper Rhine, with 10,000 more troops to be provided by Bavaria and the Bavarian *Kreis*, if these could be persuaded to join. Hanover and Saxony were invited to contribute the 20,000 needed to cover the northern sector.[52]

While the Bavarian *Kreis* did reach a closer understanding with the Franconians, both it and Swabia refused to join. Apart from the Union forces, no troops took position on the Rhine. Nonetheless, Laxenburg brought together Protestants and Catholics in a manner calculated to appeal to Dernbach, Waldeck and their allies by recognizing their collective armed status while integrating both their cross-regional grouping and the associated Ernestine dynastic defensive alliance into an organization firmly under imperial leadership. Meanwhile, the armed princes, were won over by the prospect of independent commands and the fact that Leopold authorized signatories to raise 130 RMs to fund their mobilization. Bavaria, Hanover and Saxony all joined by separate treaties in the course of 1683. With his main objective achieved, Leopold had little interest in extending the group further, as this would diminish the pool of potential winter quarters for the Alliance forces. Though the organization remained within the spirit of the reformed defence structure, neither the *Reichstag* nor the majority of the *Kreise* were formally involved. As its lynchpin, Leopold's ascendancy was assured, particularly as fear of both France and the Turks encouraged a greater willingness to cooperate with him. Further bilateral agreements augmented the forces sent by Alliance members and active *Kreise* like Swabia after Vienna came under Turkish attack in 1683.

Despite the failure to renew the Alliance when it expired in 1685, the League of Augsburg of 9 July 1686 duplicated its structure and allowed Leopold to retain control. Intended to provide 58,000 to defend south Germany against potential French aggression, the figure was soon revised to 41,000, of which only 16,000 were to be Austrians.[53] Sweden joined, promising an unspecified number on behalf of its German territories, while separate treaties with Saxony and Brandenburg ensured some protection for the north. Although commanders were appointed, no troops took position, and the League's importance remained political. The Burgundian *Kreis* had at last been included, extending collective security westward across the Rhine. The lesser territories and *Kreise* had been kept on board by the threat that Leopold would otherwise ignore them and make an exclusive league with the major princes. It was a sign of his power that he could veto Dutch membership and so prevent a repeat of 1682, when the association of the Laxenburg Alliance with The Hague Guarantee Powers appeared to endorse the right of the *Kreise* to make international treaties.[54] Leopold had consolidated his partial victory over the federalist tendencies in the *Reich*, subverting autonomous movements of the princes into vehicles for his own authority. However, this had been achieved at a price. The defence reforms remained only partially implemented, while Leopold's control over the armed princes hung precariously on his ability to manipulate their conflicting ambitions. These underlying weaknesses were exposed when French armies invaded the Rhineland late in 1688.

The heyday of the Association Movement, 1688–1714

The outbreak of the Nine Years War triggered a revival of the Association Movement and a return to its original policy of establishing a third way between dependency on the emperor and exploitation by the armed princes. Though the initial Franconian–Swabian Association of 1691 was purely defensive, the Movement grew more ideological as it came under the leadership of the second Schönborn elector of Mainz, Lothar Franz, in 1695. In contrast to his uncle over 20 years before, who regarded them as temporary substitutes for an inoperative national system of defence, Lothar Franz promoted the Associations as a permanent supplement to existing institutions to complete the 1681–2 reforms in the interests of the weaker territories.

The necessity of this was already apparent before the French attack in 1688, as Leopold's continued use of assigned billets and contributions was threatening the autonomy of many territories. This was most pronounced in the north, where the outcome of the *Kreis* assembly meetings to discuss implementation of the 1681–2 reforms had been less than satisfactory. The Duisburg meeting of the Westphalians in March–April 1682 proved particularly alarming, as the Brandenburg representative proposed that political influence should be commensurate to military contribution. The small territories whose matricular obligations amounted to only a few men should lose their full individual voting rights and be compelled to share a third of a vote each. Although this was rejected, Brandenburg collaborated with the other two executive princes to block a decision actually to form the *Kreistruppen*, compelling the unarmed members to pay them to provide substitutes in the meantime. Despite numerous disagreements over their share of these contributions, the three executives sustained their domination throughout the 1680s. Brandenburg also collaborated with the Guelphs to divide Lower Saxony on a similar basis, while Electoral Saxony continued to draw cash contributions from the weaker Upper Saxons, except for a few like Anhalt, which managed to gain exemption by sending their own contingents to Hungary. Conscious of the need to retain the support of the weaker territories, Leopold had objected to this continued extortion. He even fined the Great Elector for demanding money from the abbess of Essen despite the end of the war in 1679, but in practice he was powerless to enforce such decisions because he depended on the armed princes' auxiliaries for the Turkish War after 1683, and so left them largely in control of those areas they had established as zones of contribution during the Dutch War.[55]

The west and south had been spared this by the collective militarization of Franconia, Swabia and the Wetterau Union, but it was precisely these areas that were threatened by the outbreak of the new war. With their forces still in Hungary, these territories were dependent on the northern armed princes to defend them as the French crossed the Rhine in the autumn of 1688. Although some armed princes had Dutch subsidies, important territories like Saxony and Hanover initially lacked these and all experienced cash flow problems during mobilization. Frederick III of Brandenburg pawned his private domains to raise 600,000 tlr to fund his assistance to the Rhinelanders early in 1689, while Ernst August told Leopold that Hanoverian mobilization was costing him 120,000 tlr a month.[56] To them the current crisis merely vindicated what they had been arguing all along; the petty princelings were clearly unable to defend themselves and should pay those whose economies of scale enabled them to field effective fighting forces.

The immediate consequences was the Magdeburg Concert, formed 19–22 October 1688 by the northern and central German armed princes to defend the Rhine. While Brandenburg assisted the Dutch Republic to defend the Lower Rhine, a second army would be sent to clear the French from the Middle Rhine (Table 5.5). Arrangements were made to quarter the latter force on the Main–Tauber river lines at the expense of the local inhabitants until the start of offensive operations in the spring. The advance of the Saxons under General Flemming south of the Main at the end of the year extended

Table 5.5 The Magdeburg Concert, October 1688

Territory	Actual contingent
Lower Rhine	
Brandenburg	18,400
(under Dutch subsidy)	
Middle Rhine	
Electoral Saxony	10,000
Ernestine Dukes	1,000
Hessen-Kassel	6,000
Hanover	8,000
Münster	6,000
Brandenburg	1,500
	32,500
Total	50,900

Sources: Schnath, *Geschichte Hannovers*, vol. 1 pp. 432–7; Fester, *Armierten Stände*, pp. 70–5; Philippi, *Landgraf Karl*, pp. 113–18; Jany, *Preußische Armee*, vol. 1 pp. 360–6; Schuster & Franke, *Sächsischen Armee*, vol. 1 p. 114.

the reach of the Concert powers into Franconia and Swabia, where their help was desperately needed to expel a French raiding party under Feuquières.[57]

These arrangements were made unilaterally without reference to the emperor, who was powerless to prevent them. Unable to pay the subsidies the princes demanded, Leopold was compelled to acknowledge their division of south and west Germany into zones of extraction by sanctioning the distribution of quarters through assignations. A treaty was signed with Franconia on 6 January 1689, assigning billets worth 30,000 tlr a month until June to Electoral Saxony, which was also permitted to draw 11,000 tlr a month from the unarmed Upper Saxons and 12,000 tlr a month from districts belonging to Mainz.[58] Meanwhile, the prewar situation in the north was consolidated by the Hanover Compromise between Ernst August and Frederick III, who agreed a bilateral division of Westphalia and Lower Saxony worth 19,000 tlr a month a piece. That evening, 30 January 1689, Ernst August entertained the Brandenburg elector in his new opera house with a performance of Agostino Steffani's *Enrico Leone*, a clear reference to his pretensions to the vast north German territory of the medieval Guelph monarch, Henry the Lion.

The situation quickly got out of hand as matters slipped from Leopold's grasp. Even the armed princes could not abide by their own agreement. The Hanover Compromise broke up over who should draw money from East Frisia, while both Hanover and Brandenburg were opposed elsewhere in Westphalia by Münster. Ernst August began hinting at possible negotiations with France to force Leopold to sanction his increasingly extravagant demands, which now overlapped with areas claimed by Hessen-Kassel and Saxony. The Hanoverian contingent with the Concert's second army behaved so badly in their quarters in Hessen-Darmstadt, Fulda and Gelnhausen that many inhabitants fled over the frontier. The rivalry over resources began to affect strategy, as the Hanoverians refused to co-operate with a Hessian plan to start blockading the French in Mainz in April 1689 for fear that they would lose their present billets to the advancing Austrians. In the end, the arrival of his own troops enabled Leopold to evict the Hanoverians, but only after they had extorted 18,000 tlr in addition to free food and lodging.

However, his dependency on their auxiliaries for Hungary and votes for Archduke Joseph's election as king of the Romans forced him to extend the system of assignations, striking individual bargains where possible as the Magdeburg Concert fragmented through internal rivalry. By 1690, Hanover was drawing about 320,000 fl. annually, largely from Lower Saxony and Westphalia. Brandenburg had been assigned areas in Westphalia, plus Mecklenburg-Güstrow, Anhalt and Hamburg, worth collectively 340,000 tlr annually, while lesser parts of Westphalia like Bentheim and Rietberg were controlled by Münster. Electoral Saxony still drew 11,000 tlr a month from the unarmed Upper Saxons, plus another 50,000 tlr annually from Hanau and Frankfurt, while Leopold's recognition of a *de facto* Hessen-Kassel directorship in the Upper Rhine enabled Landgrave Carl to collect about 270,000 fl from that region.

Though the situation in the Rhine had stabilized by 1690, Leopold depended on the elector of Saxony's 12,000 men to make up the forces needed to defend the southern sector. Johann Georg III was determined that the services of these troops, whose numbers exceeded his formal obligations, should not be at the expense of ruining Saxon finances. He particularly wanted them to winter close to the front in southern Germany to spare him the cost of billeting and transit home each spring and autumn. Treaties to this effect were made with Leopold in March 1690, and again at Torgau the following year, endorsing the continued exploitation of the unarmed Upper Saxons in addition to assignations on Hanau, Frankfurt and Franconia. Leopold was trapped: he appreciated the importance of retaining the lesser territories' confidence and loyalty, but he was powerless to oppose Saxon demands. He did seize the opportunity of Johann Georg III's death on 22 April 1691 to throw doubt on the validity of the Torgau Treaty, but the Saxon commander, Hans Adam von Schöning, seized four Frankfurt villages and blockaded the city until it paid its share of the contributions.

Resentment grew amongst the Franconians and Swabians, who had fielded their *Kreistruppen* continuously since 1683 and were angry at the additional burdens placed on them without their consent. The Franconians were particularly incensed, since they had negotiated renewed promises of exemption in return for providing extra troops: Würzburg agreed to send two of its own regiments after December 1688, while Franconia promised another three on 5 July 1689 to obtain three years' freedom from further billeting. Neither of these agreements had been respected by Leopold, who continued to assign the area to the Saxons.[59]

This time the two *Kreise* were determined not to surrender the initiative and withdrew into helpless neutrality like 1677. There were already signs of growing self-confidence in Franconia at the end of 1688, when the *Kreis* compelled the Ernestines to contribute on behalf of the Henneberg counties, thus establishing an essential precondition for any successful Association that all members co-operated.[60] Bilateral talks were initiated with Swabia in winter 1690–1, leading to an agreement to raise their collective armed status by augmenting the *Kreistruppen*. A further meeting at Nuremberg led to a formal association of the two *Kreise* on the provisional basis of one year from 29 May 1691. Until then, Swabia had remained shy of all cross-regional collaborations, refusing to join either the Bavarian-sponsored Association in 1673 or the imperial-dominated groupings in the early 1680s. The combination of the two best functioning *Kreise* represented the best hope yet for a viable Association and was corroborated by the actual formation of a powerful joint army of 9,000 Franconians (7 regiments) and 10,000 Swabians (9 regiments). Having agreed to one further payment to Saxony in lieu of billets in November 1691, the two *Kreise* rejected all further attempts to impose extra burdens in them, and, following the withdrawal of Austrian regiments from the Rhine to Hungary, renewed their Association on 10 March 1692 at Heilbonn, extending it till the end of the war and increasing their forces to 12,000 men each.[61]

The growing self-confidence of the south Germans coincided with fresh attempts to establish a Third Party from amongst disgruntled northern armed princes, precipitating a major crisis for Leopold. The defection of Hanover was avoided by the problematic expedient of the ninth electoral title, but the retention of Saxon loyalty prompted even more desperate measures. Further concessions at the expense of the south Germans were now clearly out of the question, forcing Leopold to call on external assistance to pacify the new elector, Johann Georg IV. General Schöning, upon whose advice the elector depended, and who was known as an advocate of a French alliance, was abducted by Austrian agents when he went to take the waters at Teplitz in Bohemia on 4 July 1692. Bereft of advice, the indecisive elector was enticed back into the imperial camp in the Treaty of Dresden on 20 February 1693. The exploitation of the unarmed Upper Saxons, worth 100,000 tlr a year, was confirmed, although the Ernestines and other territories like Anhalt that were now providing troops were exempt. The city of Frankfurt was compelled to continue paying its 50,000 fl annually, to which Leopold added a similar amount from his own scarce resources. The bulk of the missing south German money was made good by bringing in the maritime powers, who contributed 150,000 tlr in annual subsidies, while a cavalry regiment was taken into Dutch pay that October. Another 50,000 tlr was scraped together by persuading Brandenburg, Hanover and Hessen-Kassel to relinquish shares of their own contributions, with Brandenburg being rewarded by imperial confirmation of its inheritance claim to East Frisia, Hanover obtaining Saxon recognition of the new electoral title and Hessen-Kassel receiving Leopold's backing for its control of the Upper Rhenish directory.

Johann Georg joined the Grand Alliance, committing himself to the anti-French coalition and provided his 12,000 for the Rhine in 1693. The Anglo-Dutch subsidy continued even after his successor Augustus the Strong switched the troops to Hungary in 1695. Finally, Franconia and Swabia were persuaded to pay another 150,000 fl in October 1693 and then were exempted from all further billets.[62] Leopold had won an important defensive victory, preventing the defection of the northern armed princes, but only at the cost of acknowledging the influence of the lesser princes as well as the maritime powers in war management.

A sure sign that the Association Movement was gathering pace was the ability of the Franconian–Swabian combination to overcome the kind of difficulties that had derailed earlier efforts. Part of this was simply fortuitous. Friedrich Carl, regent for the young Eberhard Ludwig of Württemberg, saw Swabia's involvement as a route to a distinct armed status for his duchy. By late 1692 he was demanding separate recognition from the maritime powers, but his capture by the French at Oetisheim on 17 September removed him and the duchy from an active role, leaving management of the Association to the majority of lesser territories that dominated the Swabian and Franconian *Kreis* Assemblies.[63] Other problems were resolved by compromise, most notably the tricky question of command. The Swabians refused to co-operate with Margrave Christian Ernst, the ambitious Franconian *Kreis* general, who had been made imperial field marshal by the Austrian government on 16 August 1691 in an effort to control events on the Upper Rhine through him as a loyal client. The lack of an effective unified command contributed to the failure of the 1692 campaign and forced the Swabians to reconsider their insistence on special rights over their troops. With imperial backing, the two *Kreise* entrusted command to Turkish Louis in April 1693. It was a well-chosen appointment. Unlike Christian Ernst, Turkish Louis enjoyed the unquestioned military reputation necessary to command respect not only in both *Kreise* but among the other German contingents on the Upper Rhine. Frederick of Brandenburg admired his ability, and, although Landgrave Carl feared for his Upper Rhenish directorship, he made no effort to supplant him as Association commander. Ambitious local rulers like the young Eberhard Ludwig felt unable to challenge him, Christian Ernst had to take a back seat, and only the supremely self-confident Max Emanuel had the presumption to try to step into his shoes while he was still alive. Moreover, as an imperial lieutenant general, he enjoyed Leopold's confidence and so had formal command over the *Reichsarmee* and attached Austrian units.[64]

Though unable to achieve the desired breakthrough into Alsace, Turkish Louis did much to consolidate the Association's collective armed status. On his suggestion both Franconia and Swabia agreed in 1694 to declare their military organization permanent, resolving to retain it after the war, albeit at the reduced establishment of 4,000 and 8,000 men respectively. Meanwhile, much was done to provide the necessary infrastructure for a collective standing army, as the *Kreis* Assemblies approved new regulations, articles of war, pay structures and organization, including the introduction of grenadier companies in the infantry regiments.[65] The *Kreise* also began to take on other prerogatives of the armed princes, making their own subsidy arrangements as they augmented their forces in 1691–2. To make up their agreed quotas, Franconia collectively hired two Würzburg regiments, totalling 2,450 men, from 1691, while Swabia paid the Württemberg regency government 155,000 fl. annually after 15 July 1691 in return for three regiments, numbering 2,720. Franconia then took the three Gotha regiments (1,600 men), previously in British pay, into its own service on 18 February 1692, having them raised to 3,279 men the next year after the Association increased its combined forces.[66] Later, in 1696, the Association followed the armed princes in joining the Grand Alliance in an attempt to gain an equal voice in the direction of the war and negotiation of a possible peace.

Though Turkish Louis played a part, much of the more assertive attitude was due to Lothar Franz von Schönborn, who had become bishop of Bamberg and Franconian co-executive prince in 1693. Like the margrave, he believed the Association should represent something more than a temporary expedient to defend south Germany, but whereas Turkish Louis still thought primarily in military terms, Schönborn was more ambitious politically. His influence grew after his election to the see of Mainz in 1695, and he began campaigning for a comprehensive reform of collective security that would end the excesses of warmaking once and for all. Like his uncle Johann Philipp, Lothar Franz championed a middle path between Habsburg hegemony and the selfishness of the armed princes, seeking to extend the Association as a permanent general guarantee for peace in the *Reich*. He was careful to stress that it should remain under overall imperial authority, but Leopold was clearly to be bound within the new system. This aspect was particularly promoted by Dr Johann Georg Kulpis (1652–98), president of the Württemberg privy council, friend of Turkish Louis and propagandist for the Association. Kulpis began publishing his arguments after 1696, including in them the preamble to his collection of Swabian military ordinances, which appeared in 1698 as evidence that the *Kreise* were just as capable of efficient and effective organization as the larger militarized territories. Rooting his case firmly within the imperial tradition, Kulpis argued for a further development of the 1555 Executive Ordinance permitting decision-making at *Kreis* level subject to retrospective action from the *Reichstag*. The political implications were clear – the initiative was to be taken away from the emperor and larger princes who dominated the *Reichstag* and returned to the smaller and medium territories who held the majority in the *Kreis* Assemblies. These arguments ideally suited Lothar Franz's personal agenda, since, as elector of Mainz and imperial chancellor, his ability to determine the *Reichstag*'s agenda would make him a vital link between it and the *Kreise*.[67]

Immediately after his accession in Mainz, Lothar Franz reversed his predecessor's policy of blocking the reactivation of the Electoral Rhenish *Kreis*, pushing instead to include it in the Association and bring in as many of the others as possible. The response remained lukewarm until defection of Savoy from the Grand Alliance in 1696 raised the possibility of the transfer of additional French troops to the Rhine front. That December a congress convened in Frankfurt attended by delegates from the Franconian, Swabian, Westphalian, Bavarian, Electoral and Upper Rhenish *Kreise*. A favourable start was made when not only Bishop Plettenberg of Münster but Frederick III agreed to co-operate, the latter even offering to end Brandenburg assignations if a wider Association could be founded. However, the larger territories refused to endorse a Franconian–Swabian request that they make up the contingents of those territories that were no longer effective members of their *Kreise*, since no one was prepared to field extra troops free of charge. Lothar Franz was compelled to abandon his more ambitious political programme and settle for a more limited military organization endorsed in the congress Recess on 23 January 1697. Although this established a permanent army of a double quota in peace (40,000 men) and triple in war (60,000) based on the 1681 matricular list, it was envisaged only as a temporary measure pending the extension of a fully revised system to the other four *Kreise*. The Association thus assumed the role of auxiliary to and not replacement of the *Reich*. The basic structure of the 1681–2 system was retained, with each *Kreis* providing its own forces at its own expense but harmonizing its supply and maintenance regulations. Due to war damage and the fact that part of their territory was still occupied by the French, the Upper and Electoral Rhinelanders were permitted to moderate their contingents to 7,000 men each, adding an unwelcome element of doubt as to the overall validity of the quotas. Turkish Louis was retained as overall commander in an acknowledgement of the Association's subordination to the existing imperial structure, but Lothar Franz ensured that the Association and not the emperor would decide any future replacement.[68]

Like the *Reichstag* in 1681–2, the Association congress had determined the basic outline but left it to the individual *Kreise* to complete the details, opening the door to the same regional tensions that had stymied the earlier reforms. Not only did the Recess have to be discussed and ratified by the six *Kreis* Assemblies but the other four *Kreise* needed to be brought on board, and all this without the active support of the emperor. The situation was exacerbated by the Rijswijk peace talks, which dampened the initial enthusiasm for further military reform, while the controversy surrounding the subsequent Religious Clause reopened old wounds and made the process of ratification and extension very difficult.

The Lower Saxons showed some interest, but this failed to transform itself into active participation because Hanover made membership dependent on recognition of its electoral title. Frederick III quickly changed his mind, preventing Upper Saxon involvement, while Burgundy was scarcely able to negotiate and Austria was dependent on Leopold. Worse, Lothar Franz ran into difficulties even in the six that had been at the Congress. Cologne refused to co-operate, forcing the electoral Rhenish Assembly to unilaterally reduce its Association quota to 4,000 men at its meeting in April 1697.[69] Lothar Franz's refusal to permit Max Emanuel to assume overall command removed the chief motive for Bavarian involvement, prompting the disgruntled elector to pull out of the June 1697 Congress, leaving the other five *Kreise* to debate the intractable issue of revision to the matricular quotas.

These difficulties prevented Lothar Franz from exploiting the groundswell of opinion among the smaller territories in areas that remained outside the original Franconian–Swabian Association. Those in the Upper Rhine had grown progressively dissatisfied with Hessen-Kassel's leadership after 1692. Hessen-Darmstadt broke away and was recognized as an armed state by Leopold in return for it fielding about 1,600 soldiers in addition to its 510 *Kreistruppen*.[70] Unable to do this themselves, the others swung behind the Elector Palatine, who wanted to reactivate the old *Kreis* executive, having partially resolved his dispute with Worms in 1690. Encouraged by the elector, Count Johann Ernst von Nassau-Weilburg led the weaker members in challenging Landgrave Carl. Inspired by the Franconian and Swabian example, the malcontents devised a plan for a proper *Kreis* army to replace the Hessian-dominated Union forces, and, having secured Palatine support, Nassau-Weilburg declared the Union dissolved as from 1 November 1696. As a result, Nassau, Fulda, Solms, Isenburg, Leiningen, Wittgenstein and some of the Westerwälders stopped paying their contributions to Hessen-Kassel, leaving Carl with the uncertain support of Hanau, Waldeck, Stolberg, Friedberg, Wetzlar, Dillenburg, Siegen, Dietz, Wied and the local imperial knights. Both he and the elector appealed to Leopold to endorse their respective positions precipitating a crisis in October–November 1696. While Lothar Franz lent diplomatic backing to Nassau-Weilburg, Carl sent troops to collect the contribution "arrears". The Palatinate responded by marching a detachment to Hanau, plundering some villages and seizing 40 Hessian soldiers. The Hessian commander, General Lippe, proposed blowing up Schloss Weilburg and seizing the count's children in retaliation, but fortunately Carl had the wisdom not to authorize it. Palatine and Mainz influence in Vienna prevailed, and Leopold ordered the landgrave to accept a final payment worth 145 RMs of the region's contributions. The Hessian directory was dissolved and the Upper Rhine joined the Association with Weilburg as its local commander.[71]

Developments in Westphalia took a similar course but with a different outcome. After 1682 Münster had patched up its differences with the other two executive princes and established a working monopoly of the *Kreis* between them. The three collaborated in placing 1,000 men in the city of Cologne threatened by the local elector after 1686. This detachment was increased to over 3,000 after 1691 in view of the French threat at the cost of 855,000 fl. annually. The three executives used their combined influence to recoup these expenses and more from the unarmed members, holding only tripartite conferences and blocking any collective mobilization. However, a growing number of Westphalians were dissatisfied with this arrangement and, like their similarly exploited neighbours in Lower Saxony, sought to break free of control by the armed princes. Territories like Lippe, Schaumburg-Lippe, Mecklenburg and Paderborn were all too weak to join the ranks of the armed princes alone since none of them could raise sufficient forces to hire to the maritime powers: the Dutch, for example, rejected an offer from Mecklenburg in 1693 on the grounds they already had enough auxiliaries from the larger territories. The convening of a Westphalian Assembly in Cologne in April–May 1697 to discuss joining the Association provided an opportunity to vent long-held frustration. Bishop Wolf-Metternich of Paderborn had already broken free by fielding his own *Kreistruppen* since 1685, and now came to the aid of the others by leading the demands to provide contingents rather than cash. They gained the support of the Jülich representative, acting on behalf of the Palatinate, but the delegates from the other two executive princes refused, arguing that the 1681–2 reforms had collapsed and it was better to replace them with contingents from the militarized territories. A second meeting in Cologne in November-December agreed a quota of 12,000 men as the region's contribution to the expanded Association and banned the arbitrary imposition of assignations upon the weaker members. However, Münster and Brandenburg continued to block the formation of an actual integrated force.[72] Though Franconia, Swabia, Westphalia, Upper and Electoral Rhine reaffirmed their commitment to the extended Association in June 1697, only the first two sent contingents into the field, and the planned autumn congress was cancelled due to conclusion of peace at Rijswijk. Despite Lothar Franz's best efforts, the Movement was breaking up. The Franconians and Swabians demobilized, dissolving their integrated army and returning the soldiers to the contributory territories. Their Assemblies did agree to garrison Philippsburg and Kehl, which the French had returned to the *Reich*, but problems over how this should be funded merely soured their relations with their neighbours. Münster and Brandenburg continued to block action in Westphalia, while the religious controversy split the reformed Upper Rhenish *Kreis*, where Hessen-Kassel saw the dispute as a way to reassert its leadership by rallying the Protestants.[73]

The loss of internal momentum eased Leopold's task of neutralizing the Association. The original Franconian–Swabian group had posed a problem for his war management but had not been a direct political challenge until Lothar Franz's leadership. The elector had always based his position on existing imperial law and otherwise acted as a loyal vassal, making it difficult for Leopold to confront him. Recognizing that the Association could contribute positively to collective security, Leopold applied to join on behalf of the Austrian *Kreis* in 1698 on the condition he was granted political leadership. Lothar Franz could not agree to this, opening the way to an imperial veto of another congress planned for July 1698. Meanwhile, Leopold pressurized Turkish Louis into resigning his command by threatening to confiscate his estates in Bohemia and circulating rumors that the Margrave was a new Wallenstein who intended to use his military position to intrigue with the enemies of the *Reich*. Swabia and Franconia held a series of fruitless meetings until the latter's Assembly decided in June 1699 to dissolve its alliance of 1691.

When measured against the extent of Lothar Franz's hopes, this outcome seems a crushing defeat, but, compared to the earlier efforts, the Associations since 1691 had been "a qualified success".[74] The Swabians and Franconians had created powerful military organizations, pointing the way for the other territorially fragmented areas and raising the fears of Louis XIV that the defence reforms of 1681–2 were now being implemented. Though the religious controversy proved a serious blow, both Franconia and Swabia remained intact and political tensions were overcome; despite its membership of the League of Corresponding Princes opposed to the Hanoverian electoral title, Würzburg remained commited to the Association. More fundamentally after the failures of the 1670s, military co-operation had been shown to work, establishing a clear precedent to be followed when the Spanish Succession crisis broke over the *Reich* after 1700.

Franconia and Swabia reactivated their alliance at Heidenheim on 23 November 1700, expressly agreeing to implement their share of the 1697 Frankfurt programme by mobilizing 6,000 men (5 rgts) and 8,200 (7 rgts) respectively. Both Assemblies ratified this decision in February and April 1701, agreeing to augment their joint forces by one-third to 18,800. As in 1691 this represented limited cross-regional co-operation for purely defenisve purposes, and both *Kreise* remained suspicious of the ambitions of Lothar Franz, Max Emanuel and Leopold alike; Franconia refused an imperial request to send troops to the Rhine in spring 1701, not wishing to take any action that might provoke France.[75]

In fact, the limited objective of armed neutrality fitted Lothar Franz's programme of reviving a wider Association as vehicle for an autonomous middle path, intended to prevent Leopold subordinating the *Reich* to

Habsburg dynastic objectives, which would unavoidably involve renewed war with France. His call for a new congress to meet in August 1701 in Heilbronn met with a good response from Franconia, Swabia, Bavaria, Electoral and Upper Rhine, and even the Austrian *Kreis*, though the executive princes blocked Westphalian participation. It helped that the elector Palatine, Johann Wilhelm, was also promoting the Movement since he helped defuse the religious controversy in the Upper Rhine and bring all the Protestants except Hessen-Kassel back into the *Kreis* structure by 1702. Though the absence of Landgrave Carl cut the *Kreis* forces to only 3,325, a final compromise with the bishop of Worms (now the elector's brother, Franz Ludwig), ended the dispute over the executive and restored the *Kreis* as one of the most active in the *Reich*. Meanwhile, Lothar Franz resumed his former pre-eminence, fighting off attempts by Leopold and Max Emanuel to take control and pervert the Association for their own ends. The Austrian *Kreis* was denied membership as was Bavarian, despite an offer of 15,000 men from that electorate.

However, the start of French operations in Cologne and the Lower Rhine exposed Mainz before any Association army had been formed. Lothar Franz was acutely aware that he lacked the resources even to finish the fortification of his capital city let alone provide a credible defence for the immediate region, leaving him open to a direct approach from Leopold.[76] After a number of false starts a deal was struck on 7 October 1701 whereby Austria provided a limited subsidy and the promise of help to obtain more money from the maritime powers, while the elector agreed to promote Habsburg claims to Spain. Immediately, Lothar Franz dropped his opposition to Austrian membership and, in his capacity as bishop of Bamberg, reversed Franconia's policy of nonco-operation by despatching 1,500 soldiers to the Rhine to help construct defensive earthworks.

Now that the Association appeared to be reduced to a convenient device to mobilize the defence of the Rhine, Leopold threw his weight behind its formation. At a congress in Nördlingen, Swabia, Franconia, electoral and Upper Rhine renewed the lapsed Frankfurt Association on 20 March 1702, agreeing to maintain troops at triple quota strength. The Austrian *Kreis* joined the next day, with all five being admitted into the Grand Alliance. Once Westphalia agreed membership on 1 August 1702, the expanded Association had a paper strength of 53,480 men. An attempt to include the Lower Saxons failed, but there was still sufficient manpower for a credible defence of the *Reich* (Table 5.6).

Although the Association backed Leopold's declaration of a *Reichskrieg* in the *Reichstag* that November, Austrian membership did not lead to a loss of political autonomy, as some have argued.[77] Lothar Franz was more successful than his uncle in preserving the integrity of the Movement, extracting a list of

Table 5.6 The Nördlingen *Kreis* Association, 1702

Kreis	Contingent
Franconia	8,000
Swabia	10,800
Upper Rhine	3,000
Electoral Rhine	6,500
Austria	16,000[1]
Westphalia	9,180
Total	53,480

Sources: Recess and supplementary agreements printed in Lünig (ed.), *Corpus iuris militaris*, vol. I pp. 402–7; Hofmann (ed.), *Quellen zum Verfassungsorganismus*, pp. 269–71.

Note:
[1] Plus 1,200 militia and 1,000 entrenchment workers.

actual regiments that Leopold promised to provide to make up his quota. The continued presence of Ludwig Wilhelm as the Association commander, plus its admittance into the Grand Alliance, consolidated its prestige and independence; the *Reich* as a whole remained outside the Alliance. The collapse of the French-sponsored Third Party after 1702 removed the only alternative vehicle for autonomous princely interests, while the onset of serious French attacks in the Rhineland and later from Bavaria made it all too clear that Louis XIV had no intention of protecting the lesser territories.

Moreover, these had no intention of permitting a return to the exploitation they had suffered in the earlier conflicts and were determined to make collective defence a reality. Though the Franconians unilaterally withdrew their soldiers when Bavaria openly joined France at the end of 1702, they remained within the Association and even augmented their own collective forces with four supernumerary regiments (3,000 men). These were used to garrison Bavaria after Blenheim, and were sent to reinforce the other Association units on the Rhine after September 1707. Swabia consistently fielded its quota throughout the war, as did the Upper Rhinelanders, and, although Trier, Cologne and the Palatinate largely failed to co-operate, Mainz provided 2,500 infantry plus additional garrison troops.[78]

However, Westphalian participation was the most significant politically given the earlier failure of the lesser territories to achieve collective armed status. Leopold had not been insensitive to their aspirations and had encouraged those that wished to arm themselves within the formal *Kreis* structure. In

1698 he backed Count Friedrich Adolf of Lippe against his estates and Münster and Brandenburg, which had previously drawn contributions from his territory, enabling the establishment of a permanent force numbering 500 regular *Kreistruppen*, backed by 1,200 militia for home defence. Thereafter, Leopold used his leverage over Frederick III during the negotiations over the Prussian royal crown to insist that the elector desist from illegal demands on the lesser Westphalians. Article IV of the Crown Treaty of November 1700 stipulated that the matter was to be resolved within 18 months, but Leopold's influence soon declined once war broke out, and he was unable to hold the new king to his bargain. Prussia continued to claim protectorate rights over Essen, Werden, Dortmund and Limburg as well as contributions from Tecklenburg, Aachen and East Frisia. However, this time the remaining Westphalians were no longer prepared to tolerate high-handed management of their affairs by the executives. The bishop of Münster swung behind the Palatine representative, who had backed the others' demands since 1697, isolating Brandenburg, which was unable to prevent some like the city of Dortmund mobilizing their own contingent as soon as the *Kreis* joined the Association in August 1701. Thanks to renewed support from Leopold and the added leverage of a formal *Reichskrieg*, the majority in the Assembly completed the mobilization orders by April 1703. By then East Frisia, Bentheim, the Westerwald counts and the cities of Dortmund and Cologne had joined Lippe and Paderborn in achieving armed status. Together with contingents from Münster and the Palatinate, the *Kreis* mobilized about 6,000 men, or half its official quota, of whom about 3,000 garrisoned Cologne during the war. They were joined by the count of Schaumburg-Lippe, who escaped his contract with Hanover, in place since 1683, and fielded his own troops from 1711, as did the new Catholic bishop of Osnabrück, Carl Joseph of Lorraine, who provided an extra regiment to Austria in addition to his *Kreis* contingent. A further sign of the Westphalians' self-confidence came in 1706, when they de-selected the Prussian general serving as their field commander and replaced him with a Palatine officer.[79]

Münster's decision to abandon its earlier insistence on contributions had played a major part in the defeat of Brandenburg opposition to mobilization, but its significance extended beyond this to indicate a wider trend. Münster had been a major militarized territory, with its bishops, especially Christoph Bernhard von Galen, exemplifying the aggressive belligerence of the armed princes. However, by 1700 it was being marginalized by its expanding secular rivals, Hanover, Prussia and Saxony. Like Mainz, Würzburg and other medium armed states, Münster was finding it harder to make an individual mark on events, and although it remained comparatively heavily militarized well into the eighteenth century, it became increasingly dependent on wider collective security. The willingness of such states to co-operate within the Association gave it military credibility and greatly increased its political effectiveness. The Nördlingen Association of 1702 thus proved so successful because it had become the refuge of precisely those territories that previously would have sought to pursue more independent policies.

This becomes clearer when we examine the position of the other small to middling territories that had been arming themselves since the late 1670s: Hessen-Darmstadt, Holstein-Gottorp, Mecklenburg, Weimar, Eisenach, Ansbach, Bayreuth, Paderborn, Lippe, East Frisia, Öttingen, Reuss, Schwarzburg, Württemberg. All these had raised permanent units to escape the exploitation of powerful neighbours, thus embarking on the same course as the larger territories, which had begun arming 20 or 30 years earlier. However, with the partial exception of Württemberg, Mecklenburg and Holstein-Gottorp all found it increasingly difficult to compete with Bavaria, Saxony, Hanover, Prussia, the Palatinate and others, which had "economies of scale", larger forces and better international connections. Some (Holstein-Gottorp, Mecklenburg, Württemberg, Ansbach, Bayreuth, Öttingen and East Frisia) managed to place one or two units each in Anglo-Dutch service, but were unable to match the brigades provided by the larger territories and so had proportionately less influence. Others were forced to subcontract to other German rulers: Hessen-Darmstadt provided the Guelph's contingent to the *Reichsarmee*, while Schwarzburg and Reuss collaborated in hiring a regiment to Franconia to meet its Association quota.[80] The problems faced by all these would-be armed princes are graphically illustrated by the case of Weimar, Eisenach and the Albertine cadet branch of Weissenfels. The three decided to provide an infantry regiment of 2,300 men for the Austrian army in Italy in return for exemption from all other military burdens, including contribution to collective defence. A secret treaty was concluded to this effect with Leopold in 1702, but since the three princes had few soldiers of their own, they had to recruit quickly at a time when demand for manpower was high. Only 1,100 men could be found, and all but 144 had succumbed to disease or deserted by October. Leopold terminated the agreement and obliged the princes to raise a new unit for the *Reichsarmee* instead.[81]

Armed status was still desired by men like the three Saxon princes, and it remained related to the imposition of absolutism, but it was now to be achieved within a collective context. In contrast to rulers like Frederick I of Prussia, all those discussed above provided their contingents to the Association forces as well as their units under Anglo-Dutch subsidy. Despite harbouring ambitions to take the European stage alongside other monarchs, most were realistic enough to know their limited resources precluded truly independent action.

Nonetheless, it still proved extremely difficult to sustain collective action through the war and even harder to continue it into the peace. Despite its mobilization, Westphalia still remained outside the core Association membership of Franconia, Swabia, Upper and Electoral Rhine. Already in 1702 it made it conditional upon joining that it could deduct the Cologne garrison from its quota. Palatine efforts to persuade the others to increase their forces failed in 1706, while Prussia refused further co-operation after its general was relieved of command. Though preferable to assignations, provision of actual contingents nonetheless proved a strain, particularly when they had to serve far afield on the Upper Rhine. After 1708 the Westphalians became less willing to contribute to defending anywhere outside their own region. The four core members responded by only retrospectively informing Westphalia of their decisions, and in March 1710 the *Kreis* decided not to attend the spring congress. Nonetheless, all three executive princes approved the 1711 Association Recess and even Prussia backed Lothar Franz's barrier project.

It was precisely such schemes that made the Association problematic for the emperor. Though the formation of what he regarded as a tame defensive bloc had suited his immediate needs in 1702, Leopold remained suspicious. Lack of resources compelled him to deploy his troops elsewhere, and Austria rarely had anything like its full quota of 16,000 men in the Upper Rhine. The vexed question of command added further difficulties. Though Leopold confirmed Turkish Louis as commander of all imperial forces in southern Germany, many others in Vienna were growing impatient with his hesitant leadership. Elector Johann Wilhelm urged that Archduke Joseph should lead the force in person, as he was entitled to as king of the Romans. Joseph was keen to have a go, "vowing to teach the French devils some manners and show them what the Austrian and *Reichstruppen* can do".[82] He did turn up at the siege of Landau to boost morale, but Ludwig Wilhelm remained too well-connected with the Association leadership for Leopold to displace. However, by 1705 his lacklustre performance was proving a serious problem, drawing censure from Marlborough and other influential figures urging a more energetic prosecution of the war. Once Joseph became emperor he grew still more impatient, especially as the margrave refused to release the Austrian regiments to be deployed to Italy. An Austrian military investigation accused the ailing general of incompetence in 1706 and he was relieved of command, dying shortly afterwards on 4 July 1707. The way was free at last for the ambitious south German princes to seize their moment of glory. Eberhard Ludwig persuaded the Swabians to make him their general, establishing Württemberg dominance of the *Kreis* military posts, while Margrave Christian Ernst, backed by Prussia, managed to replace Ludwig Wilhelm as supreme Association and imperial commander. It was not a fortuitous choice. Christian Ernst was not up to the job of defending the difficult terrain of the east bank of the Rhine with the inadequate forces at his disposal and was unable to prevent the French punching through the defences to devastate much of Swabia in May 1707.[83]

The debacle paved the way for Joseph to assert his control over the Association forces by appointing a man of his own choosing. It was a sign of his power that he was able to designate Elector Georg Ludwig of Hanover, even though he lacked formal imperial rank. This was a political move designed to reward the elector and bind him closer to the Habsburg clientele. Though his period of command, 1708–9, was not a success, it consolidated the emperor's hold over the combined forces so that when Georg resigned, Joseph could entrust them to Prince Eugene in 1710, even though the latter remained at his post on the Flanders front. Eugene devised strategy in conjunction with the Viennese *Hofkriegsrat* without reference to either the Association or the *Reichstag*, exercising authority on the spot through his deputy, the Austrian field marshal Count Gronsfeld.[84]

The Association had lost a key element of its autonomy, and with it part of its political cohesion. The development of a unified command of Association forces under Turkish Louis after 1693 had helped to hold the Movement together and keep it distinct from, but nonetheless related to, the formal structure. For instance, the presence of the margrave as Association commander assisted by generals appointed by the member *Kreise* had made the lack of a formal imperial general staff and war council less serious and indeed, helped retard discussions in the *Reichstag* over appointing new commanders for the *Reichsarmee* after 1701. After 1706 there was no one to inspire the confidence and respect of the *Kreis* members, especially since Prince Eugene remained an absentee commander. Already in 1707 the Swabians reimposed the set of restrictions that had operated before 1693 to limit Christian Ernst's control over their troops. He refused to accept these, as did Elector Georg, only heightening Swabian fears that their forces might be deployed elsewhere at a time when they needed them most. Even though confidence returned when Eberhard Ludwig replaced Gronsfeld as Eugene's deputy and *de facto* commander in 1711, the system of fully unified command had broken down, and the member Kreise remained wary of entrusting their troops to anyone but their own generals.[85]

Tension over command heightened mutual suspicion between emperor and Association. Excluded by Joseph from his bilateral talks with France in autumn 1706, the members felt they were being abandoned while the emperor pursued his dynastic ambitions elsewhere. After his failure to help them during the disasters of 1707, they no longer considered him a member, and the Austrian *Kreis* did not sign the Association recesses of 1707–10. Alarmed at rumours in April 1709 that Joseph and the maritime powers were again negotiating with France, Lothar Franz pushed to be included and insisted on the adoption of his barrier project to defend the Rhine.

The idea of a *Reichsbarriere* went back to Lothar Franz and Leopold's hopes in 1696 of reversing the *Réunions* and recovering *Reich* territory lost since 1673.[86] The Dutch had long developed a defensive network of fortified towns along their southern frontier, extending into the Lower Rhine and Meuse through their retention of towns occupied during the Thirty Years War. Although the Republic had been forced to relinquish most of these by 1679, it established new garrisons in Liège and Luxembourg in 1698. Lothar Franz's plan centred on closing the gap between Luxembourg and the Swiss frontier to provide comprehensive protection for the Middle and Upper Rhine. Parts of this were achieved at Rijswijk, which secured the return of Lorraine, Luxembourg, Kehl and Philippsburg. However, Lorraine remained indefensible without Metz, Toul, Verdun and the military corridors ceded permanently to France, while Strasbourg, Alsace and Franche Comté were necessary to protect the Upper Rhine. In pressing for these areas to be incorporated in any final peace treaty, Lothar Franz was promoting goals that which overlapped with Habsburg and Dutch objectives. The Republic wished to re-establish a solid barrier throughout the entire Spanish Netherlands, plugging the gap in Liège by controlling Huy and Liege City, and extending southeast into the Moselle–Middle Rhine region with garrisons in Bonn, Trier, Trarbach, Koblenz and Kaiserswerth. Meanwhile, both Leopold and later Joseph were keen to restore Lorraine's territorial integrity and re-establish the western protective glacis of the Burgundian *Kreis*. Not only would this relieve Austria of the burden of defending the Rhine but it would advance Habsburg interests, which were increasingly connected with the House of Lorraine. Already in 1698 Leopold was promoting the duke's brother as candidate in vacant north German bishoprics, and both Joseph and Charles VI continued to favour the family, culminating in the mariage of Duke Francis Stephen to Maria Theresa in 1736.[87]

The subsequent difficulties between the emperor, elector and the Dutch thus arose not from fundamentally divergent objectives but tactical manoeuvring to secure preferred variations of a common goal. Joseph adopted the barrier scheme particularly as the restitution of Metz, Toul and Verdun could be used to strengthen Lorraine, but believed that Lothar Franz's calls for Franche Comté and even Burgundy itself were unrealistic.

Fearful lest Joseph trade these demands for confirmation of his Italian gains, the elector tried to enlist Dutch support for his version of the barrier in 1710. By negotiating separately from the emperor, Lothar Franz unwittingly linked the constitutional ambiguities surrounding the Association's independence from imperial control to the underlying differences concerning the barrier. Joseph quickly challenged his interpretation of imperial legislation, denying the legitimacy of *Kreis* initiatives involving foreign powers. Joseph and later Charles became concerned at Dutch encroachments on *Reich* sovereignty, consistently refusing to permit them to garrison fortresses seized from Joseph Clemens in Liège and Cologne. A meeting planned for February 1711 to discuss Dutch co-operation with the Association was wrecked when the Austrians persuaded the Republic to recall its representative. Nonetheless, the Dutch did agree on 22 August 1711 to back Lothar Franz's barrier project, while another convention arranged for the four core *Kreise* to augment their forces by 16,000, of whom half would serve in the Netherlands in return for Anglo-Dutch subsidies. These schemes would have consolidated the Association's autonomy and collective armed status, but were never ratified.[88] Instead, Charles VI stole a march on the elector by signing the Association Recess on 31 August, restoring active Austrian membership and adopting the recovery of Alsace and Lorraine as his own war aims. Habsburg influence benefited from declining Dutch enthusiasm for the extended barrier. The Republic had only agreed to the 1711 treaty to keep the lesser Germans in the war and quickly lost interest in the areas south of Cologne as it concentrated its efforts to obtain a more immediate barrier in the Netherlands. This objective ran counter to Habsburg and German interests, since it was to be achieved at their expense with not only the Austrians being obliged to pay for Dutch garrisons from their Netherlands revenues, but Trier, Cologne and Liège having to surrender fortresses to plug the gaps in the line from the Channel to the Rhine. Though Charles was eventually obliged to consent to Anglo-Dutch demands on Netherlands revenues in the Barrier Treaty of 1715, he successfully backed Trier and Cologne efforts to remove the Dutch from those positions they occupied during the war. Carl Joseph of Lorraine, elector of Trier after 1711, managed to reverse his territory's growing dependency on the Dutch and recover Trarbach in 1713, while Charles gave tacit approval to Joseph Clemens after the war to evict them from Bonn. Although the Republic did compel the elector to demilitarize Huy, Liège and Bonn, its influence was clearly declining in the Rhineland after 1717.[89] Charles's adoption of the *Reichsbarriere* as his own and his opposition to Dutch designs won him sympathy within the Association. Austria signed the other recesses on 8 May 1713 and 4 January 1714, keeping the Association forces in the field as valuable support at a time when he was being abandoned by his other allies.

The Association Movement had contributed positively to the development of the *Kreise* as effective institutions, and continued to do so after its renewal in 1714, but in the longer term the membership became disillusioned at its inability to provide an independent voice for their interests. After 1735 this disillusionment affected military commitment and helps explain the declining efficiency of the *Reichsarmee*, as territories felt less compulsion to send contingents to a war the outcome of which they had little say in determining. Though the collapse of Habsburg influence following Charles VI's death in 1740 permitted more autonomy, it was no longer possible to withstand the mounting Austro-Prussian rivalry.

The decline of the Association Movement was accompanied by a general lack of interest in princely leagues. The formal defence structure, supplemented by the Association, had been shown to work in 1691–1714, and few weaker territories had any desire to enter into any other arrangement obliging them to commit additional forces. Despite the fact that most now maintained *Kreistruppen* the military gap between them and heavily armed territories like Hessen-Kassel and the secular electorates had widened with the general expansion in the forces of the more powerful princes. The opportunities for independent policies were declining, and even the larger principalities now used leagues only as a bridge to foreign subsidies and sponsorship for dynastic ambitions. With the partial exception of the Frankfurt Union of 1744, it was not until the 1780s that the lesser rulers again drew together to promote common security and imperial reform, by which time the chances of success were slight.

Chapter Six

The Reich *and the European powers, 1714–40*

The emperor in imperial and European politics, 1714–33

The early part of Charles VI's reign witnessed further Habsburg conquests in the east, which, following the other recent gains, seemed to confirm Austria as a major European power. Within the *Reich* the emperor also inherited a strong position and, despite some setbacks, managed to improve on it into the 1720s. Yet by his death on 20 October 1740, the Habsburg monarchy was nearly bankrupt, its army demoralized and its standing in the *Reich* greatly tarnished. Without this transformation, Prussia's surprise attack on Silesia in December 1740 would scarcely have been possible, and the life of the traditional imperial structure probably would have been prolonged. To understand this change we need to examine Charles's position after the War of the Spanish Succession.

The Utrecht–Rastatt Settlement of 1713–14 confirmed the shift in Habsburg geopolitics under way since 1683. In place of the traditional dualism between east (Turks) and west (Germans and French), Habsburg interests now faced the four points of the compass. Defence of the eastern frontier remained important, but this no longer meant protecting the Austrian heartlands but Hungary as far as the Danube and Carpathian Mountains. Within this area, Habsburg rule had been confirmed by the defeat of the Rákóczi Rebellion in 1711, raising Hungary's place in the monarchy beyond that of a peripheral frontier region. In the west, defence of the Rhine continued to be the emperor's primary task, but failure to obtain the *Reichsbarriere* left large stretches of the river vulnerable. Here too, direct Habsburg interest had been increased by territorial gains, for acquisition of the remainder of the Burgundian *Kreis* from Spain placed the emperor among those in the front line with France.

However, these gains also directed his attention northwards where, in the Netherlands, Austria had a significant territorial presence for the first time. Habsburg activity in northern Germany had also increased, partly in response to the recent conflict but also in reaction to the rise of Prussia. Similarly, to the south, the acquisition of Milan and other land from Spain transformed Imperial Italy from an area of limited but growing interest to one of direct concern to the dynasty. Thus, while the centre of political gravity shifted firmly eastwards into Hungary, acquisition of additional areas on the *Reich*'s periphery extended Habsburg interest to the north and south as well as reinforcing traditional involvement in the west.

Defence of the emperor's position in Germany was now complicated by the need to protect the expanded core areas of Austria and Hungary by preserving buffer zones along the peripheral regions. The desire to maintain a localized balance of power in each of these would "dictate the course of Austrian foreign policy and explain the monarchy's involvement in its remaining pre-revolutionary conflicts".[1]

It was difficult to pursue such a policy after 1714 because of the uncertain international situation. The Utrecht Settlement had expressly intended to preserve peace by establishing an European balance, but the system was inherently unstable due to the decline of traditional major powers and the rise of new states. Pockets of instability appeared on all four points of the Habsburg compass as well as influencing events within the *Reich*. To the north Sweden's decline, delineated by the 1719–21 settlement, marked the expansion of Russian power. Poland's internal collapse meanwhile permitted a further extension of Russian as well as German influence, while Ottoman defeats led to a similar clash of interests in the Balkans. The long struggles against France had weakened the Dutch, who had long played a pan-European diplomatic role in addition to interfering in Westphalian and Rhenish politics.

Events on the Habsburg periphery triggered a series of conflicts after 1716 that inevitably involved the *Reich*, at least indirectly. Formal collective defence ceased to be of overriding importance since the Turks were no longer in a position to threaten the *Reich* directly, while France abstained from further belligerence until 1733, preferring instead collusion with Britain to uphold the Utrecht Settlement against Spanish revanchism.

This did not diminish the importance of Charles's imperial role to his overall strategy, as the dynasty's fate remained closely connected with its standing in the *Reich*. At first sight this does not seem so, for the emperor's overriding consideration throughout his reign remained the future of his own hereditary lands in the absence of a male heir. Habsburg inheritance law was rewritten in the Pragmatic Sanction of 1713 to permit his daughter, Maria

Theresa (born 1717), to succeed him in the core areas should he not have a son. The decision to seek German and international recognition of this document, while entirely in keeping with European custom, gravely weakened his position, committing him to the arduous task of bargaining for agreements that ultimately proved worthless. However, contrary to the prevailing view, Charles did not neglect the *Reich*, nor was he a fundamentally weak emperor for most of his reign.[2] He remained very much in the post-Westphalian mould, continuing to balance imperial and dynastic interests to maintain his prestige as emperor, which still helped to determine his international standing as much as Austrian territorial expansion. The *Reich* remained very much part of Habsburg "core" interests, even if Charles did not rule it directly like the hereditary lands.

Charles's determination to assert and enhance his authority was more than just a reaction to the rise of Prussia and the internationalization of imperial politics; it was also a continuation of the imperial recovery begun by Leopold I. Charles was the first emperor for several generations to receive the traditional homage of the Frankfurt Ghetto, and his reassertion of old rights extended to attempts to tax the Jews and imperial knights. New areas were also developed, such as efforts to standardize coinage throughout the *Reich* during 1737–8. These efforts were ably assisted by the imperial vice chancellor, Friedrich Carl von Schönborn, nephew of Lothar Franz, till his interpretation of imperial interests diverged from Charles's and led to significant disagreements by 1734.[3]

Along with the renewed religious controversy of 1719, such problems limited the extent of Charles's achievements but did not prevent him making full use of the formal and informal means developed by his predecessors to manage the *Reich*. The *Reichstag* lent legitimacy to dynastic measures, such as the endorsement of the Pragmatic Sanction on 3 February 1732, as well as general measures like the famous restriction of artisan guilds in 1731.[4] Use of the RHR was stepped up to reinforce Charles's position as supreme arbiter, while Habsburg influence penetrated the northern *Kreise* and the Association was maintained to provide a minimum level of defence. These measures were supplemented by an intensification of patronage, boosted by the Viennese court, which reached a peak of baroque magnificence under Charles. Finally, Leopold's system of bilateral treaties was developed as an unprecedented alliance network, providing additional manpower to defend the buffer zones.[5]

International pressure continually intervened to retard Charles's progress in the *Reich*.[6] A particular stumbling block was the lack of a permanent settlement with Spain, which had not made peace with Austria or the *Reich*. While some of Charles's advisers continued to harbour hopes of gaining Spain itself, the principal threat came from the other side, especially the desire of Elizabeth

Farnese, wife of Philip V, to recover Spain's Italian possessions as independent kingdoms for her sons. Sardinia was attacked in August 1717 and followed by the invasion of Sicily by 30,000 men in July 1718. Austria diverted troops from the Balkans and hired further units from the princes, but it was clear that Charles could not defeat Spain without naval assistance. Britain and France were obvious allies, particularly as Spain supported the Jacobites and even landed 300 men in Scotland in 1719. Since the 1715 rising, George I had hired soldiers from Münster, Gotha and Wolfenbüttel to cover the Barrier fortresses, while the Dutch honoured their treaty commitments and sent 6,000 men to England.[7] More substantial help was provided to Austria from 1716 in return for Charles's toleration of Hanoverian expansion at Sweden's expense. After Austria joined the Anglo-Franco-Dutch Triple Alliance of 1717 on 2 August 1718, the Royal Navy ferried 10,000 Austrians and Germans to relieve the 7,000 Savoyards holding Sicily and then defeated the Spanish fleet at Cape Passaro. After bitter fighting, the island was recaptured along with Sardinia by summer 1720. The two were exchanged with prior British agreement, with the richer Sicily going to Charles, while Victor Amadeus had to accept bandit-infested Sardinia instead.[8]

Spanish policy had largely collapsed, but Anglo-French anxiety over the European balance prevented Charles from capitalizing further on his advantage. Preliminary international agreements in 1720–1 recognized Parma and Tuscany as imperial fiefs but compelled Charles to nominate Elizabeth Farnese's eldest son Don Carlos as heir apparent in both states.[9] Charles was determined to evade this obligation, particularly as the territories were earmarked as rewards for his chief German ally, the duke of Lorraine, whose son, Francis Stephen, was Maria Theresa's intended and a potential Habsburg candidate in a future imperial election. Assisted by the imperial vice chancellor, Charles used the excuse that the two territories were part of imperial Italy to delay the paperwork for Don Carlos's investiture until January 1723, and even then still objected to Spain garrisoning them.

Understandably put out by Charles's obstinacy, Britain and France moved closer to Spain after 1721, leaving Austria diplomatically isolated. The effects were quickly felt within the *Reich*, where ambitious princes were quick to exploit the renewed international tension to enhance their own voice in affairs. However, the situation was quite different from that which prevailed before 1714. Not only were the major subsidy donors exhausted by the long conflicts since 1672, but the "Old System" of the Grand Alliance against France had collapsed with Anglo-French *rapprochement*. Even the traditional factor of Franco-Habsburg hostility could no longer be relied upon, as French collaboration with Austria in the Quadruple Alliance of 1718–20 indicated.

France had insisted on the full restoration of the outlawed Wittelsbach electors in 1714 to sustain its credibility as a protecter of princely interests, but while it continued to pay subsidies to both Cologne and Bavaria, it no longer advanced strong support for their schemes. Experience with Max Emanuel and Joseph Clemens during the war indicated neither were particularly reliable allies, and this remained the assessment of their respective successors, Carl Albrecht (1722) and Clemens August (1723). Both rulers remained weak, able to maintain only 5,000–6,000 soldiers apiece in view of their chronic financial positions following 1714. The situation was so bad in Cologne by 1719 that Joseph Clemens feared the emperor would permit his creditors to seize his personal possessions. Both attempted to raise their profile by a family compact with the Palatinate and the Wittelsbach elector of Trier, Franz Ludwig of Pfalz-Neuburg. Formed in 1724, this quickly proved unworkable as an autonomous Wittelsbach Third Party. Conscious of the futility of defying the emperor and hoping for rewards, the Wittelsbachs edged back to the Habsburg camp. Keen to find allies in the electoral college, Charles exploited their weakness to bind them to his German alliance network, assisted in Cologne by the powerful first minister, Count Ferdinand von Plettenberg, who was a loyal member of the Habsburg clientele.[10]

Charles's chief problem was his own lack of funds, especially as he was not prepared to concede the electors' wide-ranging political demands. The problems appeared to be solved by Spain's switch to an Austrian alliance in the Treaty of Vienna on 1 May 1725, supplemented by additional secret articles on 5 November. The Spanish monarchy had grown disenchanted with Anglo-French efforts to smooth the difficulties remaining since Utrecht by further congress diplomacy. Planned for 1722, the meeting finally opened in Cambrai in 1724, and it became clear that Spanish goals might be better achieved by a direct approach to Vienna. The treaty represented a formal Austro-Spanish peace, ratified by the *Reichstag* on 7 June, and included Charles's final renunciation of claims to Spain. Austria also promised aid in recovering Gibraltar and Minorca from Britain, as well as territory in the Pyrenees lost earlier to France. In return, Spain pledged support for the Habsburgs in the next imperial election and for their candidate in a future Polish royal election, plus granted concessions to the Ostende Company established in the Austrian Netherlands to promote trade. Joint plans were devised to restore the Burgundian *Kreis* to its former extent and recover Alsace, Metz, Toul and Verdun. This was to be sealed by dynastic marriages and a 3 million fl. subsidy paid in South American silver.[11]

European and imperial politics polarized as Britain and France announced their rival Alliance of Hanover 3 July 1725, recruiting Prussia, Denmark, Sweden and the Dutch Republic by 1727. Britain sought additional bilateral defence pacts to secure Hanover in case of war, while Charles tried to widen his own network. Britain beat him to Hessen-Kassel, offering not only larger subsidies but political support for Hessian acquisition of the fortress of Rheinfels, currently held by a Habsburg client.[12] Most princes, however, preferred a closer understanding with the emperor, especially as the Spanish silver guaranteed the necessary minimum subsidy to make any agreement viable. All four Wittelsbach electors, along with Mainz, Bamberg, Würzburg and Wolfenbüttel signed defence pacts with Austria in the course of 1726. A particular coup was Prussia's defection from the Anglo-French combination by the Treaty of Wusterhausen, 12 October 1726, confirmed by that of Berlin, 23 December 1728.[13]

Princes who held out for too much found themselves spurned by both sides, particularly as Austrian ministers knew they could count on the strong residual loyalty of most rulers should war actually break out. This was the case in Württemberg, where Duke Eberhard Ludwig never seriously wavered from the Habsburg camp despite periodic negotiations with France and Charles's refusal to grant an electoral title. Even Landgrave Carl considered himself a loyal vassal, although he had agreed to defend Hanover. The case of Saxony was more problematic given Augustus's dual role as elector and king, but his demands were so unrealistic they found no response from either side: he wanted Bohemia and Silesia as a land bridge between his two states and dreamed of becoming the next emperor. However, the fact that such a comparatively powerful prince as Augustus could not hope to hold a viable middle position between the rival alliances indicated how the German territories were being marginalized by great power politics.[14]

Even Austria was ill-prepared for this potentially lethal game. The nominal size of the Habsburg army was raised from 122,945 (1722) to 190,257 (1727), but it is unlikely there were more than 125,000 effectives. In comparison, the French army stood at 229,458 in 1727. Spanish subsidies proved irregular, held up by an English naval blockade, so that only 2.5 million fl. reached Austria by 1729. Subsidy arrears to the Wittelsbach electors alone stood at 4.17 million, and although these were eventually paid, all four drifted back to France by 1729, where they found a better financial deal but still no concrete political gains.[15]

Although Austria was strengthened by a treaty with Russia in 1726, it could do little to help Spain, which returned to its Anglo-French alliance at Seville on 9 November 1729. An ultimatum was issued, demanding Charles admit Spanish garrisons into Parma and Piacenza for Don Carlos by 9 May 1730. Despite the mounting tension, the real threat of war was receding due to rifts in Anglo-French relations since 1727. Colonial and commercial rivalry contributed to this as did the conflicting policy of both partners towards the *Reich*. France's success in detaching the Wittelsbachs from Austria raised fears that it was returning to its traditional policy of building up a German alliance network. The British government edged closer to Austria, restoring good relations by 1731, when Charles conceded its demands to admit Don Carlos to Parma and Piacenza and dropped his support for the Ostende Company. Though an Austro-Hanoverian alliance was struck on 16 March 1731, a full return to the "Old System" was not possible due to Dutch hesitancy and French care not to let the break with Britain go too far.[16]

Nonetheless, the improved international situation restored stability to the Habsburg's southern buffer zone and enabled Charles to resume a higher profile in imperial Italy by intervening in Corsica. A full-scale rebellion had broken out on the island in 1729 and the Corsicans' Genoese masters appealed to the emperor as overlord to assist in restoring order. Charles welcomed the chance to enhance his influence in the region, especially as it provided a pretext to increase his Italian garrisons to pre-empt possible Spanish attack. Moreover, the Genoese appeal in April 1731 coincided with extraordinarily favourable circumstances. The emperor was on good terms with Piedmont-Sardinia, a limited defence pact had just been struck with both maritime powers and good relations had been temporarily restored with Spain. Four thousand men were despatched from the Milanese garrison in July to suppress the rebellion. The Genoese, who were paying the expenses, wished to keep the expeditionary force as small as possible, but Prince Eugene urged rein-forcements to avoid a humiliating defeat. Although numbers had risen to 12,000 by 1732, the local commander saw the impossibility of winning a guerrilla war. Experience in Hungary had taught the Habsburgs the futility of undiluted repression and the necessity of negotiation. The rebels offered sovereignty of their island to the emperor, or, if he refused, Prince Eugene, but the government preferred a less ambitious solution. The Genoese were forced to accept a compromise, decided at Corte on 13 May 1732, promising an amnesty and reforms under imperial guarantee.

It seemed the ideal settlement for Charles, reaffirming his prestige as impartial arbiter, but in reality it masked acute underlying weakness. Austrian intervention had depended on circumstances beyond its control, and once these disappeared Charles was powerless to prevent the Genoese returning to their former mismanagement of the island. It was significant that when a fresh rebellion broke out in 1734, its leader, Giacinto Paoli, turned to Spain rather than Austria for help. Nonetheless, it was another German who would be king, Baron Theodor von Neuhoff, who was chosen as monarch in March 1736. His reign lasted only until October, when he left to find further assistance and promptly landed in a Dutch debtors' prison. Unable to inter-vene because of the Polish and Turkish Wars of 1733–9, Charles remained only a nominal partner in an unusual Franco-Austrian expedition to crush the rebellion in February 1738. Anxious lest the French remain in permanent occupation, Genoa pressed Charles to send his contingent, but nothing was done before the outbreak of renewed European war in 1740 compelled Louis XV to recall his troops.[17]

Diplomatic manoeuvres also made an impression in the *Reich*, where Charles intensified efforts to secure the key princes as ratification of the Pragmatic Sanction passed through the *Reichstag* in 1731–2. The collapse of the Anglo-French alliance and the concomitant Anglo-Austrian *rapprochement* weakened France, whose German allies defected to the emperor after 1730. The earlier alliances of 1726–8 with Würzburg and Wolfenbüttel were renewed and supplemented by additional military conventions, while similar agreements were negotiated with the Ernestine dukes after 1732. Crucially, Clemens August abandoned France after lacklustre support over his candidacy in Liège and the Hildesheim issue, signing a treaty with Charles on 29 August 1731. Plettenburg had him sign the credentials for a positive vote in the *Reichstag* before the elector could change his mind, so the support of his five bishoprics went to Austria, isolating Bavaria, Saxony and the Palatinate as the only opponents.[18]

The apparently mercenary nature of these alliances seems to reinforce the standard interpretation that imperial prestige had sunk to such a point that Charles could only appeal to the princes "in cash terms".[19] Subsidies were important if the princes were to sustain their armed status without provoking domestic discontent, but attachment to the emperor remained strong, reinforced by customary loyalty, personal and dynastic ties and Charles's position as the source of all honours and political advancement. Though the scope of his alliance network exceeded that of his predecessors, it remained essentially the same policy of trading limited cash and concessions for political and military support. Moreover, despite the genuine weakness of the Pragmatic Sanction, Charles secured his objectives without recourse to such dangerous expedients as the granting of the new electoral titles demanded by Württemberg and Hessen-Kassel. For example, Wolfenbüttel's support was retained by assurances that Charles might grant a *Reichstag* vote for the cadet appendage of Blankenburg and guaranteed succession to Hanover should the current Guelph line there die out. Clemens August received a more concrete, but still traditional, reward in the form of Austrian assistance in his election as Teutonic Grand Master on 17 July 1732.

However, there were limits to this policy because of the conflicting ambitions of many princes. The classic case concerns Jülich-Berg, guaranteed by Charles as a Palatine possession in 1725 but promised to Prussia in the Treaty of Berlin 1728. Similarly, Charles supported Clemens August's attempt to end the Hanoverian occupation of Hildesheim, but could not push this too far without endangering his *rapprochement* with Britain. Aware of such difficulties, princes saw alliances with foreign powers as a means of putting additional pressure on the emperor to prefer their claims to those of their rivals. The failure of the Wittelsbach family compact of 1724 and Augustus's posturing two years later indicated there was little chance of a genuinely independent middle course. A Bavarian revival of the Wittelsbach compact in 1728 was foiled by an inability to harmonize the electors' disparate ambitions and by their chronic shortage of funds, which prevented the development of a credible military presence. Carl Albrecht's weakness was exposed in 1732 by his isolation in the *Reichstag*, forcing him to step up defensive preparations. Since these depended on additional funding, he was open to French manipulation, particularly as France offered diplomatic support for his political ambitions. Only Prussia and Hessen-Kassel were capable of holding out for comparatively better terms, but even they found their political demands ignored once the treaties had been signed.

In the face of these disappointments, it is obvious that the medium and lesser princes now stood little chance of turning international tension to real advantage. Wolfenbüttel revived the League of Corresponding Princes in 1727 in an attempt to establish a new third force between Austria and the foreign powers. Though joined by Württemberg, Gotha, Hessen-Kassel, Sweden and Denmark, the League was soon subverted by George II as a vehicle for Anglo-Hanoverian policy.[20]

German alliance policies strengthened the links between imperial and international relations, contributing to the general instability of the post-Utrecht states system. Paradoxically this furthered the interests of peace by preventing permanent polarization into stable opposing blocs. Allied to both sides, the German princes had no desire to fight each other let alone defy the emperor and their defection from one party to another usually derived from local interests little in common with wider European issues. Yet their fickle nature fuelled the prevailing uncertainty, making the threat of war seem ever present during 1725–33 and pushing forward militarization and the drive to more absolute rule in many territories.

The defence of the Rhine after 1714

The prolonged warfare of 1672–1714 made defence of the Rhine a clear priority for any emperor, yet Charles's other commitments compelled him to rely on the imperfect system developed since the Dutch War to protect the region. Failure to obtain the *Reichsbarriere* left frontline defence resting on a series of fortified points backed by local militias and mobile regular forces provided through *Kreis* mobilization and bilateral arrangements with territorial rulers.

Two of the fortresses enjoyed the dubious distinction as imperial installations (*Reichsfeste*), having been taken over as part of collective defence responsibilities in 1698. Philippsburg began its existence in 1615 as a territorial strongpoint of the bishop of Speyer, but French occupations in 1644–76 and 1688–97 emphasized the importance of securing this strategic site. The other position at Kehl had been constructed by the French in 1683 to protect the German end of the Strasbourg Rhine bridge, but was surrendered at Rijswijk and given to Turkish Louis as a reward. The *Reichstag* decision of 17 March 1698 entrusted defence of both points to the emperor, Swabia, Franconia and the Upper Rhine, pending a final resolution on the matter.[21]

This proved extremely unsatisfactory. Territorial sovereignty continued to rest with Speyer and Baden-Baden, which resented the presence of imperial garrisons as an infringement of their autonomy. Further lack of clarity was introduced by the decision to let the emperor name the commandants while the *Kreise* provided the troops. Problems began almost immediately, as the other *Kreise* refused to contribute towards the upkeep of the garrisons and repair of the fortifications. In the case of Kehl this proved catastrophic. Intended to prevent a German crossing of the Rhine, all the works faced east with little to prevent a French attack from the west. The flood waters did constant damage to the point that by 1732 the commandant feared the entire fort would be washed away.

Other stretches of the river were protected by imperial cities and territorial fortifications. Of these only Freiburg and Breisach in the Austrian Breisgau, Mainz, Ehrenbreitstein and the city of Cologne were really important, for, despite the political importance attached to Rheinfels, its strategic value was overrated, while most of the other positions were small or antiquated. The Ehrenbreitstein above Koblenz, along with Trarbach on the Moselle, were maintained by Trier, which generally needed foreign subsidies to sustain them. The great fortifications at Mainz had already become financially untenable by 1675, when the garrison mutinied through lack of pay. The elector was reluctant to admit an Austrian garrison for fear of losing politial autonomy, but the temporary loss of the city to France in 1688–9 alerted imperial generals to its strategic importance in the middle Rhine and an Austrian regiment was stationed there after its recapture.[22] The Lower Rhine was covered by the imperial city of Cologne, which was under constant threat from the local elector. Hire of a Dutch regiment in 1671–2 appeared to provide the elector with a chance to intervene and prompted the search for a less politically sensitive solution to the city's security problems. A Westphalian

Kreis garrison arrived in 1673, returning in all future crises (1684, 1686–97, 1710–13, 1734–5). Further east, defence of key cities like Frankfurt, Nuremberg, Augsburg, Ulm and Heilbronn was secured by permitting them to retain their *Kreis* contingents during emergencies.[23]

These arrangements only worked when there were sufficient field forces to parry French thrusts across the intervening open ground. Peace in 1714 removed these troops precisely when Austrian acquisition of the Netherlands heightened the Rhine's strategic importance as a line of communication with the Habsburg heartlands. Charles VI plugged the gaps by subordinating the *Kreis* Association to his security policy, using it to provide a minimum level of military preparedness, enabling him to redeploy Austria's limited forces elsewhere. The Association was renewed by congress recesses on 20 June and 19 December 1714, obliging its members to maintain their forces permanently in peacetime at the reduced strength of one and a half times their basic quota. These arrangements sustained the 1681–2 mobilization structure that Austria could activate whenever external attack threatened the *Reich*. As tension mounted in 1727, Charles persuaded the other members, including Lother Franz, to renew the Association and double their forces on 31 May – a decision made irrelevant that day by an armistice in the Mediterranean. Nonetheless, the members responded to a later imperial request by again voting a triple quota on 17 August 1730, which also only remained on paper as tension eased.[24]

Meanwhile, the December 1714 recess obliged Franconia to place 700 men in Philippsburg, while Swabia put 1,600 in Kehl and the Upper and Electoral Rhenish *Kreise* collaborated over Mainz. The arrangement broke down because Charles claimed his negotiators had exceeded their instructions by promising 2,300 men each for the two *Reichsfeste*. Meanwhile, the Associated *Kreise* grew increasingly disgruntled at the *Reichstag*'s failure to find a permanent and more equitable distribution of the burden. Despite derisory financial assistance from the other territories, they continued to maintain their garrisons as a matter of prestige and a symbol of collective armed status, with the Upper Rhinelanders even contributing to Kehl and Philippsburg in 1698–1714, although they were not obliged to. In addition, there was the fear that, if they pulled out altogether, their expenses would never be refunded, and their claims were considerable, Swabia spending 2 million fl. on Kehl alone by 1728. Therefore, Swabia, Franconia and the Upper Rhine each sent about 500 men to Kehl, Philippsburg and Mainz respectively, with detachments serving on rotation to spread the burden among the member territories.[25] In addition, Charles skilfully manipulated the ambitions of key princes within each *Kreis* to rally the others behind his policies. For example, Austrian support for the Württemberg inheritance in Mömpelgard was traded for

Eberhard Ludwig's assistance in persuading the Swabians to contribute money towards the upkeep of Breisach in 1721–2 and 1727–9 as well as Kehl. Similar assistance came from the Upper Rhine, where Charles cultivated Ernst Ludwig of Hessen-Darmstadt.[26]

Finally, the long conflicts with France had forged the *Kreise* as effective institutions capable of sustaining collective action even in adverse conditions. Significantly, the military structures survived in the Associated *Kreise* despite the penny-pinching economies of the long years of peace of 1714–33. Franconia, for instance, suffered the common problems of the larger territories wishing to separate their contingents from the integrated forces of the other members. Dissatisfied with Bamberg's directorial ambitions, Würzburg periodically detached its soldiers from the other Franconian regiments (1727–31, 1752–7), while the two Hohenzollern margraviates of Ansbach and Bayreuth regrouped their soldiers into a common regiment in 1742.[27] Both the Franconians and Swabians gradually reduced their official strength in a series of economy measures, with the former cutting their nominal triple quota from 9,200 (1714) to 7,220 (1757), while that of the latter fell from 11,704 to 7,944.[28] Only half these figures were maintained in peacetime, and even then actual strengths were often considerably below this: the Swabians were obliged by the December 1714 recess to maintain 5,900 but unilaterally cut this by 520 and in practice had only 4,400 under arms in the 1720s. The Württemberg dukes Eberhard Ludwig and Carl Alexander continually pressed for higher figures, but although the latter persuaded the others to agree in 1736, they ignored the decision after his death the next year. Eberhard Ludwig was unable to prevent the sale of the cavalry horses in 1717 to save money, and although periodic efforts were made to improve matters, including an exercise camp at Esslingen in 1729, numerous faults soon emerged in peacetime.[29] The reports of War Commissar Roth on the Swabian musters in 1737 and 1738 note typical problems in the lack of uniformity in drill and training, and the disregard for common regulations, particularly among the contingents of the smaller territories, who allowed too many of their soldiers to marry and discharged men without permission of the officers.[30]

Similar problems emerged on the Upper Rhine, which reorganized its forces to total 2,855 men after 1722. Hessen-Kassel predictably failed to co-operate, paving the way for Landgrave Ernst Ludwig of Hessen-Darmstadt, who was elected *Kreisoberst* and assumed responsibility for the provision of the contingents from Zweibrücken and the cities of Speyer and Worms. However, like the Württemberg dukes and the bishops of Bamberg, Ernst Ludwig saw the efficient management of the *Kreistruppen* as a way of earning imperial favour. This injected the energy necessary to sustain the organization throughout the years of peace and ensured that the sort of problems described above did not prevent the type of limited defensive mobilization the Association was designed to deliver. The Upper Rhenish Assembly remained in permanent session during 1730–7, while Ernst Ludwig sustained cross-regional co-operation by collaborating with Lothar Franz and his successors on the maintenance of the Mainz fortifications. Hessen-Kassel was obliged to rejoin the military structure in 1733, and although it left again in 1741, Habsburg influence was enhanced through Austrian membership through the acquisition of the Upper Rhenish county of Falkenstein from Lorraine in 1738.[31]

Outside the Association the *Kreis* structure suffered, with Upper and Lower Saxony remaining dominated by Hanover, Prussia and Saxony, while Burgundy and Austria had no existence outside Habsburg institutions. Bavaria showed some signs of activity, helped by the need of the local elector to revive good relations with the emperor. However, the Assembly meeting in 1727 only acknowledged a military obligation amounting to 3,473 infantry in the event of war and continued to use its relatively small size as an excuse to dodge all other burdens thereafter.[32]

Three years of victory, 1716–18

Charles's success in persuading the south Germans to garrison the Rhine enabled him to turn to a war of conquest against the Turks. The sultan had exploited the distraction of the wars in western and northern Europe to attack the Venetian Republic early in 1715, quickly recapturing the Morea and besieging Corfu. Few in Vienna were initially inclined to answer the beleaguered Republic's calls for help, regarding it as an unwelcome stumbling block to their own Mediterranean commercial ventures. The sultan had gone out of his way to preserve the peace with the emperor, and, given Habsburg concerns elsewhere, his continued goodwill was invaluable. Moreover, the military administration estimated the cost of only one new Balkan campaign at 16.45 million fl. or 3.5 million fl. more than the entire annual revenue.

Nonetheless, opinions were beginning to change by the end of 1715. Despite the Turkish victories of that year, and in 1711 against Russia, Austrian experts considered the Ottomans a soft target. The death of Louis XIV on 1 September 1715 finally banished the spectre of renewed war in the west, especially as the new regent, the duke of Orleans, promised not to intervene in any future war with the sultan. The "feel good factor" was reinforced by the final conclusion of the Barrier Treaty on 15 November 1715, resulting in the Anglo-Dutch transfer of the Netherlands to Austrian control, while the alliance with Britain on 25 May 1716 not only secured the Mediterranean but raised hopes of naval support against the Turks. Prince Eugene, elevated by his battlefield victories to a position of considerable political influence, also now wanted war for a variety of personal and political reasons, but chiefly to exploit what he regarded as an excellent opportunity to enhance Austrian security by destroying the Turkish threat.

The alliance with Venice was renewed on 13 April 1716 on similar terms as that of 1684, except that the Republic now guaranteed Charles's new Italian possessions. Poland was invited to join, but an extension to Russia was rejected by Vienna to deny the tsar a chance to increase his influence in the Balkans. Given that Venice was struggling even to hold the defensive, Austria was again left to fight alone. This time the emperor was not unprepared. Troops had been transferred to Hungary from garrisons in the west since September 1715, and Charles had already begun financial reforms, establishing the *Bancalität* and floating a 2 million fl. loan in the Dutch Republic. A supply and artillery train was collected and work started on additional galleys for the Danube Flotilla at a new yard in Vienna. At a formal establishment of 157,000, the army was larger than it had ever been. Two years later it had risen to no less than 162,727, a formidable total even allowing for the inevitable gap between official and actual strength. The field force stood at 80,000–90,000 with a further 40,000 covering Transylvania and the Slovenian frontier. Additional protection was provided by the new fortress of Karlsburg, begun in 1714 and already defensible by 1716, along with a new citadel at Klausenburg (Cluj), built 1715–23, both of which covered Transylvania. Despite his still shaky financial position, the emperor had never been in such a good position at the start of a Turkish war.[33]

This helps account for the novelty of the coming conflict. For the first time the emperor was about to embark on an offensive war against the Turks with high expectations that the infidel would be driven from Europe entirely. The pope also sent money, though significantly less than in the past, sustaining the atmosphere of a crusade. Nonetheless, this time the war was a more singularly Habsburg concern. The *Reichstag* was duly summoned for assistance and voted a considerable sum of money, but unlike previous wars, no official *Kreis* contingents were sent, and although not "token",[34] the contributions of the princes was below that in the past. From over half in 1664 to between 10 and 33 per cent in 1683–99, German troops formed only 18 per cent of the total army gathering in Hungary (Tables 2.1 , 3.1, 6.1).

As before, however, the contingents were sent to win imperial favour. Bavaria in particular was keen to improve relations after recent hostility, especially as Charles was refusing to complete Max Emanuel's reinvestiture on account of the renewal of the Franco-Bavarian alliance in 1714. The elector

Table 6.1 German auxiliaries in imperial service, 1716–18

Territory	Start date	Contingent	End date
Trier[1]	17 Aug 1715	4,600	1726
Baden-Durlach[2]	15 Oct 1715	2,300	1734
Württemberg[3]	24 Dec 1715	2,300	1720
Ansbach[4]	17 Mar 1717	2,300	1727
Ansbach[5]	28 Jan 1718	800	1726
Hessen-Kassel[6]	17 Apr 1717	2,300	1720
Bavaria[7]	7 June 1717	5,000	1718
Saxony[8]	18 Apr 1718	5,900	1719
Total		25,500	

Sources: As note 35.

Notes:

[1] Carl Joseph, also duke of Lorraine and bishop of Osnabrück. The 2 rgts were actually Lorrainers. They passed fully into Austrian service at the end of the contract.

[2] 3 btns permanently taken over in 1724.

[3] 1 infantry rgt. Returned home in December 1720 having served on Sicily in 1718–20.

[4] 2 infantry rgts. combined as one. Permanently taken over in 1727.

[5] 1 dragoon rgt hired for 6 years, then taken over.

[6] Actually provided 2,488 infantry. Returned to Hessen-Kassel in 1720.

[7] 3 infantry rgts, 1 dragoon rgt, 1 sqn horse grenadiers. The dragoons transferred permanently while the others returned in 1718.

[8] 6 rgts combined as 3. Returned home May 1719.

also hoped to renew his political ambitions by seeking a Habsburg bride for his eldest son, Carl Albrecht. Within a month of his formal reinvestiture on 19 May 1717, five-sevenths of the Bavarian army was pledged to support the war in Hungary. Carl Albrecht and his younger brother, Ferdinand Maria, personally accompanied the corps, stopping off in Vienna to reaffirm their new loyalty. Having been present at the Battle of Belgrade, the princes returned next year to strengthen their contacts with the imperial court. Augustus the Strong also supplied a third of his much-reduced army to secure Austrian goodwill for his position in Poland, and others sent individual regiments in return for minor favours or simply to prevent them being disbanded for want of money.[35]

Despite the usual failure of the Balkan Christians to rise, imperial operations proved outstandingly successful. Belgrade, the intended target, proved an overambitious goal in 1716, especially as drought followed by floods delayed Prince Eugene's advance. By the time he reached Peterwardein, the

Turkish main army of 120,000 was already crossing the Danube by Belgrade. When they appeared at his entrenched camp, Eugene took the unconventional approach of attacking them directly on 5 August. It nearly proved fatal, as the imperial infantry began to give way, before a flank attack by the cavalry transformed possible defeat into a resounding victory. Ottoman losses possibly reached 30,000, including those massacred in the closing stages of the engagement. As their main army retreated south, their other force abandoned the siege of Corfu, releasing pressure on the Venetians. Realizing it was now too late to attack Belgrade, Eugene turned northeast to besiege Timisoara, capital of the Banat and last Turkish enclave north of the Danube. Though an attempt to storm the place on Charles's birthday (1 October) failed, the garrison surrendered two weeks later after a relief force disintegrated en route through desertion. By the end of the year, the imperialists had overrun most of Wallachia west of the river Olt (Aluta) – the so-called Olteria or Little Wallachia.[36]

Though a successful campaign, it was now obvious that the Austrians had seriously underestimated Ottoman strength, but it was decided to continue the war the following year to consolidate the gains. The arrival of Bavarian and other reinforcements brought Eugene's army up to 100,000, strong enough to attempt the siege of Belgrade, and, assisted by the Danube Flotilla, the city was completely cut off and subjected to a regular siege. However, Eugene was running out of supplies as an Ottoman relief force approached in August. A lucky shot detonated the city's largest magazine on the 14th, killing 3,000 of the defenders. Realizing that a sortie was now unlikely, Eugene sallied forth from his trenches with 60,000 men to surprise the Turks in the early morning mist. Fortified by drink and keeping close together, the imperialists poured devastating musketry into the disordered Turkish ranks, routing them and sealing the garrison's fate. With the fall of Belgrade on 18 August, the Turkish position in Northern Serbia collapsed and the Habsburg frontier advanced south of the Danube to reach the fullest extent achieved during the Great Turkish War.

Charles had no intention of going any further. The Austrians were already beginning to doubt the wisdom of pushing deeper into the Balkan wastelands, and it was clear the Turks desired peace. This was very welcome given that Rákóczi had just arrived in Edirne, raising the spectre of renewed trouble in Hungary. Meanwhile the Turks were suspected of trying to reach a *rapprochement* with the tsar, and Spain had launched its attempt to recover its lost Italian possessions. Following long negotiations with Anglo-Dutch mediation, peace was concluded at Passarowitz (Pozarevac) on 27 July, confirming Austria's recent gains. It was not a moment too soon. Austrian units were already departing for Italy, while five days later, the emperor concluded the

Quadruple Alliance with France, Britain and the Dutch, thus committing himself to the war with Spain.[37]

The short successful war considerably extended Habsburg territory, indicating that Austria was now a major European power and raising the emperor's prestige in the *Reich*. Prince Eugene was a genuine folk hero, and even other generals became household names. Despite being a Catholic and absent as governor of Serbia, Prince Carl Alexander was feted as a hero of the siege of Belgrade when he returned to assume power in his native Württemberg in 1733. Habsburg rule was not so popular in the newly-conquered areas, and the new regional government based in Belgrade was resented by the northern Serbs, who disliked Habsburg centralism. The Wallachians of the Oltenia also objected to the loss of their autonomy by 1726 and the use of their land to supply the local garrisons.[38] Their mounting resentment weakened the emperor's ability to hold the area in a future conflict, while developments in northern Europe began to threaten his authority elsewhere.

The emperor in northern politics after 1715

The Habsburg's position in northern Germany had grown more complicated by 1715. Both Hanover and Saxony were tied to foreign crowns, enhancing their autonomy and making them more difficult to manage. Though Prussia had failed to emerge from the Great Northern War with significant territorial gains, Frederick William I had intensified his father's militarization, raising the army to 66,861 effectives by June 1729, equivalent to half the Austrian army.[39] Moreover, he showed no sign of abandoning attempts to increase Prussian influence in Franconia as well as Westphalia and Mecklenburg. The domestic dispute in Mecklenburg awaited a final resolution, while a new one was developing in East Frisia and Russian, Dutch, Danish and Swedish influence continued to penetrate the *Reich*. Charles's relative success in coping with these problems is a measure of the imperial recovery in his reign, but, like his experience in Imperial Italy, his position was partly dependent on events beyond his control.

Though often dismissed as a liability, acquisition of the Spanish Netherlands enhanced the emperor's position in the north of the *Reich*. Habsburg interest in the region was split, with Brabant, Flanders and the other western areas belonging to the geopolitical periphery while Luxembourg constituted part of the core. Austrian control of the peripheral areas was limited by Anglo-Dutch interference, which kept the Scheldt closed to commercial traffic and eventually forced the shut-down of the Ostende Company. The Barrier

Treaty of 1715 compelled the emperor to pay the Dutch to garrison key towns in addition to keeping 16,000 of his own troops there. No help was forthcoming from the *Reich*, where the princes continued to dispute whether the exposed provinces really belonged to the Burgundian *Kreis*. In contrast, Luxembourg was incontrovertibly part of the *Reich* as well as being protected by the broken country of the Ardennes. Foreign influence was excluded, as the area was not subject to the Barrier Treaty and Austrian rule was relatively popular. The area remained quiet during Belgian unrest in 1718 directed at reasserting medieval municipal autonomy and rejecting Habsburg fiscal–military demands. Order was only restored after peace with the Turks permitted the redeployment of 10,000 troops, who occupied Brussels and executed the ringleaders. Not surprisingly, Belgium featured prominently in exchange plans designed to redistribute German territory to the Habsburgs' advantage, while Luxembourg remained non-negotiable.[40]

Austrian control of the Burgundian *Kreis* and the garrison in Luxembourg raised the emperor's presence in the northern imperial institutions. Charles appreciated the value of the *Kreise* in constraining the larger territories and enforcing verdicts of the imperial courts. The revival of the Westphalian and, to a lesser extent, Lower Saxon *Kreise*, under way since the heyday of the Association Movement, reinforced the imperial recovery in the north. Increasingly, the lesser north Germans found in Charles the protection they had sought in vain from Leopold, particularly as Austria asserted control over the Association after 1714.

Westphalia is usually portrayed in a state of chronic decline, failing to hold a currency regulation meeting after 1706 or keep proper accounts from 1738, while no Assembly met between then and 1757. However, its continued membership of the Association strengthened the position of the smaller territories, who forced through an order at the Assembly on 23 May 1715, authorizing the retention of 5,000 infantry as a peacetime cadre and confirming the universal right to provide troops rather than cash. Not only were those who had armed during the war protected, but others now escaped Prussian domination: citing the recent decision, the abbess of Essen refused to renew her arrangements with Prussia and established her own force of 44 infantrymen, sustaining her autonomy until the final break up of the *Kreis* after 1795. Moreover, the bishopric of Liège, which had sought to dodge its responsibilities by leaving the *Kreis* in 1713, was compelled by the emperor to rejoin in December 1715.[41]

Austrian influence grew, as many of the smaller Westphalian counties were inherited by families closely tied to Habsburg clientele (Salm, Kaunitz, de Ligne, Arenberg, Löwenstein), while others invited imperial intervention to resolve internal disputes, permitting Charles to reinforce his position as supreme arbiter. For instance, RKG intervention in Lippe in 1734–46 ended in a successful compromise, confirming the estates' political position in return for their consent to military funding.[42] By 1734 Austria was displacing Prussia as Charles exploited Frederick William's hopes of obtaining Jülich-Berg. The king temporarily abandoned his protectorates over the lesser Westphalians in a misjudged attempt to win imperial favour, watching helplessly as Austria replaced him as the substitute for their contingents in the War of the Polish Succession. By 1735 Prussian influence was restricted to East Frisia, where the estates still relied on its support against their prince.[43]

Charles also enjoyed limited success in displacing Prussia in Lower Saxony, especially as he could rely on Hanoverian support. The latter was problematic since the Guelphs clearly regarded the *Kreis* as their own preserve and co-operated only as long as it did not infringe their vital interests. In the case of Nordhausen, collaboration proved mutually beneficial, since the town lay in Hanover's sphere of influence and they were keen to remove the Prussian garrison that had been there since 1703. Faced by combined Austro-Hanoverian pressure, Frederick William sold his protectorate rights back to the town on 22 May 1715, confirming its status as an imperial city and withdrawing his troops. Thereafter, Nordhausen collaborated with Goslar and Mühlhausen to preserve their autonomy by sending joint deputations to the *Kreis* Assemblies and fielding a combined contingent in 1735 and 1795. Mühlhausen's status survived despite a combined Prusso-Wolfenbüttel occupation in 1733–5 to enforce an imperial mandate restoring order after rioting. Intervention in Hamburg in 1705–12 also ended successfully with Charles asserting his position as overlord by brokering a workable compromise between the patricians and citizens that lasted till the end of the *Reich*.[44]

Otherwise the imperial recovery foundered where it encountered Hanoverian resistance, as illustrated by the example of Hildesheim. Exploiting the ambiguities surrounding the state of the Wittelsbach territories, which had sided with France, and using an excuse of recent rioting, Celle had occupied Hildesheim itself in January 1703 to pre-empt possible Prussian intervention and consolidate a long-standing protectorate over the Protestant inhabitants. The Catholic canons had sided with Leopold, providing a regiment to defend the Rhine in return for diplomatic pressure to evict the Celle troops in July. However, Charles was unable to remove the Hanoverians, who returned in February 1711 to enforce the old Celle protectorate, establishing a military presence that lasted with few brief interruptions until 1802.[45]

Charles was unable to do more because of his reliance on Hanover, which grew as official efforts to neutralize the north faltered after 1711. He had to tolerate Hanoverian expansion as the price of an otherwise reliable agent for imperial policy, since neither Saxony nor Prussia were suitable partners.

Hanoverian influence was moderated somewhat by Charles's cultivation of the other Guelph branch in Wolfenbüttel, beginning with his marriage to Elizabeth Christine in 1708. On 16 January 1713 he entrusted the tricky task of protecting the Mecklenburg nobles to Duke Anton Ulrich, his wife's grandfather and, as the then senior Guelph, Lower Saxon executive prince. Hanover was included in this arrangement as the Mecklenburg dispute escalated, leading to the joint Hanoverian–Wolfenbüttel military intervention in 1719.

Charles tried to retain control over Hanover by delaying the formal investiture of territory acquired since 1692, bargaining confirmation for Lauenburg (1716), Hadeln (1731) and Bremen and Verden (1733) in return for concessions, such as Hanoverian recognition of the Pragmatic Sanction. His hold over the elector was weak, as George I already realized by 1722, remarking that he would retain possession of his recent gains "whether the emperor grants the investiture or not".[46] However, as George became more English than Hanoverian, the electorate itself became a more reliable partner, especially as its territorial ambitions had largely been satisfied by 1719. True, the elector continued to occupy Hildesheim, encroach on Mecklenburg and harbour plans to secularize Osnabrück, but he was far too preoccupied with British domestic politics to do much about this. Hanoverian policy was left largely to the local privy council, composed of men firmly rooted in the *Reich* traditions. They took a legalistic view of imperial politics, regarding a functioning *Reich* as the best guarantee of the electorate's continued existence. Not surprisingly, Göttingen University soon became a bastion of pro-imperial sentiment after its foundation in 1735.[47]

Additional, although limited, assistance came from Augustus, who remained weak and in need of allies after the Polish civil war in 1717. Crown Prince Friedrich August married Charles's niece Maria Josepha in February 1718, cementing a dynastic alliance calculated to balance Habsburg ties to the Wittelsbachs. Though Saxony did not recognize the Pragmatic Sanction until 1733, it provided strong support in Charles's Turkish Wars as well as on the Rhine in 1735.

The test of the imperial recovery would be how well Charles countered Russian influence and coped with the East Frisian and Mecklenburg disputes. The latter illustrates just how far imperial justice depended on the emperor's relations with the princes. It proved extraordinarily difficult to persuade Hanover and Wolfenbüttel to leave Mecklenburg once they had enforced the original mandate protecting the nobles. Though they did comply with an RHR order in May 1719 to reduce the peacekeeping force to 1,200 men, they refused to withdraw these until their alleged expenses had been paid. The nobles were keen to retain the Guelph troops, as their presence provided an excuse to divert ducal revenue towards paying their own 5.4 million tlr demand for compensation. Matters were not helped by Carl Leopold's surreptitious return to Dömitz, from where he encouraged popular resistance to the commissioners' interim government. The practice of imperial justice thus encouraged precisely the situation it was supposed to resolve, as order broke down, peasants disobeyed their landlords, robber bands roamed the countryside and mysterious arson attacks destroyed valuable property.[48]

Both Charles and the RHR were eager to be rid of the whole business and sought a way to do so without losing face. The key obstacle was Carl Leopold, who blew his chance by insisting on nothing less than full restoration. Increasingly paranoid, the duke devised ever more fanciful plans to remove the commissioners and return to glory. Charles was reluctant to authorize his arrest, or even sanction action to prevent his levying taxes in areas under his control, for fear it would only entrench the Guelphs more firmly in the duchy. The stalemate lasted until the death of George I on 22 July 1727 extinguished the Hanoverian Commission and permitted Charles to rearrange matters, formally deposing Carl Leopold and entrusting interim government to his brother, Christian Louis, on 11 May 1728. The *Conservatorium*, or mandate to protect the nobility, was renewed but extended to include Prussia to balance the Guelphs and encourage Frederick William to adhere to his Habsburg alliance.

The change proved equally unsatisfactory, as Hanover and Wolfenbüttel refused to withdraw their troops, now demanding costs of over 1 million tlr. Christian Louis had no forces or revenues of his own and so could not establish a government to replace the defunct commission. Realizing this, Charles stepped up his support, backing Christian Louis's attempts to borrow money and hire Württemberg and Schwarzburg auxiliaries. Before this could take effect, Carl Leopold put one of his harebrained schemes into action, hoping to mediate a Franco-Russian settlement over the Polish Succession that would bring him Russian troops at French expense. Raising his standard on 13 September 1733, 6,000 peasants rallied to his cause, but the plan was suicidally unrealistic, particularly for his unfortunate supporters, whom he insisted on arming with pikes in imitation of Russian infantry he had seen 15 years before. Hanover and Wolfenbüttel rushed in reinforcements, while Prussia used its new powers to deploy 1,500 men in the south of the duchy. Resistance collapsed by 1 October, but although Hanoverian troops behaved badly, most of the captured peasants were soon released.

Nonetheless, the rising alarmed the Guelphs, who suspected Prussia of instigating it as an excuse to invade. Wolfenbüttel sold its share of the expense claim to Hanover, which in turn loaned 50,000 tlr to Christian Louis in return for control of eight districts that were not redeemed until 1768. In retaliation,

Prussia retained control of four more districts until 1787, ostensibly to collect its 230,000 tlr "expenses". At least Christian Louis now had money, with which he hired 1,800 men from Holstein, Schwarzburg-Rudolstadt and Bamberg. These bombarded and seized Schwerin castle in February 1735, reducing his brother's domain to Dömitz alone. Though reinforced by the 87 survivors of his original army who returned from Ukrainian exile in 1744, the former duke was unable to implement any of his plans before his death three years later. By then matters were clearly beyond imperial control, and the emperor was unable to prevent Christian Louis beginning his own absolutist programme after 1747. Eventually, it was Frederick the Great who intervened in 1755 to impose a settlement essentially restoring domestic arrangements to those devised by imperial lawyers in 1701. Favouring the nobility, this reactionary constitution remained in force until the socialist revolution of November 1918.

Imperial intervention in East Frisia proved no more successful.[49] The weak Cirksena dynasty had been engaged in a long-running dispute with their estates, dominated by propertied peasants and civic magistrates since the late sixteenth century. The inability of imperial institutions to find a lasting solution opened the door to foreign manipulation of East Frisian affairs, beginning with the Dutch, who guaranteed the estates' privileges and the autonomy of the town of Emden in 1611 in return for the right to garrison it and Leerort at their own expense. Military as well as fiscal affairs passed from princely control as the estates exploited the chaos of the Dutch War to consolidate their position, playing Münster against Celle. Brandenburg landed 400 marines in a surprise bloodless attack on Emden in 1682, driving out the last Celle troops and assuming a place as the estates' protectors in return for use of the town as a base for the Brandenburg navy and African company. In agreement with the estates, it took over provision of the East Frisian *Kreis* contingent in 1702–14 and was paid a retainer thereafter. Münster intervened periodically (1662, 1676–8, 1722–4), while a detachment of 200 Austrians arrived in a vain effort to keep the peace after 1678.

However, it took a natural disaster to prompt the open breach between ruler and estates. The unfortunate East Frisians were ravaged by storms and plagues of mice and locusts after 1715, culminating on Christmas Eve 1717, when the dykes broke and the North Sea flooded much of their land. The estates' mismanagement was exposed when they failed to rebuild their section of the dykes in contrast to the prompt action of their Prince Georg Albert (1708–34). Chancellor Enno Rudolph von Brenneysen went over to the attack after 1721, petitioning the RHR with the claim that the foreign garrisons had cost 5 million fl. since 1682, while the estates' debts stood at over 700,000 fl. and the country was now bankrupt. Indeed, the estates' inability to meet the foreign soldiers' current expenses of 24,000 fl. a year meant they lost control over them. The Dutch reinforced their detachment to 369 men while Prussia raised its to 550. Though Münster pulled out entirely in 1724, the others acted increasingly high-handedly. The prince won considerable popular sympathy when the sudden appearance of a Prussian detachment outside Aurich palace caused his wife to die of a heart attack.

Both sides armed as matters slipped out of control. Prussia backed the estates because they recognized its claims to succeed the Cirksena. The Emden Civic Guard was reinforced to 260 men by recruiting unemployed sailors with free beer. Despite their social origins and decision to name themselves the United Estates after the fashion of the Dutch, the democratic republican element of the so-called Emden Party was severely compromised by their use of conscription and intimidation to extend the military effort against the prince.

The imperial peacekeepers, reduced to only 40 men by lack of funds, were powerless to influence events and even found themselves disarmed by estates' troops. When Brenneysen tried to arrest Baron von Appelle, leader of the Emden Party, the situation escalated into open conflict. Violence remained restricted, however, by the limited forces available and the desire of both sides to retain a sense of legitimacy. Neither Prussia nor the Dutch felt it was worth going to war with Austria over the issue and ordered their troops to avoid confrontation with Georg Albert's forces. The prince termed his opponents rebels in order to justify force against them, and his decision was endorsed by Charles and the RHR in June 1726 as the only way to gain a hold over events. At his request, Charles also sanctioned the intervention of three Danish companies from Oldenburg, which arrived in May 1727 just in time to mop up the remaining resistance and assist the confiscation of rebel property to pay their expenses. Georg Albert's victory spared Charles, who would otherwise have had to call in Prussia to restore order.

Although the situation had stabilized, it was far from resolved. An imperial commission operated only intermittently and failed to reach a final verdict, largely through fear of antagonizing the Dutch. Georg Albert, backed by the Danish troops, remained in possession of the now much impoverished country, while the rebels retained *de facto* control of the area around Emden. Behind the scenes, Prussia negotiated with the estates through Appelle, who enjoyed Frederick William's protection. The estates confirmed the Hohenzollern succession in return for recognition of the pre-1721 constitutional arrangements, permitting Prussia to move in unopposed when the last Cirksena, Carl Edzard, died in 1744. The remaining Dutch and Danish troops withdrew and the corrupt administration was cleaned up, but otherwise the country was ruled with a light hand until the end of old Prussia in 1806.

Though Prussia was the chief beneficiary of Charles's failure in Mecklenburg and East Frisia, it was held in check by Hanover and by the continued growth of Russia. German statesmen regarded the tsar as a major threat by 1721, worse than the Turks because his empire had abandoned "barbarism" and embraced western ways.[50]

Russia had certainly learnt a lot from its first close encounter with imperial politics in Mecklenburg. Russian methods – Peter had threatened the *Renitenten* with Siberian exile – had failed to produce the desired result. On the contrary, as the Russian historian, E. V. Anisimov, aptly puts it, in "stirring up the German anthill, Peter received a serious sting, for in this region he confronted the vital interests of a number of world powers".[51] After Mecklenburg, Russia's German policy was more cautious, no longer relying on direct military intervention but using the princes as intermediaries to advance its aims. Gottorp's desire to recover Schleswig was used to help deflect possible Swedish revenge towards Denmark instead of Russia. Schleswig assumed greater importance as Russian policy became more obviously dynastic after Peter's death. Duke Carl Friedrich of Holstein-Gottorp married Anna Petrovna, daughter of the late tsar and Empress Catherine I, in 1725 in preference to a Hessen-Kassel princess. Catherine I abandoned caution with a military and naval build-up intended to recover Schleswig by force, backing down only after strong British diplomatic pressure in 1726–7.

This crisis left Russia isolated precisely when Austria's alliance with Spain was faltering in the Mediterranean. Austria had refused a string of Russian offers since 1712, not least because of Peter's controversial use of an imperial title. However, Charles VI finally accepted a Russian alliance on 6 August 1726, promising his assistance as emperor to restore Schleswig to Gottorp in return for a mutual defence pact.[52] Schleswig soon ceased to be of importance with the death of Catherine I, as neither of her immediate successors, Peter II (1727–30) and Anna Ivanovna (1730–41), desired to strengthen their Gottorp rivals, and even expelled Carl Friedrich from Russia in 1727. However, the Austrian–Russian alliance proved of lasting significance, despite constant friction from the partners' overlapping interests in Germany, Poland and the Balkans.

Gottorp claims were not completely abandoned, and were taken up again after 1741 by Empress Elizabeth, who extracted Swedish support for them in 1743 and 1758 and included them in the renewal of the Austrian alliance in 1746 and 1750. None of this yet particularly troubled the Habsburgs, who were used to promising action that could be safely postponed indefinitely. Russian and Austrian Balkan interests remained more complementary than conflicting at this stage, particularly as Russia currently pursued wars against Persia further to the east, leaving the area west of the Black Sea largely to the

Habsburgs. More immediate problems appeared in Poland, where Augustus was frequently ill after 1722, raising the question of his succession.

Austria and Russia were not well disposed towards backing another Wettin candidate, despite Crown Prince Friedrich August being Charles' brother-in-law. Russia in particular cast about for an alternative to assist its Polish policy, initially lighting on Prussia, its only loyal German ally at the end of the Great Northern War. Treaties were struck in 1720 and 1726, securing Prussian support to keep Poland weak and prevent the succession of a monarch not of Russia's choosing. The Austro-Russian alliance of 1726 upgraded Russia's German partner to none other than the emperor himself, forcing Prussia into second place. Although the three did agree to co-operate in the Alliance of the Three Black Eagles of December 1732, it was Austria and, increasingly, Russia that called the tune. Frederick William I was forced to concede Russia a free hand in the future of Courland in return for retaining some influence in Poland after 1733. The most decisive agreement, however, was the Löwenwolde Convention of 19 March 1733, whereby Austria and Russia agreed to back the Wettin candidate for want of a better alternative following Augustus's death on 1 February.

Charles increasingly lost control over events as Russia and France moved towards war. Empress Anna and her ministers were keen to settle matters in Poland quickly to be free to turn to more ambitious projects in the Balkans, forcing Charles to commit himself or lose their support altogether. Though Cardinal Fleury wanted to avoid an open breach, Louis XV pushed the candidacy of Stanislaw Leszczynski, partly from personal sympathy for a man who had become his father-in-law in 1725, and partly for want of a better candidate. Leszczynski, who had spent the intervening 20 years in French exile, had become something of a Polish national hero, helped by a series of bungled Saxon assassination attempts and by the fact that his countrymen had had time to forget his failings.[53]

The War of the Polish Succession, 1733–5

The resultant conflict proved a severe test for Charles's defence strategy, as it involved three interrelated struggles in the sensitive buffer zones of Poland, Italy and the Rhineland. Although the situation had been stabilized by 1735, the Habsburg monarchy was seriously weakened by a conflict the political importance of which far exceeded the level of actual fighting.

If Augustus had embarked on his royal adventure from a poor position, that of his son was weaker still. The Saxon army totalled only 19,800 men in June

226

1733, and even with 4,000 extra conscripts was completely incapable of enforcing Wettin rule alone. Field Marshal Lacy and 30,000 Russians crossed the Polish frontier on 11 August, their operations subsequently held up not by Polish resistance but Empress Anna's doubts as to whether she was backing the right candidate. France declared its support for Leszczynski on 4 September, and he was elected by the majority of Polish nobles eight days later. Louis XV declared war on Austria and Saxony on 10 October, spreading the war in support of his father-in-law three days later with simultaneous attacks on Kehl and Lorraine. However, a minority of nobles had already chosen the Saxon elector's Augusts II, as their King Augustus III on 5 October, and with Russian assistance Leszczynski's rule was restricted to the area around Danzig. France was unwilling to assist directly beyond sending 2,500 troops, who had already surrendered to the Russians on 23 June 1734. Fleury was only interested in securing Poland as a French *Barrière de l'est* provided it could be done without diverting resources from more important objectives. The fall of Danzig to a Russo-Saxon force on 9 September ended Leszczynski's second brief period as king and he temporarily found refuge in Königsberg, as Prussia had little desire to help its Saxon rivals.[54]

By this time the war had also spread to Italy, as France, allied to Sardinia and Spain since 1733, sent 38,000 troops to attack Milan in late October. Joined by 25,000 Sardinians, and eventually 24,000 Spanish, these proved more than enough to drive the 18,000 Austrians out of Milan The situation stabilized with the arrival of Austrian reinforcements from spring 1734, fighting the allies to a standstill in Parma and Mantua. However, Charles's troops were unable to prevent the Spanish moving south past Rome with papal permission to attack Naples in May 1734. Held by only 21,000 men, this was quickly overrun, followed by Sicily soon thereafter. The situation would probably have been even worse but for the conflicting aims of Austria's enemies. Sardinia and Spain both claimed Milan and nearly came to blows over Mantua. France was concerned to limit Spanish resurgence in Italy, while Sardinia wanted to retain at least a token Austrian presence there.

Charles's inability to defend Habsburg Italy was due in part to the need to divert forces to hold the Rhine, vital to sustain his prestige as emperor. All elements of the formal and informal defence structure were activated to assist the limited Austrian forces. The Association mobilized, agreeing a triple quota on 9 November 1733, followed by the declaration of a full *Reichskrieg* by the *Reichstag* on 9 April 1734 and the extension of the mobilization throughout the *Reich*.[55] Meanwhile contingents had started to arrive in response to Charles's network of bilateral treaties, which were extended by supplementary military conventions and fresh agreements. Charles carefully targeted princes with influence within the *Kreis* structure to ensure his bilateral arrangements complicated the Association's mobilization. The Franconian executive prince, the influential imperial vice chancellor, Friedrich Carl von Schönborn, agreed extra Bamberg and Würzburg auxiliaries in addition to promoting *Kreis* mobilization. Swabian co-operation was consolidated by a treaty with Carl Alexander, the new Catholic duke of Württemberg, who was already well integrated into the Habsburg patronage network. Hessen-Kassel was also persuaded to rejoin the Upper Rhenish *Kreis* military structure in addition to providing auxiliaries, while the agreements with Hanover and Wolfenbüttel also ensured they fielded their contingents to the *Reichsarmee*. Significantly, Prussian aid was secured without conceding Frederick William's demands for Jülich-Berg, and, to reduce the king's bargaining power, Charles rejected his offer of 40,000 men, accepting only the 10,000 he was obliged to provide under the Treaty of Berlin. The other rulers also received little material reward for their efforts and were obliged to reaffirm their support for the Pragmatic Sanction and often provide additional recruits directly to the Austrian army (see Table 6.2).

Kreis mobilization, however, was limited by the opposition of the three Wittelsbach electors to the war. Carl Albrecht of Bavaria was the most determined, already sensing Habsburg dynastic weakness and considering a bid for the imperial title and Austrian inheritance upon Charles's death.[56] Since 1732 Bavarian lawyers had been preparing arguments supporting the elector's claims and his intention of escaping his earlier (1722) recognition of the Pragmatic Sanction. His natural ally was France, particularly as French ministers had grown concerned at the poor state of his army and were prepared to pay 800,000 fl. annual subsidy provided he increased its strength to 26,000 men. A treaty was concluded on 15 November 1733, and, along with his brother, Johann Theodor, bishop of Regensburg and Freising, Carl Albrecht blocked the Bavarian *Kreis* mobilization against the efforts of pro-Austrian Salzburg. The *Kreis* Assembly decided to mobilize only 3,257 infantry instead of its official contingent of 11,682, but only Salzburg, Passau and the smaller territories sent their 1,333 men. However, Bavaria was now too weak to defy Austria openly as Max Emanuel had done. The army totalled a mere 6,204 effectives in March 1733, and although 19,600 regulars and 20,000 militia could be mobilized by January 1735, these cost a crippling 8.7 million fl. by 1737, or 5.9 million more than the French subsidies. Nearly bankrupt, Carl Albrecht felt he could no longer withstand Austrian pressure and duly despatched his 2,115 *Kreistruppen* in September 1735.

Clemens August's position proved even more parlous.[57] Ruling Münster, Paderborn, Hildesheim and Osnabrück, in addition to Cologne, he had influence in Westphalia, Lower Saxony and the Electoral Rhine and so quickly became a target of French diplomacy. France exploited a scandal at

Table 6.2 Auxiliaries for Austria, 1735

Territory	Treaty	Contingent	Returned
Prussia	1728	10,289	1735[1]
Württemberg	1733–4	8,158	1736[2]
Denmark	1732	6,195	1735[3]
Saxony	1735	6,000	1735[4]
Gotha	1733	5,000	1736[5]
Würzburg-Bamberg	1733	4,600	1736[6]
Weimar	1732	3,000	1735[7]
Hanover	1734	2,860	1736[8]
Hessen-Kassel	1733	2,400	1735[9]
Mainz	1733	2,300	1736[10]
Eisenach	1732	2,000	1738
Wolfenbüttel	1728	1,500	1735[11]
		54,302	

Sources: *Feldzüge*, vol. xix, pp. 113–19, 138–9, 285; Patze (ed.), *Geschichte Thüringens*, vol. v, pp. 302, 350–52, 431; C. v. Geispitzheim, *Historische Nachrichten von dem . . . Füsilier-Regiment . . . von Erlach* (1778, reprinted Osnabrück, 1971); Münter, "Waldeckischen Truppen", pp. 204–5; Wilson, *War, state and society*, pp. 169–76, 183, and the sources cited there.

Notes:
[1] Replaced the *Reich*'s contingent.
[2] Excluding 1,728 *Kreistruppen*.
[3] On behalf of Holstein.
[4] Provided in return for Austrian help in Poland.
[5] 800 were provided by Waldeck under subcontract, 24 August 1734.
[6] Excluding about 1,000 *Kreistruppen*.
[7] Actually sent 2,822.
[8] Excluding 2,866 serving as the *Reich*'s contingent.
[9] Excluding 1,443 serving as Upper Rhine *Kreistruppen*.
[10] Remained in garrison in Mainz and probably totalled only 1,700.
[11] Excluding 685 Lower Saxon *Kreistruppen*.

court to have Plettenberg banished, manoeuvring Clemens August into an alliance on 14 January 1734 before he could change his mind. Obliged to hold 10,000 men in readiness, the elector actually mustered 11,540 by June 1734, thanks to the still substantial forces of Münster and Paderborn. The Cologne regiments encamped at Plittersdorf near Bonn August–October 1734 in what was intended as a show of strength, but only revealed Clemens August's weakness. The supply arrangements collapsed, the tents leaked and no regiment could form up in order. By September the soldiers were deserting at the rate of 20 a day. Neither France nor Austria were impressed. When Belle-Isle invaded Trier in summer 1734 and levied contributions in Cologne enclaves as well, he simply excused himself on the grounds of his poor knowledge of German geography. The elector felt obliged to make a token effort to honour his responsibilities, sending the Paderborn contingent (1,200 men) in August, followed by those of Münster, Osnabrück and Hildesheim (another 1,200) by the end of 1734.

This failed to convince the Austrians, who turned the situation to their advantage. For once the emperor could satisfy the customary demands for winter quarters without reducing his standing in the *Reich*. Austrian and Danish troops entered the electorate, while the 10,000 Prussians occupied the Westphalian bishoprics, brawling with the Catholic civilians and generally behaving as if in occupied territory.[58] Clemens August petulantly struck back, billeting his own troops on Plettenberg's property at Nordkirchen, but was otherwise unable to do nothing for fear of more serious retaliation. The better-armed Palatinate was able to send supplies to the French army, but also refrained from overt action against the emperor, and could do nothing to prevent the billeting of a Danish contingent on its territory. Charles had neutralized the Wittelsbach threat without unnecessary violence, and there was no repeat of the open defiance of 1702–4.

However, as with other aspects of Habsburg policy, Charles's defence of the Rhine was affected by international developments. His relative success in securing German support was due in part to the absence of foreign competition. Unlike previous wars against France, Britain and the Dutch remained neutral because Fleury wisely refrained from attacking the Austrian Netherlands, negotiating a treaty to this effect with the Dutch Republic in 1733.[59]

Though German auxiliaries were not drawn to Flanders by Anglo-Dutch subsidies, this also meant there was no extra money for help in Italy. Charles could not hope to match the sums formerly paid by the maritime powers, but without additional money the princes could not mobilize more troops. As it was, many preferred to retain their remaining units for home defence, such as Ernst Ludwig, who refused to release his guard dragoon regiment on the grounds it was needed for his own outposts.[60] Shortage of funds compelled Charles to accept cash in lieu of troops from the weaker Westphalians and Lower Saxons, further reducing the effective strength of the *Kreis* contingents (Table 6.3). Though the paper strength of the Austrian army was raised from 141,713 (1732) to 205,643 (1735), no more than 157,000 were actually present, making German help crucial. Moreover, the absence of a Netherlands front enabled the French to concentrate up to 100,000 of their 280,585 troops in the Rhineland, in addition to sizeable numbers in Italy.[61]

These were more than sufficient to achieve Fleury's limited objectives of weakening Habsburg Italy and annexing Lorraine. The latter was quickly

Table 6.3 Extent of the *Kreis* mobilization by 1735

Kreis	Contingent
Swabia	7,894
Franconia	8,016
Electoral Rhine	500[1]
Upper Rhine	5,329[2]
Westphalia	3,400[3]
Upper Saxony	2,800[4]
Lower Saxony	4,951[5]
Bavaria	1,333[6]
Total	34,223

Sources: HSAS, A6: Bü. 67; A7: Bü. 42, 18 March 1736; C14: Bü. 336a; *Feldzüge*, vol. XIX, pp. 120–28; Storm, *Feldherr*, pp. 338–41; Helmes, "Fränkische Kreistruppen, 1714–1756", pp. 13–15, 32; Meissner, *Nordhausen*, pp. 59–62; Stahlberg, "Reussisches Militär", pp. 13–14; Möllmann, "Kurtrierischen Militärs", p. 68.

Notes:
[1] Field contingent from Trier.
[2] Including 1,443 from Hessen-Kassel.
[3] Paderborn 1,200, Cologne 500, others 1,700.
[4] Schwarzburg and Reuss 2,300 plus about 500 from Anhalt.
[5] Hanover 2,866, Wolfenbüttel 685, Hildesheim and Osnabrück 1,200, Mühlhausen, Goslar and Nordhausen 200.
[6] Joined by another 2,115 from Bavaria and Neuburg in September 1735.
The table excludes the Prussian and Austrian units serving as nominal contingents.

overrun after 13 September 1733, reducing the remaining French operations in the Rhineland to pressurizing Charles into negotiating. Since France could not strike at Austria, it was compelled to attack German targets, but had to limit these to symbolic objectives, such as capturing the *Reichsfeste* for fear of antagonizing the princes and provoking Anglo-Dutch intervention.[62] There was no repeat of the savage devastation that characterized Louis XIV's policy, and once Kehl fell on 28 October 1733, French forces withdrew over the Rhine. However, this failed to deter German mobilization, forcing the French to launch an attack down the Moselle valley, taking Trarbach and Trier in April 1734. A second force then broke the Ettlingen defensive lines in May, forcing the newly-assembled *Reichsarmee* under Prince Eugene to retire on Heilbronn and clearing the way for the siege of Philippsburg, which fell on 19 July.[63] Thereafter, France remained on the defensive, refraining from provocative attacks deeper into the *Reich*.

The question of Russian intervention hung over these operations from the outset, as Charles called on Anna to honour her obligations under the 1726 treaty and send the promised 30,000 men. Anna refused until her ministers had manoeuvred Charles into agreeing to back an offensive war against the Turks, which the Russians started in 1735. Even then, she unilaterally reduced the assistance to 13,000 and directed it to the Rhine rather than Italy, where Habsburg strategists originally wanted it. France and Bavaria quickly exploited the Russians' westward advance from Poland for propaganda purposes, raising the image of barbarous Moscovites as henchmen of imperial absolutism and referring directly to their earlier disorderly conduct in Mecklenburg. In fact the Russians were on their best behaviour, since Anna and her advisers used the expedition to boost their international prestige. Trained and disciplined largely along German lines, the Russians made an impressive appearance as they arrived in Swabia that August. Apart from language problems and cattle plague spread by transport oxen, the Germans had no difficulty coping with their new guests.[64]

The Russians' arrival raised hopes in Vienna of turning the tide of war, and some planned to use the Bavarians' opposition to their transit as an excuse to invade the electorate and disarm its army. However, Prince Eugene continued to regard the situation as hopeless, arguing that it was impossible to take Bavaria without a long and costly campaign. Even with the Russians on the Rhine he felt unable to take the offensive, claiming Anna's assistance came at too high a price and peace was a better option.[65]

As it was, the Russian advance did alarm the French, who opened negotiations with Charles in June 1735 when it became obvious that diplomatic efforts in St Petersburg had failed to deter Anna from intervening. Peace preliminaries were signed in Vienna with British mediation on 3 October.[66] France compelled Leszczynski to abdicate in favour of Augustus III and accept Metz, Toul, Verdun and the duchy of Bar as compensation. Lorraine would also be transferred to the ex-king once its current duke could have Tuscany after the death of the last Medici, which occurred in 1737. This paved the way for full French annexation of Lorraine along with Leszczynski's other territory upon his own death in 1766, completing Fleury's programme and ending Lorraine's association with Germany until Bismarck's Second *Reich* in 1871. Meanwhile, the Habsburgs were weakened in Italy by the transfer of Naples, Sicily and the Tuscan ports to Don Carlos as a new independent kingdom, while small parts of Milan were ceded to Piedmont–Sardinia. Retention of Parma and the eventual acquisition of Tuscany did not compensate Austria for these losses, even if they made Habsburg territory strategically more compact in the north. The Polish settlement merely confirmed the existing military situation, and although the Saxon monarch already provided military assistance for Charles, his victory benefited Russia more. Russia used its intervention to establish a firm party among the Polish nobility, who increasingly turned to the empress to protect their privileges rather than France or Austria.[67] Having decided these terms, it then took French, Austrian and British diplomats until 1739 to secure the consent of the other interested parties, prolonging a state of phoney war for nearly another four years.

Though Philippsburg and Kehl were returned by France in January 1737, and Louis XV recognized the Pragmatic Sanction, the *Reich* had suffered a serious blow with the loss of Lorraine. Most discussions of this last defence of the Rhine before 1792 conclude with a negative assessment, presenting a dismal picture of the *Reichsarmee* and blaming the outcome on Eugene's failing health and reluctance to engage the enemy.[68] The elderly imperial field marshal certainly shares some of the responsibility for the reverses, although this should not be overestimated, since, with the exception of the Russians, all the major armies were commanded by ancient veterans from the previous century: poor Count Mercy, leading the Austrians in Italy, was even deaf and blind. It is true that the French army was superior in efficiency as well as numbers in the initial stages of the war, thanks to more effective resource mobilization. Rhinelanders reported that German-speaking soldiers in the French army claimed they had plenty of supplies, were always paid on time and there was no better master than the king of France.[69] However, as the war progressed, the situation seems to have deteriorated, so that by 1735 the French resorted to drafting 7,000 militiamen to replenish their army in Italy. Frequently, the defensive posture adopted in the Rhineland was forced on their commanders by inadequate manpower as well as political considerations.

In contrast, the *Reichsarmee* improved in both numbers and effectiveness as fresh contingents arrived and the recruits grew accustomed to service. The reverses of 1733–4 were the price that had to be paid for opting for a mobilization system rather than a permanent army in 1682. Nonetheless, the *Kreis* Association ensured a minimum level of defence, sufficient to deter deep thrusts into the *Reich* despite the almost complete absence of Austrian troops before April 1734. Lorraine and Kehl were already indefensible, but Philippsburg, held by only 4,000 men, proved a tough nut to crack despite its dilapidated condition. The situation improved thereafter, and the French were unable to besiege Mainz. By autumn 1735, the Germans were sufficiently confident to launch a counterattack, as Seckendorff crossed the middle Rhine with 30,000 men, defeating a French detachment at Clausen on 20 October and forcing it to retreat up the Moselle before news of the peace preliminaries halted further operations.

Undoubtedly, the *Reichsarmee* could have achieved more, particularly from spring 1735. Eugene greatly overestimated Bavaria's capability to resist, given that it took the movement of only four cavalry regiments towards its frontier to induce Carl Albrecht to permit the Russians' transit in July. Austria successfully overran the electorate in 1741, 1743 and 1745 with fewer resources than available in 1735.[70]

As a limited holding operation, the defence of the Rhine proved successful, and the French were not given the opportunity to wreak the kind of damage they had done in earlier conflicts. However, the longer term political consequences of Austria's reverses were to prove serious, especially when they were compounded by a disastrous defeat by the Turks.

Three years of defeat, 1737–9

The Austrian government was encouraged by its recent peace negotiations with the Bourbon powers and by the continued overoptimistic assessments of Ottoman weakness. It was true that the strategic position was better following the gains of 1716–18, but Habsburg strength had been sapped by the recent setbacks in Italy and the Rhineland. Nonetheless, the emerging Eastern Question proved decisive in the calculations, as the Turks were expected to collapse quickly, creating a power vacuum in the Balkans. If Charles did not move quickly, it was feared the Russians would fill it entirely. Combined with growing political isolation, the ministers felt they had to enter the war both to check Russian expansionism and retain their last remaining ally. In the end this proved a serious miscalculation. Far from collapsing the Turks beat off three Russian attacks in 1735–7. As the delays continued into 1737, the Austrian government began to doubt the wisdom of its decision but were unable to escape the Russians' skilful diplomacy. Though the *Hofkriegsrat* president advised the army would not be ready for at least another year, the government decided on 14 June to honour its commitment to Russia. Instrumental in this had been the fear that the troops assembling in Hungary since July 1736 would succumb to malaria if they did not advance from their unhealthy cantonments.[71]

Despite his recent setbacks, the emperor was not entirely unprepared. The paper strength of the army stood at 169,000 in 1736, of which over 131,000 were effective. Due to the ongoing phoney war in the west, at least 40,000 had to remain in Italy, with a further 30,000 or so in the *Reich*, leaving only 62,550 for Hungary, but at least the financial position looked reasonably healthy. Also expecting a quick victory, the territorial estates proved surprisingly generous, pledging 6.5 million fl. collateral for foreign loans in addition to their normal tax grant of 8 million fl. The Hungarian nobles donated a further 200,000 fl., while further money was raised by the traditional expedient of a Turkish tax introduced in April 1737. The pope authorized a five-year tithe on Austrian church property to provide 1 million fl. annually in addition to 2.85 million fl. paid directly from his own coffers. However, this merely obscured the underlying weakness in the Austrian fiscal – military state. The 1716–18 Turkish war cost 43 million fl., of which the military budget covered only 22.7 million fl. While the Polish Succession conflict consumed a further 73 million fl., of which a mere 14.3 million fl. could be paid for directly. The actual value of the estates' grant was down to 6 million fl. by 1734, or 2 million fl. short of the official sum, and total revenue barely reached 20 million fl. Worse, Charles's domains were mortgaged to the tune of 100 million fl., the estates' grants were pawned to a further 31.5 million fl. and the *Bancalität*, introduced in 1714 to solve these problems, was on the verge of total collapse. Maintenance of the army in Hungary cost 5 million fl. in 1737, even before hostilities began. By diverting the domains' revenue to cover immediate outgoings, operations could be financed, but only at the cost of stopping all interest and debt repayment. State debts rocketed from 22 to 99 million fl., while the total cost of the war rose to 146 million fl. by 1739, well above the 24.2 million fl. covered by the regular military budget, and considerably above what ministers were prepared to reveal to German princes.[72]

The effect on Habsburg military effectiveness was alarming. For the first time in a major war, even the army's official establishment declined, falling in 1737 by about 8,000 on the previous year and dropping a further 3,000 in 1738. Assistance from the *Reich* became essential, but there was now no chance of mobilizing a *Reichsarmee* for a new offensive war in the east, even if Charles had desired it. After their recent exertions defending the Rhine, the territories were not prepared to sanction a redeployment to Hungary, but the *Reichstag* did vote the customary cash grant,[73] and a number of princes indicated willingness to make bilateral deals. The skill of the emperor's diplomats in manipulating princely ambition secured the services of valuable auxiliaries, and further recruits were gathered by capitalizing on the imperial privilege of recruiting anywhere in the *Reich*. However, the long-term consequences were serious. Coming after earlier broken promises, the emperor's blatant inability to honour his political concessions, or even pay the troops he hired, used up much of the Habsburg's remaining credit in the *Reich*, leaving the Austrian monarchy vulnerable when Charles died in 1740.

This was far from clear in 1737, when a number of princes agreed to send troops. The war of 1733–5 left all German rulers with inflated establishments that proved difficult to maintain in peacetime. In addition to demonstrating their loyalty to the emperor, all hoped that he would reduce their military budgets by hiring part of their armies to serve in Hungary. In most cases they were disappointed, because their emperor's catastrophic financial position prevented him honouring even the modest amounts he agreed to pay, but the princes accepted the risk, hoping that political concessions would make it worthwhile. Both Carl Albrecht and Clemens August were desperate to rebuild relations with Charles after their glaring failure to support him in the Polish War. Despite the advice of Count Törring, chief of the Bavarian *Hofkriegsrat*, that the corps would be ruined, the elector committed over half his army in the hope that Charles would remember him in his will. Similar motives lay behind Saxon involvement, but it proved a disaster for both, as the heavy losses suffered in Hungary delivered the military advantage to Prussia in 1740, as we shall see in the next chapter.[74] Whereas Wolfenbüttel and Würzburg were primarily concerned to retain imperial goodwill, the Württemberg regency government desperately needed his support to bolster their own position within the duchy after 1737. Faced with the opposition of Carl Alexander's widow, they sought imperial assistance to exclude her Catholic supporters from political power. Their subsequent bilateral arrangement with her, bypassing the imperial representative only made their dependency on Charles greater still. They also needed imperial support to defend the duchy's position in the Swabian *Kreis*, vulnerable to the machinations of other territories in the absence of a mature reigning duke, and had to find a solution to the army's funding crisis, especially as many of the officers were suspected of colluding with the duke's widow for a *coup d'état* against them. The transfer of part of the army appeared the ideal answer, with the added bonus of providing suitable employment for the young Württemberg princes. Three further regiments were placed in the vacated fortresses of Freiberg, Breisach, Philippsburg and Kehl in the hope that Charles would confirm the regent as Carl Alexander's replacement as imperial commander on the Rhine. All these hopes ended in complete disappointment. Though 4,954 men were transferred, the units that they formed were broken up and used to bring existing Austrian regiments up to strength, depriving the princes of their promising careers as imperial colonels. The three garrison regiments were left unpaid and an alternative candidate appointed commander on the Rhine. In their desperation to escape financial crisis, the government drifted towards Prussia, ending 1740 trapped into supplying Frederick the Great with additional troops for his new war against Austria.[75]

These kinds of complications encouraged the emperor to seek direct drafts of recruits rather than bilateral arrangements tied to concessions. As we have seen, this was already the preferred option during the Great Turkish War, but this time Charles went directly to the *Kreise* and key territories to recruit. Generally permission was sought from the relevant authorities either to assist imperial recruiting parties or to undertake the work themselves. However, using his authority as their direct overlord, the imperial knights were coerced into providing men under threat of sanctions against their lands. Some efforts were made to maintain goodwill, as the emperor stuck to established procedures and chose his representatives with care. The man sent to Swabia was Baron Arnoldus Franz von Tornacco, a favourite of the recently deceased Carl Alexander, who entered Austrian service in January 1738 and subsequently represented the Habsburgs in military and political negotiations in the region till 1747. Nonetheless, Austrian recruitment was increasingly resented. The numbers involved represented a heavy burden, following recent recruitment for the Polish War, and many territories found it difficult to meet their obligations. Enthusiasm for the Habsburg cause waned following further defeats, and Charles's alliance network became strained in the wake of mutual recriminations. Just how serious the situation could become is illustrated by the case of Weimar, where it was estimated that the provision of recruits and auxiliaries since 1733 had cost by 1739 800,000 tlr more than it had received, which was equivalent to ten years' state revenue! Meanwhile, heavy losses in Hungary, probably amounting to 50 per cent or more, deterred other princes from offering fresh contingents. Still, the numbers involved were considerable, and the totals summarized in Table 6.4 are probably an underestimate. No less than 18,000 men from the *Reich* passed down the Danube for the front in 1739 alone. Together with the contingents sent under bilateral treaties, the *Reich* contribution to the Habsburg war effort probably approached 30 per cent or more of the total force deployed in Hungary.[76]

Despite these reinforcements, the war proved a disaster. Though Austria and Russia agreed joint operations each year, there was little practical co-operation. Russia did try to send its main force through Poland in 1739 to be of more direct help, but otherwise it left its ally to fight largely on its own. When operations began in July 1737, the Austrians numbered only 56,700 effectives, a quarter of whom were detached to cover Transylvania and the frontier. After initial successes, including the capture of Niš, the Austrians fell back after serious reverses in Bosnia. Only 2,000 Serbs joined them, fleeing over the frontier as the Austrians retreated. However, this defeat was worse than it seemed. Casualties were relatively light and no territory was lost. As Karl Roider points out, "the chief victim was Austrian pride", defeated by an enemy considered militarily inferior.[77]

Austria accepted a French offer to mediate, as this avoided the need to deal separately with the Turks, which would have contravened the alliance with Russia. Negotiations continued into 1739 without immediate success.[78]

Table 6.4 German auxiliaries in imperial service, 1737–9

Territory	Date	Strength	Returned	Losses
Contingents				
Saxony[1]	1737	7,894	Jan 1740	*c.* 6,000
Wolfenbüttel	Mar 1737	1,555	Apr 1740	1,100
Württemberg[2]	1737–9	4,954	n.a.	n.a.
Bavaria[3]	1 Sept 1738	7,260	1740	5,400
Cologne[4]	Sept 1738	4,600	Jan 1740	*c.* 1,000
Würzburg[5]	1 Dec 1738	2,300	1740	1,300
Total		28,563		over 14,800
Recruits				
Baden-Durlach	1739	300		
Swabian Knights	1739	450		
Swabian *Kreistruppen*	1739	600		
Swabian states	1739–40	10,200		
Franconian states	1739	660		
Franconian Knights	1739	?		
Imperial cities	1739–40	2,000		
Fulda	1739	300		
Ansbach	1739	?		
Weimar	1739	300		
Total		over 14,810		

Sources: As notes 74–6.

Notes:

[1] Officially 8,000. Renegotiated to 5,565 on 1 August 1738 because of losses.

[2] 3 rgts transferred directly to the Austrian army. In addition 3,300 infantry garrisoned the four Rhineland fortresses.

[3] Extended on 12 June 1739 with a further 1,550 men added.

[4] One of the 2 rgts was provided by Münster and Paderborn. Only 242 of the 819 men sent by Paderborn returned.

[5] Initially negotiated for 1,640 infantry in July 1738 on the basis of the 1733 Austro-Würzburg treaty. After renegotiation, an enlarged infantry rgt served in 1739–40, with 305 men transferring permanently in October 1740.

Emboldened, the Turks launched energetic attacks on Austrian positions throughout the winter, while the sultan summoned Joseph Rákóczi, Ferenc II's eldest son, to Istanbul in 1737 and recognized him as "prince of Transylvania". A dilettante more interested in love intrigue than politics, Joseph lacked his father's skill, and his efforts to recruit an army of Hungarian deserters and prisoners of war failed miserably. Despite resentment at

Habsburg centralization, the Hungarians had no love for a man they had never seen. In contrast to the earlier wars, the sultan's attempt to play the "Transylvanian card" proved a damp squib, and, after living in perpetual fear of assassination, Joseph died of plague in November 1738. Turkish military operations proved more successful. Despite initial setbacks, including defeat at Korina 4 July 1738, they succeeded in recapturing most of Austrian Serbia, thanks to superior numbers and Austrian indecision.[79] Campaigning two years in a row close to the unhealthy Danube marshes had a serious effect on the Austrians: by September 1738 men were dying at the rate of 80–100 a day.

These losses placed a premium on support from the *Reich* in 1739. The primary task was now defensive, with the priority of holding on to Belgrade, the most important gain of the last war. About 15,000 men held the city, covered by a further 30,000 under Count Wallis. Count Neipperg and another 26,000 covered the Banat, while 30,000 under Lobkowitz protected Transylvania. With their forces thus scattered, the Austrians were poorly placed to match the Turkish concentration of 150,000 descending on Belgrade. Despite defeating their advance guard at Grocka on 21 July, Wallis mishandled the campaign, exhausting his men with unnecessary marches. Worse, the usual indecision was compounded this year by personal feuding amongst the generals and their insistence on referring back to Vienna for instructions before committing themselves to any action. This proved fatal. Fearing that the nervous Wallis might exceed his earlier orders to negotiate and make unwise concessions, the Vienna government gave similar powers to his rival, Neipperg, to make peace on the basis of his own assessment of the military situation. Neipperg entered the Turkish camp on 18 August. In his absence Count Schmettau took command of the city, revived morale and made successful sorties. Even Wallis moved the main force into a more advantageous position. Cut off from the outside world and unaware of these developments, Neipperg concluded a deal under French mediation, ceding Belgrade, Serbia and all other land gained in 1718 except the Banat. Vienna had no alternative but to accept this *fait accompli* or risk antagonizing France at a critical stage during ratification of the settlement of the Polish War. These terms were far better than the Turks were in a position to demand, coming as they did when their own war effort was crumbling. The treaty established the Sava–Danube river line as the Austro-Ottoman frontier, remaining unchanged, apart from relatively minor revisions in 1775 and 1790, until the annexation of Bosnia-Herzegovina in 1908. Having razed its fortifications, the Austrians evacuated Belgrade on 8 June 1740. Their army in Hungary had fallen to 36,500 effectives, and at least 80,000 Austrians and Germans had been killed in the war, while many more succumbed to disease. Abandoned by their ally and fearing war with Sweden, the Russians also made peace in 1740.[80]

The reasons for this humiliating defeat were already a source of controversy at the time, but in retrospect it is clear that underlying fiscal–military weakness was most important. Maria Theresa was convinced that the debilitating effects of the long peace of 1718–33 were to blame, allowing the estates to reassert their influence and deprive the central government of the necessary resources. Certainly, older assessments of the fiscal impact are exaggerated, based partly on inflated estimates of total revenue before the crisis. However, it seems that Roider is misguided when he downplays the financial problems and argues that the army was still "a formidable fighting force" in 1739.[81] The accumulative effect of two major wars in 1733–5 and 1737–9, pushed total state debt from 70 million fl. (1718) to 99 million fl. (1739), reversing all the savings made in the meantime. Moreover, Charles VI's increasing use of deficit finance had consumed much of the monarchy's remaining credit with bankers. Fiscal administration deteriorated to *ad hoc* emergency measures, and it is significant that there are not overall balance sheets for the years 1733–5 and 1737–9. Pay arrears for the four regiments garrisoning Tuscany stood at 225,305 fl. alone by 1739, equivalent to half their annual upkeep. Effective strength slumped to 108,000 men or 24 per cent below peacetime establishment even in 1740, while morale was so low that it was reckoned that a regiment marching from the hereditary lands would lose a tenth of its manpower to desertion by the time it reached the Netherlands.[82]

The government and public chose to blame the generals. Seckendorff, the field commander in 1737, was imprisoned on his return to Vienna, while angry mobs attacked his house. Wallis and Neipperg were arrested in 1739, and criticism was also levelled at Königsegg, who commanded in 1738. This was typical of the Habsburgs before 1740. Like the unfortunate General Arco, executed for surrendering Breisach in 1703, General Doxat de Morez met a similar fate for giving up Niš in 1737. Such treatment was unjust. Half of Doxat's small garrison were sick, and he only had sufficient fresh water for three days. Jealousy among field commanders was not unique to 1737–9. Though Neipperg's reputation took a further plunge after his defeat at Mollwitz (1741), he, like the others, had shown himself competent on occasions in the past. A trial failed to convict the imprisoned generals, who were promptly released by Maria Theresa on her accession. She abandoned the punitive search for scapegoats and took a more forgiving attitude to future military failures, to the point of indulgence towards those of her brother-in-law, Prince Charles of Lorraine. Though more humane, it scarcely did her any good. The generals and officers were demoralized by the defeat and a significant number defected to Bavaria and Prussia in 1740–41.[83]

This gives an insight into a second chief cause of the defeat, the failings of the army. The high command had seriously underestimated Turkish strength; their subsequent defeat at the hands of a supposedly inferior foe heightening their sense of failure and demoralization. The 20 years following 1718 allowed them to forget the lessons of earlier wars against the Turks. Deployment in open formations handed the advantage to their opponents, while Habsburg soldiers lacked experience of the hostile environment and unconventional enemy, who they still regarded as superhuman and capable of any atrocity. Combined with obvious failings in supply, this fear discouraged the Austrian and German soldiers, who do not seem to have shared their commanders' initial belief in a quick victory.

Defeat and demoralization undoubtedly laid the monarchy open to attack and contributed to Frederick the Great's quick victory in 1740–41, as well as doing great harm to Austria's standing in the *Reich*. Weakness in its fiscal–military system, offset by modest successes in some areas in 1733–5, were now laid bare by unmitigated defeat in Hungary and Serbia. The loss of territory, coming after that of Naples and Sicily in 1738, appeared to suggest dismemberment of the Habsburg inheritance was possible. Finally, Charles's poor treatment of the princes providing recruits and auxiliaries diminished loyalty to the traditional imperial dynasty, leading many to support an alternative after 1740.

Chapter Seven

Between civil war and partition, 1740–92

The rise of Prussia

On 16 December 1740 Frederick the Great of Prussia invaded Austrian Silesia and began a new era of German history. It is common to write of the events that followed until the end of the old *Reich* exclusively from the perspective of Austro-Prussian rivalry or "Dualism" squeezing out the "third Germany" of lesser states. Certainly these territories were politically and militarily marginalized, but they did not retreat into helpless passivity or turn their backs on the *Reich*. On the contrary, enthusiasm for the traditional structure grew as Austro-Prussian preponderance increased. Moreover, while Austria and Prussia increasingly disregarded the interests of the others, they did not themselves lose interest in the *Reich*. Austria saw it as a device to mobilize resources for its particularist intentions, especially to recover Silesia from Prussia and, when this failed, to find alternative compensation elsewhere. Prussia meanwhile came to regard the *Reich* as a bulwark against Austrian revanchism and as a substitute for international isolation. Foreign powers also remained concerned with the traditional structure, with both France and Russia seeing it as important to their wider security.

None of this German and international concern benefited the *Reich*, and indeed hastened its demise. Austrian and Prussian objectives were diametrically opposed, and their respective attempts to rally wider support split the *Reich* in what were in effect German civil wars. First, Frederick's attack triggered two Silesian wars (1740–42, 1744–5) between Prussia and Austria, which coincided with the wider struggle over Charles VI's inheritance, known as the War of the Austrian Succession (1740–48). For Austria this involved not only Prussian annexation of one of its richest provinces but also the temporary loss of the imperial title and its transfer by election to the

Bavarian Wittelsbachs in 1742–5, in a period which did lasting damage to imperial institutions. The second civil war, known as the Third Silesian War, coincided with renewed international conflict in the Seven Years War, 1756–63. Like the earlier clashes between Austria and Prussia, this was not an exclusive struggle of the two leading German powers but involved a variety of other territories that were largely unwillingly pulled into the fray. Further serious damage was inflicted on the fabric of the *Reich*, which also suffered from the underlying shift in the balance between Europe's great powers, France, England and Russia.

The wider German and international dimension to both these periods of civil war indicates that we cannot characterize the period exclusively in terms of Austro-Prussian dualism. Indeed, even to see relations between these two powers as solely antagonistic would be to miss a key threat to the traditional structure, for imperial politics after 1763 were very different from the earlier pattern. In place of the traditional danger of imperial absolutism there was now the possibility that the *Reich* might be partitioned between the old power of Austria and the new one of Prussia.

The emergence of Prussia as the second major German state alongside Austria is striking and requires some explanation, especially as it was far from obvious to contemporaries before 1740 that the Hohenzollerns rather than another dynasty would be the main challenger to Habsburg predominance. The preceding chapters have indicated that Prussian policy was far from unique before the early eighteenth century. Prussia was neither exclusively militaristic, at least not before Frederick William I's accession in 1713, nor were other territories short on aggression and grand ambitions. Though Prussia established itself early on as a major German military power, it was not until the 1720s that it gained a decisive margin over its rivals, and for much of the later seventeenth century, Bavaria, Saxony, Münster and the Guelphs had maintained roughly equivalent forces. Men like Max Emanuel of Bavaria, Ernst August of Hanover, Johann Wilhelm of the Palatinate or Christoph Bernhard von Galen in Münster had been as dynamic, scheming and ambitious as the Great Elector or any other Hohenzollern, although Prussia's unbroken line of healthy, able adult male rulers was undoubtedly significant and gave the dynasty an important advantage in an age where much was governed by the uncertainty of human biology.

Prussia had not neglected other, less violent means to advance its influence, particularly expanding its clientele network through dynastic marriages with key German families, including those of Württemberg, the Guelph duchies, Franconian Hohenzollerns and the House of Orange. It is also worth remembering that some of Germany's greatest baroque buildings were to be found not in Munich, Dresden, or even Vienna but in Berlin. Indeed, the projection of political power through such "cultural competition" did not die with Frederick I in 1713, as his grandson's resumption of royal patronage of arts and sciences as well as massive palace construction in Potsdam after 1740 reflects very much a return to traditional methods, albeit now clothed in the style of enlightened philosophy and rococo architecture, after Frederick William's spartan regime.

These comparisons indicate that we need to look beyond simple references to "Prussian militarism" or "Hohenzollern dynamism" for our explanation. Most attempts do so emphasize various combinations of three factors already encountered at various points in this book. One is the establishment of a domestic consensus by the "historic compromise" of crown and nobility, which allegedly gave such strength to Prussian absolutism and permitted the second factor, the development of the country's fiscal–military potential. The third aspect lies in the realm of international relations, especially in foreign powers' appreciation of Prussia as a potential counterweight to Austria.

While Prussia's historic compromise undoubtedly has certain unique characteristics, the establishment of a working relationship between crown and elite groups was common to German absolutism, which rested on a constant process of bargaining with key social groups. The growth of serfdom in the Hohenzollern lands east of the river Elbe was already under way before the dynasty began trading confirmation of the landlords' powers in return for their acquiescence to its political authority. The key military institution that emerged through this process, the famous "Canton system" of recruitment, had certain unique features, but was otherwise similar to other rulers' attempts to maximize their military potential with minimal fiscal or economic disruption. Whereas most sought to do this by modifying their traditional militias as a recruitment pool for their regular forces, Frederick William abolished the Prussian militia altogether in 1713, but essentially used its selection mechanisms to draft men directly into the army from the 1720s. Each regiment was assigned a canton, or district, from which it could take men to keep it up to strength. These served for life, but were released after basic training into the civilian economy for up to ten months a year to save on their maintenance and to sustain the agricultural labour force. Though the symbiosis of the Junker landlords and Prussian officer corps has been overemphasized, the same social group did benefit from the system, strengthening the identification of the nobility with the Hohenzollern state. This domestic consensus was certainly important to the growth of Hohenzollern power, but it also tied the dynasty to a relatively inflexible, conservative socio-political structure, retarding other aspects of its state building.[1]

Most accounts traditionally play down the extent of Prussian resources, often as a device to magnify the achievements of the Hohenzollerns for being able to go so far on so little. Brandenburg-Prussia certainly did lack human resources, although its total population was still larger than any other territory after that of the Habsburgs, while its surface areas in 1648 was three times the size of the next rival, Bavaria. Exploitation of these resources was certainly ruthless, but so too was that by rulers elsewhere, and we shall be careful not to overemphasise the difference between Hohenzollern rationalization and centralization and the consolidation of absolutist rule in other large territories. Prussian bureaucratic development, for instance, was far from the assured march of rational efficiency portrayed in the Borussian legend. Moreover, even by 1740, the Prussian fiscal–military state was still not capable of mounting a sustained challenge to Habsburg authority; if Frederick acted alone in invading Silesia, he did not wait long before seeking allies.

Subsidies, political backing and even military help became available because foreign powers appreciated Prussia's potential in checking their own enemies, not just Austria in the 1740s but also Poland, Denmark and Sweden at various times in the past. This already proved decisive in 1648, when France promoted Brandenburg territorial aims in the Westphalian Settlement despite the fact that it had abandoned the war eight years before. It proved significant in strengthening the electorate relative to its regional rivals, the Guelphs and Saxony, while the acquisition of full sovereignty for East Prussia in 1660 and later the royal title helped set Prussia further apart as a front runner in the race for international recognition. Undoubtedly here Prussia's geographical location helped give it a distinct advantage over Bavaria, the other obvious choice as a counterweight to Austria. Though the scattered Hohenzollern territories lay dangerously close to Sweden, Denmark and Poland, all three were declining or minor European powers, unlike Austria, which was expanding and viewed Bavaria as falling within its immediate sphere of influence.

Important as these factors undoubtedly are, they alone cannot explain the uniquely strong position enjoyed by Prussia in 1740, and for this we must also turn to its place in imperial politics. Like other territories, Prussia had benefited from its membership of the *Reich*, which helped protect its scattered possessions from external attack. Depite periodic frustration with the restrictions that this placed on their freedom of action, the Hohenzollerns needed the *Reich* and could not have survived without it. Their territorial ambitions[2] lay largely within its frontiers, not in the vulnerable kingdom of Poland to the east, and the success of these ambitions, pursued mainly through negotiation rather than aggression, depended on manipulating the existing structure, not overturning it. It is significant that the new university established at Halle in 1694 became a centre for the study of imperial law, just like Hanover's institution in Göttingen.[3]

Indeed, this comparative restraint and adherence to accepted norms gave Prussia a decisive edge over its rivals by preventing it from repeating their mistakes. Repeatedly, pursuit of unrealistic ambitions exhausted or ruined states like Bavaria or the Palatinate, while episodes when Prussia flirted with aggressive policies, such as in the 1651 Cow War, or independent military involvement in 1655–60 and 1675–9, ended in near disaster and indicated the wisdom of further abstinence. In particular, Prussia refrained from dangerous foreign adventures that threatened either to drain a territory dry, like Saxon involvement in Poland, or tie its policies to those of another European power, like Hanover's subordination to England. Perhaps most importantly, Prussia avoided direct confrontation with the emperor despite periodic threats to ally with his enemies, thus denying the Habsburgs a chance to inflict a Blenheim to cut the Hohenzollens down to size while this was still militarily possible. Geography also helped here, as the growing orientation of Habsburg interests to the south and east in Italy and the Balkans left the Hohenzollerns a freer hand in the north, where they capitalized on the constitutional framework, especially the *Kreis* and defence structure, to consolidate their influence over their weaker neighbours. Their inability to reach a compromise with the emperor over their territorial ambitions within the *Reich* proved a short-term setback but a long-term advantage, since it ultimately reinforced their distinctiveness as the leader of the German disaffected. Other rivals were either compromised by their ties to the Habsburgs or too exhausted to mount an effective opposition. Augustus the Strong's conversion to Catholicism and political alliance with Leopold I is just one important example of this, especially as it coincided with the controversy over the Hanoverian electorate and enabled Prussia to assume leadership of the German Protestants.

Finally, a special combination of circumstances left Prussia ideally placed to make its decisive strike in 1740. All immediate threats to its territory had disappeared, since Denmark, Sweden and Poland were all spent forces and Russia was not yet strong enough to pose a real danger. Its German rivals, like Bavaria and Saxony, were largely exhausted, or, in the case of Hanover, neutralized by ties to a foreign crown. Critically, the Habsburgs had never been so weak. In contrast to the 1654–8 crisis, when at least there had been a male heir, Maria Theresa was alone as a woman and the chances of her husband Francis of Lorraine being elected emperor were slim, especially given the resentment at Charles VI's mismanagement of affairs since 1733. The international defeats in Italy and the Balkans had left the monarchy weak and incapable of an immediate effective response. This situation was ideally suited to the nature of the Prussian state as it had been developed by Frederick William I. Incapable of fighting a protracted war on its limited resources, Prussia had created a disproportionately large army, establishing a war machine that was, in Dennis Showalter's words, entirely "front-loaded", that is: geared for a decisive strike to achieve a clear strategic advantage as the basis for negotiations.[4]

Silesia and the Austrian Succession, 1740–48

None of this was fully clear in 1740, when Prussia was very much an unknown quantity. Frederick William's passion for all things military was well known but thought decidedly odd, and indeed may in part stem from his stunted psychological development. The army he had expanded "was of an awkward size", too large for Prussia to be still treated as just another elector-ate, yet too small to sustain a fully independent role.[5] Apart from its brief excursion to the Rhine in 1734, it had had no combat experience since the siege of Stralsund in 1715, and it was far from certain whether it could perform as well in action as on the parade ground.

The new king, Frederick, who succeeded his father on 31 May 1740, was also regarded as a maverick; a view heightened by his decision to keep most of this father's ministers in the dark as to his intentions and to conduct his own foreign policy.[6] His apparent lack of consistency and willingness to switch alliances exceeded the bounds of old regime propriety and surprised even hardened cynical diplomats. Between June and October he tried to sell his alliance to the highest political bidder but was unable to clinch a deal with either France or England since his objectives clashed with theirs. Charles VI's death on 20 October provided an unexpected opportunity. At a meeting with his ministers and generals at Rheinsberg, it was already evident on the 28th that Frederick had made up his mind to attack Silesia. This fateful step sparked considerable controversy, as, even by the standards of the time, Prussia's claim to the province was pretty thin. In contrast to earlier German rulers, dynastic rights and prestige attached to particular pieces of lands mattered little to Frederick, who saw annexations as essential to making Prussia capable of a fully independent foreign policy. Silesia was simply where he could make the best gains at the smallest costs in 1740.[7]

This becomes obvious when we compare Prussian and Austrian military power. Frederick began preparing the invasion on 29 October, but had already started augmenting the army on 23 June, barely a month after his accession. The total increase amounted on paper to 17,654 men by December 1740, to give an official strength of 88,479, of whom 81,792 were actually present. In keeping with a maxim adhered to throughout his reign of sparing Prussia's indigenous resources as far as possible, Frederick sought the additional manpower elsewhere. He exploited the predicament of the lesser territories, whose support for Austria after 1733 led them to raise more men than they could now maintain. Trained soldiers and even entire regiments were transferred directly into the Prussian army from Württemberg, Wolfenbüttel, Eisenach, Ansbach, Gotha and Gottorp by mid-1741, although negotiations failed in Hessen-Darmstadt, Hessen-Kassel, Schwarzburg and Nassau-Usingen. Additional arrangements were made for Prussia to recruit new men to augment the existing units being transferred and to form new ones. Where such attempts met with resistance, as in Württemberg, Prussia used the excuse of pursuing deserters from the transferred units to send covert recruiting parties back to fetch more men. The augmentation was facilitated by Prussia's full treasury and lack of crown debts, factors that also made mobilization and troop concentration possible.[8]

While 29,200 Prussians massed on the Hanoverian frontier to deter intervention, 27,400 crossed into Silesia on 16 December, joined by another 14,100 reinforcements by March 1741.[9] Considering the size of Austria's Silesian garrison, it was like a sledgehammer hitting a nut. The total Habsburg army numbered only 107,892 effectives, or 31.3 per cent below establishment (157,082 men), and although this was still a good 20,000 more than the Prussian army, 60 per cent of manpower was still deployed in Hungary and Transylvania, following the recent war with the Turks. Garrisons in the hereditary lands were strengthened in the course of 1740, as were those in Italy and the Netherlands, but even with reinforcements there were only 7,359 men in Silesia by mid-December. The overall condition of the army was poor, and Silesian defences had suffered from years of neglect, when scarce resources were diverted to meet more pressing threats elsewhere. The commander of one fortress even feared to use his cannon in case the wall collapsed under the concussion of artillery fire.

Under these conditions it was scarcely surprising that Silesia was quickly overrun, except for detachments holding out in Neisse and Brieg. General Neipperg, rehabilitated after the debacle against the Turks, assembled an army of 18,000 men, including many raw recruits, and skilfully dodged Frederick in Upper Silesia to appear at his rear. Having relieved Neisse, Neipperg headed for Brieg, where he could cut Frederick's communications with Brandenburg, forcing the king to turn about and head north to meet him. The two armies were evenly matched when they met on a field of snow at Mollwitz on 10 April 1741, for although Frederick had more men (21,600), his cavalry were decidedly inferior and broke under the weight of the Austrian attack. The king fled the scene, leaving Schwerin, the former Mecklenburg general, now a Prussian field marshal, to save the day, driving the Austrians from the field with the steady fire of the Prussian infantry and light artillery.

The battle did not destroy Austria's field army, and the Prussians actually suffered higher casualties than their opponents, but the engagement proved highly significant. Neipperg's defeat ensured that "Mollwitz would not be another Mühlberg, White Mountain or Blenheim".[10] The reverse at the hands of an upstart German vassal was a major blow to Habsburg prestige, exposing the extent of the monarchy's military decline at a critical time, and by late 1741 France had moved over to backing Bavaria, Saxon and Spanish designs on other parts of the Austrian inheritance.[11] Prussian power was correspondingly magnified, particularly as Mollwitz was the first major battle won exclusively by a Prussian army since Fehrbellin in 1675, and indeed represented a more convincing victory, as the bulk of the Swedish army had remained unengaged in that action. Frederick's political credibility was confirmed and he was courted as an alliance partner by the wider anti–Habsburg coalition, beginning with the Franco-Prussian treaty of 4 June, whereby the king traded his backing for Bavaria's imperial ambitions in return for French recognition of his "claims" to Silesia.

Frederick would gladly have reversed course and rejected Franco-Bavarian offers, if he could have persuaded Maria Theresa to accept the loss of at least part of Silesia. Though the offer of Prussian recognition of the rest of her inheritance, along with military support to defend it, was tempting, she consistently refused any *rapprochement* with Frederick. Not only did she come to regard him as her personal enemy but any concession over Silesia would undermine the principle of the Pragmatic Sanction, which guaranteed her inheritance in its entirety, and so simply invite further extortion from other powers. Her intransigence compelled Frederick to continue the war, consolidating his hold on both Upper and Lower Silesia as well as the adjacent county of Glatz by 1742. The increasingly desperate situation elsewhere forced Maria Theresa to concede their loss in return for a Prussian withdrawal from the wider struggle over her inheritance, but growing suspicion of Austrian revanchism following her alliance with England, Sardinia and Saxony (Treaty of Worms, 1743) prompted Frederick to renew hostilities in 1744. After a disastrous invasion of Bohemia, Prussia scored convincing victories over the Austro-Saxon forces at Hohenfriedberg and Kesselsdorf in 1745, leading to international recognition of his new possessions in the Treaty of Dresden on 25 December.

It is not the intention of this work to follow these events in detail, particularly as they are well covered elsewhere, but to turn instead to the neglected aspect of their impact on imperial politcs. The Prussian invasion of Silesia represented a breach of imperial law and political culture, and the fact that it went unpunished did serious damage to the *Reich*. A crucial factor in Prussia's success was the initial paralysis and subsequent weakness of the key institutions intended to prevent such violent and arbitrary action. Charles VI's death was followed by a long interregnum until the election of the Bavarian Elector, Carl Albrecht, as Charles VII in January 1742. His brief and traumatic reign, which ended in his premature death in January 1745, saw the escalation of Austro-Prussian hostilities into German civil war, as both powers sought to mobilize *Reich* resources for their objectives. Imperial paralysis was associated with and exacerbated by a further internationalization of German affairs, as the controversy over Silesia and Charles VII's election coincided with renewed Anglo-French hostility. England and Spain were already at war since 1739 over colonial issues, with the latter being joined by France a year later, though a formal declaration of war did not come until 1744. Given England's ties to Hanover and France's decision to back Bavaria, it was obvious that these tensions would manifest themselves within the *Reich*.

As the following will show, the traditional structure proved remarkably resilient, assisted by the widespread opposition of the lesser territories to both the German and the European wars. The *Reich* remained formally at peace, refusing to mobilize either in support of Charles VII's private war against Austria in 1742–5 or Austria's continued struggle against France thereafter. However, Charles VII's weak rule and Austria's growing self-reliance left traditional institutions severely weakened and less able to resist later attempts to subvert them to particularist ends.

The interregnum of 1740–42 saw the first serious challenge to the Habsburg monopoly of the imperial office by a German contender since the late middle ages. However, it was clear from the outset that the situation was being manipulated by France, which played on the widespread disillusionment with the traditional ruling dynasty left by Charles VI's reverses. While many were prepared to support a change of dynasty, few wanted this if it meant war with Austria, and most hoped to preserve the territorial *status quo* as the best guarantee for peace. Hanover led the way in calling for backing for the *Reichstag*'s earlier endorsement of the Pragmatic Sanction to preserve Austria intact, even if the imperial title passed to Bavaria. Though England paid subsidies to Austria from June 1741, fear for Hanoverian security precluded a more active imperial policy, particularly as 40,000 French moved into Westphalia to threaten the electorate from the west, reinforcing the danger still posed by the Prussians to the east.

The neutralization of Hanover was important since it was still a major military power. Its forces had escaped serious damage in the campaigns of 1733–9 and numbered 19,442 at Charles VI's death. British subsidies assisted in augmenting the army by a further 5,814 by 1742, in addition to hiring 12,000 Danes and Hessians, while 12,000 English troops arrived in the Austrian Netherlands. These forces (less the Danes who were recalled) formed

250

the basis of the so-called Pragmatic army, established by 1742 to uphold Austrian territorial integrity.[12] Redeployment of the French from Westphalia, as well as Prussia's temporary withdrawal from the war in 1742, made direct Anglo-Hanoverian intervention possible. However, the inner German and wider European situation prevented a reconstruction of the old Grand Alliance, while Britain remained weaker than during the War of the Spanish Succession, unable to gain a decisive military preponderance despite naval and colonial victories.

Sardinia was persuaded to assist Austria in Italy, but the Franco-Spanish effort there was superior to that of 1733–5, and it proved difficult to hold the line even with the additional forces. Crucially, the Dutch, who had guaranteed the Pragmatic Sanction, failed to join either Britain or Austria, and although they provided auxiliaries to reinforce the Barrier garrisons, they remained reluctant participants even after the French attacked the Austrian Netherlands in 1744. Britain's weakness was exposed by the French-sponsored Jacobite rising of 1745–6, which forced the Hanoverian regime to recall units from the Netherlands, paving the way for a successful French invasion of the Dutch Republic in 1747.[13]

These difficulties restricted Anglo-Hanoverian intervention in the *Reich* to one direct effort in 1743, when George II personally led the Pragmatic army south to the river Main in an expedition that very nearly came to grief at Dettingen on 27 June. Though the combined Anglo-Hanoverian Austrian forces managed to beat off French attacks, the narrow margin of victory ensured that this action was no Blenheim, and Bavaria continued to contest Maria Theresa's inheritance. Similarly, British financial aid in 1741–8, although significant in preventing a total Austrian collapse, was insufficient to secure a decisive Habsburg victory. Increasingly, the monarchy was thrown back on its own resources, particularly those in Hungary and the military border, which contributed to an unprecedented extent.[14]

The Habsburg's loss of the imperial title compounded the lack of firm support from their traditional German and foreign allies, making it even harder to mobilize assistance from within the *Reich*. Once Charles VII had been formally elected, German military assistance became impossible, since support for Austria automatically placed a territory in opposition to its formal overlord. While opposing his claims to Habsburg territory, even Hanover voted for the Wittelsbach emperor and remained formally at peace with Bavaria.

Nonetheless, the desire for peace was such that few were prepared to take advantage of Austria's predicament. Apart from Prussia and Hanover, five territories had sufficient forces to play a role in events. With just over 5,000 men, Wolfenbüttel was the weakest and was linked diplomatically and dynastically to both Austria and Prussia as well as Hanover and so had no wish to get involved. The Palatinate had not participated in the disastrous Turkish war and still had a respectable 8,390 soldiers in 1740, but was on poor terms with Bavaria, feared Prussian designs on Jülich-Berg and was reliant on French diplomatic and financial aid. Clemens August of Cologne-Münster was similarly ill-placed to pursue an active policy, with his army and finances ruined by the policies of 1733–9. He remained suspicious of his elder brother, particularly after his election as emperor, and detested his ties to Protestant Prussia. French diplomacy secured both Wittelsbachs in the crucial period of the interregnum. Fresh subsidies enabled an increase in the Palatine army to 11,532 by 1742, while that of Cologne-Münster also rose to about 10,000, helping to intimidate Hanover and secure Charles VII's election. However, both refrained from giving Bavaria direct aid at this stage, while Clemens August permitted the transit of the Pragmatic army through his territories during 1742–3.[15]

Saxony, by contrast, was prepared to challenge Austria, abandoning its earlier alliance and laying claim to parts of the Habsburg inheritance. Yet Saxony was decisively outmanoeuvred by Prussia, for Frederick's invasion of Silesia represented not only an Austrian defeat but sealed the Hohenzollern ascendancy over the Wettins. Silesia was vital to the survival of Wettin great power ambitions, as it represented a potential land bridge between Poland and the electorate, and its loss to the rising northern rival removed the last hope of establishing Wettin absolutism in Warsaw. Critically, Saxony was in no position to compete for it, having still not recovered from first obtaining and then defending its hold on the Polish crown. Participation in the Turkish war further weakened the army, which stood at only 20,000 effectives in December 1740. It took almost a year to add another 7,800 regulars and 8,000 mobilized militia by the time Saxony entered the war alongside Bavaria and Prussia in October 1741.

By then the Prussian army was over three times as large, securing all of Silesia by July 1742 and effectively removing the reason for Saxon involvement in the war. The setback was compounded by a disastrous change of tack when Saxony reversed its alliance, providing auxiliaries to Austria in the hope of making gains from Prussia. The army was augmented to an unprecedented 45,323 by 1743, but since the Prussians now had 127,567 under arms, this merely underlined the futility of Wettin aspirations. Prussian superiority was already demonstrated in October 1744, when 60,000 troops marched through the electorate on their way to invade Bohemia as Frederick re-entered the war. Though the king's men were ostensibly "imperial auxiliaries" of Charles VII and nominally complied with transit regulations by formally requesting right of passage, they crossed the Saxon frontier without waiting for a reply.

The Saxon auxiliary corps with the Austrians shared in their defeats at Soor and Hohenfriedberg, while the state could not sustain the high level of mobilization, forcing effective strength down to 25,000. Prince Leopold von Anhalt-Dessau and a second Prussian army formally invaded the electorate in December 1745, inflicting a major defeat on its army at Kesselsdorf and occupying the capital. Prussia already showed signs of treating Saxony as a potential resource base, forcibly inducting 1,600 militiamen into its army, prefiguring more extensive exploitation during the Seven Years War.[16]

Prussian preponderance was further emphasized by Bavaria's poor performance, something that not only gave Frederick the chance to strike at Silesia unencumbered by competition, but also indicated that Wittelsbach imperial rule was seriously underresourced. Charles VII's reign undermined imperial authority and prestige because he lacked the means to sustain his new dignity, and he only made matters worse by clinging to territorial ambitions even when these were no longer realistic. As elector he had made some improvement to the Bavarian fiscal–military state, reducing the debt he inherited from Max Emanuel from 26.4 million fl. to 19.9 million fl. by 1741, despite the intervening costly mobilization during the 1730s. Yet this obscured the real damage done to the Bavarian army, particularly during the Turkish War, cutting effective regular forces from 17,960 in 1736 to under 9,000 by 1740. Mobilization in 1741 resembled a complete new foundation of the army, and the time it consumed forced the repeated postponements of the planned attack on Austria. The total strength was raised to 20,880 backed by 17,000 militia thanks to a huge injection of French aid in 1741–5, amounting to 8.8 million fl. Though 1.5 million fl. of extra funds was found from Bavaria, and a *Reichstag* grant brought another 1.6 million fl., ordinary annual revenue stood at only 1.9 million fl., whereas the army cost over 4.6 million fl. in 1742 alone. As a result total Bavarian forces rarely exceeded 20,000, including militia, leaving Charles VII dependent on French military assistance throughout his brief reign.[17]

Offensive operations only got under way in autumn 1741, with the arrival of French troops in Bavaria itself. Upper Austria was quickly overrun, followed by most of Bohemia, including Prague on 26 November, and both provinces recognized Charles VII as their new territorial sovereign. The decision to turn north to Bohemia rather than push directly east to Vienna has been criticized as a missed opportunity, but the idea that the invaders were capable of delivering the Habsburgs a knockout blow rather overestimates Franco-Bavarian power. Like the Prussian invasion of Silesia, the rapidity of their advance derived less from their own capacity than the absence of serious opposition. However, whereas Frederick had the strength to defeat a Habsburg counterattack, Charles VII had no staying power, and there was to be no Bavarian version of Mollwitz. A weak Austrian thrust was already able to recover Upper Austria in December, pushing on into Bavaria itself, while other forces advanced into Bohemia. Bavarian defeats underlined the weakness of Wittelsbach imperial rule, beginning with the surrender of the garrison in Linz on the very day of Charles's election as emperor (24 January 1742).[18]

Such setbacks seriously compromised the new emperor's attempts to capitalize on the groundswell of support within the *Reich*. His election was seen as a significant break with the past, raising the hopes of those lesser territories that had felt marginalized by the growth of Austria as an European power and the rise of the larger armed princes. Over 50 princes personally attended Charles VII's coronation, while imperial cities and counts who had long neglected *Reichstag* attendance now sent representation. The grant of 50 RMs in November 1742 exceeded the sums normally voted without a formal *Reichskrieg*, and 73 per cent was actually paid within a year, including exceptionally high amounts from the bigger territories, which were generally in arrears. Though Prussia's contribution derived from Frederick's highly partisan support for the new emperor, that of the others reflected their genuine commitment to the imperial ideal.[19]

These hopes were cruelly disappointed. The lack of a convincing Bavarian military victory deprived Charles VII of any chance of real independence. He was never able to escape from his politicized election, where the Bohemian (i.e. Habsburg) vote had been excluded, contravening the 1708 constitutional agreement. As a result, Maria Theresa refused to acknowledge the validity of his election or hand over the imperial archive in Vienna. The Austrian invasion of Bavaria in February 1742 forced Charles VII to relocate the *Reichstag* to Frankfurt, where it reopened on 27 April. This was worse than humiliating, since both Austria and the imperial city of Regensburg protested, encouraging several territories to retain their representatives in the traditional venue, thereby undermining the authority of the new institution. Moreover, Charles VII was bound by a particularly severe electoral capitulation restricting his political autonomy. The traditional obligation to recover Alsace was dropped out of deference to France, while the unwelcome presence of French troops serving as "imperial auxiliaries" provided a further reminder of his dependency.

As a weak emperor, Charles VII had no choice but to resort to expedients in his efforts to mobilize *Reich* support for his war against Austria and to compensate Bavaria for its inability to make territorial gains. For instance, in 1742 he restored Saxon overlordship over Reuss, Schwarzburg and Schönberg in return for continued Wettin military support, thus threatening the fragile political autonomy of these three weak Thuringian territories.[20] Worse, Charles VII was the first emperor seriously to consider mass secularizations in a scheme which threatened to destroy a key pillar of the traditional order. Suggested by Frederick, who was keen to broker an Austro-Bavarian compromise that would leave him with undisputed possession of Silesia, the plan would have involved Bavarian annexation of six south German bishoprics, including Augsburg. The idea was opposed by the pope and quickly leaked by Habsburg diplomats, who lost no time in exploiting its propaganda potential. Not surprisingly, Wittelsbach influence never recovered, and Bavarian candidates were defeated in crucial elections to the sees of Mainz, Speyer, Constance and Basel in 1743. The defeat in Mainz was particularly serious given this electorate's role as the traditional spokesman for the lesser territories. The successful Austrian candidate, Ostein, fulfilled a pre-election promise to Mara Theresa by formally tabling protests at Charles VII's election in the *Reichstag* on 23 September 1743. Now even the emperor's title seemed in doubt.[21]

Under these conditions, Bavarian hopes for a full *Reichskrieg* against Austria were unrealistic. Indeed, pursuit of a war by an emperor against a territory that had not formally breached imperial law placed existing institutions under great strain. Initially both Austria and Bavaria had looked to the *Kreis* structure as a framework to mobilize support, with Maria Theresa hoping to reactivate the Association. Late in 1740 Austria appealed as an Association member for help against Prussia. The then elector of Mainz, Philipp Carl von Eltz, did call for a congress to discuss the situation, but the response from the others was lukewarm at best. Friedrich Carl von Schönborn, the influential bishop of Würzburg and Bamberg struck a popular chord when he sought to steer any activation of the Association into a vehicle for armed neutrality. This was also favoured by Württemberg, then still governed by a regency that was compromised by its earlier decision to transfer troops to the Prussian army, and it proved easy for the elector Palatine to block the congresses scheduled for May and July 1741. Absence of a united front compelled the individual *Kreise* to make their own arrangements. Swabia and Franconia mobilized a triple quota of *Kreistruppen*, collectively amounting to over 13,000 men, in June 1741 to maintain their integrity, but simultaneously compromised their neutrality by agreeing vital transit rights for France in treaties brokered by Prussia.[22] As before, neutrality favoured the aggressor, since south German compliance with Franco-Prussian demands permitted the passage of the troops needed by Charles VII to invade Austria.

Increasingly it seemed imperial politics were being decided on the battle-fields of Bohemia and Silesia. Austrian defeats forced Eltz to abandon efforts to mobilize the Association for Maria Theresa and to vote for Charles VII. When the congress finally convened on 10 February 1742, it did so because Bavaria now wanted it as the basis for a potential *Reichsarmee* against Austria. The Austrian *Kreis* was naturally not invited, leaving Maria Theresa to agitate for a separate meeting, yet this was now clearly impossible, since any backing for her meant automatic opposition to the emperor. The break up of the Association only heightened Vienna's general frustration with the unsuitability of existing structures for advancing dynastic objectives: in their hour of need the *Reich* had nothing to offer the Habsburgs.

It was perhaps some small comfort that it also proved unresponsive to Wittelsbach demands. Charles VII cultivated favour amongst the weaker counts, elevating no fewer than 15 to princely status in 1742–3, but concrete support remained disappointing. The Thurn und Taxis and Öttingen families both raised dragoon regiments for the Bavarian army, as did the estates of Liège, while the imperial counts provided 1,600 infantry. A number of aristocrats defected from Austrian service, including Count Seckendorff, who also raised his own regiment. More significant aid came from Hessen-Kassel and the Palatinate, which provided 3,040 and 3,600 auxiliaries respectively from 1742, yet these were only secured by further potentially dangerous concessions, including the promise of a new Hessian electorate. Moreover, all efforts to obtain formal constitutional help failed miserably. Charles VII ordered the mobilization of all *Kreis* contingents on 28 February 1743 as a preliminary step to a full *Reichsarmee*. However, despite efforts of supporters like Öttingen-Spielberg, he was unable to obtain *Reichstag* sanction for offensive use of these forces, and the Swabians were able to reply to his demands for aid by claiming that they had already complied by mobilizing the forces to uphold their neutrality. Though Bavarian troops did occupy Philippsburg, which served as a bridgehead for French aid, they were denied access to Kehl, Mainz and other key installations, which remained garrisoned by *Kreistruppen* and territorial contingents.[23]

Just as the earlier passivity served Franco-Bavarian aggression in 1740–42, the current neutrality favoured Austria and its allies once these gained the upper hand in 1743. The Bavarians were expelled completely from their homeland in 1743, while active Anglo-Hanoverian involvement further isolated the emperor's supporters in the north. The new pro-Habsburg elector of Mainz was won over to an Anglo-Dutch alliance on 27 April 1744, receiving subsidies to strengthen his garrison to 5,000 men. That day a similar agreement was clinched with Clemens August of Cologne, extended on 4 July for his bishopric of Münster to cover a total of 10,000 troops. Following a French attempt at intimidation by plundering parts of the Rhineland, a conference was held at Bonn that agreed to the defensive mobilization of Westphalia to prevent either France or Prussia from spreading the war to north Germany, where it could threaten Hanover.[24]

These setbacks prompted France and Prussia to come to Charles VII's aid by sponsoring a new princely league known as the Frankfurt Union, which was established on 22 May 1744. Though it was dedicated to the recovery of Bavaria from temporary Austrian occupation, this league had little in common with earlier groupings, which had been intended to uphold the IPO. Instead it was a tactical grouping of Bavaria, Prussia, Hessen-Kassel and the Palatinate underwritten by secret French support, intended to advance their political ambitions, including a Hessian electorate, secularizations, annexations of imperial cities and a joint Prusso-Bavarian partition of Bohemia. Bankrolled by France, Bavaria renewed its agreements with Hessen-Kassel and the Palatinate, whereby both raised their auxiliaries to 9,000 and 5,078 respectively.[25] These assisted in the recovery of Bavaria later in 1744, but proved incapable of withstanding a new Austrian attack at the beginning of 1745. As his forces began another retreat, Charles VII died on 20 January, and his successor Elector Max III Joseph was forced to recognize the impossibility of his ambitions and sign the Treaty of Füssen 22 April, abandoning the war against Austria.[26]

The coincidence of Bavaria's collapse with Charles VII's death greatly strengthened the Habsburg position in the *Reich*. Austria ruthlessly exploited its temporary military preponderance and access to Anglo-Dutch funding to force the new Bavarian government into contributing 4,700 auxiliaries to the campaigns in the Netherlands during 1746–8 and to voting for the Habsburg imperial candidate, Francis Stephen. Max Joseph was persuaded to use his constitutional powers as imperial vicar in the new interregnum to order the western *Kreise* to deploy their troops to protect Frankfurt, venue of the new election, from potential French attacks. The Upper Rhinelanders, along with the Swabians, Franconians and Westphalians, moved their troops into position as the French advanced from the west. However, no serious attempt was made to disrupt the proceedings, and Augustus III of Saxony, the French candidate, knew he stood no chance and cast his lot along with Bavaria, Hanover, Mainz, Trier, Cologne and Bohemia for Francis on 13 September. Only Prussia and the Palatinate opposed the election, and even Frederick refused a French request to lodge a formal protest, acknowledging the Austrian victory as a *fait accompli*.

Meanwhile, Austria exploited the discomfiture of Charles VII's former supporters to extract additional help against France. Most Palatine troops managed to escape the Bavarian collapse, but 3,000 Hessian were captured at Vilshofen on 28 March, and their commander was obliged to intern these along with his other troops in Ingolstadt. Landgrave Wilhelm VIII waited until the formal expiry of his agreement with Bavaria before bowing to Austrian pressure to sign a new agreement with the maritime powers on 16 June for another 6,000 men to defend the Netherlands.[27]

However, the new emperor proved no more successful than his predecessor in persuading the *Reich* to sanction a formal effort. Under pressure from England to do more against France, Francis called for a triple quota mobilization on 14 October, the day after the *Reichstag* reopened in Regensburg. He also summoned an Association congress for 20 October in an effort to ensure that at least the most active *Kreise* contributed. Bavaria was obliged by the Treaty of Füssen to assist these efforts but deliberately encouraged the general aversion to renewed war with France. Württemberg, which feared for its dependency of Mömpelgard, surrounded by French territory, also blocked the revival of the Association. The Bavarian *Kreis* Assembly meeting at Wasserburg in February 1746 was seen as a test case for Austria's proposals. The *Kreis* did agree to the triple quota, but only sanctioned its deployment within its own frontiers, pending a final *Reichstag* decision. This provided a welcome element of delay, quickly exploited by France, which wanted to neutralize the *Reich*, especially as Prussia had also left the war in December 1745. France returned to the old expedient of building a loose block around Prussia, Bavaria, Saxony, Cologne, Württemberg and the Palatinate as a Third Party to campaign for peace. Saxony led the way by a bilateral treaty of neutrality with France on 21 April 1746, followed by the recall of its remaining auxiliaries from Austrian service. Various agreements and dynastic marriages strengthened the ties between Prussia, Bavaria, Saxony, the Palatinate and Württemberg by 1747, but this proved insufficient to prevent Austria from browbeating the lesser territories in Franconia, Swabia and the Upper Rhine into establishing an alliance on 7 February 1747 into which Austria was admitted some three weeks later. Constance led the pro-Habsburg elements of Swabia into a new congress in spring 1748, leading to a formal renewal of the Association on 1 March as a perpetual alliance. It was an empty victory, since it was achieved on the condition that the Association remained neutral in the present war, stalling all attempts to mobilize a *Reichsarmee* for aggressive action.[28]

If attempts to raise troops through the formal constitutional structure failed, clarification of imperial politics after 1745 did permit a number of territories to enter the war as auxiliaries of the Dutch. The French had overrun most of the Austrian Netherlands by 1747 and invaded the Dutch Republic on 17 April. Dutch resistance collapsed almost completely, triggering a coup that brought the stadholder William IV to power. The Dutch had sought German auxiliaries in times of crisis since 1665, but the uncertain situation during Wittelsbach imperial rule discouraged princes from responding to their requests, and both Ansbach and Hessen-Darmstadt rejected subsidy offers in 1742–3. Only Waldeck, which refused to abandon Austria and had long ties to the Republic, consented, and its prince even served as Dutch field commander from 1745.[29] In contrast, many were now pleased to answer William IV's call for reinforcements, since the Dutch were no longer associated with the enemies of the emperor. Princes like the landgrave of Hessen-Darmstadt wanted to demonstrate their loyalty to the Habsburgs without provoking France, and justified their support for the Dutch on the grounds the Republic was waging a defensive war. Many were also concerned at the growth of Austrian and Prussian forces and saw Dutch finance as a means to sustain their identity by increasing their own establishments (Table 7.1).

Table 7.1 German auxiliaries for the Dutch, 1742–8

Territory	Treaty	Contingent	Fate
Waldeck	1742	1,624 ⎫	Two-thirds retained as part of
	1744	812 ⎭	Dutch army
Gotha	1744	3,600	One-third retained
Bavaria	1746	4,698	1,500 transferred to Austria 1749, rest returned
Würzburg	1747	1,600 ⎫	
Hessen-Kassel	1747	3,040 ⎬	Returned 1749
Hessen-Darmstadt	1747	1,620 ⎭	
Hildburghausen	1747	812	Remained part of Dutch army
Wied	1747	812 ⎫	Retained and combined with the
Solms	1747	812 ⎭	Baden-Durlach rgt as brigade
Wartensleben	1747	812 ⎫	Oranien-Nassau 1752
Kirchberg	1747	812 ⎭	
Schwarzburg	1748	812	Transferred to Prussia, 1755
Wolfenbüttel	1748	4,901	Returned 1749
Baden-Durlach	1748	812 ⎫	Remained part of Dutch army
Baden-Baden	1748	812 ⎭	
Total		28,391	

Sources: STAD, A6 Nr. 1425; E8B260–64; HSAS, A202: Bü. 2298; C14: Bü 586; Tessin, *Regimenter*, pp. 572–3; Hagen, "Würzburgische Hausinfanterie . . . 1636–1756", pp. 193–7; Elster, *Braunschweig-Wolfenbüttel*, vol. II, pp. 113–22; Schmid, *Max III Joseph*, pp. 193–4, 234–5.

Note: Apart from 1 Gotha dragoon rgt all were infantry and attached light artillery.

Although the auxiliaries saved the Republic, they were of little direct help to Austria, which remained beleaguered by France and Spain. As nothing could be expected from the *Reich*, Maria Theresa fell back on her father's alliance with Russia, which was renewed in 1747 and led to a repeat of the intervention of 1735. In February 1748 35,000 Russians advanced through Poland and Bohemia as far as Kulmbach in Franconia in an operation financed by the maritime powers. The demonstration improved Austria's bargaining position at the peace conference that had now opened at Aachen, but also reinforced the growing importance of Russia to imperial politics.[30] Major operations had ceased, as all the belligerents were exhausted and no longer believed they would achieve their objectives on the battlefield. The Peace of Aix-la-Chapelle (Aachen) officially ended the war in October, essentially confirming the prewar *status quo* except with regard to Austria. Prussian possession of Silesia was confirmed, as were the Spanish gains of Parma and Piacenza in Imperial Italy. Austria was also obliged to cede a further slice of Milan to Sardinia as a reward for its wartime support. The Italian buffer built by Leopold I and Joseph I was thus further eroded, compounding the losses of 1733–5, but the loss of Silesia, recognized officially by the *Reichstag* in 1751, was far more critical and had a lasting impact on German politics.

The Reich *in the reversal of alliances, 1748–56*

The war had a profound affect on the *Reich*'s internal equilibrium, confirming that Bavaria, Saxony, the Palatinate and Hanover were no longer major German powers. The first three had been weakened by their involvement, while the crisis of 1740–2 exposed Hanover as a liability for Britain rather than an active participant in its own right. Moreover, not only had the loss of Silesia forced Habsburg political gravity further south, but Prussian predominance in the north had been reinforced through its inheritance of East Frisia on the death of its last legitimate prince in 1744. The need to integrate the new provinces into the Prussian monarchy as well as to defend Silesia against potential Austrian revenge stimulated the process of territorialization and with it separation of the Hohenzollern kingdom from the *Reich*. This had been boosted by a series of concessions wrung from Charles VII in return for Prussian support. The Wittelsbach emperor had agreed to recognize Frederick as "majesty", placing him on equal footing with foreign monarchs, as well as ending imperial interference in ennoblements within his domains, leaving the king free to dispense his own patronage without external restraint.[31]

Prussia's new status was reflected in its international position, where it replaced Bavaria as the lynchpin of French imperial policy. France had been badly affected by the war and its own inability to reform, while the poor performance of its troops in Germany, especially during their precipitous retreats in 1744–5, had reduced its standing in the *Reich*. Sponsorship of unreliable allies was stopped, and although Cologne and the Palatinate received new subsidies, payments to Bavaria were broken off in March 1750. French diplomacy became a form of power sharing with Prussia, as Louis XIV's ministers sought to use Prussian prestige and clientele to rebuild their own influence. Prussia mediated a number of agreements, including arrangements for financial compensation for the damage done in 1744–5, in pointed contrast to Austria, which left countless bills unpaid from its transit through south Germany in 1743.[32]

Prussian imperial policy became increasingly distinctive as a result, taking its place alongside Frederick's international manoeuvring as part of his general search for security against Austria. Far from disengaging from the *Reich*, Prussia remained active at all its political levels, but now operated from a position of autonomy and strength previously only enjoyed by the Habsburgs. In addition to territorial consolidation in the north, Prussian influence increasingly penetrated the south, displacing that of the Habsburgs in areas that had been traditional imperial preserves. For example, Frederick replaced the emperor as the guarantor of political stability at local and territorial levels in many areas, acting in his capacity as *de facto* leader of the *corpus evangelicorum*. Prussia confirmed local agreements (*Reversalien*) in Hessen-Kassel and Württemberg, protecting the rights of Protestant inhabitants when members of the ruling dynasty converted to Catholicism. It also brokered the Weimar–Eisenach regency crisis of 1748 and imposed the final settlement in the Mecklenburg constitutional dispute 1755. Prussia rather than the emperor arranged the 1752 treaty regulating the mutual, inheritance of Ansbach and Bayreuth, paving the way for the accession of the former to the latter in 1769. A similar agreement was brokered between Catholic Baden-Baden and Protestant Baden-Durlach in 1766, leading to their transference to a single margrave five years later. Dynastic ties were also strengthened, especially with Wolfenbüttel, Bayreuth and Württemberg to extend Prussia's regional influence into areas where it did not hold territory. These clients were carefully chosen to balance Habsburg adherents, with Anhalt and Ernestine Saxons acting as counterweights to electoral Saxony and Schwarzburg in Upper Saxony, Ansbach and Bayreuth, balancing Würzburg and Bamberg in Franconia, and Württemberg and Baden-Durlach facing the Swabian Catholics in the southwest.[33]

Although Prussia was copying methods traditionally associated with Habsburg imperial leadership, its policy was essentially negative. Prussian defence rested primarily on its own army and alliance with France, and Frederick's interest in the imperial constitution was limited to its use in restraining Austria rather than protecting his own lands. He saw no advantage in collective security, since his principal opponent lay within the system, and he certainly did not favour reform or innovation, since these merely threatened to enmesh himself as well as Maria Theresa. His highly partisan support was thus restricted to sustaining constitutional immobility as long as this served Prussian security.

As Prussian policy became more imperial and German, that of Austria became more dynastic and European. The experience of 1740–45 had been a severe blow, not just in terms of territorial losses, but in the desertion of traditional clients to the Wittelsbach cause. The imperial dignity recovered with Francis's election was no longer that which had been lost in 1740, while the re-establishment of Spanish satellites in northern Italy by 1748 undermined the network of imperial fiefs that had been consolidated since the time of Leopold I.[34] As in the case of Prussia, the shock of war accelerated the process of territorialization and with it separation from the *Reich*, altering the rough balance between imperial and dynastic interests that had sustained the recovery of the emperor's authority into the 1720s.

The imperial recovery, and with it Habsburg territorial power, had rested on manipulating possibilities offered by the existing political framework. This had bound Austria to the imperial constitution and a socially conservative client group within both Germany and the hereditary lands,[35] inhibiting the reforms necessary to unlock Habsburg resources, which had grown in the meantime through acquisition of additional land outside the *Reich*. Defeat in 1740–42 indicated that Austria could no longer rely on this system to save it in a crisis, and a new direction became obvious by 1748. The reforms associated with Minister Haugwitz were essentially traditionalist in that they sought to modify the existing territorial structure by renegotiating tax agreement with the estates, yet they also contained a modernizing element that became increasingly pronounced after the accession of Joseph II as emperor and co-regent of Austria with Maria Theresa in 1765. Once Joseph assumed full personal rule on his mother's death in 1780, the reform process became increasingly radical, spreading to a sustained attack on traditional privileges in the interests of increased state fiscal–military extraction. This disturbed the domestic consensus between the regime and its traditional clients among the elite, as well as encouraging popular hopes for wider social reforms that territorial absolutism was incapable of delivering.[36]

A similar disregard for established rules began to characterize Austria's policy within the *Reich*, as the dynastic imperative of recovering Silesia came to the fore. Rather than working within the existing structure as their predecessors had done, Maria Theresa and her husband simply tried to neutralize it to be free for their revenge against Prussia. In turn, this affected the emperor's international position, as the new direction was opposed by the Anglo-Hanoverian desire to sustain the *status quo*. British ministers were still trying to return to the Old System of an Anglo–Dutch–Austrian alliance to be modified by the inclusion of Russia to counterbalance Prussia. The Dutch reluctantly agreed to participate in order to preserve their influence in north-west Germany, and George II confidently floated a scheme in 1750 designed to secure the Habsburg hold on the imperial title by promoting the election of Archduke Joseph as king of the Romans. France and Prussia responded with countermeasures leading to intense Anglo-French competition for German clients, raising false hopes among the medium and lesser princes of a renewed opportunity to benefit from international tension. However, without a viable framework for a Third Party they were unable to improve their position, as both France and Britain stuck to bilateral arrangements where they retained the advantage. Though a new injection of foreign cash enabled them to rebuild their armies, they were left dependent on their foreign sponsors.[37]

The entire episode was an embarrassment for the Austrian government, which had only gone along with the proposal reluctantly, rightly predicting that it would stir up resentments and leave the emperor isolated. Worse, George's intentions were clearly out of step with Maria Theresa's, who, far from wishing to preserve the *status quo*, wanted to revise it to Prussia's disadvantage. The result was a gradual *rapprochement* with France, under way from 1749, which led to the famous reversal of alliances of 1754–6.[38]

The outbreak of a colonial conflict with France in America in 1754 renewed British fears for Hanoverian security and prompted the response first used in 1726 of contracting German territories to hold men in readiness. Following agreements with Hessen-Kassel, Ansbach and Würzburg, the Convention of Westminster was signed with Prussia on 16 January 1756 as a logical step to prevent a repeat of the twin Franco-Prussian threat of 1740–41.[39] Prussia's apparent defection to Britain convinced France of Frederick's unreliability and removed remaining doubts about the wisdom of an Austrian alliance. A defensive agreement was made at Versailles on 1 May 1756, whereby both promised 24,000 troops should the other be attacked by a third party. This has rightly been described as an "asymmetrical alliance" since the current colonial war was excluded with Austria only obliged to assist France if it was attacked by a continental power.[40] The treaty secured the Habsburg

Achilles heel in the Netherlands, leaving Austria free to concentrate on Prussia.

Kaunitz, the minister directing Austria's foreign policy, was already pushing to extract further advantage by converting the defensive arrangement into an offensive alliance to be extended to include Russia and Sweden for a joint partition of the Prussian monarchy. Here, however, imperial politics tended to slow the pace, as neither Austria or France wished to damage its standing in the *Reich* by appearing the aggressor. France was still bound to Prussia by its treaty of 1741, which had been renewed for ten years on 29 May 1747, and wanted to wait until this had expired. Austria also delayed, beginning military preparations but avoiding provocative troop concentrations near the Silesian frontier, since it was essential that Frederick be placed in the wrong if the emperor was to stand any chance of mobilizing German resources against him.[41]

The Seven Years War, 1756–63

Prussia obliged its opponents by invading Saxony on 29 August 1756, initiating a second German civil war. As in the case of Silesia, this clear breach of the public peace proved highly controversial. Frederick harboured annexationist plans, recommending in his secret political testament of 1752 that Prussia acquire Saxony, Mecklenburg, Ansbach, Bayreuth and Swedish Pomerania. However, these considerations were not at the forefront of his mind in 1756, as the king was now caught up in the inescapable logic of the events he had helped set in motion since his accession: he had to fight to retain Silesia. Hopes that he could avoid war altogether evaporated when he learnt that Russia was about to commit itself to the unlikely Franco-Austrian combination. The invasion of Saxony became imperative as a pre-emptive strike, achievable at minimum cost, to bring Prussia a decisive strategic advantage and so forestall a potentially disastrous protracted war.[42]

The plan nearly succeeded. Sixty-three thousand Prussians, or slightly under half the total army, quickly overran the entire electorate, entering Dresden on 9 September, but they failed to catch the bulk of the 19,000-strong Saxon army, which retreated into fortified positions at Pirna in the mountains close to the Bohemian frontier.[43] Though Frederick made a second attempt, invading Bohemia in spring 1757, the decisive advantage was to elude him, condemning his kingdom to a long war.

His action greatly eased Kaunitz's diplomacy, assisting in the conversion of the Franco-Austrian alliance into an offensive arrangement by 1 May 1757, which Russia joined on 11 January. Russian participation greatly tipped the scales in Vienna's favour, despite the fact that Empress Elizabeth was never able to deploy more than a quarter of her theoretical total strength of 437,823 men. The attack on Saxony induced its elector to place his kingdom of Poland at Russia's disposal as an operational base, and the initial assault force of 80,000 proved more than enough to seize East Prussia during 1757. Nonetheless, the war effort placed Russia under great strain and its full potential was never realized, owing to inadequate co-ordination with Austria and almost insurmountable logistical problems. The main impact was to demonstrate beyond doubt Russian military capacity and the defeats at their hands at Gross-Jägersdorf (1757), Zorndorf (1758), Kay and Kunersdorf (both 1759) left a lasting impression on Frederick and the post-war orientation of Prussian policy.[44]

French involvement had a more immediate and profound effect on imperial politics. Kaunitz's diplomatic triumph tied France to fighting a war solely in Austria's interests. The revised alliance of 1 May 1757 obliged France to send 105,000 troops in addition to subsidizing 10,000 German auxiliaries and paying 22.5 million livres direct to Austria. Prussian military potential was to be destroyed, with Silesia and Glatz being restored to Austria, and all this for only a vague promise that Maria Theresa might cede part of the Netherlands.

In addition to insulating the Netherlands against external attack, the new alliance brought security for imperial Italy, consolidating the 1748 peace and ensuring it lasted until 1792. Here Austria was assisted by the decline of Spain's ambitions, which had already been satisfied in 1748, leading to the Treaty of Naples 1759, with both Bourbon powers resolving the remaining points of contention concerning feudal jurisdictions. The absence of international tension in the region neutralized Sardinia and ensured it did not develop as an Italian Prussia capable of threatening Austria from the south. Security was further enhanced by a convention with Modena on 1 November 1757, whereby 5,000 Modenese troops took over guard duty in Austrian Lombardy to free forces to fight Prussia.[45]

If anything, the Second Treaty of Versailles was rather too good to be true. Kaunitz had not wanted such substantial French assistance, but Louis XV had insisted on sending a large army to Germany, partly because he had taken the Prussian occupation of Dresden as a personal affront, but also because he wished to put pressure on Britain by seizing Hanover.[46] This was the last thing Kaunitz wanted, since it threatened to divide the *Reich* against Austria. Aided by Hanoverian ministers, he worked for the neutrality of the electorate, but was thwarted by French demands that would have effectively turned it into their operational base. Austria's failure in Hanover meant that Prussia would not stand alone in Germany, and Britain now moved towards converting its own defensive Convention of Westminster into an active alliance. Although not completed until 1758, this process ensured that the *Reich* was caught between the two hostile novel international combinations produced by the diplomacy of 1754–6.[47]

Efforts intensified from 1756 to secure German support, as both sides courted the major and minor princes. However, whereas such competition appeared welcome only a few years before, in the light of the reversed alliances it was an unmitigated disaster. The Franco-Austrian *rapprochement* destroyed not only the Old System of Britain's continental policy, but the traditional alignment of princely support for a Habsburg defence of the Rhine. Most German courts had relied on Franco-Austrian antagonism, and all previous Third Party schemes had depended on the idea of holding the middle ground between these two seemingly irreconcilable powers. This was now clearly impossible. Worse, whereas the old tension had generally resulted in war along the Rhineland, the new alignment was producing fighting at the heart of the *Reich*.

The princes, whose primary interest was peace, were running out of options. The neutrality of the Austrian Netherlands removed the reason for Dutch intervention in imperial politics, and with it a traditional partner of many weaker territories.[48] Allied to Austria, France could intervene in Germany directly, whereas any British aid had to come by sea. There was no guarantee that Britain could offer anything beyond money, while help from Prussia was clearly out of the question. Yet an alliance with Austria was problematic for many: the Prussian invasion of Saxony had caught both Hanover and Hessen-Kassel with a large part of their armies stationed on the English south coast, where they had been moved in the invasion scare of 1756.[49] Hessen-Kassel, Wolfenbüttel and other north German territories lay within the operational radius of Hanoverian and Prussian forces, which were likely to retaliate if they chose the other side. Moreover, there were long-standing dynastic and diplomatic connections, linking them to both Britain and Prussia, that ultimately proved stronger than the limited offers made by France and Austria. A variety of northern territories had renewed these arrangements by 1757, agreeing to contribute to an army of observation assembling to protect Hanover. The intention was purely defensive and these arrangements were regarded as simply extending the Convention of Westminster rather than a breach with Austria. Yet the polarization of imperial politics had left all territories bereft of a framework for viable neutrality, and all were pulled inexorably into open conflict once they signed military conventions (Table 7.2).

Table 7.2 Britain's German allies, 1755–62

Territory	Initial treaty	Contingent	Remarks
Hessen-Kassel	18 June 1755	8,000	Renewed and extended 17 Jan 1759 to cover 21,756 men by 1762
Ansbach	6 Sept 1755	1,812	Expired 6 Sept 1756 and not renewed
Würzburg	6 Sept 1755	2,400	Terminated 1756
Prussia	16 Jan 1756		Converted into a subsidy treaty 11 April 1758, expired 1762
Hanover	8 May 1756	8,605	Additional troops taken into British pay, 1757–62
Schaumburg-Lippe	28 Aug 1756	800	Renewed Dec 1758
Gotha	17 Nov 1756	800	Unit incorporated into the Hanoverian army 25 Jan 1759
Wolfenbüttel	19 Feb 1757[1]	6,241	Renewed 14 Jan 1760 to cover 9,280 men by 1762

Source: As notes 37 and 39.

Note: Dated 5 October 1756 to predate imperial decrees against Prussia.

A similar logic was at work in the south and west, where France had a larger range of clients, whose treaties, mostly dating from 1750–52, were due to expire by 1757. France offered considerable inducements for their renewal, but most princes initially struggled to remain out of the war. Prussia's unprovoked attack had caused great alarm, and the ecclesiastical rulers feared that secularization might also be on Frederick's agenda. Clemens August even believed that a combined assault on Prussia and Hanover could permit the restoration of full Catholicism to Osnabrück, and, like several other leading churchmen, was prepared to support the war with additional troops. The Palatinate, and eventually Bavaria and Württemberg, followed suit, although the secular rulers were noticeably more reluctant and all favoured formal mediation through the *Reichstag* to defuse the crisis (Table 7.3).[50]

Austria had no intention of permitting this and instead forced through the legal process to punish Prussia for a breach of the peace and so legitimize mobilization of German resources for Austrian war aims. This began on 13 September 1756 with a *Mandata avocatoria* to the *Reichstag*, including decrees forbidding Prussian military personnel from continuing to support Frederick's

Table 7.3 German auxiliaries in Austro-French service, 1756–63

Territory	Treaty	Partner	Initial contingent	Notes
Zweibrücken	7 Apr 1756	France	6,800	Withdrawn Jan 1759
Würzburg	16 Sept 1756	Austria	2,000	Part of French army from 1 Apr 1757
Mainz	27 Sept 1756	Austria	3,728	Revised to 2,725 on 18 Jan 1761 till Feb 1763
Bavaria	1 Mar 1757	France	6,800	Withdrawn Jan 1759
Württemberg	30 Mar 1757	France	6,000	200 added 16 Apr 1757 Till Feb 1759
Württemberg	9 Feb 1759	France	2,000	Increased to 8,670 on 3 Nov 1759 till 1760
Württemberg	23 July 1760	Austria	11,000	Terminated Dec 1760
Ansbach	2 Apr 1757	France and Austria	300	Cancelled by Ansbach in Aug 1757
Palatinate	16 Apr 1757	France	6,000	Withdrawn Jan 1759
Neuwied	8 Feb 1758	France	678	Attached to the Zweibrücken rgt Withdrawn 1760
Saxony	11 Mar 1758	France and Austria	10,000	Served in W.Germany till 1763
Anhalt–Zerbst	1761	Austria	*c.* 500	Till 1767

Sources: As *note* 50 plus Bittner (ed.), *Staatsverträge*, nos 1060, 1062, 1068, 1073, 1079, 1090.

Note: Treaty dates are those of military conventions committing the territories to send contingents to the field. Many had earlier subsidy agreements to hold men in readiness. In addition to the above, Cologne made a convention on 20 March 1757 to provide supplies, plus sent 1,800 recruits directly to the French army. France also had a convention with Liège on 18 May 1757 for use of territory, while Bamberg agreed on 8 February 1757 to recruit men for the Austrian army. Grand Duke Peter of Russia agreed on 26 July 1757 on behalf of Holstein-Gottorp to hold troops in readiness for Austria.

illegal actions and releasing them from their personal oaths of loyalty, while the rest of the *Reich* was instructed not to assist the wayward king. Mobilization was initiated the next day with a formal request to the *Reichstag* to sanction peace enforcement by military action. The delegates debated the request on 20 September, predictably failing to reach a decision, since the majority actually favoured mediation. Emperor Francis forced the pace by reissuing his call on 9 October, followed the next day by a formal request for a *Reichsarmee* along with intervention from the two foreign guarantors of the IPO. French and Austrian influence now secured the necessary majority on 17 January 1757, authorizing triple quotas as a *Reichs-Exekutions-Armee* to execute the verdict against Prussia. The sanctions were extended to the expulsion of Prussian representatives from *Reich* institutions, the suspension of postal communications and travel in and out of its territory and, somewhat belatedly, an embargo on war materials in 1760.[51]

As in the case of the earlier mobilizations against external attack, implementation of these orders rested with the *Kreis* executive princes, and their response depended very much on their geographical location and the level of Austrian influence. Predictably, Upper and Lower Saxony failed to respond, since both were dominated by Prussia, Hanover and their allies. Francis assigned his Mainz and Würzburg auxiliaries as his official Austrian and Burgundian contingent, supplemented by a few cavalry regiments and frontier militia from his own army. Mobilization across the other six *Kreise* was patchy. That of Electoral Rhine was surprisingly complete, with Trier taking the rare step of providing a substantial field contingent, indicating the effectiveness of the *Kreis* structure in the absence of adverse French influence. Hessen-Kassel was noticeably absent from the Upper Rhine, but the others turned out in their usual strength. Westphalian mobilization was limited by the presence of Prussian territory in its midst and the general proximity to the north German forces subsidized by Britain. The formation of separate auxiliaries by Bavaria, Württemberg and Würzburg delayed the organization of the Bavarian, Swabian and Franconian contingents respectively. The situation in Swabia was especially serious, given Duke Carl Eugen's last-minute decision to double his original auxiliary contingent to 6,000 men in 1757 in the mistaken belief that wholehearted support for the Franco-Austrian coalition would bring him an electoral title. Problems in recruiting compounded long-term grievances in the Württemberg army over poor pay and conditions. When combined with Prussian agitation, this provoked a mutiny in Stuttgart on 21 June, as the entire army disintegrated, terrorizing the city for a day and a night. The duchy's *Kreis* contingent had to be depleted to replace deserters from the auxiliaries, who were filled out with fresh conscripts. The mutiny and subsequent poor performance of the auxiliaries in Austria and French service did lasting damage to Carl Eugen's political ambitions, which remained unfilled despite raising his total army to an unprecedented 16,000 men by 1760.[52]

Though the actual turnout of 33,000 men represented barely a quarter of the triple quota, the response to Austria's demands was actually quite strong. Apart from the territories already in the Anglo-Prussian camp, the biggest absentee was Austria itself, which alone owed another 27,919 men on its official contingents. The other territories were only collectively about 10,000 men short of their recognized obligations, and most of the missing men were accounted for by the decision of various *Kreis* executives to sanction their retention as garrisons of key cities like Frankfurt, Nuremberg and Heilbronn (Table 7.4). In any case the actual size of the *Reichsarmee* was not as important as its mere presence, which symbolized formal support for Austria's war against Prussia. This crucial point has often been missed by the many commentaries that dwell on the force's obvious practical shortcomings. Though militarily it would have made more sense to use the *Reichsarmee* in a rear echelon or as garrison troops, politically it had to be deployed in the front line against Prussia as the principal instrument to execute the formal will of the *Reich*.

The level of the response also reflected the growing success of the Franco-Austrian coalition. The decisive advantage sought by Frederick continued to prove elusive. He did turn back an Austrian attempt to relieve the Saxons in Pirna at the Battle of Lobositz on 1 October 1756, leading to the capitulation of the electorate's army two weeks later. Frederick pressed the 17,000 survivors directly into his own army, but they deserted in droves, reassembling as a 10,000-strong auxiliary corps that joined the French after March 1758. This episode has rightly been described as the king's "worst miscalculation as a man-manager", but was merely the prelude to an increasingly ruthless exploitation of Saxon human and material resources.[53] The Prussian spring offensive

Table 7.4 *Kreis* contingents, 1757

Kreis	Effectives
Austria ⎫ Burgundy ⎭	8,255
Electoral Rhine	6,462
Upper Rhine	3,041
Swabia	5,500
Bavaria	2,487
Franconia	5,674
Westphalia	1,800
Upper Saxony	
Lower Saxony	
Total	32,219

Source: As notes 51–2.

1757 failed to take Bohemia despite a bloody victory outside Prague on 6 May, while an attempt to repel an Austrian relief effort ended in total disaster at Kolin on 18 June. Kolin equalized the humiliation of Mollwitz, clearly re-establishing the reputation of the Austrian army and forcing the Prussians out of Bohemia and on to the defensive.

Success in Bohemia was matched by that in western Germany, where French intervention got under way. Like the mobilization of the *Reichsarmee*, Francis's call to the two guarantor powers to restore order was of considerable political significance. France and Sweden formally announced their intention on 30 March 1757 to uphold the IPO by sending troops against the Prussian lawbreaker. French influence secured full Swedish participation by a treaty of 22 September, whereby that country promised 20,000 men in return for financial assistance. The Pomeranian garrison was increased to 22,000, although in practice no more than 14,000 generally entered the field, while the Baltic galley fleet harried the Prussian coast. Swedish involvement did not contribute significantly to Frederick's military problems and is generally dismissed as a minor footnote to the great struggles in Saxony and Silesia. However, its presence, along with that of France, reinforced Vienna's por-trayal of the war as a legal police action within the constitutional framework, and, moreover, as Protestant guarantor, helped take the sting from Prussian propaganda depicting the conflict as a Catholic attack.[54]

France sent two armies. The first and largest totalled 129,000 men under d'Estrées, who advanced into north Germany in June 1757 to engage the 47,600-strong observation army under Cumberland.[55] The French quickly overran Prussia's Westphalian provinces as well as Wolfenbüttel and forced Cumberland to withdraw after an inconclusive engagement at Hastenbeck on 26 July. Demoralized, Cumberland abandoned Hanover and retired to the North Sea coast where he signed the Convention of Kloster Zeven on 8 September with the new French commander, the Duc de Richelieu.[56]

Richelieu was conscious that his army had outrun its supply lines, and did not want to be deflected from his official task of executing the ban against Prussia by seizing Magdeburg. Cumberland agreed to disband the observation army, but the Convention left the ultimate fate of its components undecided. France disarmed the Wolfenbüttel garrison and militia units and opened negotiations to take the auxiliaries along with those from Hessen-Kassel into its own pay to solve the problem. However, little effort was made to bring matters to a speedy conclusion, since Richelieu had entered Prussian territory by Halberstadt on 29 September and was confident of success. The Swedes secured permission from Mecklenburg-Schwerin to use its territory as a base, permitting them to advance towards Halberstadt, where the French expected to be reinforced by 18,000 Hessians and Wolfenbüttel troops pending the result of their negotiations. Coming after Kolin, the collapse of the observation army made Frederick's position appear hopeless, and he authorized a 500,000 tlr bribe to Mme de Pompadour, Louis XV's mistress, as well as a retainer to Richelieu in the hope that they would use their good offices to end the war.

Meanwhile, news of the Austrian reverse at Prague in May prompted France to send a second army of 24,000 men under Prince Soubise, who advanced through Hessen-Kassel and Thuringia, picking up the *Reichsarmee* under Hildburghausen which had collected in Franconia. Together they advanced into northeast Saxony, falling back in the face of a Prussian counterthrust, before returning to meet Frederick at the fateful battle of Rossbach on 5 November. Within two hours, 5,000 Franco-imperial soldiers were dead or wounded, while a similar number had surrendered against a Prussian loss of only 548 officers and men.

More than any other this action has shaped the historical image of the *Reich* at war and requires fuller discussion. The force that Frederick defeated was essentially French, although even this must be qualified, since a third of their infantry and a sixth of their cavalry consisted of foreign regiments serving as integral parts of their army.[57] The great bulk of the *Reichsarmee* had been detached to cover the river Saale and key points to the rear, so that only about 11,000 were actually present at the battle, of whom 3,860 were Austrians. A major reason for the debacle was inept French command, particularly at brigade level, resulting in poor liaison between the sections of the army and ending in fatal confusion before the battle even started. This prevented the execution of the tactical plan, which was basically sound, even Frederickan in its conception (see Map 5). A small detachment would pin the Prussian army by advancing towards its camp, while the main force swung round to the south to appear on the enemy flank. Soubise, a man whose principal exploits had been in the Parisian salons, merely hoped Frederick would pack his bags and go away, but Hildburghausen hoped for a battle. Poor co-ordination of the main advance resulted in the cavalry being 2 km ahead of the infantry columns by the time Frederick struck, while the infantry of the *Reichsarmee* were squeezed out by their French comrades and dropped to the rear. Worse, Soubise had set off without recalling men detached to forage or horses set out to graze, which meant that the artillery had to be manhandled by the gun crews.

Frederick's victory resulted from his skilful exploitation of these mistakes, although owed much to the initiative of General Seydlitz, who led his squadrons north of the Janus Hill to surprise the Franco-imperial cavalry. Once the engagement had begun, some of the weaknesses inherent in the *Reichsarmee* did emerge. The Swabian and Franconian heavy cavalry had only recently mustered and had not yet fully learnt how to wheel and deploy in formation, in contrast to the disciplined Prussians, who rode so tightly together that one trooper's body, whose head was shot off, was carried along by the sheer force of his comrades' attack! Such problems were a direct product of the defence structure's function as a mobilization system rather than a permanent army. Moreover, the controversy over the war had delayed the formation of many units, reducing the time available to train the raw recruits who made up over half the manpower of the smaller contingents.[58] Most of the experienced and homogenous units were absent, either because they had been detached like the Bavarians, or because their rulers were not supporting the war, like Hanover and Hessen-Kassel. As it was, the Hessen-Darmstadt regiment, whose landgrave had endorsed mobilization, remained disciplined throughout and retired in good order. However, even some of the smaller formations put up a good fight, indicating that the structural flaws in the army were not solely to blame for the defeat. One such unit was the Württemberg dragoon regiment, reduced by detachments and Carl Eugen's failure to provide his duchy's contingent to a mere 75 men from 12 different Swabian counties and imperial cities. Despite being caught by the full force of the initial attack, they stood firm until an Austrian hussar regiment charged into them, thinking they were Prussians.

The defeat of the Franco-imperial cavalry sealed the fate of the rest of the army. Disordered by the confused approach march and fleeing horsemen, the French infantry never formed up properly to meet the disciplined Prussian foot, who now appeared over the Janus Hill. Some French units that did deploy held their fire at a renewed Prussian cavalry attack because they also mistook the approaching forces, this time believing them to be retreating imperialists. Fugitives from the front of the column crashed through the imperial infantry still deploying to the rear. Having successively reformed after being hit by fleeing French cavalry, Prussian musketry and their own retreating mounted comrades, the German infantry finally broke when the enemy artillery opened up. Even then the Darmstadt regiment, along with the Würzburg auxiliaries substituting for the Austrians, retained formation and helped cover the retreating French army.

This detailed account has been necessary to dispel the persistent myths of imperial troops throwing away their weapons at the first shot, or running because, as Protestants, they did not want to fight their hero, Frederick the Great. Prussian propaganda had helped stir religious animosity within the *Reichsarmee* to the point that it became necessary to ban theological discussion within the ranks. However, Hillburghausen did not feel subsequently that it contributed to the defeat, and it is significant that the deserters questioned later did not mention either religion or Prussian sympathies as a reason for absconding. On the other hand, the decision to retain parts of some contingents for home defence caused widespread resentment amongst their comrades who had to go to the front.

However, the main fault lay in the complete breakdown in the supply arrangements, which caused the disintegration of the combined army after the battle. Some contingents had not been paid since 4 October and had had no bread since the 21st. Pay before that had been irregular, and, given that soldiers' wages were fixed at subsistence level, few men could afford the high-priced victuals still available from the sutlers. Conditions in the French army were often worse, so that its soldiers stole provisions from the imperialists. Already before the battle men of the Augsburg contingent told their officers that they would go home unless they were paid and fed. Most of the remaining supplies were lost along with the baggage train abandoned in the rout on 5 November, leaving many soldiers no option but to return home in search of food. A similar disintegration occurred almost simultaneously in the Prussian army left by Frederick to hold Silesia. Once the field force was defeated outside Breslau, the 4,000-strong garrison of the city surrendered with the honours of war on 25 November, but only 600 rejoined the main army, the rest having left to find food and shelter elsewhere.[59]

Rossbach's importance was symbolic rather than a practical demonstration of the prowess of the Prussian army; something that was in any case proved more convincingly by Frederick's stunning victory over the Austrians at Leuthen on 5 December 1757. The battle has been called the birth of German nationalism,[60] and certainly it did become a symbol to later generations seeking proof of their alleged superiority over the French. Some contemporaries also thought this way, although Frederick unquestionably did not, regarding French culture as part of the cosmopolitan enlightened environment in which he lived. Eighteenth-century concepts of German identity lacked the clearer boundaries drawn later. Officers who saw the battle as a German victory were just as capable of applying the word "nation" exclusively to an individual territorial state, and arguably, in eighteenth-century terms, the Austrians who were defeated at Leuthen were as "German" as the Prussians who triumphed at Rossbach. Indeed, as well as being feted as a German hero, Frederick was idolized at the French court by those opposed to the "unnatural" Austrian alliance. The French were hated in 1757, as indeed they had been the previous century, but only because their ill-disciplined march through Thuringia made them appear invaders rather than executors of the will of the *Reichstag*. The French occupation of western Germany in 1757–62 was relatively benevolent, and a Göttingen University professor described them as "the best enemies anyone could have".[61] A similarly ambiguous attitude developed towards the Russians, who were regarded by the Prussian rank and file as little short of barbarians, but who were well liked by the civilian population under their rule in occupied East Prussia.

What Rossbach did symbolize was the defeat of Austria's interpretation of the war, shattering the facade of the conflict as a police action against Prussia. The war now split into two halves, fragmenting the anti-Prussian coalition so painstakingly assembled by Kaunitz. Co-operation between the emperor and the two foreign guarantors broke down, reducing formal execution of the imperial ban to a mere adjunct of great power objectives. In the west the war became a thinly disguised continental dimension to the Anglo-French colonial conflict, while that in the east developed as an Austro-Russian assault on Prussia.

Rossbach demonstrated Prussia's viability as a continental ally for Britain with immediate practical results. The British government repudiated the convention of Kloster Zevern, reinforced the army on the continent with a contingent of its own troops and began paying subsidies to Prussia. The Prussian general, Ferdinand of Brunswick, replaced Cumberland and led the revitalized army in a spring offensive in 1758, temporarily clearing the French from northern Germany and removing any chance of their co-operating with the Swedes.[62] The latter were now restricted to their base in Pomerania from where they made half-hearted sorties while they waited for the Russians to inch their way westwards from East Prussia.

Finally, the battle proved a profound shock to France, prompting not only military reforms but a re-evaluation of foreign policy. As early as January 1758 France tried to cut its military involvement in Germany. The government did send 30,000 men towards Saxony again, but these had to be redirected northwards to help the main army stem Ferdinand's offensive. Thereafter, France made no further effort to co-operate with the *Reichsarmee* and began to disengage from its undertaking to assist Habsburg dynastic policy. By 1759 they realized they had committed a colossal blunder in signing up to Austria's ambitious war aims, as the destruction of Prussia now seemed contrary to French interests. French subsidy commitments to Vienna and other German courts were scaled down in March 1759, and Maria Theresa agreed to renounce all claims to direct military assistance.[63] The French effort was now restricted to Westphalia and Hessen, where it was no longer intended to uphold the IPO but to seize German bargaining counters that could be traded against potential colonial losses. Though the total force in Germany was increased from 100,000 (1758–9) to 160,000 (1761), victory remained elusive, and France eventually sued for peace, signing the Treaty of Paris with Britain on 10 February 1763.[64]

Flagging French support left Austria fighting alone, since logistical problems prevented effective co-operation with the Russians beyond the temporary success of the Kunersdorf campaign of 1759. Apart from 1760, the main Austrian effort was generally directed at attacking Prussian positions in Silesia, leaving the *Reichsarmee* to co-operate with the smaller Austrian force intended to recover Saxony. The effective strength of the *Reichsarmee* did not rise above about 25,000 men, or the level achieved in 1757, but combat efficiency improved considerably. While it did not distinguish itself, there was no repeat of the earlier disaster, and although individual detachments were defeated, units assigned to the Austrian force performed well, particularly at the battle of Freiberg on 29 October 1762, the only major engagement involving a significant proportion of the *Reichsarmee* apart from Rossbach. The *Kreis* contingents made up well over a third of the combined force attacked by Prince Henry, Frederick's brother, whose soldiers were admittedly not as good as those that had comprised the royal army in 1757. Nonetheless, they bore the brunt of some of the fiercest attacks, and although the combined force was defeated, the margin of victory was not nearly as great as at Rossbach and there was no disintegration of the retreating force.[65]

Although the improved Austro-imperial performance after 1757 was insufficient to defeat Frederick, it did force him to fight a protracted war for which Prussia was ill-equipped. The king was compelled to remain on the strategic defensive, using the advantage of his interior lines to shuttle his dwindling forces from front to front to parry his opponents' ill-co-ordinated attacks. Frederick survived only by ruthlessly exploiting the resources of his own lands and those in Saxony he continued to occupy. Additional supplies were seized by a policy of raiding Bohemia, Thuringia and Franconia whenever possible, generally in the late autumn or winter when his opponents had withdrawn to regroup, while the war economy was kept going by debasing the coinage. British subsidies, though politically important, covered only a fifth of the total expenditure.[66]

Unprecedented numbers of recruits were taken from the Cantons, while prisoners and enemy deserters were pressed into service or kept on short rations in the Magdeburg camp until they "volunteered". Many of these, along with others driven by the general economic dislocation in Germany to enlist in the Prussian forces, were grouped into the so-called Free Battalions (*Freibataillone*), used as second-line troops, raiders and eventually cannon fodder as the king's experienced regulars died out. Finally, Frederick was forced to reverse his father's policy and re-establish a militia, initially calling out 17,000 men in his northern and eastern provinces to confront the Russians and Swedes. The militia served throughout the war, although increasingly it was used to give Cantonists basic training before they were drafted to the field regiments.[67]

Such ruthlessness led contemporaries and later commentators to speculate whether Frederick had ushered in a new era of total war. Kaunitz and Maria Theresa certainly felt that their opponent's methods were unprecedented in "that the king does not just exploit his own population, money and military potential, but also all the inhabitants, money, food and other materials of innocent and neutral neighbours as far as force enables him".[68] Prussia was identified with a dangerous new form of militarism that subordinated all aspects of society to supporting an inflated military establishment, making it not only a challenge to Austria's political interests but a danger to all humanity. That this was no mere rhetoric designed to justify the war is clear from Kaunitz's consistent opposition to those in Vienna like Archduke Joseph, who stressed the advantages of copying Prussian ideas like the Canton system. Whereas Joseph believed this would strengthen the monarchy by making every civilian a potential soldier, Kaunitz opposed it precisely because he saw this aspect as the most repulsive.[69]

Ironically, by wishing to eradicate the evils of Prussian militarism, Kaunitz and Maria Theresa went further towards total war than Frederick. Austria planned to inflict punishment on Prussia far in excess of anything previously meted out to wayward German vassals. There were the traditional plans for redistribution of territory to loyal supporters, with Kaunitz himself hoping to become Prince of East Frisia, but no emperor had intended *La destruction totale* that was written into the Franco-Austrian Treaty of Versailles. True, this was defined as only the reduction of Prussia by partial territorial dismemberment to a status equivalent to the other electorates, but as the Danish minister, Count Bernstorff, observed, it was no longer a contest over the possession of a few small provinces "but about the very existence of the new monarchy", whether it could survive or expand and "whether the *Reich* should have two rulers and north Germany be controlled by a prince who has made his state into an armed camp and his people into an army".[70]

Certainly, Prussia's ability to raid deep into Franconia, levy contributions and intimidate the lesser princes indicated its adoption of great power tactics already used by Louis XIV. Indeed, Prussia's mere survival in the face of a hostile coalition confirmed its arrival as a European great power, albeit the weakest, by 1763. If the Seven Years War did usher in a new form of warfare, it was total war for limited objectives, as war aims still fell well short of the extremes sought in the twentieth century.[71]

The new destructiveness hit the *Reich* badly, particularly given the character of the conflict as a civil war fought on home soil, where the damage was the worst since the Thirty Years War. The shorter duration of the Seven Years War limited its material effect, but not its psychological impact, which was magnified by the relative absence of conflict, especially in western and northern Germany, since 1714. Increasingly, the *Reich* seemed to be at the mercy of Prussia, Austria and their respective allies. Already in 1757 Ferdinand of Brunswick had prevented his brother, the reigning duke of Wolfenbüttel, from withdrawing his contingent from the allied army.[72] Both the French and Hanoverians occupied the strategic city of Bremen at various times between 1757 and 1763, and the Westphalian and Lower Saxon bishoprics were plundered by both sides. Britain and Prussia agreed to partition the ecclesiastical states between them at an eventual peace, with Münster and Osnabrück to go to Hanover, while Frederick took Hildesheim. The plans were shelved after the accession of George III in 1760, as the new king was less concerned for Hanover and his ministers were keen to reach a compromise with France. Nonetheless, the threat to the continued existence of the *Reichskirche* was clear, and Prussia managed to extract no less than 3 million tlr from the Mainz enclave of Erfurt during the war.[73] Austria also stepped up its exploitation of German resources, for instance, forcing the Ernestine Saxons to field their Upper Saxon *Kreis* contingent from 1758 despite Prussian reprisals.[74] Maintenance of such contingents proved a growing strain for the weaker territories, with Mainz providing no less than 12,000 men in the course of the war to keep its 4,662 *Kreistruppen* and auxiliaries up to strength, a considerable burden for a state with only 336,000 inhabitants.[75]

The result was growing disillusionment with a war that had been controversial from the start. Already in spring 1758 Bavaria and the Palatinate agreed to withdraw their auxiliaries in a co-ordinated action completed by January 1759. Württemberg followed suit at the end of 1760 after political and military disagreements with the Austrian government.[76] Such unilateral actions only made matters worse by fuelling resentment and suspicion in Paris and Vienna. The French were angered when the Palatine garrison surrendered Düsseldorf to the allies under Ferdinand in spring 1758, and when it was abandoned that August, they placed their own forces in the city, refusing to admit the elector's troops. The elector of Trier was also obliged to admit the French into the Ehrenbreitstein fortress on 25 September 1759, seriously compromising his claim that he was a mere auxiliary of the emperor and not a full belligerent. Ferdinand seized on this and similar actions elsewhere as an excuse for heavy requisitioning, particularly after the temporary French military collapse at the battle of Minden on 1 August 1759. Anglo-Hanoverian units occupied Münster, disarming the small neutral garrison of that bishopric's army. The death of Clemens August on 6 February 1761 was exploited by both sides to increase their hold on their respective parts of northern Germany. The allies prevented his successor assuming office in his five vacant bishoprics, which the French now treated as enemy territory. The remaining Münster regiments sheltering in Bonn were disarmed and interned in Aachen, while the region's support for the official war effort collapsed. Clemens August had already not replaced his contingent to the *Reichsarmee*, which had been captured in stages during 1759–61, and neither did his successor, while Bavaria also stopped its cash contributions in 1761.[77]

By then most were seeking a permanent way out, which Frederick sought to encourage by launching his biggest raid yet, sending 10,000 men under the enterprising General Kleist into Franconia in November 1762. Württemberg opened negotiations, agreeing neutrality on 4 December and recalling the Swabian contingent from the Saxon frontier. It was followed by Bavaria and the Palatinate, which also signed separate armistices, and together they pressed the *Reichstag* into declaring neutrality for the entire *Reich* on 11 February. The Austrian high command was compelled to let the Palatine contingent leave the *Reichsarmee* when its general threatened to fight his way out.[78]

The withdrawal of the *Reichsarmee* was not militarily significant, since the war was already effectively over and Austria had made its own armistice with Prussia on 24 November. Politically it was decisive in symbolizing the defeat of Austria's interpretation of the war and the general disillusionment with Habsburg imperial policy.

Apart from Britain's clear victory in the colonial contest, the crucial factor in bringing the war to a close was the death of Empress Elizabeth on 6 January 1762. The new tsar, Peter III, not only signed an armistice but proceeded to ally with Prussia on 16 March, voluntarily evacuating East Prussia and providing 20,000 Russians to attack the Austrians in Silesia. This bizarre decision has less to do with the tsar's admiration for Frederick, which features prominently in most explanations, than his desire to recover his ancestral home in Schleswig from Denmark, for which a Prussian alliance was essential. Already before becoming tsar, Peter had established a Holstein corps as an autonomous German element of the Russian army with the intention of realizing this long-term ambition. In spring 1762 45,000 Russians slowly moved from Polish West Prussia through Pomerania and Mecklenburg, while the navy cruised the western Baltic. The Danes mobilized 30,500 and advanced into Lower Saxony, forcing the local territorial authorities to place their own forces on standby in what threatened to become a repeat of the disasters of 1711–15. The two armies were actually closing to contact when news arrived of Peter's murder in a palace coup that brought his German-born wife to power as Catherine II. Though she recalled the troops from Mecklenburg and Silesia, she honoured the armistice with Prussia, leaving Austria isolated, especially as Sweden left the war by separate treaty in June 1762.[79]

Austria's war effort was already flagging by the end of 1761, when it was forced to cut 20,000 men from the army establishment and issue paper money to cover the burgeoning expenditure. Frederick was in a similarly desperate state, especially as Britain did not renew its subsidy commitments when these expired in 1762. The king regarded this as an act of treachery, and it was to have a lasting effect on Anglo-Prussian relations. In fact, Britain did much to assist him throughout 1762, negotiating the withdrawal of the French from the occupied Westphalian provinces in such a way as to prevent these being seized by the Austrians before Prussian garrisons could arrive. However, Frederick misjudged Britain, failing to appreciate how important colonial issues had become after George III's accession or to realize British alarm at his apparent support for Peter III's dangerous attempt to widen the war.[80] Abandoned by their respective allies, Austria and Prussia made peace at Hubertunsburg on 18 February 1763 on the basis of the prewar territorial *status quo*.

A dangerous divergence

The long-term impact of the Seven Years War was to fuel the forces pulling the *Reich* apart, not just in the obvious sense of exacerbating Austro-Prussian rivalry, but also by promoting a twofold divergence within the traditional structure. On the one hand, the dynamic centralizing reforms within the territories increasingly set them apart from political immobility at *Kreis* and *Reich* level. On the other, the territories themselves diverged, with the continued growth of Austria and Prussia leading them to dwarf the rest. However, even at this stage there was nothing inevitable about the decay of the *Reich*, which was certainly not following a steady path of decline.

Peace in 1763 meant more than an end to Austrian hopes of recovering Silesia; it represented a defeat for the *Reich*. The ostensible purpose of the conflict had been to uphold the public peace and punish Prussia, yet the restoration of Saxony was not affected by constitutional methods through the *Reichstag* and *Reichsarmee*, but by a military stalemate and international pressure. Not only had the formal structure failed to prevent the Prussian invasion of Saxony, but Frederick was not even obliged to repay the 48 million tlr he had extorted from that unfortunate electorate. Lower Saxony, Westphalia, Hessen and Thuringia also became battlegrounds for Europe's great powers, while Austria's refusal to accept nonviolent *Reichsmediation* tarnished the emperor's reputation as impartial judge. Finally, the failure of collective security was demonstrated not so much by the famous defeat at Rossbach, but by the unilateral retreat into neutrality at the end of 1762, which set a dangerous precedent for future behaviour in unpopular wars.

The accumulative effect of Austro-Prussian tension and Wittelsbach and Habsburg imperial manipulation since 1740 was seriously to undermine the structure developed for common defence since 1681. The security of the Rhine was seriously neglected and even Swabian and Franconian collaboration waned. Both *Kreise* only retained token garrisons in Kehl and Philippsburg to maintain grounds for compensation for their earlier expenses. Most of the Kehl fortifications had collapsed into the river by 1742, and the last troops were withdrawn in 1754 after Swabia had spent over 3 million fl. since 1698 without receiving significant assistance from the rest of Germany. The tiny bishopric of Speyer had spent 500,000 fl. of its own funds on the other common fortress at Philippsburg since 1633, and the new bishop from 1770, Damian August von Limburg-Styrum, refused to co-operate any further. By this stage the works needed 1.4 million fl. worth of repairs and were so hazardous to the health of the garrison that the Franconian *Kreis* withdrew its last 106 men in November 1772. Five years later the garrison had fallen to a mere 20 Austrians and the emperor began removing the remaining equipment. The last man left on 10 October 1782 and Styrum claimed the ruinous fort reverted to him by default. Both installations had not lost their strategic importance, with an Austrian memorandum of 1792 even describing Philippsburg as "the key to the German Reich", but neither could resist a siege even if money could be found to garrison them.[81]

The situation was less serious at Mainz, where the electorate's army continued to do duty, while the decline of the Westphalian *Kreis* was offset in Cologne, where the city paid the Austrians to garrison it from 1747. However, Austria's new understanding with France disinclined the hard-pressed *Hofkriegsrat* to rebuild the Breisgau defences, which had been destroyed in the fighting of the 1740s. The regional militia system, which had acted as a valuable supplement to the *Reichsarmee*, decayed and the regular Austrian garrison fell to a single regiment by the 1770s.[82]

The mobile *Kreis* forces also decayed. Württemberg disbanded its contingent to the Swabian corps in 1763, although the duke continued to appoint officers to the nonexistent regiments. Hessen-Kassel was compelled by the RHR to rejoin the Upper Rhine military structure in 1764 but reabsorbed its contingent into its own army in 1789. The Palatinate also disbanded its contingent (1770), which had constituted the only cavalry unit, while even Hessen-Darmstadt pulled out in 1790. However, here, as elsewhere, the *Kreis* structure did not break down completely, especially where there was the political will to keep it alive. The lesser Upper Rhinelanders continued to maintain the remaining two regiments until the destruction of the *Kreis* in 1794, while, as we shall see, both Franconia and Swabia made significant contributions to the last formal war against revolutionary France. Even

Westphalia, where no Assembly met after 1757, continued to function and actually held an executive meeting in October 1786 at Prussia's request. A new member was admitted and the *Kreis* still had representatives accredited to it from the emperor, pope, Britain, France, Russia, Prussia, Bavaria and Dutch Republic on the eve of the Revolution.[83]

Nonetheless, the balance between the territories had shifted dramatically since 1740, placing a full revival of the old institutions into question. The Seven Years War was the first conflict in which major German territories had cut their military involvement prior to the peace. The Prussian occupation of Saxony only further increased the margin over the electorate established in the 1740s and indicated that even such comparatively powerful territories were being reduced to a minor role in affairs.

The futility of trying to compete was demonstrated by the Württemberg experience, where, despite fielding more troops than Sweden in 1760, Carl Eugen failed to obtain concrete concession from Austria. The end of the war removed the need for Württemberg support and the emperor swung behind the duke's estates, who appealed to the RHR against his illegal financial measures introduced to support the army. Imperial intervention restored the estate's fiscal control and secured Austrian regional influence by 1770, reducing the duchy to a minor political and military factor until the end of the century.[84]

The point was reinforced by the case of Hessen-Kassel on the opposing side. Thanks to British subsidies the army was increased to 22,000 by 1761, or nearly double its previous size, yet while this represented the equivalent to half the Prussian army before 1714, it was only a tenth of the numbers Frederick had under arms. To achieve even this, Hessian society was militarized to an extent not even reached in Prussia, but the country was exhausted for no practical result and Britain ignored the landgrave's pleas for compensation for damage done by the French.[85]

The result was a trend to demilitarization that was especially pronounced among the medium and smaller territories after 1763. Münster disbanded part of its army and slighted its citadel in 1765, while Bremen demolished its fortifications and turned them into a park. The walls and casemates of the city of Augsburg were rented out to private citizens, and although Schaumburg-Lippe built a new miniature fortress in 1761–7, it subsequently reduced its army and sold its famous cannon foundry to a bell manufacturer in 1788. After briefly playing the general, Duke Carl August of Weimar virtually disbanded his entire army as an economy measure during 1779–83.

The presence of such enlightened figures as Goethe at the head of Weimar's military reform commission, along with the general philosophical critique of standing armies, had led many to ascribe this process as a product of a new intellectual climate. The new language certainly coloured the older rhetoric of fiscal economy, but the demilitarization was also a practical acknowledgement that the lesser territories were clearly overshadowed by the two German giants. Austrian and Prussian forces continued to expand even in peacetime to reach official levels of 314,783 and 195,344 respectively by 1789 and both states built new expensive military installations in Bohemia and Silesia.[86]

Again, as with the official military structure, it would be wrong to see this as a universal pattern of decline. Territories that received fresh subsidies, particularly from Britain during the American War of Independence, 1776–83, or that experienced territorial consolidation, such as the reversion of Hanau to both Hessian landgraviates or the mergers of the two Badens (1771) and Ansbach and Bayreuth (1769), tended to consolidate and even expand their forces. The Saxon army remained highly efficient, particularly after a series of reorganizations in 1769–78, while Hanover also continued to maintain substantial numbers. However, even after the unification of Bavaria and the Palatinate after the death of Elector Max III Joseph in 1777, the combined Wittelsbach might had a paper strength of only 22,430, of whom only 19,964 were effective (1788). This, the largest of all the remaining territorial armies was thus scarcely a tenth of the size of the Prussian host, indicating just how far even the largest electorate had been marginalized by the great German powers.[87]

The divergence between the *Reich* and the territories, and between Austria and Prussia and the others, was furthered by so-called "reform" or "enlightened absolutism". Modernization took place at territorial level where governments were becoming increasingly innovative, whereas reform proposals for the *Reich* aimed essentially at restoring or reviving what had already broken down. Dynamism and flexibility at territorial level faced conservatism and immobility at that of the *Reich*.[88] Reform absolutism had its roots in earlier attempts to strengthen the territorial fiscal–military state as well as in the intellectual ideas of the enlightenment, but it was given a practical impetus by the Seven Years War. The process of reconstruction in Prussia, known as the *Rétablissement*, was intended to secure resource extraction necessary to sustain great power status. The increasingly radical programme of "Josephism" in Austria was also intended to raise military capacity by closing a perceived gap with Prussia. The lesser territories were also not short of reformers, particularly in Baden, Hessen-Kassel and especially the ecclesiastical principalities, which increasingly felt it necessary to justify their continued existence in the face of enlightened anti-clericism's reinforcement of traditional arguments for secularization.[89] However, the long-term impact merely served to widen the gap between Austria, Prussia and the Third Germany, since the material resources of the lesser territories remained roughly constant, while those of the two great powers increased significantly at Poland's expense in 1772. Since they already enjoyed a substantial margin even over Palatine-Bavaria, improved Habsburg and Hohenzollern resource mobilization only increased their lead still further.

The main controversy with these reform programmes concerns their motivation and results. They have been associated with the concept of "defensive modernization",[90] which argues that German territorial rulers were able to avoid revolution from below in 1789, 1830 and 1848 by reforming from above. The state was transformed or "objectified", becoming depersonalized, abstract, rational and secular, resting on a revised version of its traditional promotion of the "common good", underpinned by an extended client base amongst broader social groups. The chief vehicle was the bureaucracy, which not only devised and implemented the reforms, but mediated pressure from below by deflecting it through controlled change and judicial redress. As the territorial state redefined and legitimized itself, it fostered a widespread belief among intellectuals, including the political opponents of absolutism, that it did not require radical modification, since it was already "modern".

It was unable to survive the upheavals after 1789 without implementing further adaptation in the Reform Era, but it was strong enough to ensure that these changes did not destroy its fundamental characteristics or its ties to traditional, socially conservative client groups. Such an explanation is certainly helpful in explaining the survival of the territorial regimes during the collapse of the *Reich*, provided it is not portrayed as a *conscious* effort to avoid revolution. As the next chapter will indicate, even after 1789 there was little popular threat to the princely governments. The impetus to reform came not from below, nor from pressure from outside through emulation of other countries or implementation of foreign ideas, but from the inner German situation, as Austro-Prussian competition raised fears for territorial autonomy.

The threat of partition, 1763–92

As well as the tensions produced by internal divergence, the *Reich* was caught in the midst of two interrelated tripartite power struggles after 1763. The clash between France, Austria and Prussia for influence within the *Reich* was matched by Austrian and Prussian competition with Russia in Poland and the Balkans. Increasingly, Russia also intruded into imperial politics, filling the vacuum left by the withdrawal of such traditional players as Sweden, Denmark, Britain and the Dutch Republic to the point that by 1779 its influence roughly corresponded to that of France.

Such great power rivalries furthered the marginalization of the lesser German territories upon which the survival of the *Reich* increasingly depended. Yet in the intermediate term they brought peace to central Europe, since mutual suspicion, acute appreciation of their own deficiencies and an exaggerated regard for the strength of potential enemies discouraged great power conflict. Apart from the brief Austro-Prussian struggle over the Bavarian Succession in 1778–9, no war disturbed the *Reich*, while the area to the east only witnessed the Russo-Turkish War of 1768–74, in which neither of the two German great powers were directly involved, and the last Turkish War, 1787–92, in which only Austria participated in alliance with Russia. Instead of war, the great powers preferred mutually assured aggrandizement to settle their differences by partitioning neutral weak states. Poland was the primary victim, disappearing completely in three partitions between Austria, Prussia and Russia in 1772, 1793, 1795, but Turkey's inability to defend itself in 1768–74 encouraged similar plans for its European territory. If anything, this policy posed a greater danger to *Reich* integrity than European conflict, for in wartime the lesser Germans could hope that it would be in the interest of at least one of the great powers to preserve them. Alone against a combination of Austria and Prussia they stood about as little chance as Poland, and the two brief periods of Austro-Prussian *rapprochement* 1769–72 and 1790–95 caused great alarm.

Habsburg policy after 1763 appeared aggressive but was in fact defensive. The intention was no longer to attack Prussia but to seek compensation for Silesia's loss elsewhere, principally through a projected exchange of Bavaria for part of the Austrian Netherlands. This scheme was pushed by Archduke Joseph, who succeeded his father as emperor on 17 September 1765. Joseph's character was to exert a powerful influence over imperial politics in the last 25 years of peace before the storms of the Revolutionary Wars. He is generally believed to have held the *Reich* in poor regard, as "little more than a convenient adjunct of the monarchy".[91] However, Austria did not ignore the *Reich* and took steps to rebuild its prestige and clientele after the damage of the Seven Years War, exploiting every opportunity to play on the fears around by Frederick's behaviour during the conflict to foster a spectre of potential Prussian predominance. That these efforts generally failed was partly due to Joseph himself, as he lacked the tact and subtlety required to manipulate imperial politics, was ignorant of constitutional detail and was far too insensitive to princely concerns and petty interests. Moreover, the experience of two major wars with little or no German support had been traumatic for

285

Austria and accelerated the reform process already under way from 1748, which inevitably furthered the monarchy's separation from the *Reich*.

Indeed, this was now symbolized in the decision of Maria Theresa and her son to rule as co-regents after 1765. Until Maria Theresa's death on 29 November 1780, Joseph had to take third place in the direction of Habsburg affairs after his mother and her trusted minister, Kaunitz. When he could at last take charge, his personal rule merely reinforced the pre-eminence of Austrian over imperial interests. He redoubled his reforming efforts, turning them outwards in ways that fundamentally affected the traditional imperial clientele. In particular, he attempted after 1781 to remove the spiritual jurisdiction of the ecclesiastical princes that overlapped Habsburg territory and sought to nationalize their property along with that of native church foundations. In the intellectual and political environment of the time this seemed the first step towards secularization and caused great alarm.[92]

These efforts were in part driven by the belief that Austria must close the gap with Prussia in its ability to mobilize resources for war. In fact, Prussia was still comparatively weak and lacked the material means for true great power status. Its position was undermined still further by Frederick's "acute and perhaps exaggerated sense of Prussia's vulnerability" and his inability to spot the underlying weaknesses in Austria and even Russia, particularly after the harrowing experience of the Seven Years War, which heightened his anxieties.[93] His principal aims were to uphold Prussia's new status whilst avoiding another war, and he developed a three-track policy to these ends.

The first element was his continued development of the Prussian army as a "strategic deterrent". The army had demonstrated its fighting abilities during the war, but Frederick was conscious of how much his survival had depended on this and was determined to keep it at maximum readiness to deter attack and, should that fail, to achieve a quick and decisive victory. Though Prussia had survived, the war had proved that it was barely capable of protracted conflict, and all efforts were concentrated on ensuring that the army could defeat its opponents in an initial short, sharp campaign. The resulting overemphasis on drill and training was a desperate attempt to prevent anything from going wrong that ultimately confused means with ends. Despite its impressive size, the army remained a brittle machine and nothing was done to rectify this, even though it was becoming obvious to some foreign observers by the 1770s.[94]

The Seven Years War had also taught Frederick that he could not rely on the army alone and that he needed a powerful ally if he was going to survive another major conflict. Antagonism resulting from the nonrenewal of the subsidy treaty in 1762 removed Britain from his calculations, and he also seems to have underestimated the possibility of a *rapprochement* with France.

He believed reconciliation with Austria was unlikely, despite it being favoured by his brother Prince Henry and even briefly by Joseph. A temporary
understanding did follow a personal interview with the emperor at Neisse in
1769 and led to various proposals for territorial redistribution, involving not
only Poland, but Austrian designs on Bavaria and Prussian claims to Ansbach
and Bayreuth. The concrete result was the First Partition of Poland by which
Prussia annexed the land bridge of West Prussia to link Brandenburg to its
eastern duchy. However, Austria also acquired Galicia while Russia took
Polish Ukraine, counterbalancing Prussia's gains and fuelling further mutual
suspicion.[95]

Inability to reach a permanent understanding with Austria left Russia as the
only alternative. Russian military performance during the Seven Years War
and its role in ending the conflict had convinced Frederick of its importance
and he made great efforts to secure and maintain an alliance, signing a mutual
defence pact for eight years in April 1764, which was renewed (each time for
eight years) in 1769 and 1777.[96]

The third element of Prussia's policy was a safety net should either of the
other two fail. Prussia took over the mantle of constitutional defender as it was
being discarded by Joseph, extending its own quasi-imperial role, developed
after 1748, to mobilize the *Reich* to block Habsburg plans for aggrandizement.
Frederick had discovered that he could play the system to his advantage;
indeed, he could manipulate imperial politics better than the emperor, since
he was not obliged to adhere so closely to the rules. The Seven Years War had
witnessed an extension of Prussian influence over Protestant and north German territories like Mecklenburg, Anhalt and the Ernestine duchies. Frederick
benefited from the corresponding decline of Austrian influence that had
accelerated with the disillusionment with imperial war management. For
example, the city of Dortmund had backed the emperor during the war but
bowed to Prussian pressure after 1768 and supported Frederick in the imperial
institutions. What was perhaps more startling was the growth of Prussian
influence in south German and Catholic areas like Bavaria, where Frederick
was celebrated in poems and peasants had his picture alongside that of their
elector on their cottage walls.[97]

The three elements of Prussian policy came together in the War of the
Bavarian Succession, 1778–9, which constituted the only serious breach of the
public peace between 1763 and 1792. Prussia became concerned at Joseph's
plans to exploit the death of Max Joseph (30 December 1777) to seize Bavaria,
particularly after the emperor reached a preliminary understanding with the
late elector's heir, Carl Theodor of the Palatinate. Acquisition of all or part of
Bavaria would greatly increase Habsburg power in the *Reich*, even if it was
accompanied by the transferral of part of the Netherlands to the Wittelsbachs

as compensation. Frederick moved quickly, mobilizing public opinion in an extensive pamphlet war that Austria lost. His diplomats obtained the vocal objection of the duke of Zweibrücken, the next Wittelsbach heir, as well as active Saxon support after Joseph rashly ignored Saxon feudal rights in some Bavarian lordships. Both politically and strategically this was of some importance, since it helped sustain Prussian arguments that Frederick was merely acting with the best interests of the *Reich* at heart, and it removed the need to reinvade Saxony as an operational base. The Prussian army was placed on a war footing of 253,000, with an additional 12,000 in new supplementary free battalions, of which 154,000 were deployed on the Bohemian frontier. To these the Saxons added a further 22,000, and when this failed to deter Joseph, the joint army invaded on 4 July 1778.[98]

The Habsburg monarchy raised even more prodigious numbers, recruiting no less than 148,877 men in 1778–9, raising the total strength to 308,535 regulars and 70,000 frontier militia. The need to garrison the empire meant that no more than 261,665 could be deployed in the war zone, but this still represented the largest force ever assembled by an emperor within the *Reich*, while both armies were accompanied by unprecedented numbers of heavy artillery pieces.[99]

The resultant conflict is of interest as the last major German, indeed, western European clash before the French Revolutionary Wars. Despite the formidable forces there was little fighting and the operations merely exposed serious flaws on both sides. The Prussian emphasis on clockwork precision stifled initiative and led to a hesitant strategy compounded by grave logistical problems, which cost the army 40,000 deserters and casualties from disease. Lack of food forced the soldiers to plunder the new crop introduced in Bohemia to boost agricultural productivity, giving rise to the popular name "Potato War". Though losses were less serious on the Austrian side, the heavy concentration of men defending Bohemia and Moravia consumed most of the available food and exhausted the government treasury. More significantly it exposed the political failings of absolutism personified in Joseph's obvious inadequacy as a general. In his desire to emulate Prussia's earlier successes, he tried to copy Frederick's unification of political and military control in his own hands. In an age of rudimentary communications, information retrieval and resource mobilization, personal control was too much even for a man with Joseph's talents; or indeed for Frederick, who, in practice, relied heavily on his brother, who commanded half the army. Joseph lost his nerve and already on 7 July, only two days after the Prussians crossed the frontier, he was writing to his mother to request another 40,000 men, believing the situation was now desperate.[100]

Maria Theresa had always been opposed to the conflict and opened negotiations behind the emperor's back. In the end, Frederick's flagging war effort was baled out by his Russian ally, which threatened to invade Galicia unless Joseph made peace. Along with France, Russia brokered the Peace of Teschen of 13 May 1779, the significance of which far exceeded the minor territorial adjustments it sanctioned. Austria evacuated Bavaria except for a small piece of territory called the Innviertel, which it kept, but agreed to pay Saxony 6 million tlr compensation for its feudal rights and recognized Prussian claims to Ansbach and Bayreuth.[101] Otherwise, the old Westphalian Settlement was endorsed and guaranteed by Russia, which now assumed similar constitutional powers as France, effectively replacing Sweden, which was no longer in a position to intervene actively in imperial politics.

Many medium princes regarded Russian intervention as an unwelcome intrusion, particularly as its mediation displaced their attempt to regain some influence by brokering peace. Alarmed by renewed Prussian proposals to secularize the Westphalian bishoprics, Hanover had joined Cologne-Münster in promoting a potential Third Party to include the Dutch in an effort to preserve political autonomy in northwest Germany. This was paralleled by a combined effort by Hanover, Cologne, Mainz and Saxony to interpose themselves through the *Reichstag* between Austria and Prussia to resolve the conflict by constitutional means. Both initiatives collapsed, as Russian intervention bypassed the formal structure altogether.[102]

The situation grew more serious after Maria Theresa's death, which not only brought Joseph to full power, but removed the key stumbling block to an Austro-Russian *rapprochement* that was completed in 1781–3. With Russia as an ally, Joseph felt confident to restart efforts to exchange the Netherlands for Bavaria, provoking renewed international crisis by 1784.[103] Prussia was dangerously isolated as the new combination removed its chief foreign support. When the Russian Grand Duke Paul embarked on his Grand Tour of Germany in 1782, he demonstrably omitted Berlin from the itinerary.[104] Increasingly, Prussia fell back on the third strand of Frederick's policy, seeking to mobilize the *Reich* to block Austria.

Prussia rallied the support of the medium princes by skilfully exploiting their concerns and growing sense of powerlessness. Baden, Weimar and Anhalt-Dessau had floated a scheme since 1782 that was intended to revive the constitution. In contrast to previous reform initiatives, which had been directed against the spectre of imperial absolutism, this was intended to restrain both Austria and Prussia. Frederick perverted the project, converting it into a defensively oriented princely league, established as the *Fürstenbund* on 23 July 1785 with an initial membership of Prussia, Hanover and Saxony.[105]

Prussia succeeded because it paid lip service to the princes' concerns, while Austria regarded them as a threat and responded only negatively with attempts to frustrate the league's formation.

The defection of Mainz to the new group on 18 October 1785 was a serious blow to Habsburg prestige given the electorate's traditional role as leader of the Catholics and lesser territories. Archbishop Erthal's ambitions perfectly encapsulate both the aspirations of the league's members as well as their lack of realism. Like the earlier Schönborn electors, Erthal hoped to become a key power broker in the *Reich*, intending to head a reformed Catholic German National Church free from papal interference, with his own position underpinned by Prussian and Hanoverian subsidies to raise his army to 8,000.[106] Prussia had no intention of permitting such independence, and Erthal's dream, like the reform proposals generally, remained unfulfilled.

Nonetheless, the *Fürstenbund* also demonstrated the limits to Prussia's influence. Despite considerable efforts, Frederick's diplomats could not persuade other ecclesiastical rulers to follow Erthal's example apart from securing his successor designate, Dalberg, in 1787. They also failed to recruit leading Protestants like Sweden, Denmark and Hessen-Darmstadt, and although the group formally survived into the 1790s, it was clearly losing cohesion. By then it had served Prussia's purpose of providing a temporary stopgap until the king could find an alternative foreign ally, which was achieved in 1788 by Frederick's successor, Frederick William II, who signed a treaty with Britain. The cost to the *Reich* was considerable. A chance to revive the constitution had been lost and instead Prussia's clientele had been marshalled to block all initiatives at *Reich* and *Kreis* levels, leaving the imperial institutions partially paralyzed on the eve of the French Revolution. With the medium and lesser princes thus neutralized, preservation of the traditional *status quo* increasingly rested on the fickle interests of outsiders.

The key power in this respect was France, whose policy toward the *Reich* had changed since 1756. Generally, this has been seen as a switch from aggressive expansionism to a process of *Pénétration pacifique*, whereby French territory and influence was extended across the Rhine by diplomacy and an expansion of its clientele network. Thanks to Eckhard Buddruss's excellent recent study, we now have a new understanding of French imperial policy. The heavy financial toll of the Seven Years War forced a partial disengagement from the *Reich*, manifested by a reduction in subsidies to the Geman courts, which had constituted the principal means of advancing French interests. Apart from the duke of Zweibrücken, who, as heir to the entire Wittelsbach territorial complex, merited special treatment, all other rulers found their payments either terminated or cut severely. Influence in the Rhineland was sustained by diplomacy intended not to acquire additional territory, but to make the existing area more secure through an exchange of enclaves with Trier, Nassau-Saarbrücken and Zweibrücken. The crowning achievement was the peaceful absorption of Lorraine in 1766, as arranged by the Treaty of Vienna 28 years before, which consolidated France's strategic advantage along the Rhine.[107]

This policy inadvertently furthered the marginalization of the middling princes who were denied access to the funds they needed to rebuild their armies and recover their influence. Saxony, Bavaria and Württemberg all failed in their attempts to negotiate new ties to France. It also gradually distanced France from its nominal major ally, Austria, so that by the mid-1760s, French diplomacy had assumed a position roughly equidistant from both German powers. The primary objective had become maintenance of the German *status quo* by balancing both Austria and Prussia. France assumed this position not through any sense of duty towards the old Westphalian Settlement but from naked self-interest. The First Partition of Poland had weakened France's European position by handicapping its traditional partner in the east, and it wanted to prevent a further erosion by blocking potential Austro-Prussian aggrandizement within Germany. French diplomats regarded the lesser territories as *forces mortes*, or inert resources, which covered over half the total surface of the *Reich*.[108] It was imperative for France's survival as a great power to prevent the mobilization of these resources through their incorporation within either Austria or Prussia.

Accordingly, France began covertly opposing Austrian candidates in episcopal elections within the *Reichskirche* from the mid-1760s, as well as stiffening Wittelsbach resolve to resist Joseph's exchange schemes. This represented a significant reversal of pre-1757 direction, since France now placed the German *status quo* above potential territorial gains that could have come from Austrian concessions in the Netherlands. French ties to Zweibrücken proved Versailles's trump card, since its duke consistently opposed Joseph's plans. France also blocked Prussian designs, backing Austria in 1769 when it looked as if Frederick might acquire Ansbach and Bayreuth. Yet, increasingly Prussia was viewed as an unofficial partner, especially after 1778, when France realized that Frederick was doing their task for them by opposing Austrian aggrandizement. Ironically, this contributed to the prevailing uncertainty, since it removed the need for a formal alliance with Prussia and so heightened Frederick's sense of insecurity. From a French perspective, however, the policy was highly successful until 1787, when the objectives of Berlin and Versailles began to diverge.

The issue was the domestic condition of the Dutch Republic, where tension between the Orangist stadholder and the republican Patriot Party grew in the late 1770s. Matters became crossed with Joseph's attempts to promote his exchange plan by excluding foreign interference in the Austrian Netherlands. He did manage to persuade the Dutch to withdraw their garrisons from the Barrier fortresses in 1782, but his plans to promote Belgian trade by reopening the river Scheldt caused widespread concern.[109] Matters slid out of hand with skirmishing between the Patriot paramilitary free corps and units of the Dutch regular army still loyal to William V of Orange. Prussian involvement was essentially dynastic, as William V's wife was Frederick William II's sister. By 1787 the Prussian monarch had decided that military intervention was necessary to uphold Hohenzollern prestige and the traditional links to the House of Orange. This was at variance with French policy, which, like the Patriot movement, had supported the American colonists in their recent war of independence, and which now hoped to extend its influence in Dutch internal affairs by opposing the stadholder. As French military experts arrived to train the Patriot paramilitaries, 20,000 Prussian regulars collected in Cleves ready to intervene. On 13 September 1787 they crossed the frontier and all resistance collapsed by 9 October. The Prussians remained only until the following April, when the Dutch restored William's political rights and his government hired German auxiliaries to strengthen its decaying forces.

The Dutch crisis had major German and international repercussions. It signalled the collapse of French monarchical foreign policy and hastened the onset of its own domestic crisis from 1787. It also extricated Prussia from its diplomatic isolation, as its support for the Orangist faction established common ground with Britain, which had long fought to strengthen the powers of the stadholder. The Anglo-Prussian alliance of 13 August 1788 provided security against both Austria and Russia, including the potential support of a British fleet in the Baltic. Lastly, the success of Prussia's police action encouraged overconfidence when it was decided to repeat the exercise against France in 1792. For all their rhetoric of liberty and freedom, Patriot resistance had been feeble, and the Prussian corps had lost only 211 killed and (more significantly) only 218 deserters of whom a mere 15 were native Prussians.[110]

The partial disengagement of France from the *Reich* furthered Russian penetration of imperial politics, which reached new heights under Catherine II. Though providing a second prop for the traditional *status quo*, this brought the medium princes few direct benefits and left the constitution further dependent on external interference. Even Prussia suffered. Frederick had hoped to use his 1764 Russian alliance to return to his pre-1756 policy of enhancing his own power by acting as the conduit for external influence within the *Reich*. However, Catherine II was determined not to be tied to German interest and manipulated Frederick for her own ends. Like those of France, these were a form of "crisis management" to increase Russian influence by balancing Austria and Prussia.[111] However, Russia went beyond France in utilizing its influence in Germany to force Austria and Prussia into concessions in eastern Europe and the Balkans, beginning in the First Partition of Poland and continuing with subsequent annexations at Turkey's expense. Not only did Prussia become dependent on Russia, but Catherine II began to displace the emperor from his traditional role as internal peacemaker and source of patronage.

Catherine II's diplomacy in 1765–73 resolved long-standing tensions in north Germany to Russia's advantage. In return for conceding Danish possession of Schleswig, the Russian branch of the Gottorp dynasty was relocated to Denmark's German possessions of Oldenburg and Delmenhorst. At the same time, Denmark renounced all claims to Hamburg, signalling its withdrawal from imperial politics, which, while ending a constant source of friction, also removed a counterweight to Prussian influence in Lower Saxony. Meanwhile, Russia took the place of the traditional imperial guarantee for German dynastic inheritance treaties, endorsing Prussia's treaty of 1752 with Ansbach in 1769 and that of 1764 between the two Badens two years later. Russia adopted the traditional Habsburg methods of patronage, advancing its influence in key Protestant states like Württemberg and Hessen-Darmstadt by dynastic marriages and posts in its army for German cadet princes. Finally, a extensive diplomatic network was established, including from 1782 a permanent representative in Frankfurt. A sign of Russia's importance was the way its intrusion damaged both the major German powers. Not only was Prussia weakened, especially when Catherine II abandoned Frederick after 1781, but the new Russian alliance proved a liability for Joseph as well. Russian support for Habsburg policy, particularly in opposing the *Fürstenbund*, raised German fears that Joseph was now so powerful that he could push through his unconstitutional schemes. More immediately, Russia's Balkan ambitions sucked Austria into a new conflict with the Ottoman empire, which it could ill-afford.

The last Turkish War, 1787–92

The last Turkish War was a product of a classic paradox of great power politics. Austria went to war not so much out of a desire to obtain new territory but to prevent its Russian ally from making extensive gains. The origins lay in the shift in the underlying strategic balance on the *Reich*'s eastern frontier, which had been accelerating since the 1760s. A Turkish attempt to pre-empt further Russian expansion ended in disaster in 1768–74, including a complete military collapse at Khotin (Chocim) on the Dniester (1769) and the destruction of their entire fleet at Cesme in the Aegean by a Russian squadron sent from the Baltic in 1770. These defeats greatly alarmed Kaunitz, who reluctantly agreed to the Polish partition in 1772 as a means of blocking further Russian and Prussian expansion. Pressure was then applied to the sultan to cede Bukovina in 1775, an area between newly-acquired Polish Galicia and Transylvania, thus retrieving it from potential Russian occupation and consolidating the monarchy's eastern frontier.

Karl Roider has aptly summed up Austria's aims after 1775 that "a weak Turkey was a welcome neighbour; a strong Russia was not".[112] The aim continued to be to preserve the Ottoman empire and avoid another partition of Poland. Kaunitz was convinced that, if either Austria or Russia made additional gains in the Balkans, Prussia would insist on "compensation". As long as the *Reich* continued to exist, such compensation could only come from Polish land, far more valuable economically and strategically than anything Austria could obtain in the Balkans. The other option, a serious *rapprochement*, was out of the question for either Kaunitz or Maria Theresa, all the more so after Frederick opposed Austria over the Bavarian Succession in 1778–9 and received Russian diplomatic support to mediate a favourable peace. While sharing much of these views, Joseph increasingly pushed a different course. He also regarded an Ottoman collapse as undesirable but unlike the others he viewed it as inevitable. If it was going to happen, he felt Austria should protect its existing frontiers by seizing its share of the remaining Ottoman territories, and, following his understanding with Russia, Catherine II dropped her opposition to the Bavarian exchange scheme and the two prepared to co-operate in a new Turkish war.

Like the war of 1737–9, the new conflict was started by Russia with Austria joining later as an ally. In other respects, it was radically different. The German context had been transformed and Austria was now a great power pursuing its own interests across the entire continent. The emperor was no longer primarily a German–Christian champion, valiantly holding back the infidel hordes, but instead pursued war for Habsburg strategic reasons alone, defined in political realist terms alien to the whole spirit of the *Reich*. After the partition of Poland it was clear that German help would be unforthcoming, particularly as Prussia was opposed to the war. Wisely, Joseph did not even ask, thus avoiding the humiliation of the inevitable rejection. Papal assistance was no longer requested and the Turkish bells remained silent; crusading was definitely out of fashion. Venice, now earmarked for potential absorption into the expanding Habsburg monarchy, was also not approached.

Though doubting the wisdom of the war, Austrian policy-makers decided they had more to lose by remaining neutral than joining in. In addition to the by now ever-present fear of Russia, there was concern at possible Prussian intervention against Austria or in the *Reich*. The sultan had already approached Prussia for military support in 1784, although he received an unfavourable response. Prussia appeared particularly threatening when news leaked out of the "Grand Design" of the new monarch's influential minister, Erwald Count von Hertzberg, for a complex redistribution of territory in eastern Europe, which essentially expected Austria and Russia to fight for Prussian gains at Poland's expense. This seemed so alarming because of Prussia's apparent ability to put this into effect, especially after securing its British alliance in 1788. Only reassurances from Russia kept Joseph on line.

Austria mobilized a huge army, totalling around 314,000 in 1788.[113] Of these 140,000 could be deployed at the front, the largest ever mustered against the Turks. As before, Austrian calculations depended on a successful Russian advance on the Ukrainian front, and, like 1737–9, this soon got bogged down, enabling the Turks to redeploy their main force to confront the Austrians. Joseph was persuaded to remain on the defensive, and by late May 1788 53,000 out of his 66,000 men under his direct command were already ill. Between then and May 1789 a further 120,000 fell ill, of whom 33,000 died. A sudden Ottoman offensive broke through the ailing Austrians, stopping only when it outran its supply lines. Having laid waste to the region, the Turks retreated, allowing their opponents to begin a modestly successful counterattack, backed by reasonable Russian support in Moldavia. Hopes that the Balkan Christians would lend a hand proved even more unrealistic than usual, with many of the local inhabitants actually assisting the Ottoman defence, especially in Bosnia.

Faced with logistical problems that surpassed even those encountered in the war against Prussia in 1778–9, the Austrian high command doubted their ability to continue the offensive into 1789 and only launched an assault on Belgrade after direct orders from Joseph. Austro-Russian co-operation continued to improve, however, leading to a victory for the first time with a joint army at Focsani on 30 July 1789. Meanwhile, at Belgrade Joseph's army began "the most spectacular and convincing display of the technique of bombardment in the whole era of black powder".[114] Having been pelted with 187,000 rounds from the Danube flotilla and land batteries in a mere 17 hours, the defenders surrendered on 8 October. Six weeks later the Austrians took Bucharest while the Russians made further gains.

By now the international situation was looking increasingly ominous. The collapse of France into revolution removed Austria's chief western deterrent against Prussia, and Joseph began to fear that his successes would drive the Turks into the arms of Fredeick William II. His control of the Austrian Netherlands collapsed, as the local rebellion there drove out the garrison by

December 1789, while there was a danger that the insurrection might spread to Galicia and Hungary. His death on 20 February 1790 removed the final obstacle to peace, as his successor Leopold II had consistently opposed the war. A *rapprochement* with Prussia was initiated, culminating in the Convention of Reichenbach, confirming a policy of peace without annexation. This was adhered to in the Anglo-Prussian brokered Treaty of Sistova on 4 August 1791. Habsburg pride was salvaged by a special bilateral agreement with the sultan, who ceded a narrow strip 120 km along the river Unna in Bosnia, plus the strategic town of Orsova, on the Danube in Western Wallachia on the condition it was not fortified. Left in the lurch by these developments, Russia made its own peace in January 1792, defusing the subsequent Russo-Prussian antagonism by a second partition of Poland in 1793.[115]

The last Turkish War ended to Austria's disadvantage, with Russia consolidating her gains from the Turks, advancing deeper into the Balkans and encroaching on Austria's sphere of influence in Poland. Russia rather than the Ottomans now clearly represented the greater danger. Though emerging since 1686, this "eastern question" had developed partly as a consequence of Austria's own military success in 1683–1718. The setback of 1737–9 accelerated the pace by weakening both Austria and the Ottomans without seriously damaging Russia. As Austria's influence deteriorated, the emperor's eastern territorial ambitions diminished. The dreams of reaching Istanbul, present at the height of victory in 1688, had long disappeared by 1737, while by the 1750s further gains were no longer considered desirable in themselves, but merely as means of blocking Russia.

The gradual transition in German involvement is also significant. In 1664 and 1683 a Turkish War was definitely a matter for the *Reich*, the *Reichsarmee* was mobilized and considerable financial support provided . Events on the Danube affected imperial politics directly, not only in *Reichstag* discussions, but also through bilateral assistance treaties, and the sense of common danger was widespread. Even awkward rulers like the Great Elector and Frederick III/I felt obliged to forget at least part of their differences with Austria and provide troops, albeit at a price. Even though enthusiasm waned after 1687, when it was clear that it was now a conflict to extend Habsburg hegemony, imperial patriotism and general political dependency on the emperor persuaded many princes to continue supplying troops. The spectacular success at Zenta, followed by the advantageous Peace of Karlowitz, boosted Habsburg military and political prestige in the crucial run up to the great conflict over the Spanish succession. Further gains in 1716–18 compensated for the failure to obtain the entire inheritance and helped sustain the image of Habsburg might. This was shattered in 1737–9, compounding damage done in 1733–5, and in a reversal of 1699 weakened Habsburg influence just before another major conflict.

As dynastic and strategic interests predominated in what were now offensive wars, the *Reich* became less and less involved. Though individual princes still sent contingents, the conflicts were no longer a common concern beyond the money voted by the *Reichstag*. Even these forms of involvement were absent in the last war. Nonetheless, events in the Balkans still exerted an influence on the *Reich* through Austro-Prussian rivalry. Just as imperial politics had polarized, marginalizing the lesser territories, these were also squeezed out of the Turkish wars. The emperor acted primarily as head of a European power in uneasy concert with Russia after 1726. Only Prussia remained an indirect participant after 1739, first by unsuccessfully seeking Turkish assistance against Austria during the 1740s and 1750s, and later by manipulating events to extract concessions in Poland. The expansion of Austro-Prussian rivalry eastwards and the concomitant withdrawal of the lesser territories is indicative of the *Reich*'s declining influence on events.

Chapter Eight

The challenge of revolution

The Reich *and the French Revolution*

Central European history in the period of the French Revolution and Revolutionary Wars (1789–1801) is normally depicted as a clash between old and new in which the "moribund" *Reich* stood little chance of withstanding the new ideology and force of a unified national state.[1] In nowhere else does the contrast seem more pronounced than in the field of military organization: against unified, centralized France with its mass army of motivated citizens-in-arms was pitted the apparently antiquated *Reich*, with its decentralized, fragmented structure producing an army that was an object of mockery, commanded by incompetents and composed of men held together only by fear of punishment.[2] Explanations for the *Reich*'s collapse by 1806 are inseparable from accounts of the French victories, since the two are seen as different sides of the same coin; the revolutionary transformation of France enabling it to defeat the obsolete, reactionary German political system. This chapter reappraises these arguments to indicate that the *Reich* coped comparatively well with both the ideological and material challenge from France, falling less through the strength of its enemies than through a lack of political will from its main components to continue its defence.

The Revolution threatened the *Reich* in three ways. First, it represented a general assault on the traditional order and was soon recognized as such, although this did not necessarily make German rulers tremble in their buckled shoes nor wish to embark on a counterrevolutionary crusade. Secondly, it provoked popular unrest in Germany, or at least appeared to do so to contemporaries who activated the existing conflict resolution and public order mechanisms to counter it. Finally, the outbreak of the Revolutionary Wars in April 1792 posed an external threat that had to be met by peaceful compromise or military retaliation. It was this third aspect that placed the *Reich*'s continued existence into question, because it destroyed the pre-revolutionary international balance sustaining the political *status quo* and released the indigenous forces seeking to partition Germany.

The French Revolution initially struck a chord not only amongst German intellectuals but many princes, who welcomed the collapse of an old enemy and believed the crisis was the monarchy's own fault for not having emulated their own enlightened reforms. Most elites were confident in their superiority, not only at territorial level but within the wider *Reich*. On the surface the structure did indeed appear weak; the *Reichstag* met in full session only infrequently during 1788–91, while other institutions showed serious flaws. Yet despite Prussia's manipulation of the *Fürstenbund*, enthusiasm for imperial reform remained high, and the considerable pamphlet literature it generated continued to express faith in the traditional structure and its continued relevance to contemporary events. Indeed, appreciation for existing institutions grew as attitudes hardened towards events in France. The abolition of feudalism by the new French National Assembly on 11 August 1789 affected German rights in the areas annexed by Louis XIV west of the Rhine, including the Mömpelgard lordships belonging to Württemberg, as well as various territories of Nassau, Hessen-Darmstadt and other middling princes. The arrival of aristocratic refugees (*émigrés*) from August onwards spread further alarm with exaggerated tales of events in Paris, and many were given shelter by ecclesiastical princes in the Rhineland. Increasingly, revolutionary ideology and the policies of the new government were no longer regarded as internal French affairs but as a sustained attack on the established order within Europe. The abolition of German property and feudal rights far exceeded the threat posed by the *Réunions*, which had left these intact, while the French creation of a secular, national state implied an attack on the temporal jurisdiction of spiritual princes and hence a threat to one of the key pillars of the *Reich*.

These fears were magnified by the coincidence of the upheavals in France with those elsewhere. Following the suppression of serious unrest in Transylvania in 1784, renewed trouble had broken out in the Austrian Netherlands after 1787, which soon exceeded the capacity of the local Habsburg garrison to contain it. Further disturbances occurred in Liège, Aachen, Trier, Zweibrücken, Nassau, Speyer and parts of the southwest in 1789, followed by a massive peasant rising in electoral Saxony the next year.[3] The territorial authorities were understandably alarmed and suspected the trouble was due to revolutionary ideas being spread by vagrants, deserters and French agitators. This was an entirely traditional reaction and had characterized attitudes during the Reformation and an earlier populist peasant movement known as the *Bundschuh*, when Rhenish and south German governments had suspected their own inhabitants were being radicalized by subversive ideas spread by a few conspirators. The new ideology did enflame existing German social and political problems, especially through the exemplary French popular action of storming the Bastille and erecting "Liberty Trees". However, the authorities greatly exaggerated the danger and failed, at least initially, to see that German unrest was the result of existing socio-economic problems unconnected with events across the Rhine. No outbreak was truly revolutionary. Most radical was that in Liège, where the local "patriots", modelling themselves on the similarly named Dutch republicans, stormed the citadel on 18 August 1789, forcing the bishop to flee. The Belgian revolt was the most extensive, but was largely a conservative reaction to Joseph II's enlightened political and religious reforms as well as alien Habsburg rule. Regardless of their true motive, all popular action convinced the local authorities of the necessity of swift action. The *Reich*'s multi-layered structure permitted a flexible and, from the perspective of the elites, effective response, but matters overall were complicated by latent Austro-Prussian tension and worsening relations with the new French government.

The constitutional structure facilitated action at three levels. At the top, the *Reichstag* provided a convenient forum for discussion and a recognized authority to legitimize countermeasures. Opinion was divided between those who favoured violent repression and others who advocated deflecting protest through the courts and administrative review. Unfortunately for the *Reich*, the debate became intermeshed in Austro-Prussian rivalry, as the two powers supported alternative responses. Austria favoured formal conflict resolution through the imperial courts, sanctioning repression only if necessary and within the framework of the executive ordinance. These proposals found favour among those who felt that undiluted repression would be counterproductive. However, Austria had an ulterior motive, since it wished to strengthen the courts as a means of curbing princely autonomy, while some Habsburg ministers hoped to use the executive ordinance to sanction German assistance for the flagging Austrian military effort against the Belgian rebels on the grounds that the Netherlands were part of the Burgundian *Kreis*. Habsburg policy was fatally hamstrung by Joseph II's failing health and, following his death on 20 February 1790, the necessity of not provoking the princes until his successor, Leopold II, had been elected. Formal *Reich* assistance remained unforthcoming, forcing Austria back on the old expedient of bilateral agreements to procure auxiliaries from Anhalt-Zerbst, Würzburg and Bamberg.[4]

These problems strengthened Prussia's hand as it tried to rally the princes in a renewed *Fürstenbund* to oppose Leopold's election. Deliberately exaggerating the danger from below, Prussia played on the princes' anxieties to justify the direct use of force at *Kreis* level, where it had greater influence. The *Kreise* offered a second avenue for a counterrevolutionary response, being ideally placed to co-ordinate regional activity. The Upper Rhinelanders already met in October 1789, followed by their electoral neighbours and both established military cordons along their western frontiers to arrest potential revolutionary agitators. Westphalia, Franconia, Swabia and Bavaria also met to discuss possible action, but their debate soon became mired in the national controversy over the appropriate response. Bishop Erthal of Würzburg and Bamberg favoured a co-ordinated response through the territorial courts to settle justified grievances and defuse popular tension, but Prussia continued to urge repression. The financial implications of a military response soon emerged as a major issue that was to escalate once the *Reich* was pulled into armed conflict with France. Some, such as Mainz and Trier, favoured the Prussian initiative because they saw *Kreis* military action as a way of sparing their beleaguered exchequers by spreading the cost of counterrevolution among the member territories. Others objected paying for police actions required by their neighbours' misrule while their own good government left their lands tranquil. In particular, the idea that costs could be recovered from the guilty party was controversial and dependent on the success of the repression.

Matters were brought to a head by the Liège debacle of 1789–92, which demonstrated what could go wrong when the formal system of conflict resolution was not adhered to. In the heady days of August 1789, in the wake of the storming of the Bastille, the RKG failed to distinguish between the French Revolution and the largely traditional protests in Liège. Without properly considering the matter, the court ruled on 27 August that the Liège Patriots were rebels in breach of the public peace and summoned Westphalia as the relevant *Kreis* to restore order. The official response immediately became distorted by the general political controversy as Prussia moved to block intervention. Despite its talk of repression elsewhere, Prussia wanted to avoid it in Liège in case it provided a pretext for Austria to summon help for the Netherlands. Given its influence in the Westphalian *Kreis* executive, Prussia's attitude was crucial, and its contradiction of the oficial response contributed to the failure of the first armed intervention in November 1789. This policy backfired on Prussia, particularly after its recognition of the Belgian rebels' unilateral declaration of independence (10 January 1790) appeared to sanction the fragmentation of the *Reich*. Prussia withdrew its contingent from the combined Westphalian force on 15 April, forcing the RKG to extend execution of its verdict to Franconia, Swabia, Electoral and Upper Rhine four days later. Swabia and Franconia showed little enthusiasm and the 6,800 men assembled by Münster and the Rhenish electorates stood little chance of defeating the 17,000 Patriots deployed along a 20km front.

Execution of the court verdict clearly depended on the success of Austrian repression in Belgium, since the Liège rebels could not survive on their own. Indeed, they displayed the typical characteristics of the *Reich* in desiring a negotiated settlement to military confrontation. The mood of the times was against them, and Austrian troops moved in as nominal Burgundian *Kreistruppen* in January 1791 after a temporary victory over the Belgians and imposed order with token Mainz and Münster participation.

The operation exposed serious flaws, not least in the poor quality of the Westphalian and Electoral Rhenish contingents, which had been hastily mobilized with raw recruits. Worse, the financial problems emerged as a serious constraint on collective action, since few of the medium territories could sustain prolonged military activity. The Trier estates refused to contribute towards their elector's participation, and it proved impossible to enforce the RKG ruling of 11 February 1791 that expenses were to be recovered from the rebels themselves. Nonetheless, it is only in retrospect that the Liège affair appears a total failure since the action had successfully restored the *status quo* by 1792. By then the *Reich* was being overtaken by events that were to ensure that this success mattered little: the reactionary Bishop Hoensbroeck died on 3 June, followed by the occupation of his land by the French revolutionaries, temporarily from November 1792, permanently from June 1794.[5]

Apart from official *Kreis* intervention in Aachen, under way since 1786 to resolve a typical internal dispute, most counterrevolutionary repression took place at territorial level, especially in Baden, but also Mainz and to a limited extent elsewhere. Most rulers avoided violence and instead followed the growing national consensus in favour of compromise and pacification to defuse protest along traditional lines. Measures included food relief to alleviate the bad harvest of 1789, judicial redress of complaints against landlords and state official and limited public welfare measures. Collectively, they proved far more successful than violent coercion and ensured the continued broad acceptance of the existing authorities. The *Reichstag* contributed to the success of these measures by providing legal guidelines for specific territorial action. Examples include national censorship laws passed in August 1791 and the ban on "German Jacobins" in February 1793, laying them open to military sanctions should any actually be apprehended. An attempt to outlaw freemasonry was rejected, but the *Reichstag* did ban secret fraternities to prevent the "contagion" of the new ideas spreading from the universities to infect the territorial bureaucracies. No action was taken beyond this, not through *Reich* ineffectiveness, but because the princes no longer felt the danger sufficient to merit more serious measures. The response remained flexible, tailored largely to suit local circumstance as defined by the relevant authorities, and there was no perceived need to strengthen national institutions to intervene directly.[6]

The *Reich* also provided German elites with a framework to deal with their principal grievance with revolutionary France: the abolition of feudal rights on the left bank. The *Reichstag* provided a forum for peaceful resolution of tension with neighbouring states and most princes favoured its use to negotiate with France. Some did advocate a more robust response, particularly Bishop Styrum of Speyer, who argued as early as 20 August 1789 that war was justified on the grounds that the French action violated existing international treaties, while the domestic chaos provided the ideal opportunity for a German recovery of Alsace and Lorraine.[7] Though the *Reichstag* played a useful role in dampening such hot-headed calls for revenge, its attempts to mediate a more appropriate response foundered on unrealistic expectations and mutual suspicion. The princes themselves contributed by rejecting offers of financial compensation, insisting instead on full restitution of their former rights, while the French accused the Rhinelanders of fostering counter-revolution by harbouring the *émigrés*.[8]

However, neither of these problems was sufficient to prompt the disastrous war with revolutionary France, which resulted instead from factors beyond the control of Reich institutions. Probably most important was the desire of the increasingly radical French government to solve its domestic problems through foreign war, while a renewed Austro-Prussian *rapprochement*, under way since 1790, removed any chance of wider German neutrality.[9]

Austro-Prussian rapprochement, 1790–95

The two German great powers established a working relationship in the Convention of Reichenbach, July 1790, that was to last, though not without tension, until 1795. Whereas the earlier transient *rapprochement* of 1769–72 had merely highlighted the possible dangers, the new co-operation inflicted serious damage on the *Reich*. Realizing that there was now no alternative, the medium princes were driven to desperate, ultimately destructive measures, culminating in their drift to France after 1795.

Meanwhile, the Habsburgs' desire and ability to preserve the traditional structure was undermined by their changing relationship with Prussia, which derived far greater benefit from the uneasy partnership than did Austria. As a result, Austria increasingly saw its German clients as potential compensation for disappointments elsewhere and the growing need to maintain influence by equalizing Prussia's gains.

Ironically, these problems were already responsible for driving Austria into its bad bargain with Prussia in the first place. The revolt of the Netherlands from 1787 combined with the costly last Turkish War to weaken the monarchy at a time when its international position was deteriorating. Leopold II's attempts to extricate Austria from the Turkish War merely antagonized the Russians, who understandably felt they were being left in the lurch. As nothing could be expected from France after 1789, a compromise with Prussia seemed the sensible policy and met with a favourable reception in Berlin, where Hertzberg was planning another partition of Poland. The Habsburg government had little desire for a further reduction of its Polish buffer zone, but hoped to bargain concessions at its expense to exclude Prussia from Ansbach-Bayreuth and secure Frederick William II's consent to the Bavarian Netherlands exchange scheme. These terms proved unacceptable to Prussia, which inherited Ansbach-Bayreuth in 1792 by arrangement with its last margrave. Prussia then proceeded to a Second Partition of Poland by bilateral agreement with Russia on 23 January 1793, ignoring both its earlier guarantees to the Poles and its new understanding with Austria. Saxony was also excluded to frustrate a Polish attempt to preserve their integrity by offering their crown to the elector as a hereditary possession. The electorate slid unwillingly into the slipstream of Prussian policy, while Hohenzollern influence was entrenched in the *Reich* by its new and significant territorial presence in Franconia. However, Berlin was acutely aware of the need to forestall possible Austrian intervention and sought to placate its ally without the need of condoning an annexation of Bavaria by encouraging hopes of alternative compensation in Alsace and Lorraine at France's expense.

The Habsburg–Hohenzollern *rapprochement* was thus an alliance of convenience to exploit French weakness as a means of resolving their respective problems in the Netherlands, Poland and the *Reich*. Despite rhetoric to the contrary, there was little sense of sinking their differences for the sake of monarchical solidarity with Louis XVI. Austria wanted war to neutralize Prussia's advantage, while Prussia supported it in the hope it would bring the emperor sufficient gains to reconcile him to its new aggrandizement in Poland.[10]

The immediate repercussion was to force an unwilling *Reich* into renewed war with France by 1793. *Rapprochement* between the two German great powers prevented the other territories from exploiting their rivalry to advance an alternative middle path. In August 1791 the *Reichstag* declared the French expropriation of German property rights illegal, thereby creating a basis for a more radical response, but left it up to the emperor to choose between war and peace. Leopold II did try to negotiate, but by December it was already too late, as the revolutionaries now saw war as a way out of their own problems. Fear of Prussia as much as the emotional factors of hatred of revolution hindered a compromise that might have been possible before the end of 1791:

for all their radicalism at home the revolutionaries had retained much of the monarchy's traditional foreign policy and had continually proposed peaceful solutions that would have permitted Austria to complete the long-desired exchange of the Netherlands for Bavaria. The chance of any last-minute compromise was removed by a new distraction for Austrian policy-makers: as in the case of the initial response to the Revolution, the new external crisis coincided with an imperial interregnum between the death of Leopold II, 1 March, and the election of his successor, Francis II, 5 July 1792. Austria became caught up in the logic of its co-operation with Prussia at a time when the latter's desire for war coincided with renewed French aggression.[11]

From war of aggrandizement to Reichskrieg, *1792–3*

The French revolutionaries declared war on 20 April 1792, sending an army into the Austrian Netherlands nine days later. The declaration was framed solely against Francis II as king of Hungary and Bohemia, which, while technically correct, as he had not yet been elected emperor, was also an attempt by France to restrict the scope of its operations. Like Louis XIV, the revolutionaries wanted to fight the Habsburgs without involving the *Reich* in order to deny Austria the chance of mobilizing Germany's considerable resources. The question of these resources was to determine the fate of the *Reich*, since the conflict soon became as much a struggle to control them as to defeat France. Austria and Prussia were sole participants in this struggle until 1795, when they were joined by France, which began to manipulate the growing discontent of the marginalized medium princes.

Initially, Austria and Prussia sought access to German resources through mutual co-operation, but this fragile partnership did not survive the first military reverses against France, and the two became increasingly competitive. The earliest efforts centred on moves to reactivate the *Kreis* Association after 1790 to provide a framework for defence co-operation against France. Austria was the initial prime mover, and Leopold ordered the *Kreise* to review their security measures and start collaboration on 3 December 1791. Prussia backed these efforts from February 1792 as the best means of mobilizing the resources of the weaker territories. Some exposed territories like Baden were prepared to co-operate, but most feared any action would provoke France. At the national level both Hanover and Bavaria campaigned for neutrality, while within Swabia Württemberg blocked attempts to mobilize the *Kreis*, seeking instead to use it as a framework to keep southwest Germany out of any international conflict. The opposition of these princes to a war has been

305

criticized as the short-sighted product of selfish interests on the grounds that revolutionary France could only be confronted by total mobilization.[12] Such a view is greatly distorted by the benefit of hindsight, since no one could have predicted in 1792 that the motley rabble of disgruntled regulars and ill-trained patriots that fled before they engaged the Austrians in May would be turned into a formidable fighting machine capable of transforming the map of Europe. What princes saw in 1792 was what their predecessors had seen in 1700 and 1757: an attempt by the leading German powers to force them into a war they had no wish to fight, that was contrary to the spirit of the *Reich* and indeed had little to do with their interests.

Faced with this attitude, it was not surprising that attempts to reactivate the Association failed, particularly as Austro-Prussian efforts were half-hearted at best. Neither was interested at this stage in formal *Reich* participation, since this threatened to encumber their policy with constitutional constraints and their primary concern was to persuade the others to contribute cash to subsidize their war effort. This policy was the product of the peculiar mix of overconfidence and anxiety that characterized the entire German response to the French Revolution. Ministers in Berlin and Vienna tended to believe *émigré* reports that support for the new French government had dwindled to a band of fanatics in Paris, and even astute observers like Kaunitz believed "that we will win is obvious; we need only a bit of time to gather our strength". Yet underneath there were concerns that defeat could spell disaster, and Kaunitz stressed the need for a quick, convincing victory because "we cannot endure many campaigns".[13]

Invasion forces were cut from the projected 120,000, initially agreed by the Austrian and Prussian high commands, to about 85,000, intended to converge on Paris from the Netherlands, Middle and Upper Rhine. Apart from 4,500 French *émigrés*, this force included a few troops from other German territories, indicating the start of a practice that was to dominate the wider German involvement in the Revolutionary Wars. Rather than constituting an autonomous force, contingents from the smaller territories were attached by bilateral agreement to the army of one of the two German great powers. Austria extended its network of limited alliances from 1790 by an additional agreement with Mainz on 14 August 1792 for 2,069 men, while Hessen-Kassel placed 5,500 at the disposal of Prussia.

Despite these reinforcements, the invasion force was hopelessly inadequate and some of the senior commanders doubted the wisdom of the operation. After a slow start in June 1792, the main force came up against a French army at Valmy, east of Paris on 20 September. After a long cannonade in which the Prussians only lost 184 men, their commander decided to retreat. The decision made a huge psychological impact, especially in France, where Valmy was regarded as a great victory, heartening the revolutionaries' resolve and precipitating the suspension of the monarchy and its transformation into a republic, following Louis XVI's execution in January 1793. Military reforms, culminating in the famous *levée en masse* of 23 August 1793, revitalized and enlarged the French army, which resumed the offensive with great success. One part of the army struck northwards, re-invading the Netherlands and scoring a far more convincing victory over the Austrians at Jemappes (6 November 1792). The other part advanced eastwards, seizing German territory west of the Rhine along with the cities of Speyer, Worms, Mainz and Frankfurt by 23 October 1792. A Prusso-Hessian counterattack recovered Frankfurt on 2 December, followed by Mainz after a long siege (14 April–23 July 1793), thereby stabilizing the situation.[14]

Nonetheless, it was now obvious that more resources were required to achieve victory over the French, particularly as the revolutionaries now embarked on an expansionist policy embodied by their edict of fraternity of 19 November 1792, promising to liberate Europe from the feudal yoke. Already on 1 September 1792 Francis II formally requested 100 RMs, initiating debates in the *Reichstag* on a military response to France.

The reverses following Valmy caused alarm amongst the princes, who saw immediately that it would result in increased pressure from Austria and Prussia. Max Franz of Cologne-Münster, himself a Habsburg prince and uncle of Francis II, commented that "one fears the French less than these two powers", and that their advocacy of war represented a "cure worse than the malady".[15] Pamphleteers complained that Austria and Prussia had reduced the Third Germany to a "shadow empire" (*Schatten-Reich*), but the continual defeats merely convinced the princes of the inevitability of war. As before, it had proved impossible to prevent a Franco-Habsburg great power struggle from spilling over into the *Reich*. Since the combatants were already over their frontiers, the lesser territories felt that only by participating could they have any say in the future course of the conflict. Hanover led the response to Austria's call for financial assistance by demanding full mobilization instead, and in November 1792 the *Reichstag* sanctioned a triple quota as a defensive measure. Three months later the request for 100 RMs was scaled down to a grant of 30 to be paid into the imperial Operations Fund (*Reichs Operations Kasse*), while finally, on 23 March, the assembled representatives declared the existing struggle to be a *Reichskrieg*.

The attempt to control direction of the war by activating these formal mechanisms of war management was thwarted by Austro-Prussian pressure during formulation of the common objectives. In addition to the traditional purpose of restoring the Westphalian Settlement, the new *Reichskrieg* was intended to secure reparation of all costs since the start of the conflict. The second aim was imposed on the *Reich* by Austria and Prussia to legitimize their expansionist objectives of securing territorial compensation from France and as such committed the other territories to an offensive war. This tension between the defensive concerns of the majority and the annexationist designs of the two great powers coincided with incipient fragmentation of their *rapprochement* in the face of the mounting impossibility of any gains in the west. The French resumed the offensive in summer 1793, forcing the Germans back over the Rhine and recovering control of the left bank territories. Another offensive the following year shattered the Austrians at Fleurus on 26 June and secured permanent possession over the Netherlands, thereby ending once and for all any hopes of an exchange. These Austrian disappointments were magnified by Prussian successes, as Frederick William II satisfied Hohenzollern ambitions through the Second Partition of Poland in January 1793. Prussia now lost interest in continuing the war in the west, particularly as it became embroiled in suppressing a Polish revolt from spring 1794 until the third and final partition removed the kingdom from the European map in 1795. Austrian isolation was increased by Russia's initial refusal to support the war against France, leaving it increasingly reliant on what help it could extract from the *Reich*. The gradual shift in Habsburg policy was furthered by a change in the Austrian government, which also coincided with the *Reichskrieg*. Baron Thugut, the former ambassador to Turkey, became the new foreign minister on 27 March and began implementing a new hard-line attitude towards the princes with the intention of seizing control over German military potential as compensation for flagging Prussian support.[16]

The struggle over German resources, 1793–5

Competition for German resources centred on five issues. First was the imperial general staff, which offered access to the *Reichsarmee* and direction of operations on the ground. Both Austria and Prussia also sought to control territorial manpower by continuing the practice of assigning contingents directly to their own armies, while a similar struggle took place over the cash contributions to the Operations Fund. A fourth possibility lay in the reform of the executive ordinance to strengthen formal powers to tap territorial resources either centrally or through the *Kreis* structure, while the final issue was the question of a mass popular mobilization (*Volksbewaffnung*) to counter the growth in French forces.

Austria enjoyed distinct advantages in the case of the general staff, thanks to its entrenched influence in selection and appointment procedures. Only a single Prussian was among the eight officers named as active generals by the emperor on 8 April 1793. In an attempt to forestall traditional objectives on religious grounds, Francis II named the Protestant Friedrich Josias von Sachsen-Coburg as the commanding field marshal, yet this could not obscure the fact that, like six of his comrades, he held general's rank in the Austrian army. His successor in 1794, Albert von Sachsen-Teschen, was Francis II's uncle and also a member of the Habsburg clientele. Prussia responded by mobilizing the *Reichstag* to back its campaign to exert influence on the military executive. The emperor was compelled to nominate the Prussian general, Heinrich August Prince Hohenlohe-Ingelfingen, as second imperial field marshal in 1794, but this success was negated by his death two years later. Though the *Reichstag* did demonstrate its autonomy by rejecting Thugut's candidate, General Wurmser, for a new appointment in 1796, it accepted the Habsburg Archduke Charles as an imperial field marshal even though, as a Catholic, he was technically not eligible for a vacant Protestant post.[17]

The value of this Habsburg monopoly of the high command was undermined by an inability to control the contingents. Mobilization in 1793 produced four categories of troops. The first were the *Kreistruppen*, who traditionally formed the backbone of the *Reichsarmee*. However, this time only three of the ten *Kreise* formed integrated contingents and of these only Swabia mobilized in full. Württemberg opposition to the war was weakened by Carl Eugen's death on 24 October 1793, and the duchy was overruled by the Catholic pro-Habsburg majority in the *Kreis* Assembly. With Wüttemberg participation, Swabian mobilization was impressive. Already in 1792 4,400 men had been assembled on the Rhine as a defensive measure. These rose to 6,800 by 1793, and following later increases to a nominal 18,500, 11,330 were actually present by September 1795. This represented seven times the region's basic quota, and collectively the Swabians accounted for 65 per cent of the total *Kreistruppen* present in the *Reichsarmee*.[18] Though Prussia did field five cavalry squadrons in place of the traditional Ansbach-Bayreuth contingent, Franconian participation was reduced by the separate service of Würzburg and Bamberg's troops as Austrian auxiliaries since 1790, leaving 1,569 men from the smaller territories as the only integrated *Kreistruppen* during 1793–5. Similarly, Upper Rhine forces were reduced to two weak infantry regiments by the decision of the two Hessian landgraves not to combine their troops with those of the other members.[19] The absence of the Electoral Rhine was due to losses suffered in 1792, which saw the destruction of the Mainz army at the battle of Speyer on 30 September and subsequent siege of the city. Trier and Cologne also suffered casualties, and French occupation of most of their territory by 1794 prevented all three electorates from reconstituting their armies.

Though never amounting to much more than 15,000 men, the *Kreistruppen* represented a considerable effort on the part of those lesser territories that provided them. They were insufficient to constitute a fully autonomous force but their presence in the *Reichsarmee* indicated the determination of the lesser territories to maintain their autonomy. Attempts by the Austrian-dominated imperial general staff to subordinate the troops to direct Habsburg control were resisted vigorously despite threats in March 1795 to arrest Lieutenant-General Stain, the Swabian commander.[20]

The absence of other *Kreis* contingents was explained by the decision of many territories to attach their contingents directly to either the Austrian or the Prussian army. While Saxony and Hessen-Kassel sent their troops to join the Prussians, Anhalt-Zerbst, Würzburg, Bamberg, Hessen-Darmstadt, Salzburg and many others let theirs march with the Austrians. Competition for these forces mounted after 1793 and both powers sought to tie them closer to their own troops. The Prussians refused to let the Saxons act as an autonomous contingent and kept them firmly attached to their own corps on the Middle Rhine, also persuading Hessen-Darmstadt to reassign its units from the Austrian command, although they later rejoined the official *Reichsarmee* further to the south. Meanwhile, the emperor insisted that Hanover and Palatinate-Bavaria subordinate their forces to the imperial command. The latter eventually sent a reduced contingent of about 2,500, but the former refused to send any men at all on the grounds that a proper *Reichsarmee* had not been formed and that the Austrians were using those units that had assembled for unconstitutional offensives.[21]

A large number of other territories also failed to send soldiers, preferring to pay cash *Relutions* instead. Often this has been interpreted as reflecting general apathy and a lack of concern for the *Reich*, but in fact derived partly from the breakdown of the *Kreis* structure in northern Germany, partly from recruiting difficulties and also from the desire to avoid direct involvement in a war many were opposed to politically. Some of the money went via the Operations Fund to hire substitutes provided by medium territories like Hessen-Darmstadt, which provided 2,400 men from September 1793.[22] Other payments were used to subsidize the *émigré* regiments operating on the Rhine. Paderborn and Wolfenbüttel hired the 1,800 strong Corps Rohan until 1795, when it transferred to the Austrian army, while the two princes of Hohenlohe-Bartenstein and Hohenlohe-Schillingsfürst collaborated with the Condé and Mirabeau Legions on a private counterrevolutionary venture in which they sank most of their own resources. The *émigrés* embodied the worst characteristics of old regime armies in terms of discipline, composition and efficiency: apart from reactionary aristocrats, few men could be persuaded to enlist in the poorly paid, ill-equipped units, and in 1793 the Condé and Bourbon regiments comprised 329 officers, but only 1,125 other ranks! Though associated with the *Reichsarmee*, the *émigrés* proved largely unwelcome guests and were not typical of the wider imperial war effort.[23] The bulk of the *Relutions* went directly to Austria and Prussia through bilateral agreements with individual territories. Prussia drew sums equivalent to 10,000 men, mainly from the weaker north Germans, while Austria had arrangements with about 60 territories, including Gotha, Weimar, Cologne, Mecklenburg and Lippe to substitute for 12,000 *Kreistruppen*. The total value of these sums was comparatively small, amounting to only 2 million fl. by 1797, but their political importance was considerable, since they reinforced the general dependency on the two great powers.[24]

Independent auxiliaries formed the fourth element of German military involvement, but unlike previous wars payments from the maritime powers were slow in coming and did not increase the bargaining power of the medium princes. Some units were already serving the Dutch under agreements made before the war with Stadholder William V (see Table 8.1), but the chaotic conditions within the Republic precluded further arrangements and most were withdrawn following the French invasion in 1795. Britain initially refused to pay subsidies, believing victory could be achieved without their expense, but signed a number of agreements from March 1793 for German troops to reinforce its own corps with the Austrians in the

Table 8.1 Auxiliaries in Dutch service 1782–1808

Territory	Treaty	Contingent	Remarks
Münster	19 Feb 1782	1,400	Revised 30 Dec 1784
Württemberg	1 Oct 1786	1,982	With the Dutch East India Company. Unit served in the colonies till 1808.
Wolfenbüttel	24 Feb 1788	3,000	3,060 served till 1794
Ansbach-Bayreuth	6 Mar 1788	1,345	1,386 served till Apr 1794
Mecklenburg-Schwerin	5 May 1788	1,000	Till 1795

Sources: Braubach, "Politisch–militärischen Verträge", pp. 191–4; J. Prinz, *Daus Württembergische Kapregiment, 1780–1808* (Stuttgart, 1932); Elster, *Braunschweig-Wolfenbüttel*, vol. II, pp. 469–70; Bezzel, *Haustruppen des letzen Markgrafen von Ansbach-Bayreuth*, pp. 25–44; Tessin, *Regimenter*, p. 223.

Note: An additional 8 rgts recruited by Nassau, Waldeck and Gotha continued to serve as integral elememts of the Dutch army till 1795. See Table 7.1.

Netherlands. As in earlier conflicts, these treaties pulled some of the best German regiments away from service with the *Reichsarmee*, but it is unlikely that the contributory territories would otherwise have had the resources to have deployed them all on the Rhine. Service with the maritime powers kept these troops out of the reach of Austria and Prussia, but any chance that their service might enhance their princes' political position was removed by the complete allied military collapse in the Low Countries in 1795 (Table 8.2).

The third area of Austro-Prussian competition concerned the cash contributions to the imperial Operation Fund which amounted to a nominal 15 million fl., of which a third was actually paid by 1797.[25] The two powers immediately quarrelled over the division of the Fund in February 1793, with matters getting worse when Prussia demanded recompense for the 2 million tlr it allegedly expended on recovering Mainz by July.[26] The imperial general staff meanwhile diverted money to pay for the "Austrian" contingent, meaning the monarchy's own army. Prussia's failure to control the Fund led Berlin to try another approach. By November 1793 ministers there felt they could

Table 8.2 Auxiliaries in British service, 1793–7

Territory	Treaty	Contingent	Remarks
Hanover	4 Mar 1793	1,300	Increased by 5,000 in 1794. Till 1795
Wolfenbüttel	4 Mar 1793	20,263	Not implemented. Revised 7 Jan 1794 for 5,299 but only a further agreement on 8 Nov 1794 for 2,200 was put into effect. Withdrawn 1796
Baden	21 Sept 1793	754	Till 1795
Hessen-Kassel	10 Mar 1793	8,000	Added 4,000 on 23 Aug 1793, followed by 535 on 23 Mar 1794. Till 1796
Hessen-Darmstadt	5 Oct 1793	3,000	Renewed on 10 June 1796 for 2,284 till 1797
Prussia	1 Apr 1794	62,407	Terminated Oct 1794

Sources: STAD A6 Nr. 1225, 1227, 1228; G. Schreiber, *Der badische Wehrstand seit dem 17. Jahrhundert bis zu Ende der Französischen Revolutionskriege* (Karlsruhe, 1849), pp. 185–6; Presser, *Solatenhandel in Hessen*, pp. 28–9; Elster, *Braunschweig-Wolfenbüttel*, vol. II, pp. 470–72; J. M. Sherwig, *Guineas and gunpower: British foreign aid in the wars with France, 1793–1815* (Cambridge, Mass., 1969).

no longer afford both the war in the west and occupation of Poland in the east and threatened to pull out of the *Reichskrieg* unless the *Reich* provided 10 million fl. subsidies, to be supplemented by a further 3 million fl. from Austria and 9 million fl. from Britain.

Thugut grasped this as an opportunity to both discredit Prussia and soften up the *Reich* for further Austrian financial demands. He secretly offered Prussia to support an application to the *Reichstag* to take its entire field army into imperial pay until a subsidy treaty could be struck with Britain. Prussia seized on this without waiting for open Austrian support or considering the impact on its public standing. In January 1794 Prussia requested that the six western *Kreise* take over the pay and provisioning of its field army, estimated at 2–3 million fl. a month, equivalent to a massive 480 RMs a year in formal contributions. As Thugut had hoped, this met with universal hostility, especially as no one believed Prussian resources were exhausted and suspected Frederick William II of deliberately making unreasonable demands in order to justify territorial annexations in Germany as "compensation" for his efforts on behalf of the common cause. Prussia was compelled to back down. eventually finding a solution in a direct treaty with the maritime powers on 19 April, whereby they paid for its 62,400 men on the Rhine. Though this resolved its financial crisis, the arrangement was a considerable blow to Hohenzollern prestige, and even Prussian officers felt it was a disgrace that the British should have to pay them to fight the French.[27]

Thugut was unable to capitalize on his advantage, since the *Reich* remained resistant to Austrian demands. The *Reichstag* was growing restless at Habsburg manipulation and refused further money until Austria provided accounts for the imperial Operations Fund. By autumn 1793 Austrian attempts to control German resources had reached an impasse and Thugut adopted a policy of blocking further discussion of military matters, triggering a protocol dispute to paralyse the *Reichstag*, thereby denying the princes a voice in war management.

Circumstances forced a change of tack in January 1794, as Austria realized this policy was counterproductive at a time when the war was going badly and Prussia was proving increasingly unreliable. Moreover, support for the *Reichskrieg* was growing, as many princes appreciated that this was now a truly defensive war against French aggression. Thugut sought to exploit renewed calls for reform to revise the executive ordinance in order to strengthen central authority and thereby gain greater direct access to German resources. Punishment for those who defaulted on their obligations to the *Reich* was to be taken out of the hands of the *Kreis* executive and entrusted to the imperial, that is, Austrian, general staff, who were to be allowed to proceed directly by occupying the offending territory without a prior court hearing. In a further, highly controversial suggestion, defaulters were to lose their political rights within the imperial constitution (*Reichsstandschaft*), leaving them open to further exploitation. The *Reichstag* was to authorize new RMs and additional contingents for the *Reichsarmee* to legitimize Austria's extraction of greater material and manpower resources from the weaker territories. The *Relutions* system was to be abolished in a move intended more to deprive Prussia of income and influence than to augment the actual strength of the *Reichsarmee*. New methods of fund raising were to be introduced, including an emergency poll tax, the collection of ecclesiastical gold and silver and the circulation of paper money, all controlled by enhanced central direction.

These measures would have gone far to implementing the monarchical solution to the old question of defence reform, and it is testimony to the continuing strength of the *Reich* that Austria refrained from tabling them for open discussion at the *Reichstag*. Direct negotiations behind the scenes met with mounting opposition from princes who feared that the enhanced executive powers were merely a device to annex Bavaria and much of south Germany as compensation for Austria's military effort. The princes also opposed attempts at matricular reform, including demands for definitive levels for each territory, preferring instead to keep arrangements deliberately vague to deny Austria the chance to accuse them of defaulting.[28] As in the case of 1681–2, the *Reich* sacrificed military efficiency for the sake of preserving its traditional political structure, this time by blocking reform altogether.

Popular mobilization, 1794

Opposition to change was far from a blanket rejection of innovation, but was directly related to the survival of territorial political autonomy. To preserve this, several princes were prepared to take the apparently radical step of arming their subjects in a mass mobilization to confront the French. Controversial at the time, this move sparked a subsequent debate concerning the inspiration behind it, the nature of its execution and the level of effectiveness. Depending on which aspects are given greater emphasis, mass mobilization appears either as a German version of the French *levée en masse*, leading to the glorious days of "universal service" during the Wars of Liberation against Napoleon, 1813–15, or as the last gasp of a dying old order trying to press its unwilling subjects to resist the forces struggling for their own emancipation.[29]

The controversy is partly explained by the comparisons that are inevitably drawn with France, especially those that stress the novelty of the French experience and accept at face value the revolutionary rhetoric of citizens-in-arms and universal service as a patriotic duty. In fact, the French developed and extended old regime conscription into a system for replenishing the regular army. The old royal army, recruited by voluntary enlistment, had been greatly weakened by 1791 through desertion and the general political upheavals. By that time, the royal militia, established by Louis XIV in 1688 and maintained by limited, selective conscription, had been entirely replaced by the new National Guard composed of volunteers from amongst the propertied classes, somewhat similar to the British Yeomanry mobilized for home defence against French invasion in 1793. Conscious of the weakened state of the line army, the revolutionary government called for what was euphemistically termed "voluntary conscription" in 1791, based on a quota system of one recruit for every 20 national guardsmen. In fact, compulsion was largely unnecessary and most of the 100,000 extra soldiers were genuine volunteers. By 1792 the authorities had to resort to conscription by ballot to fill quotas as the volunteer units were amalgamated into the expanding line army, which grew to 350,000–400,000 by the following year. The call for a further 300,000 men in February 1793 met with disappointing results, as only half that number came forward by July.

Attitudes to conscription changed as the French government fell into the hands of the more radical Jacobins that month. The Jacobins believed they represented the true will of the people, and it suited their universalist claims to extend military service to all able-bodied males. These ideas were embodied in the famous *levée en masse* decreed on 23 August. Far from transforming every French citizen into a soldier, actual practical implementation was restricted to unmarried men aged 18–25. Though the fiction of voluntary service was maintained, most of the 300,000 new recruits had been compelled to serve by local officials seeking to fill their quotas. This huge increase boosted total strength to about 750,000, and the army was able to survive with only limited further drafts, numbering 70,000 new recruits in 1794–7. The one novelty of Jacobin legislation was a ban on substitution, but this was soon dropped to allow richer citizens to buy exemption.

True universal service was not implemented until September 1798 when a system of annual drafts of the 20–21 age group was introduced, intended to keep the army permanently up to strength. The men were supposed to be discharged once they reached 25, but this was no longer fully observed by 1806, since war had become continuous. Even now, there were still exemptions, while the system met with widespread resistance that was gradually worn down by increasing bureaucratic and police vigilance. Far from creating a symbiosis of soldiers and citizens so beloved by later extremists, fascist as well as communist, the revolution in fact completed the separation of the military and civil spheres, demilitarizing French society and concentrating all organized coercive power in the hands of a centralized state now capable of exerting far greater direct rule over its population than anything dreamed of by the monarchy.[30]

German mobilization plans differed from this French experience in two important respects. First, they were intended to create a secondary reserve force rather than inflate the size of the regular armies. Secondly, exemptions were tied to social status rather than wealth, reflecting traditional German corporate society as opposed to the emergent liberal-capitalism in France. While both had universalist claims, those in Germany were related not to new notions of universal citizenship, but to old obligations to defend a locality and serve a common ruler. German mobilization thus took place within the framework of the existing territorial militias, which were either revived or revised along the Rhine frontier in 1790–94. Most followed the pattern in Württemberg, where all males were theoretically liable for service as they were in France, but, as they always had been, under traditional German militia organizations. Those over 50 were designated home guards only to be called out in dire emergency. The rest aged over 17–50 were divided into three groups of which only the youngest was actually mobilized and trained.

There had been discussions before 1792 of the value of citizens-in-arms, but this had not gone beyond the views expressed in France in 1789–91 that the best combination was a small regular army backed by a patriotically motivated militia. The war intensified the debate and threw up some more radical opinions. One of the more extreme suggested placing Württemberg on a total war footing with all 100,000 able-bodied adult males in the army supported by the 150,000 women, who were to spin yarn for sale to pay for the war effort. Schools and ecclesiastical foundations were to be converted into gun foundries, hospitals and other military installations.[31] However, most proposed variants of the scheme actually adopted and looked to the past rather than across the Rhine, recalling peasant resistance to the French invasion of 1688 rather than invoking revolutionary Jacobin ideas. The actual mobilization may have been stimulated by the British Yeomanry of 1793: the state archives in Stuttgart contain a colourful map of the dispositions of the Württemberg militia bearing the inscription in English "God save my country".

Mobilization was in fact a traditional response to external danger and was initiated not by intellectuals but by the local authorities and the Austrian high command under General Wurmser in the light of the faltering official military effort, graphically exposed by the French firebombing of Alt Breisach on 15 September 1793. The territorial authorities began mobilizing militias in Baden, Württemberg, Trier, Mainz, Hessen-Kassel, Palatinate-Bavaria, Fürstenberg and the Austrian Breisgau, and the measures were taken up at

Table 8.3 Militia mobilization in southwest Germany, 1794

Territory	Population	Total militia	Total mobilized
Württemberg	634,711	67,100 (10.6%)	14,000 (2.2%)
Fürstenberg	90,000	6,000 (6.7%)	?
Baden	195,000	16,000 (8.2%)	5,280 (2.7%)
Breisgau and Austrian lordships	46,000	60,786 (13.2%)	14,000 (3%)
Total	1,379,711	149,886 (10.9%)	over 33,000 (2.4%)

Source: As note 32.

Note: The figures in parentheses represent the militia as a proportion of the total population.

Kreis level in the Electoral and Upper Rhine, Franconia and Swabia in January–February 1794. All announcements stressed the legality of the mobilization in accordance with established procedures, with the Württemberg decrees of 10 September 1794 referring expressly to agreements made with the estates in 1622 and 1623 (Table 8.3).[32]

Mobilization took place using exactly the same mechanisms that had been used for limited drafts to fill out the *Kreistruppen* and other regular units since 1790 and in earlier wars. Württemberg, for example, had decreed the conscription of 4,000 men on 1 October 1793, using the duchy's traditional method of selecting young single men by ballot on a quota basis in each parish. Like the French authorities, some German territories also shunned the notion of compulsion, even paying conscripts small cash bounties like genuine volunteers, and all militiamen were promised a discharge upon termination of hostilities. Mainz, Würzburg, Bavaria and others used such schemes throughout the Revolutionary Wars, as they had done in earlier conflicts, but there was no attempt to implement them on a wide scale. In other words, German practice remained rather like that in France prior to 1791 in that the regulars were kept separate from the militia, which was reserved as a home defence force.[33]

Austria took up the idea of mass mobilization at the *Reichstag*, and on 20 January 1794 the emperor singled out the Württemberg example for special commendation when he called on all inhabitants of the Rhineland to join the nearest military units for a common effort against the French. Despite the apparent radicalism, this German equivalent of the "fatherland in danger" was extremely traditionalist, contrasting solid "German patriotism" explicitly with the measures of a terroristic French government that relied on the guillotine to enforce fanaticism in its population. Thugut himself stressed that the call was "based upon the spirit of the old imperial constitution".[34]

Against Prussian claims that arming subjects was dangerous and would lead to revolution, Austria continually stressed that French terror methods and anticlericalism had created a bond between prince and people and that only tyrants need fear their own population. Some rulers and propertied Germans were decidedly uneasy about mobilizing the masses. Carl August of Weimar wrote that he would "rather pay my last écu to the elector of Saxony to have a couple of his good regiments march than arm 500 of my peasants".[35] However, most were concerned the militia would add to the general burden of an unpopular war and trigger protest on material rather than ideological grounds. There was far more to Prussian opposition than fear of revolution. As many in Berlin suspected, Thugut's championing of mass mobilization was another ploy to isolate them and gain greater access to German resources.[36]

Like the other aspects of war management, attempts to assert central control over the militias foundered on opposition in the *Reichstag*, which voted on 5 May to leave matters in the hands of the territorial authorities, thereby endorsing traditional arrangements. Again military efficiency had been sacrificed to political autonomy and none of the projected *Kreis* militias actually formed. Political considerations also affected the organization of those territorial militias that did assemble. In keeping with established practice, Württemberg militiamen were required to hand in their guns after training for safekeeping in the local town halls. Despite the latent suspicion on the part of the authorities, there were instances of genuine popular enthusiasm with particularly large numbers of volunteers joining the Württemberg cavalry and artillery detachments, while the Breisgau militia was permitted to elect its own officers. The proportion actually under arms in some areas even exceeded mobilization levels in revolutionary France.

Yet serious difficulties were also encountered with no less than 17 separate mutinies in the Württemberg militia during Duke Ludwig Eugen's 19-month reign, 1794–5. The discontent was not, however, a sign of popular revolutionary fervour or an ideological rejection of the old regime and, despite trouble, the Austrian government in the Breisgau estimated that 95 per cent of the population was still well disposed.[37] The French Revolution had given the masses a new language with which to articulate mundane grievances associated with militia conscription, boredom of drill, generational and social antagonism and high war taxation. Indeed, it seems likely that the differing response between France and Germany to calls to defend the fatherland can be put down as much to their previous experience of war as to political ideology.

Aside from the old royal militia, which had never been numerous, and ineffective attempts to draft men from maritime communities into the navy, France had had relatively little experience of conscription prior to 1792. Germans, however, were long acquainted with attempts to compel them to serve in the armed forces and probably interpreted the mobilization decrees as merely another imposition on top of high taxation and Austrian and French requisitioning.

By autumn 1794 even the authorities' enthusiasm was waning and, regarding mobilization as something of an unknown quantity, they decided to play safe when it began to prove troublesome. The Württemberg militia was disarmed and stood down by the new duke, Friedrich Eugen, in 1795, as was that in the Breisgau. The latter was reactivated in 1796, and other authorities returned to it in the desperate days of autumn 1799, when even a total call-out (*Landsturm*) was decreed in Mainz and elsewhere in the Rhineland. Some peasants waged an effective guerrilla war in the hilly, wooded country east of the Rhine, but were unable to turn the tide against the invaders.[38] Ironically, by then the princes were generally more receptive to French ideas, which had become more authoritarian and conservative since 1794. As in France, conscription now seemed the best route to a large and relatively cheap army, fusing the militia with the professional cadre of a regular force. Following the death of Friedrich Eugen, Duke Friedrich abolished the Württemberg militia altogether on 23 December 1799, and once he had removed the duchy's estates along with the rest of its traditional constitution in 1805, he implemented full conscription on the French model. In the light of a popular uprising in the nearby Tirol in 1809, Friedrich completed the Revolution's divide between civil and military spheres by confiscating all weapons still in private possession. Similar measures were implemented in other territories, including those that joined the French-sponsored *Rheinbund* (Confederation of the Rhine) after 1806, as well as Prussia and Austria, which remained outside.[39]

The failure of reform, 1794–5

Austria's failure to reform collective security in a manner that would have increased central control left Thugut no choice but to fall back on the existing system. Proposals were tabled in the *Reichstag* in May 1794 to raise the formal strength of the *Reichsarmee* to a *Quintuplum* of 200,000 men. These met with a favourable response, as many believed that only by establishing a truly autonomous force could they escape Austro-Prussian domination. Again, Austria manipulated these concerns to pursue its own objectives. Thugut knew that most territories were completely incapable of fielding five times their basic quota, since they could not even muster the existing *Triplitz*, and he intended to use the increased requirements to extort more money in *Relutions* despite his official line that these were to be abolished. Prussia voted in favour but publicly announced that it would not provide any extra soldiers.

Nonetheless, many responded positively once the measure had been passed on 9 October 1794. Saxony increased its contribution from 4,704 men in 1794 to 9,706 by the following year, while Bavaria and others also augmented their contingents. More significantly, many territories that had previously paid *Relutions* now took steps to send soldiers instead, seizing the opportunity to terminate their agreements with the two great powers. Both Lippe and Schaumburg-Lippe raised contingents, although the latter at least did not manage to join the *Reichsarmee*. Nonetheless, Westphalia now sent 2,434 *Kreistruppen*, while Münster also provided 1,200 men. Despite Prussian interference, the Upper Saxons mobilized with contributions from Weimar, Gotha, Reuss, Schwarzburg, and Nordhausen, all of which had previously paid cash instead, and Würzburg rejoined the Franconian organization and fielded its *Kreistruppen*.[40]

Many began to see greater exertions not as an attempt to defeat France but as a basis to negotiate peace from a position of strength. A number of proposals were floated for a revived *Fürstenbund* to enhance princely bargaining power both in respect of Austria and Prussia and in possible negotiations with France, which, since the fall of Robespierre in July 1794, seemed a more reasonable and stable country. Some projects were completely unrealistic. Mainz suggested an electoral alliance of itself, Cologne, Trier and Palatinate-Bavaria to raise an army of 79,000 men, yet at the time only Bavaria was not occupied by French troops!

One scheme did come to fruition. Margrave Carl Friedrich of Baden, along with his adviser, Edelsheim, Landgrave Wilhelm IX of Hessen-Kassel and the Nassau minister, Botzheim, met at Wilhelmsbad near Hanau from 28 September to 2 October 1794 and concocted a plan for a new alliance entirely free of Prussian interference. The proposed league was thrown open to medium princes to establish a common force of 40,000 men underwritten by a loan of 24 million fl. The response was hardly overwhelming. Mainz and Wolfenbüttel did join but refused to provide troops, while Palatinate-Bavaria, Mecklenburg-Schwerin, and Württemberg remained lukewarm and Hessen-Darmstadt refused outright. Only Franz Ludwig von Erthal, bishop of Würzburg and Bamberg, was truly enthusiastic, promising no less than 10,000 men. This was highly embarrassing, since he had only been invited for forms sake, as Baden and Hessen-Kassel were secretly planning secularization as compensation for their war effort. With 16,866 regular troops, Hessen-Kassel was the only member with significant forces and Wilhelm IX intended his involvement should bring him an electoral title.[41]

In the end, despite support from Catherine II, the League folded after it was publicly opposed by the emperor in November. "The Viennese court did not recognize a third party, only vassals" and its reaction was an overhasty instinctive response that regarded all such projects as inherently anti-Habsburg.[42] It would have been difficult to have embraced the Wilhelmsbad group as a means of rallying *Reich* support given its members' ulterior motives, but outright rejection was certainly a mistake and constituted the first push forcing the princes into the arms of France.

Mainz broke the deadlock by tabling a set of peace proposals on 13 October 1794, four days after the *Reichstag* had sanctioned the *Quintuplum*. It was a modest plan intended to restore the territorial *status quo* to that of 1792 and establish a mutual guarantee of noninterference in internal affairs, in return for which the *Reich* would recognize the regicidist French Republic as a full member of the international community. Thugut stalled, arguing that France was still governed by criminals who came and went with such rapidity that no one could be sure that any treaty signed with one group would be respected by the next. However, he could not prevent the *Reichstag* formally requesting on 22 December that the emperor negotiate peace on the basis of the Westphalian Settlement. Austria continued to delay matters, deflecting the peace initiative by a prolonged debate on the formation of an imperial deputation to conduct the talks.[43] This refusal to take the initiative quickly revealed itself to be a serious miscalculation, as Prussia broke ranks and signed a separate peace with France at Basel on 5 April 1795.

The Peace of Basel and its consequences, 1795–8

The Peace of Basel proved to be highly significant. Its public articles established a demilitarized zone under Prussian protection covering the northern half of the *Reich* from the Dutch frontier south to the river Main and thence to Franconia. This *Pax Borussica* was to last until a final peace settlement, effectively restricting *Reich* involvement in the war to areas south of the neutrality zone. Separate secret articles agreed that if a final treaty endorsed French annexation of Prussian territory west of the Rhine, compensation was to be found at other princes' expense to the east. These arrangements represented the first formal French sponsorship of German annexations and so heralded the reorganization of the *Reich* that was to be affected by Napoleon.

Even without the full details, the treaty sparked an immediate contro-versy.[44] Some defended Prussia's action as the necessary first step toward a general peace, accusing Austria of continuing the war for its own interests. However, most condemned Prussia for abandoning the *Reich* in its hour of need in a treacherous break of faith and responsibility, with a few going so far as to argue that only a strengthening of executive power and unquestioning submission to imperial authority could save the *Reich*. This was precisely what Austrian ministers wanted to hear and they lost no time in capitalizing on the admittedly dire situation.

It has generally been the Austrian viewpoint that has been the accepted interpretation of the Peace of Basel, although recently some historians have argued that Prussia's action was a perfectly rational move, in keeping with its general strategy since 1740 of avoiding protracted and unprofitable wars.[45] The war was becoming unpopular amongst the Berlin elite, which viewed with alarm the worsening situation in Poland, where revolt had broken out a year before. Arguably the worst was over by the time the treaty was signed, since Polish resistance had been broken by the capture of Warsaw by superior Russo-Prussian forces on 8 October 1794 and collapsed completely with the final partition in January 1795.[46] However, suspicion of Austria remained and Frederick William II mistakenly believed the emperor was already negotiating with France over a Netherlands–Bavaria exchange. Meanwhile, the strategic situation had altered significantly to Prussia's disadvantage with the allied collapse in Flanders in July 1794. The French subsequently drove into the Dutch Republic, seizing Maastricht on 4 November and crossing the frozen Waal river on 27 December. The now defenceless Republic opened negotia-tions, while, cut off from resupply, the unpaid British corps was "reduced to gangs of pillaging bandits".[47] The stadholder went into exile as the state, now styled the Batavian Republic, made peace with France on 16 May 1795, agreeing to pay an indemnity of 100 million fl. and maintain 25,000 French troops. The collapse of the Dutch had been obvious since December, and the Prussian and Hessian units with the allied army had had no choice but to withdraw into the *Reich* while they still could in January. Westphalia was now the front line, placing France in a position to threaten Prussia's north German sphere of influence for the first time directly. Under these circum-stances, neutrality seemed the wisest option.

Neutrality was to be enforced by an observation army assembled from 25,000 Prussians, 11,500 Hanoverians and about 2,000 Wolfenbüttel soldiers, initially commanded by the hereditary prince of Hohenlohe-Ingelfingen, the only Prussian member of the imperial general staff, who was soon replaced by the duke of Brunswick. Despite the Guelph presence, the zone was domi-nated by Prussia, which used the pretext of sustaining the observation army to continue its extortion of cash from the unarmed territories. None of the territories within the zone formally joined the Peace of Basel, but geography left them little choice than to observe unofficial neutrality. Where they attempted otherwise they met with Prussian opposition, like Franz Egon von Fürstenberg, bishop of Paderborn and Hildesheim, who was compelled to suspend his financial contributions to the imperial Operations Fund. However, many rulers resisted Prussian efforts to convert the zone into permanent territorial hegemony. Max Franz, whose bishopric of Münster was within the demarcation line, used the *Kreis* structure to help sustain his fragile autonomy, while the Upper Saxons kept their troops with the *Reichsarmee* in defiance of Prussian demands for their withdrawal. Only in Franconia did Prussia achieve a brief success. Hardenberg, in charge of the local Prussian administration in Ansbach-Bayreuth, annexed the imperial city of Nuremberg in September 1796 with the agreement of most of its citizens. However, his superiors in Berlin were alarmed lest it give Austria an excuse to make greater gains in Bavaria and Frederick William II restored the city's status the next month. Indiscipline among the occupying Prussian troops elsewhere in the zone deterred others from inviting annexation.[48]

Despite the realities within the zone, many outside it wished to join, as they were permitted under clause 9 of the Peace of Basel, which encouraged them to seek admittance with Prussian help within three months. The emperor warned others against following Prussia's example and only Hessen-Kassel actually made use of this option, joining by special arrangement on 28 August 1795. Baden, Württemberg and Palatinate-Bavaria opened secret negotiations with the French, but their efforts were frustrated by an Austrian counteroffensive in October that drove the French back over the Upper Rhine.[49]

Austria ruthlessly exploited its success to consolidate its hold on the south. Though he was not privy to the details, Thugut was aware that Prussia's new understanding with France guaranteed it preferential treatment at a future peace conference. He was left with no choice but to redouble Austria's military effort in the hope of equalizing Prussia's advantage by defeating France. As far as he was concerned, after Basel the gloves were off and he no longer felt obliged to adhere to the rules governing transit, billeting and contributions within the *Reich*. Austrian generals were empowered to take whatever action they felt necessary, and on 21 November Wurmser seized Mannheim to prevent the local authorities surrendering it to the French. Two Wittelsbach ministers, Salabert and Oberndorff, were arrested on grounds of treason and the unfortunate inhabitants forced to contribute 400,000 fl. to the imperial war effort. The protests of the *Reichstag* were ignored, and this deliberate show of force was intended to intimidate the south Germans into continuing to support Habsburg policy.[50]

The change in attitude in 1795 is graphically illustrated by a breakdown in payments from the Palatine civil and estates' treasuries for military requisitioning. Money extorted by France amounted to over 335,470 fl. spread fairly evenly across the period 1792–9, and while that paid to Austria came to only just over half this figure (164,856 fl.), all but 4,328 fl. fell in the period after 1795. Austria also became increasingly high-handed towards the lesser territories' contingents. For example, Prussian neutrality had caught Münster's soldiers still with the *Reichsarmee*, but when Max Franz tried to withdraw them, the Austrian generals refused to release them and they were obliged to co-operate with Habsburg forces until 1801.[51]

Moreover, Austria reordered its strategic priorities at the *Reich*'s expense to concentrate on combating the inroads the French had made into Habsburg possessions in north Italy since 1795. Taking advantage of a brief armistice on the Rhine in May 1796, Wurmser and 25,000 men were switched south over the Alps, cutting the two Austrian armies in Germany to about 140,000 in total. When these proved insufficient to prevent Moreau and Jordan with 157,000 French from crossing the Rhine, the imperial field marshal, Archduke Charles, made a strategic withdrawal, abandoning most of southwest Germany and pulling back to a central position closer to the Danube.

While this made sense given the indefensibility of the Rhine, it proved politically disastrous. Already under Prussian pressure to abandon the war, the Saxons pulled out on 21 July, depleting the Austrians' northern (right) wing by 10,000 men. The whole of Upper Saxony, including the Ernestine duchies, was sucked into the neutrality zone. Meanwhile, the situation for the southern territories in Swabia became desperate, as they were now in the French line of advance. Württemberg withdrew its *Kreistruppen* from the Swabian corps on 1 July and opened negotiations with the French, signing an armistice on 17 July, agreeing to pay 4 million livres plus deliver huge quantities of food, horses and boots to the invaders. Baden followed suit on 25 July, paying 2 million livres, with the other Swabians agreeing to pay a further 12 million livres, while 7 million livres more was to be pressed from the numerous ecclesiastical foundations in the region. Also defenceless, the Franconians offered 6 million livres in cash and 2 million livres in kind. The Austrians naturally regarded this as nothing short of treachery, and at the crack of dawn on 29 July 8,000 of their men burst into the camp of the remaining 3,000 Swabian *Kreistruppen*, disarming them and impounding their weapons.[52]

Charles's strategy worked, and, having drawn the French deep into Germany, he turned and inflicted a series of defeats on their overextended forces, driving them back over the Rhine by October. In the light of this success, many later writers have followed the official Austrian line and argued that the south German withdrawal from the war was a mistake, resulting from political short-sightedness and a lack of enthusiasm for the common cause. Instead of paying the huge sums to the French, they should have invested the money in their own war effort.[53] However, the south Germans had no way of predicting that Charles's withdrawal was a piece of strategic brilliance rather than a hasty retreat. More importantly, they sensed correctly that the *Reichskrieg* could not be won given the loss of the left bank and the neutrality of the north.

Nonetheless, the defection of the southern medium states was highly significant, representing both recognition of the futility of traditional reliance on Habsburg protection and patronage and acknowledgement that a middle course was no longer possible. Talks had continued intermittently for a viable Third Party to replace the defunct Wilhelmsbad group, but it was now obvious that this no longer stood a chance. The only alternative to Prussia and Austria was France, and Württemberg and Baden converted their armistices into full treaties on 7 and 22 August respectively. For the first time the agreements contained specific references to secularization as the means for rewarding these territories at a future final peace. Prussia also revised its arrangements with France, contracting its neutrality zone slightly northwards to a more viable demarcation line on 8 August and securing French agreement to its future annexation of Münster.[54] The tocsin was being rung for the *Reich* and the days of the lesser territories were clearly numbered.

In any event, matters were being decided in the south where Napoleon Bonaparte led a revitalized French Army of Italy in a winter campaign across the Alps into southern Austria, forcing the emperor to abandon the war by the preliminary Peace of Leoben of 18 April 1797, which included a six-month truce for the entire *Reich*. The Habsburg position continued to deteriorate after April, while the French consolidated their hold over north Italy, forcing the Austrian negotiators into greater concessions in the Treaty of Campo Formio of 18 October. Austria now acknowledged the principle of secularization as the basis of compensation, effectively abdicating its responsibilities for the *Reich* in order to save its territorial empire. France was to keep most of the left bank along with the Habsburg possessions in imperial Italy in return for secret French permission for an Austrian annexation of neutral Venice and the archbishopric of Salzburg.[55]

Francis II had signed in his capacity as Habsburg ruler rather than as emperor and now had to negotiate a full settlement on behalf of the *Reich*. Austria was increasingly isolated in Germany, and suspicion surrounding the true terms of Campo Formio appeared to be confirmed when its troops handed the Mainz fortress to the French in December. Habsburg ministers took steps to prevent the complete evaporation of their influence, especially as Thugut now appreciated the value of the *Reich* as a buffer against both France and Prussia. The annexation of Salzburg was postponed, and whereas past emperors had struggled to exclude the *Reich* from international negotiations, Francis II now welcomed its involvement. The Deputation, appointed by the *Reichstag* following the initial peace initiative in 1795, was permitted to represent the *Reich* at the peace conference that opened at Rastatt in November 1797. The move was an astute one, since it shifted the odium of what would inevitably be a bad peace from the emperor to the princes. It was also a significant indication of Habsburg weakness, since the emperor had abandoned his traditional role as defender of the *Reich* and was now sheltering behind those he was supposed to protect.[56]

France exploited German divisions to force the imperial Deputation into even greater concessions than those made at Campo Formio, and by April 1798 had secured agreement to its permanent possession of the entire left bank and the secularization of all ecclesiastical territories save the three clerical electorates. The situation now looked desperate, not just for the *Reich* but for Austria, as the territorial reorganization threatened to exceed what Thugut believed sustainable by the traditional imperial constitution. Only France and Prussia could benefit from such radical change and Austria began to look for a way out of the negotiations. The international situation began to look more promising by the end of 1798, as Napoleon's invasion of Egypt was heading for disaster, while Russia now promised Austria military assistance. When Austria refused to respond to an ultimatum, the French reopened the war in February 1799. The Rastatt conference struggled on but this too broke up in April after Austrian hussars, acting without orders, murdered the French delegates.

From war to collapse, 1799–1806

The talks had revealed the extent of the danger to the lesser territories and prompted their strong support for renewed war, especially as Russian involvement raised hopes of victory. Britain remained at war with France throughout and welcomed renewed German participation with new subsidy offers, signing agreements with Bavaria, Württemberg, Mainz and Würzburg, although only the first two actually managed to provide their troops. The *Reichstag* endorsed the *Quintuplum* and voted another 100 RMS for the Operation Fund in September 1799.[57]

This promising start masked underlying weakness. Collective security had broken down, the north continued to remain neutral and the still well-armed territories of Saxony, Hanover and Hessen-Kassel stayed out of the war. Prussia consolidated its hold on the area, temporarily occupying Hanover

April–November 1801.[58] The strain also showed in the south, where even the Swabian military organization broke down as Duke Friedrich disbanded the Württemberg *Kreistruppen* during his army restructuring in September 1798 and refused to contribute when the others reformed the corps in May 1800. It was significant that no less than 2,215 of the 5,052 Swabian soldiers were provided by the region's numerous small ecclesiastical territories.[59]

Austria and the rump smaller territories were left to fight alone on the Upper Rhine assisted only by the Russians in Switzerland and north Italy.[60] The situation worsened as Austro-Russian co-operation broke down, leading to Russia's temporary withdrawal from the war. Crushing defeats at Marengo on 14 June and Hohenlinden on 3 December 1800 compelled Francis II to make peace at Lunéville, 9 February 1801.

The treaty restated that of Campo Formio in more precise terms but with two important differences. Francis II signed in his capacity as emperor, thus formally sanctioning secularization and the loss of the left bank, which this time was confirmed in its entirety, removing the possibility that Austria might deny Prussia the chance to make gains east of the Rhine on the grounds it had not lost territory to the west. As at Rastatt, the Austrian government tried to avoid blame by entrusting the detailed territorial redistribution to a new imperial Deputation. In doing so, it squandered the last chance to seize the initiative in the question of compensation and destroyed any remaining hope that the process might take place within the existing constitutional framework. Although the emperor was represented in the Deputation in his capacity as king of Bohemia, it was clear that Europe's great powers would pay scant regard to its deliberations.[61]

The princes were left with little choice but to deal directly with France and also Russia, which now resumed its earlier role of protecting German client dynasties. The formal constitutional position enjoyed by both powers as guarantors of the Westphalian Settlement were cynically exploited to realign the *Reich*'s internal equilibrium in favour of their German allies. France made new treaties with Bavaria, Baden, Württemberg, Prussia, Hessen–Darmstadt and Mainz between July 1801 and May 1802, which, with the exception of Mainz, were followed by the movement of these territories' troops into the lands of their neighbours. The north Germans were especially vulnerable. Franz Egon von Fürstenberg wrote despairingly to his brother on 9 September 1801 that "Prussia wants to have us, Austria is not bothered about us." Hanover was occupied by Prussian troops during these crucial months and was powerless to protect its traditional sphere of influence. All the Westphalian and Lower Saxon ecclesiastical territories had been seized by Prussian forces by 1802. Defenceless territories like Oldenburg only survived thanks to their dynastic ties to Russia.[62]

France and Russia completed their joint plan for the political reorganization of the *Reich* in June 1802 and the imperial Deputation confirmed it with few changes in its Final Decision (*Reichsdeputationshauptbeschluß*) of 25 February 1803, which took effect after Franco-Russian ratification. The process of secularization and annexation that had proceeded on the ground since 1801 now received formal approval.[63] One hundred and twelve territories east of the Rhine disappeared, including all but six of the imperial cities and all the ecclesiastical states except Mainz, which was relocated to the former bishopric of Regensburg along with the rump of the old electorate around Aschaffenburg. The *Reichskirche* had been destroyed completely, with the ecclesiastical element of the old structure undermined still further by the confiscation of all church foundations within the enlarged secular states. The absorption of the new areas into the remaining medium and lesser territories accelerated the process of absolutist reform from above under way well before the war. The autonomy of towns, villages and corporate social groups was greatly eroded, furthering the transition from indirect to direct rule by the state. The reform process was thus well under way before 1806, normally taken as the start of the Reform Era, when Prussia responded to its defeat by France and the western territories were encouraged to implement changes adopted in France by Napoleon.[64]

There was virtually no resistance to these dramatic changes. The population of the annexed areas was often hostile to its new ruler, but could do nothing beyond demonstrative acts, such as the closing of doors and windows as the Prussians entered Münster on 3 August 1802. Even the militarized territories were powerless. Hanover, one of the beneficiaries of the territorial redistribution, was invaded by Napoleon in June 1803 in an effort to compel Britain to adhere to the Anglo-French Peace of Amiens (27 March 1802). The protective framework of the *Reich* was beyond repair, and Wallmoden, the Hanoverian commander, realized the futility of resisting alone and signed the convention of Altenberg, disbanding the electorate's entire army.

The reorganization of 1801–3 had swept away the old *Reich*, although it nominally remained in existence until 1806.[65] While key elements of the traditional structure were retained, including elective emperorship, the *Reichstag*, imperial courts, *Kreise* and imperial knights, the cement needed to hold them together had been removed. The redistribution of territory had been accompanied by a reassignment of voting and political rights associated with these areas. Since the enlarged electoral college[66] contained those who had acquired the most land, the new arrangements gave it an inbuilt majority, with the total votes held collectively by the electors in the College of Princes rising from 29 in 1789 to 78 out of a revised total of 131 in 1803. Moreover, the traditional association of the *Reich* with Catholicism had been broken by the destruction of the *Reichskirche*, giving the Protestants a majority for the first time.

The *Reich* was clearly moving inexorably towards a federation of sovereign princes before Francis II abdicated on 6 August 1806. Already in 1804 the emperor assumed a hereditary Austrian imperial title to counter the one Napoleon had created for himself in France. The new title symbolized Austria's disengagement from traditional imperial politics and announced its determination to concentrate on preserving its own territorial empire. Venerable institutions like the *Reichstag* and the imperial courts could do little to prevent other powerful princes consolidating their own autonomy at the expense of their surviving weaker neighbours. The imperial knights who had survived in the Rhineland, Swabia and Franconia since the 1520s disappeared in 1804 through forcible incorporation into the expanded medium states of Nassau, Hessen-Kassel, Hessen-Darmstadt, Fulda, Württemberg and Bavaria.

These acts stimulated a lively public debate on the *Reich*'s future.[67] Enthusiasm for the old constitution was far from dead, with most pamphleteers arguing for revisions to the pre-1803 structure rather than radical reform. Practical support came from those lesser territories that had survived in 1801–3 but saw that their days were clearly numbered. Counts and imperial knights banded together for mutual preservation in new cross-regional alliances, of which the Frankfurt Union of 1803–6, led by Prince Carl I of Isenburg-Birstein, was the most important.[68] However, such organizations were powerless given the lack of political will that extended now not just in Berlin and Vienna, but to the medium courts. The rulers of the enlarged secular territories had fully embraced the harsh new culture of power politics that had helped them achieve long-held ambitions of regional aggrandizement. The violence of the new attitude far exceeded that of the earlier baroque belligerence that had been more rhetorical thunder than action. The old emphasis on peaceful adherence to established norms had gone: the newly-styled elector of Württemberg declared that his favourite officers were those that sparked the most complaints as they besieged the castles of the Swabian imperial knights and dragged the occupants away in chains.[69]

On the European stage, however, the inflated principalities remained puny potentates, powerless to prevent themselves being sucked into the French orbit. During the last war fought in its existence, the *Reich* was entirely marginalized as Napoleon and his new German allies destroyed the Austro-Russian armies at Austerlitz in 1805. The subsequent Peace of Pressburg referred only to the *Confédération Germanique* and raised Bavaria and Württemberg to fully sovereign kingdoms. On 12 June 1806 16 of the largest states formally left the *Reich* and established the Confederation of the Rhine

(*Rheinbund*) with Napoleon, making Francis's formal abdication a largely irrelevant gesture.[70]

Prussia's intervention in October 1806 was prompted not by belated pangs of German conscience but by the desperate desire to escape political isolation and prove its military worth to its Russian and British allies. Austria's defeat in 1805 indicated that continued neutrality was unlikely to preserve Prussia's recent gains in northern Germany. Gambling on a limited campaign to "bloody Napoleon's nose" while awaiting Russian reinforcements, the Prussians were rudely brought into the new era by their crushing defeats at Jena and Auerstädt, triggering an almost complete political collapse.[71] Only Saxony had actively backed Prussia, but Napoleon punished both Hessen-Kassel and Wolfenbüttel for their suspect neutrality by beginning a radical reorganization of north Germany to bring it into the new *Rheinbund*. Prussia's dramatic collapse emphasizes the extent of the old order's defeat and reopens the question of accounting for the breakdown in the mechanisms that had preserved the *Reich* for so long. It is to this question that we turn in the final concluding chapter.

Chapter Nine

Conclusion: why the Reich *collapsed*

A final question

Francis II's abdication marked the formal extinction of a state that had spanned much of central and western Europe for more than a millennium. The Peace of Westphalia had represented a milestone in its long history but did not mark the start of its final decline. The imperial constitution had continued to display flexibility, absorbing both internal tensions and external pressures to enable the *Reich* to preserve its essential characteristics throughout the prolonged warfare of the later seventeenth century. Although Habsburg dynastic objectives began to diverge from wider imperial interest with the conquest of Turkish Hungary and subsequent competition for the Spanish Succession, both Joseph I and Charles VI were able to maintain the imperial recovery begun by Leopold I. Serious problems emerged in the wake of Habsburg defeats after 1733, culminating in the double calamity of Wittelsbach imperial rule and German civil war after 1740. However, even though the traditional political fabric was partly torn, new threads were still being woven in as the renaissance of institutions like the *Reichstag* after 1789 indicates.

Such a revision of the traditional historical picture as presented in this work raises one final question: if the *Reich* was not a bankrupt and decrepit structure after 1648, why did it collapse when it did? As the preceding chapter has indicated, it is impossible to consider this issue without taking account of explanations of the victories of revolutionary France, since the two are so often interrelated, as the inevitable triumph of the new over the old order. For convenience's sake, the main arguments can be grouped under social, economic, military and political factors, all of which feature with varying degrees of emphasis in the standard interpretations.

Social factors

The question of motivation dominates all discussion of the contrast between French and German society. Whereas the Revolution is held to have produced a superior kind of army by transforming society, the conservative, hierarchical German social structure resulted in a force composed of men who were at best unable to identify with their political masters and had little interest in the outcome of the conflict. The problem of motivation certainly exercised contemporaries. Laukhard expressed the view, which has featured prominently since, that German recruits, regarded as the scum of the earth by the people they were supposed to protect, had no fatherland and were fighting to defend an unequal social system, in contrast to the French volunteers, held in high regard by civilians, who were struggling to build a new society.[1]

The contrast is clearly exaggerated. As the discussion of conscription systems in the previous chapter indicated, many Frenchmen were serving involuntarily, and it must be questioned whether they all really "marched to the front primed with patriotism".[2] Certainly, as one recent discussion of this topic has concluded, "it would be absurd to suppose that when the citizen-soldiers were defeated they were somehow having an off-day and were not feeling very revolutionary".[3] Given the highly subjective nature of the evidence, the question of motivation is a complex if fascinating issue that cannot be fully resolved here. Nonetheless, it is possible to make some preliminary remarks that will also shed light on the German military experience throughout the period under consideration.

The recruitment systems employed by German armies drew in men who, in terms of social background, were not markedly dissimilar to their French opponents, although the guillotine and ideology of meritocracy saw to it that there was a difference in the case of the officers. Most German volunteers enlisted, as they had always done, to escape hunger and in the hope of a better life.[4] They remained in the ranks not solely through fear of their officers or draconian punishment, but also through the difficulty of re-entering civilian life and by the sense of pride and professional many developed over along years of service.

Contrary to popular mythology, German soldiers did not desert in droves. The Prussian army lost under 2 per cent of its total strength annually through desertion throughout most of the eighteenth century, and most other territories lost less than 5 per cent in peacetime. Although 734 men absconded from the Swabian *Kreistruppen* in 1795 without the corps ever coming into action, this was still only just over 6 per cent of the total and probably lower than the rates suffered by the French army, where looser discipline and poorer supply arrangements made desertion both easier and more compelling. No fewer than 50,000 soldiers deserted the French field army in 1793, equivalent to 8 per cent of total strength, and while precise overall figures for the German forces do not exist, they were probably in line with the experience of the Saxon corps with the Prussians (Table 9.1).[5]

The sharp end of German military discipline was felt only by a small proportion of hard cases, who drew attention to themselves by unruly and unco-operative behaviour. Punishment of their transgressions reaffirmed solidarity among those who toed the line. Such conformity itself cannot be taken solely as evidence of fear or broken spirit in an environment where each man was taught that failure to perform evolutions on the battlefield endangered himself and his comrades in the tightly packed formations used to maximize firepower. The drill necessary to instil this conviction was not as brutal or unceasing as is often supposed, rarely lasting more than four hours a day, and many regulations stressed the need for patience, so that recruits could "imbibe an early impression of love and affection for the service".[6]

To be sure, the system and the philosophies behind it were socially conservative, but were no less effective for that. Courage and honour were considered attributes only to be found in officers, while soldiers were driven

Table 9.1 Saxon losses, 1793–6

	Total, 1793–6	Percentage of total loss	Percentage of average annual strength
Category			
Killed in action	88	7.7	0.3
Died of wounds	56	4.9	0.2
Died of illness	762	66.6	2.5
Accidental deaths	8	0.7	
Captured	6	0.5	
Deserted	224	19.5	0.7
Total	1,144	100.0	
Annual strength			
1793	5,982		
1794	4,704		
1795	9,706		
1796	9,688		
Average	7,520		

Source: As note 5.

(allegedly) more by instinctive sentiments like bravery.[7] This was reflected in the social division in rewards offered by German armies for exceptional conduct, with officers receiving medals and soldiers cash bonuses. Nonetheless, ordinary soldiers were expected to, and clearly did, share in the corporate professionalism that characterized most territorial armies by the 1740s if not before. Regimental histories circulated in Prussia in the 1760s despite Frederick's best efforts to suppress them, and some, like that prepared by Ensign Geispitzheim, were explicitly intended to be read by privates as well as officers.[8] In addition to uniforms, flags and military music, group identity was reinforced by regimental traditions like special holidays celebrated by units in the Cologne army in the early eighteenth century.[9] Men looked back on a long unblemished record with pride: for instance, Württemberg Grenadier Sebastian Merck, a man of 32 years' exemplary service, was devastated when he nodded off and allowed a man in his custody to escape, describing the incident as the "worst misfortune of my life".[10]

Arguably, this was a source of weakness as much as strength. Group solidarity did not always extend beyond the individual regiment, leading to unit rivalries that helped divide armies as much as any squabbles over preferment among the senior commanders. In eighteenth-century Potsdam, for example, it was unwise for soldiers of the privileged guard battalions to stray into parts of town where men from other units were quartered.[11] Moreover, it certainly contributed to what late eighteenth-century and subsequent critics highlight as the central problem: the alienation of soldiers from civilians. Civil officials in mid-century Württemberg, for example, complained that soldiers were too haughty and insufficiently humble when asked to show their passes. Frequently, the authorities were themselves to blame, as they often backed up the military in dispute with civilians: significantly, Duke Carl Eugen rejected the complaints against his men.[12] The solution, it seemed, was to inspire all inhabitants with a genuine sense of patriotism to unite the nation against the fanatical French. Just who or what constituted the nation, of course, was a moot point, although there was arguably already a well-established sense of a national cultural community, defined by language and, increasingly, in some circles, literature. This was scarcely sufficient to inspire all but the most passionate Romantic to face the French bayonets, yet the force of nationalism must also be questioned as a factor in French success given the Revolution's need to impose linguistic uniformity by force on the Bretons and other minorities, as well as fight a civil war against regional and religious particularism that lasted until 1801.

If anything can be deduced from this it is that the late eighteenth-century German armies did reflect the society in which they lived. There was as much that bound them to civilians as separated them. Well over half were married or had long-term partners, and a large number worked in the civilian economy, since even regular soldiers generally only did duty one day in three and many were given leave up to ten months a year to save on their wages.[13] Soldiers remained a distinct group, but simply one of many in what was a highly stratified society held together by a complex network of ties that reinforced common as well as corporate identity. Like the political structure of the *Reich*, this preserved diversity alongside considerable inequality and immobility. Such a structure had shown powers to absorb change through modest adaptation, but there were limits, as the impact of the Revolution clearly showed.

Economic factors

If the Revolutionary Wars involved a struggle between old and new, they certainly did not represent a clash between a backward feudal Germany and a dynamic capitalist France. Recent research indicates a picture of mixed economic development for both countries, although one that is perhaps clearer in explaining German defeat than French victory. The French Revolution was not the result of the rise of capitalism, nor did it transform the French economy into a capitalist one, retarding growth as much as it promoted it. The structure and size of the French economy seems less important to the Revolution's military victory than its ability to exploit the resources of occupied territories beyond its frontiers.[14]

The German economy was behind that of France and certainly England in terms of industrialization, despite signs of growth in Saxony and parts of the Rhineland, but even the general image of backwardness is deceptive. As T. C. W. Blanning has pointed out, apparently reactionary forms of production, such as East Elbian serfdom, were "simultaneously archaic and progressive", combining elements of feudalism and capitalism with tied labour producing grain for commercial sale.[15] The imperial constitution only indirectly slowed economic growth and then only certain aspects of it. By preserving territorial fragmentation, the *Reich* hindered standardization of weights, measures and currencies, as well as encouraging a proliferation of tariff barriers and toll points. However, it also provided frameworks to counteract this, particularly the *Kreis* structure, which, where it worked well as in Swabia, helped promote regional and interregional economic co-operation. The territorial governments also fostered growth, although it must be questioned how far the bureaucratic cameralist schemes and state-subsidized industries had any real effect.[16] It did not take a political reorganization to start a demographic revolution, since the population of areas like Württemberg and Hessen had been expanding rapidly since before mid-century.

Economic factors are only important when considered in conjunction with territorial rather than imperial politics. Rule in both the imperial cities and the principalities rested on a bargaining process between state and key social groups, the net sum of which was a web of agreements tending towards preservation of traditional corporate society.[17] The significance for national defence was the central reliance on the territorial governments for resource mobilization. All territories, including Austria and Prussia, encountered genuine difficulties in financing their war effort, but late-century German reformed absolutism was undoubtedly more efficient at revenue extraction than the systems in place during the earlier wars against the Turks and monarchical France. Larger numbers of men were mobilized, even allowing for the intervening growth in population, and more cash flowed into both territorial and imperial military chests. Fear of unrest did inhibit governments from turning the fiscal screw, but it seems likely that neither rulers nor ruled were prepared to go back to the desperate hardship that had characterized the military effort in 1672–1714, especially not after 30 years of near-unbroken peace since 1763. A greater effort required a level of direct rule beyond the capacity of the traditional bargaining process, and only became possible with the destruction of traditional privileges in the wake of the territorial reorganization after 1801. This, rather than the Prussian defeat at Jena 1806, marks the true beginning of the German Reform Era, when the state adapted itself to changed circumstances, refounding its base in a society composed more of citizens than subjects.

Military factors

The contrast between revolutionary France and imperial Germany shows most clearly in the area of military organization, partly perhaps because this is where the two systems came most violently into contact, and partly through the widespread belief that all armies exemplify the social and political systems that produce them. The key issue here is the critique of the imperial war effort, which centres on the failings of the territorial armies as well as the *Reichsarmee* and formal defence structure.

In the former case, most discussions do not go beyond the general criticism levelled at all old regime armies.[18] The Austrian and Prussian forces are regarded as sharing the flaws of all old regime establishments: amateur aristocratic officers commanding unwilling or disinterested mercenaries, outnumbered and outfought by hordes of patriotic Frenchmen. If nothing else, the defeats inflicted on revolutionary and Napoleonic France by the unreformed forces of Britain and Russia indicate that this is a distortion.

The criticisms of the *Reich* defence structure are more serious, because they touch on what has been at the heart of this study. German collective security is widely regarded as responsible for a force that was inherently inferior to the armies of not only France, but Austria and Prussia as well. Laukhard, for example, stressed that, whereas Austria and Prussia took men from across their various dominions as well as from beyond and moulded them into a single fighting force, the very structure of the *Reichsarmee* perpetuated the debilitating diversity in equipment, organization and training that prevented it from ever being an efficient weapon.

Mobilization after 1792 was certainly creaky, especially as the problem of self-moderation had gone largely unchecked since 1763, so that some territories no longer knew how many men they were supposed to provide.[19] Nonetheless, Swabia, the most politically fragmented region of all, managed to field more men than it had ever done in the past. There were problems amongst the smaller contingents, which were certainly inferior in military terms to Prussian and Austrian regiments, although quality improved with time, as it had done in the Seven Years War.

The *Kreistruppen* formed only a small proportion of the total force pitted against France, raising the question asked by contemporaries of whether the *Reich* structure hindered Germans from reaching their full military potential. Many were convinced that the French Revolution had transformed conflict, necessitating total war as a new response. Thugut, for instance, believed that none of Austria's pervious conflicts compared "with such an all-embracing struggle that we are now in".[20] It was a life or death struggle, no longer concerned with limited objectives but the fate of entire ways of life. Others clearly agreed, like Friedrich Baron von Bock, a captain in the Westphalian *Kreistruppen* and author of a reform proposal that has drawn considerable comment from later historians.[21] Like many others, Bock criticized the selfishness of the petty princes, who were too preoccupied with preserving their autonomy to pull their weight for the common cause. Although we do not know the response of the Habsburg government to which he submitted his proposals in 1794, it was probably music to the ears of people like Thugut, whose claim that the territories were failing in their obligations was an argument for Austrian centralism.

The belief that the mini-states could not be stirred "from their lethargy" has persisted to this day – and is incorrect.[22] As discussion of resource mobilization and provision of *Kreis* contingents has shown, the smaller territories provided a disproportionate share of the common effort. The biggest defaulter on financial contributions to the imperial Operations Fund was Prussia, whereas many others made additional voluntary payments. Moreover, Prussia never deployed more than 76,000 of its 235,000 men against France and always less than its imperial and treaty requirements, pulling out altogether in 1795.[23] Austria exceeded its obligations, although arguably this was more to do with its wider objectives than a sense of duty toward the *Reich*. The lesser territories provided only three-quarters of their official contingents, but most of the shortfall is accounted for by the loss of their lands west of the Rhine, which occurred prior to formal mobilization in 1793.[24]

However, war is not merely a matter of material resources and manpower, and we need to consider how these assets were used in action. Much has been written on the novelty of French tactics and their role in the defeat of the allegedly hidebound old regime armies. In addition to greater concentration of artillery fire, the French used a more flexible approach, screening their advance with loose formations of skirmishers, who harassed and enveloped enemy positions. There was a certain reluctance in Germany to reform, despite defeats. The Austrian military commission appointed in 1791 to investigate the army's disappointing performance in the recent Turkish War sat for six years without result, and a second body established in March 1798 also "achieved little".[25]

However, German military doctrine was not devoid of innovation or the willingness to learn from opponents. Even small armies like that of Württemberg experimented with light "horse artillery" for rapid battlefield response, as well as mixed units or "legions" combining infantry and cavalry. Many had used small units of skirmishers, called *Jäger*, before, particularly those that had provided auxiliaries for Britain in America in 1777–83. The Hessian *Jäger* were at the head of the units that chased the French from Frankfurt in 1792, while the Prussian army developed specialist fusilier battalions for similar purposes after 1786.[26] The Germans did not adopt such innovations as the French use of reconnaissance balloons, keeping the one captured in September 1796, called *Hercule*, as a trophy, but they did use other ideas, such as the "optical telegraph" or semaphore, first employed on 4 August 1798 and quickly developed as an effective communication network across southwest Germany.[27]

More important than tactical differences was the French ability to concentrate their forces to gain numerical advantage on the battlefield. Despite the persistent myth that the French had a million men under arms, the forces of the Republic were outnumbered overall, but were better used by their commanders, who won virtually every engagement where they enjoyed a significant advantage in manpower, but lost where they were evenly matched or outnumbered. The German generals frittered away their superior forces in a strategy known as "cordon defence", stringing out detachments to cover a wide area. Although criticized by Archduke Charles and other innovators, most officers were reluctant to abandon a method developed through long experience in defending the Rhine and fighting the Turks.[28]

The French also enjoyed the advantage of youth. Led by men in their 30s or 40s, most French conscripts were only aged 20–25 compared with German armies, which preferred seasoned soldiers in their mid-30s or older and were often commanded by generals over 60. Difference in age was matched by one in attitude, which was probably the most important factor overall. When Archduke Charles summed up the problems of fighting the French in his *On war against the New Franks* in 1795, he might have more aptly called them the "New Turks", for they launched the kind of fierce mass attacks not seen since the Great Turkish War.[29] Stubborn opponents like the Russians, who had accepted losses of one-third of their strength as the price of victory at Kunersdorf in 1759, had still fought conventional battles. In contrast, the French displayed a new ruthlessness and aggression that alarmed and dismayed most senior German officers. War remained for them and their princely master the controlled application of force to achieve specific ends. Their military theory was concerned to limit casualties out of concern for humanity and practical reasons of state not to waste expensive, trained manpower. Both military men and political philosophers speculated that the proper application of scientific rulers could make war less costly and even less frequent. Thus, the Austrian General Mack rejected the idea that Germans should adopt French tactics, urging instead continuation of disciplined, orderly movements that were "the true way to avoid bloodshed; all firing and skirmishing cause losses of men and decide nothing".[30]

Political factors

These considerations spilled over into the political sphere in a refusal to accept radical change. Despite their distaste and fear of the Revolution, most Germans resisted the idea of the war as a cosmic showdown and argued that traditional privileges could not be ignored, even in a *Reichskrieg*. In short, they should not destroy what they were trying to protect simply in order to defeat France.

Consequently, few of the numerous reform proposals floated at this time went beyond modifications to the existing constitution. Utopian suggestions included a parliament of enlightened princes, philosophers and literary luminaries like Goethe and Wieland to replace the *Reichstag*, but still envisaged a collective political framework. More concrete proposals also wished to retain key traditional features, such an elected emperor, the *Reichstag*, *Kreise* and territorial sovereignty. For example, despite its emphasis on the necessity of creating a national spirit, Bock's military reform ideas of 1794 essentially recommended implementing in full what had been decided in 1681–2 to bind the bigger territories to collective defence by creating fully integrated *Kreis* armies. Bock still endorsed the retention of separate *Haustruppen* by major princes, and even as late as 1803 most writers interpreted the political reorganization that was now taking place as evolutionary and urged retention of the essentials of the *Reich*'s multilayered structure.[31]

Such hopes were partially justified by signs that, far from collapsing, elements of the *Reich* were reviving, despite the crisis. No *Reichstag* decision was blocked by religious controversy during 1792–1801; on the contrary, the institution acted promptly and effectively on many issues. The *Kreis* structure also displayed resilience, with Swabia preventing Württemberg from either subordinating the organization to its own objectives or leaving it altogether.

What stifled these positive signs was the coincidence of the revolutionary threat with Austro-Prussian rivalry. By 1794 at the latest the war was really a three-cornered struggle for German domination between France, Austria and Prussia, and the *Reich* could have obtained peace with the French Republic if Vienna and Berlin had desired it. The inner-German tension exacerbated the structural problems associated with collective security, which, while serious, were insufficient alone to explain the defeat. The *Reich* also suffered from its association with a series of international coalitions that proved far weaker and more disunited than those pitted against monarchical France. In particular, the internal problems of the Dutch weakened the defence of the Austrian Netherlands and enabled the French to gain a decisive strategic advantage by 1794.

Most fundamental, however, was the clash of incompatible political cultures. The pacific, introspective neutral *Reich* was pulled apart, first by the two expansive, centralizing, absolutist German great powers and then by aggressive, dynamic revolutionary France. The final straw came when the medium principalities abandoned ship and swam to the life raft of a French alliance. As the troubled waters of nineteenth-century politics were to prove, the reconstructed German Confederation was a far less watertight vessel for princely and territorial particularism than the old *Reich*.

Appendix

Major German rulers

1679–1726   Max II Emanuel
1726–45   Carl Albrecht (Emperor Charles VII, 1742–5)
1745–77   Max III Joseph
Passed to the Palatinate (see below)

Brandenburg (-Prussia)

1640–88   Frederick William, the Great Elector
1688–1713   Frederick III, from 18 January 1701 King Frederick I
1713–40   Frederick William I, the Soldier King
1740–86   Frederick II, the Great
1786–97   Frederick William II
1797–1840   Frederick William III

Cologne

1612–50   Ferdinand, duke of Bavaria
1650–88   Maximilian Heinrich, duke of Bavaria
1688–1723   Joseph Clemens, duke of Bavaria
1723–61   Clemens August, duke of Bavaria
1761–84   Maximilian Friedrich von Königsegg-Rothenfels
1784–1801   Maximilian Franz, archduke of Austria
1801–2   Anton Viktor, archduke of Austria (prevented from taking
            office by the secularization)

Hanover

1641–8   Christian Ludwig (as duke of Calenberg)
1648–65   Georg II Wilhelm (became ruler of Celle, see below)
1665–79   Johann Friedrich
1679–98   Ernst August (as elector from 1692/1708)
1698–1727   Georg Ludwig (King George I of Great Britain from 1714)
1727–60   George II
1760–1802   George III (died 1820)

Mainz

1647–73	Johann Philipp von Schönborn
1673–5	Lothar Friedrich von Metternich
1675–8	Damian Hartard von der Leyen
1679	Carl Heinrich von Metternich
1679–95	Anselm Franz von Ingelheim
1695–1729	Lothar Franz von Schönborn
1729–32	Franz Ludwig von Pfalz-Neuberg
1732–43	Philipp Carl von Eltz
1743–63	Johann Friedrich Carl von Ostein
1763–74	Emreich Carl Joseph von Breidbach zu Bürresheim
1774–1802	Friedrich Carl Joseph zu Erthal
1802–3	Carl Theodor von Dalberg

Saxony

1611–56	Johann Georg I
1656–80	Johann Georg II
1680–91	Johann Georg III
1691–4	Johann Georg IV
1694–1733	Friedrich August I (Augustus II of Poland from 1697)
1733–63	Friedrich August II (Augustus III of Poland)
1763	Friedrich Christian
1763–1827	Friedrich August III (king from 1806)

The Palatinate

1610–23	Friedrich V (died 1632)
1623–48	under Bavarian rule
1648–80	Carl Ludwig
1680–5	Carl (the last of the Simmern line)
1685–90	Philipp Wilhelm (Pfalz-Neuburg line)
1690–1716	Johann Wilhem
1716–42	Carl Philipp (last of the Pfalz-Neuburg line)
1742–99	Carl Theodor (Sulzbach line, inherited Bavaria 1777)

1799–1825   Maximilian IV Joseph (Birkenfeld line, king from
            December 1805)

Trier

1623–52   Philip Christoph von Sötern
1652–76   Carl Kaspar von der Leyen
1676–1711   Johann Hugo von Orsbeck
1711–15   Carl Joseph, duke of Lorraine (bishop of Osnabrück)
1716–29   Franz Ludwig von Pfalz-Neuburg
1729–56   Franz Georg von Schönborn
1756–68   Johann Philipp von Walderdorf
1768–1802   Clemens August, prince of Saxony

Main ecclesiastical principalities

Bamberg

1642–53   Melchior Otto Voit von Salzburg
1653–72   Philipp Valetin Voit von Rieneck
1672–83   Peter Philipp von Dernbach (bishop of Würzburg from 1675)
1683–93   Marquard Sebastian Schenk von Stauffenberg
1693–1729   Lothar Franz von Schönborn (elector of Mainz from 1695)
1729–46   Friedrich Carl von Schönborn (bishop of Würzburg)
1746–53   Johann Philipp Anton von Frankenstein
1753–7   Franz Lonrad von Stadion-Thannhausen
1757–79   Adam Friedrich von Seinsheim (bishop of Würzburg)
1779–95   Franz Ludwig von Erthal (bishop of Würzburg)
1795–1802   Christoph Franz von Buseck

Münster

1612–50   Ferdinand I (elector of Cologne, bishop of Paderborn
            from 1618)
1650–78   Christoph Bernhard von Galen, "Bomber Bernard the
            Cannon Bishop"

1678–83   Ferdinand II von Fürstenberg
1683–8   Max Heinrich (elector of Cologne)
1688–1706   Friedrich Christian von Plettenberg-Lenhausen
1706–18   Franz Arnold Josef Wolf von Metternich (bishop of
             Paderborn)
1719–61   Clemens August (elector of Cologne)
1761–84   Maximilian Friedrich zu Königsegg-Rothenfels (elector of
             Cologne)
1784–1801   Maximilian Franz (elector of Cologne)

Osnabrück

Ruled alternately by Catholic bishops and Guelph dukes
1648–61   Franz Wilhelm von Wartenberg (Catholic bishop)
1662–98   Ernst August I (Guelph duke, ruled Hanover from 1679)
1698–1715   Carl Joseph Ignaz (Catholic bishop, elector of Trier
             from 1711)
1716–28   Ernst August II (Guelph duke)
1728–61   Clemens August (Catholic bishop, elector of Cologne)
1761–4   Duke Georg, Guelph administrator
1764–1802   Frederick Duke of York (Guelph duke)

Paderborn

1618–50   Ferdinand I (elector of Cologne, bishop of Münster)
1650–61   Theodor Adolf von der Recke
1661–83   Ferdinand II von Fürstenberg (bishop of Münster
             from 1678)
1683–1704   Hermann Werner Wolf von Metternich
1704–18   Franz Arnold Wolf von Metternich (bishop of Münster
             from 1706)
1719–61   Clemens August (elector of Cologne)
1761–3   interregnum
1763–82   Wilhelm Anton von der Asseburg
1782–9   Friedrich Wilhelm von Westphalen
1789–1802   Franz Egon von Fürstenberg

Würzburg

1642–73	Johann Philipp I von Schönborn (elector of Mainz from 1647)
1673–5	Johann Hartmann von Rosenbach
1675–83	Peter Philipp von Dernbach (bishop of Bamberg)
1683–4	Konrad Wilhelm von Wernau
1684–98	Johann Gottfried II von Guttenberg
1699–1719	Johann Philipp II von Greiffenklau zu Vollraths
1719–24	Johann Philipp III Franz von Schönborn
1724–9	Christoph Franz von Hutten-Stolzenberg
1729–46	Friedrich Carl von Schönborn
1746–9	Anselm Franz von Ingelheim
1749–54	Carl Philipp Heinrich von Greiffenklau zu Vollraths
1755–79	Adam Friedrich von Seinsheim (bishop of Bamberg from 1757)
1779–95	Franz Ludwig von Erthal (bishop of Bamberg)
1795–1802	Georg Carl von Fechenbach

Main secular principalities

Celle

1648–65	Christian Ludwig (became ruler of Hanover)
1665–1705	Georg II Wilhelm (previously ruled Hanover)

Passed to Hannover

East Frisia (Ostfriesland)

1648–60	Enno Ludwig
1660–65	Georg Christian
1665–1708	Christian Eberhard
1708–34	Georg Albrecht
1734–44	Carl Edzard

To Prussia

Gotha

1640–75	Ernst I, the Pious
1675–91	Friedrich I

1691–1732	Friedrich II
1732–1772	Friedrich III
1772–1804	Ernst II
1804–22	August Emil Leopold

Hessen-Darmstadt

1626–61	Georg II
1661–78	Ludwig VI
1678	Ludwig VII
1678–1739	Ernst August
1739–68	Ludwig VIII
1768–90	Ludwig IX
1790–1830	Ludwig X

Hessen-Kassel

1637–63	Wilhelm VI
1663–70	Wilhelm VII
1670–1730	Carl
1730–51	Friedrich I (King of Sweden since 1720, territory ruled in his absence by Wilhelm VIII)
1751–60	Wilhelm VIII
1760–85	Friedrich II
1785–1806	Wilhelm IX (elector from 1803)

Holstein-Gottorp

1616–59	Friedrich III (sovereign in Schleswig after 1658)
1659–94	Christian Albrecht (territory under Danish occupation 1675–9, 1684–9)
1694–1702	Friedrich IV
1702–21	Christian August von Holstein-Eutin, regent
1721–39	Carl Friedrich
1739–45	Adolf Friedrich, regent

1745–62   Carl Ulrich, called Peter from 1741. Became Tsar Peter III of Russia in 1762

Lorraine

1625–75   Charles IV (land occupied by France 1670–97)
1675–90   Charles V
1697–1729 Leopold
1729–36   Francis (husband of Maria Theresa, emperor from 1745)
1736–66   Stanislaw Leszczynski (former king of Poland)
To France

Mecklenburg-Schwerin

1631–58   Adolf Friedrich I
1658–92   Christian (Louis)
1692–1713 Friedrich Wilhelm (Grabow line)
1713–28   Carl Leopold (deposed, died 1747)
1747–56   Christian Ludwig (adminstrator since 1728)
1756–85   Friedrich II
1785–1837 Friedrich Franz I

Pfalz-Neuburg

1614–53   Wolfgang Wilhelm
1653–90   Philipp Wilhelm (Elector Palatine from 1685)
United with the Palatinate in 1685

Weimar

1640–62   Wilhelm
1662–83   Johann Ernst I
1683–1728 Wilhelm Ernst

1728–48	Ernst August
1748–58	Ernst August Constantin
1758–75	Anna Amalia von Wolfenbüttel, regent
1775–1828	Carl August

Wolfenbüttel

1598–1666	August II
1666–1704	Rudolf August ⎫ co-rulers
1666–1714	Anton-Ulrich ⎭
1714–31	August Wilhelm
1731–5	Ludwig Rudolf
1735	Ferdinand Albrecht
1735–80	Carl I
1780–1806	Carl Wilhelm Ferdinand

Württemberg

1628–74	Eberhard III (under Austrian occupation 1634–48)
1674–7	Wilhelm Ludwig
1677–93	Friedrich Carl, regent
1693–1733	Eberhard Ludwig
1733–7	Carl Alexander
1737–8	Carl Rudolph, regent
1738–44	Carl Friedrich, regent
1744–93	Carl Eugen
1793–5	Ludwig Eugen
1795–7	Friedrich Eugen
1797–1816	Friedrich (elector from 1803, king from 1806)

Notes

Chapter One: War and German politics

1. S. Pufendorf, *Die Verfassung des deutschen Reiches* (1667, new edn. Stuttgart: H. Denzer, 1994).
2. The following is based on a reading of C. Tilly, *Coercion, capital and European states, AD 990–1992* (Oxford, 1992); M. Mann, *The sources of social power* [2 vols] (Cambridge, 1986–93); W. G. Runciman, *Substantive social theory* (Cambridge, 1989); A. Giddens, *The nation-state and violence* (Berkeley, 1985); N. Elias, *The civilizing process* (Oxford, 1994); M. Weber, *The theory of social and economic organization* (New York, 1964); J. G. Ruggie, "Continuity and transformation in the world polity. Toward a Neorealist synthesis", *World Politics* **35**, 1983, pp. 261–85. For a further guide to these ideas see E. W. Lehman, "The theory of the state versus the state of the theory", *American Sociological Review* **53**, 1988, pp. 807–23.
3. J. E. Thomson, *Mercenaries, pirates and sovereigns: state building and extraterritorial violence in early modern Europe* (Princeton, 1994).
4. Mann, *Social power*, vol. I, pp. 11, 28, 46–8.
5. Elias, *Civilizing process*, pp. 263–439. See also the broadly similar arguments of B. D. Porter, *War and the rise of the state: the military foundations of modern politics* (New York, 1994). I have discussed the relationship of this process to warfare at greater length in my "European warfare 1450–1815", in *War and Warfare, 1450–1815*, J. Black (ed.) (London, 1998).
6. For the theoretical dimension see M. Mann, "The autonomous power of the state. Its origins, mechanisms and results", in *States in history*, J. A. Hall (ed.) (Oxford, 1981), pp. 109–36.
7. W. Reinhard (ed.), *Power elites and state building* (Oxford, 1996); A. Mączak (ed.), *Klientelsysteme im Europa der frühen Neuzeit* (Munich, 1988), and his article "From aristocratic household to princely court: restructuring patronage in the sixteenth and seventeenth centuries", in *Princes, patronage and the nobility*, R. G. Asch & A. M. Birke (eds) (Oxford, 1991), pp. 315–27.
8. Good recent studies provided by M. C. t'Hart, *The making of a bourgeois state: war, politics and finance during the Dutch revolt* (Manchester, 1993); J. Brewer, *The sinews of power: war,*

money and the English state, 1688–1783 (New York, 1989); D. Parker, *Class and state in ancien régime France: the road to modernity?* (London, 1996).

9. For this process in the German territories, see M. Raeff, *The well ordered police state: social and institutional change through law in the Germanies and Russia, 1600–1800* (New Haven, 1983); G. Oestreich, *Neostoicism and the early modern state* (Cambridge, 1982); B. Wunder, *Geschichte der Bürokratie im Deutschland* (Frankfurt-on-Main, 1986).

10. For a breakdown of the German territories, see E. Wallner, "Die Kreissässigen Reichsterritorien am Vorabend des Luneville Friedens", *Mitteilungen des Instituts für Österreichischen Geschichtsforschung*, supplement vol. **11**, 1929, pp. 681–716.

11. The literature on the Reich is substantial. The best recent contributions are K. O. v. Aretin, *Das alte Reich, 1648–1806* [3 vols, only one published so far] (Stuttgart, 1993), and his *Das Reich: Friedensordung und europäisches Gleichgewicht, 1648–1806* (Stuttgart, 1992); H. Duchhardt, *Deutsche Verfassungsgeschichte, 1495–1806* (Stuttgart, 1991); M. Hughes, *Early modern Germany, 1477–1806* (London, 1992); V. Press, *Kriege und Krisen: Deutschland, 1600–1715* (Munich, 1991). Overviews of the historiography are provided by J. A. Vann, "New directions for the study of the old Reich", *JMH* **58**, 1986, supplement, pp. 3–22, and the two articles by V. Press, "Das Römisch-Deutsche Reich – ein politisches System im verfassungs- und sozialgeschichtlicher Fragestellung", in *Spezialforschung und "Gesamtgeschichte"*, G. Klingenstein & H. Lutz (eds), (Vienna, 1981), pp. 221–42, and "The Holy Roman Empire in German history", in *Politics and society in Reformation Europe*, E. I. Kouri & T. Scott (eds), (London, 1987), pp. 51–77.

12. The origins and development of this institution are well covered by P. Moraw, "Versuch über die Entstehung des Reichstags", in *Politische Ordnungen und soziale Kräfte im alten Reich*, H. Weber (ed.), (Wiesbaden, 1980), pp. 1–36; K. Härter, *Reichstag und Revolution, 1789–1806: Die Auseinandersetzung des Immerwährenden Reichstag zu Regensburg mit den Auswirkungen der Französischen Revolution auf das alte Reich* (Göttingen, 1992), pp. 32–66.

13. For the estates see D. Gerhard (ed.), *Ständische Vertretungen im 16. und 17. Jahrhundert* (Göttingen, 1969), and R. G. Asch, "Estates and princes after 1648: the consequences of the Thirty Years War", *German History* **6**, 1988, pp. 113–32, which provide good overviews of the specialist literature. The *Kreise* will be discussed at greater length on pp. 17–22.

14. S. Ogilvie & R. Scribner (eds), *Germany: a new social and economic history*, vols I & II (London, 1996), and C. Dipper, *Deutsche Geschichte, 1648–1789* (Frankfurt-am-Main, 1991), provide excellent introductions to this area.

15. For the imperial cities after 1648 see M. Neugebauer-Wölk, "Reichsstädtische Reichspolitik nach dem Westfälischen Frieden", *ZHF*, **17** (1990), pp. 27–47.

16. E. W. Zeeden, "Grundlagen und Wege der Konfesionsbildung im Deutschland im Zeitalter der Glaubungskämpfe", *HZ* **185**, 1958, pp. 244–99; W. Reinhard, "Zwang zur Konfessionalisierung? Prologemena zu einer Theorie des konfessionellen Zeitalters", *ZHF* **10**, 1983, pp. 257–77, and his "Reformation and Counter-Reformation and the early modern state. A reassessment", *Catholic Historical Review* **75**, 1989, pp. 338–404; H. Schilling, "Confessionalization in the empire: religion and societal change in Germany between 1555 and 1620", in *Religion, political culture and the emergence of early modern society* (Leiden, 1992), pp. 247–301.

17. After 1648 the electoral college comprised the rulers of Mainz (who was simultaneously the *Erzkanzler* or Arch-chancellor and chair of the *Reichstag*), Cologne, Trier,

Brandenburg, Saxony, Bavaria, Bohemia and the Palatinate. The Bohemian vote was in abeyance until 1708, when a new, ninth elector of Hanover was formally admitted.

18. G. L. Duggan, "The church as an institution of the Reich", in *The old Reich: essays on German political institutions, 1495–1806*, J. A. Vann & S. W. Rowan (eds), (Brussels, 1974), pp. 149–64; A. v. Reden-Dohna, "Problems of the small states of the empire. The example of the Swabian prelates", *JMH* **58**, 1986, supplement, pp. 76–87; L. Hüttl, "Geistlicher Fürst und geistliche Fürstentümer im Barock und Rokoko. Ein Beitrag zur Strukturanalyse von Gesellschaft, Herrschaft, Politik und Kultur des alten Reiches", *Zeitschrift für bayerische Landesgeschichte* **37**, 1974, pp. 3–48; E. J. Greipl, "Zur weltlichen Herrschaft der Fürstbischöfe in der Zeit vom Westfälischen Frieden bis zur Säkularisation", *Römische Quartalschrift* **83**, 1988, pp. 252–69.

19. The best and most recent overview is R. G. Asch, *The Thirty Years War: the Holy Roman Empire and Europe, 1618–1648* (London, 1997).

20. F. Bosbach, "Die Habsburger und die Entstehung des Dreißigjährigen Krieges: Die *Monarchia Universalis*", in *Krieg und Politik, 1618–1648*, K. Repgen (ed.) (Munich, 1988), pp. 157–68.

21. The treaty is printed in K. Zeumer (ed.), *Quellensammlung zur Geschichte der Deutschen Reichsverfassung in Mittelalter und Neuzeit* (Tübingen, 1913), pp. 395–443. For discussions see F. Dickmann, *Der Westfälische Frieden* (Münster, 1964), and G. Schmidt, "Der Westfälische Friede – eine neue Ordnung für das alte Reich?", *Der Staat*, supplement 10, 1993, pp. 45–72. The international context is covered by H. Duchhardt's two articles: "Westfälische Friede und internationales System im ancien régime", *HZ* **249**, 1989, pp. 529–43, and "Reich und europäisches Staatensystem seit dem Westfälischen Frieden", in *Alternativen zur Reichsverfassung in der frühen Neuzeit?*, V. Press (ed.) (Munich, 1991), pp. 179–87.

22. F. Hertz, "Die Rechtsprechung der höchsten Reichsgerichte im römisch-deutschen Reich und ihre politische Bedeutung", *MIÖG* **69**, 1961, pp. 331–58; I. Scheuermann (ed.), *Frieden durch Recht: Das Reichskammergericht von 1495 bis 1806* (Mainz, 1994), with extensive bibliography.

23. H. Duchhardt, "Die preußische Königskrönung von 1701. Ein europäisches Modell?", in *Herrscherweihe und Königskrönung im frühneuzeitlichen Europa* (Wiesbaden, 1983), at pp. 82–3. For the importance of dynasticism in German and international relations, see E. Luard, *The balance of power: the system of international relations, 1648–1815* (London, 1992), pp. 149–73; J. Kunisch, *Staatsverfassung und Mächtepolitik: Zur Genese von Staatenkonflikten im Zeitalter des Absolutismus* (Berlin, 1979), and his *Fürst-Gesellschaft-Krieg: Studien zur bellizistischen Disposition des absoluten Fürstenstaates* (Cologne, 1992), pp. 1–41.

24. C. Kampmann, *Reichsrebellion und kaiserliche Acht: Politische Strafjustiz im Dreißigjährigen Krieg und das Verfahren gegen Wallenstein 1634* (Münster, 1992).

25. Habsburg territory, including the still elective kingdom of Hungary, covered 320,155 km^2 in 1648, while that of the Hohenzollerns amounted to 68,159 km^2 within the Reich, plus the Duchy of East Prussia (36,960 km^2), held as a fief of the kingdom of Poland.

26. First conceptualized by H. E. Feine, "Zur Verfassungsentwicklung des Heiligen Römischen Reiches seit dem Westfälischen Frieden", *Zeitschrift der Savignystiftung für Rechtsgeschichte, Germanistische Abteilung* **52**, 1932, pp. 65–133, and later developed by V. Press, whose views are summarized in his "Österreichische Grossmachtbildung und Reichsverfassung. Zur kaiserlichen Stelling nach 1648", *MIÖG* **98**, 1990, pp. 131–54.

27. A good general overview of the *Kreise* is provided by W. Dotzauer, *Die deutschen Reichskreise in der Verfassung des alten Reiches und ihr Eigenleben (1500–1806* (Darmstadt,

1989). Two studies of individual *Kreise* also provide valuable introductions: J. A. Vann, *The Swabian Kreis: institutional growth in the Holy Roman Empire, 1648–1715* (Brussels, 1975), and B. Sicken, *Der fränkische Reichskreis: Seiner Ämter und Einrichtungen im 18. Jahrhundert* (Würzburg, 1970). Developments immediately preceding 1648 are well covered in F. Magen, "Die Reichskreise in der Epoche des Dreißigjährigen Krieges", *ZHF* **9**, 1982, pp. 409–60.

28. For an example see P. C. Hartmann, "Die Kreistage des Heiligen Römischen Reiches – Eine Vorform des Parlamentarismus? Das Beispiel des bayerischen Reichskreises (1521–1793)", *ZHF* **19**, 1991, 29–47.

29. K. R. Böhme, "Die Krone Schweden als Reichsstand 1648 bis 1720", in *Europas Mitte*, H. Duchhardt (ed.) (Bonn, 1988), pp. 33–9; P. D. Lockhart, *Denmark in the Thirty Years War, 1618–48* (Selinsgrove, 1996).

30. Wartime depreciation reduced the total population of the Hohenzollen lands, which, even in 1688, still only numbered about 1.4 million. For territorial and political development prior to 1648, see F. L. Carsten, *The origins of Prussia* (Oxford, 1954).

31. Calculated from Wallner, "Kreissässigen Reichsterritorien", pp. 702–7, according to the distribution of territory amongst the branches after 1665. Osnabrück had a population of 60,000 in the late seventeenth century and was under Guelph rule 1662–98, 1715–28, 1761–1802.

32. H. J. Adamski, *Der Welfische Schütz über die Stadt Hildesheim* (Hildesheim, 1939), pp. 6–54.

33. For the latest contribution to the debate on the losses, see J. Theibault, "The demography of the Thirty Years War re-revisited: Günther Franz and his critics", *GH* **15** (1997), pp. 1–21 which lists the earlier literature.

34. F. Redlich, "Contributions in the Thirty Years War", *Economic History Review*, 2nd series, **12**, 1959/60, pp. 247–54; J. A. Lynn, "How war fed war: the tax of violence and contributions during the *Grand Siècle*", *JMH* **65**, 1993, pp. 286–310; R. T. Ferguson, "Blood and fire: contribution policy of the French armies in Germany" (*1668–1715*) (unpublished PhD thesis, University of Minnesota, 1970).

35. These developments are traced in M. Jähns, "Zur Geschichte der Kriegsverfassung des deutschen Reiches", *Preussische Jahrbücher*, **39**, 1877, pp. 1–28, 114–40, 443–90, and H. Weigel, *Die Kriegsverfassung des alten deutschen Reiches von der Wormser Matrikel bis zur Auflösung* (Bamberg, 1912), both of which provide useful detail subject to anachronistic commentary.

36. Printed in H. H. Hofmann (ed.), *Quellen zum Verfassungsorganismus des Heiligen Römischen Reiches deutscher Nation, 1495–1806* (Darmstadt, 1976), pp. 40–51.

37. The REO was included in paragraphs 31–102 of the final document of the 1555 Augsburg *Reichstag* and is printed in J. J. Schmauss & H. C. v. Senckenberg (eds), *Neue und vollständige Sammlung der Reichsabschiede* [4 parts in 2 vols] (Frankfurt, 1747, reprint Osnabrück, 1967), vol. III, pp. 43–135. This collection contains most of the other key legislation.

Chapter Two: From Westphalia to the Réunions, 1648–84

1. For the new emperor and his election, see J. P. Spielman, *Leopold I of Austria* (London, 1977), and the useful chapter in A. Schindling & W. Ziegler (eds), *Die Kaiser der Neuzeit, 1519–1918* (Munich, 1990), pp. 169–85.

2. The best general overview of German military development is G. Papke, *Von der Miliz zum Stehenden Heer: Wehrwesen im Absolutismus* (*HDM*, vol. I, Munich, 1983). For attitudes to war, see K. Repgen, "Kriegslegitimationen in Alteuropa. Entwurf einer historischen Typologie", *HZ* **241**, 1985, pp. 27–49.

3. Two new studies trace these developments and provide good bibliographies of the specialist literature: R. Baumann, *Landsknechte: Ihre Geschichte und Kultur vom späten Mittelalter bis zum Dreißigjährigen Krieg* (Munich, 1994); P. Burschel, *Söldner im Nordwestdeutschland des 16. und 17. Jahrhunderts* (Göttingen, 1994).

4. Key documents printed in E. v. Frauenholz (ed.), *Das Heerwesen in der Zeit des Dreißigjährigen Krieges* [2 vols], vol. II, Munich, 1938–9, with overview in H. Ehlert, "Ursprünge des moderner Militärwesens. Die Nassau-oranischen Heeresreformen", *Militärgeschichtliche Mitteilungen* **38**, 1985, pp. 27–56. For the contractors see F. Redlich, *The German military enterprizer and his workforce* [2 vols]. (Wiesbaden, 1964–5).

5. E. Heischmann, *Die Anfänge des stehenden Heeres in Österreich* (Vienna, 1925); J. Zimmermann, *Militärverwaltung und Heeresaufbringung in Österreich bis 1806* (*HDM*, vol. III, Munich, 1983); G. E. Rothenberg, *The Austrian military border in Croatia, 1522–1747* (Urbana, 1960); A. v. Wrede, *Geschichte der k.u.k. Wehrmacht von 1618 bis zum Ende des XIX Jahrhunderts* [5 vols] (Vienna, 1898–1905).

6. For Bavaria see A. Kraus, *Maximilian I: Bayerns grosser Kurfürst* (Graz, 1990), pp. 63–4, 112–13, 146–55, 319; E. v. Frauenholz, *Die Eingliederung von Heer und Volk in der Staat in Bayern, 1597–1815* (Munich, 1940). Prussian development in C. v. Jany, *Geschichte der preußischen Armee von 15. Jahrhundert bis 1914* [4 vols] (Osnabrück, 1967), vol. I, especially pp. 98–106.

7. P. Hoyos, "Die kaiserliche Armee 1648–1650" in *Schriften des Heeresgeschichtlichen Museums in Wien* (Vienna, 1976), vol. VII, pp. 169–232; J. A. Mears, "The Thirty Years War, the "General Crisis" and the origins of a standing army in the Habsburg monarchy", *Central European History* **21**, 1988, 122–41.

8. Unless otherwise stated, all French strengths cited in this work are based on J. A. Lynn, "Recalculating French army growth during the *Grand Siècle*, 1610–1715", in *The military revolution debate*, C. J. Rogers (ed.), (Boulder, 1995), pp. 117–48. For the leading territorial armies see K. Staudinger, *Geschichte des kurbayerischen Heeres* [5 parts] (Munich, 1901–9); O. Bezzel, *Geschichte des kurpfälzischen Heeres von seinen Anfängen bis zur Vereinigung von Kurpfalz und Kurbayern 1777* [2 vols] (Munich, 1925–8); L. H. F. v. Sichart, *Geschichte der Königlich-hannoverschen Armee* [5 vols] (Hanover, 1866–98); O. Elster, *Geschichte der stehenden Truppen im Herzogtum Braunschweig-Wolfenbüttel, 1600–1806* [2 vols] (Leipzig, 1899–1901); O. Schuster & F. A. Franke, *Geschichte der sächsischen Armee von deren Errichtung bis auf die neueste Zeit* [3 vols] (Leipzig, 1885); G. Knüppel, *Das Heerwesen des Fürstentums Schleswig–Holstein–Gottorf, 1600–1715* (Neumünster, 1972); G. Tessin, *Mecklenburgisches Militär in Türken- und Franzosenkriegen, 1648–1718* (Cologne, 1966).

9. J. Ehlers, *Die Wehrverfassung der Stadt Hamburg im 17. und 18. Jahrhundert* (Boppard, 1966); I. Kracauer, "Das Militärwesen der Reichstadt Frankfurt im 18. Jahrhundert", *Archiv für Frankfurts Geschichte und Kunst*, NF **12**, 1920, pp. 1–180; F. Willax, "Das Verteidigungswesen Nürnbergs im 17. und 18. Jahrhundert", *Mitteilungen des Vereins für Geschichte der Stadt Nürnberg* **66**, 1979, pp. 192–247; J. Kraus, *Das Militärwesen der Reichsstadt Augsburg 1548 bis 1806* (Augsburg, 1980); T. Schwark, *Lübecks Stadtmilitär im 17. und 18. Jahrhundert* (Lübeck, 1990).

10. T. Verspohl, *Das Heerwesen des Münsterschen Fürstbischofs Christoph Bernhard von Galen, 1650–1678* (Hildeheim, 1909); C. Frhr. v. Bönninghausen, *Die Kriegerische Tätigkeit der Munsterschen Truppen, 1651–1800* (Coesfeld, 1978); F. P. Kahlenberg, *Kurmainzische Vesteidigungseinrichtungen und Baugeschichte der Festung Mainz im 17. und 18. Jahrhundert* (Mainz, 1963); R. Harms, "Landmiliz und stehendes Heer in Kurmainz namentlich im 18. Jahrhundert", *Archiv für hessische Geschichte und Altertumskunde*, NF **6**, 1909, pp. 359–430; G. Aders, *Bonn als Festung* (Bonn, 1973); Oberleutnant Möllmann, "Zur Geschichte des Kurtrierischen Militärs", *Trierisches Archiv*, supplement 1, 1901, pp. 60–87; W. Kopp, *Würzburger Wehr: Eine Chronik zur Wehrgeschichte Würzburgs* (Würzburg, 1979).

11. H. Münkler, *Im Namen des Staates. Die Begründung der Staatsraison in der frühen Neuzeit* (Frankfurt-am-Main, 1987); H. Dreitzel, *Absolutismus und ständische Verfassung in Deutschland* (Mainz, 1992); M. Behnen, "Der gerechte und der notwendige Krieg. 'Necessitas' und 'utilitas reipublicae' in der Kriegstheorie des 16. und 17. Jahrhunderts", in *Staatsverfassung und Heeresverfassung in der europäischen Geschichte der frühen Neuzeit*, J. Kunisch (ed.) (Berlin, 1986), pp. 42–106.

12. For examples, see P. H. Wilson, "The power to defend or the defence of power: the conflict between duke and estates over defence provision, Württemberg, 1677–1793", *Parliaments, Estates and Representation* **12**, 1992, pp. 25–45. Good coverage of ruler–estate disputes over military funding is provided by F. L. Carsten, *Princes and parliaments in Germany from the fifteenth to the eighteenth centuries* (Oxford, 1959).

13. Events at the *Reichstag* are well covered by A. Müller, *Der Regensburger Reichstag von 1653–54: eine Studie zur Entwicklung des Alten Reiches nach dem Westfälischen Frieden* (Frankfurt-am-Main, 1992). The JRA is printed in Schmauss & Senckenberg (eds), *Sammlung der Reichsabschiede*, vol. III, pp. 640–92. For detailed coverage of imperial politics at this stage see M. Schnettger, *Der Reichsdeputationstag 1655–1633. Kaiser und Stände zwischen Westfälischem Frieden und Immerwährendem Reichstag* (Münster).

14. M. Hughes, "Die Strafpreussen: Mecklenburg und der Bund der deutschen absolutistischen Fürsten, 1648–1719", *Parliaments, Estates and Representation* **3**, 1983, pp. 101–13. The Extensionist treaty is printed in T. v. Moerner (ed.), *Kurbrandenburgs Staatsverträge von 1601 bis 1700* (Berlin, 1867), pp. 696–701.

15. For the political aspects of this important bishop's reign, see W. Kohl, *Christoph Bernhard von Galen: Politische Geschichte des Fürstbistums Munster, 1650–1678* (Münster, 1964), and his edition of key documents, *Akten und Urkunden zur Aussenpolitik Christoph Bernhard von Galen (1650–1678)* [3 vols], (Münster, 1980–86).

16. W. Frhr. v. Tettau, "Erfurts Unterwerfung unter die mainzische Landeshoheit", *Neujahrsblätter herausgegeben von der Historischen Kommission der Provinz Sachsen* **11**, 1887, pp. 3–56; H. Querfurt, *Die Unterwerfung der Stadt Braunschweig im Jahre 1671* (Brunswick, 1953); L. Hüttl, *Friedrich Wilhelm von Brandenburg, der Großer Kurfürst, 1620–1688* (Munich, 1981), pp. 260–94, 342–8; F. Hirsch, "Die Armee des Großer Kurfürsten und ihre Unterhaltung während der Jahre 1660–1666", *HZ* **53**, 1885, pp. 229–75.

17. F. L. Carsten, "The States General and the Estates of Cleves about the middle of the seventeenth century", in *Essays in German history* (London, 1985), pp. 80–89. See also his articles, "The resistance of Cleves and Mark to the despotic policy of the Great Elector", *English Historical Review* **66**, 1951, pp. 219–41, and "The Great Elector and the foundation of Hohenzollern despotism", *EHR* **65**, 1950, pp. 175–202.

18. H. Schmidt, *Philipp Wilhelm von Pfalz-Neuburg, 1615–1690* (Düsseldorf, 1973), vol. I, pp. 64–95; A. Hanschmidt, "Kurbrandenburg als Kreisstand im Niederheinisch-Westfälischen Kreis vom Westfälischen Frieden bis zum Spanischen Erbfolgekrieg", in

Preußen, Europa und das Reich, O. Hauser (ed.) (Cologne, 1978), pp. 47–64; P. Casser, "Der Niederheinisch-Westfälische Reichskreis", in *Der Raum Westfalen*, H. Aubin & E. Schulte (eds) (Berlin, 1934), vol. II, pp. 35–72; W. Kohl (ed.), *Westfälische Geschichte* (Düsseldorf, 1983), vol. I, pp. 540–60.

19. G. Mentz, *Johann Philipp von Schönborn, Kurfürst von Mainz, Bischof von Würzburg und Worms, 1605–1673* [2 vols] (Jena, 1896–9), vol. II, pp. 13–14, 66–70, 136–8; Bezzel, *Kurpfälzischen Heeres*, vol. I, pp. 97–101; B. Erdmannsdörffer, *Deutsche Geschichte vom Westfälischen Frieden bis zum Regierungsantritt Friedrichs des Großen, 1648–1740* [2 vols] (Leipzig, 1932 edn), vol. I, pp. 361–4.

20. The historiography is covered by P. H. Wilson, "The German 'Soldier Trade' of the seventeenth and eighteenth centuries: a reassessment", *International History Review* **18**, 1996, pp. 757–92, which includes extensive references.

21. The treaty is printed in Kohl, *Akten und Urkunden*, vol. I, pp. 455–7. See also C. Brinkmann, "Charles II and the Bishop of Münster in the Anglo-Dutch War of 1665–6", *EHR* **21**, 1906, pp. 686–98. For the general background, see J. R. Jones, *The Anglo-Dutch wars of the seventeenth century* (London, 1996).

22. Kohl, *Galen*, pp. 189–243; Bönninghausen, *Münsterschen Truppen*, pp. 22–8. For the auxiliaries hired by the Dutch, see F. G. J. Ten Raa et al., *Het staatsche Leger, 1568–1795* [8 vols in 10] The Hague, 1911–59, vol. V, pp. 160–81, 499–500; Jany, *Preußische Armee*, vol. I, pp. 203–7. For the Republic's treaty with the Great Elector, see Moerner (ed.), *Kurbrandenburgs Staatsverträge*, pp. 272–7.

23. G. Pagès, *Le Grand Electeur et Louis XIV, 1660–1688* (Paris, 1905), esp. pp. 145–220; Kohl, *Galen*, pp. 244–96; J. T. O'Connor, *Negotiator out of season: the career of Wilhelm Egon von Fürstenberg, 1629–1704* (Athens Georgia, 1978), pp. 24–34; R. Pillorget, "La France et l'électorat de Trèves au temps de Charles-Gaspard de La Leyen (1652–1679)", *Revue d'histoire diplomatique* **78**, 1964, pp. 7–34, 118–47; Ten Raa, *Het Staatsche Leger*, vol. V, pp. 500–502.

24. For this and the following, see R. I. Frost, *After the deluge: Poland–Lithuania and the Second Northern War, 1655–1660* (Cambridge, 1993); S. E. Oakley, *War and peace in the Baltic, 1560–1790* (London, 1992), pp. 80–92; Kunisch, *Fürst-Gesellschaft-Krieg*, pp. 43–82.

25. Austro-Brandenburg involvement is covered by E. Opitz, *Österreich und Brandenburg im Schwedisch-Polnischen Krieg* (Boppard, 1969), with further detail in Hüttl, *Friedrich Wilhelm*, pp. 200–59, and Jany, *Preußische Armee*, vol. I, pp. 115–48. Dutch intervention is discussed by A. Tjaden, "The Dutch in the Baltic, 1544–1721", in *The Baltic in power politics, 1500–1990*, G. Rystad (ed.) (Stockholm, 1990), vol. I, pp. 61–136.

26. Knüppel, *Schleswig-Holstein-Gottorf*, especially pp. 82, 167–70; F. C. Rode, *Kriegsgeschichte Schleswig-Holsteins* (Neumünster, 1935), pp. 25–32. The duke raised an army of 5,000 with Swedish technical and financial assistance.

27. Good overviews in P. F. Sugar, *Southeastern Europe under Ottoman rule, 1354–1804* (Seattle, 1977); A. Palmer, *The decline and fall of the Ottoman empire* (London, 1992); B. Jelavich, *History of the Balkans*, vol. I (Cambridge, 1983); M. G. Hodgson, *The gunpowder empires and modern times*, vol. 3 of *The venture of Islam* (Chicago, 1974), especially pp. 126–44.

28. O. Subtelny, *Domination of eastern Europe: Native nobilities and foreign absolutism, 1500–1715* (Gloucester, 1986), especially pp. 56, 109–13, 156–66.

29. On these issues see the excellent collection of articles in R. J. W. Evans & T. V. Thomas (eds), *Crown, church and estates: central European politics in the sixteenth and seventeenth century* (New York, 1991). Also, R. Bireley SJ, "Confessional absolutism in the Habsburg lands

in the seventeenth century", in *State and society in early modern Austria*, C. Ingrao (ed.) (West Lafayette, 1994), pp. 36–53.

30. K. Vocelka, "Das Türkenbild des Christlichen Abendlands in der frühen Neuzeit", in *Österreich und die Osmanen – Prinz Eugen und seine Zeit*, E. Zöllner & K. Gutkas (eds) (Vienna, 1988), pp. 20–31; M. Grothaus, "Zum Türkenbild in der Kultur der Habsburgmonarchie zwischen dem 16. und 18. Jahrhundert", in *Habsburg-Osmanische beziehungen*, A. Tietze (ed.) (Vienna, 1985), pp. 67–89.

31. J. Dietz, *Memoirs of a mercenary: being the memoirs of Master Johann Dietz . . .* (London, 1987), p. 36. For the geography and economy of the region see the contributions by L. Mákkai and I. N. Kiss in *East central Europe in transition*, A. Maczak et al. (Cambridge, 1985).

32. J. Blum, *The end of the old order in rural Europe* (Princeton, 1978), pp. 253, 255. Figures for 1720. The combined population of Royal (92,000 km^2) and Turkish (110,000–120,000 km^2) Hungary was 1.7–1.8 million in the late seventeenth century, while Transylvania (57,000 km^2) had about 500,000 inhabitants. The larger surface areas often cited for Transylvania include parts of Hungary. Even as late as 1787 only 8 of the 77 Hungarian and Transylvanian towns had more than 15,000 inhabitants. For the logistical problems, see P. Broucek, "Logistische Fragen der Türkenkriege des 16. und 17. Jahrhunderts", in *Vorträge zur Militärgeschichte* (Herford/Bonn, 1986), vol. III, pp. 35–60.

33. For the war, see K. Peball, *Die Schlacht bei St-Gotthard-Mogersdorf 1664* (Vienna, 1964); A. v. Schempp, *Der Feldzug 1664 in Ungarn*, (Stuttgart, 1909), E. Eickhoff, *Venedig, Wien und die Osmanen: Umbruch in Südosteuropa, 1645–1700* (Munich, 1973), pp. 196–204.

34. B. Auerbach (ed.), *Recueil des instructions*, vol. 18 *Diète Germanique* (Paris, 1912), pp. 37–8; Hüttl, *Friedrich Wilhelm*, pp. 329–33.

35. H. Forst, "Die deutschen Reichstruppen im Türkenkrieg 1664", *MIÖG*, supplement vol. **6**, 1901, pp. 634–48; Schuster & Franke, *Sächsischen Armee*, vol. I, pp. 83–4; Staudinger, *Bayerischen Heeres*, vol. I, pp. 82, 507, 513; Jany, *Preußische Armee*, vol. I, pp. 201–2; Schempp, *Feldzug, 1664*, pp. 40–41, 46, 52–3, 259–60; Vann, *Swabian Kreis*, pp. 61–3, 270; P. C. Storm, *Der Schwäbische Kreis als Feldherr: Untersuchungen zur Wehrverfassung des schwäbischen Reichskreises in der Zeit von 1648–1732* (Berlin, 1974), pp. 245–6, 264, 274–5, 301–5; H. Fahrmbacher, "Vorgeschichte und Anfänge der Kurpfälzischen Armee in Jülich-Berg, 1609–1685", *Zeitschrift des Bergischen Geschichtsveriens* **42**, 1909, pp. 35–94; pp. 50–53; H. Helmes, "Übersicht zur Geschichte der fränkischen Kreistruppen, 1664–1714", *Darstellungen aus der bayerischen und Kriegs- und Heeresgeschichte* **14**, 1905, pp. 1–70; Tessin, *Mecklenburgisches Militär*, pp. 11–14. The key legislation is printed in Schmauss & Senckenberg (eds), *Sammlung der Reichsabschiede*, vol. IV, pp. 5–32.

36. The Austro-Hungarian element totalled 10,900 along with 7,400 *Kreistruppen* and the 900 survivors of the German Alliance contingents. The French, who had arrived later and suffered proportionately less from disease, still totalled 5,250. Other detachments, including the Brandenburgers, were serving to the north under General Souches to cover Hungary and so missed the battle.

37. The failure of Habsburg repression in Hungary is covered by E. Pamlényi (ed.), *A history of Hungary* (London, 1975), pp. 164–7; R. J. W. Evans, *The making of the Habsburg monarchy, 1550–1700* (Oxford, 1979), pp. 121, 235–74.

38. K. M. Setton, *Venice, Austria and the Turks in the seventeenth century* (Philadelphia, 1991), pp. 104–243; W. Kohlhaas, *Candida: die Tragödie einer abendländischen Verteidigung und ihr Nachspiel im Morea, 1645–1715* (Osnabrück, 1978); Anon., *A relation of the siege of Candia . . .* (London, 1670); F. H. Tyrell, "The siege of Candia, 1645–1668", *Journal of the Royal United Services Institute* **52**, 1908, pp. 1093–1112; Eichhoff, *Venedig*, pp. 230–64.

39. J. Bérenger, "An attempted *rapprochement* between France and the emperor: the secret treaty for the partition of the Spanish succession of 19 January 1668", in *Louis XIV and Europe*, R. Hatton (ed.) (London, 1976), pp. 132–52. For French policy since 1667 and the war generally, see P. Sonnino, *Louis XIV and the origins of the Dutch War* (Cambridge, 1988), and C. J. Ekberg, *The failure of Louis XIV's Dutch War* (Chapel Hill, NC, 1979).

40. Kohl, *Galen*, pp. 375–9; Erdmannsdörffer, *Deutsche Geschichte*, vol. I, pp. 545–7; O'Connor, *Negotiator out of season*, pp. 62–4.

41. K. Müller, "Zur Reichskriegserklärung im 17. und 18. Jahrhundert", *ZSRG* **90**, 1973, pp. 246–59, printing the relevant documents. See also K. P. Decker, *Frankreich und die Reichsstände, 1672–1675* (Bonn, 1981), p. 185.

42. For Brandenburg's policy in this period, see D. McKay, "Small-power diplomacy in the age of Louis XIV: the foreign policy of the Great Elector during the 1660s and 1670s", in *Royal and republican sovereignty in early modern Europe*, R. Oresko et al. (eds) (Cambridge, 1997), pp. 188–215. Erdmannsdörffer, *Deutsche Geschichte*, vol. I, pp. 562–3; Jany, *Preußische Armee*, vol. I, pp. 223–4; Pagès, *Le Grand Electeur et Louis XIV*, pp. 354–9; Spielman, *Leopold I*, pp. 59–60, 76–7. Further insight into Habsburg policy and military activity throughout the war is provided in C. Beese, *Markgraf Hermann von Baden (1628–1691): General, Diplomat und Minister Kaiser Leopold I* (Stuttgart, 1991), pp. 85–190.

43. A. Schindling, "Reichstag und europäischer Frieden. Leopold I., Ludwig XIV. und die Reichsverfassung nach dem Frieden von Nimwegen (1679)", *ZHF* **8**, 1981, pp. 161–3.

44. On the operations, see C. du Jarrys, Frhr. de La Roche, *Das deutsche Oberrhein während der Kriege seit dem Westphälischen Frieden bis 1801* (Stuttgart, 1842), pp. 16–20; Jany, *Preußische Armee* vol I, pp. 227–9; Elster, *Braunschweig-Wolfenbüttel* vol. I, pp. 132–52.

45. G. Benecke, *Society and politics in Germany, 1500–1750* (London, 1974), pp. 314–18, 359.

46. K. Hüsgen, "Die militärische Vertretung des Stiftes Essen durch Brandenburg-Preußen im 17. und 18. Jahrhundert", *Beiträge zur Geschichte von Stadt und Stift Essen* **30**, 1909, pp. 1–92, especially pp. 7–14; R. Fester, *Die Armirten Stände und die Reichskriegsverfassung, 1681–1697* (Frankfurt-am-Main, 1886), p. 82.

47. H. Caspary, *Staat, Finanzen, Wirtschaft und Heerwesen in Hochstift Bamberg (1653–1693)* (Bamberg, 1976), pp. 290–91, 313–19, 351.

48. HSAS, C9: Bü. 326.

49. HSAS, C9: Bü.290–94, 298–9, 305, 310–12, 316–25, 337–45, 356; K. v. Martens, *Geschichte der innerhalb der gegenwärtigen Gränzen des Königreichs Württemberg vorgefallene kriegerischen Ereignisse . . .* (Stuttgart, 1847), p. 499.

50. L. I. v. Stadlinger, *Geschichte des Württembergischen Kriegswesens* (Stuttgart, 1856), pp. 70, 322; Strack von Weissenbach, *Geschichte der Königlichen Württembergischen Artillerie* (Stuttgart, 1882), p. 64.

51. G. Schnath, *Geschichte Hannovers im Zeitalter der neunten Kur und der englischen Sukzession, 1674–1714* [5 vols] (Hildesheim, 1938–82), vol. I, pp. 80–81; W. Schmidt, "Geschichte des niedersächsischen Kreises vom Jahre 1673 bis zum Zusammenbruch der Kreisverfassung", *Niedersächsisches Jahrbuch für Landesgeschichte* **7**, 1930, pp. 1–134 (p. 55).

52. Schmidt, "Niedersächsischen Kreises", pp. 28–37, 85–7, 105–18; Dotzauer, *Reichskreise*, p. 329. Schmidt misses the significance of Celle's ulterior motives. As the Celle and Wolfenbüttel units were in fact serving as Dutch auxiliaries, they have been omitted from Table 2.2.

53. Tessin, *Mecklenburgisches Militär*, pp. 26–7; Benecke, *Society and politics*, pp. 318–20.

54. J. Güssregen, *Die Wehrverfassung der Hochstiftes Bamberg im achzehnten Jahrhundert*

(Bamberg, 1936), pp. 24–6; E. Hagen, "Die fürstlich Würzburgische Hausinfanterie von ihren Anfängen bis zum Beginne des Siebenjährigen Krieges, 1636–1756", *DBKH* **19**, 1910, pp. 69–203 (pp. 80–4); H. J. Wunschel, *Die Außenpolitik des Bischofs von Bamberg und Würzburg Peter Philipps von Dernbach* (Neustadt a.d. Aisch, 1979), pp. 56–142; Caspary, *Bamberg*, pp. 289–94, 303, 341–6; H. Patze (ed.), *Geschichte Thüringens*, vol. 5 of *Politische Geschichte in der Neuzeit* (Cologne, 1982), pp. 245, 353; A. Zernin, *Abriß der Großherzoglich-Hessischen Kriegs- und Truppen-Geschichte, 1567–1888* (Darmstadt, 1889), p. 17; F. Beck, *Geschichte der alten Hessen-Darmstädtischen Reiterregimenter . . .* (Darmstadt, 1910), pp. 19–24; stAD, A6 Nr. 1440; E8 B180/1–2.

55. H. Philippi, *Landgraf Karl von Hessen-Kassel* (Marburg, 1976), pp. 19–21, 30–9; G. Hollenberg, "Landstände und Militär in Hessen-Kassel", *Hessisches Jahrbuch für Landesgeschichte* **34**, 1984, pp. 101–27 (pp. 104–5). In all 1,400 Hessians died in Danish service.

56. By December 1678 the elector had 45,318 soldiers and mobilized militiamen costing 238,000 tlr a month, exceeding total annual tax receipts of 2.37 million tlr: Jany, *Preußische Armee*, vol. I, p. 269; S. B. Fay, "The beginning of the standing army in Prussia", *American Historical Review* **22**, 1917, pp. 763–77 (p. 77).

57. Schmidt, "Niedersächsischen Kreises", pp. 36–7; Jany, *Preußische Armee*, vol. I, pp. 253–4, 269; Philippi, *Landgraf Karl*, pp. 24–5; Hüttl, *Friedrich Wilhelm*, p. 414; Schnath, *Geschichte Hannovers*, vol. I, pp. 97–8.

58. HSAS, L6.22.2.27; L6.22.2.32; L6.22.2.49; Helmes, "Übersicht", pp. 4–11; Storm, *Feldherr*, pp. 80–84; Vann, *Swabian Kreis*, pp. 270–71.

59. The latter was due to the duke's refusal to recognize the Nijmegen Settlement, which, while restoring his duchy, would have compelled him to cede Nancy and Longwy to France and so have left him defenceless.

60. H. Schmidt, "Die Verteidigung des Oberrheins und die Sicherung Süddeutschlands im Zeitalter des Absolutismus und der Französischen Revolution", *Historisches Jahrbuch* **104**, 1984, pp. 46–62; M. Hildenbrand, "Die Kriegerischen Auseinandersetzungen im 17. und 18. Jahrhundert, 1672–1748", in *Land um Rhein und Schwarzwald*, K. Klein (ed.) (Kehl, 1978), pp. 103–11. The IPO also prohibited the construction of new fortesses on the east bank between Basel and Philippsburg. This ban remained in place until the Peace of Rijswijk in 1697.

61. J. L. Wohleb, "Die Sicherung der Heerstraßen des Südschwarzwaldes im siebzehnten Jahrhundert", *ZGO*, NF **56**, pp. 398–450; E. v. Müller, "Die Bühl-Stollhofener Lines im Jahre 1703", *ZGO*, NF **21**, 1906, pp. 99–137; G. Weber, "Die 'Eppinger Linien'", *Kraichgau. Heimatforschung im Landkreis Sinsheim* **3**, 1972, pp. 179–87; K. Lang, *Die Ettlinger Linien und ihre Geschichte* (Ettlingen, 1965).

62. Details from the Swabian *Kreis* papers, HSAS, C14: Bü.307; L6.22.4.66–7.

63. K. F. Wernet, "Der Hauensteiner Landfahnen", *ZGO*, NF **56**, 1943, pp. 301–95; O. Heinl, *Heereswesen und Volksbewaffnung in Vorderösterreich im Zeitalter Josefs II. und der Revolutionskriege* (PhD thesis, Freiburg University, printed 1941), pp. 51–2; A. v. Pfister, *Der Milizgedanke in Württemberg und die Versuche zu seiner Verwirklichung* (Stuttgart, 1883).

64. J. Lindegren, "The Swedish 'military state', 1560–1720", *Scandinavian Journal of History* **10**, 1985, pp. 305–36; K.-R. Böhme, "Building a Baltic empire. Aspects of Swedish expansion 1560–1660", and J. Glete, "Bridge and bulwark. The Swedish navy and the Baltic, 1500–1809", both in Rystad (ed.), *The Baltic in power politics*, pp. 9–59, 177–220. For the north German dimension of the Dutch War, see also H. Regelmeier, *Die politischen Beziehungen der Fürsten Norddeutschlands zu Frankreich und den nordischen*

Seemächten in den Jahren 1674 bis 1676 (Hildesheim, 1909), and N. Wimarson, "Zur Entstehungsgeschichte des Brandenburgisch-Schwedischen Krieges, 1675–1679", *Forschungen zur brandenburgischen und preussischen Geschichte* **14**, 1901, pp. 267–72.

65. Schnath, *Geschichte Hannovers*, vol. III, p. 312.

66. J. B. Wolf, *Louis XIV* (London, 1968), pp. 402–5; J. B. Collins, *The state in early modern France* (Cambridge, 1995), pp. 99–100.

67. Auerbach (ed.), *Recueil des instructions*, pp. 40–70, instructions of 31 July 1679, 8 January 1680 and 27 July 1681. See also Wolf, *Louis XIV*, pp. 403–7; O'Connor, *Negotiator out of season*, pp. 80–1.

68. For example, by Schnath, *Geschichte Hannovers*, vol. I, p. 167.

69. H. Schilling, *Höfe und Allianzen: Deutschland, 1648–1763* (Berlin, 1989), pp. 235–40; J. Stoye, *Europe unfolding, 1648–1688* (London, 1969), p. 386; Aretin, *Alles Reich*, especially pp. 408–9. For a revisionist French perspective, see F. Bluche, *Louis XIV* (Oxford, 1990), pp. 283–97.

70. B. Wunder, *Frankreich, Württemberg und der Schwäbische Kreis während der Auseinandersetzungen über die Reunionen (1679–97)* (Stuttgart, 1971); F. L. Ford, *Strasbourg in transition, 1648–1789* (Cambridge, Mass., 1958), pp. 28–75; C. Pohlmann, "Zweibrücken in der Zeit der französischen Reunion (1680–1697)", *Mitteilungen des Hist. Vereins der Pfalz* **56**, 1958, pp. 107–36; F. Textor, "Die französische 'Saarprovinz', 1680–1697", *Rheinische Vierteljahrsblätter* **10** 1940, pp. 1–76; M. Herold, "Von Saarlouis zum Mont-Royal, von der mittleren Saar zum unteren Mosel!", *RVJB* **3**, 1933, pp. 355–68; R. Pillorget, "Jean-Hugues d'Orsbeck électeur de Trèves et la politique des Réunions (1678–1688)", *Revue d'histoire diplomatique* **79**, 1965, pp. 315–37. Some French officials were murdered but otherwise there was little resistance, and existing landowners kept their property and feudal rights provided they recognized Louis as their sovereign.

71. E. Opgenoorth, "Der Große Kurfürst, das Reich und die europäischen Mächte", in Hauser (ed.), *Preußen, Europa und das Reich*, pp. 19–31, especially p. 27. Traditional interpretation in Erdmannsdörffer, *Deutsche Geschichte*, vol. I, 619–54. See also Aretin, *Altes Reich*, pp. 282–6, 305–9, whose otherwise excellent discussion is somewhat distorted by an overly censorious appraisal of the Great Elector.

72. On Dutch policy in this period, see H. H. Rowen, *The princes of Orange: the stadholders in the Dutch Republic* (Cambridge, 1988), pp. 141–4; S. B. Baxter, *William III and the defence of European Liberty, 1650–1702* (London, 1966), pp. 182–92; N. A. Robb, *William of Orange* [2 vols] (London, 1962–6), vol. II, pp. 136–7, 171–95; Ten Raa, *Het staatsche Leger*, vol. VI, pp. 86–101.

73. Schindling, "Reichstag und europäischer Frieden", pp. 166–8. The Reichstag announced its satisfaction at Leopold's withdrawal in February 1680.

74. G. Livet, "Louis XIV and the Germanies", in Hatton (ed.), *Louis XIV and Europe*, pp. 60–81 (pp. 64–5); A. Gestreich, *Absolutismus und Öffentlichkeit: politische Kommunikation in Deutschland zu Beginn des 18. Jahrhunderts* (Göttingen, 1994), pp. 79–81, 194. See also Robb, *William of Orange*, vol. I, p. 133, with similar comments on the Dutch Calvinist attitude to war.

75. Strattmann had acted as imperial negotiator at Nijmegen and was Austrian chancellor in 1683–93. On his career and influence see Spielman, *Leopold I*, pp. 103–4, and Aretin, *Altes Reich*, pp. 276–7. For the *Reichstag* in this period, see H. Angermeier, "Die Reichskriegsverfassung in der Politik der Jahre, 1679–1681" *ZSRG* **82**, 1965, pp. 190–222.

76. Here I follow Schindling, "Reichstag und europäischer Frieden", pp. 169–71, and Aretin, *Altes Reich*, pp. 294–5. For an example of the traditional view, see Schnath, *Geschichte Hannovers*, vol. I, pp. 178–93.

77. Schindling, "Reichstag und europäischer Frieden", pp. 172–7. The Truce and ratification are printed in Schmauss & Senckenberg, *Sammlung der Reichsabschiede*, vol. IV, pp. 142–56. The Laxenburg Alliance is discussed in Chapter 5.

78. Angermeier, "Reichskriegsverfassung", pp. 195–204; Hüttl, *Friedrich Wilhelm*, pp. 431–5; K. Müller. "Wien und Kurmainz, 1673–1680", *RVJB* **32**, 1968, pp. 332–60; L. Hüttl, "Die bayerisch-österreichischen Beziehungen, 1679–1683", *Mitteilungen des Österreichischen staatsarchivre* **36**, 1983, pp. 83–119. The new elector became an important figure in imperial politics and has been studied in depth by L. Hüttl, *Max Emanuel. Der Blaue Kurfürst 1679–1726* (Munich, 1976).

79. Aretin, *Altes Reich*, pp. 290–93, 410; W. Jannen Jr, " 'Das Liebe Teutschland' in the seventeenth century. Count George Frederick von Waldeck", *European Studies Review* **6**, 1976, pp. 165–95 (pp. 181–2); Wunschel, *Außenpolitik des Bischofs von Bamberg*, pp. 155–65. The Wetterau Union and Waldeck's role are discussed in detail in Chapter 5.

80. Hanschmidt, "Kurbrandenburg als Kreisstand", pp. 57–9; Angermeier, "Reichskriegs-verfassung", pp. 206–9; Fester, *Armirten Stände*, p. 41; Schnath, *Geschichte Hannovers*, vol. I, pp. 183–9. The Herzberg Plan is printed in *ibid.*, pp. 696–701.

81. The legislation is printed in Hofmann (ed.), *Quellen zum Verfassungsorganismus*, pp. 232–40, Schmauss & Senckenberg (eds), *Sammlung der Reichsabschiede*, vol. IV, pp. 137–8, 141; E. v. Frauenholz (ed.), *Das Heerwesen in der Zeit des Absolutismus* (Munich, 1940), pp. 375–80. Useful discussions in Aretin, *Altes Reich*, pp. 293–8, and B. Sicken, *Das Wehrwesen des fränkischen Reichskreises: Aufbau und Struktur (1681–1714)* (Nuremberg, 1967), pp. 30–37, 59–60.

82. H. Neuhaus, "Prinz Eugen als Reichsgeneral", in *Prinz Eugen von Savoyen und seine Zeit*, J. Kunisch (ed.) (Freiburg, 1986), pp. 163–77, and his "Das Problem der militärischen Exekutive in der Spätphase des Alten Reiches", in Kunisch (ed.), *Staatsverfassung und Heeresverfassung*, pp. 297–346; also Kohlhepp, *Militärverfassung*, pp. 49–51. The position of the *Kreis* generals is covered by Storm, *Feldherr*, pp. 182–234, and further discussed in Chapter 5 below.

Chapter Three: War on two fronts, 1683–99

1. For this and the following: I. Parvev, *Habsburgs and Ottomans between Vienna and Belgrade (1683–1739)* (New York, 1995); J. W. Stoye, *The Siege of Vienna* (London, 1964); T. M. Barker, *Double eagle and crescent: Vienna's second Turkish siege and its historical setting* (Albany, 1967); A. Arkayin, "The second siege of Vienna (1683) and its consequences", *Revue internationale d'histoire militaire* **46**, 1980, pp. 107–17, and the excellent collection of articles in *Der Sieg bei Wien 1683* (Vienna/Warsaw, 1983).

2. Estimates of the Turkish army vary wildly. Most sources agree that the fighting strength was 90,000, of whom 15,000–20,000 were elite Janissaries, with an additional 20,000 Tatars and 20,000 Hungarians under Thököly. The rest were largely baggage personnel.

3. Hanover did manage to send 600 infantry (not cavalry as usually stated) in return for special imperial confirmation of the introduction of primogeniture. For this and the other

German assistance see Schnath, *Geschichte Hannovers*, vol. i, pp. 185–97; Schuster & Franke, *Sächsischen Armee*, vol. i, pp. 101–9; Tessin, *Regimenter*, pp. 65, 89–90, 295; Philippi, *Landgraf Karl*, pp. 63–5; Helmes, "Übersicht", pp. 19–21; Sicken, *Wehrwesen*, pp. 119–20, 174; Kopp, *Würzburger Wehr*, pp. 57–8; Storm, *Feldherr*, pp. 314–19; A. Pfister, *Das Infanterieregiment Kaiser Wilhelm König von Preußen (2. Württ.) No. 120* (Stuttgart, 1881), pp. 20–25; T. Griesinger, *Geschichte des Ulanenregiments König Karl (I. Württ.) Nr. 19* (Stuttgart, 1883), pp. 7–12; G. v. Niethammer, "Aus der Geschichte des Grenadier-Regiment Königin Olga (I. Württ.) Nr. 119. Türkenkriege", *Beiheft zum Militär-Wochenblatt* 1, 1877, pp. 7–36; StAD, E8 B 180/3, covering the Hessen-Darmstadt and Union forces.

4. N. Davies, *God's playground: a history of Poland* [2 vols] (Oxford, 1981), vol. i, pp. 364–5, 470–72, 478–9; Jany, *Preußische Armee*, vol. i, pp. 137, 221–3, 285–95; Eickhoff, *Venedig*, pp. 286–304. Only 370 of the 1,500 Brandenburg cavalry provided in 1672–4 returned alive.

5. For the siege and battle see in addition to the works in *n.* 1 above: W. Hummelberger, "Wien in der Verteidigung gegen die Türken", and P. Broucek, "Der Feldzug von 1683 und der Einsatz Wiens in der Schlacht am Kahlenberg", both in Zöller & Gutkas (eds), *Österreich und die Osmanen*, pp. 42–68. There is also a useful historiographical overview by T. M. Barker, "New perspectives on the historical significance of the 'Year of the Turk' ", *Austrian History Yearbook* **19/20**, 1983–4, pp. 3–14.

6. L. Bittner, *Chronologisches Verzeichnis der Österreichischen, Staatsverträge* (Vienna, 1903), vol. i, pp. 92–3; Spielman, *Leopold I*, pp. 94–6, 18–19, 125–6; Setton, *Venice*, pp. 269–73, 279; F. W. Carter, *Dubrovnik (Ragusa): a classic city state* (London, 1972), pp. 343–6. Innocent even believed that Shiite Persia could be persuaded to join the Christian alliance.

7. R. Wittram, *Peter I: Czar und Kaiser* [2 vols] (Göttingen, 1964), vol. i, pp. 119–28; B. H. Sumner, *Peter the Great and the Ottoman empire* (Oxford, 1949), pp. 13–22; Davies, *God's playground*, vol. i, p. 487.

8. Spielman, *Leopold I*, pp. 19, 124–5; Ingrao, *Habsburg monarchy*, pp. 78, 85, 87; Pámlenyi (ed.), *Hungary*, p. 169; Subtelny, *Domination*, p. 84.

9. L. Hüttl, "Die Beziehungen zwischen Wien, München und Versailles Während des großen Türkenkrieges 1684 bis 1688", *MÖSA* **38**, 1985, pp. 81–122; Staudinger, *Bayerischen Heeres*, ii/ii, pp. 180–245. For the arrangements with the other larger territories see Schuster & Franke, *Sachsischen Armee*, vol. i, pp. 110–30; P. Haake, "Die Türkenfeldzüge August des Starken 1695 und 1696", *Neues Archiv für sächsische Geschichte* **24**, 1903, pp. 134–54; Sichart, *Hannoverschen Armee*, vol. i, pp. 188–92, pp. 471–6; Elster, *Braunschweig-Wolfenbüttel*, vol. i, pp. 181–93; Hüttl, *Friedrich Wilhelm*, pp. 459–69; Jany, *Preußische Armee*, vol. i, pp. 288–95, 381–7, 397–401.

10. For Brandenburg and Guelph casualties see Schnath, *Geschichte Hannovers*, vol. i, pp. 372–4, 512 *n*28, 639; Jany, *Preußische Armee*, vol. i, pp. 288, 294, 382–3, 386. For examples of the burden on the smaller teritories, see StAD E8 B180/3–5 relating to the deployment of Upper Rhine *Kreistruppen* and E8 B180/6 containing Hessen-Darmstadt expenditure for 1683–5.

11. Cited in Philippi, *Landgraf Karl*, pp. 98–9. For the transfers and the contributions of the smaller territories generally see Wrede, *Wehrmacht*, vol. ii, p. 416, vol. i, p. 599, 602, ii/ii, p. 954; F. Scharlach, "Fürstbischof Friedrich Christian von Plettenberg und die Münsterische Politik im Koalitionskrieg, 1688–1697", 2 parts, *Westfälische Zeitschrift* **80**, 1922, pp. 1–25; *WZ* **93**, 1937, pp. 79–127; O"Connor, *Negotiator out of season*, pp. 107–22; Hagen, "Würzburgische Hausinfanterie, 1636–1756", pp. 90–93; Tessin,

Mecklenburgisches Militär, pp. 35–6, 88–91; A. Keim, *Geschichte des Infanterie-Regiments Großherzogin (3. Großherzog. Hessisches) Nr. 117 und seiner Stämme, 1677–1902* (Berlin, 1903), pp. 2–17; O. Münter, "Die Waldeckischen Truppen von 1681 bis 1750", *Geschichtsblätter für Waldeck* **71**, 1983, pp. 179–211 (pp. 192–5).

12. R. v. Andler, "Die Württembergischen Regimenter in Griechenland, 1687–89", *WVJHLG*, NF **31**, 1922–4, pp. 217–79 (p. 226 n 80); Schirmer, *Nec asperra terrant!*, p. 37; Schuster & Franke, *Sächsischen Armee*, vol. I, p. 110. Details of the Hessen-Darmstadt Regiment (part of the Württemberg contingent) losses are in STAD E8 B 180/8–12, 181/1. The unit, nominally 1,000 strong, had only 319 effectives in June 1689.

13. HSAS, A28: Bü. 92–93; L6: 22.3.14–17; STAD E8 B180/1–12; 181/6; Schnath, *Geschichte Hannovers*, vol. I, pp. 349–54; Setton, *Venice*, pp. 292–4; Philippi, *Landgraf Karl*, pp. 93–4; Patze (ed.), *Geschichte Thüringens*, vol. V, p. 458; W. Thensius, *Die Anfänge des stehenden Heerwesens in Kursachsen unter Johann Georg III. und Johann Georg IV* (Leipzig, 1912), pp. 72–4.

14. HSAS, A5: Bü.66. The regiment (rgt) was formed by Friedrich Carl after he had been displaced as regent in 1693. For the other units, see Tessin, *Regimenter*, pp. 741–2.

15. J. Stoye, *Marsigli's Europe, 1680–1730: the life and times of Luigi Ferdinando Marsigli, soldier and virtuoso* (New Haven, 1994), pp. 36–8; Broucek, "Logistik", pp. 51–6; W. v. Wersebe, *Geschichte des hannoverschen Armee* (Hanover, 1928), p. 58; Beese, *Markgraf Hermann von Baden*, pp. 241–52.

16. Anon., *An historical description of the glorious conquest of the city of Buda . . .* (London, 1686); Dietz, *Memoirs*, pp. 36–53; Sugar, *Southeastern Europe*, pp. 199–200. Lorraine had 75,000 men in 1687, including the German auxiliaries.

17. Parvev, *Habsburgs and Ottomans*, pp. 55–88, 99; Stoye, *Marsigli*, pp. 63–4, 88. To bring him to heel, the new sultan made Jegen governor of Belgrade early in 1688. Max Emanuel had 53,000 men for the 1688 campaign, while a further 30,000 held Transylvania.

18. Pámlenyi (ed.), *Hungary*, pp. 169–70; Spielman, *Leopold I*, pp. 132–41; Subtelny, *Domination*, pp. 82–3.

19. Parvev, *Habsburgs and Ottomans*, pp. 87–96, 117; Stoye, *Marsigli*, pp. 88–99; Jelavich, *Balkans*, vol. I, pp. 92–3, 148–50. Habsburg forces were intended to total 59,000 by August 1690, but it is not clear if this target was reached.

20. Including German auxiliaries, imperial strength varied from 32,000 in 1692 to 50,000 in 1696.

21. M. Braubach, *Prinz Eugen von Savoyen* [5 vols] (Munich, 1962–5), vol. I, pp. 258–60.

22. By 1700 Austrian Habsburg territory amounted to 517,585 km^2 of which 230,155 km^2 lay within the *Reich*. The non-Habsburg territories within the *Reich* covered 438,524 km^2 For the treaty and its implementation, see Stoye, *Marsigli*, pp. 164–215.

23. Dietz, *Memoirs*, p. 57. For a similarly horrific account see Anon., *Historical description*, pp. 62–3.

24. Sichart, *Hannoverschen Armee*, vol. I, p. 348. Quote from Dietz, *Memoirs*, p. 45.

25. N. Malcolm, *Bosnia: a short history* (London, 1994), pp. 84–5; B. R. Kroener, "Prinz Eugen und die Türken", in Kunisch (ed.), *Prinz Eugen*, pp. 113–25 (pp. 119–20). Braubach, *Prinz Eugen*, vol. I, pp. 262–5 describes the raid as a deliberate attempt "to strike fear into the enemy".

26. Dietz, *Memoirs*, pp. 52–3, 64, 121–2; K. v. Seeger, *Zweitausendjahre Schwäbisches Soldatentum* (Stuttgart, 1937), pp. 41–2; K. Czok, *Am Hofe Augusts des Starken* (Stuttgart, 1990), p. 68.

27. Schuster & Franke, *Sächsischen Armee*, vol. I, pp. 109, 200, vol. III, 385; H. Bleckwenn, *Die friderizianischen Uniformen, 1753–1786* [4 vols] (Osnabrück, 1987), vol. IV, pp. 23–4; G. Kandler, "Zur Geschichte der deutschen Soldatenmusik" in B. Schwertfeger & E.O. Volkmann (eds.), *Die deutschen Soldatenkunde*, vol I, (Berlin & Leipzig, 1937), *Soldatenkunde*, vol. I, pp. 473–523. Two "Moors", Carl Thomas Martiale and Jean Baptista, were made trumpeters in the Württemberg Garde du Corps on 7 April 1752: HSAS, A202: Bü. 2260.

28. E. Wangermann, *The Austrian achievement, 1700–1800* (London, 1973), pp. 145–6.

29. G. Symcox, "Louis XIV and the outbreak of the Nine Years War", in Hatton (ed.), *Louis XIV and Europe*, pp. 178–212, quote from p. 180. See also for the following: Schnath, *Geschichte Hannovers*, vol. I, pp. 358–71, 390–95, 402–37; O'Connor, *Negotiator out of season*, pp. 125–37; Pagès, *Le Grand Electeur et Louis XIV*, pp. 530–606; G. Pfeifer, "Ein französisch-bayerischer Mediatisierungsplan 1687/88", *ZBLG* **27**, 1964, pp. 245–58. R. Place, 'Bavaria and the collapse of Louis XIV's German policy 1687–8', *JMH*, **49** (1977), 369–93.

30. Ferguson, "Blood and fire", pp. 64–169, quote from p. 78; H. Musall & A. Scheuerbrand, "Die Kriege im Zeitalter Ludwigs XIV und ihre Auswirkungen auf die Siedlungs-, Bevölkerungs und Wirtschaftsstruktur der Oberrheinlande", in *Hans Graul Festschrift* (*Heidelberger geographische Arbeiten*, vol. 40, Heidelberg, 1974), pp. 357–78; K. v. Raumer, *Die Zerstörung der Pfalz von 1689* (Munich, 1930).

31. Fester, *Armirten Stände*, pp. 79–85. The Magdeburg Concert is discussed further in Chapter 5.

32. Baxter, *William III*, pp. 222–30, provides a good overview of Anglo-Dutch policy in the war. For aspects of Savoy in this period, see the excellent G. Symcox, *Victor Amadeus II: absolutism in the Savoyard state, 1675–1730* (London, 1983).

33. G. Symcox, *The crisis of French naval power, 1688–97* (The Hague, 1974).

34. Sweden hired 6,000 men to the Dutch in 1688, later increasing these to 9,700, while Denmark provided 5,600 to England in 1689, adding another 1,940 in 1694. For these and the following figures, see J. Childs, *The British army of William III, 1689–1702* (Manchester, 1987), and his *The Nine Years War and the British army, 1688–97* (Manchester, 1991); Ten Raa, *Het Staatsche Leger*, vols VI & VII; D. French, *The British way in warfare, 1688–2000* (London, 1990), pp. 14–20; Jany, *Preußische Armee*, vol. II, pp. 360–425; P. G. M. Dickson, *Finance and government under Maria Theresia, 1740–1780* [2 vols] (Oxford, 1987), vol. II, p. 344; R. Wiebe, *Untersuchungen über die Hilfeleistung der deutschen Staaten für Wilhelm III von Oranien im Jahre 1688* (Göttingen, 1939); HSAS, A202: Bü. 2469–71.

35. A. F. Pribram (ed.), *Österreichische Staatsverträge: England* [2 vols] (Innsbrück, 1907–13), vol. I, pp. 162–90.

36. There is some discussion of these problems in W. Hubatsch, "Koalitionskriegführung in neuester Zeit, historisch-politisch betrachtet", in *Schicksalfragen der Gegenwart: Handbuch politisch-historischer Bildung*, Bundesministerium für Verteidigung, [4 vols] (Tübingen, 1957–9), vol. I, pp. 245–70. The following is based on a synthesis of the various contingent histories and the literature in *n*34 above.

37. D. W. Jones, *War and economy in the age of William III and Marlborough* (Oxford, 1988), and his article and that by J. G. A. Pocock in D. Hoak & M. Feingold (eds), *The world of William and Mary* (Stanford, CA, 1996); A. C. Carter, *Neutrality or commitment: the evolution of Dutch foreign policy, 1667–1795* (London, 1975).

38. Braubach, *Prinz Eugen*, vol. I, pp. 160–236. This work gives an excellent overview of the operations in this theatre.

39. These intrigues can be followed in the papers of the Habsburg commander in Spain, Prince Georg von Hessen-Darmstadt in STAD D4 Abt. IV Konv. 281–8. See also B. Rill, *Karl VI: Habsburg als barocke Großmacht* (Graz, 1992), especially p. 42, and Aretin, *Das Reich*, pp. 218–19.
40. J. Fayard, "Attempts to build a 'Third Party' in north Germany, 1690–1694", in Hatton (ed.), *Louis XIV and Europe*, pp. 213–40; Scharlach, "Fürstbischof Friedrich Christian von Plettenberg", part 2, pp. 79–108; Schnath, *Geschichte Hannovers*, vol. I, pp. 506–648.
41. K. Krüger, "Militär und Stadt: Ratzeburg, 1689–1695", in *Europäische Städte im Zeitalter des Barock* (Cologne, 1988), pp. 399–436.
42. See Chapter 5.
43. R. H. Thompson, *Lothar Franz von Schönborn and the diplomacy of the Electorate of Mainz* (The Hague, 1973), p. 113. For the Rijswijk Conference in general see *ibid.*, pp. 110–21; Baxter, *William III*, pp. 331–64; Spielman, *Leopold I*, pp. 156–8.
44. H. Ritter v. Srbik, *Wien und Versailles, 1692–1697* (Munich, 1944), pp. 290–92; G. W. Sante, "Die kurpfälzische Politik des Kurfürsten Johann Wilhelm, vornehmlich im Spanischen Erbfolgekrieg, 1690–1716", *HJb*, **44**, 1924, pp. 19–64; K. Müller, "Kurfürst Johann Wilhelm und die europäische Politik seiner Zeit", *Düsseldorfer Jahrbuch* **60**, 1986, pp. 1–23; M. Braubach, "Johann Wilhelm Kurfürst von der Pfalz, Herzog von Jülich und Berg (1658–1716)", *Rheinische Lebensbilder* I, 1961, pp. 83–101.

Chapter Four: Habsburg strategy in continental conflict, 1700–21

1. C. W. Ingrao, *In quest and crisis: Emperor Joseph I and the Habsburg monarchy* (West Lafayette, 1979), p. 79. The importance of Italy is discussed by L. Auer, "Zur Rolle Italiens in der Österreichischen Politik um das Spanische Erbe", *MÖSA* **31**, 1978, pp. 52–72 and "Osterreichische und europäische Politik um das Spanische Erbe", *Wiener Beiträge zur Geschichte der Neuzeit* **20**, 1993, pp. 96–109.
2. Aretin's work in this area is summarized in his *Das Reich*, pp. 76–166, 241–54, and *Altes Reich*, pp. 12–15, 310–12, on which the following is largely based.
3. G. Hanlon, *The twilight of a military tradition: Italian aristocrats and European conflicts (1560–1800)* (London, 1998). John Stoye's biography of Marsigli provides another detailed example. For the contributions see Aretin, *Das Reich*, pp. 243–4; Braubach, *Prinz Eugen*, vol. I, p. 212.
4. Baxter, *William III*, pp. 365–73; M. A. Thomson, "Louis XIV and the origins of the War of the Spanish Succession", in *William III and Louis XIV*, R. M. Hatton & J. S. Bromley (eds) (Liverpool, 1968), pp. 140–61.
5. L. & M. Frey, *A question of empire: Leopold I and the War of Spanish Succession, 1701–1705* (New York, 1983), especially pp. 3–18, 46–8, 59; Braubach, *Prinz Eugen*, vol. I, pp. 300–29; D. McKay, *Prince Eugene of Savoy* (London, 1977), pp. 58–61. A digest of the Austrian archival material relating to this and the other campaigns of the war is given by *Feldzüge des Prinzen Eugen von Savoyen* [21 vols] (issued by the Austrian Kriegs-Archiv, Vienna, 1876–96).
6. Pribram (ed.), *Staatsverträge*, vol. I, pp. 210–33; Frey, *Question of empire*, pp. 19–25; Baxter, *William III*, pp. 379–98.
7. R. E. Scouller, *The armies of Queen Anne* (Oxford, 1966), appendix C; J. B. Hattendorf,

England in the War of the Spanish Succession (New York, 1987), pp. 133–8; French, *British way*, pp. 21–31; Ten Raa, *Het staatsche Leger*, vol. VIII/3, pp. 275–88, 338–41.

8. *Feldzüge*, vol. I, pp. 499–504; Symcox, *Victor Amadeus*, pp. 168–9; H. Kamen, *The War of Succession in Spain, 1700–15* (London, 1969), pp. 59–68, 92–4. See also *n*34, p. 364.

9. Ten Raa, *Het staatsche Leger*, vol. III/3, p. 341; *Feldzüge*, vol. v, pp. 124–8; M. Braubach, *Die Bedeutung der Subsidien für die Politik im Spanischen Erbfolgekrieg* (Bonn, 1923), pp. 170–71; Hattendorf, *England*, pp. 129–32, 274–303.

10. W. S. Churchill, *Marlborough: his life and times* [4 vols] (London, 1967 edn), vol. I, p. 455; Dickson, *Finance and government*, vol. II, pp. 344–5.

11. For French diplomatic efforts, see B. Wunder, "Die bayerische 'Diversion' Ludwig XIV in den Jahren 1700–1704", *Zeitschrift für bayerische Landesgeschichte* **37**, 1974, pp. 416–78; Aretin, *Das Reich*, pp. 209–40; and the articles by Max Braubach reprinted in the collection *Diplomatie und geistiges Leben* (Bonn, 1969), pp. 128–84.

12. G. Schnath, "Die Überwältigung Braunschweig-Wolfenbüttels durch Hannover und Celle zu Beginn des Spanischen Erbfolgekrieges, März 1702", *Braunschweigisches Jahrbuch* **56**, 1975, pp. 27–100; Jany, *Preußische Armee*, vol. I, pp. 437–8. Movement is covered in Chapter, 5 while the outbreak of the Great Northern War is analyzed on pp. 129–33.

13. For the Wittelsbach military effort, see H. E. v. Gottberg, "Die Kriegerische Tätigkeit der Kurkölnischen Armee im 18. Jahrhundert", *Alt-Köln* **8**, 1914, pp. 18–22; Aders, *Bonn als Festung*, pp. 98–115; P.-C. Hartmann, "Die französischen Subsidienzahlungen an den Kurfürsten von Köln, Fürstbischof von Lüttich, Hildesheim und Regensburg, Joseph Clemens, im Spanischen Erbfolgekrieg (1701–1714)", *HJb* **92**, 1972, pp. 358–71, and his "Die Subsidien- und Finanzpolitik Kurfürst Max Emanuels von Bayern im Spanischen Erbfolgekrieg", *ZBLG* **32**, 1969, pp. 238–89. Bavarian policy is covered by Hüttl, *Max Emanuel*, pp. 281–374.

14. Hofmann, *Quellen zum Verfassungsorganismus*, pp. 272–5; A. Berney, "Der Reichstag zu Regensburg (1702–1704)", *Historische Vierteljahrschrift* **24**, 1929, pp. 389–442. The revival of the Association. Movement is covered in depth, pp. 192–6.

15. The treaties are printed in C. Jenkinson First Earl of Liverpool (ed.), *A Collection of all the treaties . . . between Great Britain and other powers* [3 vols] (London, 1785), vol. I, pp. 337–54, and Pribram (ed.), *Staatsverträge*, I 236–42. Discussions in Frey, *Question of empire*, pp. 63–8; Ingrao, *Quest and crisis*, p. 91; Rill, *Karl VI*, pp. 49–56. For the subsequent conflict in Spain see *ibid.*, pp. 57–90, and D. Francis, *The first Peninsular War, 1702–1713* (London, 1975); J. A. C. Hugill, *No peace without Spain* (Oxford, 1991).

16. B. Holl, *Hofkammerpräsident Gundaker Thomas Graf Starhernberg und die österreichische Finanzpolitik der Barockzeit (1703–1715)* (Vienna, 1976), especially pp. 39–60, 79–82, 100–6. For the Hungarian revolt, see F. Theuer, *Brennendes Land: Kuruzzenkriege* (Vienna, 1984); Á. Várkonyi, "Rákóczi's war of independence and the peasantry", in *From Hunyadi to Rákóczi* J. M. Bak & B. K. Kiraly (eds), (New York, 1982), pp. 369–91; Subtelny, *Domination*, pp. 145–55, 183–91; C. W. Ingrao, "Guerrilla warfare in early modern Europe: the *Kuruc* war (1703–11)", in *War and society in east central Europe*, B. K. Kiraly & G. E. Rothenberg (eds), (New York, 1979), pp. 47–66, and his *Quest and crisis*, pp. 126–60.

17. C. C. Sturgill, *Marshall Villars and the War of the Spanish Succession* (Lexington, 1965), pp. 17–52; Ten Raa, *Het staatsche Leger*, vol. VIII/1, pp. 358–70; Braubach, *Prinz Eugen*, vol. I, pp. 337–68, vol. II, 16–45; McKay, *Prince Eugene*, pp. 64–72; Berney, "Reichstag", pp. 397–419.

18. Frey, *Question of empire*, pp. 50–58, 68–75, 81–4; Ten Raa, *Het staatsche Leger*, vol. VIII/1, pp. 37–394.

19. Ingrao, *Quest and crisis*, pp. 12–14; Sante, "Kurpfälzische Politik", pp. 39–42; Braubach, *Prinz Eugen*, vol. I, pp. 363–8, vol. II, pp. 34–8; McKay, *Prince Eugene*, pp. 67–71; Holl, *Hofkammerpräsident*, pp. 39–132, with detail on the financial and administrative implications of the changes.

20. For the war planning see Braubach, *Prinz Eugen*, vol. II, pp. 45–54, and Churchill, *Marlborough*, vol. II, pp. 232–54. The extensive literature on Marlborough has been summarized recently by J. R. Jones, *Marlborough* (Cambridge, 1993), which provides a useful balance to Churchill's detailed but rather hagiographic account.

21. Good coverage of the campaign and battle are provided by Braubach, *Prinz Eugen*, vol. II, pp. 54–77; *Feldzüge*, vol. VI, pp. 478–525; Ten Raa, *Het staatsche Leger*, VIII/1, pp. 399–479; Churchill, *Marlborough*, II 260–376; D. Chandler, *Marlborough as a military commander*, 2nd edn (London, 1979), pp. 123–50.

22. Ten Raa, *Het Staatsche Leger*, vol. VIII/1, pp. 748–53, provides a list of these units.

23. Storm, *Feldherr*, pp. 332, 334; Churchill, *Marlborough* vol. III, pp. 44–6. Mindelheim encompased 375.5km^2 with 10,000 inhabitants. It was restored to Max Emanuel in 1714, but the duke kept a personal title.

24. R.v. Dülmen, "Bäuerlicher Protest und patriotische Bewegung. Der Volksaufstand in Bayern 1705/6", *ZBLG* **45**, 1982, pp. 331–61; C. Probst, *Lieber bayerisch sterben: Der bayerische Volksaufstand von 1705 und 1706* (Munich, 1978); Ingrao, *Quest and crisis*, pp. 29, 44–8.

25. Berney, "Reichstag", pp. 418–37; Sante, "Kurpfälzische Politik", pp. 43–5. For Swedish intervention, see pp. 136–7.

26. Ingrao, *Quest and crisis*, pp. 34–8; Braubach, *Prinz Eugen*, vol. II, pp. 95–111; McKay, *Prince Eugene*, pp. 94–7; K. Gutkas, "Die führenden Persönlichkeiten der habsburgischen Monarchie von 1683 bis 1740", in *Prinz Eugen und das barocke Österreich*, Gutkas (ed.), (Salzburg, 1985), pp. 73–86.

27. V. Press, "Josef I (1705–1711) – Kaiserpolitik zwischen Erblanden, Reich und Dynastie", in *Deutschland und Europe in der Neuzeit*, R. Melville et al. (eds) (Wiesbaden, 1988), pp. 277–97 (pp. 293–4). For Dutch influence, see M. Braubach, "Politisch–militärische Verträge zwischen den Fürstbischöfen von Münster und den Generalstaaten der Vereinigten Niederlande im 18. Jahrhundert", *WZ* **91**, 1935, pp. 150–94.

28. For this and the following, see Press, "Josef I" pp. 292–6; Ingrao, *Quest and crisis*, pp. 49–50, 72–4; HSAS, A202: Bü. 2102–4.

29. Key documents printed in Zeumer (ed.), *Quellensammlung*, pp. 470–74. On Johann Wilhelm's role, see Sante, "Kurpfälzische Politik", pp. 42–54, and Müller, "Kurfürst Johann Wilhelm", pp. 15–16.

30. A. Berney, *König Friedrich I und das Haus Habsburg (1701–1707)*, (Munich, 1927); L. & M. Frey, *Frederick I: the man and his times* (New York, 1984), especially pp. 197–207, 219–24, 232–4. Prussia's treaties are in PRO, SP108 nos 405, 406, 408, 409, and its military involvement is covered by Jany, *Preußische Armee*, vol. I, pp. 434–526. Frederick's territorial ambitions in Franconia are analyzed on pp. 134–5.

31. The Palatine treaty is in PRO, SP108 no. 234. On the other arrangements, see Braubach, *Subsidien*, pp. 40, 141–2, and his *Prinz Eugen*, vol. II, pp. 143–5; *Feldzüge*, vol. VIII, pp. 79, 84, 180; Churchill, *Marlborough*, vol. III, pp. 38–43; Elster, *Braunschweig-Wolfenbüttel*, vol. I, pp. 272, 308–9; H. L. Mikoletsky, "Die große Anliehe von 1706", *MÖSA* **7**, 1954, pp. 268–98.

32. *Feldzüge*, VII, 251–70; Braubach, *Prinz Eugen*, vol. II, pp. 153–65; Philippi, *Landgraf Karl*, pp. 336–43; Elster, *Braunschweig-Wolfenbüttel*, vol. I, pp. 309–14.

33. On this and the operations of 1707, see Braubach, *Prinz Eugen*, vol. II, pp. 165–8, 191–9; McKay, *Prince Eugene*, pp. 102–7; Churchill, *Marlborough*, vol. III, pp. 230–42.

34. Braubach, *Prinz Eugen*, vol. II, pp. 170–1; Aretin, *Das Reich*, p. 275; Ingrao, *Quest and crisis*, pp. 49, 98–9, 247.

35. Ingrao, *Quest and crisis*, pp. 99–120.

36. H. Kramer, "Der Werbungsversuch der Kurie in der Schweiz im Jahre 1708", *Zeitschrift für schweizerische Geschichte* 14, 1934, pp. 30–7.

37. Ingrao, *Quest and crisis*, p. 110. On the war and subsequent settlement see also Stoye, *Marsigli*, pp. 271–6; Aretin *Das Reich*, pp. 276–82; Press, "Josef I", pp. 286–7.

38. *Feldzüge*, vol. VII, p. 65; vol. VIII, p. 74. The impact of the French raid is discussed in Ferguson, "Blood and fire", pp. 229–46.

39. Rill, *Karl VI*, pp. 62–3. The *Reichsbarriere* project is analyzed in Chapter 5.

40. Ingrao, *Quest and crisis*, quotes from pp. 33–4, 76; Aretin, *Das Reich*, especially pp. 313–20.

41. Here I follow Press, "Josef I", pp. 290ff, and Auer, "Österreichische und europäische Politik", pp. 106–8.

42. Good overviews of Habsburg policy 1709–14, are given by Rill, *Karl VI*, pp. 87–131; Braubach, *Prinz Eugen*, vol. II, pp. 316–28; Aretin, *Das Reich*, pp. 313–20.

43. B. Wunder, "Die französisch-Württembergischen Geheimverhandlungen 1711", *Zeitschrift für Württembergische Landesgeschichte* 28, 1969, pp. 363–90; Frey, *Frederick I*, pp. 268–88; Braubach, *Diplomatie und geistiges Leben*, pp. 268–88.

44. HSAS, L5: Tom. 125 fol. 110–14 (for Württemberg); STAD, E8 B258/1–14, E1 C36/6 (for Hessen-Darmstadt); Tessin, *Mecklenburgisches Militär*, pp. 44–6; Elster, *Braunschweig-Wolfenbüttel*, vol. I, pp. 344–5; Philippi, *Landgraf Karl*, pp. 398–418; C. Frhr. v. Bönninghausen, *Die kriegerische Tätigheit der Münsterschen Truppen, 1651–1800* (Coesfeld, 1978), pp. 140–41. Landau, taken by the French in 1703, was recaptured by the *Reicharmee* in Nov 1704, but fell on 20 Aug 1713 after a siege of 56 days.

45. The standard biography is still P. Haake, *August der Starke* (Berlin, 1926), which is superior to more recent efforts like H. Schreiber, *August der Starke: Leben und Lieben im deutschen Barock* (Munich, 1981), and K. Czok, *August der Starke und Kursachsen* (Leipzig, 1989).

46. Excellent coverage of Polish politics in this period is provided by J. Lukowski, *Liberty's folly: the Polish–Lithuanian Commonwealth in the eighteenth century, 1697–1795* (London, 1991). Military aspects are covered by the articles by M. Zgórniak and E. Rostworowski in G. E. Rothenberg et al. (eds), *East central European society and war* (New York, 1982). Three zloties were equivalent to 1 tlr.

47. *Ibid.*, pp. 122–4; J. Kalisch, "Zur Polenpolitik Augusts des Starken: Reformversuche in Polen am Ausgang des 17. Jahrhunderts" (PhD thesis, Leipzig University, 1957); L. R. Lewitter, "Russia, Poland and the Baltic, 1697–1721", *Historical Journal* 11, 1968, pp. 3–34. Good coverage of all aspects in the collection of articles in *Sächsische Heimatblätter* 29, 1983, pp. 218–30.

48. Army from W. Thum, *Die Rekrutierung der Sächsischen Armee unter August dem Starken (1694–1733)* (Leipzig, 1912), especially pp. 8–30; Schuster & Franke, *Sächsischen Armee*, vol. I, pp. 138–43; Tessin, *Mecklenburgisches Militär*, p. 37, and *Regimenter*, pp. 68–71.

49. Knüppel, *Schleswig-Holstein-Gottorf*, pp. 174–82; Rode, *Kriegsgeschichte Schleswig-Holsteins*, pp. 36–7; Ten Raa, *Het staatsche Leger*, vol. VII, pp. 146–50; Schnath, *Geschichte Hanovers*, vol. I, p. 524, vol. II, pp. 272–87, vol. III; pp. 311–30; Schuster & Franke, *Sächsischen Armee*, I 146–7; Sichart, *Hannoverschen Armee*, vol. I, pp. 573–6.

50. Knüppel, *Schleswig-Holstein-Gottorf*, pp. 43–4, 54, 181–4; C. Kock, "Schleswig-Holsteiner

unter gottorfischer Fahne im Spanischen Erbfolgekrieg", *Zeitschrift der Gesellschaft für schleswig-holsteinische Geschichte* **64**, 1936, pp. 161–200, Hattendorf, *England in the War of the Spanish Succession*, pp. 282–3; Schnath, *Geschichte Hannovers*, vol. III, pp. 338–41, 609–12; R. M. Hatton, *Charles XII of Sweden* (London, 1968), especially pp. 130–42.

51. Saxon operations are covered in Schuster & Franke, *Sächsischen Armee*, vol. I, pp. 151–70.

52. Czok, *August der Starke*, pp. 50–51; Schnath, *Geschichte Hannovers*, vol. II, pp. 433–69, vol. III; p. 593, 625–7; F. Facius, *Staat, Verwaltung und Wirtschaft in Sachsen-Gotha unter Herzog Friedrich II. 1691–1732* (Gotha, 1933), pp. 56, 60, 75.

53. H. Silberborth, *Preußen und Hannover im Kampfe um die Freie Reichsstadt Nordhausen (1697–1715)* (Nordhausen, 1936); G. Meissner, *Das Kriegswesen der Reichsstadt Nordhausen, 1290–1803* (Berlin, 1939), pp. 73–4; Jany, *Preußische Armee*, vol. I, p. 532; Schnath, *Geschichte Hannovers*, vol. III, pp. 564–5.

54. J. G. Droysen, *Geschichte der preußischen Politik* (Leipzig, 1872), vol. IV, p. 163, and in similar vein C. v. Noorden, "Die preußische Politik im Spanischen Erbfolgekriege", *HZ* **18**, 1867, pp. 297–358; Erdmannsdorffer, *Deutsche Geschichte*, vol. II, pp. 133–4; Jany, *Preußische Armee*, vol. I, pp. 432–5; Braubach, *Subsidien*, pp. 104–7.

55. Frey, *Frederick I*, especially pp. 226–43, and their more compact "The foreign policy of Frederick I, King in Prussia, 1703–1711: a fatal vacillation?", *East European Quarterly* **9**, 1975, pp. 259–69.

56. K. E. Demandt, *Geschichte des Landes Hessen*, 3rd edn (Kassel, 1980), pp. 421–4 (summary of Orange inheritance); Schindling, "Kurbrandenburg", pp. 42–5; Endres, "Markgraf Christian", pp. 282–7; R. Endres, "Preussens Griff nach Franken", and M. Hanisch, "Friedrich II und die preussische Sukzession in Franken in der internationalen Diskussion", both in H. Duchhardt (ed.), *Friedrich der Große, Franken und das Reich* (Cologne, 1986), pp. 57–91.

57. Lukowski, *Liberty's folly*, pp. 125–6 and pp. 142–50 on the effects of the plague; Frey, *Frederick I*, pp. 227–8; Jany, *Preußische Armee*, vol. I, pp. 429–30.

58. Schnath, *Geschichte Hannovers*, vol. III, pp. 341–2, 588–92; Philippi, *Landgraf Karl*, p. 417; H. Duchhardt, *Protestantisches Kaisertum und altes Reich* (Wiesbaden, 1977), pp. 256–7.

59. Ingrao, *In quest and crisis*, pp. 55–65; Hatton, *Charles XII*, pp. 209–30; Schnath, *Geschichte Hannovers*, vol. III, pp. 614–35.

60. For the military situation, see P. Englund, *The battle of Poltava* (London, 1992); Hatton, *Charles XII*, pp. 231–308.

61. Pribam (ed.), *Österreichische Staatsverträge*, vol. I, pp. 252–62; Schnath, *Geschichte Hannovers*, vol. III, pp. 642–52; Hattendorf, *England in the War of the Spanish Succession*, pp. 294–5; J. F. Chance, *George I and the Northern War* (London, 1909), pp. 10–24; Bezzel, *Kurpfälzischen Heeres*, vol. I, pp. 230, 237.

62. Schnath, *Geschichte Hannovers*, vol. III, pp. 342–52, 593, 607–74; W. Mediger, "Die Gewinnung Bremens und Verdens durch Hannover im Nordischen Kriege", *Niedersächsisches Jahrbuch für Landesgeschichte* **43**, 1971, pp. 37–56; Chance, *George I and the Northern War*, pp. 28–30. The Danish force numbered 12,000, drawn largely from the army that had invaded Mecklenburg the previous year.

63. Rode, *Kriegsgeschichte Schleswig-Holsteins*, pp. 38–46; Knüppel, *Schleswig-Holstein-Gottorf*, pp. 39–40, 194–205. The Gottorp regency government was on behalf of Duke Carl Friedrich (1700–39), who was Charles XII's nephew.

64. Philippi, *Landgraf Karl*, pp. 438–84.

65. Thum, *Rekrutierung*, pp. 70–3; Schuster & Franke, *Sächsischen Armee*, pp. 182–92; B. Sicken, "Truppenstärke und Militäretat des Fürstentums Ansbach um 1730", *Jahrbuch*

des Historischen Vereins für Mittelfranken **84**, 1967–68, pp. 60–82 (pp. 65–6); Lukowski, *Liberty's folly*, pp. 141, 145.

66. Schnath, *Geschichte Hannovers*, vol. I, pp. 413–21, 774–5; vol. II, pp. 83, 284–310; vol. III, pp. 106–10, 124–31, 343–606, 696–705; Chance, *George I and the Northern War*, pp. 32–9; Schmidt, "Niedersächsischen Kreises", pp. 129–32; R. Hatton, "Frederick the Great and the House of Hanover", in *Friedrich der Große in seiner Zeit*, O. Hauser (ed.) (Cologne, 1987), pp. 151–64.

67. Schnath, *Geschichte Hannovers*, vol. III, pp. 696–705; Erdmannsdörffer, *Deutsche Geschichte*, vol. II pp. 317–20; Jany, *Preußische Armee*, vol. I, pp. 632–41; Schuster & Franke, *Sächsischen Armee*, vol. I, pp. 190–2; Rode, *Kriegsgeschichte Schleswig-Holsteins*, pp. 46–8; W. Mediger, *Mecklenburg, Russland und England-Hannover, 1706–21* (Hildesheim, 1967), pp. 179–204.

68. Lewitter, "Russia, Poland and the Baltic", pp. 16–22; Schnath, *Geschichte Hannovers*, III 674; P. Wick, *Versuche zur Errichtung des Absolutismus in Mecklenburg in der ersten Hälfte des 18. Jahrhunderts* (Berlin, 1964), p. 31.

69. Schnath, *Geschichte Hannovers*, III 690–6; Philippi, *Landgraf Karl*, pp. 408–10, 439–40, 456–7; Rill, *Karl VI*, pp. 140–46; Braubach, *Prinz Eugen*, III 296–302. Prussia was to contribute 6,000–12,000 men, Hanover 2,200–4,000, Münster 2,000, Wolfenbüttel 1,400, Hessen-Kassel 2,000, with the rest from Austria, while the Hanseatic cities provided the heavy artillery.

70. W. Mediger, *Moskaus Weg nach Europa* (Brunswick, 1952), pp. 130–37; Schnath, *Geschichte Hannovers*, II 310–15.

71. There is good coverage of all aspects of Russian policy in Wittram, *Peter I*, I 191–395, II 221–462. For the Polish settlement, see Davies, *God's playground*, I 492–502; Lukowski, *Liberty's folly*, pp. 112–13, 143–6. For the military dimension see Zgórniak, "Financial problems of the Polish military", pp. 184–6; Schuster & Franke, *Sächsischen Armee*, I 192–4.

72. Mediger, *Mecklenburg*, pp. 122–75. For the negotiations with the smaller courts see Philippi, *Landgraf Karl*, pp. 364–5; Schnath *Geschichte Hannovers*, III 636–8, 683–5; Wittram, *Peter I*, II 356–64.

73. Mecklenburg, including Schwerin and Ratzeburg, covered 14,950 km^2, and was inhabited by 300,000 people generating 300,000–400,000 tlr annually for the duke, to which the estates were obliged since 1701 to add 120,000 tlr. For this and the following see Wick, *Versuche*; Mediger, *Mecklenburg*; M. Hughes, *Law and politics in 18th century Germany: the Imperial Aulic Council in the reign of Charles VI* (Woodbridge, 1988), pp. 91–122, and his "Strafpreussen". The military dimension is covered by Tessin, *Mecklenburgisches Militär*, while an eyewitness account of the brutal repression is provided by P. H. Bruce, *Memoirs of Peter Henry Bruce Esq.* (London, 1782), pp. 190–205.

74. Ten Raa et al., *Het staatsche Leger*, vol. VII, p. 354; Tessin, *Mecklenburgisches Militär*, pp. 329–47, 124–34; Jany, *Preußische Armee*, I 443, 484, 502–3.

75. Text in Pribram (ed.), *Österreichische Staatsverträge*, I 326–48, discussed in Hatton, *George I*, pp. 185–201; and D. McKay, *Allies of convenience: diplomatic relations between Great Britain and Austria, 1714–1719* (New York, 1986).

76. Treaty texts in Liverpool (ed.), *Collection of treaties*, II 243–64 with discussion in Chance, *George I and the Northern War*, pp. 294–397, 468–70; Hatton, *George I*, pp. 216–42, and her *Charles XII*, pp. 492–4, 511–16. For the German dimension, see Mediger, "Gewinnung Bremens und Verdens", pp. 50–2; Philippi, *Landgraf Karl*, pp. 484–91. Friedrich hoped for 4,000–6,000 Württemberg troops, 2,000 from Baden-Durlach, 2,000

from Hessen-Darmstadt, 10,000 from Hessen-Kassel and 3,000 from Ansbach and Bayreuth – all Protestant territories. On the actual assistance see stAD, E8 B182/3–10.

Chapter Five: Princely leagues and associations

1. E. Bock, *Der Schwäbische Bund und seine Verfassung, 1488–1534* (Breslau, 1927); E. Fabian, *Die Entstehung des Schmalkaldischen Bundes und seine Verfassung, 1524/29–1531/35*, 2nd edn (Tübingen, 1962).
2. R. Hauswirth, *Landgraf Philipp von Hessen und Zwingli* (Tübingen, 1968); A. Keller, *Die Wiedereinsetzung des Herzogs Ulrich von Württemberg durch den Landgrafen Philipp von Hessen 1533/34* (Marburg, 1912).
3. Mentz, *Schönborn*, especially vol. II, pp. 51–5, 64, 92–4; Hagen, "Würzburgische Hausinfanterie . . . 1636–1756', pp. 75–6.
4. A. Schröcker, "Der Personalunionsplan des Lothar Franz von Schönborn und seine Verwicklichung", *Mainzer Zeitschrift*, **73–4**, 1978–9, pp. 141–5.
5. Liège 1650–88, 1694–1723; Hildesheim 1583–1612, 1723–61; Paderborn 1723–61; Regensburg 1688–1716; Freising 1688–94; Teutonic Order 1732–61.
6. Speyer 1623–1711; Osnabrück 1711–15; Worms 1716–29, 1732–68; Ellwangen 1716–29; 1732–56, 1777–1802; Augsburg 1768–1802.
7. Kohl, *Galen*; Kohl (ed.), *Westfälische Geschichte*, pp. 587–98.
8. H. E. Feine, *Die Besetzung der Reichsbistümer vom Westfälischen Frieden bis zur Säkularisation, 1648–1803* (Stuttgart, 1921), pp. 316–28.
9. stAD, E1 C43/3–4; E1 H109/1–5; Kahlenberg, *Kurmainzische Verteidigungseinrichtungen*, pp. 15–18, 67–70, 151–69.
10. For the militias see Papke in *HDM*, vol. I, pp. 63–109, and pp. 27–8 above. The complex politics of the Wetterau counts are neatly summarized by Demandt, *Hessen*, pp. 410–20, 471–80.
11. Philippi, *Landgraf Karl*, pp. 12–19; Zernin, *Abriß*, p. 17. By 1676 Hessen-Kassel had 1,000 regulars and 4,000–5,000 militia while Hessen-Darmstadt mustered 1,140 regulars 2,760 militia. On the disputed *Kreis* executive see pp. 19, 33, 100 above.
12. In addition to Jannen, "'Liebe Teutschland'", Waldeck's policies are summarized in G. Menk, *Georg Friedrich von Waldeck, 1620–1692* (Arolsen, 1992), with the military dimension covered by Münter, "Waldeckischen Truppen", and W. Hellwig, "Schützen und Soldaten", in *Waldeckische Landeskunde*, B. Martin & R. Wetekam (eds) (Korbach, 1971), pp. 481–95.
13. In addition to the works in *n*12, see Philippi, *Landgraf Karl*, pp. 46, 50–55. The treaty with Cologne is printed in Hofmann, *Quellen zum Verfassungsorganismus*, pp. 230–32.
14. Analyzed by Sicken, *Wehrwesen*, pp. 279–84. Admittedly, these suffered from the same problems of enforcement affecting imperial legislation, but nonetheless represented a statement of good practice.
15. Menk, *Waldeck*, pp. 66–8. The letter notifying the *Reichstag* of Waldeck's new status is printed in Hofmann, *Quellen zum Verfassungsorganismus*, p. 249.
16. Philippi, *Landgraf Karl*, pp. 67–9; Ten Raa, *Het staatsche Leger*, vol. VI, p. 98, incorrectly refers to this arrangement as being with Hessen-Darmstadt. The Hessen-Kassel army then numbered 6,000, or more than three times the forces of the other Union members.

17. Philippi, *Landgraf Karl*, pp. 88–92, 117, 130–38, 149–61.
18. See Table 5.1. The electorate held 467.5 km^2 of Henneberg inhabited by 20,000 people in 1802. Facius, *Staat, Verwaltung und Wirtschaft*, pp. 30–33. Patze (ed.), *Geschichte Thüringens*, vol. v, provides a good overview of Ernestine politics.
19. Thum, *Rekrutierung*, pp. 9–10, 13–14.
20. H. Müller, *Das Heerwesen im Herzogtum Sachsen-Weimar von 1702–1775* (Jena, 1936); Schuster & Franke, *Sächsische Armee*, I 200–1, vol. iii, 367.
21. Elster, *Braunschweig-Wolfenbüttel*, vol. i, pp. 23–75; Sichart, *Hannoverschen Armee*, vol. i, pp. 17–47; Schirmer, *Nec aspera terrent!*, pp. 5–11. For the distribution of the Guelph territories see p. 21 above.
22. Hüttl, *Friedrich Wilhelm*, p. 171.
23. Schirmer, *Nec aspera terrent!*, pp. 16–17; Elster, *Braunschweig-Wolfenbüttel*, vol. i, pp. 76–100. Five years later Ernst August lent his brother-in-law, Elector Palatine Carl Ludwig, a cavalry regiment to assist in defence against Lorraine incursions (*ibid.*, vol. i, p. 107).
24. Ten Raa, *Het staatsche Leger*, vol. v, pp. 499–500; Elster, *Braunschweig-Wolfenbüttel*, vol. i pp. 103–17.
25. Cited in Elster, *Braunschweig-Wolfenbüttel*, vol. i, pp. 112.
26. The others were Landsberg, Kleeburg, Birkenfeld, Lautereck, Lützelstein and Bischweiler. The Simmern line was absorbed in 1673 into the Palatine branch, which in turn passed to Neuburg in 1685. The latter died out in 1742 and its territories fell to Carl Theodor of Sulzbach, who also inherited Bavaria in 1777. On his death in 1799 the bulk of the Wittelsbach territories were united under Max Joseph of Zweibrücken-Birkenfeld.
27. M. Doeberl, "Das bayerische Hilfskorps in Kölner Diensten zur Zeit des zweiten Raubkrieges", *Forschungen zur Geschichte Bayerns* 6, 1898, pp. 18–44; Münich, *Bayerischen Armee*, p. 25; Tessin, *Regimenter*, pp. 79, 84.
28. Hagen, "Würzburgische Hausinfanterie . . . 1636–1756", p. 174; H. Stahlberg, "Reussisches Militär bis zum Ende der Befreiungskriege", *Zeitschrift für Heereskunde*, 41 (1977), 13–16; Tessin, *Regimenter*, p. 314.
29. B. Wunder, "Die Erneuerung der Reichsexekutionsordnung und die Kreisasoziationen, 1654–1674", *ZGO* **139**, 1991, pp. 494–502; Aretin, *Das Reich*, pp. 167–73. In contrast to Aretin, who stresses the confirmation by the ipo of the powers to make alliances as the stimulus for the Associations, Wunder is right to relate them to the older imperial executive ordinance.
30. J. T. Johnson, *Ideology reason and the limitation of war: religious and secular concepts, 1200–1740* (Princeton, 1975); Decker, *Frankreich und die Reichsstände*, pp. 11–16.
31. Hüttl, *Friedrich Wilhelm*, pp. 339–42.
32. B. Wunder, "Die Kreisassoziationen, 1672–1748", *ZGO* **128**, 1980, pp. 167–266. See also H. H. Hofmann, "Reichskreis und Kreisassoztiation", *ZBLG* **25**, 1962, pp. 277–413.
33. Aretin, *Das Reich*, pp. 167–208.
34. F. Jürgensmeier, "Johann Philipp von Schönborn", *Fränkische Lebensbilder* **6**, 1975, pp. 161–84; Mentz, *Schönborn*, especially vol. ii, pp. 14–15, 215–19.
35. Aretin, *Das Reich*, pp. 193–4; Fester, *Armirten Stände*, p. 22; Dotzauer, *Reichskreise*, pp. 92, 258. The founding document is printed in J. C. Lünig, *Corpus iuris Militaris des Heil. Röm. Reichs* [2 vols] (Leipzig, 1723, reprint Osnabrück, 1968), I 620–23. The original intention had been a common force of 7,000–8,000 men but the absences reduced this.
36. On this and the subsequent negotiations see Kohl (ed.), *Westfälische Geschichte*, pp. 583–5; Aretin, *Das Reich*, pp. 178–80; Dotzauer, *Reichskreise*, pp. 280–84; Elster, *Braunschweig-*

Wolfenbüttel, vol. I, p. 75; Erdmannsdörffer, *Deutsche Geschichte*, vol. I, pp. 131–5; and Moerner (ed.), *Kurbrandenburgs Staatsverträge*, pp. 153–5.

37. Treaty in Lünig, *Corpus iuris militaris*, vol. I, pp. 387–93. There is no modern study of the Alliance, but a brief overview from French sources is provided by R. Schnur, *Die Rheinbund von 1658 in der deutsche Verfassungsgeschichte* (Bonn, 1955).

38. Lünig, *Corpus iuris militaris*, vol. I, pp. 393–6, 670–81.

39. H. Duchhardt, "International relations, the law of nations, and the Germanies', in C. W. Ingrao (ed.), *State and society in early modern Austria*, (West Lafayette, Ind., 1994), pp. 28–91, 286–97; O'Connor, *Negotiator out season*, pp. 26–32.

40. Quoted by Schilling, *Höfe und Allianzen*, p. 182.

41. Sonnino, *Dutch War*, pp. 36–7, 42, 50, 98–125; Erdmansdörffer, *Deutsche Geschichte*, vol. I, pp. 493–4, 511–12; Mentz, *Schönborn*, vol. II, pp. 69–70. Spielman, *Leopold I*, p. 58, seriously underestimates the shock of the invasion of Lorraine.

42. Erdmansdörffer, *Deutsche Geschichte*, vol. I, pp. 507–10; Schilling, *Höfe und Allianzen*, pp. 180–82. Leibniz was a protégé of Johann Christian von Boyneburg who resumed his role as Schönborn's chief adviser in 1668 after a temporary fall from grace.

43. F. J. Krappmann, "Johann Philipp von Schönborn und das Leibnizsche Consilium Aegytiacum" *ZGO*, NF **45**, 1932, pp. 185–219. It seems likely that Schönborn did not know the full details of the plans. On his last scheme see Decker, *Frankreich und die Reichstände*, pp. 120–34.

44. M. Landwehr von Pragenau, "Johann Philipp von Mainz und die Marienburger Allianz von 1671–1672", *MIÖG* **16**, 1895, pp. 582–632; Thompson, *Lothar Franz von Schönborn*, pp. 45–7; Mentz, *Schönborn*, II 50–1; Decker, *Frankreich und die Reichsstände*, pp. 49–61.

45. Thompson, *Lothar Franz von Schönborn*, pp. 55–6; Philippi, *Landgraf Karl*, p. 13; Ten Raa, *Het staatsche Leger*, vol. V, pp. 348–9; Elster, *Braunschweig-Wolfenbüttel*, vol. I, p. 121. The terms of the Brunswick Union are listed in Moerner (ed.), *Kurbrandenburgs Staatsverträge*, pp. 367–70. Trier provisionally agreed to join on 31 December, promising to add 400 cavalry and 2,000 infantry, roughly equivalent to its entire army.

46. For this and the following: Decker, *Frankreich und die Reichsstände*, pp. 153–61; Dotzauer, *Reichskreise*, pp. 128–30, 327; Schmidt, "Niedersächsischen Kreises", pp. 81–4; Wunschel, *Aussenpolitik des Bischofs von Bamberg*, pp. 66–97. The Upper Saxon decision is printed in Lünig, *Corpus iuris militaris*, vol. I, pp. 632–43.

47. Erdmannsdörffer, *Deutsche Geschichte*, vol. I, pp. 525, 542. For the service of the 2,800 Saxons on the Rhine, 1673–5, see Schuster & Franke, *Sächsischen Armee*, vol. I, pp. 87–92. The Quedlinburg Association army was to comprise 3,200 Franconians, 3,955 Lower Saxons and between 3,583 and 3,900 Upper Saxons.

48. Lünig, *Corpus iuris militaris*, vol. I, pp. 413–16; Schmidt, "Niedersächisches Kreises", pp. 84–5; Dotzauer, *Reichskreise*, pp. 130–31, 327–8.

49. A. Koller, *Die Vermittlung des Friedens von Vossem (1673) durch den jülich-bergischen Vizekanzler Stratmann* (Münster, 1995); Pagès, *Le Grand Electeur et Louis XIV*, pp. 322–8. For the following see also Decker, *Frankreich und die Reichsstände*, pp. 70–84; Kohl, *Galen*, pp. 396, 407; Carsten, *Princes and parliaments*, pp. 316–18; Philippi, *Landgraf Karl*, pp. 34–5.

50. As argued by Schindling, "Development of the eternal diet", pp. 70–71, and Angermeier, "Reichskriegsverfassung", pp. 220–22.

51. As argued by Aretin, *Das Reich*, pp. 193–4, and *Altes Reich*, p. 412.

52. Printed in Hofmann (ed.), *Quellen zum Verfassungsorganismus*, pp. 243–8. Discussions in Fester, *Armierten Stände*, pp. 47–8; Sicken, *Wehrwesen*, pp. 79–82; Aretin, *Altes Reich*, pp. 298–302.

53. Printed in Lünig (ed.), *Corpus iuris militaris*, vol. I, pp. 396–402. Discussion in R. Fester, *Die Augsburger Allianz von 1686* (Munich, 1893); Sicken, *Wehrwesen*, pp. 85–6, 113. The contingents comprised 16,000 Austrians, 6,000 Burgundians (i.e. Spanish, or money in lieu), 8,000 electoral Bavarians, 2,000 Bavarian *Kreistruppen*, 4,000 Franconians, 4,000 Union and Upper Rhinelanders, 1,000–2,000 Ernestine Saxons. Holstein-Gottorp (for 1,000) and the Palatinate (1,400) joined in September 1686.

54. Dotzauer, *Reichskreise*, p. 37; Aretin, *Altes Reich*, pp. 184–93.

55. Hanschmidt, "Kurbrandenburg als Kreisstand", pp. 57–61; Schnath, *Geschichte Hannovers*, vol. I, pp. 371–2; Tessin, *Mecklenburgisches Militär*, pp. 26–36; Hüsgen, "Militärische Vertretung", pp. 12–21.

56. Hüsgen, "Militärische Vertretung", pp. 23–4; Schnath, *Geschichte Hannovers*, vol. I, pp. 467–70.

57. A. Siben, "Der Kontributionszug des französischen Generals Marquis de Feuquière durch Franken und Schwaben im Herbst 1688", *ZGO*, NF **54**, 1941, pp. 108–91; K. von Martens, *Geschichte der innerhalb der gegenwärtigen Gränzen des Königreichs Württemberg vorgefallene kriegerischen Ereignisse . . .* (Stuttgart, 1847), pp. 500–22; T. Schott, "Württemberg und die Franzosen im Jahr 1688", *Württembische Neujahrsblätter*, **5**, 1888, pp. 1–52. The Magdeburg Concert is printed in Moerner (ed.), *Kurbrandenburgs Staatsverträge*, pp. 772–5.

58. For this and the following, Fester, *Armirten Stände*, pp. 75–107, 165–8; Philippi, *Landgraf Karl*, pp. 123–49, 160–66; Schnath, *Geschichte Hannovers*, vol. I, pp. 458–70; Thensius, *Anfänge*, pp. 10–28, 134–5; Hüsgen, "Militärische Vertretung", pp. 23–6; Schuster & Franke, *Sächsischen Armee*, vol. I, pp. 113–20.

59. Wunder, *Frankreich, Württemberg und der Schwäbische Kreis*, pp. 81–164, 201–5; Sicken, *Wehrwesen*, pp. 86–7; Caspary, *Bamberg*, pp. 300–1; Fester, *Armirten Stände*, pp. 120–23.

60. Patze (ed.), *Geschichte Thüringens*, vol. V, pp. 269–70; Fester, *Armirten Stände*, pp. 122–3.

61. HSAS, C14: Bü. 334; Storm, *Feldherr*, pp. 320–22; Sicken, *Wehrwesen*, pp. 87–9, 114–15, 149–52; Stadlinger, *Kreigswesens*, pp. 73–6; Wunder, *Frankreich, Württemberg und der Schwäbische Kreis*, pp. 205–12.

62. Fester, *Armirten Stände*, pp. 112–19, 130–31, 168–70; Schnath, *Geschichte Hannovers*, vol. I, pp. 625–8; Ten Raa, *Het staatsche Leger*, vol. VII, pp. 346–7, 372. Schöning entered Brandenburg service after his release from imprisonment in 1694.

63. P. H. Wilson, *War, state and society in Württemberg, 1677–1793* (Cambridge, 1995), pp. 119–21; Philippi, *Landgraf Karl*, p. 166.

64. HSAS, C14: Bü 217; Polster, *Markgraf Christian Ernst*, pp. 32–43; Sicken, *Wehrwesen*, pp. 57–63, 140–43; Storm, *Feldherr*, pp. 196–208. In the Habsburg military hierarchy, a lieutenant general outranked a field marshal. For Christian Ernst's ambitions, see H. Rössler, "Das Opfer für das Reich. Markgraf Christian Ernst von Brandenburg-Bayreuth", *Die Plassenburg*, **4**, 1953, pp. 237–51, and R. Endres, "Markgraf Christian Ernst von Bayreuth", *Frankische Lebensbilder*, **2**, 1968, pp. 260–90.

65. HSAS, C14: Bü. 334. The *Kreis* decisions are printed in J. G. Kulpis (ed.), *Eines hochlöbl. schwäbischen Crayses alte und neue Kriegsverordnungen . . .* (Stuttgart, 1737), and Lünig (ed.), *Corpus iuris militaris*, vol. I, pp. 416–36, 502–56.

66. HSAS, C14: Bü. 307; Sicken, *Wehrwesen*, pp. 121, 176–7, 370–71.

67. R. Wines, "The imperial circles, princely diplomacy and imperial reform 1681–1714", *JMH* **39**, 1967, pp. 1–29; Fester, *Armirten Stände*, pp. 135–7. For Kulpis, see E. Marquardt, *Geschichte Württembergs* (Stuttgart, 1985), pp. 173–5.

68. The Recess is printed in Hofmann, *Quellen zum Verfassungsorganismus*, pp. 252–62. Discussions in Thompson, *Lothar Franz*, pp. 93–103; Scharlach, "Fürstbischof Friedrich Christian von Plettenberg", part II, pp. 114–16; Sicken, *Wehrwesen*, pp. 92–4. For Turkish Louis' role see C. Greiner, 'Der "Schild des Reiches". Markgraf Ludwig Wilhelm von Baden-Baden (1655–1707) und die "Reichsbarrierre" am Oberrhein', in J. Kunisch et al. (eds), *Expansion und Gleichgewicht* (Berlin, 1986), pp. 31–68.

69. Printed in Lünig (ed.), *Corpus iuris militaris*, vol. I, pp. 623–6.

70. Keim, *Infanterie-Regiments Großherzogin*, pp. 17–29; F. Beck, *Geschichte der alten Hessen-Darmstädtischen Reiterregimenter* (Darmstadt, 1910), pp. 28–9.

71. Philippi, *Landgraf Karl*, pp. 167–8, 176–7, 230–42; Thompson, *Lothar Franz*, pp. 85–7.

72. Dotzauer, *Reichskreise*, pp. 289–91; Benecke, *Society and politics*, pp. 69, 359–60; Hanschmidt, "Kurbrandenburg als Kreisstand", pp. 61–2; Casser, "Niederreinisch-Westfälische Reichskreis", pp. 58–9; Hüsgen, "Militärische Vertretung", pp. 30–34; Mürmann, "Militärwesen des ehemaligen Hochstiftes Paderborn", p. 64.

73. For this and the following: Thompson, *Lothar Franz*, pp. 86–111, 121–7; Fester, *Armierten Stände*, pp. 140–45; A. Süss, 'Geschichte des oberrheinischen kreises und der kreisassociationen in der zat des Spanischen Erbfolgekrieges (1697–1714)', *ZGO*, 103 (1955); 317–425 and 104 (1956), 10–224. Philippi, *Landgraf Karl*, pp. 237–42; Aretin, *Das Reich*, pp. 194–7. For Philippsburg and Kehl see pp. 211–14.

74. Thompson, *Lothar Franz*, p. 97.

75. For this and the following see R. Gebauer, *Die Außenpolitik der schwäbischen Reichskreises vor Ausbruch des spanischen Erbfolgekrieges (1697–1702)* (Marburg, 1969); Süss, "Oberrheinischen Kreises", pp. 342–57, 369–422; Thompson, *Lothar Franz*, pp. 134–64; Wines, "Imperial circles", pp. 14–21; Sicken, *Wehrwesen*, pp. 98–9.

76. The Mainz defence budget currently ran at an annual deficit of over 100,000 fl., while total state debts stood at 2 million fl.: A. Schröcker, "Kurmainzer Finanzen 1698", *Geschichte Landeskunde*, **9**, 1973, pp. 147–89, and his "Wirtschaft und Finanzen des Hochstiftes Bamberg und des Erzstiftes Mainz unter Lothar Franz von Schönborn (1693/95–1729)", *Mainzer Zeitschrift* **75**, 1980, pp. 104–14.

77. E.g. Süss, "Oberrheinischen Kreises", pp. 416–17.

78. Sicken, *Wehrwesen*, pp. 99–102, 179–80, 362–7; Polster, *Markgraf Christian Ernst*, pp. 67–96; Helmes, "Übersicht", pp. 16–17, 31–41; Storm, *Feldherr*, pp. 261, 324–30; Süss, "Oberrheinischen Kreises", p. 355; Harms, "Landmiliz", pp. 390–91; *Feldzüge*, vol. X, p. 526; vol. XVI, pp. 85.

79. Benecke, *Society and politics*, pp. 210–14, 223–4, 327–8; H. von Dewall, "Kurzer Abriß der Lippischen Militärgeschichte nebst Fahnengeschichte und Ranglisten von 1664 bis 1806", *Lippische Mitteilungen aus Geschichte und Landeskunde* **31**, 1962, pp. 81–112; K. Rübel, "Kreigs- und Werbewesen in Dortmund in der ersten Hälfte des 18. Jahrhunderts", *Beiträge zur Geschichte Dortmunds und der Grafschaft Mark* **7**, 1896, pp. 106–58; Dotzauer, *Reichskreise*, pp. 294–7; Hüsgen, "Militärische Vertretung", pp. 30–44. The mobilization orders are printed in Lünig (ed.), *Corpus iuris militaris*, vol. I, pp. 629–31.

80. StAD, E8 B258/1–14; 259/1–3; Sicken, *Wehrwesen*, pp. 179–80, 373.

81. *Feldzüge*, vol. IV, pp. 52–5; Tessin, *Regimenter*, pp. 301–2.

82. Cited in Sante, "Kurpfälische Politik", p. 34.

83. HSAS, C14: Bü. 217a; Storm, *Feldherr*, pp. 214–17; Polster, *Markgraf Christian Ernst*, pp. 140–85.

84. Neuhaus, "Prinz Eugen als Reichsgeneral", pp. 172–4; Braubach, *Prinz Eugen*, vol. II, pp. 350–52.

85. HSAS, C14: Bü. 217 with the Swabian instructions. See also Storm, *Feldherr*, pp. 216–26; Polster, *Markgraf Christian Ernst*, pp. 123–41.

86. For this and the following, see W. Hahlweg, "Untersuchungen zur Barrierepolitik Wilhelms III. von Oranien und der Generalstaaten im 17. und 18. Jahrhundert", *Westfälische Forschungen* **14**, 1961, pp. 48–81; Aretin, *Das Reich*, pp. 286–317; Braubach, *Diplomatie und geistiges Leben*, pp. 233–66; Ford, *Strasbourg*, pp. 62–71.

87. H. Wolf, *Die Reichskirchenpolitik des Hauses Lothringen (1680–1715)* (Stuttgart, 1994).

88. HSAS, C14: Bü. 307; Pribam (ed.), *Österreichische Staatsverträge*, vol. I, pp. 263–76.

89. Braubach, *Diplomatie und geistiges Leben*, pp. 188–96, 208–22. For the 1715 Barrier Treaty, see Pribram (ed.), *Österreichische Staatsverträge*, vol. I, pp. 286–325, and R. Geikie & I. A. Montgomery, *The Dutch Barrier, 1705–1719* (Cambridge, 1930).

Chapter Six: The Reich and the European powers, 1714–40

1. C. W. Ingrao, "Habsburg strategy and geopolitics during the eighteenth century", in *East central European society and war in the pre-revolutionary eighteenth century*, B. Király et al. (eds) (New York, 1982), pp. 49–66 (p. 54). My ideas here represent a modification of Ingrao's interpretation in the light of Aretin's work on imperial Italy and the use of core–periphery theory by political geographers. See also Ingrao's "From the Reconquest to the Revolutionary Wars: recent trends in Austrian diplomatic history, 1683–1800", *Austrian History Yearbook* **24**, 1993, pp. 201–18, and his "Conflict or consensus? Habsburg absolutism and foreign policy 1700–1748", *AHY* **19–20**, 1983–4, pp. 33–41.

2. The standard assessment is summarized by Ingrao, "Habsburg strategy", pp. 50–59. For the Pragmatic Sanction, see W. Brauneder, "Die Pragmatische Sanktion – das Grundgesetz der Monarchia Austriaca", in *Prinz Eugen und das barocke Österreich* K. Gutkas (ed.) (Salzburg, 1985), pp. 141–50, and Rill, *Karl VI*, pp. 177–87.

3. Brief overviews in Rill, *Karl VI*, pp. 221–34; Hughes, *Early modern Germany*, pp. 127–38; Duchhardt, *Deutsche Verfassungsgeschichte*, pp. 206–8.

4. Printed in Schmauss & Senckenberg (eds), *Sammlung der Reichsabschiede*, vol. IV, pp. 376–92.

5. For the court and patronage see Rill, *Karl VI*, pp. 188–206, and F. Matsche, *Die Kunst im Dienste des Staates: Die Kaiseridee Karls VI* [2 vols] (Munich, 1981). The other measures are discussed in detail below.

6. There is a sizeable literature on the international relations of this period. For overviews see, from an Austrian perspective, O. Redlich, *Das Werden einer Großmacht: Österreich von 1700 bis 1740* (Brno, 1942); Braubach, *Prinz Eugen*, vols IV & V; McKay, *Prince Eugene*, pp. 148–57, 169–79, 210–26; Rill, *Karl VI*, pp. 164–72. French policy is covered by A. M. Wilson, *French foreign policy during the administration of Cardinal Fleury, 1726–43* (Cambridge, Mass., 1936), with the British dimension in J. Black, *British foreign policy in the age of Walpole* (Edinburgh, 1985), and his *System of ambition? British foreign policy, 1660–1793* (London, 1991).

7. The arrangements were for 2,100 men from Münster, 1,000 from Gotha and 2,800 from Wolfenbüttel. Negotiations for a further 5,000 from Hessen-Kassel were abandoned after the Jacobites were defeated later in 1719. Details in PRO, SP108/254; H. Magis, "Subsidien Englands an deutsche Fürsten" *(1700 bis 1785)* (PhD thesis University of

Innsbrück, 1965), p. 69; Elster, *Braunschweig-Wolfenbüttel*, vol. ii, p. 3; Philippi, *Landgraf Karl*, p. 455.

8. His kingdom henceforth became known as Piedmont-Sardinia. See Symcox, *Victor Amadeus II*, pp. 171–84. Details of operations in Sicily can be found in HSAS, AS: Bü. 52–4, 73 and A. Pfister, "Das Regiment zu Fuss Alt-Württemberg im kaiserlichen Dienst auf Sizilien in den Jahren 1719 bis 1720", *Beiheft zum Militär-Wochenblatt* **5–6**, 1885, pp. 157–268. Treaty texts in Pribram (ed.), *Österreichische Staatsverträge*, I 349–84, and Liverpool (ed.), *Collection*, vol. ii, pp. 185–243.

9. Pribram, *Österreichische Staatsverträge*, vol. i, pp. 412–33. The subsequent Anglo-French agreements with Spain can be found in Liverpool (ed.), *Collection*, vol. ii, pp. 264–74.

10. Wittelsbach policy throughout this period is well covered by Hartmann, *Geld*, and his *Karl Albrecht – Karl VII: Glücklicher Kurfürst und unglücklicher Kaiser* (Regensburg, 1985). For Plettenberg see M. Braubach, *Kurköln: Gestalten und Ereignisse aus zwei Jahrhunderten rheinische Geschichte* (Münster, 1949).

11. Negotiations in Rill, *Karl VI*, pp. 235–48. Reichstag ratification in Schmauss & Senckenberg (eds), *Sammlung der Reichsabschiede*, vol. iv, pp. 351–8.

12. The Alliance of Hanover, also called the League of Herrenhausen, and its extensions are printed in Liverpool (ed.), *Collection*, vol. ii, pp. 274–302. The treaty with Hessen-Kassel of 12 March 1726 in PRO SP108/256 is printed in Frauenholz, *Heerwesen*, vol. iv, pp. 461–3, and covered the entire army of 12,094 men. See also discussions in G. C. Gibbs, "Britain and the Alliance of Hanover", *EHR* **73**, 1958, pp. 404–30; J. Black, "Parliament and foreign policy in the age of Walpole: the case of the Hessians", in *Knights errant and true Englishmen: British foreign policy, 1660–1800* (Edinburgh, 1989), pp. 41–54; and Philippi, *Landgraf Karl*, pp. 532–40.

13. Bittner (ed.), *Staatsverträge*, nos 763–4, 767–71.

14. Wilson, *War, state and society*, pp. 150–52; D. Münch, "Die Bezichungen zwischen Württemberg und Österreich bzw dem Kaiser 1713–1740" (PhD thesis, Innsbrück University, 1961). Sentiment in the *Reich* is discussed by Gestreich, *Absolutismus und Öffentlichkeit*, pp. 201–34.

15. For the military situation, see Dickson, *Finance and government*, vol. ii, pp. 345–6; McKay, *Prince Eugene*, pp. 213–15; Wilson, *French foreign policy*, p. 158. Details of the subsidies from Hartmann, *Geld*, pp. 112–54, and *Karl Albrecht*, pp. 127–8.

16. J. Black, *The collapse of the Anglo-French alliance, 1727–1731* (Gloucester, 1987), and his "When 'natural allies' fall out: Anglo-Austrian relations 1725–1740", *MÖSA* **36**, 1983, pp. 120–49; Treaty texts in Pribram (ed.), *Österreichische Staatsverträge*, vol. i, pp. 464–530.

17. T. E. Hall, *France and the eighteenth-century Corsican question* (New York, 1971), pp. 10–51; Braubach, *Prinz Eugen*, vol. iv, pp. 386–8; Redlich, *Werden einer Großmacht*, pp. 273–4. On the later course of events in Corsica see British Library, Add. mss. 23680 no. 2, Letters from Col. Frederick to Gen. Paoli, 1771. For Neuhoff see A. Vallance, *The summer king* (London, 1956).

18. Bittner (ed.), *Staatsverträge*, nos 781–2, 794–5, 836; Hagen, "Würzburgische Hausinfanterie . . . 1636–1756", pp. 169–70; Hartmann, *Geld*, pp. 159–68, and his *Karl Albrecht*, pp. 122–4, 130. The Hildesheim issue is covered in pp. 21, 220–1. For the general situation in the *Reich* at this point, see L. Auer, "Das Reich und der Vertrag von Sevilla, 1729–1731", *MÖSA* **22**, 1969, pp. 64–93; H. v. Zwiedineck-Südenhorst, "Die Anerkenung der pragmatischen Sanction Karls VI. durch das deutsche Reich", *MIÖG* **16**, 1895, pp. 276–341.

19. McKay, *Prince Eugene*, p. 215,

20. Philippi, *Landgraf Karl*, pp. 549–55; Wilson, *French foreign policy*, p. 193; Hughes, *Law and politics*, pp. 218–19; Auer, "Das Reich", pp. 76–8.

21. Printed in Schmauss & Senckenberg (eds), *Sammlung der Reichsabschiede*, vol. IV, pp. 183–6. The following is based on HSAS, A6: Bü. 10; C14: Bü. 624–49; H. Nopp, *Geschichte der Stadt und ehemaligen Reichsfestung Philippsburg* (Speyer, 1881); K. H. Jutz & J. M. Fieser, *Geschichte der Stadt und ehemaligen Reichsfestung Philippsburg* (Philippsburg, 1966); and the articles by A. v. Schempp, "Die Beziehung des schwäbischen Kreises und Herzogtums Württemberg zu der Reichsfeste Kehl während der ersten Hälfte des 18. Jahrhunderts", *Württembergische Vierteljahreshefte für Landesgeschichte*, NF **18**, 1909, pp. 295–334; "Kehls Ende als Reichsfeste", *WVJHLG* NF **22**, 1913, pp. 336–50.

22. Kahlenberg, *Verteidigungseinrichtungen*, throughout; F. Börckel, *Geschichte von Mainz als Festung und Garrison* (Mainz, 1913), pp. 69–70. The Nördlingen Association Treaty of 1702 exempted Trier from providing a field contingent on the grounds that its army was garrisoning the Ehrenbreitstein.

23. E. Zander, "Köln als befestige Stadt und militärischer Standoart", *Jahrbuch des Kölnischen Geschichtsvereins* **23**, 1941, pp. 1–132. See also Chapter 2 n9.

24. The 1714 recess and subsequent decisions are printed in Hofmann, *Quellen zum Verfassungsorganismus*, pp. 288–98.

25. HSAS, A5: Bü. 70, 71; A5: Bü. 13, 70; STAD, E1 H109/1–5; Helmes, "Fränkische Kreistruppen, 1714–1756", pp. 4–13; Börckel, *Mainz als Festung*, pp. 82–3; F. Beck, "Zur Geschichte der Besatzung von Mainz in der 1 Hälfte des 18 Jahrhunderts", *Quartalsbericht des Historischen Vereins für das Großherzogtum Hessen* **4**, 1910, pp. 384–98.

26. HSAS, A6: Bü. 62; STAD E1 H110/3; R. Graf v. Neipperg, *Kaiser und Schwäbischer Kreis (1714–1733)* (Stuttgart, 1991), pp. 18–27, 139–43.

27. Helmes, "Fränkische Kreistruppen, 1714–1756", pp. 12, 44–5; Hagen, "Würzburgische Hausinfanterie . . . 1636–1756", pp. 168–9.

28. The exact stages were: Franconia 9,200 (December. 1714), 8,476 (November. 1733), 8,016 (March 1735), 7,220 (May 1757). Swabia 11,704 (December. 1714), 7,944 (after 1732).

29. HSAS, A30a: Bü. 57; C14: Bü. 307, 330, 332, 334, 337; Storm, *Feldherr*, 110–11, 258, 268, 330–43.

30. HSAS, C14: Bü. 327.

31. STAD, E1C37/2, 43/3–4; Keim, *Infanterie-Regiments Großherzogin*, pp. 59–61; Tessin, *Regimenter*, pp. 247–8; Dotzauer, *Reichskreise*, p. 262.

32. Jähns, "Kriegsverfassung", p. 446; Dotzauer, *Reichskreise*, pp. 200–3. Westphalia is discussed on pp. 214–20.

33. Roider, *Austria's eastern question*, pp. 39–49; Braubach, *Prinz Eugen*, vol. III, pp. 234–364; McKay, *Prince Eugene*, pp. 158–65; C. Duffy, *The fortress in the age of Vauban and Frederick the Great, 1660–1789* (London, 1985). For the war generally see also *Feldzüge*, vols XVI & XVII; J. Odenthal, *Oesterreichs Türkenkrieg, 1716–1718* (Düsseldorf, 1938); A. v. Schempp, *Geschichte des 3. Württembergischen Infanterie-Regiments Nr. 121, 1716–1891* (Stuttgart, 1891), pp. 5–39; A. v. Pfister, *Denkwürdigkeiten aus der Württembergischen Kriegsgeschichte des 18. und 19. Jahrhunderts* (Stuttgart, 1868), pp. 1–65.

34. McKay, *Prince Eugene*, p. 160. Financial asistance totalled 50 RMS with a nominal value of 6.4 million fl. Note that the declining proportion represented by German contingents was attributable to a parallel rise in the size of the Austrian army since 1699.

35. Hartmann, *Karl Albrecht*, pp. 37–40, and his *Geld*, pp. 53–5. Note that K. Linnebach (ed.), *Deutsche Heeresgeschichte* (Hamburg, 1935), p. 209, is incorrect to maintain that Max

Emanuel's sole desire was to avoid paying his share of the war tax. For the other contingents, see Schuster & Franke, *Sächsischen Armee*, vol. I, p. 196; Philippi, *Landgraf Karl*, pp. 455–6, 463–4 492–8; HSAS, A6: Bü. 57; B. Sicken, 'Truppenstärke und Militäretat des Fürstentums Ansbach um 1730', *Jahrbuch des Historischen vereins für Mittelfranken*, 84 (1967/68), 60–82; Wrede, *Wehrmacht*, vol. I, pp. 17, 130; vol. II, pp. 607, 609; vol. III/2, p. 962.

36. This area, comprising about a third of Wallachia, was formally annexed by Austria on 24 February 1717. Only 4,000 Serbs, some Bulgarian militia and a few Macedonian volunteers joined the emperor's forces in the war.

37. Bittner (ed.), *Staatsverträge*, no. 708; Parvev, *Habsburgs and Ottomans*, pp. 173–81; Braubach, *Prinz Eugen*, vol. III, pp. 364–79.

38. H. Tüchle, *Die Kirchenpolitik des Herzogs Karl Alexander von Württemberg, 1733–1737* (Würzburg, 1937), pp. 9–12, 30–31; Jelavich, *Balkans*, vol. I, pp. 93, 105.

39. Jany, *Preußische Armee*, vol. I, pp. 660. This excludes over 1,000 artillerymen and technical troops.

40. L. Just, "Österreichs Westpolitik im 18. Jahrhundert", *RVJB* **5**, 1935, pp. 1–15, and his "Grenzsicherungspläne im Western des Reiches zur Zeit des Prinzen Eugens, 1663–1736", *RVJB* **6**, 1936, pp. 230–43. The unrest is covered by McKay, *Prince Eugene*, pp. 180–87.

41. Hüsgen, "Militärische Vertretung", pp. 56–7; Herter, *Kurkölnischen Truppen*, p. 8. Dotzauer, *Reichskreise*, p. 298 misses the significance of the 1715 decision, which is printed in Lünig (ed.), *Corpus juris militaris*, vol. I, pp. 631–2.

42. Benecke, *Society and politics*, pp. 210–14, 223–4, 327–9; F. W. Schaer, "Der Absolutismus in Lippe und Schaumburg-Lippe", *Lippische Mitteilungen* **37**, 1968, pp. 154–99. For the lesser counties, see J. Arndt, *Niederrheinisch-Westfälische Reichsgrafen-Kollegium und seine Mitglieder (1653–1806)* (Mainz, 1991).

43. Hüsgen, "Militärische Vertretung", pp. 56–7, 69–87; B. Kappelhoff, *Absolutistisches Regiment oder Ständeherrschaft? Landesherr und Landstände in Ostfriesland im ersten Drittel des 18. Jahrhunderts* (Hildesheim, 1982), pp. 83–6.

44. Schnath, *Geschichte Hannovers*, vol. III, pp. 564–5; Meissner, *Nordhausen*, pp. 59–62, 74–5; Jany, *Preußische Armee*, vol. I, p. 671; Patze (ed.), *Geschichte Thüringens*, vol. V, pp. 590–1. The Mühlhausen occupation involved 2,500 Prussians and 900 Wolfenbüttel soldiers.

45. Adamski, *Welfische Schutz über die Stadt Hildesheim*, pp. 94–111; Schnath, *Geschichte Hannovers*, vol. III, pp. 563–7, 598–601. For the Hildesheim auxiliaries, see Wrede, *Wehrmacht*, vol. II, p. 181, 605.

46. Cited in Hatton, *George I*, p. 243; see also ibid pp. 269–71, 277.

47. V. Press, "Kurhannover im System des alten Reiches, 1692–1803", in *England und Hannover* A. M. Birke & K. Kluxen (eds) (Munich, 1986), pp. 53–79; Schnath, *Geschichte Hannovers*, vol. II, pp. 293–6.

48. Wick, *Versuche*, pp. 141–4, 151, and pp. 163–4, 181–91 on the deteriorating situation in the countryside. Hanover, which had provided about 85 per cent of the peace enforcement force, claimed 800,000 tlr expenses by mid-1719. This and the following is also based on Hughes, *Law and politics*, pp. 156–271; Elster, *Braunschweig-Wolfenbüttel*, vol. II, pp. 10–112, 39–46; Jany, *Preußische Armee*, vol. I, pp. 671–2; Tessin, *Mecklenburgisches Militär*, pp. 142–3.

49. East Frisia covered 3,740 km^2 inhabited by 100,000 people, generating an annual revenue, including the estates" share, of 400,000 fl. For the following, see B. Kappelhoff,

Absolutistisches Regiment; Hughes, *Law and politics*, pp. 123–55, 240–58, 265–8; Jany, *Preußische Armee*, vol. I, pp. 284–5, 427, 645–6; vol. II, pp. 87–8.

50. Hanoverian memorandum of 26 October 1721 printed in Mediger, *Mecklenburg*, pp. 477–80 (p. 478).

51. E. v. Anisimov, "The imperial heritage of Peter the Great in the foreign policy of his early successors", in *Imperial Russian foreign policy*, H. Ragsdale (ed.) (Cambridge, 1993), pp. 21–35 (p. 27). My thanks to David Saunders for drawing my attention to this work.

52. See M. Köster, *Russische Truppen für Prinz Eugen: Politik mit militärischen Mitteln im frühen 18. Jahrhundert* (Vienna, 1986), pp. 19–30, on the formation of the alliance. For Russian policy in general see H. Bagger, "The role of the Baltic in Russian foreign policy 1721–1773", in Ragsdale (ed.), *Imperial Russian foreign policy*, pp. 36–72.

53. Wilson, *French foreign policy*, pp. 232–48; Lukowski, *Liberty's folly*, pp. 150–58; Köster, *Russische Truppen*, pp. 36–40; Anisimov, "Imperial heritage", pp. 32–3.

54. Schuster & Franke, *Sächsischen Armee*, vol. I, pp. 207–18; Lukowski, *Liberty's folly*, pp. 157–63; J. L. Sutton, *The king's honor and the king's cardinal: the War of the Polish Succession* (Lexington, 1980), pp. 112–34. For the conflict generally see *Feldzüge*, vols XIX & XX.

55. Documents printed in Schmauss & Senckenberg (eds), *Sammlung der Reichsabschiede*, vol. IV, pp. 396–417.

56. For Bavarian policy in the war, see Hartmann, *Geld*, pp. 171–90, and his *Karl Albrecht*, pp. 133–8, 148–56; Staudinger, *Bayerischen Heeres*, vol. III, pp. 318–19, 473–83; J. Black, "Anglo-Wittelsbach relations, 1730–42", *ZBLG* **55**, 1992, pp. 307–45.

57. See Hartmann, *Geld*, pp. 176–84, 194–5; M. Braubach, "Das Lager von Plittersdorf. Eine Kriegerische Episode aus dem Leben des Kurfürsten Clemens August", in *Kurkölnische Miniaturen* (Münster, 1954), pp. 157–68; Herter, *Kurkölnischen Truppen*, pp. 62–76; Bönninghausen, *Münsterischen Truppen*, pp. 143–5; Mürmann, "Militärwesen des ehemaligen Hochstiftes Paderborn", p. 64.

58. Jany, *Preußische Armee*, vol. I, pp. 675–6, and Köster, *Russische Truppen*, pp. 177–9 (who, however, misses the political events behind the trouble).

59. R. Lodge, "England's neutrality in the War of the Polish Succession", *Transactions of the Royal Historical Society*, 4th series, **14**, 1931, pp. 141–73; Carter, *Neutrality or commitment*, pp. 58–9.

60. See his letter to Prinz Eugen quoted in Beck, *Hessen-Darmstädtischen Reiterregimenter*, pp. 52–3.

61. Dickson, *Finance and government*, vol. II, pp. 347; Hartmann, *Geld*, p. 178. According to Austrian documents cited by Köster, *Russische Truppen*, p. 184 *n*42, only 42,407 of the 112,391 troops on the Rhine in July 1735 were Austrian. Total strength of Austro-German field forces there the year before had reached 78,000.

62. French aims are discussed by Sutton, *King's honor*, pp. 64–75, 135–8, and Wilson, *French foreign policy*, pp. 248–51.

63. For the siege of Kehl, see HSAS, A6: Bü. 11; A29: Bü. 168; A202: Bü. 1996; Sutton, *King's honor*, pp. 75–87. Operations around Philippsburg are in HSAS, A.6: Bü. 8–9, 27–9; A202: Bü. 2024, 2026–8, 2120, 2126; C14: Bü. 188, 334; and Lang, *Ettlingen Linien*, pp. 36–47.

64. Köster, *Russische Truppen*, pp. 45–96, 147–70, 192–215; Parvev, *Habsburgs and Ottomans*, pp. 195–200; K. Roider, *The reluctant ally: Austria's policy in the Austro-Turkish War, 1737–1739* (Baton Rouge, 1972), pp. 32–50; C. Duffy, *Russia's military way to the west: origins and nature of Russian military power, 1700–1800* (London, 1981), pp. 42–54. On relations with the Swabians see also HSAS, A6: Bü 53, and P. Fähnle, *Geschichte des ehemaligen Heilbronner Herrendorfes Flein* (Böckingen-Heilbronn, 1908), pp. 213–14.

65. Sutton, *King's honor*, pp. 175–8; Köster, *Russische Truppen*, pp. 97–124.
66. Negotiations in Köster, *Russische Truppen*, pp. 125–46; Wilson, *French foreign policy*, pp. 255–77; Sutton, *King's honor*, pp. 191–209; Rill, *Karl VI*, pp. 303–12. Peace preliminaries printed in Schmauss & Senckenberg (eds), *Sammlung der Reichsabschiede*, vol. IV, pp. 419–24.
67. Lukowski, *Liberty's folly*, pp. 163–5. In May 1735 Saxony sent 6 rgts to the Rhine and later a contingent to the Turkish War.
68. Köster, *Russische Truppen*, pp. 171–91, provides a typical summary of the standard view.
69. HSAS, A202: Bü.1996, letter from Speyer, 17 November 1733.
70. Staudinger, *Bayerischen Heeres*, vol. III, pp. 478–9. On the later invasions, see Chapter 7.
71. For this and the subsequent conflict see L. Cassels, *The struggle for the Ottoman empire, 1717–1740* (London, 1966); Parvev, *Habsburgs and Ottomans*, pp. 193–246; Roider, *Reluctant ally*, pp. 99–161; T. Tupetz, "Der Türkenfeldzug von 1739 und der Friede zu Belgrad", *HZ* **40**, 1878, pp. 1–52; Staudinger, *Bayerischen Heeres*, vol. III, pp. 510–30. For a Turkish perspective, see Ibrahim [Muteferrika], *History of the war in Bosnia during the years 1737–8 and 9* (London, 1830).
72. Dickson, *Finance and government*, vol. II, pp. 346, 403–5; G. Otruba, "Das Österreichische Wirtschaftsystem im Zeitalter des Prinz Eugens", in Kunisch (ed.), *Prinz Eugen*, pp. 57–90 (pp. 65–9); F. Schönfellner, "Probleme der Staatsfinanzen und die Gründung der Wiener Stadtbank", in Gutkas (ed.), *Prinz Eugen*, pp. 215–20; Roider, *Reluctant ally*, pp. 14–15, 23, 95–6. On 3 October 1739, the imperial vice chancellor, Rudolph Count Colloredo, told Regent Friedrich Carl von Württemberg that the war had cost 50 million fl. (HSAS, A202: Bü. 1159).
73. 50 RMS granted on 23 December 1737 and ratified by Charles on 2 January 1738. See HSAS, A202: Bü. 1159.
74. Bittner (ed.), *Staatsverträge*, nos 854, 855, 872; Hartmann, *Geld*, pp. 205–8 and *Karl Albrecht*, pp. 157–9; Staudinger, *Bayerischen Heeres*, vol. III, pp. 76–7, 485–532; Herter, *Kurkölnischen Truppen*, pp. 76–8; Bönninghausen, *Münsterschen Truppen*, pp. 148–53; F. Mürmann, 'Das Militärwesen des ehemaligen Hochstiftes Paderborn seit dem Ausgange des Dreissigjährigen Krieges', *WZ*, 95 (1939), 3–78; Elster, *Braunschweig-Wolfenbüttel*, vol. II, pp. 94–111; Schuster & Franke, *Sächsischen Armee*, vol. I, pp. 220–25; H. Helmes, "Das Regiment Würzburg im Türkenkriege des Jahres, 1739", *DBKH* **13**, 1904, pp. 60–93. Augustus III refused a request for Polish troops after the Sultan wisely recognized him as king. Venice also declined to intervene, but the dukes of Modena did send 1,500 auxiliaries: see Parvev, *Habsburgs and Ottomans*, p. 217.
75. Wilson, *War, state and society*, pp. 184–998, and the archival sources cited there. The three regiments garrisoning the fortresses totalled about 3,300 men.
76. HSAS, A30a: Bd. 7 fol. 348; A202: Bü. 2256. Charles expressly chose Tornacco because he was well liked in Württemberg, see A202: Bü. 1161, 15 May 1740. On the Austrian recruiting, see also A202: Bü. 2298; C14: Bü. 307, 586a; Bittner (ed.), *Staatsverträge*, nos 163–5; Schüssler, "Werbewesen", pp. 43, 51, 58–9, 69, 160; Patze (ed.), *Geschichte Thüringens*, vol. V, pp. 303–4; Frhr. v. Stetten-Buchenbach, "Rekrutenwebungen in reichsritterschaftlichen Gebiet im 18. Jahrhundert", *BMWB* **11**, 1903, pp. 451–66.
77. Roider, *Reluctant ally*, p. 172.
78. Ibid., pp. 118–30, 141–54; Cassels, *Struggle*, pp. 136–70; Wilson, *French foreign policy*, pp. 279–80, 319–21.
79. Cassels, *Struggle*, pp. 138–40; Parvev, *Habsburgs and Ottomans*, pp. 222–3. Joseph's presence did cause the Habsburgs to detach additional men to cover Transylvania in autumn

1738. Their main army, intended to number 100,000, totalled only 34,494 against 60,000 Turks.

80. Bittner (ed.), *Staatsverträge*, no. 875, treaty of 1 September 1739; Cassels, *Struggle*, pp. 182–201; K. A. Roider, "The perils of eighteenth-century peacemaking: Austria and the Treaty of Belgrade 1739", *CEH* **3**, 1972, pp. 195–207; Staudinger, *Bayerischen Heeres* vol. III, pp. 529–30.

81. Roider, *Austria's eastern question*, pp. 87–8, and *Reluctant ally*, p. 77.

82. Schönfellner, "Probleme der Staatsfinanzen", p. 219; Dickson, *Finance and government*, vol. II, pp. 6, 61; J. C. Allmayer-Beck, *Das Heer unter dem Doppeladler: Habsburgs Armeen, 1718–1848* (Munich, 1981), pp. 18–19.

83. C. Duffy, *The army of Maria Theresia* (New York, 1977), pp. 45, 145; Nopp, *Philippsburg*, pp. 355–8 (covering Seckendorff's career); Neipperg, for instance, is praised by the Prussian General Staff history for his performance in the 1733–5 war: *Der erste Schlesische Krieg, 1740–1742* [3 vols] (Berlin, 1890–93), vol. I, p. 81.

Chapter Seven: Between civil war and partition, 1740–92

1. For a recent synthesis of these explanations see Schilling, *Höfe und Allianzen*, pp. 376–442. For the Canton system and its socio-political significance, the essential starting point is O. Büsch, *Military system and social life in old regime, Prussia, 1713–1807* (English trans., Atlantic Highlands, 1997).

2. In Westphalia (Jülich-Berg, East Frisia, the Orange inheritance and minor territories); Lower Saxony (Mecklenburg, Nordhausen); Upper Saxony (Pomerania); Franconia (Ansbach, Bayreuth and minor lordships); Upper Rhine (Hanau); Swabia (Hohenzollern-Sigmaringen, Hohenzollern-Hechingen).

3. Schindling, "Kurbrandenburg im System des Reiches", pp. 44–5. For Göttingen's importance, see p. 221.

4. D. E. Showalter, *The wars of Frederick the Great* (London, 1996), especially pp. 94–105.

5. *Ibid.*, p. 18. For a suggestive interpretation of the king's relationship to the army see K. & K. R. Spillmann, "Friedrich Wilhelm I und die preußische Armee. Versuch einer psychohistorischen Deutung", *HZ* **246**, 1988, pp. 549–89.

6. H. M. Scott, "Prussia's royal foreign minister: Frederick the Great and the administration of Prussian diplomacy", in R. Oresko (ed.), *Royal and republican sovereignty* (Cambridge, 1997), pp. 500–26.

7. For the debate on Frederick's motives see T. Schieder, *Friedrich der Grosse: Ein Königtum der Widersprüche* (Frankfurt-am-Main, 1987), pp. 127–46. G. B. Volz, "Das Rheinsberger Protokoll vom 29. Oktober 1740", *Forschungen zur brandenburgischen und preussischen Geschichte* **29**, 1916, pp. 67–93, prints transcripts of the key meeting.

8. Jany, *Preußische Armee*, vol. II, pp. 3–11, 42, 53–4, 79–81, 115–16; Anon., *Geschichte und Nachrichten von dem . . . Fuselier Regimente von Lossow* (Halle, 1767; repr. Osnabrück, 1979); Wilson, *War, state and society*, pp. 195–8, 201, and the sources cited there. For finances, see R. Koser, "Der preußische Staatsschatz von 1740–1756", *FBPG*, **4**, 1891, pp. 529–51.

9. The strengths are from Jany, who provides the most reliable figures. For the miliary operations see Austrian Kriegs-Archiv, *Oesterreichischer Erbfolgekrieg, 1740–48* [9 vols]

(Vienna, 1896–1914); Prussian Großer Generalstab, *Der erste Schlesische Krieg, 1740–1742*, and its *Der zweite Schlesische Krieg, 1744–1745*, [3 vols] (Berlin, 1895).

10. C. W. Ingrao in his *State and society in early modern Austria*, p. 283. The Prussians lost 4,659 killed, wounded and missing to the Austrians' 4,551. The battles of Mühlberg (1574) and White Mountain (1620) were Hasburg victories over Saxon and Bohemian defiance respectively.

11. Good overviews of the international dimension are provided by M. S. Anderson, *The War of the Austrian Succession, 1740–1748* (London, 1995), and the similarly titled work by R. Browning (New York, 1993).

12. PRO, SP108/259, treaty with Hessen-Kassel, 20 May 1740. Hanoverian strengths calculated from Schirmer, *Nec aspera terrant!*, pp. 63–4, 80–84. Hanoverian policy is covered by U. Dann, *Hannover und England, 1740–1760*, (Leicester, 1991), pp. 15–80.

13. The war in Italy and the Netherlands is covered by S. Wilkinson, *The defence of Piedmont, 1742–1748* (Oxford, 1927), and J. Colin, *Les campagnes du maréchal de Saxe* [3 vols] (Paris, 1901–6).

14. Anglo-Hanoverian relations with Austria and the role of the Pragmatic Army are analyzed in the excellent study by W. Handrick, *Die Pragmatische Armee, 1741–1743: eine alliierte Armee im Kalkül des Österreichischen Erbfolgekrieges* (Munich, 1991). British aid to Austria is listed in Dickson, *Finance and government*, vol. II, pp. 392–3. The paper strength of the Austrian army rose to 203,576 by 1745 but fell continuously thereafter to 171,616 by the last year of the war. Effectives are likely to have been a good 30 per cent below these figures, although the discrepancy would have been offset by greater use of frontier militia, 45,000 of whom served during the course of the war.

15. Hartmann, *Geld*, pp. 211–15; Munich, *Bayerischen Armee*, pp. 130–32; Herter, *Kurkölnischen Truppen*, pp. 80–82; Braubach, *Kurköln*, pp. 257–69; H. Weber, *Die Politik des Kurfürsten Karl Theodor von der Pfalz während des Österreichischen Erbfolgekrieges (1742–1748)* (Bonn, 1956).

16. Schuster & Franke, *Sächsischen Armee*, vol. II, pp. 3–63; A. V. Boroviczény, *Graf von Brühl* (Vienna, 1930), pp. 189–341: D. B. Horn, "Saxony in the War of the Austrian Succession", *EHR* **44**, 1929, pp. 33–47. Prussian strengths from Jany, *Preußische Armee*, vol. II, pp. 83–4. By the time of Prusso-Saxon hostilities in 1744, the Prussian army was even larger at 131,846.

17. In addition to Hartmann, *Geld*, and *Karl Albrecht*, see F. Wagner, *Kaiser Karl VII und die grossen Mächte, 1740–1745* (Stuttgart, 1938), especially pp. 121–8. The conditions of the army and its operations are well covered by Staudinger, *Bayerischen Heeres*, vol. III.

18. E. Hillbrand, *Die Einschließung von Linz, 1741/42* (Vienna, 1970).

19. Hartmann, *Karl Albrecht*, pp. 254–62.

20. Patze (ed.), *Geschichte Thüringens*, vol. V, p. 572. The Wettins had lost these rights in 1547; Austria forced Saxony to restore full autonomy to the three territories in 1743.

21. W. v. Hofmann, "Das Säkularisationsprojekt von 1743, Kaiser Karl VII und die römische Kurie", *Riezler Festschrift: Beiträge zur bayerischen Geschichte* (Gotha, 1913), pp. 213–59; Hartmann, *Karl Albrecht*, pp. 287–93. For Ostein see E. Gatz (ed.), *Die Bischöfe des Heiliges Römisches Reiches 1648 bis 1803* (Berlin, 1990), pp. 331–4.

22. HSAS, A202: Bü. 2276; C14: Bü. 328, 338; L6.22.7.4a; Helmes, "Fränkische Kreistruppen . . . 1714–56", pp. 37–45.

23. HSAS, C14: Bü. 744. For the auxiliaries and units for the Bavarian army, see Baron v. Dalwigk, "Der Anteil der hessischen Truppen am Österreichischen Erbfolgekrieg (1740–48)", *Zeitschrift für hessische Geschichte und Landeskunde* **42**, 1908, pp. 72–139; **45**, 1911,

pp. 138–201; Staudinger, *Bayerischen Heeres*, vol. iii/ii, pp. 611–12; Nopp, *Philippsburg*, pp. 457–508.

24. Treaties in pro, SP108/261, 262, 265. See also Braubach, "Politisch-militarische Verträge", pp. 160–61, 180–83; Herter, *Kurkölnischen Truppen*, p. 81.

25. Weber, *Politik des Kurfürsten Karl Theodor*, pp. 296–9; Hartmann, *Karl Albrecht*, pp. 294–5; Demandt, *Hessen*, pp. 274–5; *Oesterreichischer Erbfolgekrieg*, vol. iv, pp. 330–32, vol. v, p. 409. French plans envisaged an even more radical reorganization of Germany but remained a project of the foreign minister d"Argenson and never became formal policy.

26. A. Schmid, *Max III Joseph und die europäischen Mächte* (Munich, 1987), pp. 13–128.

27. pro, SP108/263; Dalwigk, "Anteil der hessischen Truppen", 169–94. Hessian policy in this period is covered by W. v. Both & H. Vogel, *Landgraf Wilhelm VIII von Hessel-Kasel* (Munich, 1964), pp. 70–80. For the Bavarian auxiliaries, see W. Handrick, "Der bayerischen Löwe in Dienste des österreichischen Adlers. Das kurfürstlichen Auxiliarkorps in den Niederlanden, 1746–1749", *MGM* **50**, 1991, pp. 25–60.

28. Dotzauer, *Reichskreise*, pp. 103, 203–4; Schmid, *Max III Joseph.* pp. 161–78; Franconia, Swabia and the Upper Rhine retained their mobilized triple quota on the Rhine until after the war, but it was as much intended to sustain their own neutrality as to support the emperor.

29. Rowan, *Princes of Orange*, pp. 163–71. On the attempts to hire German troops, see stAD E8B259/6; E. Städler, *Die Ansbach-Bayreuth Truppen im Amerikanischer Unabhängigkeitskrieg, 1777–1783* (Nuremberg, 1956), p. 21. Baden-Durlach did recruit clandestinely for Sardinia despite an imperial ban in 1742–5, providing about 1,400 infantry for this pro-Habsburg state.

30. Duffy, *Russia's military way*, pp. 57–9. On the renewed problems of transit through Bavaria see Schmid, *Max III Joseph*, pp. 219–23.

31. Hartmann, *Karl Albrecht*, pp. 194, 238, 254.

32. O. C. Ebbecke, *Frankreichs Politik gegenüber dem deutschen Reiche in den Jahren, 1748–1756* (Freiburg, 1931); Braubach, *Kurköln*, pp. 253–6. For the cost of transit and the compensation payments, see hsas, A202: Bü. 2115–21; L6.22.7.23.

33. G. Haug-Mortiz, *Württembergischer Ständekonflikt und deutscher Dualismus* (Stuttgart, 1992), pp. 127–53, 215–19.

34. See Aretin, *Das Reich*, pp. 143–9, for the impact on imperial Italy.

35. Press, "Österreichische Großmachtbildung", pp. 151–2.

36. Good accounts of the reform process are provided by Dickson, *Finance and government*, vol. i, pp. 207–385, and F. A. J. Szabo, *Kaunitz and enlightened absolutism, 1753–1780* (Cambridge, 1994).

37. C. W. Eldon, *England's subsidy policy towards the continent during the Seven Years War* (Philadelphia, 1938), pp. 1–41; R. Browning, "The duke of Newcastle and the imperial election plan, 1749–1754", *Journal of British Studies* **7**, 1967–8, pp. 28–47, and his "The British orientation of Austrian foreign policy, 1749–1754", *CEH* **1**, 1968, pp. 299–323; M. Olbrich, *Die Politik des Kurfürsten Karl Theodore von der Pfalz zwischen den Kriegen (1748–1756)* (Bonn, 1966), pp. 123–89; Schmid, *Max III Joseph*, pp. 276–85; Dann, *Hanover*, pp. 81–103.

38. Recent summaries in E. Buddruss, *Die französische Deutschlandpolitik, 1756–1789* (Mainz, 1995), pp. 70–92; Showalter, *Wars of Frederick the Great*, pp. 116–36. The Franco-Russian dimension is covered by L. J. Oliva, *Misalliance: a study of French policy in Russia during the Seven Years War* (New York, 1964).

39. C. W. Eldon, "The Hanoverian subsidy treaty with Ansbach (1755)", *JMH* **12**, 1940, pp.

59–68; P. F. Doran, *Andrew Mitchell and Anglo-Prussian diplomatic relations during the Seven Years War* (New York, 1986), pp. 17–49.

40. Buddruss, *Die französische Deutschlandpolitik*, pp. 83, 290.

41. G. B. Volz & G. Küntzel (eds), *Preussische und Österreichische Acten zur Vorgeschichte des Siebenjährigen Krieges* (Leipzig, 1899); M. Lehmann, "Urkundliche Beiträge zur Geschichte des Jahres 1756", *MIÖG* **16**, 1895, pp. 480–91.

42. Schieder, *Friedrich der Große*, pp. 177–82. The 1752 Political Testament is printed in R. Dietrich (ed.), *Die politischen Testamente der Hohenzollern* (Cologne, 1986), pp. 253–461.

43. The military dimension of the war is well covered by the Prussian General Staff history, *Der Siebenjährige Krieg, 1756–1763* [12 vols] (Berlin, 1901–13), which needs to be supplemented for the period from 1761 by vols v–viii of the older edition, *Geschichte des Siebenjährigen Krieges* [8 vols] (Berlin, 1824–47), as well as the good general works of A. Schäffer, *Geschichte des Siebenjährigen Krieges* [2 vols in 3] (Berlin, 1867–74), and O. Groehler, *Die Kriege Friedrichs II*, [6th edn] (Berlin, 1990). The diplomacy and war efforts of all belligerents is further explored by the excellent collection of articles edited by B. Kroener, *Europa im Zeitalter Friedrichs des Großens* (Munich, 1989).

44. Duffy, *Russsia's military way*, pp. 61–124; D. E. Bangert, *Die russisch-österreichische militärische Zusammenarbeit im Siebenjährigen Kriege in den Jahren 1758–1759* (Boppard, 1971).

45. Aretin, *Das Reich*, pp. 151–2; Wrede, *Wehrmacht*, vol. II, p. 620; vol. III/I, p. 964.

46. For this and the following, Buddruss, *Die französische Deutschlandpolitik*, pp. 92–7; Dann, *Hannover*, pp. 104–9. The Dauphine was a Saxon princess and Louis XV regarded the Wettins as part of his own family.

47. British policy is well covered by R. Middleton, *The bells of victory: the Pitt Newcastle ministry and the conduct of the Seven Years War* (Cambridge, 1985), and the works by K. W. Schweizer, *Frederick the Great, William Pitt and Lord Bute: the Anglo-Prussian alliance, 1756–1763* (New York, 1991), and *England, Prussia and the Seven Years War* (New York, 1989).

48. A. C. Carter, *The Dutch Republic in Europe in the Seven Years War* (London, 1971). The predicament of individual territories is analyzed by C. Becker, "Von Kurkölns Beziehungen zu Frankreich und seiner wirtschaftlichen Lage im Siebenjährigen Kriege (1757–1761)", *Annalen des Historischen Vereins für den Niederrhein* **100**, 1917, pp. 43–119; T., Bitterauf, *Die kurbayerische Politik im Siebenjährigen Krieg* (Munich, 1901); H. Gerspacher, *Die badische Politik im Siebenjährigen Kriege* (Heidelberg, 1934); E. Meissner, "Das südwestdeutschen Reichsstände im Siebenjährigen Krieg", *Ellwanger Jahrbuch* **23**, 1971, pp. 117–58.

49. G. Eisentraut, "Der Briefwechsel zwischen dem Landgrafen Wilhelm VII von Hessen und seinem Generaladjutanten Generalmajor Freiherr v. Fürstenberg in den Jahren 1756/57", *ZHG* **40**, 1907, pp. 73–138. The troops returned to Germany in May 1757.

50. J. B. Knudsen, *Justus Moser and the German enlightenment* (Cambridge, 1986), pp. 67–8; L. Frhr. v. Thüna, *Die Würzburger Hilfstruppen im Dienste Oesterreichs, 1756–1763* (Würzburg, 1893); Harms, "Landmiliz", pp. 364, 378–9; Bezzel, *Kurpfälzischen Heeres*, vol. II, pp. 381–518; Staudinger, *Bayerischen Heeres*, vol. III/II, pp. 962–1193; Wilson, *War, state and society*, pp. 209–26.

51. Brabant, *Reich*, vol. I, pp. 77–94; Kohlhepp, Militärverfassung, pp. 58–64.

52. *Ibid.*, pp. 65–84; H. v. Eicken, "Die Reichsarmee im Siebenjährigen Krieg dargestellt am Kurtrierischen Regiment", *PJb* **41**, 1879, pp. 1–14, 113–35, 248–67; C. Becker, "Die Erlebnisse der Kurkölnischen Truppen im Verbande der Reichsarmee während des Siebenjährigen Krieges", *AHVN* **91**, 1911, pp. 63–108; H. Helmes, "Die fränkischen Kreistruppen im Kriegsjahre 1758 und im Frühjahrsfeldzuge 1759", *DBKH* **17**, 1908,

G. v. Niethammer, "Reichsarmee im Feldzug 1757 mit Rücksicht auf das schwäbische Kreistruppenkorps und das Kreis-Füsilier-Regiments Württemberg", *BMWB* **9**, 1879, pp. 149–204; P. H. Wilson, "Violence and the rejection of authority in eighteenth-century Germany. The case of the Swabian mutinies in 1757", *GH* **12**, 1994, pp. 1–26.

53. Duffy, *Army of Frederick the Great*, p. 253. See also H. Höhne, *Die Einstellung der sächsischen Regimenten in das preussische Armee im Jahre 1756* (Halle, 1926), and O. Grosse, *Prinz Xaver von Sachsen und das Korps bei der französischen Armee, 1758–1763* (Leipzig, 1907).

54. H. Arnold, "Schwedens Teilnahme am Siebenjährigen Kriege", *BMWB* **12**, 1908, pp. 453–82, and the similarly entitled article by K. R. Böhme in Kroener (ed.), *Europa*, pp. 193–212. Propaganda and religion are dealt with by S. Fitte, *Religion und Politik vor und während des Siebenjährigen Krieges* (Berlin, 1899), and J. Burkhardt, *Abschied vom Religionskrieg: Der Krieg und die päpstliche Diplomatie* (Tübingen, 1985).

55. For French involvement see L. Kennett, *The French armies in the Seven Years War* (Durham, North Carolina, 1967), while operations in western and northern Germany are covered by R. Savory, *His Britannic Majesty's Army in Germany during the Seven Years War* (Oxford, 1966), and R. Whitworth, *William Augustus Duke of Cumberland* (London, 1992), pp. 184–99. The French army included 2,500 Austrians and 6,300 Palatine auxiliaries; see Bezzel, *Kurpfälzischen Heeres*, vol. II, pp. 386–400.

56. Frhr. v, Dalwigk, "Der Anteil der Hessen an der Schlacht bei Hastenbeck 26. Juli 1757", *ZHG* **41**, 1907, pp. 223–41; R. Waddington, *La guerre de sept ans* [5 vols] (Paris, 1899–1914), vol. I, pp. 444–95.

57. 35 battalions of French, 6 German (including 2 provided by Zweibrücken under subsidy), 12 Swiss, plus 16 French cvalry rgts, 1 German, 1 Irish, 1 Belgian (Liege). The total strength was 32,000, Soubise having being reinforced by part of Richelieu's army in the meantime.

58. Some territorial authorities had provided their men with old or defective equipment although this does not seem to have affected units present at the battle.

59. Interrogation protocols and docments relating to the battle and disintegration of the army can be found in HSAS, C14: Bü. 87/I; K. Brodrück (ed.), *Quellenstücke in Studien über den Feldzug der Reichsarmee von 1757* (Leipzig, 1858); Boffert [sic], "Die Hohenloher in der Schlacht bei Rossbach", *WVJHLG* **3**, 1980, pp. 175–6.

60. T. C. W. Blanning, "The French Revolution and the modernization of Germany", *CEH* **22**, 1989, pp. 109–29 (p. 127).

61. Buddruss, *Die französische Deutschlandpolitik*, p. 106 *n*251.

62. For this and subsequent operations see P. Mackesy, *The coward of Minden: the affair of Lord George Sackville* (London, 1979); C. Renouard, *Geschichte des Krieges in Hannover, Hessen und Westfalen von 1757 bis 1763* [3 vols] (Kassel 1863–70).

63. Waddington, *Guerre de sept ans*, I 735; Buddruss, *Französische Deutschlandpolitik*, pp. 109–11, 126, 151–3, 292.

64. Z. E. Rashed, *The Peace of Paris 1763* (Liverpool, 1951).

65. Battle reports in HSAS, C14: Bü. 87a, with later accounts in E. Kessel, "Die Schlacht bei Freiberg am 29. Oktober 1762", *NASG* **60**, 1939, 42–65; old General Staff work, *Siebenjährigen Krieges*, VI/I 414–34, and the excellent biography by C. V. Easum, *Prince Henry of Prussia, brother of Frederick the Great* (New York, 1942).

66. Duffy, *Army of Frederick the Great*, pp. 95–9. For the management of the war, see also W. Hubatsch, *Frederick the Great: Absolutism and administration* (London, 1975), pp. 112–47, and H. C. Johnson, *Frederick the Great and his officials* (New Haven, 1975), pp. 156–87, which includes details of Prussian extortion in Mecklenburg, Pomerania and Saxony.

67. F. Wernitz, *Die preussischen Freitruppen im Siebenjährigen Krieg, 1756–1763* (Wölfersheim-Berstadt, 1994); E. Schnackenburg, "Die Freicorps Friedrichs des Grossen", *BMWB* **4**, 1883.

68. Cited in J. Kunisch, *Das Mirakel des Hauses Brandenburg: Studien zum Verhältnis von Kabinettspolitik und Kriegführung im Zeitalter des Siebenjährigen Krieges* (Munich, 1978), p. 105. See *ibid.*, pp. 17–43, for further discussion and, pp. 101–41 for the full text of the key Austrian document.

69. W. A. v. Kaunitz, "Votum über das Militare", in *Zeitgenössische Studien über die altpreußische Armee*, H. Bleckwenn (ed.) (Osnabrück, 1974), pp. 3–45. See also Szabo, *Kaunitz*, pp. 266–7, 278–94.

70. Cited by Kunisch, *Fürst-Gesellschaft-Krieg*, p. 197. On Kaunitz's ambitions see H. Carl, "Kaunitz and Ostfriesland. Aspekte adeliger Familienpolitik im Hause Kaunitz", in *Staatskanzler Wenzel Anton von Kaunitz-Rietberg, 1711–1794* G. Klingenstein & F. A. J. Szabo (eds) (Graz, 1996), pp. 401–15.

71. A point forcefully made by Showalter, *Wars of Frederick the Great*. On the nature of the conflict, see also Schieder, *Friedrich der Große*, pp. 182–224.

72. See Savory, *Army in Germany*, pp. 48–50.

73. For the damage, see A. Stoffers, "Das Hochstift Paderborn zur Zeit des Siebenjährigen Kriegen", *Zeitschrift für vaterländische Geschichte und Altertumskunde Westfalens* **69**, 1911, pp. 1–90; **70**, 1912, pp. 60–182; M. Braubach, "Politik und Kriegführung am Niederrhein während des Siebenjährigen Krieges", *Düsseldorfer Jahrbuch*, 48, 1956, pp. 65–103.

74. Patze (ed.), *Geschichte Thüringens*, vol. v, pp. 376–7, 487–8, 544–5. The contingent totalled about 1,500 men.

75. Harms, "Landmiliz", pp. 378–9. In addition, Mainz maintained approximately 1,500 garrison troops throughout the war.

76. Schmid, *Max III Joseph*, pp. 413–44; Bezzel, *Kurpfälzischen Heeres*, vol. ii, pp. 400–5; Wilson, *War, state and society*, pp. 224–6.

77. Bönninghausen, *Münsterischen Truppen*, pp. 155–74; Becker, "Kurkölns Beziehungen", p. 115; B. J. Kreuzberg, *Die politischen und wirtschaftliches Beziehungen des Kurstaates Trier zu Frankreich in der zweiten Hälfte des 18. Jahrhunderts bis zum Ausbruch der Französischen Revolution* (Bonn, 1932), pp. 17–33.

78. HSAS, C14: Bü. 77, 87a. 418; L6.22.8.2, covering the Swabians; Schmid, *Max III Joseph*, pp. 462–72; Bezzel, *Kurpfälzischen Heeres*, vol. ii, pp. 516–18.

79. On the Holstein crisis, see Rode, *Kriegsgeschichte Schleswig-Holsteins*, pp. 52–5; Bagger, "Role of the Baltic", pp. 55–9; T. Schwark, *Lübecks Stadmilitär im 17. und 18. Jahrhundert* (Lübeck, 1990), pp. 47–8, 87, 97–8.

80. Buddruss, *Die französische Deutschlandpolitik*, pp. 114–18; K. Schweizer, "The non-renewal of the Anglo-Prussian subsidy treaty 1761–1762", *Canadian Journal of History* **13**, 1979, pp. 384–98.

81. HSAS, A202: Bü. 253–6, 618–23, 826; A. v. Schempp, "Kehls Ende als Reichsfeste", *WVJHLG*, NF 22, 1913, pp. 336–50; Nopp, *Philippsburg*, pp. 500–81.

82. F. Schwarz, "Die Kölner Stadt-Soldaten am Ende der reichsstädtischen Zeit", *Jahrbuch des Köhlnischen Geschichtsvereins* **48**, 1977, pp. 151–98; Regele, "Militärgeschichte Vorderösterreichs", pp. 125–30.

83. Tessin, *Regimenter*, p. 248; Casser, "Niederrheinisch-Westfälische Reichskreise", pp. 55–61.

84. Haug-Moritz, *Württembergischer Ständekonflikt*, pp. 293–453; Wilson, *War, state and society*, pp. 226–39

85. C. W. Ingrao, *The Hessian mercenary state: ideas, institutions and reform under Frederick II, 1760–1785* (Cambridge, 1987); P. K. Taylor, *Indentured to Liberty: Peasant life and the Hessian military state, 1688–1815* (Ithaca, 1994).
86. Dickson, *Finance and government*, vol. II, p. 352; Jany, *Preußische Armee*, vol. III, p. 182. For Goethe's work in Weimar, see W. H. Bruford, *Culture and society in classical Weimar, 1775–1806* (Cambridge, 1962), pp. 107–11.
87. J. Hofmann, *Die Kursächsiche Armee 1769 bis zum Beginn des Bayeischen Erbfolgekrieges* (Leipzig, 1914); J. Niemeyer & G. Ortenburg, *Die hannoversche Armee, 1780–1803* (Beckum, 1981); O. Bezzel, *Die Haustruppen des letzten Markgrafen von Ansbach-Bayreuth unter preußischer Herrschaft* (Munich, 1939); B. Thompson Count Rumford, *Collected works* [5 vols] (Cambridge, Mass., 1968–70), vol. V, pp. 394–437.
88. For the efforts to reform imperial institutions, see Gagliardo, *Reich and Nation*, pp. 49–140, and J. Whitman, *The Legacy of Roman law in the German romantic era* (Princeton, NJ, 1990), pp. 66–91. The problems associated with the term "modernization" for this period of German history are analyzed by Blanning, "Modernization of Germany".
89. Overviews are provided by the contributions to H. M. Scott (ed.), *Enlightenment absolutism: reform and reformers in later eighteenth century Europe* (London, 1990). For examples of reform in the ecclesiastical states see Blanning, *Mainz*, pp. 96–209.
90. H.-U. Wehler, *Deutsche Gesellschaftsgeschichte*, [3 vols] (Munich, 1987–95). See also Dipper, *Deutsche Geschichte*, pp. 310–12.
91. D. Beales, *Joseph II: in the shadow of Maria Theresa, 1741–1780* (Cambridge, 1987), p. 120. For Joseph's views, see also H. Conrad (ed.), "Verfassung und politische Lage des Reiches in einer Denkschrift Josephs II von 1767–1768", in *Festschrift für Nicolaus Grass zum 60. Geburtstag*. L. Carlen & F. Steinegger (eds) [2 vols] (Innsbrück, 1974), vol. I, pp. 161–85. Good modern overviews of his reign can be found in Schindling & Ziegler (eds), *Kaiser der Neuzeit*, pp. 249–76, and T. C. W. Blanning, *Joseph II* (London, 1994). The Bavarian–Netherlands exchange schemes are discussed below.
92. Aretin, *Heiliges Römisches Reich*, vol. I, pp. 137–46, 372–427.
93. H. M. Scott, "Aping the great powers: Frederick the Great and the defence of Prussia's international position, 1763–86", *GH* **12**, 1994, pp. 286–307 (p. 289).
94. D. E. Showalter, "Hubertusberg to Auerstädt: the Prussian army in decline", *GH* **12**, 1994, pp. 308–33, and his *Wars of Frederick the Great*, pp. 328–37. On the condition of the army in this period, see also Jany, *Preußische Armee*, vol. III, pp. 1–147. An example of foreign observation is given by E. Howard-Vyse, "A British cavalry officer's report on the manoeuvres of Frederick the Great's army, 1773", *Journal of the Society for Army Historical Research* **60**, 1982, pp. 66–70. Total strength rose from 149,895 (1763), 187,670 (1777) to 194,898 (1786).
95. M. G. Müller, *Die Teilungen Polens 1772. 1793. 1795* (Munich, 1984). The German dimension is discussed by Aretin, *Das Reich*, pp. 327–36, and M. Hanisch, "Friedrich II und die preussische Sukzession in Franken in der internationalen Diskussion", in H. Duchhardt (ed.), *Friedrich der Große, Franken und das Reich* (Cologne, 1986), pp. 81–91.
96. H. M. Scott, "Frederick II, the Ottoman empire and the origins of the Russo-Prussian alliance of April 1764", *European Studies Review* **7**, 1977, pp. 153–75, and his "Aping the great powers", pp. 296–9.
97. Kohl (ed.), *Westfälische Geschichte*, p. 647; Schmid, *Max III Joseph*, pp. 503–5; Haug-Moritz, *Württembergischer Ständekonflikt*, pp. 272–91; V. Press, "Friedrich der Grosse als Reichspolitiker", in Duchhardt (ed.), *Friedrich der Große*, pp. 25–56.

98. Jany, *Preußische Armee*, vol. III, pp. 107–29; R. Mielsch, "Die kursächsische Armee im Bayerischen Erbfolgekriege, 1778/79", *NASG* **53**, 1932, pp. 73–103; **54**, 1933, pp. 46–74. Note that the Saxon army had been reorganized on 1 May 1778 at a paper strength of 21,984 and so was a good 10,000 below the number quoted in many works.

99. Detsils of Austrian mobilization are given by O. Criste, *Kriege unter Kaiser Josef II* (Vienna, 1904), pp. 47–134, 255–9. For the diplomatic dimension, see also P. P. Bernard, *Joseph II and Bavaria* (The Hague, 1965); H. Temperley, *Frederick the Great and Kaiser Joseph: an episode of war and diplomacy in the eighteenth century* (London, 1915); A. v. Arneth, *Geschichte Maria Theresias* [10 vols] (Vienna, 1863–79), vol. X, pp. 439–663; Aretin, *Heiliges Römisches Reiches*, vol. I, pp. 110–30.

100. Criste, *Kriege*, p. 95.

101. The Innviertel encompassed 1,155 km² inhabited by 80,000 people in eastern Bavaria.

102. Aretin, *Das Reich*, pp. 330–36; Kohl (ed.), *Westfälische Geschichte*, pp. 644–5, 678; M. Braubach, "Die Außenpolitik Max Friedrich von Königsegg, Kurfürst von Köln und Fürstbischof von Münster (1761–1784)", *AHVN* **115**, 1929, pp. 330–53.

103. See Bernard, *Joseph II and Bavaria*, pp. 134–218.

104. For the significance of this journey, see C. Scharf, *Katharina II., Deutschland und die Deutschen* (Mainz, 1995), pp. 315–26.

105. By July 1789 it had expanded to include Weimar, Baden, Anhalt-Dessau, Anhalt-Köthen, Anhalt-Bernberg, Mainz, Gotha, Zweibrücken, Wolfenbüttel, Hessen-Kassel, Osnabrück, Ansbach, Pfalz-Birkenfeld, Mecklenburg-Schwerin and Mecklenburg-Strelitz. See A. Kohler, "Das Reich im Spannungsfeld des preussisch-österreichischen Gegensatzes. Die Fürstenbundbestrebungen, 1783–1785", in *Fürst, Bürger, Mensch*, F. Engel-Janosi et al. (eds) (Munich, 1975), pp. 71–96; Aretin, *Heiliges Römisches Reiches*, vol. I, pp. 162–217, and his "Die Großmachte und das Klientelsystem im Reich am Ende des 18. Jahrhunderts", in Mączak (ed.), *Klientelsysteme*, pp. 63–92.

106. Blanning, *Mainz*, pp. 200–34.

107. Buddruss, *Französische Deutschlandpolitik*, pp. 180–210. The older view is summarized by L. Just, "Österreichs Westpolitik im 18. Jahrhundert", *RVJB* **5**, 1935, pp. 1–15 (pp. 9–10). For French finances see J. C. Riley, *The Seven Years War and the old regime in France: the economic and financial toll* (Princeton, 1986). French policy in the Rhineland is covered by Kreuzberg, *Beziehungen des Kurstaates Trier*, pp. 48–161.

108. E. Buddruss, "Die Deutschlandpolitik der französischen Revolution zwischen Traditionen und revolutionären Bruch", in *Revolution und konservatives Beharren: das alte Reich und die Französische Revolution*, K. O. v. Aretin & K. Härter (eds) (Mainz, 1990), pp. 145–54 (p. 148).

109. The Scheldt had been closed to commercial traffic by the Westphalian Settlement of 1648. For this and the following, see S. Schama, *Patriots and liberators: revolution in the Netherlands, 1780–1813*, 2nd edn (London, 1992), pp. 64–135; Rowan, *Princes of Orange*, pp. 205–29. French policy is covered by M. Price, *Preserving the monarchy: the comte de Vergennes, 1774–1787* (Cambridge, 1995), pp. 187–222.

110. The military aspects of the intervention are discussed by Jany, *Preußische Armee*, vol. III, pp. 209–16.

111. The term comes from Scharf, *Katharina*, p. 274. For the following, see *ibid.*, pp. 272–346; Aretin, *Das Reich*, pp. 337–52; H. M. Maurer, "Das Haus Württemberg und Rußland", *Zeitschrift für Württembergische Landesgeschichte* **48**, 1989, pp. 201–22.

112. Roider, *Austria's eastern question*, pp. 151–84, with quote from p. 154. See also Beales, *Joseph II*, pp. 277–305; K. A. Roider, *Baron Thugut and Austria's response to the French*

Revolution (Princeton, 1987), pp. 26–49; P. W. Schroeder, *The transformation of European politics, 1763–1848* (Oxford, 1994), pp. 11–24, 58–64.

113. Dickson, *Finance and government*, vol. II, pp. 352. This does not include the frontier militia. A detailed breakdown prepared by the Württemberg representative in Vienna on 16 August 1786 gives the war strength at 400,136, including militia: HSAS, A74: Bü. 202. For accounts of the war, see Criste, *Kriege unter Kaiser Josef*, pp. 143–225, and P. B. Bernard, "Austria's last Turkish War – some further thoughts", *AHY* 19–20, 1983–4, pp. 15–31.
114. Duffy, *Fortress*, p. 244.
115. Blanning, *Joseph II*, pp. 176–82; Roider, *Austria's eastern question*, pp. 182–92; Müller, *Teilungen Polens*, pp. 43–51.

Chapter Eight: The challenge of revolution

1. A. Ramm, *Germany, 1789–1919* (London, 1967), especially pp. 33–9; G. Rudé, *Revolutionary Europe, 1783–1815* (London, 1964), especially p. 193.
2. For an influential example of contemporary criticism, see F. C. Laukhard, *Schilderung der jetzigen Reichsarmee nach ihrer wahren Gesalt nebst Winken über Deutschlands künftiges Schicksal* (Cologne, 1796).
3. See the contributions in H. Berding (ed.), *Soziale Unruhen in Deutschland während der Französische Revolution* (Göttingen, 1988), and F. Petri et al. (eds), *Rheinische Geschichte* [3 vols] (Düsseldorf, 1980), vol. II, pp. 319–21. Habsburg problems in containing the Netherlands revolt are covered by Criste, *Kriege unter Josef II*, pp. 226–51.
4. For Leopold II see Schindling & Ziegler (eds), *Kaiser der Neuzeit*, pp. 277–88. Anhalt-Zerbst provided 449 men from August 1790 till 1797, while Bishop Erthal hired 2,504 Würzburgers and 626 Bambergers from June–July 1790 onwards: Wrede, *Wehrmacht*, vol. II, pp. 451, 622; Hagen, "Würzburgische Hausinfanterie vom Jahre 1757", pp. 51–63.
5. The first armed intervention, November 1789–April 1790, comprised 4,000 Prussians, 1,100 Palatine-Bavarians and 994 Münster troops. The second, April–November 1790, involved 2,900 Palatine-Bavarian, 1,214 Münster, 445 Cologne, 826 Trier and 1,450 Mainz soldiers. For the events see M. Braubach, *Max Franz von Österreich, Letzer Kurfürst von Köln und Fürstbischof von Münster* (Münster, 1925), pp. 222–33; W. Lüdtke, "Kurtrier und die revolutionären Unruhen in den Jahren, 1789–1790", *Trierer Zeitschrift* 5, 1930, pp. 21–8; E. Schulte, "Der Krieg Münsters gegen Lüttich, 1789–92", *Quellen und Forschungen zur Geschichte der Stadt Münster* 2, 1927, pp. 57–9; R. Breitling, "Die Revolution in Lüttich und der Schwäbische Kreis (1789/90)", *Besondere Beilage zum Staatsanziege für Württemberg*, 1929, pp. 257–64; O. Bezzel, *Geschichte des kurpfalzbayerischen Heeres, 1778–1803* (Munich, 1930), pp. 249–55; Bönninghausen, *Münsterschen Truppen*, pp. 176–81.
6. K. Härter, *Reichstag und Revolution, 1789–1806:. die Auseinandersetzung des Immerwährenden Reichstag zu Regensburg mit den Auswirkungen der Französischen Revolution auf das alte Reich* (Göttingen, 1992), especially pp. 287–377, and his "Der Reichstag im Revolutionsjahr 1789", in Aretin & Härter (eds), *Revolution und konservatives Beharren*, pp. 155–74. For examples of the measures in individual territories, see T. C. W. Blanning, *The French Revolution in Germany: occupation and resistance in the Rhineland, 1792–1802* (Oxford, 1983), pp. 47–58.
7. Härter, "Der Reichstag", pp. 158–9.

8. Härter, *Reichstag und Revolution*, pp. 69–166; Duchhardt, *Verfassungsgeschichte*, pp. 243–5.
9. For the wider context see T. C. W. Blanning, *The origins of the French Revolutionary Wars* (London, 1986).
10. Aretin, *Heiliges Römisches Reich*, vol. i, pp. 214–14, and his *Das Reich*, pp. 439–41; Schroeder, *Transformation of European politics*, pp. 83–125; Müller, *Teilungen Polens*, pp. 43–51.
11. S. S. Biro, *The German policy of revolutionary France: a study in French diplomacy during the War of the First Coalition* [2 vols] (Cambridge, Mass., 1957) vol. i, pp. 31–70; Härter, *Reichstag und Revolution*, pp. 167–271. For Francis II see Schindling & Ziegler (eds), *Kaiser der Neuzeit*, pp. 289–308. The French Republic declared war on Britain and the Dutch in February 1793, who then formed a coalition with Austria and Prussia.
12. For example by Ramm, *Germany, 1789–1919*, pp. 34–6. On the attempts to activate the *Kreis* Association, see Dotzauer, *Reichskreise*, pp. 103–4; Borck, *Schwäbische Reichskreis*, pp. 69–74.
13. Cited in Roider, *Thugut*, pp. 94–5.
14. T. C. W. Blanning, *The French Revolutionary Wars, 1787–1802* (London, 1996), pp. 71–101; Jany, *Preußische Armee*, vol. iii, pp. 236–59; Harms, "Landmiliz", pp. 396–7. The changes in the French army are analyzed on pp. 314–16.
15. Cited by Gagliardo, *Reich and nation*, p. 144.
16. Roider, *Thugut*, pp. 124–36.
17. Neuhaus, "Militarischen Exekutive", pp. 334–46, although he overestimates the *Reichstag*'s abdication of involvement; Härter, *Reichstag und Revolution*, pp. 385–6.
18. Borck, *Swäbische Reichskreis*, pp. 60–68, 80–92, 106–8, 113–15; Stadlinger, *Württembergischen Kriegswesens*, pp. 107–54; A. v. Schempp, "Kehl und der Schwäbische Kreis gegen Schluß des 18. Jahrhunderts", *WVJHLG*, NF 28, 1919, pp. 167–264; R. Breitling, "Kehl und die süddeutsche Kriegsvorbereitungen, 1792", *ZGO*, NF 43, 1930, pp. 107–37; Württembergischer Generalquartiermeisterstab, "Quellenstudien über die Kriegsgeschichte der Württembergischen Truppen von 1792 an", *Württembergisches Jahrbuch*, 1845, pp. 211–35. Campaign losses had reduced effective strength to 5,589 by 10 July 1796.
19. Tessin, *Regimenter*, pp. 153–6, 248; Sicken, "Streitkräfte", p. 729.
20. Borck, *Schwabische Reichskreis*, pp. 95–102; A. v. Schempp, "Kompetenzstreit zwischen den Schwäbischen Kreis und den Reichs-General-Feldmarschall Herzog Albrecht von Sachsen-Teschen im Jahre 1795", *BMWB* 9, 1908, pp. 371–96.
21. Härter, *Reichstag und Revolution*, pp. 383–4, 421. For the composition of the *Reichsarmee* and the initial operations, see Austrian Kriegs-Archiv, *Krieg gegen die Französischen Revolution, 1792–1797* [2 vols] (Vienna, 1905).
22. stAD, A6.Nr.1441, treaty of 17 September 1793, renewed 19 May 1796. On the service see Zernin, *Abriß*, pp. 35–40.
23. Mürmann, "Militärwesen des ehemaligen Hochstiftes Paderborn", pp. 35–6, 45–6, 62, 70–71; F. K. Erbprinz zu Hohenlohe-Waldenburg, "Über hohenlohisches Militärwesen", *Württembergisch Franke*, NF **40**, 1966, pp. 212–41; T. Osterritter, "Die französische emigranten Legion Mirabeau im Hohenloheschen", *WF*, NF **19**, 1938, pp. 1–5, 12; P. Lahnstein, *Ludwigsburg: aus der Geschichte einer europäischen Residenz* (Stuttgart, 1958), p. 100. All *émigré* units suffered heavy desertion and an inability to find replacement recruits. The Corps Rohan totalled only 466 men when it was taken over by the Austrians. Mirabeau's Legion had been 1,500–2,000 men in 1792 but the combined Hohenlohe–*émigré* corps never totalled much over 1,000. It was hired by the Dutch in

1794, entered Russian pay in 1799 and then transferred, along with the other *émigrés*, to mercenary service with the British in 1800–1. The other *émigré* unit maintained by the *Relations* was the 1,200-strong corps under Dumouriez, the former revolutionary general who defected in 1793.

24. Härter, *Reichstag und Revolution*, pp. 399, 420 *n*197; Aretin, *Heiliges Römisches Reich*, vol. I, pp. 297 *n*244, 363; Hüsgen, "Vertretung", pp. 87–91.

25. In addition to the 30 RMs voted in February 1793, there were further grants of 50 RMs on 27 June 1794, 50 more on 28 May 1795 and 100 on 29 January 1796. See Härter, *Reichstag und Revolution*, pp. 422–6, 435–6.

26. *Ibid.*, p. 402. In fact only 43 per cent of the besieging force were Prussians, with 27 per cent being provided by Austria and the remainder coming from Saxony, Hessen-Kassel, Hessen-Darmstadt and Palatinate-Bavaria: Jany, *Preußische Armee*, vol. III, pp. 265.

27. Sherwig, *Guineas and gunpowder*, pp. 34–53; Roider, *Thugut*, pp. 138–9; Aretin, *Heiliges Römisches Reich*, vol. I, pp. 286–93; Härter, *Reichstag und Revolution*, pp. 388–401; Jany, *Preußische Armee*, vol. III, pp. 282–6. Only 51,442 of the Prussians were combat troops, the rest were transport and logistical personnel. For the condition of Prussian finances, see W. Real, "Die preußische Staatsfinanzen und die Anbahnung des Sonderfriedens von Basel 1795", *FBPG*, NF **1**, (1991), pp. 53–100.

28. Härter, *Reichstag und Revolution*, pp. 414–22, 430–35.

29. The various viewpoints are expressed by Harms, "Landmiliz", p. 385; *HDM*, vol. II, pp. 57–60; P. Sauer, *Revolution und Volksbewaffnung: die Württembergischen Bürgerwehren im 19. Jahrhundert vor allem während der Revolution von 1848/49* (Ulm, 1976), introduction.

30. The widespread belief that the French had 1 million under arms is a myth, and the figures given in the text are based on more reliable estimates. See P. Paret, "Conscription and the end of the old regime in France and Prussia", in W. Treue (ed.), *Geschichte als Aufgabe* (Berlin, 1988), pp. 159–82; J. P. Bertaud, *The army of the French Revolution: from citizen-soldiers to instrument of power* (Princeton, 1988); S. F. Scott, *The response of the royal army to the French Revolution: the role and development of the line army, 1787–1793* (Oxford, 1978), especially pp. 169–90; J. Delmas (ed.), *De 1715 à 1871*, vol. 2 of *Histoire militaire de la France* (Paris, 1992), pp. 195–252; A. Forrest, *Conscripts and deserters: the army and French society during the Revolution and Empire* (Oxford, 1988), and his *Soldiers of the French Revolution* (Durham, 1990), pp. 58–88.

31. Pfister, *Milizgedanke*, pp. 25–38. On the prewar debate, see Kunisch, *Fürst-Gessellschaft-Krieg*, pp. 161–226.

32. Both the map and the decree are in HSAS, A28: Bü. 99. For the mobilization generally, see O. Heinl, *Heereswesen und Volksbewaffnung in Vorderösterreich im Zeitalter Josefs II. und der Revolutionskriege* (Freiburg, 1941); A. v. Pfister, "Aus den Tagen des Herzogs Ludwig Eugen von Württemberg", *WVJHLG*, NF 3, 1894, pp. 94–192; Schreiber, *Badische Wehrstand*, pp. 186–8; *HDM*, vol. III, pp. 114–16. Hessen-Kassel planned 10,000 active militiamen, 14,000 reservists and 6,000 home guard, but it is unlikely that many of these were actually mobilized. Similarly, Würzburg plans remained on paper only.

33. Stadlinger, *Württembergischen Kriegswesens*, pp. 461–2; Harms, "Landmiliz", pp. 380–84; Sicken, "Streitkräfte", pp. 697–705. For example, the Swabian scheme for 40,000 militia was decreed alongside orders adding a further 4,000 regulars and a volunteer rifle corps of 1,000–1,500 men: Borck, *Schwäbischer Reichskreis*, pp. 83–7.

34. Härter, *Reichstag und Revolution*, pp. 403–14; Aretin, *Heiliges Römisches Reich*, vol. I, pp. 292–8; Roider, *Thugut*, pp. 141–4.

35. Cited in Gagliardo, *Reich and Nation*, p. 156.

36. As Härter, *Reichstag und Revolution*, p. 407, points out, this was the true reason behind Austrian support for the mobilization and not, as widely stated elsewhere, as a substitute for the expensive Prussian army.

37. Heinl, *Volksbewaffnung*, pp. 45–56; J. Forderer, "Das Bürgermilitär in Württemberg", *Tübinger Blätter* **23**, 1932, pp. 1–27. For the proportion under arms see Table 8.3, this volume.

38. Pfister, *Milizgedanke*, pp. 38–60; Borck, *Schwäbischer Reichskreis*, pp. 164–6; Blanning, *Mainz*, p. 187.

39. The decree confiscating weapons is in HSAS, E146: Bü. 4198. For the reforms in Württemberg and elsewhere, see P. Sauer, "Die Neuorganisation des Würtembergischen Heerwesens unter Herzog. Kurfürst und König Friedrich (1797–1816)", *ZWLG* **26**, 1967, pp. 395–420; J. H. Gill, *With eagles to glory: Napoleon and his German allies in the 1809 campaign* (London, 1992).

40. For the debates see Härter, *Reichstag und Revolution*, pp. 422–30. For the contingents, see Schuster & Franke, *Sächsischen Armee*, vol. II, pp. 202, 210, 214; Dotzauer, *Reichskreise*, pp. 301–2; Bönninghausen, *Münsterschen Truppen*, pp. 184–9; Dewall, "Lippeschen Militärgeschichte", p. 89; Ulmenstein, *Schaumburg-Lippischen Truppenkorps*, p. 14; Meissner, *Nordhausen*, pp. 50–51, 62.

41. Aretin, *Heiliges Römisches Reich*, vol. I, pp. 301–18, 368–70, and his *Das Reich*, pp. 346–52; also W. Andreas (ed.), *Politischer Briefwechsel des Herzogs und Grossherzogs Carl August von Weimar, 1778–1828* [3 vols] (Stuttgart, 1954–73), vol. II, pp. 65–73. Hessian strength is taken from P. K. Taylor, "The household's most expendable people: the draft and peasant society in 18th-century Hessen-Kassel" (PhD thesis, University of Iowa 1987), p. 93. Bishop Erthal was the younger brother of Friedrich Carl Joseph von Erthal (1718–1802), archbishop of Mainz from 1774.

42. Aretin, *Heiliges Römisches Reich*, vol. I, pp. 369.

43. Roider, *Thugut*, pp. 166–7; Härter, *Reichstag und Revolution*, pp. 449–74.

44. The negotiations and treaty are covered by Biro, *German policy of revolutionary France*, pp. 312–80. For the German reaction, see Gagliardo, *Reich and nation*, pp. 166–70; Roider, *Thugut*, pp. 176–8; Borck, *Schwäbische Reichskreis*, pp. 102–9.

45. P. Dwyer, "The politics of Prussian neutrality, 1795–1805", *GH* **12**, 1994, pp. 351–73, and Showalter, "Hubertusberg to Auerstädt", pp. 322–4. B. Simms, *The impact of Napoleon. Prussian high politics, foreign policy and the crisis of the executive 1797–1806* (Cambridge, 1997).

46. Jany, *Preußische Armee*, vol. III, pp. 314–35 covers the military operations.

47. Schama, *Patriots and liberators*, p. 187.

48. Aretin, *Heiliges Römisches Reich*, vol. I, pp. 362–6; Jany, *Preußische Armee*, vol. III, pp. 300–5; Kohl (ed.), *Westfälische Geschichte*, pp. 646–7. For the Guelph contributions to the observation army, see Sichart, *Hannoverschen Armee*, vol. V, pp. 651–3; Elster, *Braunschweig-Wolfenbüttel*, II 470–72.

49. Biro, *German policy of revolutionary France*, pp. 381–5, 402–14; Borck, *Schwäbische Reichskreis*, pp. 109–12.

50. Härter, *Reichstag und Revolution*, pp. 512–13; Aretin, *Heiliges Römisches Reich*, vol. I, pp. 334–6; Roider, *Thugut*, pp. 179–97.

51. The breakdown of Palatine payments is given in the table facing p. 188 of La Roche, *Deutsche Oberrhein*. For the Münster contingent, see Bönninghausen, *Münsterschen Truppen*, pp. 186–96.

52. Biro, *German policy of revolutionary France*, pp. 586–94; Borck, *Schwäbische Reichskreis*, pp.

128–36; Stadlinger, *Württembergischen Kriegswesens*, pp. 145–54; H. Hahn, "Das Ende des Schwäbischen Kreiskontingents", *Zeitschrift für Heereskunde* **37**, 1973, pp. 52–7, 123–31; A. v. Schempp, "Die Entwafffnung und Auflösung des Schwäbischen Kreiskorps am 29. Juli 1796", *BBSW* **14**, 1911, pp. 209–15. Electoral Saxony only formally joined the neutrality zone on 29 November 1796.

53. For example, Linnebach (ed.), *Deutsche Heeresgeschichte*, p. 112. Its worth pointing out that similar criticism has been levelled at earlier payments of contributions during the wars against Louis XIV.

54. Details in Biro, *German policy of revolutionary France*, pp. 631–79.

55. Napoleon's campaign is analyzed by D. G. Chandler, *The campaigns of Napoleon* (London, 1966), pp. 53–132. This work is still the best study of Napoleonic warfare although it can now be supplemented by C. J. Esdaile, *The wars of Napoleon* (London, 1995), which also has good coverage of the campaigns against German forces. For Leoben, Campo Formio and their consequences, see Biro, *German policy of revolutionary France*, pp. 730–950.

56. For this and the following: Härter, *Reichstag und Revolution*, pp. 475–538; Gagliardo, *Reich and nation*, pp. 187–90; Roider, *Thugut*, pp. 239–91.

57. Härter, *Reichstag und Revolution*, pp. 539–66. Britain's treaties were for 12,000 Bavarians, 7,000 Württembergers, 4,000 from Mainz and 12,000 Würzburgers.

58. P. G. Dwyer, "Prussia and the armed neutrality: the invasion of Hanover in 1801", *International History Review* **15**, 1993, pp. 661–87.

59. Borck, *Schwäbische Reichskreis*, pp. 163, 168–77; Stadlinger, *Württembergischen Kriegswesens*, pp. 155–6, 471–7.

60. For the operations involving the *Reich*, see F. Dollinger, "Baar, Schwarzwald und Oberrhein im zweiten Koalitionskrieg (1799/1801)", *ZGO*, NF **54**, 1941, pp. 333–402; G. Tümbült, "Vor 100 Jahren-Die Schlachten bei Ostrach und Stockach-Liptingen", *Schriften des Vereins für Geschichte und Naturgeschichte der Baar und der angrenzenden Landesteile* **10**, 1900, pp. 68–82; J. B. Muller, "Kriegstagebuch 1799–1802", *SVGNBaL* **8**, 1893, pp. 68–115; **9**, 1896, pp. 16–78.

61. The other members were Mainz (as chair), Saxony, Brandenburg (i.e. Prussia), Württemberg, Hessen-Kassel and the Teutonic Grand Master, Archduke Charles of Austria. For the politics of this period, see K. O. v. Aretin, *Vom Deutschen Reich zum Deutschen Bund*, 2nd edn (Göttingen, 1993), pp. 84–93, and his *Heiliges Römisches Reich*, vol. I, pp. 360, 437–47; Gagliardo, *Reich and nation*, pp. 193–226; Härter, *Reichstag und Revolution*, pp. 567–98. A useful territorial perspective is provided by J. R. Dieterich, "Die Politik Landgraf Ludwigs X von Hessen-Darmstadt von 1790–1806", *Archiv für Hess. Gesch. und Altertumskunde*, NF **7**, 1910, pp. 417–53.

62. Fürstenberg cited in Kohl (ed.), *Westfälische Geschichte*, p. 647. For the fate of the north Germans, see Adamski, *Welfische Schutz*, pp. 109–11; Jany, *Preußische Armee*, vol. II, pp. 387–90.

63. The decision is printed in Zeumer (ed.), *Quellensammlung*, pp. 509–31.

64. For an example of the reorganization and reform in an individual territory, see E. Hölze, *Das alte Recht und die Revolution: eine politische Geschichte Württembergs in der Revolutionszeit, 1789–1805* (Munich, 1931), and P. Sauer, *Der Schwäbische Zar: Friedrich-Württembergs erster König* (Stuttgart, 1984). The literature in the Reform Era is summarized by L. Gall, *Von der ständischen zur bürgerlichen Gesellschaft* (Munich, 1993), especially pp. 71–81.

65. For the politics of the final years, see Aretin, *Heiliges Römisches Reich*, vol. I, pp. 454–506; Gagliardo, *Reich and nation*, pp. 227–89; O. F. Winter, "Österreichische Pläne zur Neuformierung des Reichstages 1801–1806", *MÖSA* **15**, 1962, pp. 261–335.

66. The imperial Deputation's final decision abolished the old electorates of Trier and Cologne but sanctioned new titles, raising the total to ten: Salzburg (that is, the former Habsburg grand duke of Tuscany, who had been relocated to the *Reich*), Württemberg, Baden, and Hessen-Kassel, along with the existing electorates of Saxony, Brandenburg, Bohemia, Palatinate-Bavaria, Hanover and the imperial archchancellor (former elector of Mainz).

67. See Gagliardo, *Reich and nation*, pp. 242–64. P. Burg, *Die deutsche Trias in Idee und Wirklichkeit* (Stuttgart, 1989), pp. 7–20.

68. The Union included arrangements for military co-operation similar to the earlier Wetterau Union. See A. Woringer, "Geschichte des fürstlich Isenburgischen Militärs, 1806–1816", *ZHG* **64**, 1953, pp. 79–118.

69. Aretin, *Das Reich*, pp. 48–9.

70. The key documents are printed in Zeumer (ed.), *Quellensammlung*, pp. 531–9. Further discussion of events is provided by Aretin, *Vom Deutsches Reich*, pp. 93–102.

71. Here I follow Showalter, "Hubertusberg to Auerstädt", pp. 31–2, in contrast to B. Simms, "The road to Jena: Prussian high politics 1804–06", *GH* **12**, 1994, pp. 374–94, who overemphasizes the irrational forces of the ministerial power struggles in Berlin as behind Prussia's decision in 1806. Solid analyses of Prussia's military failure are provided by F. L. Petre, *Napoleon's conquest of Prussia* (London, 1907); Jany, *Preußische Armee*, vol. III, pp. 537–565; W. O. Shannahan, *Prussian military reforms, 1786–1813* (New York, 1945).

Chapter Nine: Why the Reich collapsed

1. An example of the standard view, expressed with particular reference to Prussia, is H. Delbrück, *History and the art of war*, [4 vols], (reprint, Lincoln, 1990).

2. J. A. Lynn, *The bayonets of the Republic* (Illinois, 1984), p. 119. For a balanced discussion, see Forrest, *Soldiers of the revolution*, pp. 89–124.

3. Blanning, *French Revolutionary Wars*, p. 119.

4. It's worth remembering that the men who flocked to the French volunteer units in 1791–3 were drawn in part by the higher rates of pay and better conditions they offered than service in the old line army.

5. W. R. Fann, "Peacetime attrition in the army of Frederick William I 1713–1740", *CEH* **11**, 1978, pp. 323–34; M. Sikora, *Disziplin und Desertion: strukturprobleme militärischer Organisation im 18. Jahrhundert* (Berlin, 1996); Borck. *Schwäbische Reichskreis* p. 108; Bertaud, *Army of the French Revolution*, p. 259; Schuster & Franke, *Sächsischen Armee*, vol. II, p. 221.

6. The quote comes from the English translation of the Prussian regulations, but similar passages can be found elsewhere: *Regulations for the Prussian infantry* (London, 1757; reprinted New York, 1968), p. 120.

7. C. Duffy, *The military experience in the age of reason* (London, 1987), pp. 76, 134.

8. Geispitzheim, *Historische Nachrichten*.

9. Herter, *Kurkölnischen Truppen*, p. 46.

10. HSAS, A30c: Bü.13, documents from 1785.

11. D. Kotsch, *Potsdam: die preußische Garnisonstadt* (Brunswick, 1992), p. 81.

12. HSAS, A202: Bü. 2248, 25 April 1746.

13. For further on these issues, see P. H. Wilson, "German women and war, 1500–1800", *War in History* **3**, 1996, pp. 127–60; R. Pröve, *Stehendes Heer und städtische Gesellschaft im 18. Jahrhundert: Göttingen und seine Militärbevölkerung, 1713–1756* (Munich, 1995), and the collection edited by B. R. Kroener & R. Pröve, *Krieg und Frieden: Militär und Gesellschaft in der frühen Neuzeit* (Paderborn, 1996).

14. W. Doyle, *The origins of the French Revolution,* 2nd edn (Oxford, 1988); M. Lyons, *Napoleon Bonaparte and the legacy of the French Revolution* (Basingstoke, 1994).

15. Blanning, "Modernization of Germany", p. 114.

16. Vann, *Swabian Kreis,* pp. 207–48; W. Söll, *Die staatliche Wirtschaftspolitik in Württemberg im 17. und 18. Jahrhundert* (Tübingen, 1934).

17. Further discussion in Scribner & Ogilvie (eds), *New social and economic history,* vol. II, especially pp. 263–308, and H. U. Wehler, *Deutsche Gesellschaftsgeschichte* [3 vols] (Munich, 1987–95).

18. Most clearly expressed by G. Best, *War and society in revolutionary Europe, 1770–1870* (London, 1982).

19. For an example, Güssregen, *Bamberg,* pp. 17–19.

20. Cited by Roider, *Thugut,* p. 129.

21. A. Ernstberger, "Reichsheer und Reich", in *Gesamtdeutsche Vergangenheit: Festgabe für Heinrich Ritter von Srbik* (Munich, 1938), pp. 179–86.

22. Quote from Rothenberg, *Napoleon's great adversaries,* p. 34.

23. Prussia was obliged to field about 12,000 men under the *Triplum* and 20,000 under the *Quintuplum* as its *Kreis* contingents, plus over 10,000 substitutes in return for *Relutions.* An additional 20,000 men were to be provided under its treaty of 7 February 1792 with Austria, followed by 62,407 more in agreement with Britain, 19 April 1794, although only 51,442 of the latter were actually combat personnel. In practice, Prussia fielded 46,769 in the west in 1792; 68,018 in 1793 and about 76,000 in 1794. Extracted from Jany, *Preußische Armee,* vol. III, pp. 242, 262–3, 285, 289.

24. See the figures in Aretin, *Heiliges Römisches Reich,* vol. I, pp. 298 n247.

25. Rothenberg, *Napoleon's great adversaries,* pp. 17, 50–54. For further discussion of tactics see S. T. Ross, *From flintlock to rifle: infantry tactics, 1740–1866,* 2nd edn (London, 1996).

26. Stadlinger, *Württembergischen Kriegswesens,* pp. 449–50; Weissenbach, *Württembergischen Artillerie,* pp. 94–7; Atwood, *Hessians,* especially p. 247; P. Paret, *Yorck and the era of Prussian reform, 1807–1815* (Princeton, 1966), especially pp. 7–110.

27. For the *Hercule,* which can still be viewed today in the Heeresgeschichtliches Museum in Vienna, see the appendix by H. L. Zollner in Lang, *Ettlinger Linien,* pp. 64–7. The semaphore is described in Müller, "Kriegstagebuch ", part 1 (1893), pp. 112–13, and part 2 (1896), pp. 17, 20, 23.

28. Further comparison of tactics is provided by Blanning, *French Revolutionary Wars,* pp. 119–24.

29. For age preference, see W. R. Fann, "On the infantryman's age in eighteenth century Prussia", *Military Affairs* **41**, 1977, pp. 165–70. Archduke Charles' *Krieg gegen die Neufranken* is printed in Frhr. v. Waldstätten (ed.), *Erzherzog Karl: Ausgewählte militärische Schriften* (Berlin, 1882), pp. 1–11.

30. Quoted in Delbrück, *Art of war,* vol. IV, p. 403.

31. Full discussion of the proposals in Gagliardo, *Reich and nation,* pp. 157–64, 171–83, 242–62.

Select bibliography

For reasons of space, this list is very selective and concentrates on modern works with good bibliographies and on secondary works cited frequently in the notes. The theoretical literature that has influenced this work is included in the notes to Chapter 1.

Adamski, H. J. *Der welfische Schutz über die Stadt Hildesheim* (Hildesheim, 1939).

Angermeier, H. "Die Reichsverfassung in der Politik der Jahre 1679–1681", *ZSRG* **82**, pp. 190–222, 1965.

Aretin, K. O. Frhr. v. *Das altes Reich, 1648–1806* (Stuttgart, 1993).

Aretin, K. O. Frhr. v. *Das Reich: Friedensgarantie und europäisches Gleichgewicht, 1648–1806* (Stuttgart, 1986).

Aretin, K. O. Frhr. v. *Heiliges Römisches Reich, 1776–1806: Reichsverfassung und Staatssouveränität* [2 vols] (Wiesbaden, 1967).

Aretin, K. O. Frhr. v. *Vom Deutschen Reich zum Deutschen Bund*, 2nd edn (Göttingen, 1993).

Aretin, K. O. Frhr. v. & K. Harter (eds). *Revolution und konservatives Beharren: das alte Reich und die Französische Revolution* (Mainz, 1990).

Arneth, A. Ritter von. *Geschichte Maria Theresias* [10 vols] (Vienna, 1863–79).

Asch, R. G. *The Thirty Years War: the Holy Roman Empire and Europe, 1618–1648* (London, 1997).

Barker, T. M. *Double eagle and crescent: Vienna's second Turkish siege and its historical setting* (Albany, 1967).

Beales, D. *Joseph II: in the shadow of Maria Theresa, 1741–1780* (Cambridge, 1987).

Benecke, G. *Society and politics in Germany, 1500–1750* (London, 1974).

Berding, H. (ed.). *Soziale Unruhen in Deutschland während der Französischen Revolution* (Göttingen, 1988).

Bernard, P. P. *Joseph II and Bavaria: two eighteenth century attempts at German unification* (The Hague, 1965).

Berney, A. *König Friedrich I und das Haus Habsburg (1701–1707)* (Munich, 1927).

Bezzel, O. *Die Haustruppen des letzen Markgrafen von Ansbach-Bayreuth unter preußischer Herrschaft* (Munich, 1939).

Bezzel, O. *Geschichte des kurpfälzbayerischen Heeres, 1778–1803* (Munich, 1930).

Bezzel, O. *Geschichte des kurpfälzischen Heeres von seinen Anfängen bis zur Vereinigung von Kurpfalz und Kurbayern, 1777* [2 vols] (Munich, 1925–8).

Biro, S. S. *The German policy of revolutionary France: a study in French diplomacy during the War of the First Coalition, 1792–1797* (Cambridge, Mass., 1957).

Blanning, T. C. W. *The French Revolution in Germany: occupation and resistance in the Rhineland, 1792–1802* (Oxford, 1983).

Blanning, T. C. W. *The French Revolutionary Wars, 1787–1802* (London, 1996).

Blanning, T. C. W. *Reform and revolution in Mainz, 1743–1802* (Cambridge, 1974).

Bönninghausen, C. Frhr. v. *Die Kriegerische Tätigheit der münsterschen Truppen, 1651–1800* (Coesfeld, 1978).

Borck, H.-G. *Der Schwäbische Reichskreis im Zeitalter der Französischen Revolutionskriege (1792–1806)* (Stuttgart, 1970).

Brabant, A. *Das Heilige Römische Reich teutscher Nation im Kampf mit Friedrich dem Großen* [3 vols] (Berlin, 1904–31).

Braubach, M. *Die Bedeutung der Subsidien für die Politik im Spanischen Erbfolgekrieg* (Bonn, 1923).

Braubach, M. *Diplomatie und geistiges Leben im 17. und 18. Jahrhundert* (Bonn, 1969).

Braubach, M. *Prinz Eugen von Savoyen* [5 vols] (Munich, 1963–5).

Broucek, P., et al. *Der Sieg bei Wien 1683* (Vienna, 1983).

Browning, R. *The War of the Austrian Succession* (New York, 1993).

Buddruss, E. *Die Französische Deutschlandpolitik, 1756–1789* (Mainz, 1995).

Büsch, O. *Military system and social life in old regime Prussia, 1713–1807* (Eng. trans., Atlantic Highlands, 1997).

Carsten, F. L. *Princes and parliaments in Germany from the fifteenth to the eighteenth century* (Oxford, 1959).

Caspary, H. *Staat, Finanzen, Wirtschaft und Heerwesen im Hochstift Bamberg (1672–1693)* (Bamberg, 1976).

Criste, O. *Kriege unter Kaiser Josef II* (Vienna, 1904).

Czok, K. *August der Starken und Kursachsen*, 2nd edn (Leipzig, 1989).

Dann, U. *Hanover and Great Britain, 1740–1760* (Leicester, 1991).

Decker, K. P. *Frankreich und die Reichsstände, 1672–1675: die Ansätze zur Bildung einer "Dritten Partei" in den Anfangsjahren des Holländischen Krieges* (Bonn, 1981).

Denmandt, K. E. *Geschichte des Landes Hessen*, 3rd edn (Kassel, 1980).

Dickmann, F. *Der Westfälische Frieden* (Münster, 1964).

Dickson, P. G. M. *Finance and government under Maria Theresa, 1740–1780* [2 vols] (Oxford, 1987).

Dotzauer, W. *Die deutschen Reichskreise in der Verfassung des alten Reiches und ihr Eigenleben (1500–1806)* (Munich, 1989).

Duchhardt, H. *Altes Reich und europäische Staatenwelt, 1648–1806* (Munich, 1990).

Duchhardt, H. *Deutsche Verfassungsgeschichte, 1495–1806* (Stuttgart, 1991).

Duchhardt, H. (ed.). *Friedrich der Große, Franken und das Reich* (Cologne, 1986).

Duffy, C. *Frederick the Great: a military life* (London, 1985).

Duffy, C. *The army of Frederick the Great*, 2nd edn (Chicago, 1996).

Ebbecke, O. C. *Frankreichs Politik gegenüber dem deutschen Reiche in den Jahren, 1748–1756* (Freiburg, 1931).

Eickhoff, E. *Venedig, Wien und die Osmanen: Umbruch in Südosteuropa, 1645–1700* (Munich, 1973).

Eldon, C. W. *England's subsidy policy towards the Continent during the Seven Years War* (Philadelphia, 1938).

Elster, O. *Geschichte der stehenden Truppen im Herzogtum Braunschweig-Wolfenbüttel, 1600–1806* [2 vols] (Leipzig, 1899–1901).

Erdmannsdörffer, B. *Deutsche Geschichte vom Westfälischen Frieden bis zum Regierungsantritt Friedrichs des Großen, 1648–1740* [2 vols] (Leipzig, 1932 edn).

Evans, R. J. W. *The making of the Habsburg monarchy, 1550–1700* (Oxford, 1979).

Ferguson, R. T. "Blood and fire: contribution policy of the French armies in Germany (1668–1715)" (unpublished PhD thesis, University of Minnesota, 1970).

Fester, R. *Die armirten Stände und die Reichskriegsverfassung, 1681–1697* (Frankfurt-am-Main, 1986).

Fester, R. *Die Augsburger Allianz von 1686* (Munich, 1893).

Frauenholz, E. v. *Entwicklungsgeschichte des deutschen Heerwesens* [6 vols] (Munich, 1935–48).

Frey, L. & M. *A question of empire: Leopold I and the war of Spanish succession, 1701–1705* (Bloomington, 1980).

Frey, L. & M. *Frederick I: the man and his times* (New York, 1984).

Gebauer, R. *Die Außenpolitik der Schwäbischen Reichskreises vor Ausbruch des Spanischen Erbfolgekrieges (1697–1702)* (Marburg, 1969).

Gespacher, H. *Die badische Politik im Siebenjährigen Krieg* (Heidelberg, 1934).

Groehler, O. *Die Kriege Friedrichs II*, 6th edn (Berlin, 1990).

Großer Generalstab (Prussia), *Die Kriege Friedrichs des Großen* [19 vols] (Berlin, 1890–1914).

Güssregen, J. *Die Wehrverfassung der Hochstiftes Bamberg im 18. Jahrhundert* (Bamberg, 1936).

Hacke, P. *August der Starke* (Berlin, 1926).

Handbuch zur deutschen Militärgeschichte, 1648–1939 [11 vols] (issued by the Militärgeschichtliches Forschungsamt, Freiburg, 1983).

Handrick, W. *Die Pragmatische Armee, 1741–1743: eine alliierte Armee im Kalkül des Österreichischen Erbfolgekrieges* (Munich, 1991).

Härter, K. *Reichstag und Revolution, 1789–1806* (Göttingen, 1992).

Hartmann, P.-C. *Geld als Instrument europäischer Machtpolitik im Zeitalter des Merkantilismus, 1715–1740* (Munich, 1978).

Hartmann, P.-C. *Karl Albrecht, Karl VII: Glücklicher Kurfürst, unglücklicher Kaiser* (Regensburg, 1985).

Hatton, R. M. (ed.) *Louis XIV and Europe* (London, 1976).

Haug-Moritz, G. *Württembergischer Ständekonflikt und deutscher Dualismus* (Stuttgart, 1992).

Hauser, O. (ed.) *Preußen, Europe und das Reich* (Cologne, 1987).

Heinl, O. *Heerwesen und Volksbewaffnung in Vorderösterreich im Zeitalter Josefs II und der Revolutionskriege* (Freiburg, 1941).

Herter, E. *Geschichte der Kurkölnischen Truppen in der Zeit vom Badener Frieden bis zum Beginn des Siebenjährigen Krieges* (Bonn, 1914).

Holl, B. *Hofkammerpräsident Gundaker Thomas Graf Starhemberg und die österreichische Finanzpolitik der Barockzeit (1703–1715)* (Vienna, 1976).

Hughes, M. *Law and politics in eighteenth century Germany: the imperial Aulic Council in the reign of Charles VI* (Woolbridge, 1988).

Hüsgen, K. "Die militärische Vertretung des Stiftes Essen durch Brandenburg-Preußen im 17. und 18. Jahrhundert", *Beiträge zur Geschichte von Stadt und Stift Essen* **30**, pp. 1–92, 1909.

Hüttl, L. *Friedrich Wilhelm von Brandenburg, der Große Kurfürst, 1620–1688* (Munich, 1981).

Huttl, L. *Max Emanuel. Der blaue Kurfürst 1679–1726* (Munich, 1976).

Ingrao, C. W. *In quest and crisis: Emperor Joseph I and the Habsburg monarchy* (West Lafayette, 1979).

Ingrao, C. W. *The Habsburg monarchy, 1618–1815* (Cambridge, 1994).

Ingrao, C. W. *The Hessian mercenary state: ideas, institutions and reform under Frederick II, 1760–1785* (Cambridge, 1987).

Jähns, M. "Zur Geschichte der Kriegsverfassung des deutschen Reiches", *PJb* **39**, pp. 1–28, 114–40, 443–90.

Jany, C. v. *Geschichte der Preußischen Armee vom 15. Jahrhundert bis 1914* [4 vols] (Osnabrück, 1967).

Kahlenberg, F. P. *Kurmainzische Verteidigungseinrichtungen und Baugeschichte der Festung Mainz im 17. und 18. Jahrhundert* (Mainz, 1963).

Kappelhoff, B. *Absolutistisches Regiment oder Ständeherrrschaft? Landesherr und Landstände im Ostfriesland im ersten Drittel des 18. Jahrhunderts* (Hildesheim, 1982).

Knüppel, G. *Das Heerwesen des Fürstentums Schleswig-Holstein-Gottorf, 1600–1715* (Neumünster, 1972).

Kohl, W. *Christoph Bernhard von Galen: Politische Geschichte der Fürstbistums Münster, 1650–1678* (Münster, 1964).

Kohl, W. (ed.). *Westfälische Geschichte*, vol. 1 (Düsseldorf, 1983).

Kohlhepp, A. G. W. *Die Militärverfassung des deutschen Reiches zur Zeit des Siebenjährigen Krieges* (Greifswald, 1914).

Koller, A. *Die Vermittlung des Friedens von Vossem (1673) durch den jülich-bergischen Vizekanzler Stratmann* (Münster, 1995).

Kopp, W. *Würzburger Wehr: eine Chronik zur Wehrgeschichte Würzburgs* (Würzburg, 1979).

Köster, M. *Russische Truppen für Prinz Eugen: Politik mit militärischen Mitteln im Frühen 18. Jahrhundert* (Vienna, 1986).

Kreuzberg, B. J. *Die politischen und Wirtschaftlichen Bezeihungen des Kurstaates Trier zu Frankreich in der zweiten Hälfte des 18. Jahrhunderts bis zum Ausbruch der Französischen Revolution* (Bonn, 1932).

Kriegs-Archiv, Kriegsgeschichtliche Abteilung (Austria). *Feldzüge des Prinzen Eugen von Savoyen* [21 vols] (Vienna, 1879–96).

Kriegs-Archiv, Kriegsgeschichtliche Abteilung (Austria). *Kriege gegen die Französischen Revolution 1792–1797* [2 vols] (Vienna, 1905).

Kriegs-Archiv, Kriegsgeschichtliche Abteilung (Austria). *Oesterreichische Erbfolgekrieg 1740–48* [9 vols] (Vienna, 1896–1914).

Kroener, B. R. (ed.). *Europa im Zeitalter Friedrich des Großen: Wirtschaft, Gesellschaft, Kriege* (Munich, 1989).

Kroener, B. R. & R. Pröve (eds). *Krieg und Frieden: Militär und Gesellschaft in der Frühen Neuzeit* (Paderborn, 1996).

Kunisch, J. *Das Mirakel des Hauses Brandenburg: Studien zum Verhältnis von Kabinettspolitik und Kriegführung im Zeitalter des Siebenjährigen Krieges* (Munich, 1978).

Kunisch, J. *Fürst-Gesellschaft-Krieg: Studien zur bellizistischen Disposition des absoluten Fürstenstaates* (Cologne, 1992).

Kunisch, J. (ed.). *Prinz Eugen von Savoyen und seine Zeit* (Freiburg, 1986).

Kunisch, J. (ed.). *Staatsverfassung und Heeresverfassung in der europäischen Geschichte der frühen Neuzeit* (Berlin, 1986).

Linnebach, K. (ed.). *Deutsche Heeresgeschichte* (Hamburg, 1935).

Luard, E. *The balance of power: the system of international relations, 1648–1815* (London, 1992).

Mediger, W. *Mecklenburg, Russland und England-Hannover, 1706–21* [2 vols] (Hildesheim, 1967).

Mentz, G. *Johann Philipp von Schönborn: Kurfürst von Mainz, Bischof von Würzburg und Worms: 1605–1673* [2 vols] (Jena, 1896–9).

Müller, A. *Der Regensburger Reichstag von 1653/54* (Frankfurt-on-Main, 1992).

Müller, M. G. *Die Teilungen Polens 1772. 1793. 1795* (Munich, 1984).

400

Neipperg, R. Graf v. *Kaiser und Schwäbischer Kreis (1714–1733)* (Stuttgart, 1991).

Neuhaus, H. *Das Reich in der früher Neuzeit* (Munich, 1997).

Oakley, S. P. *War and peace in the Baltic, 1560–1790* (London, 1992).

O'Connor, J. T. *Negotiator out of season: the career of Wilhelm Egon von Fürstenberg, 1629–1704* (Athens, Geo., 1978).

Odenthal, E. *Österreichs Türkenkrieg, 1716–18* (Düsseldorf, 1938).

Oestreich, G. *Neostoicism and the early modern state* (Cambridge, 1982).

Ogilvie, S. & B. Scribner (eds). *Germany: a new social and economic history* [2 vols] (London, 1996).

Opitz, E. *Österreich und Brandenburg im Schwedisch-Polnischen Krieg* (Boppard, 1969).

Pagès, G. *Le Grand Electeur et Louis XIV, 1660–1688* (Paris, 1905).

Parvev, I. *Habsburgs and Ottomans: between Vienna and Belgrade (1683–1739)* (Boulder, 1995).

Patze H. & W. Schlesinger (eds). *Politische Geschichte in der Neuzeit*, vol. 5 of *Geschichte Thüringens* (in 2 parts, Cologne, 1982).

Peball, K. *Die Schlacht bei St-Gotthard-Mogersdorf, 1664* (Vienna, 1964).

Philippi, H. *Landgraf Karl I von Hessen-Kassel* (Marburg, 1976).

Polster, H. *Der Margraf Christian Ernst von Brandenburg-Bayreuth und seine Rolle in den Reichskriegen (1689–1707)* (Erlangen, 1935).

Press, V. *Kriege und Krisen: Deutschland, 1600–1715* (Munich, 1993).

Querfurth, H. *Die Unterwerfung der Stadt Braunschweig im Jahre 1671* (Brunswick, 1953).

Raumer, K. v. *Die Zerstörung der Pfalz von 1689* (Munich, 1930).

Redlich, F. *The German military enterprizer and his workforce* [2 vols] (Wiesbaden, 1964–5).

Regelmeier, H. *Die polititschen Bezeihungen der Fürsten Norddeutschlands zu Frankreich und den nordischen Seemächten in den Jahren 1674 bis 1676* (Hildesheim, 1909).

Rill, B. *Karl VI: Habsburg als barocke Großmacht* (Graz, 1992).

Rode, F. C. *Kriegsgeschichte Schleswig-Holsteins* (Neumünster, 1935).

Roider, K. A. *Austria's eastern question, 1700–1790* (Princeton, 1982).

Roider, K. A. *Baron Thugut and Austria's response to the French Revolution* (Princeton, 1987).

Roider, K. A. *The reluctant ally: Austria's policy in the Austrian Turkish War, 1737–1739* (Baton Rouge, 1972).

Rothenberg, G. E. *Napoleon's great adversaries: the Archduke Charles and the Austrian army, 1792–1814* (London, 1982).

Scharf, C. *Katharina II, Deutschland und die Deutschen* (Mainz, 1995).

Schempp, A. v. *Der Feldzug von 1664 in Ungarn* (Stuttgart, 1909).

Scheuermann, I. (ed.). *Frieden durch Recht: das Reichskammergericht von 1495 bis 1806* (Mainz, 1994).

Schieder, T. *Friedrich der Grosse: ein Königtum der Widersprüche* (Frankfurt-am-Main, 1986).

Schilling, H. *Höfe und Allianzen: Deutschland, 1648–1763* (Berlin, 1989).

Schilling, L. *Kaunitz und das Renversment des alliances. Studien zur außenpolitischen Konzeption Wenzel Antons von Kaunitz* (Berlin, 1994).

Schindling, A. "Reichstag und europäischer Frieden. Leopold I., Ludwig XIV und die Reichsverfassung nach dem Frieden von Nimwegen (1679)", *ZHF*, 8 (1981), 159–77.

Schindling, A. & W. Ziegler (eds) *Die Kaiser der Neuzeit, 1519–1918* (Munich, 1990).

Schirmer, F. *Nec aspera terrant! Eine Heereskunde der hannoverschen Armee von 1631 bis 1803* (Hanover, 1929).

Schmid, A. *Max III: Josef und die europäischen Mächte. Die Außenpolitik des Kurfürstentums Bayern, 1745–1765* (Munich, 1987).

Schnath, G. *Geschichte Hannovers im Zeitalter der neunten Kur und der englischen Sukzession, 1674–1714* [5 vols] (Hildesheim, 1938–82).

Schnettger, M. *Der Reichsdeputationstag 1655–1663. Kaiser und stände zwischen Westfalischen Frieden und Immerwährendem Reichstag* (Munster, 1996).

Schnur, R. *Der Rheinbund von 1658 in der deutschen Verfassungsgeschichte* (Bonn, 1955).

Schroeder, P. W. *The transformation of European politics, 1763–1848* (Oxford, 1994).

Schulte, A. *Markgraf Ludwig Wilhelm von Baden und der Reichskrieg gegen Frankreich 1693–1697* [2 vols] (Heidelberg, 1901).

Schuster, O. & F. A. Franke. *Geschichte der sächsischen Armee von deren Errichtung bis auf die neueste Zeit* [3 vols] (Leipzig, 1885).

Schwark, T. *Lübecks Stadtmilitär im 17. und 18. Jahrhundert* (Lübeck, 1990).

Schweizer, K. W. *England, Prussia and the Seven Years War* (Lewiston, New York, 1989).

Setton, K. M. *Venice, Austria and the Turks in the seventeenth century* (Philadelphia, 1991).

Showalter, D. E. *The wars of Frederick the Great* (London, 1996).

Sichart, L. H. F. v. *Geschichte der königlich-hannoverschen Armee* [5 vols] (Hanover, 1866–98).

Sicken, B. *Das Wehrwesen des fränkischen Reichskreises: Aufbach und Struktur (1681–1714)* [2 vols] (Nuremberg, 1967).

Simms, B. *The impact of Napoleon. Prussian high politics, foreign policy and the crisis of the executive 1797–1806* (Cambridge, 1997).

Sonnino, P. *Louis XIV and the origins of the Dutch War* (Cambridge, 1988).

Spielman, J. P. *Leopold I of Austria* (London, 1977).

Stadlinger, L. I. v. *Geschichte des württembergischen Kriegswesens* (Stuttgart, 1856).

Städtler, E. *Die Ansbach-Bayreuth Truppen im Amerikanischen Unabhänigheitskrieg, 1777–1783* (Nuremberg, 1956).

Staudinger, K. *Geschichte des kurbayerischen Heeres* [5 vols] (Munich, 1901–9).

Storm, P. C. *Der Schwäbische Kreis als Feldherr: Untersuchungen zur Wehrverfassung des Schwäbischen Reichskreises in der Zeit von 1648–1732* (Berlin, 1974).

Subtelny, O. *Domination of eastern Europe: native nobilities and foreign absolutism, 1500–1800* (Gloucester, 1986).

Sutton, J. L. *The king's honor and the king's cardinal: the War of the Polish Succession* (Lexington, 1980).

Ten Raa, F. G. J. et al. *Het staatsche Leger, 1568–1795* [8 vols in 11 parts] (The Hague, 1911–59).

Tessin, G. *Die Regimenter der europäischen Staaten im ancien régime des XVI bis XVIII Jahrhunderts* (Osnabrück, 1986).

Tessin, G. *Mecklenburgisches Militär in Türken- und Franzosenkriegen, 1648–1718* (Cologne, 1966).

Thensis, W. *Die Anfänge des stehenden Heerwesens in Kursachsen unter Johann Georg III und Johann Georg IV* (Leipzig, 1912).

Thompson, R. H. *Lothar Franz von Schönborn and the diplomacy of the Electorate of Mainz* (The Hague, 1973).

Thum, W. *Die Rekrutierung der sächsichen Armee unter August dem Starken (1694–1733)* (Leipzig, 1912).

Vann, J. A. *The Swabian Kreis: institutional growth in the Holy Roman Empire, 1648–1715* (Brussels, 1975).

Vann, J. A. & S. W. Rowan (eds). *The old Reich: essays on German political institutions, 1495–1806* (Brussels, 1974).

Wehler, H. U. *Deutsche Gesellschaftsgeschichte* [3 vols] (Munich, 1987–95).

Weigel, H. *Die Kriegsverfassung des alten deutschen Reiches von der Wormser Matrikel bis zur Auflösung* (Bamberg, 1912).

Wersebe, W. v. *Geschichte der hannoverschen Armee* (Hannover, 1928).

Wick, P. *Versuche zur Einrichtung des Absolutismus in Mecklenburg in der ersten Hälfte des 18. Jahrhunderts* (Berlin, 1964).

Wilson, P. H. The German "soldier trade" of the seventeenth and eighteenth centuries: a reassessment. *International History Review* **18**, pp. 757–92, 1996.

Wilson, P. H. *War, state and society in Württemberg, 1677–1793* (Cambridge, 1995).

Wrede, A. v. *Geschichte der K. v. K. Wehrmacht von 1618 bis zum Ende des XIX Jahrhunderts* [5 vols] (Vienna, 1898–1905).

Wunder, B. *Frankreich, Württemberg und der Schwäbischen Kreis während der Auseinundersetzung über die Reunionen (1679–97)* (Stuttgart, 1971).

Wünschel, H. J. *Die Außenpolitik des Bischofs von Bamberg und Würzburg Peter Philipp von Dernbach* (Neustadt, 1979).

[Zernin, A.] *Abriß der Großherzoglich-Hessischen Kriegs- und Truppen-Geschichte, 1567–1888*, 2nd edn (Darmstadt, 1889).

Zollner, E. & K. Gutkas (eds). *Österreich und die Osmanen – Prinz Eugen und seine Zeit* (Vienna, 1988).

Index